ALSO BY THE MOOSEWOOD COLLECTIVE

*New Recipes from Moosewood Restaurant*

# Sundays at
# MOOSEWOOD
# RESTAURANT

*by the Moosewood Collective*

A **FIRESIDE BOOK** PUBLISHED BY SIMON & SCHUSTER
NEW YORK LONDON TORONTO SYDNEY TOKYO SINGAPORE

*Simon and Schuster/Fireside*

*Simon & Schuster Building*

*Rockefeller Center*

*1230 Avenue of the Americas*

*New York, New York 10020*

Copyright © 1990 by Vegetable Kingdom, Inc.

Illustrations Copyright © 1990 by Martin Berman

**Designed by Bonni Leon**

**Illustrations by Martin Berman**

Manufactured in the United States of America

5   7   9   10   8   6   4

9   10                    PBK

Library of Congress Cataloging in Publication Data

Sundays at Moosewood Restaurant/by the Moosewood Collective.

p.   cm.

"A Fireside book."

Includes bibliographical references and index.

1. Moosewood Restaurant.   2. Vegetarian cookery.   3. Cookery

(Natural foods)   4. Cookery, International.   I. Moosewood

Restaurant.   II. Moosewood Collective.

TX837.S915   1990

641.5'636 — dc20                                                    90-36863

CIP

ISBN 0-671-67989-9

0-671-67990-2 PBK

# *Acknowledgments*

*Heartfelt thanks to Michael Aman for his unbelievable patience, skill, flexibility, and humor. To the Moosewood employees, without whom we couldn't have pulled this off. To Carole Lalli, our editor, for her willingness to work with an author with nineteen heads without ever losing her own. To Kerri Conan for her enthusiasm, diplomacy, and meticulous attentiveness. Finally, to our agents, Elise and Arnold Goodman, for being vigilant and enthusiastic advocates and conscientious supporters.*

*Thanks to Thabo Raphoto and to Judy Barringer for talking to me about Africa and African foods, giving me both information and inspiration. And warm thanks to Rick, because he is steadfast and generous.*

*Nancy Lazarus*

*Thanks to Anaïs Salibian, whose eloquent compassion inspired and sustained me, and to my wonderful family for their good company.*

*Laura Ward Branca*

*I want to acknowledge Colette Rector Walls for her participation in searching out and creating recipes.*

*Tom Walls*

*I would like to thank Ahdi, Ruby, Andi, Scott, Nana, and Juda, whose child care made it possible for me to do research and cook, Robin Lee for her wonderful books, and Jimmy for taking me to the tropics.*

*Ned Asta*

*I would like to thank my husband, Jano, for his support and for always loving my cooking.*

*Eliana Parra*

*I would like to thank David Deutsch for his loving support and enthusiastic recipe tasting.*

*David Hirsch*

*Nan Salamon deserves much thanks for her companionship as a fellow dancer and traveler through the Balkans, and I would also like to thank all those family and friends who have cooked, danced, laughed, cried, and eaten with me over the years.*

*Maureen Vivino*

*These generous people shared Finnish hospitality and gave other much appreciated help: Salli and Ray Matta, Toini and Onni Kaartinen, Mary Kuhlman, Michael Aman, and Tony Del Plato.*

*Susan Harville*

*Acknowledgments to Artie, who gave me my first Indian cookbook, and to Ira, who has been eating my cooking ever since.*

*Linda Dickinson*

*Grazie di Zia Maria, Cugina Anna, Luna, Aunt Blanche e Mama. Grazie specialmente per Susan.*

*Anthony Del Plato*

*I would like to thank my mother, whose wonderful cooking has always inspired me, and my father for truly loving Japanese food even before it became popular. Also thanks to my many astute tasters: Ashley, Gene, Allan, Tazio, Ned, Ruby, Juda, Therese, and Jody. Thank you to Yvonne Fisher for being so supportive and funny. And I would especially like to thank Junco Tsunashima for all those many hysterical hours in my kitchen teaching me so much about Japanese cooking.*

*Andi Gladstone*

Thanks to my mother, Davina Stein, who spent hours compiling her favorite recipes—her last gift to me. And thanks to my father, Milt Stein, whose gift of laughter endures. Special thanks to Tom and Aaron for sharing love and baseball with me.

*Wynelle Stein*

A special thanks to Robin, Noah, and Fouad for their support and for being such willing and enthusiastic tasters, and to my mom, whose example influenced my love of cooking.

*Lisa Wichman*

Thanks to my mom, Olga, and my cousin, Ann, and thanks also to Jürg Butler for his sweet-hearted encouragement.

*Maggie Pitkin*

I wish to thank Lisa Wichman for her enthusiastic and enduring support, Robin and Noah Wichman for their helpful suggestions and comments, and all members of my family for all the pleasant memories stirred up during work on my chapter.

*Fouad Makki*

I would like to thank my children, Danica and Brendan, for their courage and enthusiasm in tasting new and unusual dishes.

*Kip Wilcox*

Thanks first and foremost to Sally for tasting and good criticism, to Keith and Marty, Ward and Leslie for their criticisms and contributions, and to my mother who taught me about discrimination and balance. Apologies to Tony, my son. You can't have macaroni and cheese every night.

*Bob Love*

Thanks to my mother for inspiring me to present the food of the South; any and all of the aunts, uncles, and cousins of the Wade family who ever cooked a meal; and to fellow Moosewood chef and friend, Penny Condon, for creating a delicious jambalaya one Sunday night.

*Sara Wade Robbins*

Thanks to my mom, Rose Adler, for a passion for food; to my friend, Cindy Anderson, for knowing poetry from pedantry; and to my brother Sam, for reading, writing, editing, and eating—voraciously.

*Joan Adler*

# Contents

GENERAL INTRODUCTION 10

THE CUISINES

# *General Introduction*

Moosewood is a small, casual, collectively owned and operated restaurant in downtown Ithaca, a small city in the Finger Lakes region of New York State. Our town is more international than most communities of its size, perhaps because Cornell University and Ithaca College are here. At Moosewood, we've never been interested in following stylish trends; our focus has always been on carefully prepared, artfully presented foods with a healthful, vegetarian emphasis. Since our opening in 1973, Moosewood has offered a different menu at each meal. We draw from our established repertoire of dishes, most of which are a blend of familiar and exotic influences, and we also continually develop new recipes.

Sundays at Moosewood are different from the rest of the week. Sunday night is "ethnic night," when we serve foods from one particular ethnic, national, or regional cuisine. On Sundays we stretch a little. We experiment and take chances. Sometimes we venture into relatively unknown territory. It's fun for us. Occasionally we ask a friend who knows the cuisine well to act as a consultant, answering questions, offering hints and suggestions, and helping us keep within the tradition of the culinary style we're trying.

We have seen a growing interest in international cooking. We regularly get calls for food advice. A couple of years ago, most questions were about tofu, tempeh, yogurt, and even whole wheat flour. More recently, we've been hearing questions about such things as how to use okra, where to get specific fresh chiles, can a food processor be used instead of a mortar and pestle to mash plantains, and what would be good chutney ingredients to accompany an eggplant curry. Couscous, goat cheese, porcini mushrooms, and cilantro are increasingly easy to find in our supermarkets. There are more "foreign food" restaurants in small cities and towns in the U.S., and it is evident to us that lots of people want to try something exciting at home, too. It used to be that we could take obscure cookbooks right off the shelf at our public library; now we usually have to reserve them.

Previously unfamiliar foods are now readily available, and more and more exotic flavors are becoming commonplace. This is part of an age-old, evolutionary process. Foodstuffs, styles, and techniques unknown in some part of the world were introduced by newcomers, often through migration or conquest, and then adapted and incorporated. Often within a generation, the new food became an integral part of the traditional cuisine. Incredible networks of culinary exchanges have formed. Today, cuisines are changing faster and faster, and at Moosewood we're happy to be a part of that process.

At the same time, the preparing and serving of foods is one of the most interesting and carefully preserved identifiers of a culture. Traditional food is a balm for the uncertainties and confusion of a new life; the most usual common bond among immigrants is the sharing of food. At Moosewood, all of us have discovered time and again the integral connection that food has to culture, heritage, the retelling of history through family stories, and the celebration of rituals and seasons of the year.

We find it healthy and exciting to foster an appetite for and interest in other cuisines and cultures. Such exchange might eventually result in a new hybrid of ethnic cooking and perhaps a more homogenous world culture. Some of the wonderful ethnic idiosyncracies are doubtless lost in the process, but we have tried to capture and preserve the lasting value that is common to all ethnic and regional cuisines—the food reminds us of our connection to people and to the earth.

We've always looked on our Sundays at Moosewood as special days. Both the menu planner and the dessert maker research new dishes. Because we're not open for Sunday lunch, the cooks have more time to prepare the evening meal. The menu planner might shop for ingredients we don't normally have on hand or help the cooks with unusual techniques or preparations. We often make extra side dishes or condiments and offer a special salad, in addition to our regular salads. Sometimes we bake a bread particularly representative of the cuisine. We might play ethnic background music or write the menu in two languages.

*Sundays at Moosewood Restaurant* evolved from our desire to expand and share our repertoire of ethnic and regional dishes. It contains a collection of recipes from eighteen different or regional cuisines and an extensive guide to ingredients, techniques, and equipment. Each chapter was compiled and written by one of the Moosewood cooks, who chose a particular country or region of the world for his or her focus. Some of us selected the cuisine related to our family backgrounds. Others remembered places we had lived, studied, or traveled, where we had tasted exotic foods and unusual spices and gathered recipes. A few of us picked a country that has simply caught our fancy or intrigued us. We've collaborated to present this healthful, delicious array of dishes that combine the characteristic, traditional foods of a place or a people with our own innovations and adaptations.

Although not the same as being there, cookbooks, we find, can provide a taste and a glimpse of a foreign place. We make no claims about comprehensively covering the "world" of ethnic cooking, but the wide spectrum these eighteen chapters explore contains diversity and contrast. Some chapters cover vast, populous territories such as China or Africa and others focus on smaller areas such as Provence or Finland. The dishes range from classic, authentic recipes, true to their traditional sources, to original creations of our own, inspired by traditional dishes.

From cultures known for spicy hot food such as Mexico and Southeast Asia, to Jewish and Eastern European cultures renowned for dairy products, to those that have an intrinsic vegetarian emphasis such as India and Japan, this book includes tastes for every palate and more variety than pattern. Here you can take a fresh look at a familiar cuisine like Italy's or New England's or explore a culinary tradition generally little known to us such as that of the Eritrean highlands.

We have always looked to ethnic foods for new ideas for vegetarian dishes. Restraints such as religious and ethical restrictions or limited natural resources have often been the basis for the development of vegetarian cuisines. Although we have no such restrictions imposed on us, at Moosewood we simply prefer a meatless cuisine. We often create new versions of recipes that originally included or even featured meat. Sometimes we substitute ingredients accessible to us for technically "correct" ingredients that are difficult to obtain, expensive, or particularly time consuming to prepare. For these reasons, we recommend such foods as brined artichoke hearts and dried shiitake mushrooms, rather than fresh. At times our penchant for creating lighter, more nutritious dishes prompts our innovations, although many ethnic foods already are naturally healthful (corn and beans, rice and tofu, vegetables and pasta). Occasionally, we offer techniques utilizing nontraditional equipment or appliances that help to simplify preparation and make these dishes feasible within our busy lives and schedules.

Some of the ingredients may be unfamiliar. We hope this will not intimidate even the novice cook but will instead kindle a spark of interest. Our chapter, Guide to Ingredients, Techniques, and Equipment, contains a wealth of alphabetically arranged entries that include tips from our experience. Page references appear in the main text next to ingredients or procedures that we consider obscure or particularly crucial. In addition, the Guide covers much more that is not directly referenced in the text. If you are uncertain about any ingredient or technique, we encourage you to look first in the Guide for help. Even the most seasoned, knowledgeable cook may discover some useful or interesting fact by browsing through it.

The recipes are easy to follow, and we use consistent methods and procedures. Most of them are neither difficult nor time consuming. A few may take some extra preparation or special attention but are included because we felt them well worth the effort. You may choose to prepare the more intricate, involved recipes only for special occasions, which is indeed an age-old tradition in itself.

As we worked on *Sundays at Moosewood Restaurant,* we discovered a world of still largely untapped possibilities in the realm of cross-cultural menu-planning. In some of the chapters in the book you will see similarities in the spices, foodstuffs, and methods of preparation, such as those between the Caribbean and Southern U.S. or British and Finnish. But you might want to combine more divergent cuisines to suit your taste. Try Southeast Asia and Africa South of the Sahara. Try a Chilean drink with an Armenian dessert. We have taken a deliberate step toward experimenting with and combining elements and dishes of different cuisines and expect you will too. Honoring the knowledge of the past and using it in the present is the very process of keeping tradition alive.

NANCY LAZARUS

*Africa*

*South*

*of the*

*Sahara*

# INTRODUCTION

Africa is a land of contrasts. The coasts are lined with warm sandy beaches lush with greenery and brilliant flowers or with rocky shores backed by high, forbidding cliffs. Rugged, snow-peaked mountains and steep escarpments with rushing waterfalls overlook its vast plains. Rain forests give way to the savannahs and the most magnificent deserts on earth. Africa is a melange of old and new, modern and traditional. A young man walking down the street in Accra or Abidjan might be wearing blue jeans, a dashiki, a business suit, or a *kenta* cloth wrap. He might return home to his high-rise apartment and watch the evening news on television, or head home to his village and his family's compound of thatched-roof dwellings and listen to the news from the talking drums. On the radio, you can tune in to King Sunny Ade and His African Beats, traditional Mandinke Kora musicians, or to Janet Jackson and Kenny Rogers. Polygamy vies with monogamy and fertility rites with birth control. On the roads, Toyotas face off with donkey-pulled carts.

Africa is, in fact, much larger than most of us think of it. Our Mercator-based maps significantly distort the relative sizes of land masses around the equator and approaching the poles, making Europe's 4 million square miles seem to be about the same size as Africa's 11.5 million. North America appears to be larger than Africa even though the fifteen nations of West Africa alone (the bottom half of the western "bulge") are roughly the size of the United States.

There are fifty-four countries in Africa and hundreds of languages and dialects spoken there. The Sahara divides the continent both geographically and culturally. The countries north of the Sahara, which extend along the Mediterranean from Western Sahara to Egypt and into northern Sudan, represent an Islamic tradition different from the countries to the south. Sub-Saharan Africa is described regionally as West, Central, East, and

Southern Africa. We Americans look to West Africa in tracing one of the major enriching influences of our culture and the ancestral home of most black Americans. Most of these recipes have been drawn from the cuisines of West Africa.

West Africa has an acute sense of history. While Europe was mired in the Dark Ages, learning and culture were flourishing in the great kingdom of Ghana. The Songhai Empire, a vast state that in 1500 A.D. stretched from the Atlantic Ocean to what is now central Nigeria, had a strong centralized government. The early West African civilizations had stable political systems, rich cultural traditions, large urban settlements, and trading, mining, and agricultural industries. They produced an original tradition of art, including the great bronzes of Benin, the wood carvings and masks of Nigeria and Ghana, and the elaborately woven silks, wools, and cottons of Mali.

By the eighteenth century, the slave trade, the missionary movement, and European colonialism had begun to eclipse traditional sub-Saharan African society and culture. In the twentieth century, active resistance to colonialism led to the struggle for independence, which has largely been achieved. Today, African nations are regaining control over their governments and economies. Traditional values and cultures, the social, political, and economic influences of the West, and hopes and plans for equity and prosperity are all part of African life now.

Although all the nations of Africa are politically independent of the colonial powers, most Africans view South Africa as their last colonial nation. South Africa achieved independence from Britain in 1910, but through apartheid the constitution has systematically excluded the black majority from the political process, and so a form of colonialism prevails.

When I was first introduced to sub-Saharan African foods, I experienced a feeling of familiarity with it, a kind of déjà vu. Just as I began to fantasize happily about some former life in Mali, I realized that of course I was familiar with this food. The aromas, flavors, ingredients, and cooking techniques were those of my childhood friends and neighbors in central Florida. Long ago West African ingredients and cooking methods became assimilated in Southern, Creole, Soul, and Cajun cooking. The five million Africans brought to the Americas during the slave trade greatly influenced the cuisine in the new land. Caribbean and Brazilian cuisines can even be described as West African with French and Latin influences.

Many foods that are familiar in the U.S. were brought here from Africa: black-eyed peas, pigeon peas, nutmeg, sesame, coffee, kola, watermelon, millet (originally from India), and okra, whose seeds are reported to have been brought by slaves who hid them in their hair. Among the plants introduced to Africa from the New World were maize, cassava, pineapples, papaya, and chiles. Peanuts were native to Brazil, introduced to Africa by the Portuguese, and then brought to Virginia by slaves.

Just as the flavors of Africa emerge in American cooking, so too the rhythms of Africa pulse through jazz, rock and roll, blues, zydeco, and reggae. The conga, rhumba, mambo, tango, and Charleston are all derived from traditional ritual dances in various parts of sub-Saharan Africa. The samba is the traditional wedding dance of Angola. Drums, the xylophone, and the marimba came to us from Africa. Syncopation, improvisation, polymeter, vocal harmony, responsorial singing, and unity of song and dance originated in Africa.

Many American words are derived from African languages, including: tote, meaning to carry *(tota)*; cat, meaning person *(cat)*; dig, meaning understand *(dega)*; hip, meaning aware *(hipi)*; guy, meaning young man *(goy)*; OK *(yaw kay)*; and, my favorite, jukebox from the Senegalese *juke,* meaning to have a wild time.

Travelers in West Africa describe African people as exceptionally warm and hospitable and express delight with their spontaneous and infectious friendliness. Often, in the next breath, they describe their first African meal, usually with vivid descriptions of their own physical responses to the intense hotness of the food. When I asked Thabo Raphoto, a South African friend, what he could tell me about West African food, he responded immediately with a smile, a sparkle in his eye, and, "Oh, the West Africans! They do not believe they've eaten unless they've severely burned the insides of their mouths!"

In his book, *Through African Doors,* Janheinz Jahn described his first night in West Africa in a Yoruba home where he was graciously welcomed and served a cool drink after his tiring trip. Then he was ushered into the dining room for a meal. He was far from prepared for his first bite. Determined to learn to taste the flavor through the fire, he persisted, forcing himself to swallow several small bites. At that point he said, "I had to stop. My mouth was completely scalded, and there was a buzzing in my ears. I felt rather faint, held my breath, wiped my nose, wiped the tears out of my eyes . . ." His compassionate host, no longer able to politely pretend that everything was fine, said, "But it has been prepared specially mild for your sake!"

West African markets are brilliant with color, bustling with activity, and filled with familiar and exotic foodstuffs. West African food is lively with ginger, dried red chiles, and garlic—rich and fiery. Meals usually contain fruits, vegetables, and flavorings that we North Americans have never tasted. African cooks readily improvise according to which spices are at hand, what fruits and vegetables are in season, and, always, the preferences of their guests.

Although the emphasis here is on West Africa, I've also drawn from the cuisines of East and Southern Africa, with their Asian influences, primarily Malay and Indian. These foods are often scented with cinnamon and mace, and can be called upon when you want delicate aromas and pungent and sweet flavors. It is not unusual for Southern African recipes to call for curry spices, chutney, pickled mangos, coconut milk, or fresh green chiles.

The cuisines of East and Southern Africa share many ingredients with that of West Africa. Pumpkins, yams, sweet potatoes, peanuts, corn, cabbage, and coconuts are used extensively in all regions. Tender greens are often added to stews just before serving. There are hundreds of African greens, some we've heard of and many more that aren't available here. The tender greens of sweet potatoes, pumpkins, and squash are favorites —try some. Suitable substitutes include spinach, sorrel, beet and turnip greens, chard, and collards.

Peanuts, called groundnuts, have become an essential of African cooking since their introduction to West Africa from Brazil in the early sixteenth century by the Portuguese. Groundnuts are eaten whole, pounded into peanut butter, crushed into a coarse powder, and also cultivated for their oil. They are incorporated into sauces, soups, stews, and fritters. Goobers are called *nguba* in Fulani (the Congo).

Yams are a mainstay of the African diet. Their name is derived from the verb "to eat" in several African languages (*"nyami"* in Fulani). Yams are native to West Africa, where they are revered as a symbol of survival and given ceremonial status, much as corn is among North American Indians, and are always served on holidays and special occasions. These true yams are not the orange-fleshed sweet potato grown in the U.S. There are many variations of true yams, but generally they have white flesh and bark-like skin. Yams are not readily available in the U.S., so these recipes call for sweet potatoes, which are good in themselves, but not, please, to be confused with yams.

Hot sauces are found throughout Africa and are as widely used as catsup is in the U.S. Pili pili is perhaps the most widespread hot sauce in Africa. It is a simple tomato-cayenne-horseradish sauce. Tabasco or any basic hot sauce will do with African food. The Chilean Pebre (see page 158) and either of the Mexican salsas (see pages 458 and 459) in this book are quite compatible with African foods.

Most characteristic in West Africa is a one-dish meal consisting of a starch (rice, millet, maize porridge, or "fufu," which is pounded plantains, yams, or cassava) served with a spicy stew or soup. In Senegal, a dinner often begins with a plate of appetizers— deviled eggs, ripe tomatoes or grated carrots vinaigrette, fresh fruits, and smooth, creamy potato salads are all favorites. In West Africa today, spicy hot meals often end with very simple, cooling desserts. Chilled fruit salads of diced fresh pineapples, guavas, and sectioned oranges, topped with thinly sliced bananas and a very cold vanilla custard are the perfect ending.

For a splendid pan-African feast, select dishes from both African sections of this book, but also freely select from the Caribbean and Southern United States sections (because of the strong West African influence upon these cuisines) and from the India and Southeast Asia sections (because of these regions' influences on the cuisines of Southern and East Africa).

S O U P S

# West African
# Peanut Soup

If you're a person who loves peanuts, but thinks they were made to eat at baseball games or on bread with jelly, think again and get ready for a culinary adventure.

This peanut soup is rich and spicy. The chopped scallions or chives are an integral element, not just a garnish.

### SERVES 6 TO 8

2 cups chopped onions
1 tablespoon peanut or vegetable oil
½ teaspoon cayenne or other ground
 dried chiles (or to taste)
1 teaspoon grated peeled fresh ginger
 root
1 cup chopped carrots
2 cups chopped sweet potatoes (up to 1
 cup white potatoes can be
 substituted)

4 cups vegetable stock (see page 685) or
 water

_____

2 cups tomato juice
1 cup smooth peanut butter
1 tablespoon sugar (optional)
1 cup chopped scallions or chives

Sauté the onions in the oil until just translucent. Stir in the cayenne and fresh ginger. Add the carrots and sauté a couple more minutes. Mix in the potatoes and stock or water, bring the soup to a boil, and then simmer for about 15 minutes, until the vegetables are tender.

In a blender or food processor, purée the vegetables with the cooking liquid and the tomato juice. Return the purée to a soup pot. Stir in the peanut butter until smooth. Taste the soup. Its sweetness will depend upon the sweetness of the carrots and sweet potatoes. If it's not there naturally, add just a little sugar to enhance the other flavors.

Reheat the soup gently, using a heat diffuser if needed to prevent scorching. Add more water, stock, or tomato juice for a thinner soup.

Serve topped with plenty of chopped scallions or chives.

# Cape Verde
# Vegetable Soup

Coastal West Africa is a land of green mountains, white sands, turquoise skies with immense thunderclouds, spectacular sunsets, and dark, starry nights. Cape Verde is the westernmost point on the continent. It was created by volcanic activity and southwesterly winds keep it warm and lush. This soup tastes fresh and uncomplicated and makes a good beginning for any African meal. Served with crisp French bread and fresh fruit, it is a satisfying lunch or supper.

### SERVES 6

1 cup chopped onions
2 garlic cloves, minced or pressed
2 tablespoons peanut oil
pinch of summer savory or thyme
¼ teaspoon ground dried red chiles (or
   to taste)

_____

2 cups diced potatoes
2 cups sliced cabbage (cut into 1-inch
   lengths)

1 cup sliced okra
3 cups chopped fresh tomatoes (or 2
   cups canned tomatoes with juice)
3 cups water
1 teaspoon salt
1 tablespoon minced fresh cilantro
juice of 1 lemon

_____

chopped fresh parsley
chopped fresh cilantro

Sauté the onions and garlic in the oil for 10 minutes. Add the summer savory or thyme and the ground chiles and sauté gently, stirring often, for another 5 minutes. Add the rest of the ingredients, except the lemon juice, and bring to a boil. Reduce the heat and simmer until the vegetables are tender, about 20 minutes. Add the lemon juice.

Serve topped with chopped fresh parsley or more fresh cilantro or both.

# East African Sweet Pea Soup

 This rich, spicy soup is typical of Indian fare in East and Southern Africa. There is a large Indian population in Nairobi, the cosmopolitan capital of Kenya. Nairobi is called "the city of flowers" because many of its streets are lined with the rainbow colors of bougainvillea, hibiscus, oleanders, and jacaranda. "Nairobi" is Masai for "place of cool waters." Cool water and poppadums (see page 675) seem the best accompaniment for this tasty, satisfying soup.

**SERVES 6**

*2 cups chopped onions*
*1 teaspoon minced or pressed garlic*
*1 tablespoon vegetable oil*

*½ teaspoon grated fresh peeled ginger root*
*1 teaspoon salt*
*½ teaspoon ground black pepper*
*⅛ teaspoon cayenne or other ground dried chiles*
*1 teaspoon ground coriander seeds*

*1 teaspoon ground cumin seeds*
*¼ teaspoon ground cardamom*
*⅛ teaspoon ground cloves*
*¼ teaspoon cinnamon*
*1 teaspoon turmeric*

*2 tomatoes, chopped*
*1 sweet potato, diced (about 2 cups)*
*3½ cups water*
*3 cups fresh green peas (or 1 pound frozen)*

Sauté the onions and garlic gently in oil in a covered pot, stirring frequently, for 5 to 10 minutes, until the onions are just translucent. Mix in the ginger, salt, and all the spices and sauté for a couple of minutes, stirring often. Add the tomatoes and sweet potato. Stir well. Add 1½ cups of water and stir to dissolve the spices and deglaze the bottom of the pot. Bring the soup to a boil. Reduce the heat and simmer, covered, for 5 minutes. Add 2 cups of the peas and simmer, covered, for another 10 minutes, or until the peas and sweet potato are tender.

Remove the soup from the heat and add the remaining 2 cups of water. Purée the soup in a blender or food processor until smooth. Return to the pot, add the remaining cup of peas, and gently reheat.

## MAIN DISHES

# *Groundnut Stew*

All over West Africa, today and every day, thousands of ground-nut stews will be cooked and eaten. A few of them might be indistinguishable from others, but the rest will all be different. Very thick here, almost a soup there. Fiery hot or mildly piquant with lots of fresh ginger root, a hint of ground dried ginger, or no ginger at all. Garlic or not. Maybe one of those stews was made with only okra, others with many different vegetables, including some that most of us in the United States have never tasted or dreamed of. The liquid used may be coconut milk, water, stock, or fruit or vegetable juices.

West African groundnut stew was the first African dish served at Moosewood, and it's a great favorite. This recipe is for my own favorite version, made with cabbage, sweet potatoes, and okra, as in the maffes of Senegal and Mali. Make it with eggplant and plenty of ginger, and it will be *hkatenkwan* as in Ghana. Served with tender steamed greens, it is *dovi* in Zimbabwe. Experiment to find your favorite version. Just be sure to remember the groundnuts and cayenne.

Always serve groundnut stew on one of the West African starches—rice, millet, or stiff porridge *(ugali)*. And alongside serve any of the following: hard-boiled eggs, chopped scallions, chopped fresh parsley or cilantro, cubed papaya, sliced bananas, mangos, pineapples, or oranges, grated coconut, whole or crushed peanuts.

2 cups chopped onions

2 tablespoons peanut or vegetable oil

½ teaspoon cayenne or other ground
  dried chiles

1 teaspoon pressed garlic cloves

2 cups chopped cabbage

3 cups cubed sweet potatoes (1-inch
  cubes)

3 cups tomato juice

1 cup apple or apricot juice

1 teaspoon salt

1 teaspoon grated peeled fresh ginger
  root

1 tablespoon chopped fresh cilantro
  (optional)

2 chopped tomatoes

1½–2 cups chopped okra

½ cup peanut butter (see page 673)

Sauté the onions in the oil for about 10 minutes. Stir in the cayenne and garlic and sauté for a couple more minutes. Add the cabbage and sweet potatoes and sauté, covered, for a few minutes. Mix in the juices, salt, ginger, cilantro, and tomatoes. Cover and simmer for about 15 minutes, until the sweet potatoes are tender. Add the okra and simmer for 5 minutes more. Stir in the peanut butter, place the pan on a heat diffuser, and simmer gently until ready to serve. Add more juice or water if the stew is too thick.

# Senegalese Seafood Stew

The main attraction in the many fishing villages along the coast of West Africa is the arrival of the fishing boats after a long day at sea. Most of the fishing is traditional—done with man-powered boats and hand-controlled nets. In Senegal (the Wolof first called this land *Su nu Gal,* "our canoes"), much of the fishing is done in fleets of long, wooden pirogues. All along the coast, when the fishermen return, they're eagerly greeted by women and children who help unload the boats and nets.

This seafood stew is peppery and exotic. The bananas taste like some strange and unusual vegetable, not recognizable as our familiar and most popular fruit in the United States.

### SERVES 6 TO 8

1 teaspoon salt
2 green (unripe) bananas, sliced into
  ½-inch rounds
_____

4 cups chopped onions
2 garlic cloves, minced or pressed
2 tablespoons olive oil
½ teaspoon cayenne or other ground
  dried chiles (or to taste)
¼ teaspoon summer savory or thyme
2 potatoes, chopped
2 sweet potatoes, peeled and chopped
¼ small head of cabbage, chopped
  (about 2 cups)

1 cup chopped fresh parsley
4 cups chopped fresh tomatoes (or 3
  cups chopped canned tomatoes with
  juice)
3 cups vegetable stock (see page 685) or
  water
_____

1 pound fresh shrimp, rinsed, shelled,
  and deveined
1 pound fresh fish fillets, cut into
  chunks
salt to taste

Dissolve the salt in enough water to cover the sliced bananas. Soak the banana rounds in the salt water for about 15 minutes and then drain them and set aside.

Meanwhile, in a large saucepan, sauté the onions and garlic in the olive oil until the onions are just translucent. Stir in the cayenne and summer savory or thyme and sauté for a couple more minutes. Add the potatoes, sweet potatoes, cabbage, parsley, tomatoes, and stock or water. Bring the stew to a simmer and cook for 15 minutes.

Add the bananas, shrimp, and fish. Simmer gently for another 10 minutes or until the fish is opaque and the shrimp are pink. Add more stock, water, or tomato juice if the stew is too thick. Add salt to taste.

Serve Senegalese Seafood Stew on rice or Steamed Millet (see page 34) or with Ugali (see page 35). Garnish with wedges of lemon or lime.

*Variation* To make a soup, add more stock or water. Serve with plenty of crisp French bread and fresh fruit.

# Casamance Stew

The sea and rivers of West Africa are abundantly blessed with fish, an important food source. This stew is inspired by Yassa, a popular specialty of Casamance, the southernmost coastal region of Senegal. Yassa is a spicy marinated dish prepared with poultry or fish. I've added sweet potatoes, because I think it's even more delicious with that soft sweetness providing a counterpoint to the lemony tang of the onions and fish.

The fish caught in West Africa's warm, shallow waters tend to be firmer and more substantial than our usual cod or flounder, so look for a firm, even chewy, fish that won't be lost in this tasty stew.

### SERVES 6

**MARINADE**

½ cup fresh lemon or lime juice

½ cup white vinegar

2 tablespoons tamari soy sauce

2 tablespoons peanut oil

1 teaspoon freshly ground black pepper

3 large garlic cloves, minced

2 or more seeded chiles, minced

1½ pounds firm fish steaks or fillets, such as monkfish

4 cups sliced onions

2 cups 1-inch cubed sweet potatoes

1 tablespoon peanut oil

1 red bell pepper, chopped (optional)

salt to taste

Combine the marinade ingredients. Rinse the fish well. If you're using a large fillet, cut it into serving-sized pieces. In a large glass bowl, layer about half of the onion slices. Pour some marinade over them. Then add the fish and the rest of the onions and marinade. Cover and refrigerate for at least 2 hours, but preferably overnight or all day.

When you're ready to cook, lift the fillets out of the marinade and set them aside. Pour the marinade off the onions and set the marinade aside. Cover the cubed sweet potatoes with cool, salted water, bring them to a boil, and then simmer for a few minutes until they are just barely tender. Drain any excess liquid. Meanwhile, in a heavy, nonreactive skillet, gently sauté the onions in the peanut oil for about 20 minutes, until lightly browned. Add the red bell pepper, if used, for the last 5 minutes of sautéing. Combine the sautéed onions and bell pepper with drained sweet potatoes and marinade and simmer for about 20 minutes.

While the vegetables simmer, briefly grill, broil, or sauté the fish until lightly browned on both sides. Add the fish to the simmering vegetables and continue to simmer for 15 minutes more or until the fish is just cooked through. Salt to taste.

Serve Casamance Stew in wide, shallow bowls on plenty of rice or Steamed Millet (see page 34). If you like, garnish with chopped fresh parsley, cilantro, or scallions. Extra tamari at the table might be appreciated. Gombo (see page 37) and Maize Pudding (see page 38) or Banana Chutney (see page 43) would make this meal a feast.

# Capetown Fruit and Vegetable Curry

 The culinary traditions of Southern Africa not only include the dishes of the African continent, but also the influences of the colonial powers and the immigrants from Malaysia and the Indies. This sweet and savory curry incorporates all of those influences.

### SERVES 6

4 cups coarsely chopped onions
2 tablespoons peanut or vegetable oil
2 garlic cloves, minced
1 teaspoon grated peeled fresh ginger
   root

**CURRY SPICES**

1 1/2 tablespoons ground cumin seeds
1 1/2 tablespoons ground coriander seeds
1 1/2 teaspoons cinnamon
1 teaspoon turmeric
1/2 teaspoon cayenne or other ground
   dried red chiles
1/2 teaspoon ground fennel seeds
1/4 teaspoon ground cardamom
1/4 teaspoon ground cloves

————————————————

2 medium zucchini, quartered
   lengthwise and sliced

1 1/2 cups water
1 cup cut green beans
2 firm tart green pears or apples, cored
   and cubed
1/2 red bell pepper, coarsely chopped
1 cup chopped dried apricots
   (unsulfured)
1/2 cup currants or raisins
1/2 cup apricot conserve
fresh lemon juice (optional)

————————————————

6 cups cooked brown rice

————————————————

1 cup raw or roasted peanuts
2 bananas

Sauté the onions in the peanut oil for 10 minutes. Stir in the garlic, ginger root, and curry spices and continue to sauté, stirring constantly for about 3 minutes.

Add the zucchini and water and stir well so that the spices won't stick to the bottom of the pan. Cover the pan and simmer for 10 minutes. Mix in the green beans, pears, red bell peppers, and dried apricots. Simmer gently, covered, for about 30 minutes. Stir occasionally and add a little more water if needed to prevent sticking. When the fruit and vegetables are quite tender, stir in the currants and the apricot conserve. Taste the curry and adjust the flavor to your liking. Add cayenne or Garam Masala (see page 293) if it's not spicy enough, lemon juice if you'd like more tartness, or more apricot conserve to intensify the sweetness. Keep the curry warm on a heat diffuser, to prevent scorching, until ready to serve.

Serve on a bed of rice, topped with peanuts and sliced bananas, with Minted Cucumber-Yogurt Refresher (see page 42) alongside.

# Tofu Bobotie

Bobotie is one of the dishes described as most typically South African. In much of Africa today, meat is a luxury. That was also true for the Malay cooks of South Africa in the seventeenth and eighteenth centuries, who developed bobotie as a delicious way to "stretch" meat with bread. Now bobotie is a widespread supper dish regularly enjoyed by all the racial groups of South Africa at home and in restaurants.

I first heard of bobotie from Russell Groener and Beverly Oskowitz, South Africans who visited Ithaca. They had been out of their country for several months and were feeling a little homesick. So I jumped at the chance (and had the audacity) to cook an experimental tofu bobotie for them. How satisfying it was when they declared it authentic, ate it all up, and asked for the recipe. Now it's a regular favorite at my house and at Moosewood.

2 cakes tofu, frozen (see page 684)

3 cups chopped onions

2 teaspoons minced garlic

2 tablespoons peanut or vegetable oil

---

1 tablespoon ground cumin seeds

1 tablespoon ground coriander seeds

1/4 teaspoon ground fennel seeds

5 whole cloves, ground

1 teaspoon cinnamon

2 teaspoons turmeric

1/2 teaspoon ground black pepper

2 tablespoons white vinegar

3 tablespoons tamari soy sauce

1/3 cup homemade* or commercial
  chutney (peach, apricot, or mango)

---

1 1/2 cups whole wheat bread chunks

1/2 cup milk

---

1 tablespoon dark sesame oil

1/2 cup raisins or currants

1/2 cup almonds, coarsely chopped

---

3 bay leaves

1 egg

3/4 cup milk

Remove the frozen tofu from the freezer and allow it to thaw; then crumble it and set aside.

In a covered saucepan, cook the onions and garlic in the oil on medium heat, stirring occasionally, for 20 to 30 minutes, until quite soft. Add the curry spices (cumin through black pepper in the ingredient list) and sauté for a couple of minutes, stirring constantly. Mix in the vinegar, soy sauce, and chutney and remove the pan from the heat.

Preheat the oven to 350°.

In a large mixing bowl, soak the bread in 1/2 cup of milk for a few minutes and then mash it with a fork or your fingers. Stir in the crumbled tofu. Drizzle on the sesame oil and mix well. Add the raisins, almonds, and onion-spice mixture. Stir well.

Oil a baking dish, about 12x8 inches, or a large pie pan. Spread the bobotie evenly into the baking dish. Tuck the bay leaves in here and there, leaving the stems sticking out. Whisk the egg and 3/4 cup of milk together to make a custard. Pour the custard over the top of the bobotie. Bake, covered, at 350°, for 15 minutes. Then uncover and bake until the custard is set, about 15 minutes more. Remove the bay leaves after baking.

Serve bobotie on brown rice and with more chutney on the side. Minted Cucumber-Yogurt Refresher (see page 42) and steamed vegetables are a good accompaniment.

---

* See New Recipes from Moosewood Restaurant, page 215.

# GRAINS,
# SIDE DISHES,
# AND
# CONDIMENTS

## Steamed Millet

There are many types of millet native to Africa, producing grains in a range of sizes and a variety of colors, including pink and green. To further confuse things, other seed-like grains, such as sorghum, are often referred to as millet. The cooking time and water-to-grain ratio given in this recipe are suitable for the millet available in the United States, which is a small, pale yellow, round grain. Be sure to get hulled millet, not bird seed!

Steamed millet is light and fluffy, something like couscous, yet firm. It has a pleasant, rather earthy flavor. Millet has had an undeserved reputation in this country as a heavy, mushy grain, but I think that this must be because so many cookbooks instruct us to use four parts water to one part millet, more than twice as much water as needed! Try this recipe and I think you'll be delighted with the results.

### SERVES 6 TO 8

3½ cups cold water                    2 cups millet
1 teaspoon salt

In a heavy saucepan, stir together the water, salt, and millet. Cover and bring to a boil. Reduce the heat, stir, cover, and simmer gently. After about 20 minutes, stir to fluff the millet and taste it. If it's dry yet still a little crunchy, add about ¼ cup of boiling water and continue to steam, covered, for about 10 minutes more.

Serve millet with any West African stew or as a side dish with any African meal. For a richer flavor, add a little butter or margarine just before serving. Millet, like rice, is also good in fillings for stuffed vegetables or as pilaf.

# Ugali

•

# Stiff Porridge

Maize or American Indian corn was introduced to Africa from North America. It has become a staple starch in Africa, particularly Southern Africa, where it is called "mealie." It is drier and starchier than the sweet corn we know. Ground, it is called "mealie meal." Mealie meal is most commonly made into porridge, which is a major part of the African diet. Stiff mealie meal mush or porridge is called *putu* by the Bantus, *fufu* in West Africa, *pap* by the Dutch, *nsima* in Malawi and Zambia, *bidia* in Zaire, *oshifima* in Namibia, and *ugali* in Kenya and Tanzania.

African slaves brought this method of cooking maize back to the Americas. Ugali is similar to the corn pones and cornmeal mush of Southern United States and the coocoos of the Caribbean.

To eat ugali in a traditional African manner, pull off a bite-sized chunk from the communal bowl of ugali placed in the middle of the table. Form the chunk into a small ball, flatten it, make an indentation in it with your thumb, and use it to scoop up your stew—an edible spoon! In much of West Africa, it's the Muslim-influenced custom to use only your right hand to touch food.

Ugali can also be spread on a plate or in a bowl and then topped with stew. Or, roll the ugali into small balls and drop them into individual servings of soup or stew just before serving.

1 cup water

1 teaspoon salt

1 cup milk

1 cup white cornmeal (see note)

Bring the water and salt to a boil in a saucepan. In a bowl, stir the milk into the cornmeal until smooth. Slowly pour the cornmeal paste into the boiling water, stirring constantly for a couple of minutes, until it thickens. Place the pan on a heat diffuser and continue to cook the ugali for 10 to 15 minutes. Once a minute, stir it briskly and then smooth it over the bottom of the pan again. After a while, the ugali will be "stiff" and pull away from the sides of the pan. The length of time this takes varies with different cornmeals.

When the porridge is done, turn it into a cool, damp bowl. With dampened hands, shape it into a smooth ball and serve immediately.

> *Note: White cornmeal is best for stiff porridge, but if it's unavailable, substitute yellow cornmeal for a less authentic, but still delicious, ugali.*

# Abidjan Cabbage Salad

This cool, crunchy salad is welcome with any West African stew. Serve it with avocados, deviled eggs, and baguettes for a delightful luncheon.

## SERVES 6

4 cups thinly sliced cabbage

1 cup shredded carrot

1 cup pineapple chunks (fresh or
    canned)

juice of 1 lemon

juice of 1 orange

¼ teaspoon salt

⅓–½ cup vegetable oil

Pile the cabbage, carrots, and pineapple into a large bowl. Mix the dressing either by whisking all the ingredients until creamy or by slowly drizzling the oil into the juices while whirling in a blender or food processor. Thoroughly mix the salad and dressing.

Serve immediately or refrigerate until ready to serve.

# *Gombo*

•

## *Okra Side Dish*

*Gombo* means okra in Swahili. This okra dish is served as a relish or side vegetable with any African meal. Gombo is delicious with eggs for breakfast or supper.

### SERVES 4 TO 6

*1 cup finely chopped onions*
*3 garlic cloves, minced*
*1 tablespoon peanut oil*
*2 cups finely chopped okra (10-ounce package frozen) (see note)*

*2 chiles, stemmed, seeded, and thinly sliced*
*2 tomatoes, chopped*
*1 teaspoon salt*

In a nonreactive saucepan, sauté the onions and garlic in the oil for 10 minutes. Add the okra and chiles and sauté, stirring frequently, for 5 minutes. Add the tomatoes and salt, cover, and simmer for about 30 minutes.

*Note: When using frozen okra, it is easier to chop it while it is still frozen.*

# Maize Pudding

This maize pudding is a sumptuous steamed fresh sweet corn pudding that is quickly and easily prepared for the oven. It's especially good with spicy-hot West African dishes and with Hoppin' John (see page 620)—called Thiebou Nop Niébé in Senegal—or West Indian Rice and Peas with Tempeh (see page 132).

Maize pudding is perfect for Thanksgiving dinner.

### SERVES 6 TO 8

*4 cups cut corn, fresh or thawed frozen*
   *(20-ounce package)*
*3 eggs*
*2 tablespoons peanut or vegetable oil*
*½ teaspoon salt*
*1 tablespoon molasses*

*1 tablespoon sugar*
*1 tablespoon baking powder*
*¼ teaspoon nutmeg or mace*
*¼ teaspoon ground allspice*
*¼ cup flour*

Generously oil a 9x5x3-inch loaf pan or similarly sized casserole dish. Maize pudding bakes in a boiling water bath, so have ready a larger baking pan that the maize pudding pan fits into comfortably.

Preheat the oven to 375°.

In a blender or food processor, purée 2 cups of the corn with the eggs, oil, salt, molasses, and sugar until smooth. In a separate bowl or cup, stir the baking powder, nutmeg or mace, and allspice into the flour. With the blender whirling, gradually sprinkle the flour mixture into the corn mixture. When that is well blended, add the rest of the corn and whirl just long enough to break up the corn a little. The texture of the batter should be coarse.

Pour the batter into the oiled baking pan and cover it with aluminum foil, sealing the edges tightly. Place the baking pan into a larger baking pan and pour boiling water into the larger pan until it reaches halfway up the side of the maize pudding pan. Bake for about 1½ hours, until a knife inserted in the middle comes out clean.

To serve, either spoon the maize pudding directly from the baking pan or, about 5 minutes after taking it from the oven, loosen the edges by sliding a knife around the inside rim of the baking pan. Invert it onto a serving platter. Serve warm.

# *Peanut Sauce*

So many African meals and snacks are spiced up with peanut sauces that I've included one here for you to use in any number of ways. Peanut sauce is used as a base for stews or soups, as an accompaniment to starches, and as a dip for fritters and grilled or deep-fried vegetables. In Nigeria, Ghana, and Sierra Leone, roasted poultry is rarely served without peanut sauce. Peanut sauce makes a quick and nutritious meal served on rice or millet and steamed vegetables (try cabbage, broccoli, and carrots).

## YIELDS 4 CUPS

2 cups chopped onions
1 tablespoon peanut oil
¼ teaspoon cayenne or other ground
    dried chiles (or to taste)
¼ teaspoon ground ginger

1 very ripe banana, mashed
1 cup tomato juice
½ cup apple or apricot juice
½ cup peanut butter (see page 673)
½ teaspoon salt (or to taste)

Sauté the onions in the oil until translucent. Mix in the cayenne, ginger, and mashed banana and sauté, stirring often, for 5 minutes. Add the juices and simmer for 10 minutes. Stir in the peanut butter and salt to taste. Keep the peanut sauce warm on a heat diffuser until ready to serve.

Make a double batch of peanut sauce and refrigerate the leftovers. Peanut sauce will keep refrigerated for two to three weeks. Reheat gently before serving.

*Note: Deep-frying is an art, but one that once learned produces delicious, light, not greasy, foods. What you're aiming for is a high enough temperature to seal the outside of the food, without overcooking it before the inside is done. If the temperature is too low, the food will cook, but will be sodden with oil. If you have a thermometer, maintain a temperature of between 350° and 375° for most foods. If you don't have a thermometer, one way to test the temperature is to drop in a 1-inch cube of bread. It should turn golden brown in 45 to 60 seconds. Because it is important to maintain the temperature, either use deep oil (several inches) or fry only a few items at a time.*

*Peanut, soybean, and safflower oils are all good for deep-frying because they have a high smoking temperature, so you can fry at a higher temperature without scorching the oil and less oil penetrates the food. After frying, the oil should be cooled, strained, and stored in the refrigerator. It can be reused until it darkens or smokes at too low a temperature, which will eventually happen because of impurities from frying.*

# Fried Sweet Potatoes
## or Plantains

 Fried sweet potatoes, plantains, and yams are found throughout Africa. Vendors tend bubbling black cauldrons in the noisy, colorful marketplaces frying fritters or these tasty snacks. People eat these treats on the spot or wrap them in cloth and hurry them home to family and friends.

Usually fried sweet potatoes or plantains are just sprinkled with salt or with hot sauce (Tabasco is perfect) and salt. Sometimes they are coated with cayenne and/or powdered ginger before frying and then salted. For sweet snacks they're sprinkled with sugar and cinnamon or topped with chocolate sauce.

*peanut, soybean, or safflower oil for*     *sweet potatoes or ripe plantains*
  *deep-frying (see note)*

Heat the oil in a heavy saucepan until it's very hot, but not smoking, about 350°. Slice the sweet potatoes or peeled plantains into ¼-inch rounds. Fry the slices, a few at a time, until they are golden and crisp on the outside but still soft on the inside. Turn them if necessary to brown on both sides. If fried too long, the golden color won't darken much, but the inside will toughen, so try a couple of test pieces first to determine the optimum timing. Remove them with a slotted spoon and drain on paper towels.

# Minted Cucumber-Yogurt Refresher

 This simple raita is delicious, refreshing, easy to prepare, and just the thing for curries or other spicy dishes. It's also good with anything else for summer suppers or picnics.

### SERVES 4 TO 6

2 cucumbers, peeled, seeded, and
   shredded, diced, or sliced
1 cup plain yogurt
1 scallion (white and green parts),
   minced or thinly sliced

1 tablespoon chopped fresh mint ($\frac{1}{2}$
   teaspoon dried)

Combine all the ingredients. For the best flavor refrigerate for at least an hour before serving. Serve chilled.

# *Banana Chutney*

This simple banana condiment is simply delicious. Its fullness of flavor is dependent upon very ripe bananas that are soft and sweet with dark brown or black skins. If you must use slightly green or just ripe bananas, add a little sugar. A hint of cinnamon or allspice is also nice in this chutney.

Serve banana chutney with curries or Tofu Bobotie (see page 32). Enjoy it also as a welcome complement to fiery West African dishes. My family likes it best spread on toast for breakfast.

### YIELDS 1 ½ CUPS

*2 or 3 very ripe bananas (1 ½ cups mashed)*
*2 tablespoons fresh lemon juice*

*1 teaspoon freshly grated lemon rind*
*2 pinches ground cloves*

Mash the bananas with a fork or potato masher, but not too thoroughly. Leave a few lumps. Place the mashed bananas in a small, nonreactive saucepan. Add the lemon juice, lemon rind, and cloves. Bring the mixture to a boil and then simmer gently, stirring occasionally, for about 15 minutes. Use a heat diffuser if needed to prevent sticking. While simmering, the bananas will slowly heave up into mounds and then spout little puffs of steam, like simmering oatmeal.

Pour the chutney into a clean jar, cover, and refrigerate. It will keep in the refrigerator for a couple of weeks.

# E X T R A S

## *Rusks*

Rusks are hard, very dry biscuits, originally prepared in South

Africa by the Dutch for traveling long distances in a hot climate.

Rusks were a bread that wouldn't spoil. Now, all over South

Africa, rusks are eaten as snacks, dipped in coffee, tea, or milk. In the cities, many different varieties of commercially baked rusks are available. There are raisin, chocolate chip, almond, peanut, and probably soon, oat-bran rusks.

Rusks can become habit-forming. My family now wants a steady supply to have for breakfast and to take along on outings for snacks. My favorite rusks are the basic version below. If you like them as much as we do, maybe soon you'll be trying some variations of your own.

2 cups unbleached white flour

2 cups whole wheat bread flour (see
    note)

1/3 cup sugar

1/2 teaspoon salt

2 teaspoons baking powder

1 teaspoon cinnamon

1/2 cup melted butter

2 eggs

3/4 cup buttermilk

2 teaspoons pure vanilla extract

2 teaspoons pure almond extract

Preheat the oven to 400°.

In a large mixing bowl, thoroughly mix the dry ingredients. Combine all the wet ingredients, pour them into the dry ingredients, and stir until you have a soft dough, similar to biscuit dough.

Turn the dough onto a well-floured surface and roll or pat it to about a 1/2-inch thickness. Cut the dough into rectangles about 2 x 4 inches.

Bake the rusks about 2 inches apart on buttered baking sheets for about 25 minutes until the tops are crisping and browning a little. Now, eat a few "soft" rusks warm from the oven.

Loosely pile the rusks on a baking sheet and keep them in a 200° oven all day or all night (about twelve hours) to dry. The finished rusks should be very dry and hard. Cool and store in an airtight container. Rusks will keep for weeks.

## Variations

Oatmeal-raisin rusks: reduce the white flour to 1 1/2 cups and add 2 cups rolled oats and
    1/2 cup currants or chopped raisins.

Almond rusks: Add 1 cup chopped almonds and omit the cinnamon.

Peanut rusks: Add 1 cup coarsely chopped peanuts.

Anise rusks: Omit the cinnamon and almond extract and add 2 teaspoons pure anise
    extract or 1 tablespoon anisette.

> Note: Coarsely ground whole wheat flour provides the best texture. If you're using whole wheat pastry flour, add a couple of tablespoons of wheat germ or bran.

# South African Milk Tart

·

# Melktert

 Melkterts are the quintessential Afrikaans dessert. The melktert is to South Africa as apple pie is to America.

The crust given here is light and puffy. I suggest rolling it out to fit a baking sheet or pizza pan, but if you use a smaller or larger pan, it will still be fine—thicker, thinner, larger, smaller, oddly shaped, or crudely made are all okay. In South Africa, melktert is sometimes made with puff pastry.

**SERVES 12**

**CRUST**

2½ cups unbleached white flour, plus extra for rolling

2 teaspoons baking powder

¼ teaspoon salt

1 cup butter

1 cup sour cream

**CUSTARD**

2 cups milk

½ cup sugar

¼ cup unbleached white flour

5 eggs

¼ teaspoon salt

1 teaspoon pure vanilla extract

1 teaspoon pure almond extract

_____

2 teaspoons cinnamon

½ cup brown sugar

Preheat the oven to 400°.

For the crust, combine the flour, baking powder, and salt in a large bowl. Cut in the butter with a pastry cutter or knife until the flour resembles coarse cornmeal. Stir in the sour cream to form a soft dough. Dust the dough with flour and form it into a ball.

On a generously floured surface, roll out the dough to fit an 11x13-inch baking sheet or a 14-inch round pizza pan. It will be thicker than a usual pie crust. Carefully lift the dough and lay it out flat on the unoiled pan. Crimp the edges by pinching them to form a rim. Pierce the dough with a fork in several places. Bake for 25 to 30 minutes until crisp and golden.

Meanwhile, make the custard by heating the milk to boiling. Combine the sugar, flour, eggs, and salt in a blender. When the milk begins to foam, pour it slowly into the whirling blender. Pour the custard back into the saucepan. Cook over medium heat, stirring constantly, for 3 to 5 minutes, until thickened. Remove from the heat, and stir in the vanilla and almond extracts. Set aside.

When the crust has baked, spread the custard filling evenly over it. Generously sprinkle the top with cinnamon and brown sugar. Return the tart to the oven for about 15 minutes, until the brown sugar melts and the top of the custard is firm.

Serve the milk tart warm or cold.

# *Ginger Soft Drink*

Many variations of homemade ginger beers (soft drinks) are brewed all over sub-Saharan Africa. Fresh ginger makes a spicy drink, cooling in summer, warming in winter, and always refreshing and energizing. Fruit juices other than the citrus called for below, such as pineapple, apricot, or guava, make interesting variations in its flavor. When using other fruits, I always add the juice of a couple of limes or lemons.

This recipe makes a concentrate that can be diluted with plain or sparkling water. Make a batch and try it—if you like it, you'll love it.

### YIELDS 3 QUARTS OF CONCENTRATE

| | |
|---|---|
| *6 cups boiling water* | |
| *1 cup grated peeled fresh ginger root* | *½ cup fresh lime or lemon juice* |
| *1 cup sugar* | *1 cup orange juice* |
| *2 teaspoons whole cloves* | *8 cups cool water* |
| *4 cinnamon sticks* | |

Pour the boiling water over the grated ginger root, sugar, cloves, and cinnamon in a large nonreactive pot or bowl (enamel, glass, or stainless steel). Cover and set aside in a warm place, in the sun if possible, for at least an hour.

Strain the liquid through a fine sieve or a cloth. Add the juices and water. Set aside in a warm place for another hour or so. Gently strain the liquid again, taking care not to disturb the sediment at the bottom. Store in the refrigerator in a large nonreactive container. A glass gallon jar or jug works well.

Serve warm, chilled, or on ice, either as is or diluted with water or sparkling water. A squeeze of fresh lime juice in each glass of ginger drink is the cat's meow.

LAURA WARD BRANCA

# Armenia

## and the

## Middle

## East

# INTRODUCTION

*And three apples fell from the sky; one for the*

*one who told this story, one for the one who*

*listened to it, and one for the rest of the world,*

*to make us all happy.*

*—Old Folk Tale*

I'm an African-Armenian American born in Brooklyn, New York. I began working at Moosewood in 1979 and became a member of the collective in 1980. I have two sons, Matt and Dan.

It seems fitting that I begin with my various group identities. Both sides of my lineage have histories of persecution, forced removal from their homelands, and the struggle to gain a foothold and voice in a new culture. Both the Africans and the Armenians are survivors of a diaspora. In tracing their painful journeys I have rediscovered that we indeed have rich histories and ancient roots and that our peoples have contributed much worth honoring, sharing, and passing along to those who follow.

My mother, Mary Sangigian Ward, is a first generation Armenian-American. Her family's story follows. This chapter is dedicated to her and includes many of her reminiscences and recipes.

My father, Theodore Ward, was born in Thibodeaux, Louisiana, one of eleven children of Louise Pierre Ward and John Ward, who was born a slave and became a teacher. My father was a pioneer among black playwrights, creating thirty-one plays, numerous short stories, poems, and librettos in his lifetime of eighty years. He was also an excellent cook, and our family might eat my mother's dolma, pilav, and *madzoon* (yogurt) one night, and his chicken fricassee and peach pie the next.

Culture is not inherited through one's genes. It has to be intentionally, consciously transmitted by one person to another, or it will die. If we don't sing the songs, tell the stories, and make the foods that are dear to us, our children won't know what they've missed, but I think they'll miss it just the same. I'm forever grateful to my people for having survived, and I'm especially thankful for my parents, because they knew how important it was to share their histories with me and my sister, Elise, along with their deep-seated belief in the goodness of all people and their unshakable faith in the possibility of peace and prosperity for the world.

I in my turn want to share a little of the Armenian side of the family with you and to express my admiration for the beautiful peoples of the Middle East, among whom many Armenians found refuge and safe new homes.

The region called the Middle East begins on the southern and eastern shores of the Mediterranean and Aegean seas, encompassing the Fertile Crescent of the Levant, where it is said that agriculture began. It stretches eastward through what was once Mesopotamia, the "Cradle of Civilization," which lies between the Tigris and Euphrates rivers and is now known as Iraq. The Middle East reaches across the Persian Gulf and Iran to Afghanistan, and south to include the lands on the eastern shore of the Red Sea and the northwestern shore of the Indian Ocean. The Middle East curves around to the south and west to include the countries of North Africa along the southern Mediterranean shore. In the north, the Middle East is bounded by the Black Sea, Turkey, Soviet Armenia, and the Caspian Sea. Here in ancient Armenia, Noah's ark came to rest on Mount Ararat, still the powerful source of spiritual inspiration to Armenians no matter where we have made our homes since the diaspora.

Ancient Armenia encompassed a large portion of what is now eastern Turkey, a section of northwestern Iran, and a region in the north that stretched from the Black Sea to the Caspian Sea. Strategically located along significant military and trade routes, Armenia was overrun repeatedly throughout the centuries. Yet, despite subjugation and plunder, the Armenian culture flourished with extraordinary expression through unusual architecture, metalworking, ceramics, the weaving of fine fabrics and carpets, and extensive literature, arts, and sciences. The Armenian language is an independent branch of the Indo-European languages and has its own alphabet. Armenia was the first nation in the world to embrace Christianity as its official religion, in 381 A.D., and this religious faith has been a source of remarkable strength and unity for the people.

My grandparents, Verzhin (Virginia) Chalian Sangigian and Khatchatour Sangigian, were born in Armenia in the late nineteenth century. My grandfather came from the town of Zeitoon, famous for the endurance and fighting spirit of its fierce warriors. My grandmother came from Marash, another city whose people made a heroic resistance against the Turks. They were both fortunate to have escaped the Turkish Massacres and mass deportations that occurred between 1894 and 1923, which took the lives of most in their families and, indeed, close to two million Armenians. The Armenians have resettled throughout the countries of the Middle East, North Africa, Europe, and the United States, some even as far away as Singapore and Rangoon. What had been Russian

Armenia became a republic of the U.S.S.R. in 1918. The cities of Marash and Zeitoon were within the area of historic Armenia that was swallowed up by Turkey.

My grandmother's family were merchants in Marash and, unlike the majority of Armenians, who are members of the Armenian Orthodox Church, they were Roman Catholics. There's a photograph in my mother's album of a family gathering of these handsome, olive-skinned people. Each man wears a fez, baggy pantaloons, and a snug jacket. My great-grandfather has a huge moustache and an incredible snarling scowl on his face. The women are beautiful, petite, and dark, except for my great-grandmother, who had blue eyes. My grandmother is the tiny infant in the photo. At the age of five, she and several other little girls and boys were sent by their parents out of Armenia to Recanati, Italy, in order to escape the massacres. They never saw their families again.

The children were brought up in Catholic boarding schools with boys and girls on opposite sides of a huge courtyard. There my grandmother learned to write poetry and to appreciate Italian opera; she was taught to embroider, make lace, and sew a fine seam. On the assumption that she would marry a man of some means, she learned how to instruct her future servants about what to prepare for supper. She expected to limit her food preparation to tasting the sauce and telling the cook to make some adjustments.

In 1910 she came to the United States on the promise of marrying an Armenian husband. The marriage was arranged, probably through the Armenian Benevolent Association. They settled in Bridgeport, Connecticut, where there was a small colony of Armenians from Zeitoon.

My grandfather was a silversmith, continuing a tradition of metalworking that Armenians began by mining and smelting metals on the slopes of Ararat 5,000 years ago. We don't know how he came to the United States, but we know that he traveled all across this country and went as far as Vancouver. He was a highly principled person involved in Armenian political activities aimed at humanitarian relief and self-determination for Armenians back home. My grandfather had no formal education, yet with my grandmother's help he taught himself to read and write English as well as the Turkish and Armenian he had spoken all his life. In turn, he taught her to speak Turkish. He read the Armenian newspapers and spent his spare money on his cherished Armenian history books. It's very likely that it was he who taught his wife how to cook Armenian food, because, of course, she had grown up speaking Italian and eating Italian food.

My mother, Mary, was the eldest of their seven children. She was christened Mariam Sangigian, and the Italian midwife who delivered her wrote her name as Mariano Sangigiano on her birth certificate. But like all the members of her family and so many other immigrants and their children, her name was Americanized.

Grandma made the family's clothes and Grandpa cobbled their shoes and cut their hair. Grandma identified herself as an Armenian, but also maintained her connections to and affinity for Italians all her life. Grandpa, however, always remained strongly identified as an Armenian and never assimilated. Once when she was very young and away from home, my mother received a letter from him. He knew that she could understand spoken Armenian, though she couldn't read the Armenian alphabet. He couldn't express himself very well in English, but he could write using this alphabet. He wrote the letter in Armenian by painstakingly spelling the words phonetically, using the English alphabet. My mother has long since forgotten the content of that letter but not the ingenuity of his effort to bridge two cultures to communicate with her.

When my mother reminisces about her childhood, the foods eaten are always recalled along with the people and occasions. Her family ate a lot of fish. They also ate meat, but never in large portions; inexpensive cuts of beef and lamb were roasted along with vegetables or used to flavor stews and soups. My mother grew up on vegetables, fruits, whole grains, and *madzoon,* and these are still her diet today.

Once the family had moved to New York City, at Christmastime they often attended midnight mass. After the beautiful candlelit service, Grandma would take the children over to see Auntie Tina, one of her classmates from boarding school, for nuts, cakes, and late-night good times. At New Year's, Armenians enjoy an ancient tradition: a pudding called anoush abour, prepared from wheat, apricots, almonds, and raisins to represent the four seasons.

The family's favorite summertime drink was called tan or ayran, a refreshing mixture of *madzoon* and ice water. My mother's afternoon snacks were things like crusty bread toasted in the oven with butter or olive oil, or slices of eggplant, scored with a knife, rubbed with olive oil, sprinkled with minced garlic, and then roasted in the oven. Marvelous! There was a cold, unheated room in the apartment where crocks of tourshu, or pickled vegetables, stood. She would run in there after school and tear off leaves of whole pickled cabbage. Sweet treats were rare, perhaps an occasional ice-cream cone, halvah, chewy St. John's bread, or apricot leather. The family bought keteh, crispy bread rings, stacked on wooden sticks, from Armenian vendors on Twenty-third Street in Manhattan. They drank Turkish coffee, and afterward Grandma told each person's fortune by inverting demitasse cups and reading the pattern left by the grounds. Grandpa kept a bottle of raki in the house, an extremely potent distilled liquor made from raisins and anise seed, and red wine was served with meals.

Grandma had a truly adventurous and daring spirit. During Prohibition when my mother was a young girl, she remembers coming home from school and discovering a strong aroma coming from the family's apartment building. Upstairs, Grandma was operating a homemade raki still in the kitchen. "Mama!" my mother cried, "you can smell this out on the street, all over the neighborhood. The police are gonna arrest you!" But Grandma went on undaunted.

Another time, my mother arrived home and, as she entered the building, she thought she heard gun shots in rapid fire. Grandma came reeling and running down the stairs, her white apron covered with crimson stains, clutching her sides and her heart and groaning, wild-eyed. "Mama! Who shot you?" She was too overcome to answer. Together they bravely climbed the stairs after the shots had stopped. There in the kitchen the cupboard doors stood open where twenty bottles of red wine had popped their corks at Grandma. She had corked them too soon, and the wine had continued to ferment on the shelves till one hot day the pressure built up and forced them to open fire on her in a grisly assault.

Grandma tasted everything as she prepared a meal. And like her, I pop bits of raw vegetables, shreds of cheese, a spoonful of broth or sauce into my mouth, testing with my fingers and teeth to see if the food is tender and done. By the time I've nibbled browned bits of onion and adjusted the spices and everything has been seasoned exactly to my taste, I'm seldom hungry enough to eat any more. Grandma too would put the food on the table and be quite unable to eat.

I also inherited my grandmother's style of cooking. With the exception of tricky cakes or pastry, I don't like to measure, time, or use recipes. Developing the recipes here has been a difficult process, but I know that "a pinch of this and a handful of that" is unnervingly vague and bewildering for people who have no idea how a new dish is supposed to look or taste. However, I encourage you to experiment with the seasonings and make your own adjustments as you go. By becoming familiar with the ingredients and seasonings characteristic of the Middle East, you can then design your own dishes with them. Most of the dishes in this chapter are inspired by and derived from many versions I've tried and then adapted to my liking. I don't claim that they're all strictly authentic.

It's true that some Middle Easterners use alcohol, and that Armenians produce wine, brandy, cognac, and raki from their wonderful vineyards and orchards. However, the Middle East is largely Islamic, and it's against Islamic dietary laws to use alcohol, so many recipes don't call for it. None of the ones in this chapter do.

You will find that many North African, Balkan, and Sephardic dishes in our book are very compatible with the foods included in this chapter. The ingredients and cooking methods are similar, and with a little cross-cultural menu planning you can create exciting combinations.

Nothing stings quite like the sense that aspects of one's culture have been stolen and claimed by others. If I've failed to accurately give the national origin of these recipes, forgive me for not giving credit where credit is due. This area of the world has been a crossroads where cultural customs and favorite foods were carried off by travelers and transplanted, fortunately for us, to such unlikely places as Bridgeport, Brooklyn, and Ithaca.

# Mezze *or* Maza

*When you want to eat, just spread this magic cloth and you will eat forever.*

*—Old Folk Tale*

*Mezze* or *Maza* are appetizers. They are served throughout Middle Eastern communities, either before a larger meal or as a meal themselves. *Mezze* can be eaten any time of the day or night accompanied by drinks. Literally all of the dishes in this chapter could be served as *mezze* in smaller quantities or scaled-down versions so that people will have room to sample a little of everything. The possible array of *mezze* is limited only by your resources and your imagination.

Typically, *mezze* include plain yogurt and a bowl or platter of fresh herbs. Scallions, chives, mint, tarragon, parsley, dill, and coriander, either in sprigs or chopped, are served with pita bread. Sometimes almonds or walnuts are chopped up and mixed with the herbs, or the nuts might be offered separately in little bowls.

You can try combinations of puréed dips, marinated beans and vegetables, soups, salads, olives, pickles and relishes, pilavs and grain salads, cheese, hot miniature stuffed pastries, stuffed vegetables and vine leaves, cold fish, perhaps served with a taratour sauce and lemon wedges, hard-boiled eggs, steamed vegetables with garlicky dressings, fresh and dried fruits, and dainty sweet pastries. Frequently, hearty, vegetable-filled omelets called eggah are served warm or chilled and cut into small pieces. Hot croquettes like felafels or ta'amia are always popular, served with tahini dressing or a hot sauce.

Sumptuous repasts like these can be expensive and are time consuming to prepare. Bear in mind that the creation of a fabulous array of *mezze* was usually the result of many women in an extended family working together and sharing wisdom, advice, and a little gossip. It's fun cooking this way with friends.

To serve *mezze,* spread a cloth before low couches or cushions, or use large trays, either with folding legs or balanced on low stools. The traditional trays are copper, brass, or silver and beautifully ornamented with etched or embossed designs and inlayed with a metal of contrasting color. Set the trays with assorted dishes within arm's reach of all of your guests. Bring them water and a clean hand towel and offer them food. When they politely refuse, as is the custom, wheedle and tempt them until they weaken. The *mezze* table along with strong Turkish coffee, spearmint tea, or iced fruit drinks will lure you into the pleasures of cheerful conversation and sensual delights that can last for hours. This is life as it should be lived, lingering and savoring the fruits of loving hands.

# *Sample* Mezze *Menus*

These sample *mezze* menus include dishes from this chapter and the North African, Jewish, and Eastern European chapters. Items in roman can be purchased, items in italic can be found in this book, and those with an asterisk can be prepared ahead and served cold.

### ELABORATE MEZZE

Pita

Yogurt

Olives

*Syrian Salad**

*Sambussa*

*Davina's Fish Koklaten*

Pickled Vegetables

*Rice Pilav with Orzo*

*Roasted Chile and Tomato Relish**

*Fritada Espinaca**

*Halvah Shortbread**

*Turkish Coffee*

### WARM WEATHER MEZZE *(everything made ahead and served cold)*

Pita

Olives and Pepperoncini

*Black Bean Ful*

Hard-Cooked Eggs

Tabouli

Cold Baked or Poached Fish

Steamed Peppers, Carrots, Asparagus, and Potatoes

*Taratour Sauce*

*Fig and Apricot Conserve*

Plain Yogurt

### SPICY SOUTHERN MEZZE

Pita and Chopped Nuts

Marinated Artichoke Hearts*

*Puréed White Bean Dip**

*Roasted Chile and Tomato Relish**

*Topig with Tahini Dressing**

*Baked Fish Nicosia*

*Oven-Roasted Vegetables*

*Stuffed Figs and Dates**

**Pita, Scallions, and Olives**
*Miniature Beureks with Parsley-Cheese Filling*
*Jajoukh°*
*Fried Batilgian*
*Bulghur Pilav*
*Fassoulia*
*Slovenian Almond Apricot Bread°*
**Spearmint Tea**

**Green Salad with** *Feta Garlic Dressing°*
*Stewed Batilgian*
**Stuffed Grape Leaves**
*Macedonian Cottage Cheese Croquettes*
*Bulghur Pilav*
*Ukrainian Almond Crescents°*

TYPICAL FAVORITE MEZZE

**Pita**
*Lebanese Vegetable Soup*
**Hummus°**
**Falafels with** *Tahini Dressing*
**Grape Leaves with Tahini Dressing**
**Green Olives and Pepperoncini**
*Eggplant Coucharas*
*Shereh Pilav*
*Paklava°*
*Turkish Coffee*

# Roasted Chile and Tomato Relish

Chiles vary a lot in appearance, size, and intensity. This relish is intended to be spicy but not unbearable. I know of no way to predict how hot yours will turn out to be. If you're cautious, you can combine the tomatoes, sweet pepper, and other ingredients first, and then add the minced chiles little by little until you reach the desired hotness. See the introduction to the Mexican chapter for methods of handling hot peppers.

**SERVES 6 AS AN APPETIZER**
**YIELDS 2½ CUPS**

*2 green chiles (2–3 inches long)*
*1 small bell pepper (green, red, or*
  *yellow)*
*2 large ripe tomatoes*
*3 tablespoons olive oil*
*2–3 tablespoons fresh lemon juice*

*1 teaspoon ground cumin seeds*
*1 teaspoon ground fennel seeds*
*½ cup chopped fresh parsley*
*salt to taste*

Roast or bake the chiles and bell pepper to remove the outer skins.

*To roast:* Using a long-handled serving fork, hold each chile or pepper in the flame of a gas stove burner. Slowly turn to char the skin.

*To bake:* Place the chiles and pepper in a 550° oven for about 15 to 20 minutes. Turn them several times until they are evenly charred.

Place the roasted or baked chiles and pepper in a covered bowl to cool for several minutes. The steam that gathers in the bowl will help make the skins easy to peel. Split the chiles and pepper and peel off the charred outer layer. Remove the stems and seeds.

Finely mince the chiles and dice the bell pepper. Dice the tomatoes and combine them with the chiles and pepper, oil, lemon juice, spices, and parsley. Salt to taste.

Serve chilled on little plates with wedges of warm pita bread to scoop up the relish.

# Topig

·

# Little Balls

This is my adaptation of a dish served during Lent. The little balls are prepared in large batches for church luncheons. They can be made in various sizes, and some versions are wrapped in big handkerchiefs or cheesecloth and dropped into boiling water. This untraditional recipe calls for coating with beaten egg and browning them in a skillet. They're a little time consuming but delicious, and the combination of nuts and whole grain makes them high in protein. They're good hot or cold as appetizers with Tahini Dressing (see page 68) or yogurt or served with green salad, soup, and Roasted Chile and Tomato Relish (see page 61).

### SERVES 6 TO 8

*1 cup raw bulghur*
*2 cups boiling water*
*3 potatoes, peeled and chopped*

---

*2 cups chopped onions*
*⅓ cup olive oil*
*½ cup pine nuts*
*½ cup walnuts, finely chopped*
*1 teaspoon cinnamon*
*1 teaspoon ground allspice*

*salt and ground black pepper to taste*
*1 cup raisins or currants*

---

*1 tablespoon honey*

---

*1 egg beaten with a dash of salt and cinnamon*

---

*¼ cup butter for frying*
*2 tablespoons olive oil for frying*

Cover the bulghur with the boiling water and let it steam, covered, until the water is absorbed and the grain is tender. Boil the potatoes until tender.

Meanwhile, sauté the onions in ⅓ cup olive oil. When they are translucent and soft, mix in the nuts and spices. Add the raisins and sauté, stirring frequently. When the mixture is hot, remove it from the heat.

Drain the potatoes and mash them. Combine them with the bulghur, onion-nut mixture, and honey. Add more salt, honey, and spices to taste. When cool enough, form into little balls, about two inches in diameter.

Dip each ball into the egg, salt, and cinnamon mixture. Heat the butter and oil in a heavy skillet on medium-high heat and brown the topigs on all sides.

Serve hot or cold with yogurt and a lemon wedge or with Tahini Dressing.

## *Puréed White Bean Dip*

Rich and smooth in texture, this can be served as a first course or as a lovely addition to the *mezze* table. It looks very exotic when the pale dip is drizzled with a highly aromatic extra-virgin olive oil colored red by the paprika, studded with capers, and served in a red, green, or blue ceramic dish.

### Serves 4 to 6

2 cups dried white beans (navy, pea, or
    great northern)
6 cups salted water (or half water and
    half vegetable stock, see page 685)

――――――――――――――――

1/3 cup extra-virgin olive oil
1/3 cup fresh lemon juice
4 garlic cloves, pressed
1/2 teaspoon ground cumin seeds

salt and ground black pepper to taste
1/4 teaspoon cayenne

――――――――――――――――

2 tablespoons capers
2 tablespoons olive oil mixed with 1/2
    teaspoon sweet Hungarian paprika
lemon wedges
warmed pita bread, cut into wedges

Soak the beans overnight and then drain them. Cover with 6 cups of salted water and cook about an hour until very tender. Drain the beans, reserving the cooking liquid; you should have about 5 or 6 cups of beans. Purée the beans in batches in a blender or food processor with the oil, lemon juice, and garlic. Add a little of the reserved cooking liquid if necessary for a creamy and smooth consistency. Add the cumin, salt, pepper, and cayenne.

Spread the dip in a shallow dish or serve in individual small bowls. Garnish with a sprinkling of capers and a drizzle of the paprika–olive oil. Serve with lemon wedges and warmed pita bread.

# Black Bean Ful

Years ago two of my friends and I had spent three days in a grueling July heat wave painting a house in Allentown, Pennsylvania. Upon completion, we celebrated our liberation, clean and free at last, by feasting at a wonderful Middle Eastern restaurant the name of which I've forgotten. This was my introduction to Black Bean Ful, which is really a misnomer for this wonderful stuff.

Traditionally, ful is an Egyptian dish made with fava beans. If you can find fresh green favas, try them. Evidently, good favas must have been hard to come by in Allentown, so these folks substituted black turtle beans.

I've forgotten everything else we ate that evening but the pleasure of the cool, dimly lit room and the dish of tender black beans, the brilliant red of summer tomatoes, and the liberal garnishing of parsley and lemon.

### SERVES 6

2 cups dried black turtle beans (or 4–5 cups fresh favas)
8 cups water

_____

1/4–1/2 cup olive oil
4–5 garlic cloves, pressed
1/2 cup fresh lemon juice (or to taste)
salt and freshly ground black pepper to taste

1 1/2 cups chopped fresh tomatoes
1 cup chopped fresh parsley

_____

1 lemon, cut into 6 wedges

_____

several hard-boiled eggs, sliced or in wedges (optional)

Soak the dried black turtle beans in the water for several hours or overnight.

Cook the soaked beans in fresh water to cover for 1 1/2 to 2 hours until tender (cook fresh favas until just tender). Drain the cooked beans while they're still hot and toss them with the olive oil, garlic, and lemon juice. The warm beans will readily absorb the flavors. Add plenty of salt and black pepper to taste. Stir in half of the tomatoes and parsley.

Taste the ful. It should be lemony and garlicky, not bland. Add more lemon if necessary. Turn the ful into a warm serving bowl and top it with the rest of the tomatoes and parsley and garnish it with lemon wedges and hard-boiled eggs if you like.

Served warm, the aroma of the garlic, olive oil, and lemon will be intoxicating, but the dish is excellent chilled or at room temperature as well. Ful can be served as an appetizer or side dish with Dolma (see page 72) or sarma, or for a simple lunch with the hard-boiled egg and tossed salad.

# *Jajoukh*

•

# *Cucumbers in Yogurt*

A wonderfully refreshing side salad, this jajoukh is more highly seasoned than some more traditional versions. Cucumbers in yogurt appear in many cuisines, from India and West Africa to Greece and Finland. No fewer than five of my colleagues submitted delicious variations on the theme. But I have a reputation for Armenian stubbornness and I made sure this recipe would be included.

### SERVES 4 TO 6

*2 cucumbers, peeled and thinly sliced*
*3 tablespoons chopped fresh parsley*
*1 tablespoon dried dill (3 tablespoons chopped fresh)*
*1½ cups plain yogurt*
*2–3 tablespoons fresh lemon juice (or to taste)*

*1 tablespoon olive oil*
*3 large garlic cloves, minced or pressed*
*1 teaspoon freshly ground black pepper*
*¾ teaspoon salt*

Toss all ingredients together and chill.

# Syrian Salad

1 head romaine lettuce

1 cucumber, thinly sliced

5 radishes, thinly sliced

1 red bell pepper, seeded and sliced

1 green bell pepper, seeded and sliced

2 large tomatoes, cut into wedges

2 scallions, chopped

1 small red onion, sliced

3 ounces feta cheese, sliced or crumbled

½ cup stemmed fresh parsley, coarsely
chopped

several black olives

2 tablespoons capers (optional)

DRESSING

¼ cup olive oil

juice of 1 lemon

1 tablespoon wine vinegar

1 garlic clove, pressed

salt and freshly ground black pepper to
taste

pinch of dried mint

Rinse the romaine, tear it into bite-sized pieces, and place it in a salad bowl. Arrange the other vegetables attractively over the romaine, topping with the feta, parsley, olives, and capers, if desired.

Combine the oil, lemon juice, vinegar, garlic, salt, pepper, and mint. Drizzle the dressing over the salad.

# *Taratour Sauce*

This is an "eggless mayonnaise" that's good on baked or broiled fish or served with steamed and raw vegetables. Carrots, bell peppers, potatoes, and artichokes are especially good with Taratour Sauce. It's rich and garlicky, and you may like just a dab, or a dollop. This recipe makes a large quantity, and it will keep well in the refrigerator for ten days.

### YIELDS 4 GENEROUS CUPS

*4 garlic cloves, pressed*
*1 teaspoon Dijon mustard*
*juice of 2 lemons*
*1 cup olive oil*
*1½ cups pine nuts or blanched almonds*
  *(or a combination of both)*

*2 cups water*
*2 cups crumbled, soft French or Italian*
  *bread*
*salt and freshly ground black pepper to*
  *taste*

In a blender, grind the garlic, mustard, lemon juice, olive oil, and nuts with 1 cup of the water. Add the bread and slowly pour in the remaining cup of water, blending until the ingredients form a thick sauce the consistency of mayonnaise. Season with salt and pepper.

Serve the sauce, at room temperature or chilled, on baked fish or steamed vegetables.

# Feta Garlic Dressing

A brilliant invention created by Linda Dickinson, the "dean" of Moosewood cooking, Feta Garlic Dressing is quickly becoming the favorite salad dressing of the Moosewood cognoscenti. Serve it on crisp greens and raw vegetables and then pass the after-dinner mints—this isn't for the fainthearted.

### YIELDS ABOUT 3½ CUPS

1 cup olive oil

2–3 tablespoons vinegar

2–3 garlic cloves, pressed

1 teaspoon dried dill weed

salt and freshly ground black pepper to taste

1½ cups grated feta cheese

1 cup milk or buttermilk

In a blender or food processor, whirl all the ingredients except the milk, or buttermilk, for one minute. With the blender running, slowly pour in the milk. As soon as the dressing thickens, turn off the blender or the dressing will separate and become runny. It should be thick and creamy. Chill at least 30 minutes so the flavors meld.

Refrigerated and tightly covered, Feta Garlic Dressing will stay fresh for three or four days. If the dressing separates, simple reblend it.

# Tahini Dressing

### YIELDS 3½ CUPS

¼ cup extra-virgin olive oil

¾ cup soy or other vegetable oil

¼ cup red wine vinegar

¼ cup fresh lemon juice

5 garlic cloves, chopped

¼ teaspoon cayenne

1½ teaspoons ground cumin seeds

1 teaspoon salt

1 cup tahini

——————————————————

1 cup water

Place all the ingredients except the water in a blender or food processor and begin to whirl them together. Gradually add the water and blend until you have a thick, creamy dressing. Refrigerated and tightly sealed, this dressing will keep for several weeks.

# S O U P S

## *Lebanese Vegetable Soup*

This soup has a spicy kick to it. I dedicate it to my friend Anaiis

Salibian, whose family came to North America by way of Beirut.

Lebanese Vegetable Soup is quick to make if you have cooked

chick peas on hand. If not, remember to soak the chick peas ahead of time.

### SERVES 8 GENEROUSLY

*1 large Spanish onion, chopped (about
    2 cups)*

*2 tablespoons olive oil*

*3 medium-large carrots, chopped (2½
    cups)*

*¼ teaspoon ground red pepper*

*1 teaspoon ground coriander seeds*

*2–4 garlic cloves, minced*

*1½ cups chopped potatoes*

*1 teaspoon salt (or to taste)*

*4–5 cups vegetable stock (see note)*

*2 large tomatoes, chopped*

*10 artichoke hearts, cut into eighths (2
    14-ounce cans)*

*¾ cup canned or cooked chick peas (see
    page 653) and the reserved cooking
    liquid*

*¼ cup chopped fresh parsley*

*2 lemons, cut into wedges*

> *Note: For stock, use a combination of vegetable stock (see page 685), the chick
> pea cooking liquid, and the artichoke heart brine or some fresh lemon juice.*

In a large soup pot, sauté the onions in the olive oil for about 5 minutes. Stir in the carrots. Cover. Stir again after 3 minutes. Add the ground red pepper, coriander, and garlic. Cover and cook for a few more minutes. Add the potatoes, salt, and 2 cups of the stock.

Cover the pot and bring the soup to a boil. Reduce the heat and simmer until the potatoes are nearly tender. Be careful not to overcook them. Gently stir in the tomatoes, artichoke hearts, and cooked chick peas. Salt to taste. Cover and simmer for 3 or 4 minutes, just to heat the tomatoes. Add the remaining 2 to 3 cups of stock or even more if a brothier soup is desired. Heat gently. It is important not to overcook or boil this soup. The potatoes, tomatoes, and artichokes should be heated just enough to blend the flavors or they might lose their shape and disintegrate. If this happens, garnish with more chopped fresh tomatoes. The soup will still taste delicious.

Sprinkle each serving with fresh parsley and garnish with a wedge of fresh lemon.

# Turkish Spinach and Lentil Soup

This is a very hearty soup, high in protein because of the combination of lentils and bulghur. Rosemary is liberally used in Turkish, Armenian, and Greek cooking, and I love it. I suggest starting with a small pinch and then adding more as you like.

1 cup dried lentils
5 cups vegetable stock (see page 685) or
    water (more if needed)
1 teaspoon salt

_____

1/4 cup olive oil
2 cups chopped onions
3 garlic cloves, pressed
1/4 teaspoon cayenne
2 bay leaves
1/2 cup raw bulghur

1/4 cup chopped fresh parsley
2 cups chopped tomatoes
1/4 cup tomato paste
pinch of dried rosemary (or to taste)
salt and freshly ground black pepper to
    taste

_____

2 cups stemmed, cleaned, and coarsely
    chopped fresh spinach

_____

chopped fresh parsley

Rinse the lentils. Bring them to a boil in the salted stock or water. Reduce the heat and simmer, covered, for 40 minutes.

Meanwhile, heat the olive oil in a heavy soup pot. Sauté the onions until translucent. Add the garlic, cayenne, bay leaves, and raw bulghur. Stir the mixture on medium heat until the onions and bulghur are lightly browned.

Mix in the parsley and tomatoes. When the tomatoes begin to give up their juice, gently stir in the tomato paste.

Pour the lentils and their liquid into the soup pot with the onions and bulghur. Simmer the soup for 15 minutes. Add the rosemary, salt, and pepper to taste. If the lentils and bulghur have absorbed too much liquid, add more stock, water, or tomato juice. Remove the bay leaves.

Just before serving, stir in the fresh spinach and let it wilt in the hot soup. Garnish with more fresh parsley and serve with crusty bread.

# ENTRÉES

## *Dolma*

·

## *Stuffed Vegetables*

"Dolma" is a word commonly used for both stuffed vegetables and stuffed grape leaves. In our family we referred to stuffed grape leaves and cabbage as "sarma," while "dolma" meant stuffed vegetables.

Dazzling red tomatoes, green and red peppers, green and yellow squash, filled with savory herbed pilav of rice, pine nuts, and walnuts are simmered in a lemony tomato sauce. My mother's stuffed vegetables are always awaited with happy anticipation. She serves dolma with her tart homemade yogurt *(madzoon)* and plenty of lemon wedges.

Dolma can be served in combination with Jajoukh (see page 65) and Fried Batilgian (see page 80). This recipe makes a large amount, enough for each person to have an assortment of two or three vegetables.

### SERVES 8

*3 cups uncooked brown rice*
*1 tablespoon olive oil*
*4¹/₂ cups water*
*pinch of salt*

---

*¹/₄ cup olive oil*
*2 large Spanish onions, chopped*
*6 large garlic cloves, pressed*
*²/₃ cup chopped fresh basil*
*1¹/₂ tablespoons dried basil*
*1¹/₂ tablespoons dried marjoram*

---

*6 ounces tomato paste*
*2 28-ounce cans whole tomatoes,*
*    chopped, and their juice*
*3–4 bay leaves*

*salt and freshly ground black pepper to*
*    taste*

---

*2 or 3 medium zucchinis*
*6 large tomatoes*
*3 green bell peppers*
*3 red bell peppers*

---

*2 cups walnuts, ground or chopped*
*1–2 cups pine nuts (or to taste)*
*juice of 1¹/₂ lemons*
*salt and ground black pepper to taste*

---

*lemon wedges*
*chopped fresh parsley*

Sauté the rice in a tablespoon of olive oil for a couple of minutes. Add the water. Cover and bring to a boil. Add a pinch of salt. Simmer on very low heat until tender. The rice can be slightly underdone; it will continue to cook in the stuffed vegetables.

In ¼ cup of olive oil, sauté the onions, garlic, and herbs until the onions are just translucent. Remove half of the onions and set them aside for the pilav filling. Add the tomato paste, the canned tomatoes and their juice, and the bay leaves to the remaining onions. Add salt and pepper to taste and simmer gently for 10 minutes.

Meanwhile, prepare the vegetables to be stuffed. It is easiest to scoop them out using a small spoon like a grapefruit spoon, an apple corer, or a vegetable reamer. Hold the vegetable firmly in your palm as you hollow it out, being careful not to break through the outer shell or bottom. Cut the zucchinis crosswise into sections about 3 inches tall. Hollow out each section, leaving a ¼-inch shell on the sides and bottom. Cut holes about 2 inches in diameter in the tops of the tomatoes; discard the tops. Carefully scoop out the tomatoes. Chop the tomato pulp and add it to the sauce. Rub the insides of the tomato shells with a little salt and lemon juice (this will help them hold their shapes). Without removing the stems, slice the tops off the peppers about ½ inch down. Remove the seeds from the peppers and their tops, which will be used as lids.

In a large mixing bowl, combine the cooked rice, sautéed onions, walnuts, and pine nuts. Add the lemon juice and season to taste with salt and black pepper.

Stuff the vegetables with the pilav. Put an inch of the sauce in the bottom of a large soup pot or Dutch oven and arrange the vegetables stuffed side up. Put the lids on the peppers. If your pot is deep enough, add another layer of vegetables on top of the first. If not, you may need two pots. Pour the remaining sauce into the pan. It should nearly cover the vegetables. Otherwise, add a little water and lemon juice. Cover tightly and gently simmer the dolma for 45 to 50 minutes, until tender.

Remove bay leaves and serve garnished with lemon wedges and parsley.

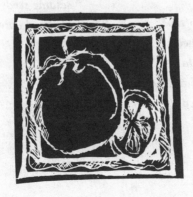

# *Beurek with Parsley-Cheese Filling*

These are savory, cheese-filled pastries. There are many, many ways to make beurek. Beurek dough can be made with baking powder or yeast, or prepared filo leaves can be used. Almost every city in the Middle East has its own special version and some of the pastry requires such time-consuming, painstaking preparation you could make a career out of it.

Somewhere in the Middle East, women are kneading, rolling, cutting, brushing, stacking, yacking, broiling, toiling, buttering, and trimming. Meanwhile, back in Ithaca, I make this simple yeasted dough that is easy to work with and the results are great. Why sweat?

### SERVES 8

**DOUGH**

¾ cup warm water

1 package dry yeast (about 1
  tablespoon)

1 teaspoon honey

2 tablespoons melted butter

1 teaspoon salt

2 cups unbleached white flour

**FILLING**

8 ounces cream cheese, softened

1 cup grated Muenster cheese

1 cup shredded mozzarella

1 cup grated feta (or about 4 ounces
  other sharp cheese, such as
  Parmesan)

2 eggs

3 garlic cloves, pressed

¾ cup chopped fresh parsley

¼ cup chopped fresh basil

freshly ground black pepper

_____

1 egg

sesame seeds (optional)

chopped chives (optional)

Combine the warm water, yeast, and honey in a mixing bowl and set aside for a few minutes, until the yeast has softened and dissolved. Add the melted butter and salt. Thoroughly stir in 1¾ cups of flour. Knead until the dough forms a ball. Continue kneading on a lightly floured surface until the dough is smooth and elastic, adding more flour if necessary. Place the dough in a lightly buttered or oiled bowl, cover with a damp cloth, and let it rise in a warm spot, for about one hour, until doubled in size.

While the dough is rising, combine the cheeses by mashing the cream cheese well with a fork or potato masher and mixing in the other cheeses. Stir in the rest of the filling ingredients.

When the dough has doubled, divide it into eight pieces. Roll the pieces of dough into smooth balls, place them on a lightly floured board, and cover for 15 minutes.

Preheat the oven to 375°.

Roll out each ball of dough into a circle about 7 inches in diameter. Place a generous ⅓ cup of cheese filling on the lower half of each circle. Moisten the lower edge of the dough with water. Fold the upper half down over the filling and press the edges together with a wet fork to seal.

Arrange the beureks on a buttered baking sheet so that their edges do not overlap. Seal any holes by pinching the dough together. Beat the egg with a tablespoon of water and brush it on the pastries to give them a nice glaze. Sprinkle the beureks with sesame seeds or chopped chives, if you like.

Bake the beureks for 15 to 20 minutes, until golden brown with slightly crisp edges. Serve hot.

*Note: To make smaller beureks, divide the dough into twelve pieces. Roll out each ball into a circle about 4 inches in diameter. Fill with about 2 tablespoons of cheese filling. Bake at 375° for 10 to 12 minutes.*

# Baked Fish Nicosia

These fish fillets stay tender and moist while the exotically spiced bread-crumb topping gets crisp and golden. The cumin, coriander, garlic, lemon, and olive oil are flavors substantial enough to stand up against even a strong tasting fish like bluefish or fresh sardines, but I recommend you try it first with scrod.

SERVES 6

TOPPING

½ cup extra-virgin olive oil

4 garlic cloves, pressed

pinch of cayenne

2 teaspoons ground cumin seeds

1 teaspoon ground coriander seeds

salt to taste

3 cups whole wheat bread crumbs (see page 654)

½ cup chopped fresh basil

_____

2 pounds firm, white, fish fillets

_____

2 medium tomatoes, chopped

2 garlic cloves, pressed

½ cup chopped fresh parsley

juice of 2 lemons (about ¼ cup)

salt and freshly ground black pepper to taste

_____

lemon wedges

Heat the olive oil in a heavy skillet. Add the garlic and let it sizzle for a minute. Add the cayenne, cumin, coriander, and salt to taste. Stir for a minute more. Don't let the spices burn. Add the bread crumbs and stir so that they are blended with the spices and coated with the oil. Continue to sauté, breaking up any lumps, until the bread crumbs are golden and crisp. Add the chopped basil and toss for another minute. Remove from the heat.

Rinse the fish fillets in cold water, pat them dry with paper towels, and place them, skin side down, in an oiled baking dish. Spread the chopped tomatoes evenly over the fish. Sprinkle on the garlic, parsley, and then the lemon juice. Add a little salt and pepper. Top with the seasoned bread crumbs, completely covering the fish.

Bake, uncovered, at 350° for about 20 minutes, until the fish flakes easily with a fork. Garnish with lemon wedges.

This dish goes well with Rice Pilav with Orzo (see page 83) or Bulghur Pilav (see page 82), Sautéed Vegetables (see page 81), and green salad.

# Imam Bayildi

•

# The Imam Fainted

"The Imam Fainted" when he was presented with this stuffed eggplant. I don't guarantee your guests will swoon in ecstasy, but some folk really do love their eggplant.

SERVES 4 TO 6

3 small to medium eggplants

1 tablespoon olive oil

3 cups chopped or thinly sliced onions

1 tablespoon butter

1/4 cup olive oil

2 garlic cloves, pressed

1 cup chopped fresh parsley

2 cups whole wheat bread crumbs (see

1/2 cup chopped fresh basil (2

page 654)

tablespoons dried)

4 or 5 ripe tomatoes, chopped

2 lemons, cut into wedges

salt to taste

Cut the eggplants in half lengthwise, score their flesh in a crisscross pattern, and sprinkle salt on the cut surfaces. Lay them face down in a colander to allow the bitter juices to drain. After 1/2 hour, squeeze them, rinse them in cold water, squeeze again, and pat dry.

Sauté the onions in 1/4 cup of olive oil until softened. Add the parsley and basil. Remove the onions from the skillet and combine them with the tomatoes. Salt to taste.

Oil a large baking pan and preheat the oven to 350°.

Heat a tablespoon of olive oil and a tablespoon of butter in the skillet. Sauté the garlic and bread crumbs, stirring constantly, until the oil is evenly distributed, there are no lumps, and the crumbs are golden brown. Salt to taste.

Rub the eggplant halves with a little oil and lightly salt them. Mound each half with the vegetable mixture and top with the bread crumbs. Add enough water to barely cover the bottom of the baking pan, arrange the stuffed eggplants, and cover the pan tightly with aluminum foil. Bake for one hour. Remove the foil and bake for another 20 minutes, until browned.

Garnish each eggplant half with a lemon wedge. Serve with Rice Pilav with Orzo (see page 83) or Bulghur Pilav (see page 82).

# Oven-Roasted Vegetables

These savory, satisfying, lightly browned vegetables fill the kitchen with the heady fragrance of rosemary and garlic. They're incredibly good and make a wonderful accompaniment to a main dish of fish or eggplant.

### SERVES 4 TO 6

2 large Spanish onions or 8 small whole
    onions (about 1½ inches in
    diameter)
4 large, sweet carrots or 12 whole
    tender baby carrots
8−10 small potatoes (not Idaho or
    Russet baking potatoes)

_____

2 tablespoons olive oil

2 tablespoons melted butter
4 garlic cloves, minced
1 teaspoon crushed dried rosemary
    (1 teaspoon minced fresh leaves)
1 tablespoon minced fresh marjoram
    (1½ teaspoons dried)

_____

salt and freshly ground black pepper to
    taste

Preheat the oven to 375°.

Peel all the vegetables. If using large onions, cut each onion into eighths by slicing it lengthwise into quarters and then cut each quarter crosswise. If using large carrots, halve them lengthwise and then cut them into 1-inch sections. Quarter the potatoes.

Arrange the vegetables in a large oiled baking dish and toss in the oil, butter, garlic, and herbs. Cover tightly with aluminum foil and bake for 35 minutes.

Uncover and turn the vegetables with a large spoon. Add salt and black pepper and roast at 425° for approximately 30 minutes or until the carrots and potatoes are thoroughly cooked and the edges of the vegetables have browned.

# Stewed Batilgian

*Batilgian* (pronounced bottle-john) is the Armenian word for eggplant. This simple, economical dish is similar to ratatouille but lighter. My mother serves it hot as a stew or chilled as a refreshing side dish, and it's one of my favorites. It tastes even better the next day.

### SERVES 4

*1 large Spanish onion or 2–3 small onions, chopped*

*3 tablespoons olive oil*

*4 celery stalks, cut into 1-inch pieces*

*2 cups green beans, cut into 2-inch pieces*

*3 bay leaves*

*3 garlic cloves, pressed*

*2 tablespoons finely chopped fresh basil (2 teaspoons dried)*

---

*1 large eggplant, cubed*

*salt and ground black pepper*

*2 tablespooons olive oil*

*28-ounce can tomatoes with juice (or 4 cups chopped fresh tomatoes and 1 cup tomato juice or water)*

---

*2 tablespoons fresh lemon juice*

*2 tablespoons capers (optional)*

---

*lemon wedges*

In a large saucepan or Dutch oven, sauté the onions in 3 tablespoons of oil on medium heat until translucent. Stir in the celery, cover, and cook for 5 minutes. Add the green beans, bay leaves, garlic, and basil. Cover and continue to cook for about 7 more minutes.

Without stirring, add the eggplant on top of the other vegetables—this will prevent it from scorching. Sprinkle the eggplant with salt and pepper and drizzle 2 tablespoons of oil on top. Pour in the tomatoes and their juice. The liquid will not quite cover the eggplant at first, but eventually the eggplant will cook down.

Cover tightly and simmer on low heat or on a heat diffuser for 20 minutes. Occasionally stir carefully to prevent the vegetables from sticking to the bottom, but be sure not to stir the eggplant down to the bottom before its juices are released, because it burns easily. After about 20 minutes, mix the eggplant down into the stew, adding a little more liquid if necessary. Cover and simmer until the eggplant is very tender and dark. Add more salt and pepper, lemon juice, and capers if you like. Remove the bay leaves.

This stew is finished when all the vegetables are tender and the liquid is slightly thickened. Serve in bowls and top each serving with a wedge of lemon.

# Fried Batilgian

Eggplant can soak up a tremendous amount of oil when fried. These eggplant slices are first dipped in beaten egg; they cook through very quickly in less oil and form a nice crisp edge. Try them with Jajoukh (see page 65), and either Rice Pilav with Orzo (see page 83) or Bulghur Pilav (see page 82).

SERVES 6

*¼ cup vegetable oil*
*¼ cup olive oil*

---

*1 large eggplant, sliced into ½-inch*
*    rounds*

*2 eggs, beaten*

---

*salt to taste*

Heat the vegetable and olive oils in a heavy skillet on high heat until the oil sizzles, then lower the heat to medium. Dip the slices of eggplant in the beaten egg and fry for about 4 minutes on each side, until browned. The egg coating will be crisp and the eggplant tender. You may need to reduce the heat a bit during the last few minutes of frying. Use a spatula or tongs to flip the slices in order to avoid piercing them.

Drain the Fried Batilgian on paper towels, sprinkle with a little salt, and serve immediately.

# Sautéed Vegetables

Easy, unadorned, colorful, and delicious. These are nice alongside Beurek with Parsley-Cheese Filling (see page 74).

(see page 74)

SERVES 6

2 cups diced eggplant (½-inch cubes)
1 large yellow bell pepper
1 large red bell pepper
1 large green bell pepper
1 small zucchini

6 mushrooms
¼ cup olive oil
1–2 garlic cloves, pressed
salt to taste

Sprinkle the diced eggplant with salt and set it aside. After about 20 minutes, rinse with cold water and pat dry with paper towels. Meanwhile, stem and seed the peppers and cut them into 1-inch strips. Dice the zucchini and slice the mushrooms.

Heat the olive oil in a large, heavy skillet. Sauté the eggplant until lightly browned on all sides. Stir in the peppers and zucchini and sauté for about 3 minutes. Add the mushrooms and garlic and stir-fry until the mushrooms are tender. Salt to taste.

# Bulghur Pilav

I first became aware of pilav through "Hadji Baban," an Armenian nonsense nursery rhyme that accompanies a tickling game to amuse a little child. Beginning at the little person's hand (*tatig*), let your fingers "tiptoe" up her little arm (*tsevig*) until the rhyme is at an end and you tickle her under her chin!

**Through rain and snow, Hadji Baban comes home. He wants to make pilav, but there's no oil. And there's no place for his friend, "Bald Martyros."**

| | |
|---|---|
| *Ans-rev´ goo-kah´* | *Pi-lav´ ge-pe´* |
| *Tzoun´ goo-kah´* | *Yegh´ chi-gah´* |
| *Had´-ji Ba´-ban* | *Kel´ Mar-ty-ros´-sin* |
| *Dun´-a goo-kah´* | *Degh´ chi´-gah´* |

This pilav is the staple of the Armenian diet. It's chewy, fluffy, and lighter in texture than brown rice and rich in B vitamins and iron. Many people of the Caucasus live to be over a hundred years old, and this fabulous grain has got to be a contributing factor to their health and vitality. As we rediscover the virtues of whole grains, perhaps bulghur will become an American staple as well.

Here's the way I love it, with savory sautéed onions and herbs.

### SERVES 4

| | |
|---|---|
| *1 medium onion, chopped* | *1 bay leaf* |
| *2 tablespoons olive oil* | *pinch of rosemary or marjoram* |
| *pinch of salt and freshly ground black* | *(optional)* |
| *pepper* | *1½ cups raw bulghur* |
| *1–2 teaspoons dried basil* | *2 cups warm water* |

In a covered saucepan, sauté the onions in the olive oil for a few minutes, stirring occasionally. Add the salt, pepper, basil, bay leaf, and rosemary or marjoram. Cover and cook for about 10 minutes, until the onions are translucent and beginning to brown.

Stir in the bulghur. Toast for about 2 minutes, until the bulghur begins to darken. Add the water, cover tightly, and bring to a boil. Reduce the heat to very low. Let the bulghur steam for about 15 minutes. Each grain should be separate and tender, but chewy. Add a little more hot water if the bulghur seems underdone, but be sparing or it will become mushy. Remove the bay leaf and serve hot.

## Rice Pilav with Orzo

Rice Pilav is prepared in a variety of ways, from Greece to India and developed to a high art in Iraq and Iran. The most elaborate dishes involve nuts, vegetables, diced apricots, and dates.

This is a very simple pilav that combines brown rice, though it is untraditional, and orzo, a pasta shaped like large grains of rice.

If you like, this pilav can be colored golden yellow by adding a pinch of turmeric while sautéing the rice.

### SERVES 4 TO 6

*2 tablespoons olive oil*
*1 medium onion, chopped*
*1½ teaspoons dried marjoram*
*pinch of dried rosemary (optional)*
*pinch of turmeric (optional)*
*pinch of salt and freshly ground black*
  *pepper*

*½ cup dried orzo, riso, or Rosa Marina*
  *(pasta shaped like rice) (see note)*
*1 cup long-grain brown rice*

—————————————————

*2¾ cups water*

Heat the oil in a saucepan. Stir in the chopped onions. Cover and sauté until lightly browned. Add the marjoram, rosemary, turmeric, and salt and pepper. Stir in the pasta and sauté until it browns a little. Add the rice and sauté for 2 or 3 more minutes, stirring occasionally.

Pour in the water and stir once. Cover the rice and bring it to a boil. Turn the heat down very low and simmer for 35 to 40 minutes or until the water is absorbed and the rice is tender.

*Note: Vermicelli broken into small pieces can be used instead of orzo, in which case the dish is called Shereh Pilav.*

# DESSERTS

## *Halvah Shortbread*

My mother sometimes reminisces about visits to see Grandma's friend Vartig Hanoum in her flat on Barnum Avenue in Bridgeport. A thoroughly proper Victorian lady of great dignity and bearing, she dressed in shirtwaists with high-boned collars and wore pince-nez. "Vartig" (the diminutive of Vartanoush) means "Sweet Little Rose" and "Hanoum" was the title given her indicating that she'd made a pilgrimage to the Holy Land. It was there that she acquired the two tiny crosses tattooed on the web of thin skin between the thumb and index finger on each of her hands.

My mother was a little in awe of Vartig Hanoum, and she remembers warmly the fragrance of tea brewing and the rich cookies she served.

### YIELDS 16 TO 20 PIE-SHAPED WEDGES

¾ cup butter, softened
½ cup tahini
pinch of salt
1¼ cups brown sugar

2 cups unbleached pastry flour
½ cup toasted pecans or walnuts,
    chopped or ground
a few pecan or walnut halves

Preheat the oven to 375°.

With a food processor or by hand, cream the butter with the tahini. Add the salt and brown sugar. Blend until smooth. Sprinkle in the flour, blending well. Mix in the chopped nuts. The dough will be very stiff.

Lightly butter two 7-inch pie plates or shallow baking pans. Press the dough to evenly cover the bottom and sides of the pie plates to a thickness of no more than ¼ inch. Press a few whole nuts into the surface to decorate.

Bake the shortbread for 15 minutes and then check it frequently, every couple of minutes, and remove it from the oven as soon as the edges are golden brown. Be careful not to overbake it.

While it's still warm, cut each shortbread into 8 or 10 wedges in the pan; don't wait until it's cool or it will crumble.

This shortbread is wonderful with spearmint or spiced tea or with espresso or Turkish Coffee (see page 445).

## Almond Shortbread

Prepare Almond Shortbread following the same basic procedure as for Halvah Shortbread but use the ingredients listed below.

If using a food processor, add the almond paste and almond extract before adding the flour. If preparing by hand, first mash the almond paste with the almond extract. Then combine it with the creamed butter, almond butter, and sugar mixture before adding the flour.

¾ cup butter, softened
½ cup almond butter or tahini
pinch of salt
1½ cups brown sugar
1 package almond paste (3½ ounces),
   at room temperature

½ teaspoon pure almond extract
2 cups unbleached pastry flour
½ cup toasted chopped almonds
a few whole almonds

# *Paklava*

When my son Dan was in first grade, he asked me to make a treat and bring his grandma Mary along to share something of Armenian culture with his class. I made a tray of paklava for the occasion. His grandma brought a map to show the changes in Armenia's territory. She recited the Armenian alphabet and words for parts of the body, then read the class my children's favorite story, the tale of "Nazzar the Brave":

> *Nazzar the Brave*
> *Who fear does not know*
> *Killed a thousand*
> *In a single blow!*

At first, each child tried a small piece of paklava to spare our feelings. Then they had seconds and thirds and emptied the tray.

Paklava is traditionally made in a round baking pan called a *tepsi*. This recipe makes enough for an 11x17-inch baking tray. Paklava keeps unrefrigerated for days, but I doubt it'll be around that long.

### YIELDS ABOUT 24 2½-INCH SQUARES

4 cups ground walnuts
2 cups ground almonds
1 cup brown sugar
2 teaspoons cinnamon
1 teaspoon ground allspice

―――――――――――――

1¼ cups butter, melted
1-pound package filo pastry
SYRUP

2 cups sugar

1 cup honey
1½ cups water
2 tablespoons freshly grated lemon rind
2 tablespoons freshly grated orange rind
2 teaspoons cinnamon
1 teaspoon ground allspice
juice of 1 orange

Preheat the oven to 350°.

Combine the nuts, sugar, and spices in a mixing bowl. Set up your work area with the bowl of nut filling, the pan of melted butter, a pastry brush, and an 11x17-inch baking sheet with shallow sides. Unfold the package of filo and place it next to the baking sheet.

Brush the baking sheet with melted butter. Carefully place a leaf of filo on it. The filo should be smooth and unwrinkled; if it is larger than your pan, let the edges hang over the sides. Brush the leaf with butter or, if it's easier for you, butter the top sheet of filo on the stack and then lift it onto the baking sheet. Repeat this process with four leaves. Sprinkle some of the nut filling evenly on the pastry. Cover with 2 more leaves of buttered filo. Sprinkle with nuts. Continue this procedure until the nut filling is used up.

Fold any overhanging borders up and over the top of the nut filling. Top the paklava with five more leaves of buttered filo. Carefully tuck any overhanging edges in under the paklava.

With the sharp knife, score the paklava into diamond or square shapes about 3 inches across. Cut down to, but not through the bottom layer. Bake for about one hour, until the paklava is golden.

While the paklava is baking, combine the syrup ingredients. Boil for 15 to 20 minutes, until the syrup has thickened. Either let the syrup cool a little and then pour it over the hot paklava when you remove it from the oven, or let the paklava cool a little and then pour the boiling syrup over it. The pastry will crackle as you pour it on. I like to cut through the pieces again so the syrup can reach the bottom layers of nuts.

Serve paklava at room temperature.

# Fig and Apricot Conserve

This is an intensely sweet Syrian dessert of dried fruits and nuts. A version somewhat more tart can be achieved by substituting sun-dried unsulphured apricot halves and Black Mission figs for the Turkish varieties used here, and by eliminating the honey. This is good accompanied by plain yogurt.

### YIELDS ABOUT 5 CUPS

*½ cup honey*
*1 ½ cups water*
*1 cup dried whole unsulphured Turkish apricots, halved (see note)*
*2 cups dried Turkish figs, stemmed and halved (see note)*
*½ cup raisins*
*½ teaspoon spearmint, fresh or dry, chopped or crushed leaves*

*½ teaspoon anise seeds*
*juice of 1 lemon*

_____

*½ cup walnut halves*
*½ cup slivered almonds*
*fresh mint sprigs*
*plain yogurt*
*orange slices (optional)*

In a saucepan, bring the honey and water to a boil. Add the halved apricots and figs and simmer for 5 minutes, stirring occasionally. Add the raisins, spearmint, and anise seeds. Continue to cook for about 20 minutes. When the figs are thick and tender and the liquid has become a very thick syrup, stir in the lemon juice.

Serve hot, chilled, or at room temperature in little shallow dishes or custard cups garnished with 2 or 3 walnut halves, a few slivered almonds, and a sprig of fresh mint. Or serve plain yogurt in cups with a tablespoon or two of the conserve on top, garnished with the nuts and mint or an orange slice, if desired.

*Note: Turkish apricots are sold whole and are small, plump, very sweet, and somewhat moist. Sun-dried unsulphured apricot halves are large, tart, flat, and have a fibrous, leathery texture. Turkish figs are very sugary, sticky, and moist inside, while Black Mission figs are moist outside and milder in flavor.*

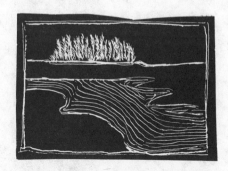

T O M   W A L L S

*British*

*Isles*

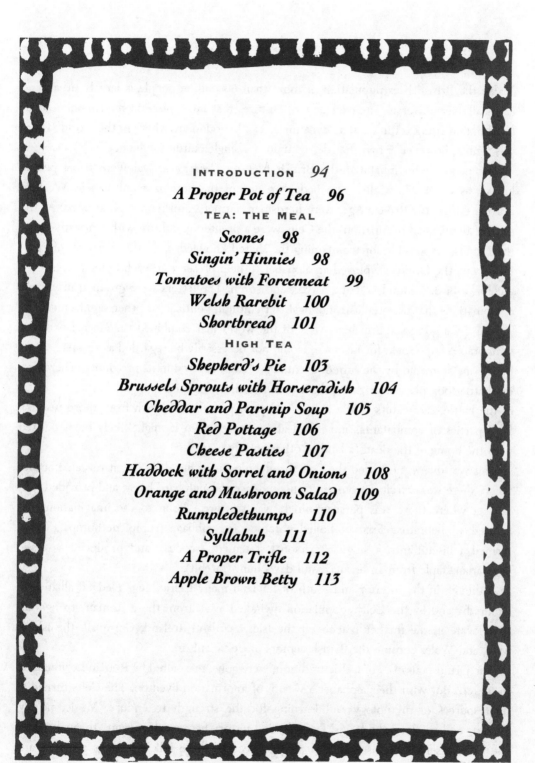

# INTRODUCTION

Today the British Isles population of more than 60 million people is largely urban and ethnically very diverse. The exchange of cultures that takes place in metropolitan areas like London is as exciting and as dynamic as can be found anywhere in the world. There was a time, however, when the Isles contained a single cultural influence.

The people who inhabited the British Isles on Caesar's arrival were tribal people known as Celts. The Celts, who had been one of the dominant cultures in Western Europe during the Bronze Age, were herdsmen, farmers, and renowned artisans. At the time of the Roman occupation, the Celts were a preliterate culture with a priestly caste, the Druids, responsible for maintaining the shared knowledge. As that body of information grew, the Druids employed an alphabet to help preserve it; each letter represented a color, a bird, a sound, a deity, a tree, and so on. The letters were grouped in various combinations that denoted astronomical, agricultural, political, or other significance.

The Celts possessed a magical view of the world that combined the eternal with the temporal. A large rock, for instance, would not necessarily be regarded as an inert object but as one animated by the sum of events that have occurred in its proximity. Therefore, if a battle took place near the rock, it then became associated with the battle, the cause of the battle, the results of the battle (and perhaps a moral drawn from those results), both parties of combatants, and if a death occurred then it might likely be associated with the home of the dead (a land of otherworldly power).

This worldview motivated the Celt throughout his or her daily life; it revealed beauty where there was scarcity, promised transcendence through hard labor, and provided self-respect where there was persecution. It was this great boon to the imagination that created a celebratory feast of boiled potatoes and cabbage (rumpledethumps), transformed a biscuit into a singular personal statement (scones), and produced a classic vegetarian staple from an unsuccessful day's hunt (rarebit).

Although in the interior and south of England many Celtic kings pledged alliance to Rome, by and by the Celtic population dwindled away from those Roman strongholds to relocate in the further reaches of the Isles. Scotland, Ireland, Cornwall, the Isle of Man, and Wales became the British centers of Celtic culture.

The Druids, curators of Celtic tradition, were gone, massacred by Roman Legionnaires in 61 A.D. But with their alphabet a wealth of information lived on. The Celts turned to its resources of mythology and learning for the strength to endure. Music, poetry, dancing and riddling, the foods, festivals, and history became the avenue through which the Celts asserted themselves as a people. Because these folk traditions survived and flourished, we needn't rely on potsherds, burial mounds, or the sometimes myopic observations of the Romans for knowledge of the Celts. Today, while little influence of the Romans or the numerous Teutonic conquerors is obvious, the Celtic spirit animates the art, music, literature, and food of the British Isles.

## Whisky for Breakfast

Until the late seventeenth century in Great Britain, beer or whisky was the popular beverage of choice. In 1662 the high-living monarch Charles II, who was experiencing personal cash-flow problems, married an extremely well-heeled princess from Portugal, Catherine of Braganza. The Portuguese dominated trade in the Far East, and tea was very popular among the aristocracy. When Catherine brought her taste for it to the English court, it soon became fashionable there as well.

The merchant class, quick to catch on, opened Tea Gardens all over London "... every skettle-ally half a mile out of town was embellished with green arbours and shady retreats ... [where one was] beguiled with cakes and ale, tea and shrimp, strawberries and cream, syllabubs and junkets."* Before long, the middle class, the working class—anyone with any class at all—had given up whisky for breakfast.

## Tea: The Beverage

Although a hot beverage might be steeped from the buds, leaves, bark, and roots of a wide variety of plants, this discussion of tea refers to the young leaves and buds of *Camellia sinensis,* a plant native to Southeast Asia, which has been used since 28 B.C. The teas of *C. sinensis* are identified by variety, grade, and place of origin. Variety refers to the type of fermentation and firing processes used to cure the tea leaves. Green tea is fired immediately after picking, oolong leaves have fermented only a short time before firing, and black tea is fired after it has fully fermented. The grade depends on the condition of the leaf.

In Great Britain, black teas are the most popular. Broadly speaking, "high grown"

---

* W. S. Scott, *Bygone Pleasures of London,* Marsland Publications, London, 1948.

black teas, those grown in the high altitudes, have the most agreeable flavor. The British are accustomed to a higher quality tea than we are here in the States, where the largest selling teas, by far, are those of the lowest grade. In defense of low-grade teas, I must say they are very cheap, and I have a large box in my cupboard right next to the higher quality, more snoot-worthy varieties.

The most popular black teas are grown in Sri Lanka (formerly Ceylon), India, and China. Teas from Ceylon are strong and dark; Assam tea, grown in India, is heavy and pungent, Darjeeling is a delicate amber-colored tea flavored with bergamot grown in the foothills of the Indian Himalayas; China produces the strong black Keemun tea as well as some very nice oolong teas, also popular in Great Britain: Formosa oolong and Lapsang souchong, with its distinctive smoky flavor.

# A Proper Pot of Tea

Use one teaspoon of leaves or one teabag per cup, and add one more for the pot.

Start with cold tap water. Hot tap water's been sitting in the water heater and lost its oxygen content, which makes the tea taste flat; boiling the water too long creates the same problem, so heat it to the "just boiling" point.

Brew the tea in a ceramic or glass pot; metal will bring out the tannic acid in the tea and make it bitter. Warm the pot by swishing hot water through it before brewing the tea to ensure that the cold surface of the pot won't reduce the temperature of the water. The brewing water needs to be right near the boiling point in order to brew the tea properly.

Pour the steaming water directly on the tea leaves. Keep the lid on your pot or the temperature will drop. Brew for at least 3 minutes; less will make the tea too weak. Allow a longer brewing period if you like a stronger flavor, but not longer than 5 minutes, or the tea will become bitter. Don't dip your tea bag, the leaves must remain in the water while brewing. Strain or otherwise remove the leaves when brewing has finished.

# TEA: THE MEAL

*A British-style tea has lately become a popular light meal with the power-lunch crowd and is now featured at fashionable restaurants on both sides of the Atlantic. Typically available for tea: scones with double cream (a British cream cheese) and jam (when served in combination with tea, this is known as a "cream tea"), cucumber sandwiches and the like, rarebit, fruitcake, and for a tony tea: sorbet, torten, and pastries.*

# Scones

There are as many scone recipes as there are cookbooks. A scone should be quick and easy to make and provide a simple, crunchy medium for your favorite topping. This is a recipe from before the days of baking powder. Without the bitter taste that often accompanies baking powder, one can savor the natural flavor of the wheat.

## YIELDS 8 SCONES

1 1/2 tablespoons butter (at room temperature)
2 cups unbleached white flour
1 1/2 tablespoons sugar

1/4 teaspoon salt
1/2 cup raisins
3/4 cup milk

Preheat the oven to 450°.

In a mixing bowl, combine the butter and flour, rubbing the lumps of butter between your fingers and thumbs. Stir in the sugar, salt, and raisins. Slowly stir in the milk, adding just enough to make a smooth, but not sticky, dough.

On a lightly floured surface, roll the dough out to a 1/2-inch thickness. Cut out 2-inch rounds and place them on a buttered baking pan. Keep rolling out the scraps until all the dough is used up. Bake for about 20 minutes, until just beginning to brown.

Serve the scones hot from the oven, split and topped with butter, jam, honey, or cream cheese.

> *Note: In a recipe such as this one, using unleavened dough baked at a high temperature, it is important that the oven heat evenly and that the oven rack is not too close to the heat source. Many ovens heat significantly hotter than the setting indicates. If you have problems, use an oven thermometer.*

# Singin' Hinnies

For a quick breakfast or brunch, here's a Celtic alternative to French toast or pancakes.

1 ¼ cups unbleached white flour (may
   be part whole wheat flour)
1 teaspoon baking powder
⅛ teaspoon salt
2 tablespoons butter

⅓ cup currants
⅓–½ cup milk

_____

oil for frying

In a mixing bowl, combine the flour, baking powder, and salt. Cut in the butter until the mixture resembles coarse meal. Stir in the currants. Add just enough milk, a little at a time, to make a firm dough that is like a pie crust.

Roll out onto a well-floured surface to a ¼-inch thickness. Cut into rounds about 2½ inches in diameter.

Coat the bottom of a heavy frying pan with oil. On low heat, fry the cakes for 4 to 5 minutes on each side, until nicely browned. Serve piping hot, spread with butter and jam.

# Tomatoes with Forcemeat

The term "forcemeat" comes from medieval times. People of limited means used minced vegetables, herbs, nuts, and fruits to supplement meats that were often in short supply.

## SERVES 6 AS A SIDE DISH OR LUNCHEON ENTRÉE

6 large ripe fresh tomatoes

_____

1 medium onion, finely chopped
¼ cup butter
6 ounces finely chopped mushrooms
5 leaves fresh sage, minced (½ teaspoon
   dried)
¼ teaspoon minced fresh rosemary
   (pinch of dried)

¼ cup chopped fresh parsley
salt and freshly ground black pepper to
   taste
1 cup cooked brown rice
¼ cup raisins
½ teaspoon sweet Hungarian paprika

_____

bread crumbs

Slice the tops off the tomatoes and scoop out the pulp. Chop the pulp and set aside.

Sauté the onions in the butter for 2 or 3 minutes. Add the mushrooms and sauté a minute more. Stir in the tomato pulp, sage, rosemary, parsley, and salt and pepper. Cook on low heat for 5 minutes. Add the rice, raisins, and paprika. Cook for a few more minutes, remove from the heat, and let cool for a few minutes.

Stuff the tomatoes and mound any extra filling on top. Place in a buttered casserole dish and sprinkle the tops with bread crumbs. Bake at 375° for 25 minutes.

# *Welsh Rarebit*

Around the turn of the century, an American artist named Winsor McCay—an authentic Celtic name—did a great comic strip called "Dreams of the Rarebit Fiend." (This is the same guy who did "Little Nemo.") It usually featured some poor soul who'd dreamt he'd gone to work without his pants on. He'd awaken and moan, "What a dreadful dream! Oh, that rarebit! I swear, I'll never eat Welsh rarebit again!"

They say Welsh Rarebit is an Englishman's wry comment on the Welshman's prowess as a hunter. However, hors d'oeuvres were known in the past as "fore bits" and the savories that followed the meal were referred to as "rear bits," so a little imagination reveals a less rancorous origin.

**SERVES 4 GENEROUSLY**

**6 cups grated sharp cheddar cheese**
  **(about 20 ounces)**
**6 ounces beer, at room temperature**
**2 egg yolks, beaten**
**⅛ teaspoon cayenne**
**1 teaspoon Dijon mustard**

**¾ cup walnuts**
**2 apples**
**16 broccoli spears**
**8 slices bread**

Heat the grated cheese in the top of a double boiler. Mix the warm beer with the beaten egg yolks. When the cheese has melted, slowly stir in the egg-beer mixture. Add the cayenne and mustard. Stir until smooth.

Chop and toast the walnuts. Slice the apples thinly. Steam the broccoli spears until tender but still bright green. Toast the bread.

For each serving of rarebit, start with two slices of toast. The general idea is to cover the toast with broccoli and apples, pour cheese sauce over them, and top with walnuts. However, I like to put apple slices between two slices of toast, top with broccoli spears, cover with cheese, and garnish with nuts.

## *Shortbread*

Delicate and pure, this shortbread is the ultimate, melt-in-your-mouth butter cookie, perfect at teatime.

YIELDS 16 WEDGES

*¼ pound butter*
*¼ cup confectioners' sugar*
*¾ cup unbleached white flour*

*⅜ cup cornstarch*
*¼ teaspoon pure almond or vanilla*
*    extract (optional)*

Preheat the oven to 300°.

Cream the butter. Stir in the sugar until well blended. Sift in the flour and cornstarch. Add the almond or vanilla extract, if you wish. Stir until the mixture just begins to come together. Take care not to overwork the dough because this will make the cookie tough and shortbread should be delicate.

Pat the dough into a circle about ½-inch thick on a lightly oiled cookie sheet. Punch a bunch of holes in the dough with a fork. Bake for 50 to 60 minutes, until just beginning to turn golden, but not brown. Cut into wedges while still warm.

# HIGH TEA

*Although many folks imagine high tea to be a fancy-shmancy variety of teatime, the term originally referred to a meal held at the end of the workday by working-class people. Eventually it was taken up by the upper classes, who were always on the lookout for something new and different, then spread to the middle class, who indulged their inclination to emulate the upper class.*

# Shepherd's Pie

Shepherd's Pie is an extremely popular meal among the British working class. At Moosewood we serve a dish called "The Blue Plate Special," which consists of tofu "meatloaf," mashed potatoes, and mushroom gravy. My vegetarian Shepherd's Pie "anglicizes" the Blue Plate for a meal hearty enough to satisfy the wind-chapped, bone-weary herdsman. Serve with pickled beets and a warm stout.

### SERVES 4

#### TOFU LAYER

1 cake tofu, frozen, thawed, and
   shredded (see page 684)

---

1 large onion, chopped
2 tablespoons vegetable oil
1/4 teaspoon thyme
1/2 teaspoon ground coriander seeds
pinch of freshly ground black pepper
1/2 cup walnuts, toasted and chopped
juice of 1/2 lemon (about 1 tablespoon)
1–2 tablespoons tamari soy sauce to
   taste

#### POTATO LAYER

4 large potatoes, peeled and cubed
3 tablespoons butter or margarine
1/2 cup milk
salt to taste

#### MUSHROOM GRAVY

2 tablespoons vegetable oil
1/2 pound mushrooms, sliced
3 tablespoons tamari soy sauce
pinch of freshly ground black pepper
1 1/2 cups hot potato water
2 tablespoons cornstarch dissolved in
   1/2 cup water

This Shepherd's Pie is a casserole combining three elements: a tofu sauté, mashed potatoes, and mushroom gravy. If you perform the three operations concurrently, you will shorten the preparation time considerably. Start the freeze-thaw tofu procedure at least the day before you expect to make the casserole.

For the tofu layer, sauté the chopped onions in the oil with the thyme, coriander, and black pepper until the onions are translucent. Stir in the chopped walnuts and shredded tofu. When heated through, stir in lemon juice and soy sauce. Remove from the heat.

To make the mashed potatoes, place the cubed potatoes in a saucepan and cover with lightly salted water. Bring to a boil, and then simmer until the potatoes are soft. Drain, saving the hot potato water to use in the gravy. Mash the potatoes with the butter and milk. Salt to taste.

For the gravy, heat the oil in a skillet. Stir in the mushrooms, soy sauce, and black pepper. Sauté, stirring occasionally, until the mushrooms are tender. Add 1½ cups of the potato water and bring to a boil. Slowly stir in the cornstarch mixture and cook at a low boil, continuing to stir, until the gravy is clear and thick.

Oil a 9-inch square casserole dish or use a 10-inch round cast-iron skillet. Layer the tofu mixture, then the mushroom gravy, and then the mashed potatoes. Dot the top with butter or margarine. Bake at 400° for 15 to 20 minutes until the top becomes golden.

*Variation* For the nondairy diet, just substitute margarine for butter and use some of the water left over from boiling the potatoes in place of the milk when mashing the potatoes.

# Brussels Sprouts with Horseradish

 This recipe introduced us to the pleasures of fresh horseradish. It's easy to use and a singular gustatory experience. Brussels sprouts, little bite-sized cabbages, are very popular in Great Britain. This dish will put to rest the notion that British food is bland.

### SERVES 6 TO 8

*1½ pounds Brussels sprouts*
*3 large carrots*
*3 leeks, thoroughly washed (see page 667)*

*2 tablespoons butter*
*⅓ cup vegetable oil*

*3 tablespoons grated fresh or prepared horseradish*
*3 tablespoons cider vinegar*
*1 teaspoon dried dill weed (1 tablespoon fresh)*
*½ teaspoon salt*
*freshly ground black pepper to taste*

Trim off the tough outer leaves of the Brussels sprouts. Cut the carrots into 1-inch-thick slices and the leeks into ½-inch pieces. Steam the vegetables until tender, for 10 to 12 minutes (see page 681). Drain.

Meanwhile, melt the butter in a heavy saucepan. Stir in the remaining ingredients. Toss well with the hot, drained vegetables and serve immediately.

# Cheddar and Parsnip Soup

The Tuatha Dé Danann were a race of warriors and sorcerers who, during the fifth mythological age, occupied Ireland. When they were defeated by the Sons of Mil, the ancestors of the historical occupants, they retreated to a kingdom underground, where they remain. It is perhaps a blessing of the Tuatha that the British should enjoy so many root vegetables, like the parsnip in this soup, the plant that seeks nourishment from the earth.

Cheddar was a local farmhouse cheese that became the single most popular cheese in the world. There are many cheeses of renown in Great Britain. Unfortunately they aren't readily available elsewhere. If you have the opportunity to visit, make a point of dropping by the local cheese shops. Otherwise, content yourself with the creamy Blue Stilton, the smooth and pungent Double Gloucester, and this delicious soup.

### SERVES 6

1 medium onion, chopped
1 teaspoon salt
2 tablespoons vegetable oil
2–3 teaspoons caraway seeds
5 medium parsnips, peeled and cubed
   (about 1 pound)

3 medium potatoes, peeled and cubed
   (about 1¼ pounds)

3 cups water

¼ teaspoon ground fennel seeds
3 cups medium sharp cheddar, grated
   (about 8 ounces)
3 cups milk

chopped fresh parsley or a sprig of dill

In a 3-quart saucepan, sauté the onion with the salt in the oil on low heat until the onions become translucent, about 10 minutes. Mix in the caraway seeds and parsnips. Stir and simmer them gently for about 5 minutes.

Add the potatoes and water. Bring the soup to a boil. Moderately simmer for about 10 to 15 minutes, until the potatoes are tender and easily pierced with a fork. Remove the soup from the heat.

Stir in the fennel and the cheese. When the cheese has melted, pour in the milk. Allow the soup to cool for 5 to 10 minutes. Then in a blender or food processor, purée the soup in batches. Gently reheat it, being careful not to let it boil. Serve hot.

# Red Pottage

 Here's a hearty soup without any dairy products that goes nicely with Cheese Pasties (see page 107) and adds color to your meal. Pronounce with a glottal stop (pah' idge) to achieve an authentic Cockney effect.

## SERVES 6 TO 8

1¾ cups dried kidney beans
7 cups water
1 medium beet, peeled and cubed

_____

1 cup chopped onions
2 tablespoons vegetable oil
1 cup chopped celery

salt and freshly ground black pepper to taste
⅛ teaspoon cayenne
2½ cups undrained canned whole tomatoes (28-ounce can)
1 tablespoon fresh lemon juice

Sort and rinse the beans. In a medium saucepan, bring the water and the beans to a boil. Cover and simmer gently for 1½ hours. Add the chopped beets and continue to simmer another ½ hour or until both the beans and beets are tender. Add more water, if needed, to keep the beans covered in liquid.

Meanwhile, sauté the onions in the oil until translucent. Add the celery, salt, black pepper, and cayenne and continue cooking until the celery is tender. Add the tomatoes and lemon juice. Lower the heat and gently simmer until the tomatoes are well stewed.

Stir the stewed vegetables into the beans. In a blender or food processor, purée in batches until smooth. The soup will be thick and creamy. Carefully reheat the blended soup, stirring frequently. Adjust the salt and pepper to taste.

Serve garnished with a mint leaf and a dollop of sour cream or with croutons.

# Cheese Pasties

"You can't please everyone." As holidays approach, I experience the transcendent wisdom of this homily most deeply. Among my friends and family there is such a jumble of cultures, religions, philosophies, and habits that even the most well-intentioned host is bound to offend, overlook, and otherwise fall short. However, it seems that if one shoots enough arrows into the air, one of them is bound to hit the target. So it was with Cheese Pasties.

Pasties are a savory turnover the miners of Cornwall allegedly carry down into the earth with them. Nanny, my friend Jeff's grandmother, made them in the traditional way with meat, potatoes, leeks, turnips, flour, and lard. We made them in Jeff's honor one Christmas Eve and satisfied every Cornish corpuscle in his body. Although we vegetarians found them attractive, one can't fully appreciate food solely from a visual perspective. So with a little experimentation and several Christmas Eves down the road, we have come up with a delicious vegetarian pasty that satisfies everyone in the room and still remains faithful to the spirit of Nanny's original.

### YIELDS 6 PASTIES

**CRUST**

3 cups unbleached white flour

1 teaspoon salt

1 cup butter

3 tablespoons ice water

**FILLING**

2 celery stalks, diced (about 1 cup)

1 small turnip, diced (about ¾ cup)

1 leek, washed and chopped (about ⅔ cup; see page 667) (or ½ cup chopped scallions)

1⅓ cups diced carrots

4 cups grated cheddar cheese (12 ounces)

pinch of mace

¼ teaspoon freshly ground black pepper

¼ teaspoon cayenne

To make the crust, sift the flour with the salt. Cut the butter into the flour with your fingers until the mixture resembles coarse meal. Sprinkle on ice water while you stir with a fork until the dough hangs together. Form into a ball and refrigerate for 15 to 30 minutes. Don't chill too long or you will have trouble working the dough.

In a large bowl, mix together all the filling ingredients.

Preheat the oven to 375°.

Cut the ball of dough into six equal pieces. Roll out each piece to about ⅛ inch thick. Cut a 9-inch circle out of each pastry piece.

Place ⅙ of the filling in the middle of each pastry circle. Pack it down so that it will fit. Pull one edge over the filling to make a half-circle. Seal the two edges together like a turnover. Turn the edges over all around and press with a fork or your fingers to double seal. Cut slits in the top of each pastie so that steam can escape.

Bake for 15 minutes at 375°, then reduce the heat to 350° and bake for 15 to 20 minutes more, until lightly golden. Let the pasties rest for at least 5 minutes out of the oven before serving.

Make plenty. Pasties are even better when reheated the following day.

## *Haddock with Sorrel and Onions*

Sorrel, or sourgrass, is an herb indigenous to Great Britain that grows abundantly in the United States as well. With its fresh lemony taste, sorrel combines extremely well with fish. It is a common weed that adds a simple elegance.

**SERVES 4**

*¼ cup butter*
*2 medium onions, sliced into ⅛-inch-thick rings (about 2 cups)*
*½ teaspoon ground mace*
*½ cup chopped fresh sorrel*

*1½ pounds haddock or other lean white fish fillets*
*salt and freshly ground black pepper to taste*

*1 lemon, cut into wedges*

Preheat the oven to 350°.

Melt the butter in a small skillet. Add the onion rings and sauté on medium heat until soft, 5 to 10 minutes. Add the mace, stir in the sorrel, and remove from the heat.

Lay out the fish fillets in an oiled baking dish. Sprinkle with salt and black pepper and smother with the onion-sorrel mixture. Cover the dish and bake for about 25 minutes, until the fish flakes easily with a fork.

Serve with lemon wedges.

# Orange and Mushroom Salad

An unusual combination of thinly sliced orange sections and mushrooms, served on greens with a vinaigrette, and garnished with chopped toasted walnuts. Very nice and refreshing.

### SERVES 4 TO 6

1/4 cup olive oil
1/8 cup cider vinegar
1 tablespoon fresh lemon juice
1 garlic clove, peeled and halved
salt and freshly ground black pepper to
    taste

1/2 pound mushrooms (2–3 cups sliced)
juice of 1 orange
2 seedless (navel) oranges
1 head leaf lettuce
1/4 cup chopped walnuts, toasted

In a small bowl, combine the oil, vinegar, lemon juice, garlic, salt, and pepper. Set aside.

Wash and slice the mushrooms and place them in a bowl. Toss the mushrooms in the orange juice and salt lightly. Peel and section the navel oranges, add them to the mushrooms, and set aside for several minutes.

Tear the lettuce into bite-sized pieces and place in a large salad bowl. Place the mushrooms and oranges on the bed of lettuce.

Remove the garlic halves from the dressing. Whisk the dressing well and pour it over the salad. Sprinkle on the toasted walnuts and serve.

> *Note: You may also prepare this salad (without the lettuce and walnuts) an hour or two in advance and let it marinate in the refrigerator. The mushrooms will be even more flavorful and tender.*

# *Rumpledethumps*

The diet of northern European peasantry relied heavily upon the potato ever since it was imported from Peru in the sixteenth century. In Celtic Britain it was taboo to harvest any potatoes before the festival of Lugnasa, and so the event was met with great anticipation. Colcannon, a potato and cabbage dish—variations of which are legion—is traditionally served on Lugnasa. All members of the family must share the dish or risk offending the agricultural spirit that protects the crop. After the first bite everyone shouts, "Death to the Red Hag!" thus driving away the specter of starvation.

Rumpledethumps is a colcannon that includes broccoli and cheddar cheese; it serves equally well as a luncheon or side dish. There are over one zillion known varieties of colcannon, and I have tried them all. This one is best.

### SERVES 6

5 large potatoes (2–2½ pounds)
2½ cups chopped cabbage
2 leeks, washed and chopped (see page 667)
2½ cups coarsely chopped broccoli
6 tablespoons butter

¼ teaspoon mace
salt and freshly ground black pepper to taste
¾ cup milk
1½ cups grated cheddar cheese

Peel the potatoes, cut them into chunks, and boil them in salted water for 15 minutes. Meanwhile, steam the cabbage, leeks, and broccoli (see page 681). Melt 2 tablespoons of the butter and stir in the mace. Mix this seasoned butter and salt and pepper to taste into the steamed vegetables.

Drain the potatoes and mash with 2 more tablespoons butter, the milk, and salt and pepper to taste. Stir in the seasoned vegetables and mix evenly. Spread in an oiled 13x9-inch baking pan. Melt the remaining 2 tablespoons of butter and drizzle it over the potato mixture. Sprinkle the top with the grated cheese. Place under the broiler for 3 to 4 minutes or until the cheese is browned and bubbly.

If you'd like to prepare Rumpledethumps ahead of time, omit the cheese topping, cover the baking pan tightly, and refrigerate. Later, bake, covered with foil, for 30 minutes at 350°. Uncover, sprinkle with the cheese, and place Rumpledethumps under the broiler for a few minutes to brown.

# Syllabub

Syllabubs are a festive old English dessert drink. In the earliest versions, a cow was milked directly into a bowl of sweetened wine, ale, or cider. There are two types of syllabub: a liquid alcoholic whip like the one below, and a solid or everlasting syllabub that resembles a citrus mousse.

### SERVES 8 TO 10

*1 fifth claret (Bordeaux, but any dry, red wine will do)*
*½ pound superfine sugar (see note) (or less if you prefer a not-so-sweet drink)*

*1 pint heavy cream*
*½ cup sherry (optional)*
*juice of 2 oranges*
*grated peel of 1 orange and 1 lemon*

Mix the claret and 5 heaping teaspoons of the superfine sugar in a glass or pottery bowl and blend well until the sugar dissolves. Fill wineglasses half full with the claret mix.

Mix the remaining sugar you're using with the rest of the ingredients in a deep, wide bowl and beat well with a mixer until frothy and just solid, but not stiff like whipped cream. Top the sweetened claret in each glass with froth and serve immediately.

*Note: Superfine sugar is a rapid dissolving sugar, widely available.*

# A Proper Trifle

You notice I use the term "proper" here, and I used it also to describe the tea-brewing instructions. It's been my experience that Brits tend to be a little set in their ways. Not to say that they are rigid or tradition bound, mind you. There are just certain ways of doing things that are typically British: proper.

In England, the proper trifle contains just enough custard to bind the fruit and cake; however, an Irish acquaintance tells us that the discriminating diner always chooses the trifle with the most custard.

### YIELDS 8 SERVINGS

**A PROPER CUSTARD**

1 ½ cups heavy cream

5 egg yolks

3 tablespoons superfine (see note on page 111) or granulated sugar

1 ½ teaspoons cornstarch

**CAKE/FRUIT LAYER**

5 cups broken pieces pound cake or sponge cake

raspberry jam

⅛–¼ cup sherry

1 ½ cups fresh or frozen raspberries or blackberries

1 large banana (optional)

**TOPPING**

½ pint heavy cream, whipped

¼ cup slivered almonds, lightly toasted

To make the custard, heat the cream in a small saucepan, taking care that it does not scorch. In the meantime, whisk the egg yolks, sugar, and cornstarch in a bowl. When the cream is hot, pour it into the bowl with the egg mixture, stirring constantly. Return the custard to the saucepan and stir constantly on low heat until thickened, but do not let it boil. Remove it from the heat and cool.

To assemble the trifle, spread the pieces of cake with a very thin layer of jam. Put the pieces in a large bowl. (Clear glass or crystal is traditional.) Sprinkle the sherry and berries over the cake and stir. Don't bother to thaw frozen berries; there's less mess if they're frozen. Peel and thinly slice the banana. Stir it in with the cake and berries. Drizzle the custard over the top. Don't expect to cover and completely encase the cake and fruit mix.

Spread the whipped cream over the trifle. Sprinkle the almonds on top. Cover and chill for at least 4 hours.

# *Apple Brown Betty*

My mother, Betty, was a rosy-cheeked, freckle-faced, Irish lassie who was raised in the apple-growing region of southwestern Michigan. Although no one calls her Apple Brown Betty, you may, if you like.

SERVES 6

2 tablespoons butter
3 cups whole wheat bread crumbs
  (about 5 slices)

---

1 lemon
¼ cup sugar
¼ teaspoon freshly grated nutmeg

¼ teaspoon cinnamon
2 tablespoons water
5 large Granny Smith baking apples, or
  other tart variety
2 tablespoons butter

---

heavy cream (optional)

Preheat the oven to 450°.

Liberally butter a 2-quart round baking dish. Melt 2 tablespoons of butter, pour it on the bread crumbs, and mix well. Set aside.

Grate the lemon rind. In a small bowl mix the grated rind with the sugar, nutmeg, and cinnamon. Set aside.

Squeeze the juice of the lemon into a small bowl, add the water, and set aside.

Peel, core, and slice the apples thinly. Place ⅓ of the bread crumbs in the bottom of the baking dish. Cover with ½ of the apples. Sprinkle ½ of the sugar-lemon mixture on top of the apples. Cover with another ⅓ of the bread crumbs, then the remaining apples. Sprinkle the rest of the sugar-lemon mixture on top of the apples. Pour over the lemon water and cover with the rest of the bread crumbs. Dot with 2 tablespoons of butter.

Cover the dish and place it in the 450° oven. Immediately reduce the heat to 350°. Bake for 35 to 40 minutes, then remove the cover and bake for 10 to 15 minutes longer, until browned. Allow to cool for 15 minutes. Loosen the edges with a knife, then turn out, upside down, onto a plate.

Serve warm. If you wish, serve with a little pitcher of heavy cream, which may be poured over individual servings.

NED ASTA

# *The*

# *Caribbean*

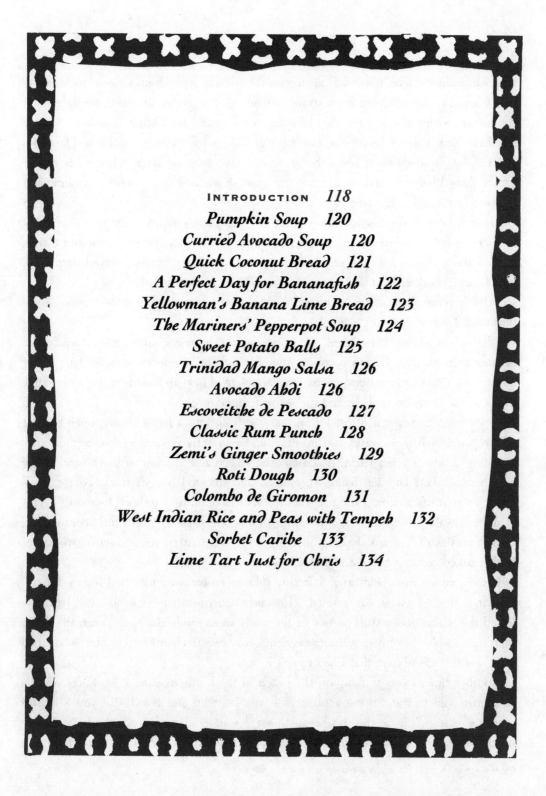

# INTRODUCTION

One winter in the late '60s, while sitting on the subway going from Queens to Manhattan, I became overwhelmed by a strange feeling as I marveled at some deeply tanned commuters sitting across from me. I began to recognize this feeling as *jealousy*. Where did these New Yorkers become so tan? I began to have incessant tropical island fantasies and to plot my own flight from the gray city. Twenty years later, when each winter comes along I become anxious to leave my snow shovel and down booties at home and escape to an island in the tropics.

My first taste of the tropics and its warmth, calm, and serenity came on a seven-day boat cruise from Puerto Rico through the Virgin Islands. My friends Demi and Carlos steered the cruiser while the rest of the crew (four of us) relaxed, played dominoes, fished, read, snorkeled, and ate exotic foods for dinner at each port.

I vividly remember sitting on the top deck of the boat staring out into a vast ocean of turquoise. I was stunned by the color.

Of the few islands I've visited, St. Lucia has the hottest climate; it's closer to the equator than Mexico, Puerto Rico, or Anguilla, and the temperature never falls below 60°. On St. Lucia's plantations, cocoa trees are planted next to banana trees, where they thrive in the screened sunlight and the warm temperatures.

In Castries, the capital of St. Lucia, one can walk into a large, sunny, open market where people sell their wares and produce under brightly colored umbrellas. The surrounding buildings are a worn, peach-colored stucco and in front of them vendors lay out their blankets and sell fruits, vegetables, and spices. I bought thick, coarse, raw-looking scrolls of cinnamon and beautiful black ovals of nutmeg webbed by reddish veins of mace. I walked between huge mounds of pumpkin, papaya, breadfruit, avocado, and many varieties of bananas. I was pulled this way and that by the seductive aromas of freshly baked coconut bread and sliced limes and pineapples.

Once a young man held open a freshly split green-brown cocoa pod for me to see. "What is this?" I asked. "It's weird." He said, "Cocoa-cocoa—you like it." I timidly licked the white, gooey stuff on one of the many seeds inside the pod. When the white pulp had dissolved in my mouth, it was deliciously sweet! Then I bit the almond-shaped seed, and it was so bitter that I had to spit it out.

Another time, I was walking on the beach in the southern part of St. Lucia when a local man said to me, "Bring a plate with you later on and I will give you a lobster dinner so cheap." So as the sun began to set, I wandered away from the large seaside hotel where I was staying to the beach where "Sugar Ray" was cooking large crayfish in old coffee cans over a small, but steady, driftwood fire. There, other tourists were scattered about, plates in hand, eagerly awaiting Sugar Ray's simple feast. I'll never forget those sunset dinners, and I learned a valuable lesson: for the most delicious food and the best company, get away from the big, expensive resorts and seek out the native vendors.

Nerville, our guide and driver, took us one day to the rain forest by Mount Houlon and the incredible Piton Mountains. We walked single file and when the path got too muddy, Nerville would pick huge, thick leaves and lay them down so that we could continue. I had never seen such lavish green ferns, some of them seven feet tall— swaying, delicate, lacy ferns, the dew glittering on each frond. And there were flowers —flowers I'd only dreamt about, flowers with fantastic pointed shapes, psychedelic orchids, and succulents drooping over the precipices. We gathered bouquets to bring back to our rooms. Never had I gazed upon such rare and glorious combinations; this was better than any fantasy I'd ever had in the subway.

One fine day on a two-hour tour from the very populated Sint Maarten (Dutch side of St. Martin), I stumbled upon the island of Anguilla and fell in love with it. Now, whenever I vacation in the Caribbean, I stay at a guest house, Casa Nadine, in The Valley, the less touristy, interior part of Anguilla.

Most of my early impressions of the tropical world were of rich saturated color— warm, white, powdery sand, coral-pink sunsets over the aqua sea, and leisurely meals of exotic island foods. I've also gained tremendous respect for the kind and generous Anguillans and the quiet peace of their wholesome way of life.

# Pumpkin Soup

Pumpkin was one of the first vegetables I tasted when in St. Lucia. My friend Jimmy and I were served a cup of simple pumpkin soup before the entrée.

**SERVES 6**

2 pounds pumpkin or winter squash, peeled, seeded, and cubed (about 5 cups)

3 garlic cloves

2 onions, chopped

2–3 bay leaves

¼ teaspoon marjoram

¼ teaspoon celery seeds

2 fresh tomatoes, chopped (or 1 cup chopped canned tomatoes)

5 cups vegetable stock (see page 685)

⅓ cup dry white wine

1 tablespoon honey

1 teaspoon cinnamon

salt and freshly ground black pepper to taste

_____

1 cup heavy cream

Place all the ingredients, except the cream, in a large saucepan. Simmer until the pumpkin is soft. Remove the bay leaves.

Purée the mixture in a blender or food processor in several batches. Return the purée to the saucepan on low heat and gradually stir in the cream. Heat through but do not let the soup come to a boil.

# Curried Avocado Soup

This cool soup was inspired by Amy, who has a bakery near Blowing Point where the small ferry docks as it enters Anguilla.

**SERVES 4 TO 6**

2 medium-ripe Haas (dark-skinned)
  avocados
2¼ cups vegetable stock (see page 685)
1–1½ teaspoons curry powder
¾ teaspoon salt

⅛–¼ teaspoon white pepper
½ cup heavy cream

_____

2 tablespoons fresh lemon juice

Split the avocados in half with a knife and remove the pits. Set aside one half. Scoop out the insides of the other three halves with a spoon and blend with 1 cup of the stock in a blender until smooth. Stir in the curry powder, salt, pepper, cream, and remaining stock. Chill.

When ready to serve, garnish the soup with thin avocado slices that have been cut from the remaining avocado half and dipped in lemon juice. Or if you're a "garni queen" like I am—a large pink hibiscus!

## Quick Coconut Bread

This easy bread isn't exactly like putting a straw in a coconut, but almost. If you have the time, you can use fresh coconut to grate and to make the coconut milk (see page 660). If not, a good-quality canned coconut milk and unsweetened grated coconut is just as delicious.

### YIELDS 2 LOAVES

4 cups flour
⅓ cup sugar
2 teaspoons baking powder
¼ teaspoon salt

_____

1 egg, beaten

1 cup canned or fresh coconut milk or
  milk
½ cup butter or margarine, melted
1 teaspoon pure vanilla extract
2 cups grated unsweetened coconut
1 cup currants or raisins (optional)

Preheat the oven to 350°.

Sift the dry ingredients into a mixing bowl. Blend in the egg, milk, butter, and vanilla. Mix in the grated coconut and the currants or raisins if used. Turn out onto a floured board and knead slightly. Shape into two loaves and pat into two buttered medium loaf pans. Bake for 40 to 45 minutes, until a toothpick in the center comes out clean.

# A Perfect Day for Bananafish

 On a voyage through the islands, most of our lunchtime meals were frozen foods prepared in Puerto Rico. Bananas appeared in casseroles, desserts, soups, and snacks. Carlos, our Puerto Rican navigator, laughed when I remarked, "What a banana-oriented culture this is!" I hadn't eaten this many bananas or plantains in my entire life. A couple of years later I was lucky enough to be in St. Lucia (one of the Windward Islands) and see acres of banana trees, the banana bunches growing upward toward the sun. No account of island foods would be complete without a special tribute to these wonderful fruits.

### SERVES 6 TO 8

*2 pounds flounder, cod, or perch*

*2 garlic cloves, pressed*

*1 teaspoon fresh thyme (1 1/4 teaspoons dried)*

*juice of 1 lime*

*salt and freshly ground black pepper to taste*

*3 yellow plantains*

*4–5 cups salted water*

*2 medium onions, finely chopped*

*1/3 cup finely chopped celery*

*2 tablespoons butter*

*1 cup diced fresh tomatoes*

*2 tablespoons tomato paste*

*2 garlic cloves, pressed*

*1 teaspoon fresh thyme*

*juice of 1 lime*

*2 eggs, well beaten*

*1 cup grated sharp cheddar cheese*

Place the fish fillets in a nonreactive casserole dish or shallow bowl. Combine the garlic, thyme, lime juice, salt, and pepper and pour half of this mixture over the fish, reserving the other half. Cover the dish and set aside to marinate.

Peel the plantains and thinly slice. Bring the salted water to a boil and drop in the plantain slices. Boil them for 20 to 25 minutes until tender and easily pierced.

Sauté the onions and celery in the butter until the onions are translucent. Add the tomatoes, tomato paste, garlic, thyme, lime juice, and reserved marinade; cook for a few minutes more.

Oil an ovenproof baking dish. Place a layer of plantain slices on the bottom and top them with a layer of fish fillets. Pour on half of the tomato sauce, half of the beaten eggs, and sprinkle on half of the cheese. Repeat the layers, ending with the cheese.

Bake, covered, at 350° for 30 minutes, then uncovered for 10 minutes. Allow the casserole to set for 5 to 10 minutes before serving.

## *Yellowman's Banana Lime Bread*

 In St. Lucia and Anguilla, I made friends with some local people after repeated visits to the same beaches. I won't forget their great nicknames: Merit, Rah's Bucket, Campbell Soup, Sugar Ray, the Ram, So-Lar, Freakout, Domino, Splif, and Gorgeous.

This tasty bread is named after Yellowman.

### YIELDS 1 LOAF

**BATTER**

¾ cup brown sugar, packed

½ cup butter, softened

2 eggs, lightly beaten

1 cup mashed bananas (about
   3 bananas)

3 tablespoons milk (or plain yogurt)

1 tablespoon fresh lime juice

½ teaspoon salt

½ teaspoon ground ginger

¾ cup unsweetened grated coconut,
   toasted (see note)

2 cups unbleached white flour

1 teaspoon baking powder

**GLAZE**

¼ cup brown sugar

1 tablespoon butter

1 tablespoon rum

3 tablespoons fresh lime juice

_____

¼ cup unsweetened grated coconut,
   toasted

Preheat the oven to 350° and butter a 9x5x3-inch loaf pan.

To make the batter, in a large mixing bowl, cream the sugar and butter. Stir in the eggs, bananas, milk or yogurt, and lime juice. Add the salt, ginger, and grated coconut

*Note: Spread the grated coconut on an unoiled baking tray and toast in a 300° oven or toaster oven for less than a minute. Be careful not to let it burn—it's delicate.*

and mix well. Sift the flour and baking powder together in a separate bowl. Add the dry ingredients to the wet ingredients and mix them until smooth. Pour the batter into the buttered loaf pan and bake for an hour, or until a knife inserted in the center comes out clean. Cool the bread for about 10 minutes before removing it from the pan.

Meanwhile, for the glaze, combine the brown sugar, butter, rum, and lime juice in a small saucepan on low heat, stirring constantly for about 5 minutes, until it becomes a thin syrup. Pour this glaze over the loaf, spreading it with a spatula or spoon to coat the top and sides. Sprinkle toasted grated coconut evenly over the glazed loaf.

# The Mariners' Pepperpot Soup

 On Anguilla in the port of Road Bay is a popular restaurant called The Mariners'. Out in the bay is an old shipwreck. My friend Jimmy and I paddled out to explore the wreck and afterward treated ourselves to The Mariners' zesty pepperpot soup.

SERVES 6 TO 8

*1 large onion, chopped*
*4 garlic cloves, minced*
*2 tablespoons vegetable oil*

---

*2 celery stalks, chopped*
*2 carrots, peeled and chopped*
*1 large green bell pepper, chopped*
*1 large red bell pepper, chopped*
*2 tomatoes, coarsely chopped*
*1 teaspoon sweet Hungarian paprika*
*½ teaspoon ground black pepper (or to taste)*

*1 teaspoon salt*
*¾ teaspoon cinnamon*
*¼ teaspoon ground cloves*

---

*6 cups vegetable stock (see page 685)*
*½ cup dry white wine*
*1 cup cooked brown rice*

---

*minced fresh parsley*

In a soup pot, sauté the onion and garlic in the oil until the onion is translucent, 5 to 10 minutes. Add the celery, carrots, peppers, tomatoes, and spices. Sauté for another 5 minutes, stirring often to prevent sticking. Add the stock, wine, and rice and simmer until the vegetables are tender, about 25 minutes. Garnish with fresh parsley.

# Sweet Potato Balls

 About a fifteen-minute walk from the house where I stay on Anguilla is a friendly little snack bar owned by Phyllis Hodges called the Tasty Tit. Here I sip dark English beer and eat a lunch of sweet potato balls. Then I'm ready for an afternoon of exploring one of Anguilla's incredible beaches.

### YIELDS ABOUT 20 BALLS

*1 pound sweet potatoes*
*1 egg, beaten*
*1 small onion, minced*
*1 tablespoon milk*
*1 tablespoon butter*
*¾ teaspoon grated peeled fresh ginger root*
*2 tablespoons unbleached white flour*

*1 tablespoon chopped fresh parsley*
*pinch of cayenne*
*salt and freshly ground black pepper to taste*

*¼ cup vegetable oil*
*2 cups whole wheat bread crumbs (see page 654)*

Cook the sweet potatoes. Either bake them and scoop out the insides, or peel them and then steam or boil and drain.

Mash the cooked sweet potatoes and mix together with all the ingredients except the oil and bread crumbs. Heat the oil in a heavy skillet on medium heat. Place the bread crumbs in a bowl. Form little balls by dropping a heaping tablespoon of the sweet potato mixture into the bread crumbs, dredging each ball through the bread crumbs. Fry several balls at a time in the hot oil, rolling them around occasionally to brown on all sides. When golden brown, drain them on paper towels and serve immediately, or keep them warm in the oven until you're ready to serve.

Try dipping the sweet potato balls in Pebre (see page 158), a wonderful taste complement.

*Variation* Stuff each sweet potato ball with an olive or a little cube of sharp cheese by poking the olive or cheese into the center with your finger. Roll the balls in the bread crumbs and fry as above.

# Trinidad Mango Salsa

## YIELDS 1 ½ CUPS

*1 ripe mango or papaya*
*1 red chile, minced*
*1 garlic clove, minced*

*salt and ground black pepper to taste*
*juice of 1 lime*

Peel the mango or papaya, discard the stone or seeds, and chop the fruit. Combine it with the remaining ingredients.

Spoon the salsa into a jar, cover tightly, and refrigerate. It will keep for a month.

Use Trinidad Mango Salsa as a condiment with vegetables or fish, or serve it with chips.

# Avocado Ahdi

## SERVES 4

*2 small avocados*
*½ cup finely chopped red bell pepper*
*¼ cup finely chopped green bell pepper*
*¼ cup finely diced carrots*
*¼ cup finely chopped cucumbers*
*¼ cup finely chopped tomatoes*
*¼ cup finely chopped red onions*

*10 whole Spanish olives, finely chopped*
*juice of 1 lime*
*½ teaspoon salt*
*freshly ground black pepper to taste*
*Tabasco or other hot sauce to taste*

*chopped fresh cilantro*

Cut the avocados in half lengthwise very carefully, discard the pits and carefully scoop out the shells with a tablespoon. Reserve the shells. Chop the flesh finely and set aside.

Combine the chopped vegetables and olives and season with lime juice, salt, black pepper, and Tabasco. Add the avocado and toss lightly. Take care not to break up the avocados too much while tossing or the salad will look muddy.

Gently mound the salad into the avocado shells or on a bed of fresh spinach leaves. Garnish lightly with cilantro.

# Escoveitche de Pescado

On Anguilla I often relax and exchange stories with people at Roy's Place, a restaurant/bar that features wonderfully fresh fish caught only minutes before it's served. Many times I've watched the fishermen dock their boats near Roy's to unload yellowtail snapper, conch, and crayfish. Anguillans are famous boat builders and are very proud of their bright, individually decorated boats.

One night after enjoying a few rum punches with my friends, I decided to approach some local fishermen and barter for the night's catch. I got much more than I bargained for—the fish was huge and barely dead. Barefoot and clad only in my bikini, I teetered up the steep, rocky hill carrying this big snapper in the dark.

This was only the beginning, because once at the guest house, Casa Nadine, I had to scale, gut, and divide it. The scales were the size and width of dimes and I was equipped with only a butter knife. Thirty minutes into this unfamiliar procedure, my entire body was covered with silver, glittering fish scales. When Hudson, the proprietor of Casa Nadine, entered the communal kitchen and saw me pathetically struggling with the huge snapper, he became nearly hysterical with laughter. Once he'd recovered, he lent me a hand, and we managed to serve up a delicious meal of fish steaks.

## SERVES 6

1½ pounds fish steaks or fillets
   (snapper, swordfish, cod, yellowtail,
   bluefish, etc.)
2–3 limes

**MARINADE**
½ cup olive oil
½ cup water
½ cup white vinegar
½ teaspoon freshly ground black pepper

¼ teaspoon salt
3 medium onions, thinly sliced
1 small red bell pepper, chopped

___

½ cup vegetable oil
¼ teaspoon ground allspice
1½ cups unbleached white flour

___

½ cup coarsely chopped Spanish olives

Rinse and pat dry the fish steaks or fillets. Place them in a nonreactive casserole dish or a shallow bowl. Squeeze the limes and pour the juice over the fish. Refrigerate, turning the fish occasionally to coat it with lime juice.

Combine the marinade ingredients in a saucepan. Simmer on low heat for 45 minutes.

Heat the vegetable oil on medium-high heat in a frying pan. Combine the allspice and flour in a bowl. Evenly coat each fish steak with the flour mixture. Brown on both sides, then reduce the heat and cook for 10 to 15 minutes more until the fish is just done—don't overcook.

When the fish is done, put it back into the casserole dish, sprinkle on the olives, pour the marinade over it, cover, and refrigerate for several hours or overnight.

Serve cold.

# *Classic Rum Punch*

 One teeny weeny island off the coast of Anguilla is called Scilly Cay. It is owned by a man named Gorgeous and his dog, Dracula. You arrive at Scilly Cay after a three-minute motorboat ride from Anguilla's northeast shore. I was mesmerized by this tiny (only one acre), calm, remote island. As you stroll the beach or sit gazing at his beautiful conch shell sculptures, Gorgeous will mix up a classic Caribbean rum punch, usually dark rum and a combination of fruit juice and ice.

## SERVES 4 TO 6

*16 ounces orange juice*
*16 ounces pineapple juice*
*2 ounces fresh lime juice (or fresh lemon juice)*

*2 ounces grenadine*
*8–12 ounces dark rum*

Combine all of the ingredients. Serve over ice, garnished with slices of orange, lime, or lemon.

# Zemi's Ginger Smoothies

There's a beautiful vegetarian healthfood restaurant called Zemi's on the beach in Phillipsburg, Sint Maarten, that I visited daily for Nancy's fresh fruit smoothies. With this recipe I have re-created my favorites, Zemi's Ginger Smoothies.

Here are three smoothies, each one using banana and grated ginger root as its base. Choose your favorite. I prefer to serve smoothies at room temperature. And, of course, the fresher the fruit, the better the drink will taste. If you have the time, using fresh, homemade coconut milk will make these smoothies even more delectable.

## SERVES 1

### ORANGE-PINEAPPLE SMOOTHIE

½ cup orange juice

¼ cup pineapple juice

½ banana

¼–½ teaspoon grated peeled fresh ginger root

½ cup crushed ice (or 2 small ice cubes)

### APPLE-COCONUT SMOOTHIE

¾ cup apple juice

pinch of unsweetened grated coconut (or 1 tablespoon coconut milk [see page 660])

½ banana

¼ teaspoon grated peeled fresh ginger root

½ cup crushed ice (or 2 small ice cubes)

### ORANGE-PINEAPPLE-COCONUT SMOOTHIE

¼ cup orange juice

¼ cup pineapple juice

1 tablespoon coconut milk

½ banana

¼ teaspoon grated peeled fresh ginger root

½ cup crushed ice (or 2 small ice cubes)

Blend all the ingredients in a blender or food processor until smooth.

# Roti Dough

I was sitting on the French side of St. Martin, when I noticed a small stand with little wooden tables and chairs and lots of people eating these wonderful, handy turnovers with all kinds of fillings. I had to have one. Here's my recipe for roti dough. I've used it with both sweet and savory fillings. Try it filled with Colombo de Giromon (see page 131).

YIELDS DOUGH FOR 4 ROTIS

*2 cups unbleached white flour*
*½ teaspoon baking soda*
*½ teaspoon salt*

*½– ¾ cup milk*
*vegetable oil or ghee (see page 294)*

In a large bowl sift together the flour, baking soda, and salt. Stir in ½ cup milk. Add more milk as needed, one tablespoon at a time, until a stiff dough is formed. Knead the dough well on a floured board. Shape it into four equal balls. Roll out each ball to form an 8- or 9-inch circle. Brush each circle with vegetable oil or ghee and then form it into a ball again. Cover the balls of dough and let them sit for 15 to 20 minutes at room temperature.

Roll out the balls of dough once more to their original size. Heat a cast-iron frying pan. Place a roti in the pan and cook it for one minute. Turn and brush it with a thin layer of vegetable oil. Turn the roti a couple of times until both sides are lightly browned. Remove it from the frying pan and let it cool until the roti can be handled. Pat it between the palms of your hands (ouch!) until supple. Repeat with the rest of the rotis. Keep the rotis warm and moist by covering them with a cloth.

Place about ¾ cup of Colombo de Giromon, or other filling, in the center of each roti. Fold the bottom half up first, then fold over the two sides, and last the top half to form a rectangular package. Either eat them right away, or place them in a baking dish, covered with a damp cloth, and bake, tightly covered with foil, at 350° for 15 to 20 minutes.

Rotis are good served with a side dish of spicy black beans and slices of ripe avocado.

# Colombo de Giromon

·

## Curried Vegetables

SERVES 4 TO 6 AS AN ENTRÉE
YIELDS FILLING FOR 4 ROTIS (SEE PAGE 130)

4 cups water

½ cup dry white wine

1 heaping teaspoon whole peppercorns,
   tied in cheesecloth (or ¾ teaspoon
   freshly ground black pepper)

2 pounds pumpkin or winter squash,
   peeled, seeded, and cubed (about
   5 cups)

½ red bell pepper, chopped

½ green bell pepper, chopped

**COLOMBO SEASONING**

¼ teaspoon cayenne

2 teaspoons ground coriander seeds

2 teaspoons dry mustard

4–5 garlic cloves, pressed

¼ teaspoon turmeric

½–1 teaspoon water

_____

¼ cup peanut oil

3 small onions, chopped

1 teaspoon unbleached white flour

½ cup coconut milk (see page 660)

2 tablespoons fresh lime or lemon juice

2 tablespoons dark rum

1 scallion, chopped

salt and freshly ground black pepper to
   taste

Combine the water, wine, and peppercorns or black pepper in a saucepan and bring to a boil. Reduce the heat to a simmer, add the pumpkin and red and green peppers, and cook until very soft. Strain the pumpkin and peppers and reserve one cup of the cooking liquid. Remove the peppercorns tied in cheesecloth.

Vigorously blend all of the Colombo Seasoning ingredients to a paste.

Heat the oil in a large skillet on medium heat, add the onions, and sauté for a few minutes. Stir in the Colombo Seasoning paste and flour. Add the cup of reserved cooking liquid, stirring occasionally, until the sauce thickens. Add the coconut milk, lime juice, rum, and scallion. Stir in the pumpkin mixture and cook for 5 minutes more. Season to taste with salt and pepper.

This makes enough filling for four rotis or it can be served over rice for a tasty entrée.

# West Indian Rice and Peas
## with Tempeh

This is my Moosewoodized version of West Indian Rice and Peas.

SERVES 6

2 cups uncooked brown rice
1/2 cup unsweetened grated coconut
2 1/2 tablespoons vegetable oil
4 cups water
1/2 stick cinnamon

___

2 cups fresh or frozen black-eyed peas
   (10-ounce package frozen or 1 cup
   dried, soaked at least 5 hours)
3 bay leaves

___

1 medium onion, chopped

3 garlic cloves, minced or pressed
1/4 cup vegetable oil
1/2–1 small chile, sliced (or 1/4 teaspoon
   cayenne) (or to taste)
1/2 red or green bell pepper, chopped
8 ounces tempeh, cubed
generous pinch of ground fennel seeds
1 teaspoon salt (or to taste)
1/2 teaspoon ground black pepper

___

2 scallions, chopped

Sauté the rice and coconut in the 2½ tablespoons of oil for 2 to 3 minutes, stirring constantly. Add the water and cinnamon stick. Cover the pot and bring it to a rapid boil. Don't lift the lid to see if the water is boiling. Just notice when steam begins to escape. Traditionally, the lid is never lifted while cooking rice. When steam escapes, reduce the heat and simmer about 40 minutes.

Meanwhile, cook the fresh or frozen black-eyed peas with the bay leaves in salted, boiling water until tender. The cooking time will vary with different peas. If you're using soaked dried black-eyed peas, it will take about 30 minutes. Frozen black-eyed peas will take about 20 minutes. When the peas are done, drain them and remove the bay leaves. Keep them warm until the rice and tempeh are ready.

While the rice and peas are cooking, sauté the onion and garlic with the ¼ cup oil in a cast-iron skillet for a few minutes, until the onions soften. Stir in the chile or cayenne and the bell pepper and continue to sauté for a couple of minutes. Add the tempeh, fennel, salt, and pepper and lower the heat. Stir frequently and cook, covered, until the tempeh is golden brown and a little crisp.

Combine everything, mixing together well. Adjust the seasonings and serve hot, topped with the chopped scallions.

## *Sorbet Caribe*

In January '88, my son Tazio was born and I skipped two years of tropical winter vacations. Hopefully, we can share the sights, smells, and feelings of the Caribbean in the near future. Until then, Tazio is content to eat the sweet fried plantains (one of his favorites) and taste the avocado soup. He delights in desserts like Sorbet Caribe and Banana Smoothies and sucks on the mango pits for a long time, reciting, "Bango-Bango, Mommy, Bango." Why correct him? I hope he's getting primed for a future trip to one of those "banana-oriented cultures"!

### SERVES 4

*2 very ripe bananas, sliced and frozen*
*3 ounces pineapple juice*
*3 ounces frozen pineapple juice (freeze it*
  *in an ice cube tray for convenience)*

*2 tablespoons unsweetened shredded*
  *coconut*

Place the frozen banana slices, fresh and frozen pineapple juice, and coconut in a blender or food processor. Purée until the mixture is smooth and resembles soft ice cream or a slush.

Serve immediately in chilled bowls.

# Lime Tart
# Just for Chris

In the backyard of Anguilla's Casa Nadine was Chris's tropical garden full of lime trees and other luscious fruits and vegetables. Chris told me on my first visit that I was always welcome to come and pick anything I liked, and I often did. When I returned to the island a year later, I learned that she had died. I'll never forget her limes or her generosity. So this tart is for Chris.

### YIELDS 8 TO 10 SERVINGS

**PASTRY**

7 tablespoons butter
1 1/3 cups unbleached white flour
pinch of salt
1/4 teaspoon pure vanilla extract
1/4 cup sugar
3–4 tablespoons ice water

**FILLING**

1/2 cup fresh lime juice (about 4 limes)
5 tablespoons butter

1/2 cup sugar
5 eggs, well beaten
1/4 teaspoon pure vanilla extract

———————————————

1 banana, sliced (optional)
1 lime sliced into very thin rounds
   (optional)
unsweetened flaked or shredded coconut
   (optional)

To make the pastry, cut the butter into small pieces and work it into the flour with a pastry cutter, two knives, or your fingertips. Mix in the salt, vanilla, and sugar and then just enough ice water to bind the dough. With your fingers, press the dough into the bottom and sides of a 9-inch drop-bottom tart pan. Chill the crust for one hour or overnight.

Preheat the oven to 425°.

Line the chilled crust with waxed paper and fill it with dried beans or rice to prevent the crust from buckling during baking. Bake at 425° for 15 minutes. Carefully remove the beans and waxed paper.

Lower the oven temperature to 350°.

For the filling, mix together the lime juice, butter, and sugar in a nonreactive saucepan and heat until the butter melts and the mixture is just warm. Pour the beaten eggs slowly into this mixture in a steady stream, whisking constantly. Continue to stir on low heat until the mixture thickens into a custard. Stir in the vanilla. Pour the custard into the baked crust and bake for 30 to 35 minutes or until the custard sets.

Sprinkle coconut in a ring around the edge before you chill the tart. Just before serving, garnish with banana or lime slices in a ring around the top. Serve chilled.

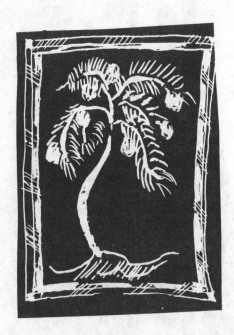

ELIANA PARRA

# Chile

# INTRODUCTION

Chile, whose name is derived from *tchili,* a native word for "snow," is a long and narrow country on the west coast of South America. It is over 2,600 miles long, roughly equivalent to the distance from Baja, Mexico, to Alaska, and its width averages only 110 miles.

The imposing Andes Mountains lie on Chile's eastern border; its western border on the Pacific Ocean is lined by lower coastal mountains. In the far north is an area of true desert, one of the driest regions on the earth, while Chile's southern tip extends into the frigid climate of the Antarctic.

The varied geography and climate allow for a wide range of agriculture. Chile's rich soil produces many fruits, including kiwis, apples, oranges, melons, water pears, strawberries, pawpaw, peaches, apricots, raspberries, watermelons, and chirimoyas. The north produces guavas, lemons, and olives, and in the *norte chico* (the near north) a vine is cultivated for making *pisco,* a type of liquor. In the central southern region, wheat, barley, grapes, and the sugar beet are grown. Ranching is important throughout Chile, especially in the south.

The sea plays a big part in the Chilean diet and also in its economy. Chile has one of the world's largest fishing industries. Spider crabs, oysters, sea urchins, lobsters, sardines, albacore, anchovies, salmon, and the conger eel are all important exports.

Immigration came more slowly to Chile than to many South American countries. This is partly attributable to the natural geographical barriers and partly to the intimidating nature of the Araucanian warriors. The Araucanians were native peoples who controlled most of the southern half of Chile. The active resistance of the Araucanians to foreign occupation lasted into the late nineteenth century.

The Indian tribes in the north of Chile were part of the vast Inca civilization, which extended south from Peru throughout the northern Andes. The Incas' sophistication in government and technology was unsurpassed by any Indian nation in the Western Hemisphere. By the early sixteenth century, however, the stability of the Inca empire was weakened by a fraternal dispute for the throne. Thus when the first Spanish explorer, Francisco Pizarro, arrived in Peru in 1532, he was welcomed by King Atahualpa as a possible ally.

In 1536, a colleague of Pizarro's, Diego de Almagro, led a gold-hunting expedition south from Peru and declared Chile under Spanish rulership. When his search for gold proved futile, de Almagro returned to Peru. In 1541, Pizarro sent another officer to

Chile, Pedro de Valdavia, and despite fierce resistance from the Araucanians, he succeeded in founding the cities of Santiago, La Serena, Concepción, La Imperial, and Villa Rica. The struggle between the Spanish and native occupants of Chile lasted hundreds of years. Finally, on September 18, 1818, Chile declared itself independent of Spain.

Modern Chile is largely an urban culture. Of the over 12 million people, 83 percent reside in the cities; more than 30 percent live in Santiago alone. Over half of the population is mestizo (of mixed Spanish and Indian blood), only 2 percent is of purely native background. One third of Chile's population is composed of people of European descent: German, British, Italian, Swiss, Austrian, Yugoslavian, and French.

## Festivals and Holidays

In the countryside there are many festivals celebrating agricultural harvests, rodeos, and local religious traditions. People from all over Chile arrive by the busloads to attend. The foods, crafts, and dress differ according to the region. In the north they serve stews, while in the south barbecues are cooked on hot stones, and on the coast they serve virtually every type of seafood. At the festivals, the local people wear traditional costumes of native or Spanish origin. The Mapuches, a prominent Indian tribe, wear blankets and ponchos adorned with silver accessories. Some festivals feature religious processions; people dance and sing as they carry a religious figure, such as the Virgin Tirana, throughout the town.

Up and down the streets musicians play such instruments as *guitarrones* (large, stringed instruments), guitars, *zampoñas* (shepherd's pipes), *quenas* (rustic flutes), *charangos* (five-stringed guitars made from the shell of an armadillo), and the *trutruca* (a Mapuche instrument made out of a long piece of bamboo with a bull's horn at the end of it).

September 18 is our Independence Day, and we celebrate by dancing the traditional Chilean dance, La Cueca. Everywhere in the country you will find *fondas* or *ramadas*. These framework structures, with walls and ceiling made of pine or eucalyptus branches, are built especially for this occasion. People will go to these places to eat empanadas, drink wine, and dance all night long. Everyone wears his or her most colorful clothes, and for the formal *cueca salon* some people wear the traditional Spanish costume of black jacket, white blouse, red waistband, and long black skirt or trousers.

On Christmas we gather with our relatives and friends for a midnight supper. The women spend the entire day cooking in preparation while the children play and the men fuss over the traditional drink, Cola de Mono. By 10 P.M. many large tables are loaded with food and we anxiously await supper.

We celebrate New Year's Eve with our families, much the same as Christmas. Just as in the United States, around 11:30 P.M. the radios and TVs begin to count down the minutes and seconds, and at the stroke of midnight people start to hug each other. Some people cry for those who are no longer there, or for the year that's gone by, hoping that the new year will be better. Others laugh and teenagers light firecrackers. Then it is time to eat. After supper everyone goes to a local dance hall where there is live music. In the Southern Hemisphere, New Year's occurs in the summertime, so in Chile people are moving up and down the streets celebrating, dancing, and having a wonderful time all night long.

## A New Country

My years growing up in Chile truly were sunny and filled with music, dancing, and feasting. Then in 1973, the government of Salvador Allende was overthrown and replaced by a military junta. A period of extreme political oppression followed, during which time my husband, Jano, was imprisoned. After Jano was released from jail, he was continually sought out and questioned by the police. We were very afraid that he would be taken from us again. In 1976, the newly elected president of the United States, Jimmy Carter, enacted a policy admitting 300 refugee families from Chile. Although we were a young couple and our son, Alejandro, was only two years old, we knew we must say goodbye to our family and friends and seek refuge in another country.

We were lucky to arrive in Ithaca, a nice, cosmopolitan town, where there was a large, supportive community. An organization called Friends of Chile helped us to enroll in school and adjust to this new culture. A few years later, after the birth of my daughter, Katalina, I began working at Moosewood, where there was a group of people that became like my family. Now I have the opportunity to write this chapter and share with you some delicious Chilean recipes and special memories of my family and country.

# SOPAS
## S O U P S

In Chile, businesses and schools close for a couple of hours in the middle of the day, and everyone stops to enjoy a leisurely lunch, which is the main meal of the day and is usually eaten at home. When I was growing up, lunch was the central family time. This was very important to my father, and he insisted that everything be done just right. We children should come to the table, clean and smiling and calm, prepared to relate stories of our successes in school. During the lengthy series of lunch courses and rambling adult conversations, we shouldn't betray any impatience to be doing anything else. My mother, who did the cooking, might have preferred a smaller, more abbreviated meal, but she indulged my father's wishes with only a little teasing.

My father insisted that lunch always begin with soup, "Even if it is just an onion boiled in water." Although mother made many delicious traditional soups, we often found it more interesting when she did just boil an onion in water, and then add noodles or cabbage or whatever other leftovers she might find. A little breathless, but with a serene smile, she would present these spontaneous, one-of-a-kind soups to begin a traditional luncheon.

# Sopa de Ajo

·

# Garlic Soup

For this soup the stock should be rich, so use half again as many vegetables as the basic vegetable stock recipe calls for and add a few garlic cloves.

### SERVES 4

*2 medium tomatoes*

*6 garlic cloves, pressed*

*4 slices French, Italian, or whole wheat bread*

*3 tablespoons olive oil*

*2 tablespoons chopped fresh basil*

*4 cups vegetable stock (see page 685)*

Blanch the tomatoes in boiling water for 5 minutes and then peel them. Cut each tomato into 4 slices. Set aside.

Spread the pressed garlic on both sides of each slice of bread. In a heavy skillet sauté each slice of bread in the oil until browned on both sides.

Place each slice of bread in a shallow soup bowl. Top each one with 2 tomato slices. Add a pinch of fresh basil and a few drops of olive oil to each bowl. Add one cup of very hot stock to each bowl. Serve immediately.

# Sopa de Camarones

•

## Shrimp Soup

SERVES 6

2½ cups shrimp, cleaned and deveined
4 cups vegetable stock (see page 685) or
    water

---

3 garlic cloves, minced or pressed
2 medium potatoes, diced
2 carrots, diced
⅛ teaspoon cayenne
3 tablespoons vegetable oil

---

¾ cup heavy cream
1 tablespoon fresh lemon juice

---

¼ cup dry white wine
1 tablespoon chopped fresh parsley
salt to taste

---

1 cup garlicky croutons (see page 661)
1 hard-boiled egg, chopped (optional)

Cook the shrimp in the vegetable stock or water for 5 minutes. Drain the shrimp, reserving the cooking liquid, and set it aside.

In a soup pot, sauté the garlic, potatoes, carrots, and cayenne in the oil for 2 minutes. Add enough of the reserved shrimp liquid to cover the vegetables and simmer, covered, for about 15 minutes, until tender. Drain, reserving the liquid.

In a blender, purée about half of the vegetables, the liquid from simmering the vegetables, about one cup of the shrimp, the heavy cream, and the lemon juice. Return the vegetable-shrimp purée to the soup pot. Stir in the remaining vegetables and drained shrimp, the white wine, and enough of the shrimp liquid to achieve the consistency you like. Simmer the soup on low heat for a couple of minutes, being careful not to boil it. Mix in the parsley and salt to taste.

Garnish each serving with garlicky croutons. Add chopped egg if you like.

## ENTRADAS
### FIRST COURSES

# *Ensalada Olimpica*

This is a summer dish that usually accompanies an entrée. When we were little my mother made it for us, but we did not like cooked vegetables. Now I ask myself, "Why?" It is delicious.

### SERVES 6

*1 medium head cauliflower, cut into florets*

*2 avocados, pitted and peeled*
*4 hard-boiled eggs*
*¼ cup softened cream cheese*
*1 cup lemony mayonnaise (homemade or commercial—if using commercial mayonnaise, add some fresh lemon juice)*

*¼ cup chopped green bell pepper*
*½ cup chopped celery*
*salt and freshly ground black pepper to taste*

*lemon wedges*

Steam the cauliflower florets (see page 681) until just tender. Rinse them immediately with cold water and then drain well.

Slice the avocados and eggs. Whisk the cream cheese together with the mayonnaise until smooth.

In a large bowl, toss all of the ingredients very lightly with the mayonnaise–cream cheese mixture until evenly coated. Add salt and pepper to taste. Serve chilled with lemon wedges.

# Huevos Rellenos con Callampas

•

## Stuffed Eggs with Mushrooms

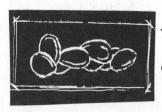 These stuffed eggs are often served at parties or as the first course of a meal.

**SERVES 6**

6 hard-boiled eggs

_____

1 small onion, minced
2 tablespoons butter
1 cup chopped fresh mushrooms
salt and freshly ground black pepper to
    taste
½ teaspoon Dijon mustard (optional)

SALSA BLANCA
1 tablespoon butter
1 tablespoon unbleached white flour
1 cup hot milk
salt and freshly ground black pepper

_____

½ cup freshly grated Parmesan cheese

Peel the hard-boiled eggs. Halve them lengthwise and separate the yolks. In a mixing bowl, mash the yolks with a fork.

Sauté the onions in the butter for a few minutes, until they are just beginning to soften. Stir in the chopped mushrooms, salt, and black pepper and cook for another 5 minutes. Add the onion mixture and mustard to the mashed egg yolks and stir until well blended.

Meanwhile, prepare the salsa blanca. Melt the butter in a saucepan. Whisk in the flour; cook the mixture for a minute or two without letting it brown. Slowly add the hot milk, whisking constantly, until the sauce thickens. Add salt and pepper to taste.

Arrange the egg whites in a buttered baking dish. Generously stuff them with the egg yolk mixture. Pour the salsa blanca over the stuffed eggs, sprinkle them with grated Parmesan, and bake at 350° for about 10 to 15 minutes, until hot.

# Tomates Claudia

·

## Stuffed Tomatoes

In the summer we enjoyed tomatoes fresh from our grandparents' garden. My mother searched out the largest ones for stuffed tomatoes like these.

SERVES 6

6 tomatoes

_____

1 cup cottage cheese
½ cup minced onion
3 tablespoons fresh lemon juice
¼ cup Spanish olives, chopped
¼ cup chopped fresh parsley
⅓ cup mayonnaise (homemade or
  commercial)

¾ cup whole wheat bread crumbs (see
  page 654)
½ teaspoon salt
½ teaspoon freshly ground black pepper

_____

6 leaves Romaine lettuce

Cut off the tops of the tomatoes and carefully hollow out each tomato to form a serving shell. Reserve the pulp for a sauce, stew, or soup.

In a bowl, mix together the remaining ingredients except for the lettuce. Stuff each tomato with the filling mixture. Place a lettuce leaf on each plate and top it with a stuffed tomato.

# PLATOS PRINCIPALES
## MAIN DISHES

## *Empanadas de Papas*

•

## *Potato Pastries*

Twice a week in Chile every community closes one or two blocks of a street to traffic for the Ferias, the farmer's market. There, local people sell produce, clothing, shoes, and empanadas and other foods. When my husband's parents came to the U.S. for a long visit, we made and sold empanadas every Saturday at the Ithaca Farmer's Market.

Empanadas are Chile's most popular food. At the soccer stadium vendors selling empanadas carry big baskets of them around the stands. Soccer is the most popular sport in Chile, and even more so in my family, because my father-in-law was once a professional soccer player. Here in Ithaca the tradition continues. My husband, Jano, played with an international soccer team, and my son, Alejandro, now fifteen years old, toured Europe with Teams U.S.A. this past summer. Sometimes we make a special trip to Rochester, nearly one hundred miles from Ithaca, just to see Chilean soccer broadcast on TV.

Empanadas are a traditional Chilean dish but are usually made with meat. I created this recipe as a vegetarian alternative.

SERVES 8

FILLING

4 medium potatoes, peeled and cubed

2 small onions, finely chopped
1/2 cup chopped green bell pepper
3 tablespoons vegetable oil
1/2 teaspoon ground cumin seeds
1/2 teaspoon ground black pepper
1 teaspoon salt
1/2 teaspoon cayenne
1 cup corn, fresh, frozen, or canned
  (drained)
1/2 cup chopped pimientos

1 cup cream cheese, softened to room
  temperature
1 cup grated mild cheddar or Monterey
  Jack cheese

DOUGH

1 cup warm water
1/2 tablespoon vinegar
1 teaspoon salt
3 1/2 cups unbleached white flour
3 tablespoons melted butter or
  margarine, or vegetable oil

vegetable oil for frying

To make the filling, in a small pot, cook the potatoes in water to cover until soft.
Drain them well and mash them with a potato masher or wooden spoon.

In a large frying pan, sauté the onions and bell peppers in the oil. Season with the
cumin, black pepper, salt, and cayenne. When the vegetables begin to soften, stir in the
corn. Continue to sauté until all the vegetables are tender, then transfer them to a large
bowl and add the pimientos. While the vegetables are still hot, vigorously mix in the
mashed potatoes, cream cheese, and cheddar cheese.

For the dough, in a large bowl, mix together the water, vinegar, and salt. Add the
flour and melted butter. Mix well and work the dough a bit with your hands. Turn the
dough out onto a flat surface and form it into a large, long roll. Cut it into eight equal
pieces. With a lightly floured rolling pin, roll out each piece into a 6- or 7-inch circle.
Place about 1/2 cup of filling on each circle leaving about a 1/2-inch border. Wet the edge
of half of each circle to help the dough seal well. Then fold the dough over the filling to
form semicircles and crimp the edges with the tines of a fork.

In about one inch of oil, heated to 360°, fry both sides of each pastry until golden
brown. Drain the empanadas on paper towels.

Serve with Pebre (see page 158).

# Torta de Papas

•

# Potato Omelet

 This is a dish my mother often made. On those afternoons, when we came home from school, the house was filled with the aroma of torta. There on the table, with a nice salad and a big bowl of Pebre, was Torta de Papas. We'd change out of our school uniforms and go to the bakery around the corner to buy some fresh bread. Then we'd sit down at the table and enjoy this tasty Torta de Papas.

SERVES 4

4 medium potatoes
1 cup vegetable oil

_____

4 eggs

1 tablespoon chopped fresh parsley
salt and freshly ground black pepper, to
    taste

Wash the potatoes and peel them if you wish. Slice them into ¼-inch rounds.

Heat the oil in a heavy frying pan until very hot, but not smoking. Fry the potatoes on high heat for 5 minutes, turning them a couple of times until golden brown. Then remove the potatoes to several layers of paper towels to drain.

In a bowl, beat the eggs well with the parsley, salt, and pepper. Add the drained potatoes and set aside.

Pour off all but about 3 tablespoons of the oil from the frying pan. Reheat it if necessary. Slowly pour the egg-potato mixture into the pan. Distribute the potatoes evenly, cover the pan, and cook the omelet for 4 minutes on medium-low heat. Flip the omelet, cover, and cook for another 4 minutes.

Serve topped with Pebre (see page 158).

# Repollo Relleno

•

# Stuffed Cabbage

I usually only eat cabbage when it is very finely chopped in a fresh salad. I was happy to discover this recipe that presents cabbage in another way that I enjoy just as much.

SERVES 6

*1 medium cabbage*

*½ cup chopped onions*
*2 garlic cloves, minced*
*3 tablespoons vegetable oil*
*salt and ground black pepper to taste*

*5 slices bread*
*½ cup milk*
*4 eggs*
*1 cup freshly grated Parmesan cheese*

Core the cabbage and remove the tough outer leaves. Place the whole cabbage in a large pot and boil it in water to cover until the outer leaves are just softening and easy to pull off. Remove the cabbage from the water; carefully peel off 10 outer leaves and set them aside. Leave the cooking liquid in the pot and set it aside. Chop enough of the remaining cabbage to make 2 cups of chopped cabbage.

Sauté the onions, garlic, and chopped cabbage in the oil with the salt and pepper for about 10 minutes, stirring occasionally.

While you are sautéing the vegetables, place the bread in a bowl and pour in the milk. When the bread has absorbed the milk, add the eggs and Parmesan and mix well with your hands. Then add the sautéed vegetables and mix again very well.

Drape a cheesecloth over a large bowl. Then line the sides and bottom of the bowl with overlapping cabbage leaves. Save a few leaves. Fill the cabbage-lined bowl with the vegetable mixture and cover it with the last few cabbage leaves. Lift the four corners of the cheesecloth and tie them down snugly.

Place the Repollo Relleno—the stuffed cabbage—in the pot with the cabbage water so that it is completely submerged. Bring it to a boil, then lower the heat and simmer for 35 minutes.

When ready to serve, cut the cheesecloth casing and invert the Repollo Relleno onto a platter of Spanish rice (see note).

I suggest you serve this with a simple tomato-avocado salad, Ensalada de Porotos Verdes (see page 159), or Ensalada Esmeralda (see page 461).

---

*Note: You can make a simple Spanish rice by sautéing ½ cup chopped onions until translucent and mixing them with ½ cup chopped tomatoes, ½ cup chopped green or black Spanish olives, and salt and freshly ground black pepper to taste. Then simply stir the vegetables into 3 cups of cooked rice.*

---

## Pastel de Choclo

•

## Corn and Tofu Casserole

I always associate this very traditional dish with my family's reunions at my grandparents' house outside Santiago, which was surrounded by huge cornfields. Everyone worked together to prepare the corn and assemble all the parts of this complicated casserole. Traditionally, Pastel de Choclo is made with beef and chicken; this is my simplified vegetarian version.

2 medium onions, finely chopped

3 garlic cloves, pressed

1 tablespoon sweet Hungarian paprika

2–3 teaspoons ground black pepper (or to taste)

1 tablespoon ground cumin seeds

2 teaspoons salt (or to taste)

2 tablespoons olive oil

3 cakes pressed tofu, grated or crumbled (see page 684)

1 cup chopped tomatoes

¼ teaspoon dried oregano

———————————————

2 hard-boiled eggs, peeled and thinly sliced

¾ cup pitted whole black olives

½ cup raisins

———————————————

2 16-ounce cans cut corn, drained (or 2 10-ounce packages frozen corn, defrosted and drained)

2 eggs

¼ cup chopped fresh basil (1 tablespoon dried)

¼ teaspoon salt

Sauté the onions and garlic with the spices and seasonings in the olive oil. When the onions are translucent, add the tofu, tomatoes, and oregano and continue to cook, covered, for 15 to 20 minutes. Stir occasionally.

Spread this mixture smoothly into an oiled 8x12-inch baking dish. Top with the egg slices, evenly distribute the olives in rows pressing them gently into the mixture, and sprinkle with the raisins.

In a blender or food processor, purée the corn with the raw eggs, basil, and salt. Pour this evenly over the top of the mixture in the baking dish.

Bake, uncovered, at 350° for 45 minutes. The pastel should bake like a frittata and be lightly browned on top but still moist.

# Pescado a la Crema

•

# Fish with Cream Sauce

We often took our vacations at El Tabo, a bathing resort on the Pacific Coast where we ate fish almost every day. This typical Chilean fish dish is very well liked at Moosewood.

### SERVES 6 TO 8

*2 pounds fresh fish fillets*
*salt and freshly ground black pepper to*
    *taste*
*1 medium onion, thinly sliced*
*¼ cup chopped fresh parsley*
*2 tablespoons fresh lemon juice*
*3 tablespoons butter*

*SAUCE*

*4 egg yolks*
*1 cup heavy cream or half-and-half*
*½ cup fresh lemon juice*
*1 tablespoon Dijon mustard*

———————————————

*¼ cup butter*
*6 slices bread*

Butter a baking pan and arrange the fish fillets on the bottom skin side down. Season with salt and pepper to taste and top with the onion slices, parsley, and lemon juice. Dot with butter. Bake, covered, for 20 minutes at 400°.

Meanwhile, make the sauce. In a small saucepan, beat the egg yolks. Add the cream, lemon juice, and mustard. On low heat, allow the sauce to thicken, stirring constantly.

In a large skillet, melt ¼ cup of butter. Fry the bread on both sides until browned.

On each plate, place a slice of bread, then a serving of fish, and ladle some sauce on top. Serve with rice or potatoes and Ensalada de Porotos Verdes (see page 159).

# Torta Pascualina

·

## Spinach Torte

Torta Pascualina originated in Spain. Many immigrants arrived in Chile after World War II: Germans, Italians, Jews, Arabs, and, of course, Spaniards. Consequently, we enjoy a variety of international cuisines.

SERVES 8 TO 10

**FILLING**

1 medium onion, chopped

3 garlic cloves, minced or pressed

3 tablespoons vegetable oil

1¼ pounds fresh spinach, cleaned, stemmed, and chopped (about 8 cups)

1 cup grated Parmesan cheese

4 ounces softened cream cheese

3 eggs

⅛ teaspoon nutmeg (or to taste)

salt and freshly ground black pepper to taste

**DOUGH**

4½ cups unbleached white flour

1¼ teaspoons salt

⅓ cup vegetable oil

1−1¼ cups water

_____

vegetable oil

6 eggs

1 beaten egg yolk

For the filling, in a medium pan sauté the onion and garlic in the oil until the onion is translucent. Add the spinach and continue to sauté for about 5 minutes. Remove the vegetables from the heat and drain any excess liquid. Thoroughly mix in the Parmesan, cream cheese, and 3 eggs. Add the nutmeg, salt, and pepper to taste. Set the filling aside while preparing the dough.

For the dough, place the flour and salt in a large bowl and combine well. Stir in the oil and enough water to make a smooth dough that will not stick to your hands. Divide the dough into six pieces. Choose a baking pan that has a rim and measures about 10x15 inches or 13 inches square. Roll each piece of dough into a shape slightly larger than the pan.

Preheat the oven to 350°.

Oil the baking pan. Brush three of the sheets of dough with oil and layer them in the pan. They should overlap the pan by at least an inch. Spread the filling on top of the third layer of dough. Make six evenly spaced indentations in the filling and crack a raw egg into each one. Fold the overlapping edges up and over the filling. Brush the remaining 3 sheets of dough with oil and layer them on top. Brush the top of the torta with the beaten egg yolk.

Bake for 20 to 30 minutes, or until golden.

Serve hot or at room temperature.

# ENSALADAS
### S A L A D S

## *Pebre*

•

## *Salsa de Cilantro*

On Sundays in Chile, my whole family enjoys a very peaceful day together. The day starts with my mother going to the Feria, where she buys the goods she needs to begin preparing lunch. Because visitors will drop by throughout the day, she always makes a large quantity of food. I remember my mother and aunts in the kitchen chopping vegetables to fill big bowls with Pebre, Chile's most popular side dish; it is always on the table and is eaten with everything.

### YIELDS ABOUT 3 CUPS

⅓ cup minced onions or scallions
½ cup finely chopped fresh cilantro
4 medium tomatoes, finely chopped
2 tablespoons Tabasco or other hot
   sauce
2 tablespoons vegetable oil

1 tablespoon vinegar
1 tablespoon fresh lemon juice
1 garlic clove, pressed or minced
   (optional)
salt and ground black pepper to taste

Mix all of the ingredients together in a medium bowl and refrigerate.

If you're using onions instead of scallions, you may want to minimize the "bite" of the raw onion. If so, sprinkle the minced onions with salt and let them sit for a few minutes. Then press them gently in a sieve and rinse them well in running water.

This sauce will keep, refrigerated, for three or four days.

Pebre is a perfect complement to any Chilean main dish.

## *Ensalada de Porotos Verdes*

•

## *Green Bean and Tomato Salad*

 This is a common summer salad that is easy to make and can accompany any of the main dishes.

SERVES 4

| | |
|---|---|
| *1–1½ pounds fresh green beans* | *1 teaspoon salt* |
| | *2 garlic cloves, minced* |
| *juice of 1 lemon* | |
| *3 tablespoons vegetable oil* | *2 large tomatoes, cut into wedges* |

Wash and trim the green beans. Cut them diagonally into 1½-inch pieces. Cook the beans in boiling water to cover for about 10 to 15 minutes, until just tender. Drain the beans and set them aside to cool. Combine the lemon juice, oil, salt, and garlic. In a bowl, combine the cooked green beans and tomato wedges. Toss them with the dressing.

This versatile side dish is served in Chile, especially in the summer, when green beans and tomatoes are abundant.

# DULCES
## SWEETS

*It is Aunt Rosa who makes the pastries for my family's special occasions. She has made pastries since she was a young woman. When we were children she always made our birthday cakes, and she made all the wedding cakes for everyone in the family. Paradoxically, she never had a wedding cake of her own; from a very young age she had to work to help my grandparents, and when they grew old she took care of them. She is now seventy-seven years old, but she is not alone, because she has all of us who love her very much.*

*When I was little, every summer we went to the beach with Aunt Rosa, where she made pastries for an American woman who owned a pastry shop. My aunt called her "La Gringa Hona." Aunt Rosa also had a big clientele of wealthy vacationers to whom we delivered pastries. If there were any pastries left over, at teatime we'd sell them from house to house. Sometimes we'd ring a doorbell and dogs would chase us. Occasionally I'd be embarrassed, but most of the time it was fun. People loved my Aunt Rosa's pastries and it was nice to return home with all the pastries sold.*

*I have so many nice memories of my Aunt Rosa. She is so sweet and strong. She still works, making pastries for family affairs. Everytime someone from Chile comes to the U.S., Aunt Rosa sends me a box of dulces, and my children, husband, and friends finish them the same day. They are delicious!*

# *Pan de Navidad*

·

# *Christmas Bread*

This is a traditional bread made for Christmas. Employers often give their workers an *aguinaldo,* a small package containing one pan de Navidad and a bottle of wine.

YIELDS 8 SERVINGS

4 cups unbleached white flour
1 cup sugar
2 teaspoons baking powder
1 cup diced dried assorted fruits, about
    6 ounces (peaches, pears, apples,
    raisins, prunes, apricots, dates,
    currants)
½ cup chopped almonds
½ cup chopped walnuts

1 teaspoon cinnamon
pinch of ground cloves
½ teaspoon freshly grated nutmeg
3 eggs, beaten
2 tablespoons butter, melted
½ cup milk
2 tablespoons cognac
sugar for sprinkling

Preheat the oven to 350°.

Sift the flour, sugar and baking powder into a bowl. Add the fruit, nuts, and spices. Stir until mixed. Fold in the eggs, melted butter, milk, and cognac. Gently work the dough for a minute or two until it holds together in a single mass. Smooth the batter into a buttered 10-inch pie plate. Sprinkle a bit of sugar on top and bake for fifty minutes to one hour until a knife inserted in the center comes out clean.

# Empanadas de Peras

•

## Pear Pastries

This is one of my Aunt Rosa's pastries. When we were children, my sister and I stood by the table and pestered her while she made empanadas. Sometimes we'd beg her to let us roll out some dough, and she'd give us enough dough to make some little empanadas.

### YIELDS 16 SMALL EMPANADAS

FILLING

3 cups dried pears (1 1/2 pounds)
4 1/2 cups water
1/2 cup sugar
1/2 teaspoon cinnamon
1/4 teaspoon ground cloves

DOUGH

1 1/2 cups unbleached white flour

1/4 teaspoon salt
1/2 cup butter, at room temperature
2 egg yolks
5—8 tablespoons ice water

_____

1 egg yolk beaten with 2 tablespoons
water

In a covered pot, simmer the pears in the water for 30 to 40 minutes, until soft; drain, saving the liquid. When the pears are cool, whirl them in a blender or food processor, with enough reserved liquid to make a thick purée. Stop the blender occasionally and push down the pears. The pear purée should be about the consistency of mashed potatoes.

Heat 1/2 cup of the leftover pear liquid in a saucepan. Stir in the sugar and cook for about 5 minutes, until the sugar begins to caramelize. Add the pear purée, cinnamon, and cloves, stirring well. Remove the filling from the heat and allow it to cool. The cooling can be hastened by placing the pan into a sink filled with cold water and stirring occasionally.

Meanwhile, prepare the dough. Sift the flour and salt into a large bowl. Cut in the butter with a pastry cutter, knives, or your fingers until the mixture resembles a coarse meal. Beat 2 egg yolks with 3 tablespoons of ice water. With a fork, gently mix the beaten yolks into the flour mixture. Add more water as needed until the dough forms a ball. Chill the dough for 10 minutes.

Preheat the oven to 350°.

Divide the dough into sixteen equal balls. On a floured surface, roll out each ball of dough into a 3- or 4-inch circle. Brush the edge of each circle with the beaten egg yolk mixture and place 2 to 3 tablespoons of the filling in the center. Fold the dough over the filling to form a semi-circle, and, using the tines of a fork, crimp the edges to seal the empanada. Pierce the top of each empanada twice with a fork and brush it with the egg-yolk mixture. With a spatula, carefully lift the empanadas onto a lightly oiled baking sheet. Bake for 30 to 40 minutes, until puffed and golden.

# Galletas de Nueces

•

# Walnut Cookies

British immigrants brought the custom of teatime to Chile, and because they took tea at 11 A.M., we refer to our teatime as *la hora de once* (the hour of eleven), even though we take tea at 6 P.M. We set the table very nicely, and Aunt Rosa's treats are the first thing on the table. Here is one of her most delicious cookies.

### YIELDS 50 COOKIES

*1¼ cups butter, at room temperature*
*1 cup confectioners' sugar*
*2½ cups unbleached white flour*

*2 teaspoons pure vanilla extract*
*1 cup chopped walnuts*

Preheat the oven to 350°.

Cream the butter and sugar until light and fluffy. Then add the flour, vanilla, and walnuts and mix well. The batter will resemble crumbly pie dough.

Using your hands, take small amounts of dough and work them into balls, then place them onto an unbuttered baking sheet. Bake for 15 to 20 minutes.

# *Manjar*

•

# *Milk Custard*

 I remember my aunt cooking a big batch of manjar outside in the yard. She poured a few gallons of milk into a big copper pot and heated it over a wood fire. On manjar days, we played around that part of the yard, always aware of the steaming pot. At first Aunt Rosa came out and stirred it just once in a while, but when it was getting close to the end, she would stay and stir it all the time. We'd stay right there with her, dreaming and thinking that she was making magic: all that white milk would be transformed into delicious, brown, thick manjar. When it was just cool enough, she gave us our first little taste of it.

Manjar is intensely sweet, and in Chile it is used in a variety of ways with baked goods —to fill pastries and "jelly rolls," to frost cakes and cookies, and as a sweet spread (like jam) for bread, muffins, or biscuits. Manjar has become a favorite dessert for many of us at Moosewood; sometimes we top fresh fruit salad with a dollop of manjar and a touch of whipped cream.

### YIELDS 2 CUPS

*8 cups milk*                                    *2 cups sugar*

Boil the milk, pour it into another saucepan, add the sugar, and allow it to simmer for 2 hours. That's right . . . 2 hours! Stir once in a while. When the mixture begins to thicken, stir more often to prevent the custard from sticking to the bottom of the pan. Although this may seem a bit tedious at first, the custard will slowly get darker and tastier as it thickens, and you will find yourself enchanted by the gradual transformation.

# Kuchen de Manzanas

•

## Apple Kuchen

My father's father, Julio Galaz, lived all alone in the countryside near Santiago. We enjoyed visiting him. During the day, we'd ride his horses and donkeys. In the evening, we'd sit in his living room and listen to tangos on his old crank Victrola. As we left, he'd bring us a huge basket of apples from his orchard. At home, my mother would use the apples to make kuchen, a favorite German dessert. German cooking became popular after World War II with the influx of many German immigrants and today is part of Chilean cuisine.

### SERVES 8

BATTER

2½ tablespoons softened butter

3 tablespoons confectioners' sugar

2 eggs

½ teaspoon pure vanilla extract

⅓ cup unbleached white flour

1 teaspoon baking powder

_____

3 medium apples, peeled and thinly
  sliced

½ teaspoon cinnamon

TOPPING

1 cup milk

3 tablespoons unbleached white flour

2 tablespoons sugar

2 eggs, separated

½ teaspoon pure vanilla extract

For the batter, cream the butter until smooth. Beat in the confectioners' sugar. Add the eggs and vanilla. While constantly beating, add the flour and baking powder and beat for a few more minutes. Spread the batter in a buttered 10-inch pie plate. Arrange the apple slices on top and sprinkle on the cinnamon.

Preheat the oven to 350°.

In a saucepan, heat the milk and then stir in the flour and sugar until dissolved. Cook on low heat until thickened. Stir in the egg yolks and remove the pan from the heat. In a separate bowl, beat the egg whites until stiff. Fold in the egg whites and vanilla and mix thoroughly. Spread the topping over the apples and bake the kuchen for 30 to 35 minutes, or until the topping is set and lightly browned.

# BEBIDAS
## BEVERAGES

## Cola de Mono

•

## Tail of the Monkey

During the Christmas holidays there is not a house in Chile without Cola de Mono. In our house, my father makes it. In the morning, he begins boiling the milk, and by evening he's filled dozens of bottles. Then he calls us, one by one, and asks, "What do you think it needs?" But he knows it is perfect. He just wants to hear, "It's delicious!"

### YIELDS 12 SERVINGS

*6 cups milk*
*1 cup sugar*
*2 cinnamon sticks (or 1 teaspoon*
*cinnamon)*

*¼ cup instant coffee*
*2 cups tequila*
*1 teaspoon pure vanilla extract*

Bring the milk, sugar, and cinnamon to a boil. Dissolve the coffee in the hot milk mixture. Let it cool in the refrigerator. When the drink is well chilled, add the tequila and vanilla. Pour it into capped bottles and return it to the refrigerator.

Serve Cola de Mono very cold.

Cola de Mono will keep in the refrigerator for two to three weeks.

# *Vino Caliente*

•

## *Hot Spiced Wine*

In the winter, when you invite friends over, welcome them from the cold with this wonderful, warm, sweet drink.

### SERVES 4 TO 6

*1 bottle dry red wine (¾ liter)*
*3 tablespoons sugar*
*4 whole cloves*

*2 cinnamon sticks*
*1 orange, sliced into rounds*
*2 tablespoons cognac, rum, or tequila*

Heat the wine with the sugar, cloves, cinnamon, and orange slices, stirring occasionally to dissolve the sugar. When the sugar has dissolved and the wine is hot, but not boiling, remove it from the heat and add the cognac. Let it sit for 10 minutes. Serve hot.

This is a warming drink for the winter season.

DAVID HIRSCH

# *China*

# INTRODUCTION

When I was growing up in New York City, my family had a routine dining schedule; each day of the week had its prescribed menu. Every Wednesday we ate veal cutlets and spaghetti, one of my favorites. Thursday we had hamburgers and mashed potatoes. Friday was a day to linger outside because the menu included boiled beef and vegetable soup. Saturday night was an evening off for a hard-working mom. Often we were treated to a visit to Ling's Restaurant on Utopia Parkway, in Bayside, Queens. This was my introduction to Chinese cuisine. Ling's was part of the trinity of Chinese, Italian, and Jewish restaurants that seemed to regularly appear on many blocks of the boroughs of the city back then. Ling's occupied a storefront on a block with a candy store, pizzeria, Hebrew National Deli, bakery, five-and-ten, and a drugstore. Stepping into Ling's, with its muted lighting, ornately carved screens, and painted scrolls depicting dragons, temples, and mist-shrouded mountains, I felt I was entering a strange and foreign world.

Instead of a standard American meal—entrée with a side dish of vegetables—here was food that was combined and cooked in a far different fashion. Everything was prepared, seasoned, and sauced in ways that were mysterious and exotic. I liked the way it tasted, all thrown together (so to speak).

My parents, brother, sister, and I were not very daring or experimental diners, inevitably ordering wonton soup, egg rolls, chow mein, fried rice, lo mein, and a couple of other favorites. As predictable as this was, it stood out from the very routine dining schedule at home. In retrospect, I see that this was an initiation to the enjoyment of vegetables for a kid who had become adept at all kinds of ruses and schemes to avoid eating my greens. How could you pick the vegetables out of an egg roll?

Since then, regional cuisines of China have become more widely known, adding a diversity that has greatly expanded the hybrid Chinese-American cuisine of two or three decades ago.

The small collection of recipes in this chapter presents some favorite, well-known Chinese or Chinese-inspired dishes that are only a glimpse at the cuisine of a country with over a billion people and more than a hundred ethnic groups. Regional differences have contributed to what we conceive of as a single Chinese style of cooking. But all the regions have their culinary significance.

South China, Canton in particular, has a reputation for "haute cuisine." For a Chinese restaurant in the U.S., having a great chef from the south is equivalent to importing a French chef. It is certainly the Chinese cuisine with which most Americans are familiar, as the Cantonese were the first to emigrate in large numbers. The abundance of seafood, fish, and agricultural products in the semi-tropical south and a history of innovative cooks have contributed to this reputation.

Eastern China, home of the Yangtze River Valley and Shanghai, is a prime rice-growing area that also exports soy sauce and Shaohsing rice wine. Braising of food is a common technique here. Buddhist vegetarian cooking, which has had somewhat limited exposure in this country, is reputed to have reached its best form in eastern China.

In the northern wheat-growing areas, rice is supplanted by noodles, crêpes, dumplings, pancakes, and steamed breads. Garlic, onions, scallions, and leeks are popular as seasonings. Many banquet dishes originated at the Imperial Court in Beijing.

Before modern transportation, the west, including Szechuan and Hunan, was isolated from the rest of China by mountain ranges. The generous use of chiles and the multiplicity of flavors in much of the cooking have sparked the palates of many a diner. Besides the perky effect on the taste buds, chiles act as a food preservative and an air conditioner (through the cooling effects of perspiration) in an exceedingly humid climate with few mechanical conveniences. And in times of scarcity, when the food supply is low, chiles add interest and zest to a meal that is predominantly rice.

In all areas of China today, restaurants and home cooks serve foods common to the whole country as well as regional specialties. It has become difficult to strictly define regional schools of cooking in China because a dish from one region may become popular in another and it will be adapted to the local cuisine. Cosmopolitan Hong Kong is the outstanding example of this cross-cultural style.

As in most Asian cultures, the regions of China have in common the use of vegetables as an integral part of every meal. With very little available arable land, the agricultural emphasis in most of China has always been toward more efficient food crops rather than livestock. Rice, soybeans, tofu, wheat, gluten, and other grains and legumes have been developed as protein sources for millennia.

In China, tradition dictates that meals are prepared with a harmonious balance of all the elements that food can offer—taste, fragrance, texture, appearance, and nutrition.

Taste can be the simple, natural, or delicate flavor of Spinach and Leek Soup or more complicated with complementary opposites like the lightly sweet and sour Batter-Fried Fish with Garlic Sauce. Choosing a "taste" for a dish involves the selection of spices or seasonings that will enhance but not mask desired flavors.

Fragrance builds to taste. The aromatic impact of garlic, ginger, and other spices are enjoyed before the first bite, as in Hot Pepper Green Beans.

Texture: here the range of possibilities—crisp, smooth, soft, slippery, crunchy—could all be used to describe Mu Shu Pancakes.

Appearance offers a wide range of options: the color, shape, and size of food. Most dishes are prepared so they can be eaten with chopsticks or a spoon. Chinese cooks will adhere to a uniformity of shape and size in a particular dish. For example, all the vegetables in a noodle dish will be shredded, whereas everything in a dish with peanuts will be diced to roughly peanut size. Multidish meals will offer a variety of "shapely" appearances with the full gamut of chunks, slices, shreds, rounds, and dices.

The nutritional value of foods is preserved by the quick cooking on high heat that characterizes much of Chinese cooking. Vitamins and minerals lost in longer cooking techniques are retained. Multidish meals where grains, legumes, vegetables, and fish are all consumed in one sitting provide excellent protein combinations.

## Menu Planning

Preparing a meal also involves considerations of a practical nature. If there's one cook and one wok, it's necessary to limit the number of dishes that have to be cooked at the last minute. Inspired by Ling's, I offer an easy reference for menu planning:

| COLUMN A (last minute) | COLUMN B (can be completed in advance) |
|---|---|
| Fried Wontons | Spinach and Leek Soup |
| Vegetable Pancakes | Wonton Soup |
| Buddha's Garden | Marinated Vegetables and Bean Thread |
| Batter-Fried Fish with Garlic Sauce | Five-spice Tofu |
| Mu Shu Vegetables | Sesame Noodles |
| Hot Pepper Green Beans | Baked Tofu |
| | Stuffed Tofu |
| | Ginger Ice Cream |
| | Almond Cookies |

Choosing just one from Column A and either one or several from Column B would simplify a cook's life. As the various elements of taste, texture, and appearance may be contrasted and harmonized in a single dish, so too would the variety of dishes in a whole meal.

In China, the ordering of dishes at banquets or smaller gatherings differs from the presentation in the United States. Tea is served before and after dining. Soup is a principal beverage throughout the meal. Leafy salads are virtually unknown. However, dishes roughly translated as "cold mix," such as Marinated Vegetables and Bean Thread, form warm weather meals. Food is eaten family style, diners taking small amounts of a wide variety of dishes. Desserts, as we know them, do not finish a meal. However, sweet snacks are served with tea and between meals. Fresh fruit in season is typically served at the end of a meal.

## Methods and Techniques of Chinese Cooking

*Cutting:* Properly cut foods will cook quickly, uniformly, and present an attractive appearance. Sharp knives or cleavers, though seemingly more fearsome, are really safer than dull ones, which always seem to slide around on vegetables, and possibly into your fingers or hands. A good sharp knife will quickly pierce hard vegetables and requires only attentiveness. Hold the food to be cut in place with one hand, curling the fingers down and under, so your fingertips are protected.

*Slicing:* Hold food perpendicular to blade, make cuts ⅛ inch apart.

*Diagonal Slicing:* Hold food at a 45-degree angle to blade, make cuts ⅛ inch apart.

*Shred (like julienne strips):* Cut ⅛-inch slices again, so they measure ⅛ x 1 or 2 inches long. You can stack the long slices on top of each other for quicker cutting crosswise into the desired length.

*Mince:* Cut shreds at right angles into very small pieces.

*Dice:* Larger than mince, ¼ inch to ½ inch square.

*Oblique or Roll Cutting:* Gives more surfaces to cook and absorb flavors. Good for hard, firm vegetables like carrots, parsnips, or broccoli stems. Cut as for diagonal slicing. Roll the vegetable ¼ turn so that the cut surface faces upward. Cut again on the diagonal through the previously cut surface. Roll the vegetable ¼ turn and continue this process until the vegetable is completely cut.

*Stir-frying:* This is a quick cooking technique using a small amount of oil, high heat, and a continuous stirring and tossing of food. Flavors, juices, nutrients, and natural color are all preserved by this process. For successful stir-frying:

a) Have all ingredients prepared beforehand and near the stove. Check the recipe and line up all the seasonings, vegetables, sauce mixes, and so on in the order they'll be cooked. Combine items that will be placed in the wok at the same time. If not, the onions will be burning while you're searching for the soy sauce!

b) Place the wok on a burner with medium-high to high heat. After a moment, add the oil called for in the recipe and swirl it to coat the bottom of the wok. When the oil has warmed, add various seasonings as directed in the recipe, typically garlic, ginger, or chiles. Stir-fry a moment to help season the oil before adding the other ingredients.

Experience is the best way to judge how long to cook vegetables. "Hard" vegetables, such as cauliflower, carrots, green beans, onions, celery, and broccoli will take longer than "medium-hard" asparagus, cabbage, eggplant, mushrooms, or zucchini; or "soft" greens like spinach, bok choy, mustard, and kale, or tomatoes, tofu, bean sprouts, peas, snow peas, and scallions.

Maintain a high heat and add water or stock only if necessary to prevent scorching. Electric ranges will not cool down fast enough if lower heat is necessary. It's better to move the wok to another burner that has been preset to a medium heat. Vegetables that contain little juice (cauliflower, green beans, broccoli) will need a bit of stock or water added and a couple minutes of steaming with the lid on. It's best to keep the initial cooking period relatively dry so the vegetables will retain crispness.

Sauce ingredients, if any, are usually added at the end and cooked only until the cornstarch or other thickener has done its part and the sauce is heated. Remove the vegetables from the wok when they're slightly crunchier than desired as they will continue to cook for several minutes on their own. Note that the times in the following recipes are only suggestions. Stove heat, vegetable size, and the quantity cooked in the wok may all alter the actual cooking time. Let the color and texture of the vegetables be your guide for determining when they're cooked just right.

***The Wok:*** The wok is essential cookware for Chinese and other Asian cuisines. Wok cookery may have begun as a fuel-saving device. In a country where resources have always been precious, it remains a quick, labor-saving method. Actual cooking time is short; the majority of labor spent in meal preparation is in the cutting and assembling of ingredients. Heavy iron skillets can do in a pinch, but the advantages of a wok are many. It can be used for stir-frying, deep-frying, and steaming. The rounded, semi-spherical shape distributes heat evenly throughout the bottom and sides, catches splattering oil, and allows for the the vigorous tossing and stirring of food that could fly out of a flat skillet.

Woks made of carbon steel conduct heat and stay seasoned better than those of aluminum, stainless steel, or copper. Seasoning instructions, telling how to protectively seal the surface, always come with new woks. To keep a wok well seasoned, never scrub it with steel wool or metal scrubbers; use sponges or plastic scrubbers and soak only if necessary with a mild dishwashing soap. Dry the wok immediately after washing and apply a bit of oil with a paper towel to avoid surface oxidation. Reseasoning the wok will only be necessary if food is badly burned onto the surface and has to be scrubbed off with abrasives.

Flat-bottomed woks are necessary for use with electric ranges because the heat elements need to be in direct contact with the cookware. Round-bottom woks come with a ring that allows the wok to sit over a gas burner. Woks usually come equipped with a cover, and frequently a wooden handle, which facilitates quick moves. A Chinese spatula, which looks like a small shovel, is an excellent tool for wok cooking and works more efficiently than a spoon.

# Chinese Vegetable Stock

Soups that are brothy and have no added legumes or grains need to have a rich, concentrated stock that is flavorful on its own. This stock is seasoned with Chinese ingredients to create a strong base for vegetarian soups.

Double the amount of ingredients and there'll be enough to freeze three 6-cup portions of stock, the amount needed for both soups in this chapter, or six 1-cup portions for sauces plus two 6-cup portions for soup.

### YIELDS 9 CUPS

*4 dried shiitake mushrooms*
*hot water to cover*

_____

*2 medium onions*
*2 large carrots, peeled*
*2 celery stalks*
*1 leek, thoroughly rinsed (see page 667)*
*  (or add 1 more medium onion)*
*1 tablespoon vegetable oil*

*4 thin slices fresh ginger root (about the*
*  size of a quarter)*
*2 whole garlic cloves*
*¼ teaspoon whole black peppercorns*
*¼ teaspoon whole Szechuan peppercorns*

_____

*1 tablespoon tamari soy sauce*
*8 cups water*

Cover the shiitake mushrooms with hot water and soak for about 20 minutes. Meanwhile, coarsely chop the onions, carrots, celery, and leek.

In a soup pot, heat the vegetable oil for a moment. Add the chopped vegetables and the remaining ingredients, except the soaking mushrooms, soy sauce, and water. Stir-fry for 3 or 4 minutes. Add the soy sauce, water, and the mushrooms with their soaking liquid. Bring the stock to a boil and then lower the heat and simmer, covered, for about an hour. Strain. Cool to room temperature.

Freeze any stock that you won't be using within two or three days. Any stock you plan to use soon, but not immediately, should be refrigerated.

# *Wontons*

Piquant with scallions, garlic, and ginger, this recipe makes enough wontons either for a couple of batches of soup or for soup and an appetizer for another day. A good dish to make when you can draft family or friends to form an assembly line for quick wonton production.

YIELDS ABOUT 50 WONTONS

2 tablespoons peanut oil
1½ tablespoons grated peeled fresh
    ginger root
2 medium garlic cloves, minced or
    pressed
2 cakes tofu, frozen, thawed, and
    crumbled, about 2 cups (see page
    684)

½ cup finely chopped scallions
2 teaspoons dark sesame oil
2 tablespoons tamari soy sauce

———————————————

50 wonton wrappers (see page 686)
bowl of lukewarm water
cornstarch for dusting

Heat the peanut oil in a wok or heavy skillet. Sizzle the grated ginger root and the garlic in the oil for just a moment, then add the crumbled tofu and stir-fry for a few minutes. Add the scallions, sesame oil, and soy sauce and stir well. Set this filling aside to cool for a few minutes.

Set up a work area with a stack of wonton wrappers, a small bowl of lukewarm water, the filling, and a platter dusted with cornstarch for the filled and folded wontons. Place a wonton wrapper flat in front of you in a diamond position. Drop a heaping teaspoon of filling on the center of the wonton wrapper. Dip your fingertips in the water and moisten all four edges of the wonton wrapper. Pull the top corner down to the bottom corner, folding the wrapper over the filling to make a triangle. Press the edges firmly to seal. Bring the left and right corners together above the pocket of filling. Overlap the tips of these corners, moisten with water, and press together. Place the completed wonton on the cornstarch-dusted platter and go on to the next one.

*For soup:* Drop the wontons into boiling water and cook until just tender, about 5 minutes. Drain. This recipe will yield about 10 servings for soup.

*To fry:* Heat 2 to 3 cups of oil in a wok or deep fryer until hot. Deep-fry the wontons in batches until golden, about 2 or 3 minutes on each side. Drain. Serve with Duck Sauce or Dipping Sauce (see pages 180 or 181).

Uncooked wontons will keep in the freezer for at least 2 months if well wrapped. Thaw them before frying, but drop them still frozen into boiling water or simmering soup and cook 2 minutes longer than when fresh. If you prefer to make fewer wontons, this recipe can be halved.

# *Duck Sauce*

Serve both this and the Dipping Sauce that follows with Wontons (see page 179) or Vegetable Pancakes (see page 185). We like to use all-fruit preserves that contain fruit concentrates as the only sweetener.

YIELDS 1 ¼ CUPS

*½ cup all-fruit peach or apricot preserves*
*¼ cup white or cider vinegar*

*1 tablespoon grated peeled fresh ginger root*
*⅓ cup finely chopped scallions*

Combine the preserves, vinegar, and ginger in a saucepan and heat to a simmer. Simmer gently, stirring occasionally, for 5 minutes. Remove from the heat and stir in the chopped scallions. Duck sauce will keep for a couple of weeks in the refrigerator.

# Dipping Sauce

*1 tablespoon tamari soy sauce*
*1 teaspoon dark sesame oil*
*1 teaspoon rice vinegar*

*¼ teaspoon chili oil*
*¼ teaspoon honey or sugar*
*1 tablespoon water*

Combine all the ingredients in a bowl. Dipping sauce will keep indefinitely if stored in the refrigerator.

# Wonton Soup

A classic. If you've already prepared the wontons and stock, the final preparation is very quick.

SERVES 6

*1½ cups shredded bok choy or celery cabbage*
*1 tablespoon peanut oil*
*6 cups Chinese Vegetable Stock (see page 178)*

*salt and ground black pepper to taste*

*25 Wontons (see page 179)*
*3 scallions, thinly sliced on the diagonal*

In a soup pot, sauté the bok choy in the oil for one minute. Add the stock and bring it to a boil. Lower the heat and simmer until the bok choy is just tender, about 5 minutes. Add salt and pepper to taste.

Meanwhile, in a separate pot, bring about 2 quarts of water to a boil. Drop the wontons into the boiling water and cook until just tender, about 5 minutes. Drain the cooked wontons and add them to the soup. Serve garnished with scallions.

# Spinach and Leek Soup

A light and delicate soup, with the flavors of the vegetables predominating.

### SERVES 4 TO 6 AS AN APPETIZER

1½ tablespoons peanut or vegetable oil
2 garlic cloves, pressed or minced
2 large leeks (white and tender green
    parts), well rinsed and sliced
    diagonally (see page 667)
1 medium carrot, cut into matchsticks

6 cups Chinese Vegetable Stock (see
    page 178) or other flavorful vegetable
    stock (see page 685), warmed
2 tablespoons tamari soy sauce
1 tablespoon rice vinegar
salt and ground black pepper to taste

10 ounces fresh spinach, washed and
    stemmed
½ cup canned water chestnuts, drained,
    rinsed, and sliced

strips of Five-spice Tofu (see page 189)

Heat a wok or heavy soup pot on high heat for half a minute and add the oil. Swirl the oil to coat the bottom and add the garlic, leeks, and carrot matchsticks. Lower the heat to a simmer and cook, covered, for 10 minutes, stirring occasionally.

Uncover the wok, increase the heat to high, and add the spinach and water chestnuts. Stir-fry for 2 minutes until the spinach is wilted. Lower the heat to medium. Add the warm stock, soy sauce, and rice vinegar. Season to taste with salt and pepper.

Heat through but do not boil. Serve immediately; garnish with strips of Five-spice Tofu.

This soup is light and delicate, an excellent appetizer.

# Sesame Noodles

 Noodles are traditionally served at birthday celebrations, left uncut, to symbolize long life. If you can get fresh Chinese noodles, so much the better.

In this dish, Chinese sesame paste adds a rich, nutty flavor and smoothness to the sauce. It's made from roasted, ground sesame seeds and is quite different in taste from Middle Eastern tahini. Use unsweetened, smooth peanut butter if sesame paste is unavailable. Once opened, jars of sesame paste can be refrigerated indefinitely. To use, pour off and reserve the oil at the top of the jar. Spoon out the desired amount of paste, and then return the reserved oil to the jar. The oil will keep the paste from drying out.

Serve sesame noodles as an appetizer, side dish, or warm weather luncheon.

### SERVES 4 TO 6 AS AN APPETIZER OR SIDE DISH

**SAUCE**

2 garlic cloves, minced or pressed

2 tablespoons Chinese sesame paste

1 tablespoon dark sesame oil

3 tablespoons tamari soy sauce

2 tablespoons rice wine

1 1/2 tablespoons rice vinegar

1 tablespoon honey

1/2 teaspoon chili paste

pinch of five-spice powder

1 scallion, chopped

2 tablespoons chopped fresh cilantro
 (optional)

---

8 ounces dried wheat noodles, linguini,
 or soba noodles (see page 680)

fresh mung bean sprouts

unsalted roasted peanuts

1 scallion, finely sliced on the diagonal

In a blender or food processor, purée all the sauce ingredients until free of lumps. Cook the noodles until tender and drain immediately; toss with the sauce. Serve at room temperature, topped with crisp, mung bean sprouts, peanuts, and scallions.

*Note: If you're not serving this soon after preparation, the noodles might clump together. Should this happen, stir in a little warm water and soy sauce just before serving.*

# Marinated Vegetables
and Bean Thread

This "salad" is at its best visually when served at once, but it can also be quite delicious after marinating a few hours or overnight. The savory dressing has a double garlic flavor, combining raw garlic and oil seasoned with garlic.

### SERVES 6

2 ounces cellophane noodles (mung bean thread) (see page 656)
2½ cups boiling water

DRESSING

¼ cup thinly sliced scallions
1 tablespoon grated peeled fresh ginger root
1 tablespoon minced or pressed garlic
2 tablespoons vegetable oil
2 whole "stars" of star anise
1 garlic clove, halved
2 tablespoons tamari soy sauce
2 tablespoons water

1 tablespoon red wine vinegar
1 teaspoon dark sesame oil
½ teaspoon molasses
¼ teaspoon freshly ground black pepper or cayenne

1 medium carrot, julienned
1 red and 1 green bell pepper, julienned
1½ cups snow peas (or green beans cut in half diagonally)
about 1 teaspoon dark sesame oil
1 scallion, thinly sliced

Cover the mung bean thread with the boiling water and allow it to sit for 20 minutes.

Meanwhile, to make the dressing, place the scallions, ginger, and minced garlic in a bowl and set aside. Heat the oil in a small skillet. Add the star anise sections and the garlic clove and cook on medium heat, turning the garlic over until it is just golden, about 3 to 4 minutes. Discard the garlic and star anise and pour the seasoned oil over the scallion-ginger mixture. Add the rest of the dressing ingredients and set aside.

Steam or blanch each vegetable until tender but still crisp (see page 681).

Thoroughly drain the bean thread. Snip the strands with scissors in one or two places so they're easier to eat. Toss the bean thread with about ⅓ of the dressing and arrange nest-like on a platter. Mix the rest of the dressing with the drained, steamed vegetables, and arrange them in the center of the nest of bean thread. Garnish with a drizzle of sesame oil and top with sliced scallions.

# Vegetable Pancakes

In these pancakes Chinese seasonings are used to create a hybrid, Western-style dish that is an ideal appetizer, light lunch, or brunch.

**YIELDS ABOUT 14 3-INCH PANCAKES**
**SERVES 4 TO 6**

*½ cup finely chopped green or red bell pepper*
*1 cup finely chopped cabbage*
*¾ cup chopped scallions*
*1 cup grated carrots*
*½ cup canned water chestnuts, drained, rinsed, and finely chopped*
*3 eggs, lightly beaten*

*1 tablespoon toasted sesame seeds*
*1 tablespoon tamari soy sauce*
*½ teaspoon salt*
*½ cup unbleached white flour*
*scant tablespoon baking powder*

—————————————————

*peanut or vegetable oil for frying*

The pepper, cabbage, and scallions may be chopped by hand or with a food processor. Try to achieve ¼-inch pieces. The carrots will cook better grated rather than chopped.

In a large bowl, mix together all the ingredients, except the oil, until well blended. Thoroughly coat the bottom of a large, heavy skillet with about a tablespoon of oil. Heat the oil until a drop of water sizzles on the hot surface. Pour about ¼ cup of batter into the hot skillet for each pancake. Cook the pancakes on medium heat for 2 or 3 minutes on each side, until nicely browned. Add more oil to the skillet as needed for subsequent batches.

Serve at once, either plain or with Duck Sauce or Dipping Sauce (see pages 180 or 181).

# *Hot Pepper Green Beans*

Fresh chiles, black beans, garlic, and vinegar have a nice affinity. They combine here to add zest to a quickly prepared vegetable dish, typical of Hunan cooking, with its use of hot peppers and a clinging, highly seasoned sauce.

### SERVES 4 TO 6

*1 pound fresh green beans, stemmed*

*4 garlic cloves, minced or pressed*
*1/2 cup chopped scallions*
*2 fresh chiles, seeded and finely chopped*
  *(or to taste)*
*1 tablespoon fermented black beans,*
  *rinsed (see note)*

*3 tablespoons rice vinegar*
*2 tablespoons tamari soy sauce*
*1 1/2 teaspoons cornstarch*
*1 tablespoon brown sugar*
*2–3 tablespoons rice wine*

*3 tablespoons peanut or vegetable oil*

Blanch the green beans for 2 minutes (see page 653).

In a small bowl, combine the garlic, scallions, chiles, and fermented black beans. In another small bowl combine the vinegar, soy sauce, cornstarch, sugar, and rice wine.

Heat the oil in a wok, add the black bean mixture, and stir-fry for a minute. Add the green beans and stir-fry for about 5 minutes. Mix in the rice vinegar mixture and continue to stir-fry just until the beans are coated. Serve at once.

---

*Note: Fermented black beans are black soybeans preserved by fermentation with salt and spices. Frequently teamed up with garlic, they add a distinctive aroma and taste. Rinse before using. They are sold in Asian food stores, packed in plastic bags, which can be refrigerated indefinitely once opened.*

---

# Baked Tofu Variations

Tofu has been popular in China for more than two thousand years, dating back to the Western Han Dynasty. At first it was predominantly a family dish. However, it now appears among fancier Chinese banquet foods and enjoys an international reputation.

We bake a lot of tofu at Moosewood. Baked tofu is firm, chewy, and will absorb the flavors of the marinade. The tofu made with a simple marinade is one of our favorites and works well as an addition to dishes that have a complex flavor of their own. The savory variation could more easily be served on its own. Use it in salads, sandwiches, soups, or to accompany other dishes and provide the central protein component of a meal. The third or "tasty" variation is a Moosewoodized Asian hybrid that adds the richness of tahini and the tanginess of miso.

## SERVES 6

2 cakes tofu (12 ounces each), pressed
  (see page 684)

### SIMPLE

1 tablespoon dark sesame oil
2½ tablespoons tamari soy sauce
2½ tablespoons water

### SAVORY

2 tablespoons dark sesame oil
2 tablespoons tamari soy sauce
1 tablespoon rice wine, sake, or dry
  sherry
1 tablespoon rice or cider vinegar
1 garlic clove, minced or pressed

2 tablespoons finely minced onion
1 teaspoon grated or minced peeled
  fresh ginger root
3 tablespoons water
¼–½ teaspoon hot chili paste
  (optional)

### TASTY

1 large or 2 small scallions, finely
  chopped
2 tablespoons miso
⅓ cup tahini
3 tablespoons water

For Simple or Savory tofu, preheat the oven to 375°. Combine the marinade ingredients in a ceramic, glass, enameled, or stainless steel 9-inch baking dish. Cut the tofu into cubes or triangles. For cubes, cut each cake like a Rubik's Cube: into three slices horizontally and then three slices from front to back and three slices from side to side. For triangles, cut each cake into three slices horizontally, stack the slices, and cut down through them from corner to corner on each diagonal. Place the pieces of tofu into the baking dish with the marinade.

Bake, turning the tofu two or three times during the baking. A rubber spatula is handy for turning the tofu without breaking it. Tofu in the Simple marinade should bake for about 35 minutes or until browned and most of the marinade is absorbed or evaporated. Tofu in the Savory marinade may take a little longer, about 45 minutes, for the same results.

For Tasty tofu, preheat the oven to 375°. Combine the scallions, miso, tahini, and water. Cut the cake of tofu horizontally into ¼-inch slices. Spread the top of each slice of tofu with the miso-tahini mixture. Oil a 10x12-inch baking dish. Place the tofu in the baking dish in stacks of two slices, miso-tahini up.

Bake for about 20 minutes, until the topping is browned and crusty. Cut diagonally into triangles and serve as appetizers or as a side dish.

# Five-spice Tofu

Because there's no oil in the preparation, this tofu is very low-fat. It can be used to add spiced flavor and protein to a variety of soups, stir-fries, sandwiches, omelets, and stews.

Method One is faster if you want to use the tofu relatively soon. Method Two is the more traditional process and requires no baking.

### YIELDS 4 5-INCH BLOCKS

2 cakes tofu (12 ounces each),
    preferably firm, or, if soft, pressed
    (see page 684)

MARINADE

3 tablespoons tamari soy sauce
¾ cup water
¼ teaspoon five-spice powder (see note)
2 whole "stars" of star anise
1 teaspoon molasses

For Method One, combine the marinade ingredients in a glass, ceramic, or stainless steel baking dish about 9 inches square. Cut each cake of tofu in half horizontally. Place the slices of tofu in the baking dish and spoon some marinade over them. Bake at 350° for one hour, turning the tofu over after 30 minutes. Cool and drain before storing the tofu. It will keep, refrigerated and covered with plastic wrap, for a week.

For Method Two, cut each cake of tofu in half horizontally. Combine the marinade ingredients in a saucepan or pot wide enough to fit the four pieces of tofu in a single layer. Bring the marinade to a boil. Add the tofu. Simmer, uncovered, on very low heat for 10 minutes. Remove the pan from the heat and marinate the tofu for 3 hours or overnight, turning 2 or 3 times. Cool and drain before storing. The tofu will keep, refrigerated and covered with plastic wrap, for a week.

*Note: Five spice powder is a blend of star anise, fennel seeds, black peppercorns, cloves, and cinnamon. It is available in spice shops and Asian grocery stores.*

# Mu Shu Vegetables

Thinly sliced or shredded stir-fried vegetables make up the filling for Mandarin pancakes. Day lily buds and tree ears provide added flavor and textural interest.

Day lily buds, also called golden needles, are actually dried flower buds. Tree ears, often called cloud ears, are a fungus harvested from tree bark. They have an unusual, slippery yet crunchy texture and a light, smoky flavor. Both day lily buds and tree ears are available dried in many Asian groceries.

Hoisin sauce, a sweet, spicy, ketchup-like condiment traditionally served with Mu Shu dishes, is sold in Asian groceries and in the Asian section of many supermarkets. It contains wheat flour, soy beans, sugar, rice, vinegar, salt, and spices, and is available in jars and cans. If purchased canned, transfer it to a glass jar where it will keep refrigerated indefinitely.

### SERVES 4

¼ cup dried day lily buds (golden needles)

2 tablespoons dried tree ears

1 cup boiling water

**SAUCE**

2 tablespoons tamari soy sauce

1 heaping tablespoon Hoisin sauce

1 tablespoon rice wine or sherry

2 tablespoons vegetable stock (see page 685) or water

½–1 teaspoon hot chili paste (optional)

**SAUTÉ**

3 tablespoons vegetable oil

1 tablespoon grated peeled fresh ginger root

3 garlic cloves, minced or pressed

1 medium onion, thinly sliced

½ small cabbage, shredded

2 bell peppers (1 red and 1 green), thinly sliced

2 medium carrots, grated

2 cups bean sprouts

2 cakes Five-spice Tofu (see page 189), cut into julienne strips

_____

6 scallions, thinly sliced

12 Mandarin Pancakes (see page 191)

1 cup Hoisin sauce

Place the day lily buds and tree ears in separate bowls and soak each with ½ cup of boiling water for 30 minutes. Drain the day lily buds and cut off the stem ends. Drain the tree ears and cut off any woody spots. Rinse briefly, squeeze dry, and set aside.

Mix together the sauce ingredients. Set aside.

Heat a wok on medium-high heat for 30 seconds. Add the vegetable oil and heat for 30 seconds before adding the ginger and garlic. Stir-fry for one minute. Add the onion and cabbage and stir-fry for 2 minutes, lowering the heat a bit if the vegetables stick or begin to brown. Add the peppers and stir-fry for a minute before adding the carrots and bean sprouts. Stir-fry for 30 seconds. Finally, add the day lily buds, tree ears, Five-spice Tofu, and the sauce for the sauté. Stir-fry until heated through, about 3 minutes.

Transfer the Mu Shu Vegetables to a platter, top with sliced scallions, and serve with warm Mandarin Pancakes and Hoisin sauce. Spread each pancake with about a teaspoon of Hoisin sauce and a couple of heaping tablespoons of Mu Shu Vegetables. Roll the pancake up and eat with your hands. Knives and forks are recommended for the fastidious.

## *Mandarin Pancakes*

Traditionally, these tortilla-like pancakes are served with Mu Shu dishes and Peking Duck. If you're feeling pressed for time and/or lazy, wheat flour tortillas from the market make an acceptable, though not nearly as good, substitute. Steam them for 3 or 4 minutes to warm them.

### SERVES 4

*2 cups unbleached white flour*  *1 tablespoon dark sesame oil*
*¾ cup boiling water*

Mound the flour in a mixing bowl. Gradually add boiling water while mixing with a spoon to form a smooth dough. Knead the dough in the bowl for 4 to 5 minutes. Form it into a ball, cover it with a towel, and let it rest for 20 minutes.

Knead the dough on a lightly floured surface for a couple of minutes. Shape it into a long cylinder, 1½ inches in diameter by about 14 inches long. Cut this cylinder into twelve equal pieces, each a little more than an inch wide. Flatten each piece between the palms of your hands to form a round slice 2½ inches in diameter. Lightly brush one side of each slice with sesame oil and then place the oiled side of a second slice against it. In other words, you will have six pairs, oiled face to oiled face. Using a rolling pin, gently roll out each pancake pair to an 8-inch round. Thinness is important or the pancake will be chewy.

Heat a cast-iron skillet on medium heat for 2 to 3 minutes. Cook each pancake pair in the unoiled pan for a couple of minutes on each side or until just speckled brown. Place it on a plate to cool for a few seconds before peeling the pancakes apart (what fun!). Stack them on a plate covered with a damp cloth.

If you're preparing these in advance, you can cover and refrigerate them for one week or freeze them for up to three months. Reheat the pancakes in a steamer before serving.

# Batter-Fried Fish with Garlic Sauce

Crisp fish with an aromatic, lightly sweet, and tangy sauce. Serve with rice, Spinach and Leek Soup (see page 182), and steamed vegetables.

### SERVES 4 TO 6

*2 pounds firm-fleshed scrod, haddock, bluefish, or monkfish fillets, cut into bite-sized pieces*
*2 tablespoons cornstarch*
**BATTER**
*2 eggs*
*1 cup cold water*
*1 cup flour*
*1 teaspoon baking powder*
*2 garlic cloves, minced or pressed*
*1 tablespoon tamari soy sauce*
*2 teaspoons sesame seeds*

---

*4 cups vegetable or peanut oil for frying*
**GARLIC SAUCE**
*4 garlic cloves, minced or pressed*

*1 tablespoon grated or minced peeled fresh ginger root*
*1 tablespoon brown sugar*
*3 tablespoons tamari soy sauce*
*1 teaspoon rice wine or cider vinegar*
*¾ cup Chinese Vegetable Stock (see page 178), vegetable stock (see page 685) or water*
*pinch of cayenne (or to taste)*
*pinch of ground black pepper*

---

*1 tablespoon cornstarch dissolved in ¼ cup cooled vegetable stock or water*

---

*½ cup chopped scallions*

Dust the fish with cornstarch and set aside.

In a large bowl, lightly beat the eggs, adding the cold water. Sift in the flour and baking powder. Stir until smooth. Add the remaining batter ingredients. Put the fish in the batter, making sure all the pieces are coated.

Heat the oil in a wok or deep fryer until it reaches 375°. Cook the fish in batches, carefully sliding in 8 to 10 pieces at a time, turning them now and then. Fry until golden and crisp, about 3 to 4 minutes. Remove the pieces to a paper towel–covered platter and place it in a warm oven until all the fish is cooked.

Pour the oil from the wok, leaving a very thin film. Stir-fry the garlic and ginger for half a minute. Add the remaining sauce ingredients except the cornstarch mixture and the scallions. When the liquid begins boiling, add the cornstarch mixture and simmer, stirring, for one minute. Transfer the fish to a serving platter, pour the sauce over the top, and sprinkle with the scallions, or serve the sauce on the side and dip the fish into it as you eat.

Serve immediately.

# Stuffed Tofu

A gingery, crunchy nut and smoky mushroom filling adds interest to smooth tofu simmered with rice wine, stock, and soy sauce.

### SERVES 4

2 cakes tofu (12 ounces each)
**FILLING**
5 dried shiitake mushrooms
1 cup hot water
¼ cup toasted walnuts, chopped
1 tablespoon grated peeled fresh ginger
    root
1½ tablespoons chopped scallions
1½ tablespoons finely chopped green
    pepper
1 teaspoon molasses
pinch of five-spice powder

salt to taste
ground black pepper or cayenne to taste
**SAUCE**
¼ cup tamari soy sauce
¼ cup rice wine or dry sherry
mushroom-soaking liquid
1 tablespoon peanut or vegetable oil
1½ teaspoons cornstarch mixed with ½
    cup vegetable stock (see page 685) or
    water
¼ teaspoon hot chili paste (optional)

Press the tofu (see page 684).

Cover the mushrooms with one cup of hot water and soak them for 20 minutes. Drain, reserving the liquid, and squeeze any excess water from the mushrooms. Trim off and discard the stems from the mushrooms. Chop the caps into ¼-inch pieces and combine them with the remaining filling ingredients, reserving half of the grated ginger for later.

The tofu we use measures about 3 inches by 3 inches by 2 inches after pressing. Cut each cake of pressed tofu in half laterally, so that you have four square slices. Now cut each slice in half diagonally to make a total of eight triangles. The aim is to have triangles of tofu approximately 1 inch thick, a good size for stuffing. You will be stuffing the long, diagonal side. Cut a slit in the tofu, being careful not to break through the other edges. Spoon into each about ⅛ of the filling. Any leftover filling may be used to top the completed dish.

Mix together the soy sauce, rice wine, and reserved mushroom liquid. If you don't have a full cup of this mixture, add enough water to make one cup of sauce. Heat a skillet or saucepan large enough to hold all eight triangles in one layer. Add the oil and 1½ teaspoons of reserved grated ginger. Sauté the ginger for half a minute and then pour the sauce into the pan. Add the stuffed tofu and heat to a simmer. Simmer the tofu for about 20 minutes, turning once. Remove the tofu to a warm platter.

Whisk the cornstarch mixed with stock or water into the simmering sauce. Add chili paste if desired. Remove the sauce from the heat as soon as it thickens. Pour the hot sauce over the stuffed tofu and serve immediately.

# Buddha's Garden

Through the ages, Buddhist beliefs have created a vegetarian diet for many Chinese. Excellent Chinese vegetarian restaurants exist in metropolitan areas where extensive menus feature dishes such as "mock roast pork" or "chicken." Stella Fessler, author of *Chinese Vegetarian Cooking,* states " . . . it is not simply a matter of replacing the meat. It is instead an effort to show off the great culinary art of China to make the impossible possible."

Wheat gluten is used as a protein source in much of Chinese vegetarian cooking. It's a wheat product that has been repeatedly rinsed and kneaded, washing off the starch and retaining the somewhat elastic gluten. The result is a bland, chewy, firm substance that readily absorbs the seasonings and flavors it is cooked with. Fresh, canned, and frozen gluten are available. Healthfood stores frequently sell fresh seitan, a Japanese type of gluten. If you have trouble finding this, one of the baked tofu variations could be substituted.

Mixed vegetable stir-fries are more appealing when an array of color and texture is presented. Other seasonal vegetables than the ones listed here can be used, but try to retain the range from crunchy to soft and the multicolored spectrum.

## SERVES 4

### SAUCE

3 tablespoons oyster sauce (see note)

1 tablespoon tamari soy sauce

1 teaspoon honey

1 cup vegetable stock (see page 685) or Chinese Vegetable Stock (see page 178)

1/8 teaspoon ground black pepper

1 tablespoon cornstarch dissolved in 2 tablespoons cold water

### SAUTÉ

3 tablespoons peanut or vegetable oil

1 1/2 tablespoons minced or pressed garlic cloves

1 tablespoon grated peeled fresh ginger root

1 medium carrot, thinly sliced on the diagonal

2 cups small, whole mushrooms

1 cup asparagus, cut on the diagonal into 1-inch pieces

1 1/2 cups red and green bell peppers, thinly sliced

1 small zucchini or summer squash, thinly sliced on the diagonal

8 ounces wheat gluten, thinly sliced

1 cup scallion pieces (white and green parts, cut on the diagonal, about 1 1/2 inches long)

Mix the sauce ingredients in a bowl and set aside.

Place a wok on medium-high heat. Add the oil, swirling it around to coat the bottom. Stir-fry the garlic and ginger for half a minute and then add the carrots. Stir-fry for one minute and add the mushrooms. Stir-fry for a minute and add the asparagus. If scorching threatens, lower the heat and/or add 3 or 4 tablespoons of stock or water. After cooking the asparagus for one minute, add the peppers and squash and stir-fry for another minute. Add the wheat gluten and scallions and cook for just a couple of minutes to heat the gluten.

Add the sauce mix and, stirring continuously, heat carefully, just until the sauce bubbles. Remove from the heat and serve with rice, Tamari Roasted Nuts (see page 198), and Seasoned Chili Oil (see page 197).

> *Note: Oyster sauce is a savory condiment of cooked and puréed oysters, soy sauce, salt, spices, and sugar. It will keep refrigerated indefinitely. For a strictly vegetarian preparation, additional soy sauce may be used in place of oyster sauce.*

## *Seasoned Chili Oil*

This homemade condiment combines the tastes of sesame oil, chiles, and flavorful spices.

YIELDS ½ CUP

*¼ cup vegetable oil*
*¼ cup dark sesame oil*
*½–1 teaspoon red pepper flakes (or 1 tablespoon chopped chiles)*

*½ teaspoon roasted Szechuan peppercorns*
*2 slices fresh ginger root (about ¼ inch thick)*

Gently heat the vegetable oil. Add the remaining ingredients and then remove the pan from the heat. Let the mixture steep, covered, for a few hours or overnight. Strain. Refrigerated, this seasoned oil will keep indefinitely.

# Tamari Roasted Nuts

A snack or garnish for a sauté. Use one kind of nut or any combination of the suggested nuts.

2 cups raw shelled nuts (cashews, almonds, pecans, walnuts, hazelnuts)

3 tablespoons tamari soy sauce

Preheat the oven to 350°.

Spread the nuts on a baking sheet and bake for 5 minutes. Drizzle the soy sauce on the nuts and stir them well. Return the baking sheet to the oven for 5 more minutes. Then turn off the oven. Stir the nuts again and leave them in the oven for a final 5 minutes.

The nuts will become dry and crisp. The baking sheet will look like a disaster, but fear not, because the soy sauce easily rinses off.

Allow the nuts to cool. Store them in a covered container to retain their crispness.

# Ginger Ice Cream

This dessert is rich, creamy, and refreshing with a bit of a zip from the fresh ginger.

Crystallized ginger is candied ginger root, usually available at Asian markets in plastic bags. It will keep indefinitely in a cool place.

SERVES 4 TO 6

special equipment: ice cream maker

½ cup water
⅓ cup sugar
2 tablespoons grated peeled fresh ginger root

1¼ cups milk

1 cup heavy cream
⅓ cup sugar
3 egg yolks
1 tablespoon finely chopped crystallized ginger

In a saucepan, simmer the water, sugar, and ginger for 3 to 4 minutes, stirring occasionally, to make a light syrup. Set aside to cool for 5 minutes.

In another saucepan, scald (but do not boil) the milk and cream. Remove the pan from the heat and stir in ⅓ cup of sugar and the ginger syrup. Set it aside for 15 minutes to allow the flavors to blend.

Strain the ginger solids from the milk mixture and discard them.

Whisk in the egg yolks and crystallized ginger. Return the mixture to the heat, either in a double boiler or on a heat diffuser. Heat gently, stirring constantly, until the mixture becomes a thin custard. It will thicken slightly but should *not* be heated to a simmer or boil.

Cool and prepare according to your ice cream–maker directions.

# *Almond Cookies*

A crisp, lightly sweet, delightful accompaniment to Ginger Ice Cream (see page 198). My childhood Chinese restaurant, Ling's, used to include little waxed paper packages of almond cookies with all their takeouts. Yummy!

### YIELDS 20 TO 30 COOKIES

2¾ cups unbleached white flour

1 cup sugar

½ teaspoon baking soda

¼ teaspoon salt

1 cup butter or margarine, cut into small pieces

2 eggs, lightly beaten

2 teaspoons pure almond extract

20–30 whole raw, shelled almonds

Mix the dry ingredients in a bowl. Cut in the butter, using a pastry cutter, two knives, or your fingers. The final result should be crumbly, with no pieces of butter larger than baby peas. Stir in the eggs and the almond extract.

Preheat the oven to 325°.

Roll pieces of dough between your lightly floured palms to form 1-inch balls. Place them 1½ inches apart on an unoiled baking sheet. Press an almond into the center of each cookie, lightly flattening the top. Bake for 15 to 20 minutes, until the bottoms just begin to brown.

MAUREEN VIVINO

# Eastern Europe

# INTRODUCTION

*Ajde, Jano, kolo da igramo.*
*Ajde, Jano, konja da prodamo.*
*Ajde Jano, ajde duso, kucu da prodamo.*
*Da prodamo samo da igramo.*

Somehow, the simple, sincere sentiment expressed in this Serbian dance-song captures for me the spirit of Eastern Europe. It speaks of a circle dance, or *kolo,* which might be danced at any festival or town gathering. *Kolos* are easy dances meant to join together the old and young, fostering a sense of community. The voice in the song tells Jano that he would sell his house and his horse—in fact he would sell everything—just to dance the *kolo.* This sense of abandon and zest for life is the thread which invisibly connects the countries of Eastern Europe. For although each country has its own distinct national characteristics, all share a variety of common influences, historical and geographical.

My first interest in this area of the world began when I was introduced to the folk dances and traditional music of the region. At first the intricate footwork and asymmetric rhythms intrigued and challenged me. But soon I became fascinated with the subtleties of styling and the endless variations on a theme. You can take a simple step-together-step and, depending on how much you bend your knees or whether you stamp or step lightly on the balls of your feet, look like a Hungarian doing a *csárdás* or a Croatian doing a *drmes.* And, yes, there is a difference.

Before long I was a confirmed fanatic. The dance tunes which had all sounded foreign and similar in the beginning I now easily identified as Hungarian, Romanian, Bulgarian,

Macedonian, or Croatian. My ear became attuned to the various instruments: the Hungarian *cymbalom,* the Romanian *furulya,* the Bulgarian *gajde* or bagpipe, the Macedonian *kaval* or flute, and the Croatian *tamburitza* or mandolin. I learned traditional dances: Hungarian *csárdás,* Romanian *invirtitas,* Bulgarian *kopanicas,* Macedonian *lesnotos,* and Croatian *kolos.* Finally, I had to go see for myself the lands and people who had cultivated this extraordinary heritage of traditional music and dance. So I went to Eastern Europe and feasted.

The Eastern European landscape is spectacular and full of variety. Mountains rise out of the Black Sea and the Adriatic Sea and are scattered throughout the countries. They provided a refuge to the natives during the many invasions and political struggles that interrupted the otherwise peaceful lives of these agrarian herders and peasants. The mountains also served as natural boundaries that separated, or sometimes isolated, certain groups of people, who were able to preserve unique social customs and lifestyles as a result. So Transylvania is a region unto itself, the Kapanci and nomadic Vlachs are not quite Bulgarian, the Calasari are a special breed of Romanians, and the Macedonians speak a language quite different from the Serbo-Croatian common throughout the rest of Yugoslavia.

Although my own heritage is Irish-Italian, I felt right at home traveling in the Balkans. To my imagination, Ireland and Eastern Europe always seemed related somehow. It has to do with folklore, mysticism, village churches, steep and narrow mountain roads overrun with goats and sheep, and the way poteen and slivovic begin to taste the same after the second or third glass. The Slovakian woodcutters believe in fairies and the "little people" and next to the Irish they are the world's greatest potato consumers. The Irish jig and the Bulgarian *pravo* have the same unusual 6/8 meter. Not long ago I discovered that perhaps it's not so odd that Gaelic music strangely resembles that of the Balkans. Apparently, the Celtic tribe, the Scordisae, founded Belgrade and other surrounding Balkan areas some considerable time ago, and the traces of connection linger on.

Eastern Europe has a complex history and mingling of diverse peoples. Borders, political and religious influences, and domination by foreign powers shifted continually over the centuries. Most of the regions had no recognized political identity until late in the nineteenth century, when the nations of Bulgaria, Hungary, Romania, and Czechoslovakia eventually took shape. The name Yugoslavia did not appear until 1929, and the present-day union of its six provinces—Serbia, Croatia, Macedonia, Bosnia-Herzegovina, Montenegro, and Slovenia—was not formed until 1945.

## Yugoslavia

The land that became Yugoslavia was originally settled by Thracian or Illyric peoples who were subjugated by the Romans in the second century B.C. During the Dark Ages, the country was then inhabited by migrating Slavs who, despite their common background, developed opposing religions and political views determined largely by where they settled. The conflict between the Hapsburgs and the Ottoman Turks and the subsequent five centuries of Turkish rule also left a lasting impression on Yugoslavia. The effects can be seen in both the architecture and the cookery. Appetizers called *meze,* ranging from slices of feta cheese to pickled vegetables and spiced meats, are all remnants of Turkish influence.

The cuisine of Yugoslavia differs somewhat from region to region, but there is an emphasis throughout on fresh fruits and vegetables, sour cream or *kajmak,* seafood, and sweet desserts such as kadaif or baklava. The salmon trout of Lake Ohrid in Macedonia is a world-renowned specialty and is often prepared stuffed with prunes or simmered in a lemon-raisin sauce.

## Bulgaria

Bulgaria is an inextricable mixture of sixth-century Slavic peoples and an Asiatic nomadic tribe, the Bulgars. The Bulgarians prevailed against the Byzantine Empire and invasions by the Hungarian Magyars but, like the peoples of Yugoslavia, fell under Turkish rule for nearly 500 years. The subjugation by the Turks insulated Bulgaria from the developments of Renaissance Europe and held it in a sort of medieval status until the seventeenth century.

The early Bulgars found the rich soil ideal for cultivating vegetables and grains. Wheat, barley, corn, lentils, and beans are all consumed in large quantities, and white beans are considered the national vegetable. Salads, relishes, and stews often feature leeks, tomatoes, eggplant, okra, or squash. Walnut, almond, and hazelnut trees are everywhere, and plums are both abundant and indispensable for making the potent clear plum brandy, slivovic, the national drink. Interestingly, Bulgarians prefer sunflower oil to olive oil and yogurt to sour cream. Mint, dill, and thyme are all used extensively, although in general Bulgarian dishes are rather lightly seasoned.

# Hungary

Hungary was settled by nomadic horsemen from Russia's Ural Mountains. These Magyars directly contributed to the distinctive charm and simplicity of Hungarian cooking. The devotion to sour cream, flavorful paprikashes, and *tarhonya,* a dried dough resembling grain, all date back to the customs of the Magyars. Hungary was not without foreign influence, however. The Italian queen Beatrice introduced pastry making and the French queen Ann brought her knowledge of garlic and sweet cream into the Hungarian court. The years of domination by the Turks and Austrians also left their mark, but the rich, spicy essence of Hungarian cuisine remained as unchanged as the *bogrács,* or cauldron, still used today.

Paprika, probably introduced via the Turks, became the hallmark of Hungarian food. The red peppers were easily cultivated in the indigenous alluvial soil and are now grown extensively for export worldwide. The city of Szeged is the country's paprika capital and produces a wide variety of paprika—the best is mild and sweet.

# Romania

Originally called Dacia, Romania was settled by Thracian tribes who crossed the Danube and were later ruled by the Romans for over 150 years. The Latin love for wine and convivial dining became an inseparable part of Romanian life. Staples of the Romanian diet are a polenta-like cornmeal porridge called *mamaliga,* cabbage and sauerkraut, *ghiveciu* or stew, and *sarmale,* a type of stuffed cabbage leaf. Romanians also show a distinct fondness for garlic, onions, and rye or dark breads.

# Czechoslovakia

The foundation of Czechoslovakian cooking is perhaps the country's favorite dumplings, *knedliky,* which can be made with flour, bread cubes, potatoes, cottage cheese, or semolina. They are made in many textures, shapes, and sizes—firm, light, tiny, large, plain, filled, round, or oval. Often the *knedliky* are garnished with butter, nuts, sugar, or spices. They are served with absolutely everything.

Grain crops in Czechoslovakia are of an exceptional quality, so baked goods and pastries have received well-deserved attention. Elaborate cakes, streusels, braided doughs, and *kolácky* are famous creations that have likely ruined many a fine figure. A surprising number of Viennese delicacies, fruit-studded cookies, layered cream cakes, and sponge cakes among them, originated in Bohemian kitchens.

Throughout Eastern Europe, food, music, and dance are intimately woven into an everyday spirit of hospitality and festivity. Open-air food markets abound and provide an arena for social exchange as well as a marketplace for groceries. Local gossip is as important as the price of peppers. Holidays are celebrated with special rituals and dishes. People line the streets in colorful folk costumes to dance and sing together. Wandering caravans of gypsies with their own traditions of improvisational melodies often frequent the festivals. They leave their wagons on the outskirts of towns and meander through the streets all over Hungary, Romania, and Bulgaria. There is always a fortune-teller among them. The bustling, rollicking atmosphere carries along even the most casual observer, and the sound of a band of *gajdas* vibrates the ground you stand on.

Amid the festivities, endless trays of *čevapčiči* or grilled meatballs, salads, dips, roasted vegetables, baklava, and sweet cakes are constantly replenished. The people are as robust and daring as the food. A wedding celebration may last for several days. At a local holiday festival in Ohrid I once saw fifteen well-built young men effortlessly form a pyramid *standing* on each other's shoulders just for show. I knew they must have practiced that little stunt, but I could not believe my eyes when the last and lightest boy climbed up the backs of the other men and balanced at the top effortlessly, just long enough for me to come to my senses and snap a picture.

There is a Serbo–Croatian *žito,* or sweetcake, that is made to celebrate Krsna Slava, a family holiday. The grain in the cake is said to represent life itself and the honey its sweetness. This is what I discovered in Eastern Europe. You smile at the people, breathe in the sweetness, and it stays lodged in your memory forever. Like gypsy melodies in the night, which have no boundaries of race or nation, there is a dynamic, timeless heritage that links all of Eastern Europe, at least in my heart.

S O U P S

## *Croatian Sour Soup*

•

## *Kisela Juha*

At Croatian festivals, the folk costumes are white with dazzling, detailed embroidery in red or other bright colors, and the women wear an intricate web or maze of coins sewn into their vests or blouses.

Perhaps the most popular dance is the *drmes,* a shaking dance that uses tiny bouncing steps repeated in a lively rhythm and danced in a closed circle. At times the dancers practically fly around the circle, coins jangling in time to the music. Other times, the *drmes* may continue for a full twenty minutes or more, alternating between a slower, smooth walking step to catch your breath and the quicker bouncing step.

Festivals almost always extend late into the night, and besides baked goods and roasted vegetables and meats, there is always a cauldron of steaming soup to warm the chill of night. This one, from the Dalmatian coastal region, incorporates sauerkraut, a staple of Croatian cookery. The sauerkraut serves as both vegetable and principal flavor and lends its characteristic sour taste.

The combination of sauerkraut and sour cream may seem odd at first, but handled with a bit of finesse, it can be unusual and stimulating without the "clash" you might expect.

*1 medium potato, diced*

---

*1 cup diced onions*
*1 teaspoon sweet Hungarian paprika*
*2 tablespoons vegetable oil*
*2 garlic cloves, minced or pressed*
*¼ teaspoon ground fennel seeds*
*1 bay leaf*
*1 carrot, diced*
*1 small parsnip, diced*
*1 celery stalk, chopped*

*2 tablespoons whole wheat pastry flour
(or unbleached white flour)*
*¼ teaspoon salt*
*½ teaspoon freshly ground black pepper*
*2 tablespoons cider vinegar*
*5 cups vegetable stock, heated (see page
685)*
*½ cup sauerkraut, drained*

---

*sour cream (optional)*
*minced chives (optional)*

Simmer the diced potatoes in salted water until tender, but still firm. Drain and set them aside, covered. The potato water can be reserved and used as part of the vegetable stock needed later.

Meanwhile, sauté the onions and paprika in the oil for a few minutes. Add the garlic and sauté for a few minutes more. Mix in the fennel, bay leaf, carrots, parsnips, and celery and sauté for 5 minutes longer, stirring occasionally.

Sift the flour into the vegetables and simmer on low heat for a couple of minutes, stirring constantly. Add the salt, black pepper, vinegar, and heated vegetable stock. Continue to simmer for about 10 minutes and then stir in the cooked potatoes and the sauerkraut.

Garnish each bowl of soup with a generous dollop of sour cream or a sprinkling of chives and serve with black bread or marbled rye and sweet butter.

# Creamy Hungarian
# Bean Soup

•

## Bab Leves

Hungary is a land brimming with pride in its heritage, something often expressed in the native dance and music. The intricate couple dances, like the *csárdás, forgatos,* or *szekey tancok,* put the jitterbug to shame, and the men's boot-slapping *verbunk* is a tribute to agility and vigor that must be witnessed to be appreciated.

Most things Magyar (Hungarian) have an ineffable quality about them that can make the culture seem as impregnable as the language. But the food, while unique, is basically straightforward and accessible and prepared with readily available ingredients and familiar cooking techniques.

This soup is hearty enough to satisfy the most robust appetite without sacrificing its delicate flavor. It is sure to delight the sensitive palate. Serve it with pumpernickel or other dark bread.

SERVES 4

1 cup navy beans
_____

1 small onion, chopped
1 leek, rinsed and chopped (see page
    667)
2 tablespoons vegetable oil
1 medium carrot, diced
2–3 large garlic cloves, minced
1 teaspoon salt (or to taste)

¹⁄₄ teaspoon ground black pepper
1¹⁄₂ teaspoons sweet Hungarian paprika
3 tablespoons unbleached white flour
_____

¹⁄₄ cup sour cream
2 teaspoons cider vinegar (or 1–2
    tablespoons fresh lemon juice)
2 tablespoons chopped fresh parsley

Soak the navy beans in plenty of water before cooking them. Soak them overnight and the cooking time will be about 1 hour. Or use the quick boiling method (see page 652).

Drain the soaked beans and place them in a 4-quart pot. Add water to an inch above the level of the beans. Bring them to a rolling boil and then simmer, covered, until tender. Replenish the water occasionally, keeping the beans covered with about an inch of water.

In a separate saucepan, when the beans are almost fully cooked, sauté the onion and leek in the oil until the onion is translucent. Add the carrot and garlic and continue to sauté for several more minutes. Mix in the salt, pepper, and paprika. Sprinkle the flour into the vegetables, stir well, and cook for a few minutes more. Ladle out 2 cups of the hot bean water and slowly stir it into the vegetable mixture until smooth and thickened. Add the vegetables to the pot of cooked beans, stirring constantly.

Remove the soup from the heat and whisk in the sour cream and then the vinegar or lemon juice. Gently reheat the soup for about 10 minutes, stirring frequently. Just before serving, add the parsley.

If the soup is too thick, thin it by adding a little hot water or vegetable stock. If it is too thin, thicken it by cooking a few minutes longer.

# *Spicy Bulgarian Tomato Dumpling Soup*

•

## *Domatene Supa*

Bulgaria is a country of picturesque towns, bustling cities, and breathtaking mountains and plateaus. Its old capital, Veliko Turnovo, is almost bewildering in its beauty. The town rises out of the cliffs above the Yantra River like a long-since-abandoned set from some ancient play. Houses and old inns are stacked one above the other. Towers, tunnels, steep stone footpaths, monasteries, and archaic columns perch on precipices or nestle in the cliffs, and the stone bridges appear to have been hurled across the river by the sudden whim of some invisible artisan. Visiting Veliko Turnovo is like walking through a romantic dream. A quiet serenity permeates the town. The place is unforgettable.

So is the food. I enjoyed most of my meals in Veliko Turnovo in small inns overlooking the water. The food was fresh and simple. It was summertime, and luscious tomatoes were in abundance. This tomato soup with its characteristic semolina dumplings topped with a sharp cheese called *kashkaval* was a popular offering on almost every menu. The semolina makes the dumplings chewier than all-flour dumplings and adds a nice flavor as well. My variation calls for couscous rather than the traditional semolina meal used in Bulgaria. Prepare the soup in a pot with at least a 10-inch diameter to allow all the dumplings room to rise to the top.

### SERVES 6

#### SOUP

1 large onion, diced
4 garlic cloves, minced
3 tablespoons olive oil
6 cups chopped fresh tomatoes (or drained canned tomatoes)

---

2–3 teaspoons hot chili powder
2 tablespoons unbleached white flour, sifted
1 teaspoon salt
½ teaspoon freshly ground black pepper
4 cups vegetable stock (see page 685), tomato juice, or water

#### DUMPLINGS

2 tablespoons butter, at room temperature
2 eggs, separated
¼ cup quick-cooking couscous
¼ cup boiling water
¾ cup unbleached white flour, sifted
¼ teaspoon salt
2 teaspoons fresh dill weed (1 teaspoon dried)
⅓ cup milk or vegetable stock

---

chopped fresh parsley
grated sharp cheddar cheese or kashkaval if available (optional)

In a medium soup pot, sauté the onions and garlic in the oil, stirring frequently, until the onions begin to soften. Add the tomatoes and cook until the onions are golden and the tomatoes soft.

Stir in the chili powder, flour, salt, and pepper and mix well to coat the vegetables evenly. Pour in the stock slowly while whisking diligently to completely dissolve the flour. Coarsely blend the soup in a blender or food processor and return it to the pot. Bring the soup to a boil, then reduce the heat and simmer it gently for 20 to 30 minutes.

While the soup simmers, prepare the dumplings. Cream the butter with the egg yolks until smooth. Place the couscous in a small bowl. Pour the boiling water over the couscous, cover the bowl with a plate or pot lid, and allow it to steam for 5 minutes. Add the steamed couscous and the flour, salt, dill, and milk or stock to the butter mixture and blend well. In a separate bowl, beat the egg whites until stiff and then fold them into the couscous mixture.

Drop the dumpling batter into the simmering soup by rounded tablespoons and cook, covered, for about 15 minutes. The dumplings will rise to the top; scoop one out and test it to be sure it is thoroughly cooked. Serve immediately, topped with fresh parsley and cheddar cheese, if desired.

## MAIN DISHES

# *Croatian Mushroom-Stuffed Tomatoes*

•

## *Rajčice sa Gljivama*

Vegetables play a large role in Croatian cooking and are frequently served as an entrée at midday. A favorite presentation, with obvious Near Eastern origins, is a stuffed vegetable filled with a savory mixture and topped with a traditional sharp cheese called *kashkaval* that is much like our cheddar.

SERVES 6

6 medium-large ripe tomatoes

1 small onion, diced
2 tablespoons vegetable oil
1 pound mushrooms, sliced (about 4 cups)
1/4 teaspoon salt
freshly ground black pepper to taste
1 teaspoon dried marjoram

1 tablespoon sweet Hungarian paprika
1/4 cup chopped fresh parsley
2 tablespoons whole wheat or unbleached white flour
2 eggs, well beaten

1/4 cup grated sharp cheddar cheese
1/4 cup bread crumbs

With a sharp knife, cut a small hole in the stem end of each tomato and then gently scoop out most of the tomato pulp with a teaspoon. Be careful not to puncture the sides or bottom of the tomatoes. The tomato innards can be saved for stock or used in another recipe, such as Spicy Bulgarian Tomato Dumpling Soup (see page 212).

In a medium skillet, sauté the onions in the oil until translucent. Add the sliced mushrooms, seasonings, and herbs. Sauté, stirring occasionally, until the mushrooms release their juice. Then simmer until the liquid is reduced, about 5 to 8 minutes. Sprinkle with the flour and stir well. Mix in the eggs to coat the mushrooms and cook for a few minutes more.

Preheat the oven to 400°.

Season the inside of the hollowed tomatoes lightly with salt and pepper. This will help the tomatoes to retain their shape. Stuff the tomatoes with the mushroom mixture and place them in a buttered 9x13-inch baking pan. Combine the grated cheese and bread crumbs; top each tomato with about 1½ tablespoons of this mixture. Add ½ cup of water to the bottom of the baking pan and bake the tomatoes, covered, for 20 minutes. Uncover and bake for 5 more minutes, until the cheese is bubbly and lightly browned.

Serve hot with a side dish of rice and a crisp garden salad.

# Bosnian "Meatballs" in Yogurt Sauce

•

## Bosanske Ćufte

Bosanske Ćufte would traditionally be made with skewered ground beef and marinated vegetables and cooked briefly over an open-fire grill. This vegetarian version can be stuffed into pita bread with raw onions and tomatoes or simply offered as an appetizer with the yogurt sauce as a dip. For a more substantial meal, serve Bosanske Ćufte on a bed of noodles with garlic butter or yogurt sauce, topped with a mild grated cheese such as Monterey Jack and with a colorful mixture of marinated vegetables* on the side.

### YIELDS ABOUT 24 2-INCH BALLS

2 large onions, diced
2 garlic cloves, minced
3 tablespoons vegetable oil
3 medium carrots, grated
salt and ground black pepper to taste

1 teaspoon ground fennel seeds
1/8 teaspoon cayenne (or to taste)
1/2 teaspoon caraway seeds, ground
2 teaspoons dried basil
1/4 cup chopped fresh parsley

2 eggs, beaten
1 1/4 cups bread crumbs (preferably whole wheat, see page 654)
1 cup almonds, toasted lightly and ground
2 tablespoons Dijon mustard
1 tablespoon dark sesame oil
1/4 cup tamari soy sauce

3 cakes tofu, pressed (see page 684)
SAUCE
4 eggs, beaten
2 cups plain yogurt
1–2 teaspoons caraway seeds, ground
1 tablespoon fresh dill, chopped
salt and freshly ground black pepper to taste

* See Vegetable Marinade in *New Recipes from Moosewood Restaurant*, page 56.

Sauté the onions and garlic in the oil for about 6 minutes, until the onions begin to turn golden. Add the carrots, salt, and black pepper and continue to cook for about 4 minutes, stirring occasionally. Set aside to cool.

Meanwhile, mix together the eggs, bread crumbs, almonds, mustard, sesame oil, and soy sauce. Stir the herbs and spices into the bread-crumb mixture. Crumble the pressed tofu into the mixture and knead it with your hands until well combined. Drain the sautéed vegetables and stir them into the mix. The mixture should be moist and sticky and easy to roll into balls.

Form about 24 balls, place them on an oiled baking sheet, and bake them at 350° for 30 minutes, until nicely browned on the outside.

The traditional yogurt sauce is very simple. Just mix together all the ingredients. Heat the sauce gently for about 15 minutes, stirring constantly until it thickens. Be patient. If the heat is too high or you don't stir enough, the eggs might curdle. Keep adding ground caraway until you're happy with the flavor (Croatians like it strong). This sauce provides a light and tangy contrast to the balls.

# Bulgarian Red Pepper Stew

Bulgarian cookery has a Slavic heritage with a distinctly Turkish influence. It boasts one of the most healthful diets in Eastern Europe with an emphasis on grains, vegetables, fruits, nuts, and yogurt, combined creatively to provide a rich repertoire of dishes. It's no wonder that Bulgarians are well known for lives of vigorous longevity.

This stew is a heart-warming, vibrant red. The lentils make a thick sauce, and the beans add texture. This is a dish to enjoy during those first chill evenings of autumn or in the dead of winter, with your chair pulled up to the wood stove.

Although sour cream is by far the favorite throughout most of Eastern Europe, Bulgarians show a strong preference for yogurt in its stead. Bulgarian yogurt has a thick, creamy texture and mild tanginess unmatched by any I have tasted elsewhere. Often made from sheep's or goat's milk, it is lower in fat and a more healthful addition to the diet than sour cream.

SERVES 6

½ cup dried lentils
½ cup dried navy pea beans

---

2 large onions, chopped
3 tablespoons vegetable oil or butter
6 medium red bell peppers, seeded and
    chopped
2 teaspoons dried basil
1 teaspoon dried marjoram
¼ teaspoon dried thyme
¼ teaspoon cayenne (or to taste)

¼ teaspoon salt
⅛ teaspoon ground black pepper
3–3½ cups vegetable stock (see page
    685) or water
¼ cup dry red wine
2 tablespoons dry sherry
¼ cup tomato paste
½ cup plain yogurt (or sour cream
    if preferred)
2 tablespoons chopped fresh parsley

Cover the lentils and navy beans with plenty of cold water and soak them for at least 4 hours or overnight. Drain and set them aside.

In a large deep saucepan, sauté the onions in the oil until golden. Stir in the bell peppers and sauté them for about 5 minutes more. Add the basil, marjoram, thyme, cayenne, salt, and pepper and continue to sauté for another minute or two. Pour in 3 cups of stock or water and the wine and sherry. Add the drained lentils and beans. Bring the stew to a boil, then lower the heat and simmer gently, covered, for about 1½ hours, until the lentils thicken and the beans are tender. Mix in the tomato paste and cook for several minutes longer. If the stew seems too thick, stir in more stock or water.

Garnish each bowl with a dollop of yogurt and a sprinkling of parsley. The colors will be a sight to behold. Serve with a crisp green salad and whole wheat bread spread with melted garlic butter.

# Macedonian Sweet-and-Savory Strudel

•

## Domaca Gibanica

Strudels are one of Eastern Europe's most striking contributions to elegant cookery. Made with thin, light sheets of filo, which are buttered and layered, strudels are rich, delicate, and versatile and can be served as appetizer, main course, or dessert. This strudel combines the sweet and the savory to make a meal in itself.

### YIELDS 8 SERVINGS

2 cups chopped onions
3 tablespoons vegetable oil
4 cups grated carrots
⅓ cup currants (or to taste)
½ teaspoon ground black pepper

4 eggs, lightly beaten
2 tablespoons unbleached white flour
2 tablespoons chopped fresh parsley
2 tablespoons chopped fresh dill (1½ teaspoons dried)

---

2 cups grated feta cheese (about 10 ounces)
1½ cups cottage cheese
8 ounces cream cheese, at room temperature

½ pound filo dough (see page 664)
⅓–½ cup butter, melted

---

2 teaspoons caraway seeds

Sauté the onions in the oil until translucent. Add the grated carrots and cook them for about 5 minutes, stirring often to prevent scorching. Mix in the currants and black pepper, simmer for a couple of minutes longer, and then drain the excess juices.

In a large bowl, combine the cheeses, eggs, flour, parsley, and dill. Stir the sautéed vegetables into the cheese mixture and mix thoroughly.

Preheat the oven to 350°.

To assemble the strudel, unfold the stack of filo sheets next to a 9x13-inch baking pan and place the melted butter nearby. Try to work quickly in a draft-free setting, otherwise the light, delicate filo will dry out quickly and become crumbly and more difficult to use. With a pastry brush or small paint brush, butter the baking pan. Take about six sheets of filo from the stack and, in one smooth movement, lift them and lay them flat in the pan; the edges may drape over the sides. Spread the filling evenly over the stacked sheets. Then brush the edges of the filo with butter and fold them in over the top of the filling. Cover the filling with two sheets of filo; brush the top sheet with butter. Repeat with three more pairs of filo sheets. Tuck the edges inside the pan. Scatter the caraway seeds over the top.

Bake the strudel for 45 minutes, until golden brown. Let the strudel rest for 10 minutes before slicing it to serve.

A nice complement to this strudel is a baked apple topped with a drizzle of apricot brandy.

# *Transylvanian Eggplant Casserole*

Transylvania is a region that has been influenced by both Romania and Hungary but has maintained an identity all its own. Traditional costumes, dances, and cuisine are all imbued with a distinctive style that can only be described as Transylvanian, and although it is difficult to pinpoint what makes it so unique, I can say that there is something of the gypsy in it.

This casserole is an adaptation of a recipe that would ordinarily include a layer of cooked veal or beef, but it is quite delightful without it. It has become a regular favorite at Moosewood.

SERVES 6

2 medium eggplants, cut crosswise into
  ½-inch slices

---

2 cups chopped onions
3 tablespoons vegetable oil
4 cups sliced mushrooms (about 1
  pound)
4 fresh tomatoes, chopped
1½ teaspoons dried marjoram
¾ teaspoon dried thyme
1 teaspoon sweet Hungarian paprika
salt and freshly ground black pepper to
  taste

---

4½ cups cooked brown rice

¼ cup fresh lemon juice (or to taste)
¼ cup chopped fresh parsley
2 tablespoons pine nuts

---

4 eggs, well beaten (optional)
½ cup bread crumbs (preferably whole
  wheat, see page 654)
⅔ cup pine nuts, ground
2–3 tablespoons vegetable oil or melted
  butter

---

chopped fresh parsley
red bell pepper slivers

Place the eggplant slices on an oiled baking sheet, salt them lightly, and cover them with aluminum foil. Bake at 400° until tender, 20 to 25 minutes.

Meanwhile, sauté the onions in the oil until translucent. Add the mushrooms and continue to cook, covered, on medium heat until the mushrooms have released their juices and become soft. Stir in the tomatoes, marjoram, thyme, paprika, salt, and black pepper. Cover and simmer for 5 minutes. Remove from the heat and drain off most of the juice. Set aside.

Combine the rice, lemon juice, parsley, and pine nuts. To assemble the casserole, oil a 9x13x2½-inch baking dish. Spread half of the rice mixture on the bottom and cover with half of the eggplant slices. Spoon half of the sautéed vegetables on top of the eggplant layer. Repeat this process using the remaining rice, eggplant, and vegetables.

Pour the eggs evenly over the top of the casserole so that they drizzle down into it. Combine the bread crumbs and nuts and sauté them on low heat in the oil or butter for about 4 minutes, stirring constantly. Top the casserole with the nut mixture and bake it, covered, at 350° for about 30 minutes. Then uncover and bake for 10 minutes until the top is crisp and the casserole still moist. Garnish with parsley and peppers.

*Note: The eggs may be omitted, in which case serve the casserole in large, shallow bowls instead of on plates, because it will not hold together quite as well.*

# Croatian Vegetable-Cheese Musaka

•

## Musaka Sarajevo

The city of Sarajevo is nothing short of splendid. Once a medieval town, it has become Bosnia–Herzegovina's cultural capital. A walk through the city streets reveals a juxtaposition and blending of Eastern and Western influences in the architecture, streets, shops, and customs. Croatia endured several centuries of Turkish occupation, which largely accounts for the penetrating Eastern influence. Even then Sarajevo was renowned as the most beautiful city in the Ottoman Empire.

This recipe is reminiscent of a dish I enjoyed in one of the tiny restaurants on the edge of the city one gusty summer evening. I remember particularly the succulent mushrooms. The Slavonian forests are rich in mushrooms as delicious as they are widespread. They have become both an integral ingredient of the local cuisine and a commercial export commodity.

Musaka is found all throughout Eastern Europe and Greece; best known is the Greek version with eggplant, lamb, tomato sauce, and a thick béchamel topping. This lighter version from Croatia includes mushrooms, squash, noodles, and feta cheese, all abundant in that region. The tamari soy sauce, although not traditional, adds depth and color to the mushroom sauce.

SERVES 8

2 large onions, chopped

3 tablespoons vegetable oil

1½ pounds mushrooms, sliced

¼ cup dry white wine

3 tablespoons tamari soy sauce

2 teaspoons dried basil (2 tablespoons fresh)

2 teaspoons dried dill weed (2 tablespoons fresh)

1 teaspoon salt

½ teaspoon freshly ground black pepper

————————————————

3–4 medium yellow summer squash or zucchini, sliced into ½-inch rounds

2 tablespoons vegetable oil

————————————————

1½ tablespoons cornstarch dissolved in 2 tablespoons cold water

3 cups grated feta cheese (1¼ pounds)

6 eggs, lightly beaten

¼ teaspoon ground black pepper

————————————————

1½ cups tomato juice

⅔ pound lasagne noodles

½ cup bread crumbs (preferably whole wheat, see page 654)

1 teaspoon sweet Hungarian paprika

In a large soup pot or skillet, sauté the onions in 3 tablespoons of oil until translucent. Add the mushrooms and continue to sauté for several minutes, stirring frequently. Mix in the wine, soy sauce, herbs, salt, and pepper and simmer, covered, stirring occasionally, for about 20 minutes, until the mushrooms are brown and have released their juices.

Meanwhile, brush the squash rounds with oil and bake them, uncovered, at 450° on an oiled baking sheet for about 10 minutes, until tender but still firm.

When the mushrooms have cooked, remove them from the heat and stir in the cornstarch mixture. Return to the heat for a few minutes, stirring continuously, until the mixture begins to thicken. Set aside.

Combine the feta, eggs, and black pepper in a medium bowl.

Assemble the musaka. Coat the bottom of a deep, oiled, 12-inch square baking pan with about ½ cup of tomato juice. Arrange a layer of uncooked, dry lasagne noodles (believe it or not, they will cook in the casserole), ⅓ cup tomato juice, half of the mushroom sauce, an overlapping layer of all the summer squash slices, and all of the bread crumbs. Continue to layer ⅓ cup tomato juice, noodles, the rest of the tomato juice, the rest of the mushroom sauce, and top with the feta mixture.

Sprinkle paprika over the musaka and bake it at 350° for 45 minutes, until golden and bubbly. Allow the casserole to set for 5 to 10 minutes before serving.

Musaka Sarajevo is nice with Serbian Cucumber-Pepper Salad (see page 228) or a tossed salad vinaigrette and a bottle of dry white wine.

# Fish in Sour Cream Sauce

•

## Som sa Kiselim Vrhnjem

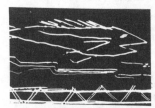

Mealtimes in Eastern Europe are quite different from ours in America. There are often four meals: a very early continental, light breakfast of strong coffee, fruit, and biscuits; a midmorning snack; the main meal at about 2 or 3 o'clock in the afternoon; and a light evening meal at about 7 or 8 P.M. Shops often close with the main meal in midafternoon and reopen for a few hours later in the evening. This dish would be appropriate for *ručak,* the main meal of the day.

### SERVES 4 TO 6

1 onion, chopped

2 tablespoons vegetable oil or butter

3 tablespoons unbleached white flour

2 teaspoons salt

¼ teaspoon freshly ground black pepper

½ teaspoon dried marjoram

1½ tablespoons sweet Hungarian
  paprika

¼ cup dry white wine

2 tablespoons fresh dill (1½ teaspoons
  dried)

2 pounds fillets of cod or other firm
  white fish

2 large garlic cloves, peeled and halved
  lengthwise

2½ cups sour cream

½ cup milk

a few red onion rings

2 sprigs of fresh dill

Sauté the onion in the oil until tender and translucent. Stir in the flour, salt, pepper, marjoram, and paprika and cook for several minutes, until the onions are nicely coated. Reduce the heat and whisk in the sour cream and milk. Simmer for about 5 minutes, stirring occasionally. Add the wine and dill and heat gently, being careful not to boil the sauce.

Meanwhile, rub the fish fillets with the cut side of the garlic cloves and place them in an oiled baking pan. Bake, covered, at 375° for about 20 minutes, until the fish is flaky and still moist.

Pour the sauce over the baked fish and garnish it with red onion rings and fresh dill. Serve with baked potatoes and buttered, steamed carrots.

## SALADS AND
## SIDE DISHES

# Macedonian Cottage Cheese
# Croquettes

•

# Kroketi od Sira-Skute

I remember eating these tasty cheese balls with slices of roasted green banana peppers and a salad of fresh cucumbers, tomatoes, and red onion. In Eastern Europe, midmorning meals are often light snacks, quickly prepared as a pause for refreshment. Many of the dishes, therefore, show a flair for simplicity as well as taste.

Although I have suggested using cottage cheese to make the croquettes, other cheeses would also be possible. There is one Yugoslavian cheese that is perfect for *kroketi*. It is a semi-soft, mild cheese made from cow's milk, originally produced by Trappist Monks at Mariastern Monastery in Bosnia. Today you can buy it throughout all of Yugoslavia. Unfortunately, I have never found it anywhere in the United States. You may, however, like to experiment with soft farmer cheeses made from cow's or sheep's milk. Like the Macedonians, you should prepare the croquettes with whatever soft, mild cheese is on hand.

Kroketi od Sira-Skute can be served with a tart applesauce or with a side dish of fresh sliced tomatoes topped with sour cream and minced chives. If left over, *kroketi* can be reheated nicely in the oven.

*½ pound cottage cheese, drained*
*⅓ cup butter, softened*
*2 eggs*
*½ teaspoon salt*
*freshly ground black pepper to taste*
*2 garlic cloves, pressed*
*1 tablespoon chopped fresh dill*

*1 cup unbleached white or whole wheat*
  *pastry flour*

*2 eggs, lightly beaten*
*1 cup bread crumbs*
*vegetable oil for frying*

Mix together the cottage cheese, butter, and 2 eggs in a large bowl. Add the salt, pepper, garlic, dill, and flour and combine well. The mixture should be thick and easily shaped into balls. You may need to add more flour, depending on the consistency of your cottage cheese.

Form croquettes by patting and rolling the mixture in your hands. Dip the *kroketi* into the 2 lightly beaten eggs and then roll them in the bread crumbs.

Fry the *kroketi* for about 5 minutes in a large, heavy iron skillet in ½ inch of oil on medium heat. Fry them in several batches or use two skillets. Gently turn the *kroketi* with a spatula as they fry to prevent sticking and to help them brown evenly. Drain the browned *kroketi* briefly on absorbent paper. Serve hot.

If you prefer, the *kroketi* can be baked on an oiled baking sheet at 425° for 15 to 20 minutes. They will be less crisp but still quite tasty.

## *Romanian Marinated Mushrooms*

Mushrooms are a favorite Romanian food and they appear in all guises: stuffed, baked, sautéed, and marinated. This recipe works best with small, bite-sized mushrooms, and although the dish may be served after chilling overnight, it is actually best after marinating for several days to a week. Any leftover marinade may be used for dipping with hearty pieces of black bread.

Don't worry about removing the bay leaves. They're considered good luck for whoever finds them.

SERVES 8 TO 10

10 cups mushrooms, whole if small, or
   sliced in half (about 2½ pounds)

¼ cup olive oil

3 tablespoons fresh lemon juice

———————————————

2 tablespoons olive oil

1 cup sliced onions

3 garlic cloves, minced

½ teaspoon freshly ground black pepper

¼ teaspoon dried thyme

½ teaspoon dried marjoram

3 bay leaves

———————————————

2 cups canned tomatoes (28-ounce can)
   with juice reserved

½ cup red wine vinegar

⅛ teaspoon cayenne

salt to taste

½ teaspoon sugar (optional)

———————————————

1 lemon, cut into 6 wedges

chopped fresh parsley

In a large frying pan or skillet, sauté the mushrooms in ¼ cup of oil until just tender, before they begin to shrink noticeably. Drain the mushrooms, transfer them to a bowl, and toss them immediately with the lemon juice; set aside.

Add 2 tablespoons of oil to the skillet and cook the onions until they begin to turn translucent. Add the garlic and continue to sauté for several minutes longer, until the onions are golden but not browned. Stir in the pepper, thyme, marjoram, and bay leaves and sauté for one more minute.

Drain the tomatoes and reserve ⅓ cup of the juice. Coarsely chop the tomatoes and mix them into the onions along with the reserved tomato juice, vinegar, cayenne, salt, and sugar, if desired. Simmer on low heat, covered, for 20 to 25 minutes, stirring occasionally.

Allow the marinade to cool for several minutes and then pour it over the mushrooms. Adjust the seasonings and chill, covered, for at least 12 hours. Bring the dish to room temperature before serving.

Garnish with lemon wedges and parsley. A bowl of fresh green grapes will add a Romanian touch to the table, and black bread with a creamy, mild cheese is a nice taste complement.

# Serbian Cucumber-Pepper Salad

•

## Srpska Salat

Throughout Yugoslavia, fresh green salads come in almost every form imaginable and are a regular part of the main course. Cucumbers and peppers are predominant favorites in Serbia.

This simple, crisp, dish may be made richer by the addition of sour cream. Cooked shrimp might be added as a traditional garnish to make a more substantial dish.

Raw yellow onions are a common ingredient in salads and relishes throughout Eastern Europe, but some people find their flavor too strong or difficult to digest; milder red onions may be substituted.

### SERVES 6 TO 8

3 green bell peppers, seeded and
  chopped
3 red bell peppers, seeded and chopped
2 medium cucumbers, peeled, cut in
  half lengthwise, seeded, and sliced
  into crescents
1 small onion, finely chopped (red,
  yellow, or white)
¼ cup chopped fresh parsley

⅛ teaspoon sweet Hungarian paprika
1 teaspoon dried basil
½ teaspoon dried marjoram
¼ teaspoon dried oregano
salt and freshly ground black pepper to
  taste

4 large leaves of romaine lettuce
3 hard-boiled eggs, peeled and halved

¼–⅓ cup olive oil
2–3 tablespoons fresh lemon juice (or to
  taste)

Place the chopped peppers in a stainless steel bowl and scald them with boiling water for about one minute. Drain the peppers well and mix in the cucumbers, onions, and parsley.

In a separate bowl, whisk the olive oil, lemon juice, paprika, basil, marjoram, oregano, salt, and black pepper. Pour the dressing over the vegetables, mix well, and chill for several hours.

Arrange the leaves of romaine on a platter, mound the marinated cucumber-pepper salad in the center, and garnish with hard-boiled eggs.

# *Romanian Carrots with Sour Cream*

•

## *Morcov mode Taranesc*

This is a Romanian peasant-style dish. It is as quick and easy as it is flavorful and nutritious, and makes a lovely addition to any meal.

SERVES 4 TO 6

8–10 medium carrots, peeled and cut
   on the diagonal into ½-inch rounds

¼ cup butter
1 tablespoon unbleached white flour
1 cup sour cream or plain yogurt
¼ cup chopped fresh parsley

2 tablespoons chopped chives
1 tablespoon chopped fresh dill
   (¾ teaspoon dried)
¼ teaspoon ground fennel seeds
salt and freshly ground black pepper to
   taste

In a large pot, cook the carrots in boiling water to cover until tender, about 5 to 7 minutes; drain and set aside. Keep the carrots covered if you plan to serve them warm or plunge them into cold water for several minutes and then drain them if you prefer them chilled.

In a medium saucepan, melt the butter and stir in the flour. Cook for a few minutes on medium heat, stirring regularly. Whisk in the sour cream or yogurt until smooth and blended. Add the remaining ingredients and gently simmer for several minutes longer, until heated through.

Pour the sauce over the carrots and serve them hot or cold, depending on the season and your mood. If serving the dish cold, it is best to chill it for at least 2 hours.

# Czechoslovakian Apple and Carrot Confetti

Modern Czechoslovakia is a union of two closely related Slavonic peoples, the Czechs, long associated with the Austrian Empire, and the Slovaks, attached for centuries to Hungary. Consequently, the culinary traditions were quite different and have created an interesting blend. Some of the most popular dishes are made with rather humble, basic ingredients.

This only adds to their appeal, as this colorful side dish demonstrates.

Apple and Carrot Confetti is a light and refreshing side dish or snack that takes almost no time to prepare. The amount of sugar needed, if any, will depend on the tartness of the apples and your preference for sweet or tart. Although I never add any sugar when I make this dish (I haven't a sweet tooth in my head), believe me, the traditional Czechoslovakian cook would not dream of omitting it.

### SERVES 4 TO 6

*¼ cup fresh lemon juice*
*2 tablespoons fresh orange juice*
*4 apples (enough for 2 cups grated)*
*2 cups grated carrots*
*1 tablespoon grated lemon rind*

*2 tablespoons currants*
*¼ teaspoon salt (or to taste)*
*2–3 tablespoons sugar (optional)*

*mint leaves*

Combine the lemon juice and orange juice. Grate the apples directly into the juices or they will turn brown quickly. Toss the apples with the rest of the ingredients and serve immediately, garnished with fresh mint leaves.

# DESSERTS

## *Ukrainian Almond Crescents*

*Rogaliki,* which means "little horns," are a specialty of the southern Ukraine. They are flaky pastries stuffed with sugar and nuts, and I warn you, they can be addictive. Although I am seldom interested in sweets, these are "devilish horns," tempting even me to eat just one more!

### YIELDS 24 PASTRIES

**PASTRY**
*2–2½ cups unbleached white flour*
*1 package dry yeast (about*
   *1 tablespoon)*
*1 cup sweet butter, at room temperature*
*2 egg yolks, beaten*
*¾ cup sour cream*

**FILLING**
*2 cups almonds, toasted and coarsely*
   *ground*
*⅔–¾ cup brown sugar, firmly packed*
*2 egg whites*
*pinch of salt*

For the pastry, mix together the flour and yeast in a medium bowl. Cut in the butter with a pastry fork until the mixture resembles coarse meal. Stir in the egg yolks and sour cream and mix well. The mixture will still be crumbly. Form the dough into a ball using your hands, working it as little as possible. The less you knead, the more tender the pastry will be. The dough will be tacky. Wrap it in waxed paper and chill it for at least 2 hours.

Prepared the filling by combining the ground almonds and sugar in a small bowl. Beat together the egg whites and salt until stiff, but not dry, and carefully fold them into the nut mixture.

Preheat the oven to 375°. When the dough is thoroughly chilled, divide it into three balls. Using a floured rolling pin, roll out three circles about ⅛ inch thick. Work on a well-floured surface to prevent the dough from sticking. Cut each circle into eight pie-shaped wedges and spread the wedges with the filling. Starting at the wide end, roll each wedge up like a little croissant and then pull the ends into a curve to form a "horn." Make sure the point is on the bottom so the "horns" will not open up while baking.

Place the almond crescents on a lightly oiled baking sheet and bake for about 30 to 40 minutes, until golden and puffed.

And may Temperance be your guide from here.

# *Albanian Walnut Cake*
# *with Lemon Glaze*

Albania borders the Adriatic Sea, Greece, and Yugoslavia, and is just a short ferry ride to southern Italy. Although the country has absorbed influences from nearby regions, Albania has maintained its cultural integrity in its folk traditions, celebratory rituals, and cookery. This dessert is a wonderful example of their well-known moist cakes, which are rich, without a doubt, but not overly sweet.

## CAKE

½ cup butter, at room temperature

¾ cup sugar

2 eggs, lightly beaten

⅓ cup plain yogurt

⅓ cup buttermilk (or additional ⅓ cup yogurt)

2 cups unbleached white flour

1 teaspoon baking powder

1 teaspoon baking soda

½ teaspoon cinnamon

1 tablespoon freshly grated lemon rind

1 cup walnuts, toasted and finely chopped

## GLAZE

¾ cup water

1 cup sugar

1 cinnamon stick (or ½ teaspoon ground cinnamon)

¼ cup fresh lemon juice

¼ teaspoon ground allspice

dash of ground cloves

Preheat the oven to 350°.

For the cake, cream together the butter and sugar until light and fluffy and then mix in the eggs. Blend the yogurt with the buttermilk. Sift together the dry ingredients and add them alternately with the yogurt mixture into the egg mixture. Stir in the lemon rind and walnuts.

Pour the batter into a buttered 9x13-inch baking pan and bake for 30 to 40 minutes, until a toothpick inserted in the center comes out mostly clean. The cake should still be moist.

Meanwhile, make the glaze by simmering together all the ingredients, covered, for about 15 minutes. Remove the cinnamon stick. When the cake is done, remove it from the oven, turn the oven off, pour the glaze over the hot cake, and return it to the oven for about 10 minutes. Cut the cake into squares and serve it warm or cool.

For the rich at heart, a dollop of freshly whipped cream or a scoop of vanilla ice cream may add just the right touch. In Albania, as in much of Eastern Europe, desserts, or "sweets" as they are called, are almost invariably accompanied by tiny cups of strong, freshly brewed coffee—even stronger-tasting than espresso. It packs a wallop, but has an alluring charm, and is a perfect contrast to the sweets. And if you prefer no caffeine, find a good brand of decaffeinated espresso and drink up.

# Macedonian
# Pear and Fig Strudel

Language can be a funny thing, especially when you are learning it by the seat of your pants as you travel. I remember overhearing a conversation in Macedonian about electric pears—I was certain that was what they said since they repeated it several times. Electric pears. I could not imagine what they meant. A new hallucinogen? Then suddenly it clicked. Lightbulbs. Of course, electric pears. I had a good laugh at myself. Here then is a pear and fig strudel to rival the world-famous baklava. I hope you get a charge out of it.

### YIELDS 12 TO 16 SERVINGS

*1 pound dried figs, stemmed*
  *(about 4 cups)*
*1²/₃ cups unsweetened pear juice*

_____

*10 ripe pears*
*1 teaspoon cinnamon*
*¹/₂ teaspoon allspice*

_____

*¹/₂ pound filo dough (see page 664)*
*¹/₂ cup melted butter*
*1 cup toasted whole wheat bread crumbs*
  *(see page 654)*

_____

*¹/₂ cup honey (or to taste)*
*¹/₂ cup chopped toasted hazelnuts*

Cover the figs with pear juice and bring them to a boil. Lower the heat and simmer, covered, for about 25 minutes, until the figs are tender. In a blender or food processor, purée the figs and their cooking juice to make about 3¹/₂ cups of smooth fig paste.

Meanwhile, peel and core the pears and chop them into bite-sized pieces. In a large bowl combine the fig paste, pears, cinnamon, and allspice.

Preheat the oven to 375°.

To assemble the strudel, butter a 9x14-inch baking pan and layer ten sheets of filo, two at a time, brushing butter on every second sheet and sprinkling it with bread crumbs. Spread the pear filling evenly on the top sheet of filo. Cover it with ten more sheets of filo, layered as before with butter and bread crumbs.

Score the top sheets of filo into pieces approximately 3 inches square. This will make it easier to cut the strudel later and will prevent the top layer from crumbling as you cut it. Be careful not to score the top layers all the way through to the filling, however, or the filling juices will bubble up as the strudel bakes.

Bake the strudel for about 35 to 40 minutes, until golden brown and crisp. Allow it to cool for 15 minutes. Then heat the honey gently, stirring constantly, until warm and more fluid. Drizzle it evenly over the strudel and top with the nuts. Use a sharp knife to cut the strudel.

## BREADS

# *Hungarian Pumpernickel Bread*

Breads are a staple of Hungarian dining. The country grows wheat of an exceptionally fine quality which is milled into a very rich and glutenous flour that is a joy to cook with. Fragrant breads, dumplings, noodles, and thin pancakes abound in a Hungarian kitchen. This is a wholesome, everyday bread and a perfect companion for a hearty soup or stew.

**BREAD**

**2 packages dry yeast (2 tablespoons)**

**¼ cup warm water**

---

**½ cup light molasses**

**1–2 tablespoons freshly grated orange peel**

**2 teaspoons caraway seeds**

**1½ teaspoons salt**

**2 cups buttermilk**

---

**3 cups rye flour (see note)**

**2½–3½ cups whole wheat flour**

**GLAZE**

**¼ cup water**

**1 tablespoon molasses**

Dissolve the yeast in the warm water in a large mixing bowl.

In a saucepan, heat the molasses, orange peel, caraway, and salt to boiling, stirring constantly. Remove it from the heat, stir in the buttermilk, and allow it to cool for several minutes, until lukewarm. Add the molasses mixture to the yeast. Gradually add the rye flour and beat the batter 200 strokes. Stir in 2½ cups of the whole wheat flour, until the batter is stiff. Cover with a cloth and allow to rest for 15 minutes.

Knead the dough on a floured surface for about 5 minutes. The dough will be sticky, so flour your hands well. Add at least ½ cup of the remaining whole wheat flour and more as necessary as you knead the bread, until the dough is moist but workable. Place the dough in an oiled bowl, cover it with a cloth, and let it rise in a warm place (see note) for an hour. Punch down the dough, form it into two round loaves, and score an X in the center of each loaf with a sharp knife. Place the loaves on an oiled baking pan, about 4 inches apart, and let them rise for about 45 minutes.

In a small pot, bring the water and molasses for the glaze to a boil and then simmer for 5 minutes. Allow to cool for about 10 minutes.

When the loaves have risen, preheat the oven to 350°. Brush the tops and sides with roughly half of the glaze. Reserve the remaining glaze. Bake the bread for about 50 minutes. Glaze it once more as soon as you remove it from the oven.

This bread is especially nice with sharp cheddar and slices of fresh tomato.

---

*Notes: There is a dark rye flour sometimes referred to as "pumpernickel rye" that is especially nice for this type of bread. Look for it at markets that specialize in whole grains.*

*To create a warm, draft-free environment where the bread can rise, boil several pots of water and place them in your oven with the bowl of dough. The oven is insulated and will retain the warmth produced by the pots of hot water.*

---

# *Slovenian Almond-Apricot Bread*

Apricot trees were planted all across Slovenia and Croatia, so apricots became a favorite fruit used in fillings, marmalade, and brandy throughout the region. Here is a fruit-nut bread that makes excellent breakfast or snack fare. The recipe came from a grandmotherly woman I met while traveling in Yugoslavia. She asked me where I was from, and when I answered, "Pennsylvania," she beamed and said, "Pennslovenia? Why that's almost like where I'm from!" I smiled and nodded in agreement.

### YIELDS 1 LOAF

*1 ½ cups water*
*1 ½ cups dried unsulfured apricots, chopped*
*2 tablespoons butter*
*½ cup maple syrup*
*1 egg, beaten*
*1 teaspoon pure vanilla extract*
*1 teaspoon freshly grated orange rind*

*1 ½ cups unbleached white flour*
*1 cup whole wheat flour*
*1 teaspoon salt*
*1 teaspoon baking soda*
*½ teaspoon baking powder*

*1 cup toasted, chopped almonds*

In a medium saucepan, bring the water and apricots to a boil and then simmer until very soft, for at least 10 minutes. Add the butter, maple syrup, egg, vanilla, and orange rind and stir well until the butter melts. Remove the mixture from the heat.

Preheat the oven to 350°.

Sift together the flours, salt, soda, and baking powder. Fold the dry ingredients into the apricot mixture. Add the chopped almonds and blend well.

Spread the batter evenly into an oiled medium loaf pan. Bake for one hour and 15 minutes, until a knife inserted in the center comes out clean. Allow the bread to cool for several minutes before removing it from the pan.

This bread is moist and flavorful enough to enjoy plain, but it is also delicious with sweet butter or cream cheese and a slightly tart fruit marmalade or apricot jam.

# Black Bread

My first afternoon in Macedonia, I secured by chance a comfortable room in the home of a large family who lived in the country. The personal warmth and congeniality of this family's simple lifestyle undoubtedly outdid the glitz of a stay at the most luxurious of hotels. The two oldest children befriended me almost instantly, and later that evening their mother offered us a rich, moist black bread and brewed fresh coffee. The bread was spectacular, but the coffee was out of my league. I had never tasted anything so bittersweet or strong.

After a few sips, I realized to my dismay that the mercifully tiny cup was almost half full of coffee grounds. No one else seemed to notice. So I mustered my meager reserves of courage and politely swallowed as much as I could without noticeably gagging. We finished the treat, and everyone else turned over their cups onto their saucers, so I did likewise. Then they all held up their cups to display the insides. It was then I realized that this custom was a kind of contest to have the cleanest cup. Several were clean as a whistle, and the rest had light films of coffee grounds on the bottom. My cup was a total lost cause. Its white china inside was coated top to bottom with a thick, brown sludge. I blushed, and we all laughed good-naturedly. This was one custom that would take a little practice. At first I approached it as a challenge to my adaptability (and my stomach lining), but eventually I actually enjoyed this powerful drink.

The black bread, on the other hand, I loved immediately. Here it is, as inviting as the twinkle of an eye.

## YIELDS 2 LOAVES

2 medium potatoes, scrubbed and
   quartered

3 1-ounce squares unsweetened baker's
   chocolate
2 tablespoons butter or vegetable oil
1/4 cup dark molasses (not blackstrap)

3 1/2 tablespoons mild-tasting honey
2 teaspoons whole caraway seeds
1/2 teaspoon cinnamon
1/2 teaspoon nutmeg, preferably freshly
   ground
1/2 cup freshly brewed coffee or decaf

2 packages dry yeast (about 2
   tablespoons)
½ cup warm water
1 teaspoon sugar

_____

1 cup cornmeal
2 cups rye flour

2 cups whole wheat flour
2 cups unbleached white flour
1 tablespoon salt

_____

1 tablespoon molasses combined with 1
   tablespoon water

Boil the potatoes until soft. Drain the potatoes, reserving a cup of the potato water. Mash the potatoes with a fork or masher to yield one cup.

In a small saucepan, melt the chocolate and butter on low heat, stirring constantly. In a large bowl, combine the melted chocolate with the mashed potatoes. Add the molasses, honey, caraway seeds, cinnamon, nutmeg, coffee, and the cup of the reserved potato water. Mix thoroughly.

In a small bowl combine the yeast, warm water, and one teaspoon of sugar. Set aside until the yeast bubbles, about 5 minutes.

Pour the activated yeast into the cooled potato mixture and combine. Add the cornmeal, rye flour, whole wheat flour, white flour, and the salt. Mix well. The dough will be somewhat lumpy. Turn the dough out onto a well-floured surface, cover it, and let it rest for 15 minutes. Meanwhile, clean, dry, and butter or oil the large bowl.

Knead the dough for about 5 minutes, adding more white flour as necessary to prevent sticking. Form it into a ball, place it in the buttered bowl, and turn it to coat all sides. Cover and let rise until doubled in a warm, draft-free place for about 1 to 1½ hours. Knead gently for one minute and let rise again until doubled, about 40 minutes. Form the dough into two round loaves and place them in buttered 9-inch round pie pans or on a large baking sheet. Cover them and let rise until almost doubled, about ½ hour.

Preheat the oven to 350°.

Brush the loaves with the molasses and water glaze. With a sharp knife, cut a shallow X in the top of each loaf. Bake for 45 minutes or until the bread sounds hollow when tapped on the bottom.

This bread is rich and moist. It is wonderful with sweet butter, a sharp cheese, or with soup.

*Variation* If you would like a sweeter, dessert bread, just increase the honey or sugar by one tablespoon, add ¼ cup currants, and omit the caraway seeds.

SUSAN HARVILLE

# *Finland*

# INTRODUCTION

Finland today is a highly industrialized, socially progressive, modern state with one of the highest standards of living in the world. It is widely associated with the products of its assertive design—modern, spare furniture; glittering crystals; bright ceramics; boldly printed textiles; and soaring architecture of characteristically pure lines and rugged materials.

And yet, despite the striking modernism of today's Finland, there remains a strong sense of the past—almost a fairy-tale atmosphere. There are vast, dense forests of fragrant pine and spruce where bears might live. Jingling sleighs are pulled by reindeer through the snowy landscape to old country houses of carved wood. The wisps of wood smoke from the chimneys assure of warmth inside where pots of steaming porridge wait. The rippling lights of the aurora borealis evoke ancient mystery and natural magic.

The Finns still live close to nature—and how could they not? The forceful climate and impressive geography are impossible to ignore. One-third of Finland is above the Arctic Circle, making it the northernmost country in the world. In Lapland, the northernmost region of Finland, it is dark for fifty-one continuous days in winter, and there are seventy-three straight days of continuous sunlight in summer. Even on the southern coast where the Finnish population of less than 5 million is concentrated, the sun is above the horizon only six hours a day in winter, while in summer it sits low on the horizon all night with only a brief twilight.

Ice was the dominant force in creating the topography of present-day Finland, leaving rugged, ancient rock of the oldest geological formation known. Glacial ice pushed up rocky ridges, hills, and cliffs and dug out scarps. The hollows carved in the rock filled with water, creating 187,888 lakes. Finland's land area is the size of New England, New York, and New Jersey combined, but it is a fretwork with more lakes in relation to its size than any other country. The lakes are dotted with islands and connected by winding, labyrinthine rivers. The thousands of miles of ragged coastline are laced by 30,000 islands. There is water everywhere. The nineteenth-century Finnish poet Zachris Topelius called Finland "daughter of the sea."

Two-thirds of Finland's surface is covered by dark blue-green forests of pine, spruce, and birch. The deep forests have long been the basis of the economy as well as the omnipresent feature of the landscape. Pine woods even creep into downtown Helsinki.

Today, a majority of the Finnish population lives in towns and cities, but they moved there in relatively recent times, and most Finns are only reluctant urbanites with strong ties to the countryside, where they feel more at home. By law and custom there is public access to all outdoors, and the vigorous Finns make good use of it. In the old days skiing was a necessity, but now it's a very popular winter sport at which Finns of all ages excel. In summer, people hike into the forests to search for wild berries and mushrooms. A large segment of the population has country cottages, usually on a sparsely populated lake (there is one lake per twenty-six people in Finland) where they enjoy the long, long days of warmth and sunlight in the land of the midnight sun.

The geographic position of Finland has been the ruling factor in its turbulent history. Squeezed between Sweden, with a Western tradition, and Russia, with an Eastern culture, Finland was long the battlefield between the two powerful empires. Beginning in the thirteenth century, Sweden dominated Finland for six centuries, which left a strong legacy on educational and cultural institutions, religion, political and legal systems, and cuisine.

Then came one hundred years of Russian colonial rule that ended in 1917 when, in the wake of the Bolshevik revolution, Finland declared its independence. The nineteenth century had been a period of emerging nationalism in Finland. Finnish, once the language of the common people, became the language of education and government, replacing Swedish. *The Kalevala,* a collection of epic Finnish folk poems, was published in 1835 and became a source of national pride and identity.

Finland has remained autonomous against great odds. Before the Winter War in 1939–40, Karelia, the easternmost region of Finland, extended halfway to Leningrad from the present Finnish-Russian border. Under the terms of a peace agreement, this large area became Russian territory. Virtually the entire population of Karelians (425,000) chose to leave their homes and move west to live within Finland's new borders. It was a time of extreme national hardship, yet other Finns shared their homes with the Karelians until new ones could be built for them. The distinctive cuisine of Karelia thus spread throughout Finland.

At first glance Finnish cuisine seems like one of the most unlikely from which to borrow for a vegetarian diet. The short growing season of an Arctic climate and the scarcity of good farmland in Finland doesn't produce a wide range of fruits and vegetables. The Finns do eat a great deal of fish, as is quite natural in such a watery place. However, I don't eat fish myself or recommend it to others, so I've not included fish recipes in this chapter.

In fact, the Finnish cuisine has much to recommend it to vegetarians. In the traditional diet, meat was a rarity. The solid foundation of the Finnish diet is cereal and bread; barley, oats, buckwheat, and rye flourish in a cold climate. There also is an emphasis on dairy protein. Milk and sour milk products are important staples. Fresh fruits and vegetables are cherished during their brief growing season and celebrated in special dishes. We can learn from the Finns how to make the most of root vegetables and other winter storage vegetables. Finland is agriculturally independent despite the hardships.

In the Arctic climate, food preservation methods of salting, souring, drying, and pickling evolved into a national preference for sour, fermented, salty tastes. To this add the flavorful influences of Russian and Swedish cuisines. Russian grand cuisine (as it was before 1917) is still very popular in Finland, and the Swedish smörgåsbord (*voileipapoyta* in Finland) has long been assimilated.

Finnish cuisine is plain, hearty, and wholesome. Although imported bananas and avocados are available now in markets in Finland, the Finns prefer the good old, tried and true, traditional dishes that taste of the past.

I feel a personal connection to Finnish food from my own past. Twenty years ago I left graduate school, for what I supposed to be a short break, to travel and visit friends. I wanted a chance to look around, assess my options, and perhaps test myself in new ways. I found a nice little place with a garden and some big old barns in the country outside of Ithaca. Here in the rural farming community of Spencer, New York, I hoped to encounter *real* life.

There was certainly nothing unique about this longing back then. Millions of my peers pursued their own searches for meaningful fulfillment. It was standard practice. What was a bit unique was that I found myself in a region where many Finnish immigrants had settled since 1910. A Finnish lifestyle was still practiced by many. A few of the older people hadn't learned to speak English. Most social occasions were celebrated with Finnish-style hospitality.

One day a couple of weeks after I'd moved in, a farmer came by to try to sell me a goat he had on the back of his truck. The price was reasonable, but my life was unsettled. To be polite and because I'd never seen one, I took a look, and saw a perfect, noble, archetypal, Picasso-esque goat with long, curved horns and an intelligent, disdainful stare. I was intimidated, not by the farmer's sales pitch, but by the silent challenge I saw in the goat's yellow eyes. I accepted her dare, and soon I was hooked.

Getting to know animals was the most fascinating and profound experience I'd had. I acquired more animals. After a while I realized that if my friendship—my cosmic interspecies connection—to Freddy, Curley, and Loopy was to be respected, I had no choice but to become a vegetarian. Soon I was going to livestock auctions to outbid the buyers from meat packing companies in order to rescue some veal calves to bring home.

My tolerant Finnish neighbors cheerfully offered advice, encouragement, and even manual labor. I got help putting up fences, learning to milk cows, growing grain crops, assisting at difficult calvings, and making cheese and yogurt. They offered tools, bread recipes, garden seeds, and invitations to soothe weary muscles in their saunas. I learned to dance the *schottische* at a Finnish midsummer party. I tasted many ethnic foods with flavors new to me.

When the animal population of goats, sheep, cows, horses, ponies, dogs, cats, chickens, and so on at my farm had reached a couple hundred, I took a job at the newly opened Moosewood Restaurant to help pay the feed bills. At Moosewood I found many like-minded people and a developing whole-foods cuisine. As our vegetarian repertoire at Moosewood grew in the following years, we often experimented with variations of traditional ethnic foods.

Sunday nights were devoted to ethnic menus. For the first Finnish night at Moose-wood we planned an ambitious smörgåsbord and decorated the restaurant with pine boughs. To my surprise, my neighbors advertised the event in the local Finnish language newspaper and many Finns, experienced and knowledgeable in the cuisine, came to sample the foods. Knowing how nostalgic Finns can be about their traditional foods, it was with some trepidation that we presented our versions of some age-old dishes. But all was well. Nothing was too far off the mark or else, with the usual quiet steadiness and reserve of the Finnish folk, they didn't let on. They had come to support and applaud our foray into their proud cultural heritage.

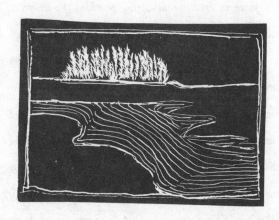

# BREADS

### L E I P I Ā

*Bread is the real glory of Finnish cuisine, a wide-ranging variety of some of the world's best. Most typically, Finnish breads are dark, dense, whole grain, and extremely nutritious. Historically, bread has been the mainstay of the Finnish diet and continues to be revered. Nothing symbolizes home as well as a loaf of sourdough rye bread.*

*Rye grows better than any other grain in the sparse northern soil of low fertility. The seed survives extended periods of extreme cold and it germinates and begins to grow as the ground thaws. Oats and barley also thrive in this climate, but wheat is largely imported.*

*In the old days, bread was made only of rye and water. The dough was allowed to ferment, creating gases that provided the leavening to make the bread rise and also gave the bread a sour taste, which Finns love. Baking was done in a wide, very deep oven built into the wall. Heat was supplied by lighting a wood fire on the floor of the oven and then carefully tending it for several hours.*

*Not surprisingly, bread was baked in large quantities. In western Finland, hundreds of loaves were made at a time, but only twice a year. These dense, nutritious rye loaves were shaped into flat wheels with holes in their centers so that they could be stacked on poles, dried and stored, suspended from the ceiling. At the same time, in Karelia in eastern Finland, bread was baked as often as every day in moist round loaves of sourdough rye.*

*There is much less home baking today than there was a generation ago,* but bread-baking is certainly not a lost art in Finland. There is a deep appreciation for beautiful bread, and a large basket filled with several kinds is offered at every meal.

In the recipes that follow, yeast is used as a leavening, saving several days in the bread-baking process, and wheat flour is added to the rye because it makes the dough easier to handle.

# Finnish Rye Bread

•

## Suomalaisruisleipä

This is a simple, basic, staff-of-life bread. It will have a more or less sour taste depending on whether it is made with beer, buttermilk, potato water, or milk, in that order. Made without any of the artificial colorings and flavorings usually added to commercially prepared rye breads, these dense loaves are a light gray-brown and exude the good, earthy taste of rye, which is loved by Scandinavians.

### YIELDS 2 ROUND LOAVES

1½ cups beer, buttermilk, milk, or potato water (reserved from cooking potatoes)
2 tablespoons butter or margarine
1 teaspoon salt
1 package dry yeast (about 1 tablespoon)

½ cup warm water
1 tablespoon sugar
2 cups dark rye flour, rye meal (see note), or light rye flour
3½–4 cups unbleached white flour

Note: Rye meal is unsifted rye flour that contains the rye bran.

Heat 1½ cups of liquid to lukewarm. Stir in the butter and salt. Set aside to cool.

Dissolve the yeast in the warm water (a temperature comfortable on the inside of the wrist) with the sugar. Let it stand for 5 minutes until the yeast bubbles.

Stir the yeast mixture into the cooled liquid. Add the rye flour and beat until smooth. Add the white flour, a cup at a time, stirring after each addition until enough is added to make a stiff dough. Dust a work surface with white flour. Form the dough into a rough ball, place it on the work surface, cover it with a damp cloth, and let it rest for 15 minutes. Generously butter a large bowl or pot.

Adding only as much flour as necessary to prevent sticking, knead the bread dough until smooth, about 5 minutes. (The gluten in rye is more fragile than in wheat. It needs a resting time to recuperate and reform and does not require as lengthy or vigorous a kneading.) Form the dough into a smooth ball and place it in the buttered bowl, turning it to coat all sides with butter. Cover it and let it rise in a warm spot until doubled in size, for about 2 hours.

Punch down the dough, gently knead it for one minute, and divide it into two parts. Form each half into a round loaf and place the loaves in two lightly buttered 9-inch round cake pans or on a large, buttered baking sheet. Press a hole through the center of each loaf to give it a traditional shape if you wish. Cover and let rise until almost doubled in size, about ½ hour.

Preheat the oven to 375°. Brush the loaves with water and gently puncture the surface all over with the tines of a fork, in a design if you wish.

Bake for about 30 minutes or until the bread is golden brown and sounds hollow when tapped on the bottom. While it is hot, brush it with butter to glaze, and then let it cool on a rack.

# Holiday Rye Bread

•

## Joululimppa

During the holiday season, Finns take a break from the everyday sour rye breads with this slightly sweet, extremely flavorful and fragrant bread. It is similar to Swedish-style rye bread and is sometimes called Oulunlimppu, named for the city of Oulu in northwest Finland where many Swedish-speaking Finns live.

Joululimppu is a fine accompaniment to any Finnish meal, or a loaf can be the centerpiece of a light meal along with apple cider and a mild cheese, such as Havarti, Gouda, or Edam. I especially enjoy this dense and fragrant bread toasted and buttered for breakfast.

### YIELDS 3 LOAVES

2 cups buttermilk (or 2 cups fresh milk mixed with 2 tablespoons vinegar or fresh lemon juice)

1/2 cup molasses

1/4 cup butter or margarine

2 teaspoons salt

1 teaspoon fennel seeds

1 teaspoon caraway seeds

2 packages dry yeast (about 2 tablespoons)

1/2 cup warm water

grated rind of 1 orange

1 cup rye flakes (available in healthfood stores) or wheat germ

2 cups dark or light rye flour

3 1/2–4 1/2 cups unbleached white or whole wheat flour or a combination

GLAZE

1 tablespoon molasses

2 tablespoons water

Heat the buttermilk, molasses, butter or margarine, salt, fennel seeds, and caraway seeds until the butter melts. Set aside to cool.

Dissolve the yeast in the warm water. Let it stand for 5 minutes until the yeast bubbles. Add the yeast to the cooled buttermilk mixture along with the grated orange rind, rye flakes or wheat germ, and rye flour. Beat well until smooth. Add 3 to 3 1/2 cups of wheat flour, stirring in a cup at a time, until the dough will not readily absorb more flour. The dough will be rough.

Flour a work surface with the remaining wheat flour and turn the dough out onto it. Cover the dough with a damp cloth and let it rest for 15 minutes. (The gluten in rye is more fragile than in wheat. It needs a resting time to recuperate and reform and does not require as lengthy or vigorous a kneading.)

Gently knead the dough for 5 to 10 minutes until smooth. Form the dough into a ball and place it in a large buttered bowl or pot, turning it to coat all sides with butter. Cover it and let it rise in a warm spot until doubled in size, about an hour.

Punch down the dough and gently knead it for one minute. Form the dough into three round loaves and place in lightly buttered 9-inch round cake pans or on buttered baking sheets. Cover and let rise until almost doubled in size, 45 minutes to an hour.

Preheat the oven to 375°. Combine the water and molasses; brush the tops with half of this mixture to glaze. Then lightly pierce the loaves all over with a fork.

Bake for 35 to 45 minutes, until the bread sounds hollow when tapped on the bottom. While the bread is hot, brush it with the remaining glaze. Remove the loaves from pans and cool on racks.

## *Finnish Sweet Bread*

•

## *Pulla*

It's common in Scandinavia to have three coffee times a day— morning, afternoon, and late evening. The "coffeetable" is an institution—the focus of all social gatherings. Even an unex- pected, drop-in guest can always count on being offered coffee, accompanied by Pulla, a yeasted, cardamom-flavored coffeebread.

On more special occasions such as birthdays, anniversaries, sauna parties, or to entertain very special guests, an elaborate coffeetable is provided, which traditionally includes seven baked items—Pulla, a plain and a fancy cake, and four varieties of cookies.

There is even an etiquette on how to sample each of these in three or four courses with four cups of coffee.

The custom of the formal coffeetable is preserved by Finnish Americans, who will proudly display Pulla, cakes, and cookies on the beautiful frosted-glass platters and intricately woven tablecloths for which Finland is famous—inherited treasures all.

In Spencer, New York, where I once lived, moist and rich Pulla is the most sought after item at every bake sale, which I suspect is true in other communities with fine Finnish bakers. Usually Pulla is formed into long braids, but it is the basic sweet bread of all Scandinavia and can be made in many shapes.

### YIELDS 3 LOAVES

2 cups milk
1/2 cup brown sugar
1 teaspoon salt
1 1/2 teaspoons ground cardamom
_____

2 packages dry yeast (about
  2 tablespoons)
1/2 cup warm water
1 tablespoon sugar
_____

4 eggs, beaten

3 cups whole wheat flour
6 cups unbleached white flour
  (approximately)
1/2 cup melted butter
GLAZE

1 egg, beaten
2 tablespoons milk
1/2 cup pearlized sugar (see note) or
  crushed sugar cubes (optional)
1/2 cup chopped or sliced almonds
  (optional)

In a large pan, heat the milk, sugar, salt, and cardamom to lukewarm. Cool. Dissolve the yeast in the warm water with one tablespoon of sugar and let it stand for 5 minutes until bubbles form. Pour the yeast mixture and eggs into the cooled milk and mix well. Add the whole wheat flour and beat until smooth. Stir in half of the white flour and beat. Beat in the melted butter. Add enough remaining flour as is necessary to form a firm dough. Generously dust a work surface with white flour. Knead the dough for 5 to 10 minutes, until it is very smooth. Add more flour, if necessary, to prevent the dough from sticking to the surface and your fingers.

> Note: Pearlized sugar is large crystals of sugar, often used to decorate sugar cookies, and can be found in the baking sections of supermarkets.

Form the dough into a ball and place it in a large buttered bowl or pot, turning it to coat all sides with butter. Cover it with a damp cloth and let it rise in a warm place until doubled in size, about 1½ hours.

Punch down the dough and divide it into thirds. Divide each third into three portions and roll each portion into strands about 2 feet long. Braid three strands into a long straight loaf and place it on a buttered baking sheet. Repeat this process to make two more braided loaves. Cover the loaves and let them rise until almost doubled, about 45 minutes.

Preheat the oven to 375°. Brush the braids with the milk and egg glaze and sprinkle with sugar and/or almonds, if desired. Bake for about 25 minutes, until light golden. A knife inserted in the center should come out clean. Do not overbake or the bread will be dry.

Serve plain with coffee or with butter and jam and coffee. If you have any left after a few days it will be best toasted.

*Variation I* After the first rising, punch down the dough and divide it into thirds. Roll each third of the dough into a rectangle about 1 x 2 feet. Top with softened butter, sprinkle with cinnamon, nutmeg, brown sugar, and raisins and/or nuts. Roll up along the longer side, jelly-roll fashion, and form into a ring, folded side down, on a buttered baking pan. Cut slices about ⅔ of the way through the ring every 3 to 4 inches all around. Slightly twist each wedge a bit, alternating in and out. Let the rings rise until almost doubled in size and brush them with the glaze. This may need to bake 5 to 10 minutes longer than braids.

*Variation II* After the first rising, punch down the dough and divide it into thirds. Roll each third of the dough into a large circle. Coat it with softened butter and sprinkle it with cinnamon, nutmeg, and brown sugar. Peel and thinly slice 2 apples and place the slices on one half of the circle. Fold the other half over the apples, like an omelet, and press the edges together. Bend this half circle into a crescent moon shape on a buttered baking pan. Cover and let it rise until almost doubled in size. Brush with the glaze and bake for 30 to 35 minutes until golden. Sprinkle with powdered sugar.

# Oat Bran Muffins

•

## Omenapyörykät

Oat bran muffins have not been part of traditional Finnish baking, but they do seem to be on their way to becoming classics in the U.S. Here, they are enhanced by apple and prune, a classic Scandinavian combination. They are very quick and easy to prepare and quite tasty, fairly lowfat and low cholesterol, and two of them provide the daily requisite of oat bran.

### YIELDS 12 MUFFINS

1 cup peeled chopped apple (about 1 apple)
1 cup chopped pitted prunes

___

½ cup maple syrup
½ cup plain nonfat yogurt
¼ cup vegetable oil

2 egg whites or 1 egg (optional)

___

½ teaspoon salt (optional)
1 teaspoon cinnamon
2 teaspoons freshly grated orange peel
2 cups oat bran
2 teaspoons baking powder

Preheat the oven to 400°. Line a muffin tin with paper muffin cups.

Prepare the apples and prunes and set them aside, so that they'll be ready to stir into the batter at the last minute.

Whisk together the maple syrup, yogurt, oil, and egg. Combine the dry ingredients in a medium mixing bowl. Fold the liquid mixture into the dry ingredients until just wet. Stir in the chopped apples and prunes.

Divide the batter among the muffin cups. The cups should be filled almost to the top, which is unusual, but this heavy muffin does not rise much as it bakes.

Bake the muffins for about 20 minutes or until they are golden and a knife inserted in the center comes out clean.

# SANDWICHES
## V o i l e i p i ā

Sandwiches are an important part of the cuisine of Finland. They're served at breakfast and lunch and as an appetizer at dinner. Usually several kinds will be presented—almost a mini-version of a smörgåsbord. Most often they are open faced and beautifully garnished with morsels of vegetables, fruits, eggs, or herbs.

Start building a sandwich with a thin slice of one of the great Scandinavian breads, the heavier the better, preferably rye, or a whole-grain crispbread. Vegetable Pâté (see page 258) and Blue Cheese Balls (see page 257) make delicious spreads. Even simpler, spread the bread with butter, cream cheese, cottage cheese, or shredded smoked cheese mixed with mayonnaise, sour cream, or yogurt.

Garnish the sandwiches with any of the following: thinly sliced mushrooms, fresh or pickled; cucumber or radish slices; paper-thin fans of red onion or chopped chives or scallions; sliced or chopped hard-boiled egg; sauerkraut or shredded vegetables such as beet, carrot, or daikon radish; slices of cherry tomato; slivers of pickle; fresh dill sprigs; caraway or fennel seeds; grated or sliced pear or apple; chopped dried apricot or prune.

Finnish cooking (like Finnish people) can be somewhat dour. It seems to me that sandwiches compose a comparatively casual, even exuberant, branch of the cuisine. Finnish cooks may have old favorites among sandwich toppings, but they don't worry much about being traditional. Sandwich combinations are chosen in an inventive and fanciful way, with an eye to the decorative.

# Blue Cheese Balls

•

## Juustotahna

These intensely flavored cheese balls are delicious spread on Finn Crisp crackers or thinly sliced rye bread. They make a good appetizer, smörgåsbord item, or an addition to a Finnish salad plate.

### YIELDS 16 TO 18 WALNUT-SIZED BALLS

*1½ cups crumbled blue cheese (such as Roquefort, Gorgonzola, or Danish Blue)*
*¾ cup unsalted butter, at room temperature*

*¼ teaspoon Tabasco or other hot sauce*
*1 tablespoon minced onion*
*1 cup finely chopped toasted almonds*

Mash the blue cheese with a fork until smooth. Add the butter, Tabasco, and onion. Blend well. Form into walnut-sized balls. Roll the balls in the chopped almonds. The cheese mixture will be a bit soft and sticky, but you should be able to perfect the shape of the balls once they have almonds on them. Mound the balls in a pretty bowl, cover, and chill.

Serve on a cheese board with crackers or bread and sliced cherry tomatoes or radishes.

# Vegetable Pâté

•

# Kasvipasteija

A pâté to spread on bread or crackers or serve as an appetizer dip is almost a must for the "bread and butter" table. Most people can't guess the ingredients in this high-protein Vegetable Pâté, but it's interesting and tasty and soon becomes addictive, as you dip in just one more and one more cracker.

## YIELDS 3 CUPS

2 cakes Five-spice Tofu (see page 189)
  (or 1 cake fresh tofu)

---

2 cups steamed green beans (about
  1 pound raw) (see page 681)
1/2 cup toasted walnuts
1 tablespoon tamari soy sauce
3 tablespoons mayonnaise or plain
  yogurt
2 teaspoons prepared mustard
1 cup plus 2 tablespoons finely minced
  onions

2 teaspoons vegetable oil
1/2 teaspoon dried thyme
1/2 teaspoon dried sage
1/4 teaspoon ground coriander seeds

---

1 kosher dill pickle, minced (about
  1/4 cup)
freshly ground black pepper

If using fresh tofu, blanch and press it (see page 684).

Grate the Five-spice Tofu or pressed fresh tofu on the coarsest side of a hand grater; it should yield about 2 cups. Put the tofu in a mixing bowl and set aside.

In a food processor or in batches in a blender, combine the green beans, walnuts, soy sauce, mayonnaise or yogurt, and mustard until well blended, but not quite puréed. Add this mixture to the grated tofu along with 2 tablespoons of the minced onions.

Sauté the remaining cup of onions in the oil with the thyme, sage, and coriander for about 5 minutes, until the onion is translucent. Stir the onions into the pâté mixture in the bowl.

Add the pickle and plenty of fresh black pepper. Mix thoroughly. Refrigerate until well chilled.

Serve with crackers or with raw vegetable sticks as a dip, or spread on thin slices of rye bread topped with slices of fresh tomato.

S O U P S

# *Yellow Split Pea Soup*

•

## *Hernerakkaa*

This smooth, thick, very filling soup is a favorite all over Scandinavia. It is often served at traditional wedding suppers, probably because of its nourishing, restorative powers. I recommend Yellow Split Pea Soup even for an ordinary day, accompanied by a dark, sour rye bread or oat bread, pickled beets and cucumbers, ice cold beer, and tiny, delicate pancakes with fresh berries for dessert.

### SERVES 6 GENEROUSLY

2 cups dried yellow split peas

8 cups water or vegetable stock (see
   page 685)

2 medium potatoes

2 large carrots

3 celery stalks

1 large onion

1 turnip, peeled

2 parsnips, peeled

———————————————

2–3 teaspoons dry mustard (or 2–3
   tablespoons prepared mustard) (or to
   taste)

dash of allspice

1 teaspoon ground cumin seeds

1 teaspoon dried marjoram

1 teaspoon dried thyme

2 teaspoons salt (or to taste)

plenty of freshly ground black pepper

———————————————

1 cup heavy cream (optional)

dark bread croutons or cubes of toast
   (optional)

Rinse the split peas. In a large soup pot, bring the split peas and the water or stock to a boil. Coarsely chop the vegetables and add them to the water as it comes to a boil. Lower the heat and simmer for about 1½ hours or until the peas are very soft and almost disintegrating. Use a heat diffuser, if needed, to prevent scorching.

Purée the soup in batches in a blender or food processor, until it is quite smooth and an even yellowish color. The puréed soup will be very thick. Add the spices and herbs and season with salt and pepper to taste. Reheat gently.

If you are using heavy cream, whip it until stiff. Serve the soup steaming hot, garnished with croutons or cubes of toast and dollops of whipped cream.

## Juurikasviksiakeitto

## Root Vegetable Purées

Humble, unassuming, root vegetables are quite important in Finnish cuisine because they are the only ones available for much of the year. Their undeserved dreary reputations are forgotten, however, with a taste of these sprightly, attractive soups with interesting, unexpected flavors. They have satisfying, creamy textures but are actually very light in fats, cholesterol, and calories.

SERVES 4

## RUTABAGA AND CARROT SOUP

*(A very thick, attractive orange soup with a bright sweet taste and a citrus bite. Yields 4 cups.)*

1 medium onion, chopped
1 tablespoon vegetable oil or butter
3 small carrrots, peeled and chopped
1 small rutabaga, peeled and chopped (about 2 cups)
½ teaspoon salt
1 cup vegetable stock (see page 685) or water
½ teaspoon ground ginger
¼ teaspoon nutmeg
2 cups orange juice
freshly ground black pepper to taste

unsweetened whipped cream (optional)
dollop of Cranberry Sauce (see page 275) (optional)

## TURNIP AND PEAR SOUP

*(This is creamy white, thick, and both sweet and sharp. Yields 4 cups.)*

1 medium onion, chopped
1 tablespoon vegetable oil or butter
3 medium-large turnips, peeled and chopped (3 cups)
3 large ripe pears, peeled, cored, and chopped (about 3 cups)
1 teaspoon dried thyme
½ teaspoon salt
1¼ cups vegetable stock (see page 685) or water
¼ teaspoon nutmeg
1½–2 cups pear or apple juice
freshly ground black pepper to taste

shredded daikon radish (optional)
a few raspberries (optional)

## POTATO, CELERIAC, AND PARSNIP SOUP

*A thick and creamy potato soup with a slight anise flavor. Yields 5 cups.)*

1 medium onion, chopped
1 tablespoon vegetable oil or butter
2 potatoes, peeled and chopped (about 2 cups)
2 parsnips, peeled and chopped (about 2 cups)
1 large celeriac (celery root), peeled and chopped (about 1 heaping cup)
1 teaspoon salt
1 teaspoon dill
1 teaspoon ground fennel seeds
2 cups vegetable stock (see page 685) or water
2 cups buttermilk or milk
freshly ground black pepper to taste

sprigs of fresh dill (optional)
lightly toasted fennel seeds (optional)

In a large saucepan, sauté the onion in oil or butter for about 5 minutes, until translucent but not browned. Add the chopped root vegetables and fruit (if used) along with the salt and herbs. Sauté for another 10 minutes or so, stirring occasionally.

Add the vegetable stock or water and cook, covered, on low heat for 20 to 30 minutes, until the vegetables are soft and tender. Add the spices. In a blender or food processor, purée the soup with juice or milk, as indicated, until smooth and thick. Season with black pepper to taste. Serve with optional garnishes, if desired.

# Cherry Soup

•

## Kirsikkakeitto

Beautiful, glistening red soup is the reward for a day of cherry picking, if picking cherries itself is not reward enough. Cherry soup is the ultimate manifestation of the ephemeral, halcyon days of midsummer, but if you live in midtown Manhattan or Helsinki or it's January and you can't wait until July, then second best is using frozen cherries, reducing the liquid slightly and cooking them for only about 10 minutes. You should be able to find unsweetened, pitted, whole sweet cherries in the frozen food section of your supermarket.

Serve as a first course for Carrot Pancake (see page 268) or Mushroom Pie (see page 269), or with a heavy rye bread and Blue Cheese Balls (see page 257), or serve as dessert, which is how the Finns like it.

### SERVES 6 TO 8

*4 cups fresh ripe cherries (about 2½ pounds) or unsweetened frozen cherries*

*1 cinnamon stick*

*4 cups water*

*juice of 2 lemons (or to taste)*

*3 tablespoons sugar or honey (or to taste)*

*½ cup Cherry Heering liqueur or white wine (or to taste)*

*1 cup heavy cream, whipped, or sour cream or plain yogurt*

Wash the cherries, removing the stems and pits. In a large nonreactive pot (stainless steel or enamel), bring to a boil the cherries, cinnamon stick, and water. Continue to cook at a low boil for 15 to 20 minutes or until the cherries have lost their color. Remove the cinnamon and discard. Drain the cherries, reserving the liquid. Set aside half of the cherries. Purée the remaining cherries and the reserved liquid in two or three batches in a blender or food processor. Return the purée to the soup pot and add the lemon juice, sugar or honey, and the cherry liqueur or wine. Reheat the soup, adding the reserved cherries.

Serve hot or chilled, topped with a dollop of whipped cream, sour cream, or yogurt.

# Russian Salad

·

# Venäläinensalaatti

Outside of Russia this salad is usually called Russian salad and is a favorite throughout Scandinavia. It's often made with the addition of pickled or salted herring and is a standard item on a smörgåsbord. It is substantial and interesting enough that it makes a good main dish at a summer picnic or a centerpiece on a winter salad plate.

### SERVES 6 TO 8

2 cups peeled, diced, and cooked
  potatoes
2 cups peeled, diced, and cooked carrots
1 cup peeled, diced tart apple
1 cup minced dill pickles
1/3 cup minced onion (or to taste)
2 cups cooked, peeled, and diced beets

**DRESSING**
2/3 cup heavy cream, whipped (or 1 cup
  sour cream)

2 tablespoons fresh lemon juice or cider
  vinegar
dash of salt, sugar, and freshly ground
  black pepper

_____

hard-boiled eggs, sliced (optional)

Mix the diced potatoes, carrots, apple, pickles, and onion in a large serving bowl. Chill. Combine all the dressing ingredients and chill. Add the beets to the other vegetables just before serving so the salad will be the proper light pink color. Serve the dressing in a small serving bowl, mound it on top of the salad, or fold it into the salad just before serving. Decorate with slices of hard-boiled egg, if you wish.

# Cucumber–Sour Cream Salad

•

## Kurkkusalaatti

Squeezing the excess moisture from the cucumbers before dressing them gives this salad a full taste and crunchy texture that is very refreshing. It's at its best when really well chilled for a few hours after making it, but it will keep well for several days. Fresh dill, usually available all year, is preferable in this dish.

### SERVES 4 TO 6

4 large unwaxed cucumbers
1 tablespoon salt

_____

2/3 cup sour cream or plain yogurt
2 tablespoons vegetable oil
2 tablespoons white vinegar

3 tablespoons minced fresh dill
   (2–3 teaspoons dried)
1/2 teaspoon sugar
salt and freshly ground black pepper to
   taste

Rinse the cucumbers, but do not peel them; cut off the ends. Using the tines of a fork, score the peel lengthwise. Slice into rounds, as thin as you can. Sprinkle with the tablespoon of salt and toss in a colander. Let the cucumbers stand and drain at room temperature for one hour. Rinse well to remove the salt. Squeeze the cucumber slices dry in a clean tea towel. They will be almost transparent.

Combine the remaining ingredients and fold into the cucumbers. Chill well before serving. Garnish with a sprig of dill.

# Beet and Horseradish Salad

•

## Punajuurisalaatti

Even if you think you don't like horseradish, you'll probably like this fuchsia-colored salad. It is the perfect accompaniment to Mushroom Pie (see page 269) or Cabbage and Tofu over Rice (see page 272), and it almost always appears on a smörgåsbord.

SERVES 4

3 medium beets
3 tablespoons sour cream or plain
    yogurt
1½–2 tablespoons freshly grated
    horseradish root (or 1 tablespoon
    prepared horseradish)

¼ teaspoon salt
¼ teaspoon sugar
dash of freshly ground black pepper

beet greens or lettuce

Cut off the stems of the beet greens about an inch above the beets and, if the greens are fresh and in good condition, wash and dry them and save them in the refrigerator. Clean the beets but do not remove the roots and do not peel them. Boil the beets in water to cover until they are easily pierced with a fork.

When the cooked beets are cool, cut off the ends, rub off the peel, and cut them into julienne strips. You should have about 2 cups. Blend the sour cream or yogurt with the horseradish, salt, sugar, and pepper. Add the beets and stir gently. Chill.

Cut the beet greens or lettuce into strips. Arrange the greens around the outside edge of a bowl and mound the Beet and Horseradish Salad in the center.

# Grated Turnip and Apple Salad

•

## Nauris-Omenasalaatti

 Simple and refreshing, sharp and sweet, this salad is very quickly prepared, especially if you use a food processor. Use as a smörgåsbord item or for a pleasing contrast to a rich main dish such as Cauliflower Rye Casserole (see page 271).

**SERVES 4 TO 6**

1 cup peeled and grated raw turnips or
  rutabaga (about 2 medium turnips
  or ¼ rutabaga)
1 cup peeled and grated tart green
  apples
½ cup chopped fresh parsley

juice of 1 large lemon
1 tablespoon vegetable oil
salt and freshly ground black pepper to
  taste

Combine everything, toss, cover, and chill.

# Cucumber-Yogurt Dressing

•

## Kurkku-Viili Kastike

This low-calorie, heart-healthy dressing is very flavorful on salad greens, or use it to dress steamed carrots or cauliflower or cold, boiled potatoes. If there is dill in the other foods you plan to serve, omit it here.

### YIELDS 1 ½ CUPS

1 medium cucumber, peeled, seeded,
   and coarsely chopped (about ⅔ cup)
⅔ cup plain nonfat yogurt
2 tablespoons minced onion
1 tablespoon vegetable oil

2 teaspoons vinegar
¼ teaspoon salt (optional)
2 teaspoons chopped fresh dill
   (½ teaspoon dried) (optional)

Combine everything in a blender or food processor and purée until creamy and smooth. Chill. The dressing will keep refrigerated for at least one week.

## MAIN DISHES

# Carrot Pancake

•

# Porkkanapannukakku

Pancakes are popular in many guises throughout Scandinavia. After much practice, traditional cooks become incredibly adept at turning out mounds of tiny pancakes. The rest of us appreciate the ease of oven-baking just one big pancake.

For a satisfying winter supper, broil some tofu "hot dogs" to serve with this slightly sweet, puffy Carrot Pancake. Serve the pancake from the skillet in which it is baked; cut it into wedges and garnish with sour cream and hot applesauce or Cranberry Sauce. Or, if you can find them, serve it with lingonberries, as is customary in Finland.

### SERVES 4

1 1/2 cups grated carrot
1/2 cup finely minced or grated onion
1/2 cup bread crumbs (see page 654) or
    wheat germ (or a combination)

_____

4 large eggs
3/4 cup milk
1/2 cup flour (white, whole wheat, or
    rye, or a combination)

1–1 1/2 teaspoons salt
scant 1/2 teaspoon thyme
scant 1/2 teaspoon nutmeg
1/4 teaspoon ground cumin seeds
plenty of freshly ground black pepper

_____

sour cream
applesauce or Cranberry Sauce (see page
    275)

In a mixing bowl, combine the carrots, onions, and bread crumbs or wheat germ. Toss to mix evenly.

Preheat the oven to 450°.

In a blender or by hand, combine the eggs, milk, flour, and seasonings until smooth. You may need to scrape down the sides of the blender jar once or twice. In a large bowl, combine the carrot mixture and the contents of the blender.

Heat about a tablespoon of oil in a heavy 9- to 10½-inch skillet. When the skillet is quite hot, pour in the pancake mixture, making sure the carrots are evenly distributed. Place the skillet in the hot oven. After 20 minutes, lower the temperature to 350° and continue to bake for another 10 to 15 minutes. The pancake should be light brown, puffy, and crisp.

Serve immediately.

# Mushroom Pie

•

# Sienipiirakka

 Finland is a heavily forested country where many different kinds of mushrooms grow—more than a hundred edible varieties.

Mushrooms are eaten fresh and they are dried, smoked, and pickled for preservation. Finnish people are avid and knowledgeable mushroom gatherers, and during mushroom season, which begins at the end of August, many make outings into the forests to collect prized wild varieties.

Fresh or reconstituted dried mushrooms, or a combination, may be used in this pie. Domestic commercial white mushrooms are fine, but if you can find (and afford) chanterelles, porcini, cremini, or any other rich-flavored mushroom, use them for at least a portion of the amount called for; this will give you a more pungent and woodsy-tasting dish. The natural acids in sour cream make this crust exceptionally tender and flaky.

FILLING
2½ cups chopped onions
3 tablespoons butter
8 cups chopped mushrooms
1 teaspoon dried thyme
½ teaspoon salt
lots of freshly ground black pepper
8 ounces cream cheese
CRUST
2½ cups unbleached white flour

2 teaspoons baking powder
¼ teaspoon salt
1 cup butter
1 cup sour cream
flour for coating the dough and board
   for rolling
GLAZE
1 egg
1 tablespoon milk

To make the filling, sauté the onions in the butter in a large skillet. When the onions are soft and translucent, add the mushrooms and thyme and sauté for a few more minutes, until the mushrooms release their juices. Add the seasonings. Cut the cream cheese into small pieces and then stir it into the mushrooms until it melts. Remove from the heat and set aside until the crust is ready.

Preheat the oven to 400°.

For the crust, combine the flour, baking powder, and salt in a large mixing bowl. Using an electric mixer or by hand, cut in the butter just enough to achieve an evenly textured crumbly mix. Stir in the sour cream to form a soft dough. Generously dust the dough with flour and form it into a ball.

On a heavily floured board, roll out ⅔ of the dough to fit a 10-inch pie plate. Trim the edges. Fill with the mushroom mixture. Roll out the remaining dough about ¼ inch thick (thicker than a usual pie crust) and cut into strips 1 inch wide. Weave the strips into a lattice over the filling. This is a bit of trouble but well worth the effort, as you'll see. Fold the ends of the lattice strips under the bottom crust, pinch the edges together, and flute.

For the glaze, beat the egg and milk. With a pastry brush, thoroughly coat the pie crust. (You'll have more than you need—give leftovers to the cat.)

Bake the pie for 25 to 35 minutes, until the crust is puffy and golden.

Serve with Glazed Onions (see page 274) and Beet and Horseradish Salad (see page 265).

# Cauliflower Rye Casserole

•

## Kukkakaalialaatikko

Beatrice Ojakangas, the doyenne of Finnish-American food writers, jokes that because it's so widely used and enjoyed, perhaps the cauliflower should be named the national flower of Finland. Here cauliflower, along with rye, caraway, mustard, and beer, all give a sour tang to a Finnish-inspired casserole—sort of a baked cheese fondue.

### SERVES 4

| | |
|---|---|
| 1 cup beer | 3 cups grated extra sharp cheddar |
| 3 cups rye bread cubes (about 4 slices) | cheese |

| | |
|---|---|
| 1 head cauliflower, cut into bite-sized | 4 eggs |
| florets | 1 teaspoon dry mustard |
| 2 tablespoons butter | 1/2 teaspoon ground coriander seeds |
| 1 teaspoon caraway seeds | freshly ground black pepper to taste |

At least an hour before cooking, pour the beer into a shallow bowl to sit until it becomes flat. Dry the bread cubes on a baking sheet in a 300° oven until they are crisp but not browned, probably about 15 to 20 minutes.

Sauté the cauliflower in the butter with the caraway seeds until just barely tender. Combine the bread cubes and cauliflower with the grated cheese. Spread the mixture into a buttered 2-quart casserole dish.

Mix the eggs, mustard, coriander, and black pepper in a blender or by hand with the flat beer and pour the mixture into the casserole dish. Bake at 350° for 30 to 45 minutes until puffed and golden.

# Cabbage and Tofu over Rice

•

## Kaali ja Tofu paalle Riisi

Preparing and eating traditional foods is the most usual way immigrants have of keeping their cultural heritage. Finnish immigrants in America have also maintained another ancient and important Finnish ethnic bond in the sauna—a hot-air bath that pleasurably relaxes body and mind.

When Finns settle in the country, they first build the little cabin that will be the sauna and use it as temporary living quarters while building the main house. Usually heated with a wood-burning stove topped with hot rocks, the sauna in Finland traditionally was used on farms for bathing, as a clean and quiet place for healing, for childbirth, and for cleansing rituals before other rites of passage. It was also used for preparing and processing foods.

In America, the sauna ritual has become largely social. On the customary Friday or Saturday night, Finnish immigrants will gather with friends and neighbors at one of their saunas to participate in a centuries-old activity reaffirming their Finnish identity. After the repose of the hot sauna, and perhaps a quick dip in a cool lake or a brisk roll in the snow, everyone gathers to enjoy traditional Finnish food.

Sometimes food was cooked thriftily using the heat from the sauna. Cabbage, in particular, benefits from a long, slow cooking, becoming sweeter. This is a "Moosewood-ized" version of a Finnish favorite. What I like best about this dish is that it has the appeal of sweet-and-sour stuffed cabbage but is much easier and faster to prepare.

**TOFU AND MARINADE**

2 12-ounce cakes tofu, pressed (see page
    684)

1 tablespoon vegetable oil

2½ tablespoons tamari soy sauce

2½ tablespoons water

1 tablespoon Worcestershire Sauce (see
    page 686)

½ teaspoon ground allspice

**CABBAGE**

1 medium onion, chopped

2 tablespoons vegetable oil

4 cups shredded cabbage (about ½
    medium head)

**SAUCE**

2 tablespoons tomato paste

1 tablespoon vinegar

1 teaspoon dried dill

1 teaspoon salt

½ teaspoon sweet Hungarian paprika

freshly ground black pepper

¼ cup water

---

1 tablespoon currants

cooked rice (or use barley, mashed
    potatoes, or egg noodles)

1 dill pickle, minced

sour cream

Bake the tofu following the instructions on page 187. Use the ingredients listed above for the marinade, and follow the instructions for the Simple variation of Baked Tofu.

To prepare the cabbage, sauté the onion in the oil in a large heavy skillet. When the onion is almost translucent, add the cabbage. Stirring occasionally, sauté until the cabbage is somewhat reduced, about 5 minutes, but do not let the onion brown.

Combine the sauce ingredients and pour them over the cabbage. Add the currants and stir to coat the cabbage evenly with the sauce. Remove from the heat. Cover the skillet with a lid or aluminum foil. Bake in a 375° oven for about 30 minutes.

Serve the cabbage over rice, barley, mashed potatoes, or (although it's not Finnish style) egg noodles. Top with minced pickle and the baked tofu. Add a spoonful of sour cream, if desired.

# SIDE DISHES

## *Glazed Onions*

•

## *Sipulia*

These tangy and sweet onions served as a side dish nicely complement an entrée such as Mushroom Pie (see page 269) or Carrot Pancake (see page 268).

### SERVES 4

*1 pound boiling onions (about 1½–2 inches in diameter)*

*2 tablespoons butter*

*1 tablespoon molasses*

*2 teaspoons prepared mustard*

*½ teaspoon ground rosemary*

*1–2 teaspoons tamari soy sauce*

Blanch the peeled onions for 5 minutes in boiling salted water. Drain them, pat them dry, and set aside.

Melt the butter in a skillet. Add the remaining ingredients and stir until smooth. Add the onions and sauté on low heat, occasionally basting the onions with the glaze. Turn the onions over at least once. After about 10 minutes, the glaze will be somewhat reduced and thickened and the onions golden brown. Serve immediately.

## *Cranberry Sauce*

·

## *Karpalokastike*

The lingonberries that accompany so many Finnish dishes, especially pancakes, are difficult to find in this country, but cranberries make a fine substitute.

YIELDS 2 CUPS

*12 ounces fresh cranberries (about 4 cups)*
*1/2–2/3 cup maple syrup*
*grated rind and juice of one orange (about 1/2 cup)*

*1/2 teaspoon ground ginger*
*1/2 teaspoon ground cardamom*
*dash of cinnamon*

Wash and drain the cranberries. Remove any soft or discolored cranberries and any leaves or stems.

Combine all the ingredients in a medium saucepan and cook on medium heat for 10 to 15 minutes, stirring, until the cranberries have popped and the sauce is thick.

Serve hot or cold.

# DESSERTS

## *Blueberry Yogurt Pie*

·

## *Mustikkapiiras*

Finland is heavily forested and quite sparsely populated, and yet most Finns like to spend a few weeks in the summer getting *even farther* away from it all—deeper into the untrammeled pine woods. A favorite vacation activity is picking wild berries that grow so abundantly in cold climates.

Historically, berries have been an important source of vitamins in the Finn's northland diet and are still highly prized as a delicious symbol of summer.

Midsummer Eve (Juhannus-June 24) is the longest day of the year. Finnish people like to be out in the countryside celebrating with bonfires, singing, and feasting. This tart-sweet Blueberry Yogurt Pie might be part of the feast (and it's very quickly prepared if you take your blender out into the deep woods).

CRUST

1/3 cup butter or margarine

1/4 cup sugar

1 egg

1 cup unbleached white flour

1/2 teaspoon baking powder

FILLING

2 eggs

3 tablespoons sugar

1 cup plain yogurt

3 tablespoons fresh lemon juice

1 teaspoon pure vanilla extract

_____

2 cups blueberries, fresh or frozen

Butter and flour a 9- or 10-inch pie pan. Preheat the oven to 350°.

Using an electric mixer or by hand, cream the butter and sugar. Add the egg and blend well. Combine the flour and baking powder and mix them into the wet ingredients to form a soft dough. With flour-dusted fingers, pat the sticky dough into the bottom of the buttered and floured pie pan. Push the dough up to cover the sides of the pan. Refrigerate for at least as long as it takes to make the filling.

Mix all the filling ingredients, except the blueberries, until smooth. Put the berries into the pie shell and gently pour in the filling so the berries are coated and evenly distributed.

Bake for 50 to 60 minutes, until the crust is browned and the custard has set. Chill well.

# Dried Fruit Pudding

·

## Sekahedelmāpuuro

 This is a wholesome, unsweetened pudding enjoyed equally by adults and children. It is a simple and homey dessert, but with the fruit pudding and whipped cream arranged in four or five layers in a pretty glass bowl, it looks quite festive.

### SERVES 6

2 cups mixed dried fruit (apricots, prunes, pears, apples)

3 or more cups fruit juice (juice of any of the above fruits or cranberry juice or a combination)

½ teaspoon nutmeg

1 teaspoon cinnamon

pinch of ground cloves

3 tablespoons quick-cooking tapioca

_____

1 cup heavy cream

1 teaspoon pure vanilla extract

1 tablespoon maple syrup, honey, or confectioners' sugar

Core and coarsely chop the pears. Leave the other fruit uncut. Stew the fruit in 3 cups of fruit juice with the nutmeg, cinnamon, and cloves on low heat for ½ hour. Drain, reserving the liquid. Set aside a few fruits of each kind.

Measure the reserved juice and add more if necessary to make 2 cups. In a saucepan, stir the tapioca into the juice and let it stand for 5 minutes. Bring the tapioca to a boil and cook it a few minutes, stirring constantly. Remove the pan from the heat and let it stand for 20 minutes. Combine the tapioca pudding and the cooked fruit. Chill.

Whip the cream with the vanilla and sweetening until stiff. In a large clear glass bowl or in individual dessert glasses, layer the chilled fruit pudding and the whipped cream, ending with whipped cream on top. Decorate with the reserved fruits.

# Apple Cake

•

## Omenakakku

This moist but fluffy almond cake is halfway to being a custard with a tart poached apple half in the center of each piece.

YIELDS 8 SERVINGS

2½ cups cold water
juice of ½ lemon
4 tart, firm, baking apples (such as
    Greening, Granny Smith, or Mutzu)
3 eggs

pinch of salt
½ cup butter, at room temperature
⅔ cup sugar
⅔ cup ground almonds

Put the water and lemon juice into a large, nonreactive saucepan. Halve, core, and peel the apples and drop them into the lemon water to prevent discoloring. Add another ½ cup of water, if necessary, to cover the apples. Cover the pan and bring it to a boil quickly. Reduce the heat and simmer, uncovered, for 3 to 5 minutes, until the apples are just barely tender. Remove the apples from the pan and drain them.

Preheat the oven to 350°. Butter a 10-inch pie plate.

Taking care not to get any yolks into the whites, separate the eggs. Put the egg whites into a mixing bowl with a pinch of salt. Whip them until stiff peaks form.

In another mixing bowl, cream the butter and sugar until smooth. Stir in the egg yolks and almonds. Mix a spoonful of the whipped egg whites into the creamed mixture and then gently fold in the rest of the egg whites, using a rubber spatula.

Place the apple halves, flat side down, in the buttered pie plate. Pour the almond topping mixture over the apples and gently smooth the batter between the apples (the tops of the apple domes will peek through).

Bake for about 35 to 40 minutes, until golden brown. Serve at room temperature.

LINDA DICKINSON

# *India*

# INTRODUCTION

The subcontinent of India is a huge kite-shaped peninsula stretching more than 2,000 miles from west to east and north to south. It embraces many different climatic regions, ranging from the lofty Himalayan and Hindu Kush mountains, through fertile plains and arid deserts, to steamy coastal jungles. The Indus River valley was home to a flourishing civilization as early as 2000 B.C. Since then, wave after wave of different peoples have come to India to conquer or simply make their homes, resulting in an almost incredible diversity of cultures, religions, languages, and food.

The wide range of climatic conditions in India accounts in part for the variety of the cuisine. Rice grows well in the heavier rainfall areas of southern and eastern India where a meal without rice would be almost unthinkable. Bread is a staple in the dry north where wheat and barley are grown. It would not be unusual in many regions, however, for both rice and bread to be served. In coastal areas, fish and seafood are popular, and tropical fruits grow in abundance. In the mountainous regions farther inland, fruits such as apples, apricots, peaches, and strawberries are cultivated; it would be difficult to think of any fruit or vegetable common in the United States that isn't grown in some part of India.

Beyond the wealth of fruits and vegetables, it is the abundance of spices that has so greatly influenced the character of Indian cuisine. Spices have long been valued for their medicinal and preservative properties, as well as for their use as seasonings. India's spice bounty has played a large role in its history. The Malabar Coast was an important trading center in the time of King Solomon. The Phoenicians, the Greeks, the Romans, the Chinese all made their way to ancient India. Later, the tales of riches to be made in the spice trade lured European explorers to risk demons, dragons, and falling off the edge of the world to seek new routes to India's golden shores.

## Vegetarianism in India

In India today the majority of the people are vegetarians. This is due partly to economic constraints, but to a greater degree, it is because of religious beliefs. Vegetarianism is basic to the Hindu concept of ahimsa, nonviolence toward, and reverence for, all life. This concept was strengthened in the sixth century B.C. by the development of Buddhism and Jainism, both of which hold ahimsa as a fundamental principle. Three hundred years later, the reign of the Emperor Ashoka was a landmark in the spread of vegetarianism. After an especially bloody conquest, Ashoka began to feel remorse and started following the tenets of Buddhism. He gave up hunting, a favored royal pastime, forbade the killing of many animals, and reduced the amount of meat used in the royal kitchens to next to nothing. Following his example, many among the upper class became vegetarians.

In view of the long cultural traditions supporting ahimsa, it is not surprising that vegetarianism is so widespread in India today. However, different religious sects restrict different foods and not only meat. Many Indians do not eat eggs, as they might contain embryonic life. Some avoid beets, tomatoes, and other red vegetables and fruits because of their resemblance to flesh, or shun garlic and onions because they "inflame the passions." Many Jains subsist mainly on rice, legumes, and leafy greens, rather than disturb the worms and other soil-dwelling creatures that might be dug up with root crops. In contrast, other Indian vegetarians refer to fish as "fruit of the sea" and find it acceptable fare. The inventiveness and variety of vegetarian cuisine in India today is due largely to this religious diversity.

I was introduced to Indian cooking twenty years ago while I was living in Cambridge, Massachusetts. One evening I came home to find the house filled with a wonderful aroma and one of my housemates, Kathy, busy in the kitchen. She said she was preparing an Indian dinner. But how would she know how to do that? Her simple answer, "I have an Indian cookbook." I was more than a little skeptical about the likely results of her efforts. However, when dinner arrived, it was delicious—spicy and totally exotic to me. I was amazed that such food could be produced by simply following recipes. In fact, I still didn't quite believe it.

It wasn't until I received an Indian cookbook for my birthday that I attempted to prepare an Indian meal on my own. I carefully selected a curry recipe that sounded good but not too difficult, went on a shopping expedition to find all the spices required, and then locked myself in the kitchen to work. Later, as my housemates and I sat around the table with tears streaming down our faces (we were not accustomed to spicy food), the meal was declared a success—they all loved it!

It became a welcome custom in our house that I would prepare an Indian dinner, and we would light incense, dress in our most colorful tie-dyes and batiks, and put Ravi Shankar on the stereo. As I gained confidence, I added more dishes to the menus, such as a special rice dish or a raita. I came to love my Indian cookbook and to understand that I really could follow recipes and produce good food from a totally unfamiliar cuisine.

In 1973, I left Cambridge and moved to Ithaca where I took a job waiting on tables at Moosewood. One day I happened to mention that I had some knowledge of Indian cooking and—presto—I became a professional cook. My cookbook moved into the restaurant and is now tattered and splattered and, frankly, smells bad, but I love it still.

## Assembling an Indian Meal

In a traditional Indian meal, all the courses are served at once on a metal tray called a *thali,* or in southern India on a banana leaf. Each person's *thali* is placed either on a low table or the floor. The center of the tray holds a mound of rice or bread, and around this are small bowls containing the other dishes. The main dishes are on the right, and the supporting dishes—chutneys, raitas, and relishes—on the left. The food is eaten with the fingers of the right hand, and at the end of the meal, bowls of water are brought for washing and a dish of paan (betel nuts, lime paste, and assorted spices, used as digestives and breath fresheners) is passed among the guests.

Since Indians prefer to eat small portions of several dishes, a traditional dinner might include five to ten different foods. In the beginning, however, it is best to concentrate on just one or two main dishes, and set out some simple accompaniments such as plain yogurt, raisins, fresh fruit, and a variety of toasted nuts and coconut. Poppadums, thin lentil-based wafers, are available in Asian groceries and many supermarkets and need only be cooked in an inch of hot oil for a few seconds before being served. Chutneys may be purchased or prepared ahead of time. Once you feel more comfortable with the cuisine, increase the number of dishes at a meal. Try to achieve a harmonious balance of contrasting tastes, colors, and textures. For example, serve a cooling raita with a spicy curry, a sweet and tangy chutney with a savory rice dish, or a vibrant red tomato salad with golden pooris.

## Spices

Spicing lies at the heart of Indian cooking: no other cuisine uses as many spices and seasonings with such sophistication. In addition to flavoring food, spices are used to add color and aroma and to thicken sauces. Some spices act as preservatives, a practical attribute in hot climates where there is little refrigeration.

In Indian cooking, any blend of spices used for seasoning is called a *masala*. The flavor of one spice may predominate, but more often a harmonious blending of tastes is the goal. Used properly, the seasonings will complement, not overwhelm, the taste of the food being prepared. A *masala* may consist entirely of dried spices or may be "wet," combining fresh or dried spices with ingredients such as coconut milk, yogurt, lemon juice, onions, or tamarind.

Proper cooking releases the full flavor and aroma of spices and allows the spice flavors to blend with the other ingredients. Uncooked spices often have a harsh, "raw" taste and can cause digestive discomfort. Generally, spices are added early in the cooking process. When spices are added to uncooked dishes, such as raitas, or are added near the end of cooking, as in dals, they should first be toasted or sautéed in a little oil or ghee.

Since spicing is so essential to Indian cooking you need a variety of spices, and they should be as fresh as possible. If you can't recall how many years ago you bought a particular spice or can't identify one by its aroma, get rid of it. Ideally, to ensure full flavor, it is best to buy small quantities of whole spices and grind them just before they're used, though this may not always be practical. Many spices contain volatile oils that start to dissipate once the spice is ground. All spices, whether whole or ground, stay fresh longer when stored in a tightly sealed container in a cool, dry, dark spot.

Every traditional Indian kitchen is equipped with a grinding stone or mortar and pestle. In my experience, mortars and pestles don't really work, or perhaps I lack patience or skill. Many seem to be sold for decorative purposes only—so decorate and then buy yourself an electric spice grinder or coffee grinder and use it for spices only. They are quite inexpensive and do the job. Sometimes a blender will work, especially if you are making a wet *masala,* but it is difficult to grind a small amount of spice in one.

Following is a list of spices, herbs, and seasonings called for in this chapter. Many will be familiar to you and may already be residing in your house. For those that you don't have, a little shopping may be in order—spices have distinctive flavors and aromas and generally have no substitutes.

# Indian Spices

**Black Mustard (Brassica juncea)** Mustard is an annual herb of the cabbage family native to India and China. The leaves of the plant are eaten as a vegetable, and the seeds are an important spice. The seeds of black mustard are small, round, dark brown to black in color, and are not as pungent as the more familiar yellow mustard seeds. Before black mustard seeds are added to food, they are commonly heated in oil or ghee until they "pop," releasing their nutty flavor. In other regions, the seeds are first roasted and then ground to a powder before being used. The whole seeds are often used in pickling as they have preservative properties.

Mustard seeds are also pressed to produce mustard oil, a golden oil with a heady aroma. Mustard oil is popular for deep-frying and cooking vegetables throughout northern and eastern India. It is also renowned for its medicinal properties and is used as a massage oil to relieve aching muscles and arthritic pain.

Whole black mustard seeds and mustard oil are available in Indian groceries and other specialty shops.

**Cardamom (Elettaria cardamomum)** Cardamom seeds come in small pods that grow on eight-foot bushes of the ginger family, native to southern India and Sri Lanka. There are two types of cardamom; one comes in green pods about the size of a pea, and the other has larger, dark brown pods with a nutty flavor. The green pod variety, which is most commonly used in India, is often bleached white for export. However, in Indian cuisine, the stronger-flavored unbleached green cardamom is preferred. Cardamom seeds, whole pods, and ground cardamom are all available, and both the green and brown pod varieties may be found in Indian grocery stores. Four green pods yield approximately a quarter teaspoon of seeds.

Whole pods are often used to impart a mild flavor to rice dishes and beverages or may be sucked as a breath freshener. The ground seeds have a stronger flavor, and are popular in Indian sweets.

**Chiles (Capsicum)** Chiles are the pungent fruit pods of the annual pepper plant, native to the Americas. Chiles were introduced to India by the Portuguese in the sixteenth century and were an immediate hit—India now produces over a quarter of a million tons annually.

In some Indian dishes, it is important to use fresh chiles for the texture or appearance they give. In other dishes, they are mainly used for their heat value; in these recipes, cayenne, the powder made from dried ripe chiles, may be substituted for fresh chiles. For more information on different chile types and on handling fresh chiles, please see page 452.

**Cilantro (Coriandrum sativum)** Cilantro is the fresh leaf of the coriander plant, a hardy annual of the parsley family. Cilantro, which might be called fresh green coriander in Indian stores, is an herb, while the dried seeds of the plant are a spice. Cilantro is grown extensively in northern India and is popular in fresh (uncooked) chutneys and as a garnish.

**Cinnamon (Cinnamomum zylanicum or Cinnamomum cassia)** Both true cinnamon and cassia, also called Indian cinnamon, are the bark of a tree in the laurel family. True cinnamon, which is native to Sri Lanka, has a somewhat more delicate flavor than cassia, but the two may be used interchangeably in Indian cooking. Cinnamon, in either stick or ground form, is used to add a sweet, aromatic flavor to rice dishes, dals, and vegetables. However, it is not used as commonly in desserts as in the West. In India, it is often used to relieve heartburn and nausea and to freshen the breath.

**Cloves (Szygium aromaticum)** Cloves are the dried flowerbuds of an evergreen tree native to the Molucca Islands of Indonesia. Clove trees have clusters of brilliant red flowers with a penetrating fragrance and thrive only by the sea in tropical climates. Small amounts of clove are used to season many savory dishes, fruit chutneys, and beverages. Clove tea is supposed to relieve stomach disorders, while clove oil is useful in relieving toothaches and headaches.

**Coriander (Coriandrum sativum)** Coriander seeds are technically the fruit of a hardy annual of the parsley family native to southern Europe and the Middle East. Coriander's mild, sweet flavor complements many foods, making it an invaluable ingredient in Indian cooking. Coriander seeds are often lightly roasted before grinding, both to bring out their full flavor and to facilitate the grinding process. Coriander is reputed to stimulate the appetite and to relieve stomachaches. It has been used since ancient times and is mentioned in the Bible and in Sanskrit literature.

**Cumin (Cuminum cyminum)** Cumin seeds come from a tender annual of the parsley family, native to the Middle East and eastern Mediterranean regions. The yellowish-brown, aromatic seeds, known in India as white cumin, are widely used in curries and other savory dishes. Roasted cumin seeds, either crushed or whole, are often used as a garnish on raitas, dals, and steamed vegetables.

A more rare variety, known as black cumin, grows in Iran and Kashmir. Black cumin seeds are smaller, have a more delicate flavor, and are available in Indian groceries. In this book, cumin refers to the more widely available white cumin.

Cumin is thought to be good for the heart and is considered a digestive.

**Fennel (Foeniculum vulgare)** Fennel is a hardy perennial native to the Mediterranean region and cultivated mainly for its seeds. Fennel seeds have a sweet licorice flavor and are used in vegetable dishes, beverages, and some desserts. Anise seeds, which have a very similar flavor, may be substituted for fennel in Indian cooking. Roasted fennel seeds are often eaten after meals in India to aid digestion and to freshen the breath, and tea made with mint and fennel is said to be good for upset stomachs.

**Ginger (Zingiber officinale)** Ginger is the aromatic rhizome of a tropical perennial thought to be native to Southeast Asia. The fresh root is used extensively in Indian vegetarian cooking. It gives heat to and thickens sauces, heightens the flavor of vegetables, and neutralizes fishy odors in seafood. It has also been used for thousands of years as a medicinal—it is said to aid digestion, relieve nausea, help fight colds, and, in general, promote cleansing of the system.

**Saffron (Crocus sativus)** Saffron is the dried flower stigmas of a variety of autumn-blooming crocus thought to be native to Greece and Asia Minor. Saffron has been cultivated for centuries and has long been valued for its culinary uses and for its reputed therapeutic properties. In the past, saffron was commonly used as a dye; because of its expense that is no longer true, but it is still used to color bridal veils in India.

To prepare saffron for use, Indian cooks generally dissolve the threads in a small amount of hot milk, or dry-roast the threads briefly so they will crumble more easily. Saffron is widely used to add color, flavor, and aroma to rice dishes and desserts.

**Tamarind (Tamarindus indica)** Tamarind is the pod of a small tropical tree native to India and east Africa. The pods are three to eight inches long, shaped like pea pods, and contain a dark brown, sticky flesh that is intensely sour. In addition to its use as a souring agent, tamarind is valued for its distinctive flavor and the deep brown color it lends to sauces. It is rich in vitamins and is said to help reduce fevers.

Tamarind is available in Asian markets in pods, compressed blocks of pulp, small jars of concentrate, and sometimes in liquid or powdered forms. Any of the first three forms is suitable for Indian cooking. To use the pods, first peel off the outer shell and then soak the pods in boiling water for about fifteen minutes. Mash the pulp and press it through a fine strainer; discard the fibrous material that remains and use the tamarind liquid. Use the same technique with compressed tamarind, although it may need to soak longer to soften. Tamarind concentrate may either be added directly to the food you are preparing or first dissolved in a little hot water. One teaspoon of tamarind concentrate and one cubic inch of compressed tamarind are roughly equivalent.

*Turmeric (Curcuma longa)* Turmeric is a perennial plant of the ginger family, native to India and Southeast Asia. As with ginger, the underground rhizomes are used; these are boiled, dried, and finally ground to produce a bright yellow powder. Turmeric is an important spice in India, sacred to Hindus and used in various religious ceremonies and rituals. It is a major ingredient in curry powders, is used extensively in vegetable and legume dishes, and adds a warm golden color to soups and sauces. Indians also use turmeric as a cosmetic and dye. It is reputed to be a blood purifier, and because it has antiseptic properties, it is used to treat cuts and bruises and some skin disorders.

In India, recipes might list the spices and seasonings to be used, but give no quantities for them. This is based on the assumption that all cooks prefer to suit their own palates and will know what amount of seasoning is right. The recipes that follow are seasoned to my taste—generally not too spicy—so feel free to make adjustments to please yourself.

# Garam Masala

•

## Spice Mix

Garam (hot) masala is a north Indian specialty that traditionally includes cardamom, cinnamon, cloves, coriander, cumin, and black peppercorns, but in greatly varying proportions depending on the recipe. The most common optional ingredients include nutmeg, mace, fennel seeds, and saffron.

Garam masala is used to enhance the other seasonings of the dish. Because the spices are roasted before they're ground, garam masala is not "harsh" and is usually added near the end of cooking time. Often it is first briefly heated in ghee, then stirred into an uncooked or previously cooked dish, such as raita or dal. Because garam masala doesn't need long cooking, it is very useful for adding pizzazz at the last minute to any dish.

While it is available prepared commercially, garam masala is easily and better prepared at home. By making your own you are assured of freshness, you have control over the hotness of the mix, and your home is filled with the aroma of roasting spices.

This recipe has some "bite"; if you find it too hot, reduce the amount of peppercorns.

*2 3-inch cinnamon sticks*  *2 teaspoons cardamom seeds*
*¼ cup coriander seeds*  *2 teaspoons whole cloves*
*2 tablespoons cumin seeds*  *1 teaspoon fennel seeds*
*2 tablespoons black peppercorns*

Using a rolling pin, crush the cinnamon sticks into small pieces. Place all of the spices on a baking tray and heat in a 200° oven for 30 minutes. Stir the spices once or twice while they are baking.

Remove the spices from the oven, let them cool briefly, then pulverize them in batches in a spice or coffee grinder, or all at once in a blender. This process may take longer in a blender, but it will still work fine. Repeatedly stop the blender and push down the spices with a rubber spatula. Blend until all the spices are well ground.

Store garam masala in a tightly sealed container in a cool, dark place. It is best if used within three months.

# *Ghee*

•

## *Indian-Style Clarified Butter*

Ghee is made by evaporating the moisture in butter and separating the milk solids from the pure butterfat. It differs from French-style clarified butter in that it is cooked longer and the milk solids are browned, which imparts a pleasant, nutty flavor. Ghee has a much higher smoking point than butter and so can even be used for deep-frying.

Ghee has been used in India since ancient times. It was a holy food of the Vedic Aryans and still is widely used in religious rituals and ceremonies. Due to its expense, ghee is not as commonly used in India today as in the past but is still considered essential in certain dishes and is the preferred cooking medium of many vegetarians.

Ghee can be purchased in Indian groceries, but it is expensive and may not be absolutely fresh. If you do choose to buy ghee, make certain you get *usli* (which means "real" or "pure") ghee, not *vanaspati* ghee, which is a form of vegetable shortening.

YIELDS 1 ½ CUPS

*1 pound unsalted butter*

Cut the butter into large cubes and heat it in a heavy 2- to 3-quart saucepan on low heat until completely melted. Increase the heat to medium. As the butter begins to boil, a white frothy foam will cover its surface, and the butter will begin to make sizzling or crackling noises. These sounds are caused by the evaporation of the moisture in the butter. Continue to cook on medium heat, stirring occasionally, for about 10 minutes, or until the crackling sounds have stopped and the foam on top has subsided.

At this point, the butter must be carefully watched and stirred constantly. Foam will again cover its surface and the milk solids on the bottom of the pan will begin to brown. This can happen very quickly, so close attention must be paid at this point. When the solids have turned a medium golden brown, remove the pan from the heat. Allow the ghee to cool slightly, then pour it through a fine sieve or several layers of cheesecloth into a glass jar. Avoid getting any of the brown sediment into the jar, because it can cause the ghee to spoil. You will have a clear, golden liquid which solidifies as it cools. If the milk solids have become overly brown (as happens sometimes), the ghee will still be usable. It will just be a darker color and somewhat stronger in flavor than is ideal.

Ghee will keep for about six weeks at room temperature, for four months refrigerated, or indefinitely in the freezer.

*Variation* For flavored ghee, add 2 teaspoons cumin seeds or peppercorns or 3 slices fresh ginger root to the melted butter at the beginning of the process.

# Indian Cheese

•

## Chenna and Paneer

 Milk was considered by the ancient Indians to be the primary food of man and the Indian reverence for and love of milk and milk products has not diminished since then. Milk, yogurt, usli ghee, and cheese are all important in Indian cooking and, for vegetarians, comprise a major source of dietary protein.

Indians make fresh, unripened cheese by bringing milk to a boil, adding a curdling agent, and draining the resulting curds from the whey. Chenna is the name for the freshly made cheese curds; when these are compressed into a solid block the result is called paneer. Chenna, similar in texture to pot cheese, is most noted for its use in sweets, while paneer is used in savory dishes. Like tofu, these cheeses are not strongly flavored, but absorb the flavors of the foods and sauces with which they are cooked. Both chenna and paneer can be made in advance and stored tightly wrapped in plastic in the refrigerator. Use them within four days for freshest flavor.

# Chenna

YIELDS 1 ½ CUPS

**2 quarts whole milk**                    **3–4 tablespoons strained, fresh lemon juice**

In a large, heavy saucepan, bring the milk to a rolling boil, stirring often to prevent sticking. Remove from the heat and stir in 3 tablespoons of lemon juice. Return the pan to low heat and stir gently until white curds separate from the yellowish whey. If this doesn't happen within 15 or 20 seconds, add an additional tablespoon of lemon juice.

Pour the curds into a strainer or colander lined with a piece of thin, damp cloth or several thicknesses of cheesecloth. Let it drain until cool enough to handle, then gather up the cloth and squeeze out any remaining liquid. Now you have chenna.

# Paneer

To make paneer, the chenna must be compressed to form a firm shallow block. With the cheesecloth still wrapped around the chenna, flatten it with your hands and then push in at the sides to form a 5-inch square or 4- by 6-inch rectangle. Place a heavy weight on top (a large pot filled with water works well) and leave it in place for 30 minutes to one hour. Longer pressing time yields a firmer cheese. Unwrap the paneer and cut it into small cubes, rectangles, or diamonds.

*Variation* For zestier paneer, add a tablespoon or two of chopped cilantro or some chopped chiles to the curds before pressing.

# *Mulligatawny*

This soup was originally developed by Indian cooks to suit British taste. It has since become quite popular with Indians, who have developed hundreds of variations to please themselves. Here is my version, with just the right amount of spice to prepare you for fiery things to come.

### SERVES 4 TO 6

1 1/2 cups chopped onions

1 celery stalk, chopped

2 tablespoons vegetable oil or ghee (see page 294)

1 small chile, seeded and chopped (or a pinch of cayenne to taste)

1 teaspoon turmeric

1 tablespoon ground coriander seeds

4 cups water or vegetable stock (see page 685)

1/2 teaspoon salt

1 medium carrot, chopped

1 large potato, cut into small cubes

_____

1 medium red or green bell pepper, seeded and chopped

1 firm tomato, chopped

1/2 cup unsweetened grated coconut

1 cup coconut milk

_____

2–4 tablespoons fresh lemon or lime juice

2 teaspoons chopped fresh cilantro (optional)

In a medium soup pot, sauté the onions and celery in the oil or ghee. When the onions are becoming translucent, add the chile, turmeric, and ground coriander. Sauté for a minute, stirring to prevent the spices from burning. Add the water or stock, salt, carrot, and potato. Bring to a boil, then reduce the heat, cover the pot, and simmer the vegetables for 10 minutes.

Add the pepper, tomato, grated coconut, and coconut milk. Simmer gently for another 10 minutes or until the vegetables are tender. Then add the lemon or lime juice and cilantro. Adjust the seasonings.

Serve at once or, even better, let it sit for an hour or so to bring out the flavors and then reheat gently and serve.

# *Lightly Spiced Tomato Soup*

This is a very fast and easy recipe. Serve it chilled in hot weather, hot in chilly weather.

### SERVES 4 TO 6

*1 cup finely chopped onions*
*1–2 tablespoons vegetable oil*
*1 small chile, seeded and minced (or a pinch of cayenne)*
*1 teaspoon ground cumin seeds*
*½ teaspoon turmeric*
*¼ teaspoon ground cardamom*

*⅛ teaspoon ground cloves*
*6 cups tomato juice (46-ounce can)*
*1 cup water or vegetable stock (see page 685)*

_____

*plain yogurt*
*poppadums (see page 675)*

In a small soup pot, sauté the onion in oil until translucent. Add the chile and spices and sauté another minute, stirring constantly. Add the tomato juice and water and simmer for about 20 minutes to blend the flavors.

Serve topped with a spoonful of yogurt and with poppadums on the side.

*Variation* For a more hearty cold-weather soup, add one cup of cooked rice while the soup is simmering.

# Savory Stuffed Bread

This is not a typical Indian bread in that it uses a yeasted dough and is baked. It is, however, quite delicious and makes a welcome, if not traditional, addition to any meal. Savory Stuffed Bread is a satisfying snack, or for a light meal, serve it with a soup and A Classic Raita (see page 318) or Tomato Kachumber (see page 315). This bread freezes very well, so make a double batch and keep some on hand.

YIELDS SIX 5-INCH BREADS

**DOUGH**

*1 teaspoon dry yeast (about ¹/₂ package)*
*1 teaspoon honey or brown sugar*
*³/₄ cup warm water*

---

*1 tablespoon melted ghee (see page 294) or oil*
*¹/₂ teaspoon salt*
*1 cup whole wheat flour*
*1–1¹/₂ cups unbleached white flour*

**FILLING**

*1¹/₄ cups diced onions*
*2 tablespoons oil or ghee*
*³/₄ cup diced carrots*
*1¹/₂ cups finely chopped cauliflower*

*1 teaspoon garam masala (see page 293) (or substitute an additional ¹/₂ teaspoon each ground cumin and coriander seeds)*
*1 teaspoon ground coriander seeds*
*¹/₂ teaspoon ground cumin seeds*
*¹/₈ teaspoon cayenne*
*¹/₈ teaspoon ground cardamom*
*pinch of ground cloves*
*salt to taste*
*1 tablespoon chopped fresh cilantro (optional)*

---

*melted ghee or butter*

Dissolve the yeast and honey or sugar in the warm water and set it aside for about 10 minutes or until the mixture starts to foam.

In a medium bowl, combine the yeast mixture, ghee, salt, and whole wheat flour and mix well. Stir in enough white flour to form a workable dough. Turn it out onto a floured surface and knead it for 5 to 10 minutes, adding more flour as necessary. The dough should be smooth and elastic when finished.

Place the dough in an oiled bowl, and then turn it over so that all sides are oiled. Cover it with a cloth and set it aside in a warm place to rise until doubled in bulk, about 40 to 50 minutes.

While the dough is rising, prepare the vegetables for the filling. In a heavy skillet, sauté the onions in the oil or ghee until translucent. Add the carrots and cook for 3 or 4 minutes. Stir in the cauliflower and all the seasonings except the cilantro. Cook on low heat until the vegetables are very tender, covering the pan if necessary to prevent sticking. It is important that the vegetable mixture not be juicy, so if you use a cover, remove it for a few minutes near the end of the cooking time to allow any excess moisture to evaporate. Stir in the cilantro, if desired, and set the vegetables aside to cool.

When the dough has doubled, punch it down, turn it out onto a floured surface, and knead it for one minute. Cut the dough into six equal pieces. Roll each piece into a small ball between your palms.

On a floured working surface with a floured rolling pin, roll each ball of dough into a 5-inch round. Mound ⅙ of the filling in the center of the round. Then, working your way around the circle, stretch the edges of the dough up and over the filling, completely covering it. Pat the dough down gently with your hand and then carefully roll it out again to form a 5-inch circle. It's fine if a few bits of the vegetables peek through the dough, but the filling should still be basically enclosed.

Preheat the oven to 450°.

Place the stuffed breads on an oiled 12x18-inch baking sheet. Cover the tray with the cloth and set it aside for 10 minutes.

Bake the breads for 10 to 15 minutes. They should feel firm to the touch and sound slightly hollow when tapped with the fingertips. Let them cool slightly and then brush the tops with melted butter or ghee before serving.

*Variation* Vegetables other than the ones listed above may be used in the filling. Green or red peppers, potatoes, and green beans work well, but avoid juicy vegetables such as tomatoes.

# Sweet Potato Bread

 This dough can be used to make either golden, deep-fried puffs called pooris or flaky, layered breads called parathas. Why not try them both?

YIELDS 12 POORIS OR 8 PARATHAS

¾ cup cooked and mashed sweet
   potatoes
1 tablespoon oil or melted ghee (see
   page 294)
¼ teaspoon salt
¾ teaspoon cinnamon

½ cup whole wheat flour
1–1½ cups unbleached white flour, as
   needed
oil for deep-frying pooris, or oil or
   melted ghee for cooking parathas

In a medium bowl, combine the sweet potatoes, oil or ghee, salt, and cinnamon and mix well. Stir in all of the whole wheat flour and enough of the white flour to form a workable dough. Turn the dough out onto a floured surface and knead it, adding flour as necessary, until at least one cup of white flour has been incorporated. The dough will be sticky at first, so you may find it helpful to oil your hands before starting to knead. The dough should be kneaded for 5 to 10 minutes and should feel smooth and elastic when you are finished. Cover the dough with plastic wrap and set it aside to rest for at least 30 minutes (at this point, the dough may be tightly wrapped in plastic and refrigerated for up to 3 days. Let the dough return to room temperature before attempting to work with it.)

For pooris, divide the dough into six equal pieces. Cut each of these pieces in half and roll between your palms to form twelve small balls. On a lightly floured surface, roll out each ball into a 5-inch round. Set aside each round as you are finished and cover with plastic wrap. Do not overlap the rounds because they will tend to stick together.

Heat 2 inches of vegetable oil to 375° in a medium pan. Carefully slip a poori into the oil. As the poori rises to the surface, gently push it down with a slotted spoon. Do this several times, gently pushing and then releasing. Turn the poori over and cook the other side until puffed and golden, only 15 or 20 seconds. Remove from the oil and drain on paper towels. Repeat this procedure with the remaining rounds of dough. Serve immediately, while still piping hot.

For parathas, cut the dough into quarters and then cut each quarter in half. Roll in your hands to form eight balls. On a lightly floured surface, roll each ball into a 6-inch circle. Brush the top of each circle with oil or melted ghee and fold in half. Brush the resulting half moon with oil or ghee and again fold it in half. Sprinkle lightly with flour and roll out to form a 6-inch triangle. Repeat this process with the remaining balls of dough.

Heat a heavy frying pan or griddle on medium heat for 2 or 3 minutes. Place a paratha in the pan and cook for about 2 minutes or until brown flecks appear on the bottom of the bread. Brush the top with oil or ghee and turn over. Again cook until brown flecks appear on the bottom of the bread, brush the top with oil or ghee, and turn over. Cook for approximately one minute more and then remove it from the pan. The parathas may be kept warm in the oven until all of them are cooked.

## MAIN DISHES

# *Eggplant, Red Pepper, and Spinach Curry*

Dark green spinach and vivid red peppers make for a bright, attractive dish. Zucchini or winter squash can be substituted for the eggplant.

*1 medium eggplant, cut into 1-inch
   cubes*

*salt*

-----

*1 large Spanish onion, chopped*

*2 tablespoons vegetable oil or ghee (see
   page 294)*

*1 tablespoon grated peeled fresh ginger
   root*

*1 tablespoon ground cumin seeds*

*2 teaspoons ground coriander seeds*

*1 teaspoon cinnamon*

*½ teaspoon turmeric*

*⅛ teaspoon cayenne*

*⅛ teaspoon ground cardamom*

*½ teaspoon salt*

-----

*½ cup coconut milk or apple juice*

*1 cup water*

-----

*10 ounces spinach, washed and
   stemmed*

*2 red bell peppers, cut into 1-inch
   squares*

*1 tablespoon fresh lemon juice*

*salt to taste*

-----

*cooked rice*

*toasted cashews*

Sprinkle the eggplant cubes with salt, place them in a colander, and set aside for 20 to 30 minutes.

In a medium pot, sauté the onion in the oil or ghee until translucent. Add the spices and sauté for another minute or two, stirring constantly to prevent burning.

Rinse the salt off the eggplant cubes and add them to the pot along with the coconut milk or apple juice and the water. Cover and simmer on low heat for 10 to 15 minutes or until the eggplant is almost tender.

Meanwhile, in another pot, cook the spinach in a small amount of water until limp but still bright green. Drain in a colander (save this liquid to add to the curry if it seems too dry). When the spinach is cool enough to handle, chop it.

Add the bell pepper squares to the eggplant mixture, cook for 5 minutes, and then stir in the chopped spinach, lemon juice, and additional salt, if desired. Simmer for another 2 or 3 minutes—the peppers should be tender but not mushy and the spinach still quite green.

Serve on rice and top with toasted cashews. This is good with Spicy Chick Peas (see page 316), Tomato-Apricot Chutney (see page 317), and A Classic Raita (see page 318).

# Baked Stuffed Potatoes

I grew up on a small dairy farm in central New York where we also raised potatoes. We ate potatoes almost every day, and my oldest sister was once our county's Potato Queen, but this is one dish my mother never made. (To the best of my knowledge, no mother in India has ever made it either.)

SERVES 4

4 medium or 2 large baking potatoes

1 cup chopped onions
¾ cup diced carrots
2 tablespoons vegetable oil or ghee (see page 294)
¾ cup chopped red or green bell pepper (1 medium)
1 teaspoon ground coriander seeds

½ teaspoon turmeric
⅛ teaspoon ground cardamom
pinch of ground cloves

4 ounces cream cheese, at room temperature
salt and freshly ground black pepper to taste
Spicy Yogurt Sauce (see page 312)

Scrub the potatoes and bake them in a 400° oven for one hour or until done.

While the potatoes are baking, prepare the filling. Sauté the onions and carrots in the oil or ghee until they are tender, for about 10 minutes. Add the bell pepper and spices and continue to sauté for another minute or two, stirring. Add a little water to the pan to prevent sticking, cover it, and cook for another 5 minutes, or until the bell pepper is just tender. Stir in the cream cheese and add salt and pepper to taste. Set aside.

When the potatoes are baked and cool enough to handle, make a lengthwise cut in the top of each one and scoop out at least half of the contents. If you are using large potatoes, cut them in half lengthwise and scoop them out, leaving about ½ inch of

*Note: Baked Stuffed Potatoes can be prepared ahead. After stuffing the potatoes, wrap them well and refrigerate for up to two days. When ready to serve, bake them in a 350° oven for about 45 minutes.*

potato clinging to the skin. Mash the scooped-out potato and then add it to the vegetable–cream cheese mixture. Lower the oven heat to 350°. Fill the potato shells with this mixture and place them in an oiled baking dish. Cover with foil and bake for 20 minutes.

Serve topped with Spicy Yogurt Sauce. Baked Stuffed Potatoes (see page 305) served with Dal (see page 314) and your favorite chutney make a complete meal.

# Vegetable Biryani

A hearty casserole combining golden saffron rice with savory sautéed vegetables.

### SERVES 6

1 1/2 cups long-grain brown rice or
   brown Basmati rice
1 tablespoon vegetable oil, butter, or
   ghee (see page 294)
generous pinch of saffron
pinch of turmeric
1/2 teaspoon salt
2 1/4 cups hot water

————————————————

1 cup chopped onions
2 tablespoons vegetable oil or ghee
2 teaspoons grated peeled fresh ginger
   root
1 1/2 teaspoons ground cumin seeds
1 1/2 teaspoons ground coriander seeds
1/2 teaspoon cinnamon

pinch of cayenne (or to taste)

————————————————

1/2 cup water
1 small sweet potato (or 1 medium
   carrot, diced)
2 cups small cauliflower florets
1 medium red or green bell pepper,
   diced
1 tomato, diced
1/2 cup green peas (fresh or frozen)
1/3 cup raisins
3/4 cup canned or cooked chick peas (see
   page 653) (optional)
salt to taste

————————————————

toasted cashews or almonds

In a saucepan with a tight-fitting lid, sauté the rice briefly in one tablespoon of oil or ghee, stirring to coat each kernel. Crumble in the saffron. Add the turmeric, salt, and the hot water. Bring the rice to a boil, cover the pan, and reduce the heat. Simmer for 30 minutes.

While the rice is cooking, prepare the vegetables. Sauté the onions in 2 tablespoons of oil or ghee for 5 minutes. Mix in the ginger, cumin, coriander, cinnamon, and cayenne and cook for a minute, stirring constantly.

Add ½ cup water, the sweet potato or carrot, and the cauliflower. Cover the pan and cook on low heat for 3 or 4 minutes. Stir in the bell pepper, tomato, peas, raisins, and chick peas. Continue to simmer until the vegetables are barely tender, adding a little more water if necessary to prevent sticking. Add salt to taste.

Butter a 2½-quart casserole dish and spread half of the rice in the bottom. Top it with the vegetable mixture and then the remaining rice. Cover the dish tightly and bake at 350° for about 30 minutes.

Garnish with toasted cashews or almonds. Vegetable Biryani is also good with plain yogurt, hard-boiled eggs, your favorite chutney, or Fiery Onion Relish (see page 313).

# *Patrani Machi*

In this dish, fish is topped with a coconut-cilantro chutney, wrapped in leaves, and baked. Here lettuce leaves substitute for the traditional banana leaves. This is a popular dish around Bombay where fish and coconuts are fresh and abundant.

### SERVES 6 TO 8

**CHUTNEY**

1 cup unsweetened grated coconut
   (preferably fresh)
1–2 small chiles
3 garlic cloves, coarsely chopped
1 tablespoon chopped fresh ginger root
½ cup chopped fresh cilantro
¼ cup fresh lime juice
1½ teaspoons ground cumin seeds
½ teaspoon salt
1 teaspoon brown sugar (optional)

2 pounds firm, white-fleshed fish fillets
6–8 large lettuce leaves for wrapping
   (leaf lettuce works well)
¼ cup melted butter or ghee (see page 294)
2 tablespoons fresh lime juice

1 lime, sliced

In the bowl of a food processor or in a blender, combine the chutney ingredients and process until quite smooth. If using a blender, it may be necessary to add one or two tablespoons of water and to blend the ingredients in batches.

Rinse the fish and cut it into 6 to 8 serving-sized pieces. Place each piece at the bottom of a lettuce leaf and spread a generous spoonful of the chutney on top. Fold the rest of the leaf down over the fish and tuck in the edges to form a packet.

Place the packets in an oiled baking dish and drizzle the butter or ghee and 2 tablespoons of lime juice over them. Bake, covered, at 350° for 30 to 40 minutes, until the lettuce looks wilted and browned. The lettuce may be eaten or not, as desired.

Serve with rice and Tomato Kachumber (see page 315) and garnish each serving with a slice of lime. Or serve the fish accompanied by a simple side dish of cherry tomatoes stir-fried with some oil and minced garlic.

> *Note: If you are pressed for time or are out of lettuce leaves, you can simply spread the chutney on top of the fish and bake it for approximately 10 minutes less. The chutney can be served by itself to accompany any Indian meal. Parsley can be used in place of the cilantro.*

## ACCOMPANIMENTS

# *Things to Do with Paneer*

*Paneer, a mildly flavored and slightly crumbly homemade cheese, is a versatile source of protein in the Indian diet. The basic recipe for paneer can be found on page 296. In India, paneer is usually cut into cubes or rectangles and sautéed or deep-fried. Sometimes it is simply crumbled into sauces to thicken them. Baked paneer is out of the ordinary since most Indians do not have ovens, but baking has its advantages. It is fast, easy, and requires little oil.*

# Sautéed Paneer

Cut the paneer into small cubes and sauté them in about ½ inch of oil, stirring until golden on all sides and hot and creamy on the inside, for about 5 minutes. Dusting the paneer with flour or using a nonstick pan for sautéing will help prevent it from sticking.

Sautéed paneer can be used in various ways. It can be eaten as a snack dipped in Fiery Onion Relish (see page 313) or Sweet-and-Sour Tamarind Sauce (see page 312). It can be used as a garnish for other dishes, such as Eggplant, Red Pepper, and Spinach Curry (see page 303). Or the sautéed paneer can be added to Spicy Yogurt Sauce (see page 312) and served on rice, topped with steamed green peas to make a delicious and easy entrée.

# Baked Paneer

In this recipe, the usually mild and unassuming paneer takes on a character that is anything but mild. Serve it with crackers or bread as an appetizer or by itself to enliven less flavorful dishes.

SERVES 6 TO 8

paneer made from 8 cups milk (see page 296)

1 tomato, coarsely chopped
3 large garlic cloves, chopped
3 scallions, chopped
2 teaspoons grated peeled fresh ginger root
1½ tablespoons fresh lemon juice

3 tablespoons plain yogurt
½ teaspoon salt
¼ teaspoon cayenne (or 1 stemmed chile)
1 tablespoon chopped fresh cilantro
1 teaspoon garam masala (see page 293) (or substitute ½ teaspoon each ground cumin and ground coriander seeds)

Cut the paneer into small cubes (½ to ¾ inch). Place them on an oiled baking sheet or casserole pan.

Blend all of the remaining ingredients in a blender or food processor until smooth. Pour the sauce over the paneer. Bake at 400° for about 15 to 20 minutes, until the sauce is hot and bubbly.

# Zucchini-Tofu Koftas

These could be served as an appetizer or afternoon snack or as a side dish at dinner. Tofu, while not a traditional food, is gaining acceptance in India as a lowfat, vegetarian source of protein.

YIELDS ABOUT 24 WALNUT-SIZED BALLS

2 cups grated zucchini, packed (about 1 medium zucchini)
6 large garlic cloves, pressed or minced
2 tablespoons vegetable oil

1 teaspoon dried mint (1 tablespoon fresh)
1 teaspoon salt
1/4 teaspoon cayenne (or to taste)

1 tablespoon ground fennel seeds
4 teaspoons ground cumin seeds
1 teaspoon cinnamon
1 teaspoon turmeric

2 blocks tofu, pressed (see page 684)
2 tablespoons unbleached white flour
1/2 cup chopped cashews, walnuts, or pistachios

In a heavy skillet, sauté the zucchini and garlic in the oil, stirring often, until most of the moisture has evaporated, about 5 to 10 minutes. Add the spices and cook for one more minute, stirring constantly. Place in a bowl. Crumble in the tofu, add the flour and nuts, and mix well.

Form the mix into walnut-sized balls. Place on an oiled baking sheet and bake at 350° until firm, about 20 to 30 minutes.

These are especially good with Sweet-and-Sour Tamarind Sauce (see page 312).

# Cauliflower Pakoras

These tasty fritters are made by coating bits of cauliflower with a chick pea batter and deep-frying them. They are always popular at Moosewood and at home.

### SERVES 4 TO 6

**BATTER**

¾ cup chick pea flour (see page 657)

1 tablespoon ground coriander seeds

¾ teaspoon salt

½ teaspoon whole cumin seeds
(optional, but nice)

pinch of cayenne (optional)

⅔ cup warm water

1 teaspoon vegetable oil

_____

1 small head of cauliflower

vegetable oil for deep-frying

In a medium bowl, whisk together the batter ingredients until smooth. Set aside in a warm place for 20 to 30 minutes.

Wash the cauliflower and break it into florets; cut very large ones in half.

Heat oil for deep-frying, 2 inches deep, in a medium saucepan to approximately 375°. If you don't have a thermometer, test the temperature by dropping a small piece of cauliflower into the oil. It should quickly rise to the surface, bubbling vigorously.

Coat each floret with the batter and then lower it carefully into the hot oil. Chopsticks work well for this. Cook several florets at a time but don't overcrowd the pot. After 3 or 4 minutes, the florets should be golden brown and tender but not too soft; I recommend that the cook try one or two to be sure they are cooked to perfection. Don't let the oil get too hot, or the fritters will be too brown and crisp.

Remove the florets with a Chinese strainer or slotted spoon, drain on paper towels, and either serve immediately or keep warm in the oven while subsequent batches are being prepared.

Leftover batter may be refrigerated for one or two days without harm, although you may need to add a little more water before using it.

These are great just as they are, but are also excellent with Sweet-and-Sour Tamarind Sauce (see page 312) or Fiery Onion Relish (see page 313).

*Variation* To make onion pakoras, cut a Spanish onion into ⅓-inch slices. Separate the rings and coat them with the batter. Deep-fry until crisp.

# Spicy Yogurt Sauce

This fast and easy sauce is essential with Baked Stuffed Potatoes (see page 305) and also makes a great topping for plain steamed vegetables. Try it!

(see page 305)

SERVES 4

1 cup chopped onions
1–2 chiles, minced
2 tablespoons vegetable oil
1 teaspoon ground cumin seeds
1 teaspoon ground coriander seeds

1 large tomato, chopped (about 1 cup)
2 teaspoons unbleached white flour
1 cup plain yogurt
salt to taste

Sauté the onions and chiles in the oil until tender, about 10 minutes. Add the cumin and coriander and sauté for a minute, stirring constantly. Stir in the tomato and flour and cook for 2 minutes. Finally, stir in the yogurt. Heat the sauce thoroughly, but do not allow it to boil or the yogurt will curdle. Add salt to taste and serve.

# Sweet-and-Sour Tamarind Sauce

Tamarind is popular with Indian cooks for its fruity, piquant flavor. This versatile sauce is a northern Indian specialty. If you're the adventurous sort, try a little over vanilla ice cream.

YIELDS 1 ¼ CUPS

1 golf ball–sized piece dried tamarind
    pulp (or 4 teaspoons tamarind
    concentrate)

½ cup raisins
1 tablespoon grated peeled fresh ginger
    root

1 tablespoon vegetable oil
½ teaspoon ground cumin seeds
½ teaspoon cinnamon
¼ teaspoon freshly ground black pepper
¼ teaspoon ground fennel seeds

⅛ teaspoon ground cardamom
¼ cup water

_____

pinch of salt

If you're using tamarind pulp, prepare it by soaking it in one cup of boiling water for at least 15 minutes, until softened. Pour it into a fine sieve and mash the tamarind, pushing the pulp and liquid through the sieve into a small bowl and discarding the seeds and skin. If using tamarind concentrate, dissolve in ¾ cup hot water and set aside.

In a small pan, sauté the raisins and ginger in the oil for about 5 minutes or until the raisins puff up. Add the spices and sauté for one minute. Remove from the heat and stir in the water.

Pour the mixture into a blender. Add the tamarind liquid and a pinch of salt and purée until fairly smooth.

This sauce will keep for two to three weeks refrigerated.

## *Fiery Onion Relish*

This popular condiment is often found on the tables in Indian restaurants. It is also very nice at home for adding extra "kick" to any meal.

### YIELDS 1 CUP

1 cup minced onions
4 teaspoons fresh lemon or lime juice
½ teaspoon sweet Hungarian paprika

¼–½ teaspoon cayenne
salt to taste

If you prefer less pungency from the onion, soak it in salted water to cover for about 30 minutes and then drain and rinse it.

Combine all of the ingredients and set them aside for about 30 minutes while the flavors blend.

This relish should be spicy hot, so add as much cayenne as you dare! Refrigerated, this will keep for several days.

# *Dal*

*Dal* is the Indian name for any member of the legume family—lentils, split peas, chick peas, and beans. Dals are an important source of protein in the Indian vegetarian diet. Lentils are the most commonly eaten legume, but unlike the brown lentils sold here, they are available hulled and so cook into a smooth purée. Split, hulled mung beans are also popular and produce a beautiful golden dal. They can be found in Indian grocery stores, or you can substitute yellow split peas. Red lentils also cook into a golden purée, but check them carefully for tiny stones.

I prefer a fairly dry dal, but many Indians make quite saucy ones. Choose the texture you prefer, taking into account the consistency of the other dishes in the meal. Dal could also be served as a soup by adding an additional cup or two of water and adjusting the seasonings as needed.

### SERVES 6

*1½ cups red or brown lentils, yellow or green split peas, or split, hulled mung beans*
*4 cups water*
*2 dried chiles, whole*
*¼ teaspoon turmeric*
*½ teaspoon salt*

_____

*2 tablespoons ghee (see page 294) or vegetable oil*

*½ teaspoon cumin seeds*
*1 cup chopped onions*
*1 teaspoon grated peeled fresh ginger root*
*1 tablespoon fresh lemon juice*
*½–1 teaspoon garam masala (see page 293)*
*salt to taste*

Wash the lentils, peas, or beans in several changes of cold water. In a medium pot, cover them with the water and add the whole dried chiles, turmeric, and salt. Bring to a boil, reduce the heat, and simmer, stirring often, until very tender. This will take about 30 minutes for red lentils, 45 minutes for peas, or an hour or more for mung beans. It may be necessary to add more water to prevent sticking, but only ½ cup at a time, because the final consistency should be fairly thick. Use a heat diffuser if necessary.

When the lentils are almost cooked, heat the ghee or oil in a small pan, add the cumin seeds, and cook for 10 or 15 seconds. Stir in the onions and ginger and cook until the onions begin to brown, about 5 or 10 minutes.

When the lentils are tender, remove and discard the hot peppers. Stir in the onion mixture, lemon juice, garam masala, and salt to taste. Serve, passing additional garam masala to sprinkle on top, if desired.

### Variations

**Spinach Dal:** Add 4 cups of chopped, fresh spinach to the onions after they have sautéed for about 5 minutes and then cook for 5 minutes more.

**Tomato Dal:** Add 1 cup chopped tomatoes to the onions after they have sautéed for about 5 minutes and then cook for 5 minutes more.

**Spinach-Tomato Dal:** Add both spinach and tomatoes.

# *Tomato Kachumber*

This light and refreshing salad makes a good side dish for Patrani Machi (see page 307) or any Indian feast.

SERVES 4 TO 6

*2 large tomatoes, cut into thin wedges*
*2 scallions, chopped*
*2 teaspoons chopped fresh mint leaves*
*½ teaspoon grated peeled fresh ginger root*
*4 teaspoons fresh lime or lemon juice*

*4 teaspoons vegetable oil*
*¼ teaspoon black mustard seeds*
*salt to taste*

Combine the tomatoes, scallions, mint, ginger, and lemon or lime juice in a medium bowl.

Heat the vegetable oil in a small pan or skillet and add the mustard seeds. When the seeds begin to pop (have a lid handy to contain them), remove the pan from the heat. Pour the oil and seeds over the tomato mixture, add salt to taste, and lightly toss. Let the salad marinate for about 30 minutes before serving.

# Spicy Chick Peas

A tangy side dish, good with curries and rice. Tamarind provides this dish with a dark, rich sauce and an exotic flavor.

### SERVES 6 AS A SIDE DISH

*1 cup chopped onions*
*3 garlic cloves, coarsely chopped*
*1–2 small chiles, coarsely chopped*
*1 tablespoon vegetable oil*
*2 teaspoons tamarind concentrate (or 1*
  *walnut-sized piece dried tamarind)*
*½ cup hot water*

*1 cup chopped tomatoes*
*1 tablespoon grated peeled fresh ginger*
  *root*
*½ teaspoon salt*

*2 cups canned or cooked chick peas (see*
  *page 653)*

Sauté the onions, garlic, and chiles in the oil until the onions turn golden, approximately 10 minutes.

If using tamarind concentrate, dissolve it in the hot water. If using tamarind pulp, prepare it by soaking it in the hot water for at least 15 minutes, until softened. Mash it through a fine sieve, reserving the liquid and discarding the seeds and skin. Purée the onion mixture, tamarind liquid, and all the remaining ingredients except the chick peas in a blender or food processor, until quite smooth.

Pour this mixture into a heavy, nonreactive saucepan. Add the chick peas and simmer, uncovered, on low heat for 20 to 30 minutes, until the sauce becomes dark and thick.

Serve hot or at room temperature.

# Tomato-Apricot Chutney

Not much to look at, but delicious tasting. This chutney is perfect for those hard winter tomatoes. Or, try this with green tomatoes for an equally delicious but different chutney.

### YIELDS 2 CUPS

1 tablespoon minced garlic
1 tablespoon grated peeled fresh ginger
   root
¾ teaspoon cinnamon
¼ teaspoon ground cardamom
¼ teaspoon ground cloves
1 tablespoon vegetable oil

———————————————

3 cups chopped firm tomatoes (3–5
   tomatoes)

1 cup chopped dried apricots (preferably
   unsulphured)
2 tablespoons honey
2 tablespoons cider vinegar
¼ teaspoon salt

———————————————

more honey and/or vinegar to taste

In a heavy nonreactive saucepan, sauté the garlic, ginger, and other spices for one minute in the oil, stirring constantly. Add all the remaining ingredients and simmer, uncovered, on low heat until the apricots are soft and the chutney is quite thick, about 30 minutes. Depending on the sweetness of the apricots and the tartness of the tomatoes, another teaspoon or two of either honey or vinegar may be needed. Chill before serving.

This chutney will keep for several weeks if tightly covered and stored in the refrigerator. It can also be frozen.

# A Classic Raita

Raitas combine fruits or vegetables with yogurt to provide cooling accompaniments to spicy dishes.

## SERVES 4 TO 6

1 medium tomato, diced
1 small cucumber, peeled and chopped
1 scallion (white and green), finely
    chopped
1 teaspoon finely chopped fresh mint

¼ teaspoon toasted cumin seeds
1½ cups firm plain yogurt
salt and freshly ground black pepper to
    taste

Combine all the ingredients. Chill for at least 30 minutes before serving.

## *Mango with Yogurt*

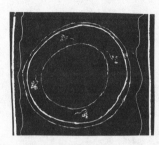

Many tropical fruits grow in India, and fresh fruit is often served

with meals. Mangoes have grown in India for thousands of years

and hundreds of different varieties are available. Mangoes rip-

ened in the Indian sun are reputed to be the sweetest in the world. But you can create a delicious and cooling finish for a spicy meal even with those available in this country.

I have discovered that maple syrup nicely complements the flavor of mangoes, so I recommend it here, although it is not a traditional sweetener in India.

### SERVES 4 TO 5

*1 large, perfectly ripe mango*
*1 cup plain yogurt*
*⅛ teaspoon ground cardamom*
*maple syrup (or other sweetener) to*
*    taste*

*finely chopped walnuts or pistachios*
*fresh mint leaves (optional)*

Peel the mango. This can be a little messy with a really ripe mango, so hold it over the bowl to catch the juices. Cut the flesh into small cubes, avoiding the fibrous area near the pit. Squeeze the juice out from this area and add it to the cubed flesh.

Mix in the yogurt and ground cardamom and then sweeten to taste. Refrigerate for about 30 minutes to allow the flavors to blend.

Serve in attractive little bowls, with a sprinkling of finely chopped nuts on top, and garnish each one with a mint leaf.

*Variation* This could be made into a raita simply by omitting the sweetener and adding a pinch of cayenne or some minced chile.

# Cheese and Nut
# Dessert Balls

 This tasty dessert uses as its base chenna, an Indian cheese easily made at home.

### YIELDS ABOUT A DOZEN WALNUT-SIZED CHEESE BALLS

| | |
|---|---|
| 1½ cups chenna (see page 297) | 2–4 teaspoons orange juice |
| | ⅛ teaspoon cinnamon |
| ⅓ cup confectioners' sugar | ½ cup finely chopped almonds or |
| ¾ teaspoon grated orange rind | pistachios |

Place the chenna in a bowl and add the remaining ingredients, except the nuts. Mash until smooth with a spoon or your fingers. Form the mixture into a dozen or so walnut-sized balls and roll each ball in the chopped nuts to coat. Chill until ready to serve.

If you've used freshly made chenna, these dessert balls will keep for 3 or 4 days if tightly wrapped and refrigerated.

Try these with Spiced Tea (recipe follows).

# Spiced Tea

Spicy, yet soothing, this tea has become a favorite of mine. It is good any time of the day, but you might want to use decaffeinated black tea if you are sensitive to caffeine and plan to serve it late in the evening.

### SERVES 4

*4 cups water*
*1 3-inch cinnamon stick*
*1-inch piece fresh ginger root, cut into*
*4 slices*
*10 cardamom pods (or ½ teaspoon*
*cardamom seeds)*
*½ teaspoon black peppercorns*

*½ teaspoon whole cloves*
*1 teaspoon whole coriander seeds*

———————————

*3 teabags of black tea*
*1 cup milk*
*honey or other sweetener to taste*

Bring the water and spices to a boil in a saucepan. Reduce the heat, cover, and simmer for 20 minutes.

Add the teabags and milk and simmer for an additional 3 or 4 minutes. Remove the teabags, sweeten to taste, and serve, pouring the tea through a strainer to catch any floating spices.

This tea gets stronger the longer it sits, so if you want a stronger spice flavor, let it sit for a while and then reheat. Add more teabags if you desire a stronger black tea taste.

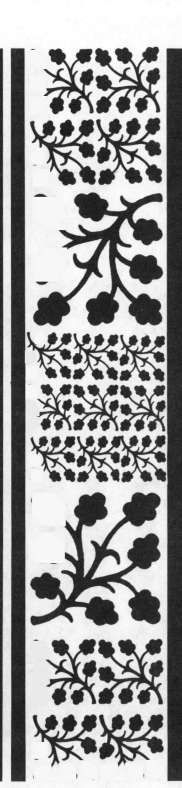

ANTHONY DEL PLATO

# *Italy*

# INTRODUCTION

Italian food is the best food in the world. I was only half conscious of my good fortune while I was growing up; then, Italian food was just food to me. Little did I realize that along with all those inspired dishes proudly presented by my mother, I was also partaking of the habits and lore of Italian culture.

My mother is an Italian immigrant who came to this country as a war bride. As with most immigrants, her experience was in many ways typical and in other ways unique. Grottaglia, Puglia, the small town in southern Italy where my mother was raised, was named for the many grottos lining the narrow canyon that snakes around the edge of town. During bombings in World War II, the people of Grottaglia were safer than those in other areas, because they could hide in the caves.

Through the long war years my mother's family was poor but resourceful. Being the oldest daughter in a family with nine children, it was her task to forage for wild plants, stretching the family's food, and then to help prepare meals. Many of the typical ingredients were scarce and unaffordable, but she nevertheless prepared dishes traditional to the region, just as she'd been taught by her mother and grandmother.

My father is a first generation Italian-American from Brooklyn who was with the U.S. Army Air Corps stationed outside Grottaglia after the liberation of Italy. Many of the GIs courted local girls—my parents were chaperoned at all times by one or more of my mother's seven brothers—but my father is still remembered in my mother's town as the only one who returned to marry his sweetheart.

When my mother immigrated to Brooklyn in 1947, she was away from her family and village for the first time in her life. She maintained her emotional ties to home, her "Italianness," in part through food. Although she enjoyed the abundance she found in America, she missed a few Italian vegetables, and most of the great cheeses of Italy were hard to come by, even in Brooklyn. She still relied on her ability to transform a few simple ingredients into a beautiful meal.

I was born about a year after my parents settled in Brooklyn, and my younger brothers followed in short order. Italian was my language at home as Ma didn't learn to speak English until I was about eight years old. The first English words she learned were the names of foods.

Often, while my mother was cooking traditional foods, she would tell us stories about her town in Italy and our family there. Or she would speak of other meals, remembered foods. Italians constantly talk about food. Even today when my mother telephones to

Italy and talks to her sister (who owns Ristorante delle Ceramiche in Grottaglia), the conversation revolves around the two big topics—family and food.

There is a definite link between food and family in the Italian mind. Marcella Hazan, who certainly knows what's what on this topic, has written, "The Italian comes to his table with the same open heart with which a child falls into his mother's arms, with the same easy feeling of being in the right place." This is true because food is shared as a gift that expresses love. The fact that the family is so strong and important in Italy is, I believe, largely a result of the Italian art of eating.

Every day in most Italian towns there's much commotion on the streets around noon. Everyone is lively and bustling. Traffic zooms by. Schoolchildren run and shriek and doors slam. But by 12:30 the stores, the schools, the churches, and the museums are closed, and there's a hush on the empty streets and sidewalks. Everyone has stopped somewhere to enact the daily ritual celebrating food and family that is the midday meal —*pranzo di mezzogiorno.* This is changing somewhat in big cities and will probably not be so true in the future; yet today, most people throughout Italy go home and spend a leisurely couple of hours with their families.

What the daily repetition of *mezzogiorno* does for family is inestimable, but it also has a lot to do with the Italian outlook on life. A leisurely, exquisite, and nurturing meal at the center of every day restores equanimity and provides serene pleasure. It offers a daily occasion for reflection on the bounty and goodness of life.

The foods served in homes for *mezzogiorno* are likely to be quite traditional and regional. Italy is still a country of fierce attachments to foods of the home region. Comprehensive cookbooks written in Italian are often divided into twenty-one chapters, corresponding to the twenty-one regions of Italy. There is no such thing as Italian food to an Italian—but Tuscan, Ligurian, Campanian, and Lombardian cooking, for example, and to subdivide it even further, Florentine, Genovese, Neapolitan, and Milanese.

I once pointed out to my Aunt Maria, a professional chef in Italy, that a dozen or so of the recipes for tomato sauces in one of her cookbooks looked very similar. Both horrified and amused by my American naivety, she said, "No, no, no. Don't you see? This one is from Puglia and this one is from Calabria—they can't possibly be alike!"

It's difficult for Americans to grasp these differences, but Italy, which is three-quarters the size of the state of California, has more local cuisines than the United States. Some foods may be associated with a single small town. One reason for this regionalism is that until the country was united, a little over one hundred years ago, it consisted of separate, independent, and often warring states, which correspond to Italy's regions today. Each state had its own distinct history, culture, customs, dialect, and classical cuisines.

Many of the regions have been geographically isolated until quite recently. The Apennine Mountains zigzag down the spine of the Italian peninsula, dividing it into isolated valleys, high mountain areas, and coastal strips. The climate varies from temperate to subtropical. Ranging from high Alpine meadows to rocky, arid coastlines, the geographic diversity makes Italy seem a much larger country than it really is.

Some areas have experienced recent and rapid changes in the traditional way of life, while other places remain virtually unchanged. The glittering, hard-edged style of Milan is a long, long way from the ancient, hard life of shepherds on Sardinia. The tradition-bound fishermen of Liguria don't ever pull their boats in on the expensive, hot sands of the nearby jet-set resorts for a light lunch at a trendy restaurant.

A rough division can be made between north and south, using the ancient Via Salaria (Road of Salt), an important ancient trade route that stretches from Rome, near the west coast, straight across the peninsula to the salty Adriatic.

The northern regions, Val d'Aosta, Piedmont, Lombardy, Trentino-Alto Adige, Veneto, Friuli-Venezia Giulia, Liguria, and Emilia-Romagna are largely fertile, industrialized, and populous. The principal cities are sophisticated and stylish Milan, bustling Genoa, serene and exotic Venice, and Bologna, considered the culinary capital of the north. The cuisine is one of abundance—butter, fresh egg pastas, rice, meats, cheeses, and mushrooms. Common flavorings are sage and rosemary. In general, life in the north is more cultured, more cosmopolitan, and a bit more outward-looking than life in the south.

The south, after centuries of foreign occupation, is more sparsely settled and more conservative. The southern regions—Sicily, Calabria, Basilicata, Apulia, Campania, Molise, and southern Abruzzi—historically have suffered poverty and hunger, and yet the people are known for vivacious exuberance. The principal cities are all seaports—Bari, Brindisi, Taranto, Polermo, Salerno, and Naples, considered the culinary capital of the south. The traditional cuisine features olive oil, cheeses made from sheep's milk, fish rather than meat, an inventive use of vegetables, and an incredible variety of dried pastas. Foods are more highly seasoned than in the north, using garlic, fresh herbs, and hot peppers; the influences of Greece, the Middle East, and North Africa are apparent. Southern cuisine has been sadly misrepresented in restaurants in the United States by thick, oregano-infused tomato sauces and heavy, wet, meatball sandwiches. Actually, it is vivid, sunny, and light-handed.

The cooking of the Italian central regions—Tuscany, Umbria, Marches, Latium, and northern Abruzzi—partakes of both north and south. Although olive oil is commonly used, butter is also popular. There are both fresh and dried pastas as well as gnocchi. The characteristic flavoring is a soffrito, a sauce base of sautéed onion, carrot, and celery.

Florence and Sienna are beautiful tourist meccas, with many famous specialties, and Rome, in the center of Italy and still considered by many the central crossroads of the world, has an all-embracing cuisine. Rome is the chief place in Italy where some foreign cuisines and the specialties of other regions are well received.

Unfortunately, many of the regional differences, which make Italy so fascinating, are rapidly disappearing. Where once it was a matter of slowly and cautiously negotiating a winding, narrow road up, down, and around geographical roadblocks, now one can travel at extremely high speeds on straight, uninterrupted *autostradas* carved through mountains and spanning improbable chasms. Not only the time between destinations but the actual distance has been considerably shortened.

Since the 1950s, television has done much to unify Italy linguistically and culturally. On my last trip there, whenever my toddler son, Emilio, was introduced, someone (sometimes even strangers in restaurants or train stations) would spontaneously break into a comic song about a baby Emilio. We eventually discovered that this was the theme song of a popular TV program.

The general prosperity in Italy today acts as a unifier, giving Italians the ability to travel more, eat out more, install modern new kitchens with the latest appliances, and shop at the new supermarkets. Paradoxically, there is less time to devote to the domestic arts. As more and more women work outside the home, fast-food cafeterias and sandwich shops proliferate in the cities, and even the smaller food markets now sell instant risotto and quick-cooking polenta.

Despite the regionalism of cuisine and the encroaching monotony of public fare, the most important characteristics of Italian food are the same everywhere, and they never change. Classic Italian cooking, known as *cucina casalinga* (home-style cooking), is solidly based in the peasant tradition of the agricultural past. It has always remained the informal cooking of hard-working people, rarely a technically difficult or highly refined style. The Italian art of cooking and eating is accessible to all. The identity of each separate ingredient is respected, and its special essence is unmistakably preserved rather than blended, disguised, subverted, or complicated. Each dish is prepared in a direct and simple way. The balancing of different dishes within a meal provides enough complexity to make the cuisine spectacular.

Freshness and quality are important in a cuisine that depends so much on the character of the materials. The meal really begins with the native products in the marketplace ("recipe" is a Latin word meaning "procure"). In Italy so many foods are good in themselves without artifice—honest fruits and vegetables, worthy breads, honored olive oils, cheeses to be grateful for, and the best pastas.

*"Mangia!"* is an Italian word that means "Eat!" It is used constantly all over Italy, and it was certainly one of the first words I ever learned. Mothers say it to their children, cooks make the invitation to everyone gathered at the table, hosts exhort the guests to *"Mangia!"* It refers to more than simply the dish presented at the moment. *"Mangia!"* means "Eat and enjoy this food, relish all food, taste as much as you can, eat up life, eat and be well."

## About Olive Oil

In Italy, olive oil is revered as one of the basic staffs of life. Like fine wines, olive oils differ depending on the variety of olives and the climate, soil, and weather conditions where the olives were grown. Oil made from the same trees differs from year to year. Some of the best olive oils come from Tuscany, Sicily, Puglia, and Liguria. They each have particular flavor characteristics. Other fine olive oils are produced in Greece, Spain, and France. Experiment to see which you prefer.

Carefully read the tempting and beautiful labels on olive oil bottles and cans, with their pictures of castles and orchards, tigers and saints. There are three basic grades that must be designated on the labels on European olive oils. (There are no such regulations in the United States for including those distinguishing grades on the label.)

**Extra-virgin** is the designation for oil made from the highest quality olives that have been hand picked and pressed only once by purely physical or mechanical means. *Spemuto a freddo* (cold pressed) and *prima spremitura* (first pressed) are other terms to look for on a label. Extra-virgin olive oil is often made in small amounts on private country estates. It has a strong, fruity flavor and aroma, is rather viscous and green in color, and sometimes is cloudy. It has the lowest acidity. Extra-virgin oil has a low smoking point, making it unsuitable for most cooking, and it's quite expensive, but used raw a little goes a long way and it's worth the price.

**Virgin olive oil** is made from riper and lower grade olives but produced in the same way. This oil has a blander taste and, generally, a yellower color. It is better for cooking than extra-virgin oil because it stands up well to heat and is much cheaper. It can be as much as four times more acidic than extra-virgin oil.

*Pure olive oil* is the most common designation. It is made from the lower grade olives and from successive, heated pressings of the residual pulp from the other oils. This oil is usually made in large, modern factories using the enormous pressure of a hydraulic press and a high-speed centrifuge. It is further refined and rectified with chemicals to make it deodorized, paler, and blander. Pure olive oil can safely be heated to 400°, making it suitable for all cooking. It is very practical for everyday use.

Refrigeration is not recommended for olive oil. It can be stored for up to a year in a cool, dark place in a sealed glass bottle.

Some of the best news about olive oil is that it's healthful; as a monosaturated fat, it may help lower cholesterol levels in the blood.

## Traditional Italian Courses

The Italian meal often follows a traditional, formal sequence of courses. Diverse and complementary tastes and textures are orchestrated to follow one another to create a harmonious whole. Quality is more important than quantity, and, in fact, moderation is as critical an element as any. The sizes and importance of the courses are likely to be equal, rather than the English-American style of building up to a large principle course. There is no main course in the Italian meal.

*Antipasto* ("before the meal"): It is somewhat like an appetizer, but not exactly. Usually it is just a little something or two, prepared ahead, which will both whet the appetite and dull the sharp edge of hunger. Many dishes served as an antipasto can also be used as a second course or as contorno. Antipasto can be an inventive part of the meal.

*Primo Piatto* (first course) or *Minestra* ("soup," but used to mean any first course): This is almost always a pasta, risotto, or a soup. Italian culinary genius is most evident here.

*Secondo Piatto* (second course): A modest piece of meat or fish, eggs, or a hearty vegetable dish. Italians are not big meat eaters, as a rule, but small amounts of meat are used to flavor many dishes, and moderate-sized portions are typical for *secondi*.

*Contorno* ("outline" or "contour," in the sense that it accompanies or follows the first or second course): Usually a vegetable side dish or a salad.

*Formaggio* (cheese): Cheese is often accompanied by bread or fruit or a special wine.

*Dolce* (dessert): This is usually fresh fruit, but even if dessert is a fancy confection, fruit will also most likely be served.

*Espresso* (coffee): A course in its own right, often served with brandy or grappa.

Not every simple family meal includes the entire course sequence, and some complex, formal meals might be further elaborated by serving multiples of each course. There is great flexibility possible within the form.

In this chapter, I've included a large selection of antipastos and first courses, which I consider the glories of the cuisine, and only one each (although splendid ones) of *secondo* and *contorno*. Baked Eggplant Sandwiches is a fine antipasto but may also serve as a *secondo,* to follow Summer Corkscrew Pasta, for instance. Marinated Tomato Salad or Stuffed Artichokes function equally well as *antipasto* or as *contorno*. Many dishes from other cuisines in this book will also work well in these categories. You might choose a simply prepared fish as *secondo*. Suitable second courses can be chosen from among our stews, stuffed vegetables, egg dishes, and bean dishes, as seen in the following sample menus.

Tomato and Mozzarella Antipasto
Saffron Butterflies
Stuffed Eggplant Provençale
Jewish Fassoulia (Sephardic Green Beans)
Fresh Pears

Marinated Roasted Red Pepper Strips
New England Autumn Gold Squash Soup
Risotto with Dried Porcini
Jewish Fritada de Espinaca
Pecorino
Figs

Mushrooms Roasted with Pine Nuts
Basic Risotto
Bulgarian Red Pepper Stew
Tossed Green Salad
Parmesan Cheese
Grapes

Stuffed Artichokes
Pasta with Sun-Dried Tomato Pesto
Middle Eastern Black Bean Ful
Spinach with Pine Nuts and Raisins
Baked Stuffed Peaches

The easiest and most usual solution for vegetarian menu planning is simply to eliminate the second course and serve a more abundant helping of the first course. Americans think of pasta as a main dish and even Italians are beginning to accept it as such, too. Crespelle would certainly qualify as a special dish central to a meal. A hearty soup like Bean and Kale Minestre can easily anchor a meal preceded by a piquant antipasto such as Caponata with Rosemary Focaccia and followed by a crisp green salad.

The important thing is an imaginative and harmoniously combined sequence of courses to provide continuous variety and interest. Each course is savored. This may make the

Italian meal seem a bit lengthy, but an old proverb teaches that *"A tavola non s'in vecchia"* —At the table one never grows old.

ANTIPASTO

# Sicilian Eggplant Relish

•

## Caponata

In Sicily, caponata is often served with every meal. There are many interpretations of this omnipresent sweet and sour relish.

It is sometimes made with fewer vegetables, sometimes without pine nuts or olives, with sugar and raisins, or with canned or dried tomatoes, but always with eggplant and celery. It is often recommended that each ingredient be sautéed separately in fresh oil in a clean pan. This recipe is our favorite because of its fresh taste and ease of preparation.

Caponata is extremely versatile—it makes a good sandwich filling or pasta topping, an interesting antipasto served with Rosemary Focaccia (recipe follows) or other bread or crackers, and a welcome side dish, especially as a counterpoint to a rich but bland entrée. Use it to stuff tomatoes or artichokes. I can think of no better lunch than some caponata with a piece of sharp cheese, a hunk of crusty bread, and a glass of wine.

With so many uses we recommend making more than you need for immediate use. Caponata can be placed in sterilized jars, refrigerated, and kept for weeks.

### YIELDS 6 TO 8 CUPS

2 small eggplants, unpeeled, chopped into ¹/₂-inch cubes (5—6 cups)

1 large onion, chopped
¹/₂ cup olive oil (more if needed)
4 celery stalks, sliced

2 large red or green bell peppers, chopped
1 heaping tablespoon minced garlic cloves

3 tomatoes, chopped

1 cup sliced, pitted black olives (6-ounce can)
¹/₄ cup pine nuts, toasted
1 tablespoon rinsed and dried capers (optional)
3—4 tablespoons red wine vinegar
¹/₂ teaspoon salt (or to taste)
freshly ground black pepper to taste

Soak the cubed eggplant in salted water to cover for at least 15 minutes and then rinse and dry.

Meanwhile, in a large cast-iron skillet, sauté the onion in 2 or 3 tablespoons of the olive oil. After a couple of minutes, add the celery. Sauté, stirring frequently, until the celery is brightly colored and still somewhat firm; remove the onions and celery to a large mixing bowl.

Add a couple more tablespoons of olive oil to the skillet, and sauté the peppers, stirring frequently. When the peppers are almost done, add the garlic and sauté for 1 minute. Add the tomatoes and sauté for just 1 minute more; add this to the bowl with the onion mixture.

Add the rest of the oil to the skillet, and sauté the eggplant (2 batches may be required) until tender and golden. Add the rest of the ingredients to the mixing bowl while the eggplant cooks. Add the sautéed eggplant. Mix well.

Serve hot, chilled, or at room temperature.

# Rosemary Focaccia

•

## Focaccia al Rosmarino

Focaccia is a rustic flat bread of Etruscan origin that predates the Neopolitan pizza by centuries. It is popular all over Italy. There are many delicious versions—sometimes thick and chewy, sometimes almost cracker-thin and crisp. A very popular version is simply topped with oil and lots of coarse salt. Make a variation with cherry tomatoes, black olives, and onions and shape it into small, individual rounds to take on a picnic. The simpler herbal versions make wonderful breads to dip into Caponata (see page 333) or Tapenade (see page 539) as an antipasto. This is also a fine bread to use for Tomato Crostini (see page 342). All focaccia is best served warm, fresh from the oven.

This assertively flavored and most fragrant version of focaccia is a favorite in the central regions of Italy where wild rosemary grows to waist-high bushes.

### YIELDS 6 TO 8 SERVINGS

*2 tablespoons dried or fresh rosemary leaves*

*1 cup boiling water*

*1 package dry yeast (about 1 tablespoon)*

*1 teaspoon sugar*

_____

*1 teaspoon salt*

*3 tablespoons olive or rosemary oil (recipe follows)*

*1¼ cups whole wheat flour*

*1–1½ cups unbleached white bread flour*

_____

*1 teaspoon coarse or Kosher salt*

*3–4 fresh rosemary sprigs (if available)*

Crush the rosemary leaves with a pestle or chop them finely. Pour the boiling water over the rosemary leaves in a large mixing bowl. Let the water cool to a temperature comfortable on the inside of the wrist. Add the yeast and sugar.

After about 5 minutes, when the yeast is bubbling, add the salt and one tablespoon of the olive oil. Stir in the whole wheat flour. Add only as much white bread flour as you need to make the dough pull away from the sides of the bowl. Knead the dough for 5 to 10 minutes, until it is smooth and springy. As you knead the dough, add just enough flour to prevent sticking. The dough should remain rather soft.

Oil a large bowl. Place the dough in the bowl, turning it once to oil both sides. Cover the bowl with a damp cloth and set it aside in a warm place for about 1½ hours or until doubled in size.

Punch down the dough and knead it for a minute or two. Oil a large baking sheet with olive oil. Stretch and pat the dough on the baking sheet to roughly form a 12x12-inch square. Cover the pan and let the dough rise again for about 45 minutes.

Preheat the oven to 375°. Make indentations with your fingertips about every 2 inches, dimpling the dough all over. Sprinkle coarse salt over the top. Lightly press in fresh rosemary sprigs. Drizzle the dough with the remaining 2 tablespoons olive oil. Bake for about 25 minutes, or until golden. Serve warm, cut or broken into pieces.

## Variations

Top with a small onion, sliced paper thin. Lightly press the onion slivers into the dough before the second rising.

Top with sliced rounds of cherry tomato and black olive and thinly sliced red onion, pressing them into the dough before the second rising.

Use sage instead of rosemary. Use 14 or 15 fresh sage leaves, minced, or 1 tablespoon dried sage leaves, crumbled.

Omit the rosemary. Knead in 2 to 3 tablespoons of minced fresh herbs—basil, oregano, parsley, chives, savory—whatever you have.

Combine any herbs and any toppings.

## ROSEMARY OIL

*HERE'S an easy way to preserve fresh rosemary and to create an aromatic and flavorful oil to use when making Rosemary Focaccia (see page 335) and many other dishes, such as Armenian Oven-Roasted Vegetables (see page 78). Put several small branches of fresh rosemary into an empty olive oil bottle or other glass bottle. Fill the bottle with olive oil. After a couple of days, the resins in the rosemary will seep into the oil to turn it a darker green. Then, each time you use some of the rosemary-flavored oil, simply refill the bottle with more olive oil to keep the rosemary covered.*

# Mushrooms Roasted with Pine Nuts

•

## Funghi Arrosti con Pignoli

 Mushrooms Roasted with Pine Nuts works well as a vegetable side dish, especially in a fall or winter menu such as Polenta Gnocchi with Gorgonzola and Roasted Red Pepper Sauce (see pages 347 and 348). They are also very good served as an antipasto.

SERVES 6 AS A SIDE DISH

18 large mushrooms
1/3 cup olive oil
juice of 1/2 lemon

---

2 large garlic cloves, minced
1/3 cup pine nuts

1/3 cup bread crumbs (whole wheat or Italian bread) (see page 654)
1/2 teaspoon red pepper flakes
freshly ground black pepper to taste
salt to taste

Wipe the mushrooms clean if necessary. Gently pull the stems out of the caps and set them aside. Coat a 10-inch pie plate or some other shallow bake-and-serve dish with some of the olive oil. Dip the mushroom caps into the lemon juice and place them stem side up, snugly fit together in the dish.

Dice the mushroom stems. Sauté them in the rest of the olive oil along with the garlic, until the garlic turns golden. Stir in the pine nuts and the bread crumbs. Add the red pepper flakes, plenty of black pepper and salt to taste. Remove from the heat.

Spoon the sautéed mixture into the mushroom caps, sprinkling any extra on top. Bake uncovered at 400° for 15 to 20 minutes. Serve hot.

> *Note: This dish can be prepared ahead, covered with plastic wrap, and refrigerated until baking time.*

# Stuffed Artichokes

•

## Carciofi Ripiene

Artichokes prepared with a sprinkling of this tasty stuffing on each leaf don't require any rich dipping sauce. They are best served hot, but are fine the next day cold or at room temperature. Serve as an antipasto or as a side dish with something cheesy and rich such as Crespelle (see page 353) or Fettucini with Creamy Gorgonzola Sauce (see page 368).

### SERVES 6

6 artichokes

1 tablespoon vinegar or fresh lemon
  juice

1 cup crisply toasted bread crumbs (see
  page 654)

1 cup freshly grated Parmesan cheese

1 cup chopped fresh parsley

juice of 1 lemon

3–4 tablespoons olive oil

Cut off the stems and thorny top ends of the artichokes. In a large nonreactive pot, bring to a boil enough water to cover the artichokes. Add the vinegar or lemon juice to the boiling water. Add the artichokes and cook (see page 650) until just tender (they will cook further after stuffing and, if overcooked, will fall apart). Drain and rinse with cold water, then drain well again.

Combine the bread crumbs, cheese, and parsley.

With your fingers, carefully and delicately pull the artichoke leaves away from the center, widening the opening in the center enough so that you can pull the tiny center leaves from over the artichoke heart. With a spoon, scrape off the fuzzy choke, taking care not to damage the tender precious heart just beneath it.

Sprinkle the bread crumb mixture into the center cavity and between the leaves of each artichoke. Carefully push the artichoke leaves back into a more closed position.

Place the artichokes in a bake-and-serve dish and sprinkle with the lemon juice and olive oil. Bake, uncovered, at 325° for 20 to 30 minutes until hot. Serve immediately.

*Note: This dish can be prepared ahead, covered, and refrigerated until baking.*

# Baked Eggplant Sandwiches

•

## Tramezzino di Melanzane

Baked Eggplant Sandwiches are an always popular antipasto—the perfect thing to serve while the pasta is cooking. They can be mounded on a big platter and served at the table or cut into halves or quarters and eaten out of hand. They're also satisfying with a glass of wine for a light luncheon or a late night snack.

### SERVES 6 TO 8 AS AN ANTIPASTO

2 small eggplants, sliced into ½-inch
  rounds
salt

_____

1 cup bread crumbs (see page 654)
¼ cup grated Parmesan cheese (or other
  sharp, dry cheese)

2 tablespoons chopped fresh parsley
freshly ground black pepper to taste

_____

½ pound provolone or mozzarella,
  thinly sliced
1 cup unbleached white flour
3 eggs, beaten

Lightly salt the eggplant slices and set them aside for at least 20 minutes.

Mix together the bread crumbs, grated cheese, parsley, and black pepper.

Preheat oven to 350°.

The key to assembling the sandwiches efficiently is organization. Set up your work area in the following order: a plate with the sliced provolone or mozzarella, a plate with the eggplant slices, a bowl of flour, a bowl of beaten eggs, a bowl with the bread-crumb mixture, and an oiled baking sheet.

For each sandwich, place a slice of cheese between 2 slices of eggplant. Hold the sandwich firmly and coat both sides with flour. Dip the sandwich first into the eggs and then into the bread crumbs to coat both sides. You may find it easiest to use one hand for dipping into the eggs and the other hand for dipping into the bread crumbs. Place the finished sandwich on the baking sheet. Continue assembling the sandwiches until you have used all of the eggplant slices. The sandwiches can be prepared for baking several hours ahead and refrigerated.

Bake the sandwiches for 35 to 40 minutes, until easily pierced with a fork.

Baked Eggplant Sandwiches are at their best while still bubbly hot but can be eaten at room temperature also. They reheat nicely wrapped in aluminum foil.

# TOMATOES, TOMATOES

•

## POMODORI, POMODORI

*THESE four tomato dishes exemplify what is best about Italian cuisine: they are simple and good. In an uncomplicated dish the flavor depends on the quality of the raw materials. The cook must show as much skill at the market as in the kitchen. Only the best oil or cheese will do, and only fresh summer tomatoes. Any of these dishes is excellent as an antipasto or for a light luncheon. They are rustic and casual and yet could have a place in a sophisticated, orchestrated meal. These combinations of ingredients have been popular in Italy for hundreds of years, but the recipes should be read as broad outlines, not as if they were written in stone.*

# Marinated Tomato Salad

This is a refreshing salad to serve after a cheesy pasta, or for lunch with a piece of cheese and some bread to sop up the juices.

### SERVES 4 TO 6

*3 tomatoes, cut into wedges*
*1 tablespoon extra-virgin olive oil*
*1 garlic clove, minced*
*2–3 leaves fresh basil, minced*

*2 teaspoons balsamic vinegar*
*salt*
*plenty of freshly ground black pepper*

Combine everything and serve at room temperature.

# Tomato and Mozzarella Antipasto

### SERVES 6

*1–2 balls fresh mozzarella (about 12*
*ounces), sliced*
*1–2 tomatoes, about the same size as*
*mozzarella balls, sliced*
*shredded lettuce (optional)*

*1 tablespoon chopped fresh basil*
*salt*
*freshly ground black pepper*
*extra-virgin olive oil*

Arrange mozzarella and tomato slices alternately in overlapping rows or rings on a large serving platter on top of shredded lettuce, if you wish. Top with basil, salt, and pepper. Drizzle on oil to taste.

*Winter Variation* Use ordinary mozzarella rather than fresh. Use 1 to 2 tablespoons chopped fresh parsley instead of basil. Sprinkle on a little red wine vinegar in addition to the oil. Use the best fresh tomatoes you can find and sprinkle minced sundried tomatoes and a few capers over everything.

# Bread and Tomato Salad

A coarse, whole wheat peasant bread from an Italian bakery would be a good choice for this salad, but garden variety "Italian bread" is also fine, better if stale.

### SERVES 2 TO 4

2 cups dry bread cubes (about ½-inch cubes)

2 garlic cloves, minced

3 tablespoons olive oil

2 heaping cups chopped tomatoes

1 tablespoon chopped fresh basil or parsley

1 tablespoon fresh lemon juice or vinegar

salt and freshly ground black pepper to taste

In a large cast-iron skillet, sauté the bread cubes and garlic in olive oil until the garlic is beginning to color and most of the oil has been absorbed by the bread. Put the bread in a serving dish and add the tomatoes. Press down with the back of a wooden spoon to release some tomato juices into the bread. Add the remaining ingredients and mix.

# Tomato Crostini

I've eaten these open-faced sandwiches standing at the sink in the kitchen at home in Brooklyn and as an elegant antipasto in trattorias in Italy. I give you general directions here for putting the crostini together, because whatever amounts you choose will be just right.

Put thick slices of bread on a baking sheet in a 350° oven for about 20 minutes or so until the bread is crisp and dry, but not browned. Cut a garlic clove in half and rub its cut side on the bread (about ½ clove per slice). Roughly chop fresh tomatoes and lightly squeeze them over the bread to release their juices. Closely pack the tomatoes on top of the bread. Sprinkle the crostini very lightly with oregano and drizzle with some extra-virgin olive oil. Serve whole or cut into pieces.

## Rice and Endive Soup

·

## Riso e Indivia

This chunky soup has a lot of body and texture but a very light, fresh, almost lemony flavor.

SERVES 8

1 cup uncooked rice (about 2 cups cooked)

---

1 ½ cups chopped onions
2 celery stalks, sliced
2 small carrots, peeled and cut into half moons
3–4 tablespoons olive oil
3–4 cups vegetable stock (see page 685) or water
10–12 fresh, ripe plum tomatoes, chopped (or 28-ounce can whole plum tomatoes, crushed, with the juice)
1 head curly endive, chopped

---

½ cup chopped fresh parsley
1 ½ tablespoons chopped fresh basil (optional but recommended)
salt and freshly ground black pepper to taste
fresh grated Parmesan (optional)

Cook the rice (see page 676).

Meanwhile, sauté the onions, celery, and carrots in the olive oil until tender.

Add the stock, tomatoes, and endive. Simmer for about 15 minutes. Stir in the cooked rice. Stir in the parsley and basil, if using. Add salt and pepper to taste.

Top the soup with the Parmesan cheese if you like.

# Bean and Kale Minestra

•

# Incavolata

Incavolata is a rustic, hearty, coarse-textured soup of beans and kale, flavored with sage and garlic, and thickened with corn-meal. It's a meal in itself served with fresh tomatoes and olives and a glass of red wine.

### SERVES 6 TO 8

*½ pound kale (about 4 cups chopped)*

---

*4 large garlic cloves, minced or pressed*
*1 tablespoon olive oil*
*6 cups cooked cannellini (white kidney beans) or cranberry beans (2 cups dried beans, cooked, see page 652)*
*4–5 cups bean water, vegetable stock (see page 685), or water*
*2 heaping tablespoons tomato paste*

*6 fresh sage leaves (½ teaspoon dried)*
*1 teaspoon salt (or to taste)*
*freshly ground black pepper*

---

*½ cup finely ground cornmeal (optional)*
*2 tablespoons fresh lemon juice (or to taste)*

---

*freshly grated Parmesan cheese*

Remove the stems from the kale and coarsely chop the leaves. Soak the leaves in a bowl of cold water while you prepare the soup.

In a soup pot, sauté the garlic in the olive oil for just half a minute. Add about half of the cooked beans and part of the water or stock to the pot. Purée the rest of the beans and stock in a blender or food processor along with the tomato paste and sage. Stir the puréed beans into the soup. Add salt and pepper to taste.

Drain the kale. Mix it into the soup and simmer for at least half an hour, until tender.

Mix the cornmeal with the lemon juice and enough water to make one cup. Pour this paste slowly into the simmering soup while stirring constantly to prevent lumps from forming. Simmer the soup for another 10 to 15 minutes, stirring occasionally. Use a heat diffuser, if necessary, to prevent scorching. Taste for salt and pepper and adjust the seasonings. Serve the soup immediately, topped with freshly grated Parmesan.

# *Pasta e Fagioli*

There is such a variety of bean dishes in Tuscany that Tuscans have been called "bean eaters." To be a bean-eater in Tuscany seemed a fine thing to us when we visited our friend Luna at her fifteenth-century stone farmhouse in the Chianti region. The house is perched atop a cypress-lined ridge, surrounded by silvery olive trees, fields of red poppies in spring, and graceful, curved rows of grapevines.

From the walled and terraced hillside garden we enjoyed breathtaking views of the classically beautiful landscape, little changed since it had served as the harmonious background in Renaissance painting. We picked tiny zucchini and tender new chard and pulled up slender young carrots that had been planted in a huge, old pottery urn. Best of all, we showed our two-year-old son, Emilio, how to pick (and pluck from their pods to consume on the spot) fat, ripe fava beans.

We snipped fistfuls of fresh herbs and hurried, hungry, back to the kitchen anticipating our meal. The setting was incomparable, the Chianti Classico was rare and perfect, and the pasta e fagiole, so quickly prepared, was the best we'd ever tasted. It was devoured in minutes.

Most of the time, pasta e fagioli is not quite this romantic a dish for us. More often it is a hearty, unpretentious, family-style meal for a wintery Ithaca day. Fresh fava beans are rarely available here and the vegetables are not always this freshly picked. But pasta e fagiole is exactly the kind of dish that can be improvised and changed according to inspiration and what's available. The way we make it, thick and hearty, it should probably be listed with pasta sauces rather than soups. We combine the pasta and bean soup at the last minute in individual bowls. We would serve this soup as a first course only with a very light second course. We usually eat it as a meal in itself with salad. We like to make a big batch of the fagioli part and keep it in the refrigerator to heat up when we cook pasta for several quick meals. Pasta e fagioli is Emilio's favorite dish.

### SERVES 6

3 tablespoons olive oil

1 large onion, chopped

2 carrots, sliced into half moons

2 celery stalks, sliced

2 garlic cloves, minced

2 small zucchini, sliced into half moons

½ pound spinach (or 5 leaves of chard, tough stems removed, and coarsely chopped)

3 cups chopped plum tomatoes with liquid (28-ounce can)

15-ounce can canellini (white kidney beans) with liquid (or 1 cup cooked dried beans, see page 652)

¼ cup chopped fresh parsley

2 tablespoons chopped fresh basil leaves (1 teaspoon dried)

oregano (optional)

freshly ground black pepper to taste

___

1 pound short, chunky pasta (ziti, spirals, or shells)

___

grated Parmesan (optional)

olive oil (optional)

Heat the olive oil in a large pot. Sauté the onion, carrots, and celery for a few minutes. Add the garlic, zucchini, and any dried herbs you're using. Sauté, stirring occasionally. A few minutes later add the spinach or chard and cook until just wilted. Mix in the tomatoes and white beans. Add water to make it the consistency you like. Flavor with parsley, fresh herbs, and black pepper. Simmer gently for 15 to 20 minutes while you cook the pasta.

Cook the pasta al dente in a large pot of boiling water. Drain.

In individual pasta bowls, serve pasta topped with the "bean soup." If desired, top with grated Parmesan and drizzle on a little olive oil.

---

*Note: Substitute or add any fresh vegetables you like: green or red bell peppers, summer squash, green beans, etc. Also, the addition of a chopped fresh tomato at the end is nice. Use fresh, rather than dried, herbs when you can.*

---

# *Polenta Gnocchi with Gorgonzola*

Versatile polenta makes an attractive presentation here in little bite-sized gnocchi arranged in an overlapping pattern. Quick baking at a high temperature gives it a toothsome crust and the buttery blue-veined Gorgonzola melted over the top adds its unique flavor.

This dish can be enjoyed plain, served as a hot antipasto, or with sauce as an entrée. Mushroom sauce is often paired with polenta. Polenta Gnocchi with Gorgonzola has a special affinity for Roasted Red Pepper Sauce we think. Here's a wonderful winter menu:

Mushrooms Roasted with Pine Nuts (see page 337)

Polenta Gnocchi with Gorgonzola (see page 347) and Roasted Red Pepper Sauce (see page 348)

Simple spinach salad

Red wine

Pears

Roasted chestnuts

The thirty minutes needed to stand at the stove and cook (and frequently stir) the polenta could seem long and maybe boring, so we recommend that you bring a book or plan to do another kitchen chore at the same time (such as preparing roasted red peppers for Salsa di Peperoni Arrosti).

### SERVES 6

*6 cups water*
*2 cups cornmeal (1 cup each of finely*
*and coarsely ground cornmeal is*
*ideal)*

*2 teaspoons salt*

*2 tablespoons melted butter*
*½ pound Gorgonzola cheese*

In a large saucepan or heavy soup pot, slowly pour water into the cornmeal, stirring constantly, until you have a lump-free paste. Stir in the rest of the water and the salt. Cook on medium-low heat for 20 to 30 minutes, stirring very frequently, until thick and smooth. Be especially vigilant during the last 10 minutes to prevent scorching. When the polenta is done, a spoon will stand up in the middle and the whole mass will cling together and pull away from the sides of the pan.

Remove the polenta from the heat and slop it out onto a countertop (or large baking sheet or cutting board) that has been wet down with cold water to prevent sticking. Smooth out the polenta with a large spoon or spatula or your hands (wet and cooled with cold water) to about ½-inch thickness. Let it cool for at least ½ hour. It can be left half a day, covered with a cloth.

Brush the bottom and sides of a baking dish with some of the melted butter. Brush the rest of the butter on the top of the polenta. Cut the polenta into small rounds (1½–2 inches). We use a sherry glass; a biscuit cutter would work well also.

Remove all the little four-sided pieces of polenta from between the cut rounds and place them in the baking dish. Then, on top of these, make an overlapping row of rounds leaning up against the side of the dish. Lean the next overlapping row of rounds on the first row (like roof tiles at a 45° angle) and so on until the dish is filled. Crumble the Gorgonzola over the top. Bake right away, or cover and refrigerate until baking time.

Bake at 450° for about 20 minutes or until the cheese melts and the gnocchi are crusty. Serve at once.

# *Roasted Red Pepper Sauce*

•

# *Salsa di Peperoni Arrosti*

During fall and winter months, when tomatoes are not at their best, ripe red peppers are usually available, and here they are used in a light but surprisingly full and rich-tasting sauce. A combination of red, yellow, and green peppers is festive, but the red peppers should predominate.

We like Roasted Red Pepper Sauce with Polenta Gnocchi with Gorgonzola (see page 347). It is also very nice over pasta. We recommend a short and thick pasta such as penne, ziti, spirals, or rigatoni. Undercook the pasta, drain it, and put it into the pot of hot sauce to finish cooking with the sauce for 2 to 3 minutes. Pass grated pecorino or Parmesan at the table.

Roasted Red Pepper Sauce will keep nicely in the refrigerator in a covered sterilized jar for a couple of weeks.

SERVES 6

*6 huge or 9 medium red bell peppers*
*1 onion, chopped*
*3 tablespoons olive oil*
*3 garlic cloves, finely diced or pressed*
*3 fresh tomatoes, finely chopped (or 6*
  *canned whole Italian plum tomatoes*
  *with enough juice to make 1 1/2 cups)*

*2 tablespoons chopped fresh basil (1*
  *teaspoon dried)*
*freshly ground black pepper to taste*

_____

*1/4 cup chopped fresh parsley*

Place the peppers directly on the racks in a preheated 500° oven for about 20 minutes, turning two or three times to get all sides evenly charred. Cover the bottom of the oven with aluminum foil to catch any drips in case a pepper splits open. Peppers should be roasted until their skins are charred (black and blistered). When the peppers are all charred, put them immediately into a covered bowl. Allowing the peppers to cool down in their own steam makes them easy to peel.

When the peppers are cool enough to handle comfortably, peel off the skins. They should flake off in large pieces. Don't worry about removing every little fleck of blackened skin though, and do not wash the peppers or you will lose much of the special roasted flavor. Remove the stems, thick inner membranes, and seeds. Slice into thin strips. Cut the long strips in half lengthwise. You should have at least 2 cups. Set aside.

In a large skillet, sauté the onions in the olive oil for a few minutes. Add the garlic and sauté a few minutes more. When the onions are translucent, add the tomatoes, basil, and black pepper. Stir in the red pepper strips and cook for a few minutes. Purée about 1/3 of the sauce in a blender or food processor and then return it to the pan. Add the parsley.

Serve hot.

*Note: Roast more peppers than you need for this recipe to have a few to slice into olive oil and keep in the refrigerator to keep on hand for an antipasto, salad garnish, sandwich filling, or midnight snack.*

# *Risotto*

Rice holds a very important place in the cuisine of northern Italy, even edging out pasta in some regions. The classic and ubiquitous rice dish is risotto.

Risotto can range from a simple *primo piatto,* as it is most often used in Italy, to an elaborate main course containing several ingredients. It is uniquely and seductively delicious. The characteristically firm and flavorful rice is suspended in a creamy smooth base.

Risotto is made with an extremely glutinous short-grained rice grown in the Po River valley and is known for its ability to absorb a lot of liquid quickly and still remain firm. The most common variety is Arborio rice, which is now widely available in this country.

Risotto is nutritious, economical, and quite versatile, and it can be prepared in under 30 minutes. Following is my version of the basic risotto and a number of variations.

### SERVES 4 AS PRIMO PIATTO, 2 AS A MAIN DISH

### BASIC RISOTTO

*5 cups vegetable stock (see page 685)*
*2 tablespoons vegetable oil or butter or*
   *a combination of both*
*1 small yellow onion, finely minced*

*1 ½ cups Arborio rice*
*½ cup dry white wine*
*⅓ cup freshly grated Parmesan cheese*

Bring the stock to a boil in a small saucepan. Lower the heat and maintain a simmer.

Meanwhile, heat the oil or butter in a large, heavy saucepan on medium heat. Sauté the onion, stirring occasionally, for 2 or 3 minutes, until translucent but not browned. Add the rice and stir for one minute to thoroughly coat the rice with oil. Use a wooden spoon for stirring so as not to break the rice kernels.

Add the wine and stir constantly until it is absorbed. Pour in the simmering stock, ½ cup at a time, stirring after each addition. Continue adding liquid as the rice dries out, about every 2 minutes. It should take about 18 to 20 minutes to cook the rice. Reduce the amount of stock added toward the end and increase the frequency, tasting every couple of minutes until the rice is tender but al dente.

Remove the risotto from the heat and quickly stir in the last ¼ cup of stock and the grated cheese. Serve immediately.

*Variations*

**RISOTTO WITH PEAS:** Follow Basic Risotto recipe, adding one minced celery stalk with the onion. Add one cup of briefly blanched fresh or frozen peas with the last ¼ cup of stock.

**RISOTTO WITH ASPARAGUS:** Cut ½ pound of asparagus spears into ½-inch pieces, discarding the tough bottom parts. Reserve the tips separately. Follow the Basic Risotto recipe, but add the asparagus pieces after the first addition of stock. Add the tips 5 minutes later. You could replace half of the Parmesan cheese with a milder, softer cheese such as mascarpone or mozzarella.

**RISOTTO WITH DRIED PORCINI:** Begin by soaking ¾ ounce of dried porcini mushrooms in one cup of boiling water for ½ hour. Strain the cup of liquid through a coffee filter or several thicknesses of paper towel and add it to 4 cups of vegetable stock. Chop the mushrooms. Follow the Basic Risotto recipe, but add a pinch of rosemary with the onion. Marsala is strongly recommended for the ½ cup of wine. Add the mushrooms after the first addition of stock.

**RISOTTOS WITH VEGETABLE PURÉES:** Follow the Basic Risotto recipe, adding about a cup of any puréed vegetable with the last ¼ cup of stock. Broccoli, green beans, winter squash, and carrots are all good. (I find that jars of commercially prepared puréed baby food are very convenient and just the right size.)

You might want to further jazz up the broccoli version by adding ¼ cup of thinly sliced fresh fennel bulb with the first addition of stock. To the green bean version you could add ¼ cup of chopped, oil-packed, sun-dried tomatoes with the first addition of stock. Minced red sweet pepper could be sautéed with the onion in the winter squash risotto. Add one cup of finely shredded radiccio after the first addition of stock in a carrot risotto.

*Other Variations*

Add any vegetable that suits your fancy (spinach or chopped artichokes are classics).

Add both peas and asparagus to Basic Risotto.

Replace part or all of the Parmesan with a different cheese such as Fontina, Gorgonzola, or Asiago.

Add puréed winter squash and sautéed minced red sweet peppers to Risotto with Dried Porcini.

Add a pinch of saffron or 3 chopped plum tomatoes, or both, to Risotto with Peas.

Add 3 to 4 tablespoons of pesto to Basic Risotto.

Add chopped fresh parsley to any risotto.

Add ½ cup halved seedless red grapes to Basic Risotto.

# *Brown Rice Mock Risotto*

Brown rice cannot be substituted in place of Arborio rice to make an authentic risotto because it does not release the starch necessary to create the creamy coating so characteristic of risotto, nor do the rice kernels remain as firm as Arborio. And, even using a risotto technique, brown rice still requires 35 to 45 minutes to fully cook. Brown rice is suited to slow boiling in a lidded pot.

However, if you prefer brown rice, try this simulated risotto: sauté minced onion in oil or butter as in Basic Risotto. Add 2 cups of brown rice and sauté for one minute. Add 5 cups of vegetable stock (or ½ cup wine and 4½ cups stock). Tightly cover the pot and bring the liquid to a boil. Then reduce the heat and simmer gently for about 35 to 45 minutes, until the liquid is absorbed and the rice is tender. Add grated Parmesan cheese plus either about 2 tablespoons of sweet butter, ¼ cup of heavy cream, or about 2 ounces of a creamy cheese such as mascarpone to simulate the velvety texture of risotto. It won't really be risotto, but it's a very nice rice dish.

# Crespelle

Crespelle, sometimes called crespoline or manicotti, are thin but fluffy crêpes. Here they are wrapped around a cheese and spinach filling and topped with a light, quickly cooked tomato sauce. These take a bit of effort but are easier than you might expect. In Brooklyn, as in Italy, this is a dish to please a special guest or for Sunday dinner with the whole family.

The sauce and the filling are both easy and foolproof. The crêpes are not at all difficult to make with a well-seasoned crêpe pan, but a bit trickier with an ordinary skillet.

The crêpes can be made in advance and refrigerated for several days or they can be frozen. You might want to double the recipe and freeze half so that next time you'll be way ahead. If using frozen crêpes, defrost them, wrapped, in the refrigerator.

SERVES 6 TO 9
YIELDS 18 TO 20 FILLED CRÊPES

CRESPELLE

4 eggs

2 tablespoons vegetable oil

pinch of salt

1 ½ cups unbleached white flour

2⅔ cups milk and water in any proportion (half of each is usual)

1–2 tablespoons vegetable oil or melted butter for cooking the crêpes

SAUCE

¼ cup olive oil

3 cups chopped onions

3 celery stalks, thinly sliced

4 large garlic cloves, minced

8 fresh basil leaves, chopped (½ teaspoon dried)

1 teaspoon chopped fresh oregano (1 teaspoon dried)

2 28-ounce cans Italian plum tomatoes

salt and freshly ground black pepper to taste

FILLING

3 tablespoons olive oil

2 cups chopped onions

3 large garlic cloves, minced

10 ounces fresh spinach (about 4 cups), stemmed and chopped (or 10-ounce package frozen spinach defrosted, drained, and chopped)

2 cups coarsely grated mozzarella cheese (½ pound)

½ cup grated sharp Parmesan or Pecorino cheese

3 pounds ricotta cheese

¼ teaspoon nutmeg (freshly grated preferred)

salt and freshly ground black pepper to taste

To make the crespelle, beat the eggs, gradually adding the oil, salt, and flour, until smooth. Add the milk and water and blend. This can be done by hand or in a blender or food processor. Set the batter aside to rest for at least ½ hour. (This should be enough time to prepare the sauce and filling, if you wish.)

Heat a small skillet or crêpe pan and brush with a little oil or butter. Pour in just enough batter to coat the bottom of the pan (a bit less than ¼ cup); swirl the batter around by tilting the pan. Add milk or water if the batter is thicker than heavy cream. Cook one side for a minute, until set and golden. Turn the pancake over and cook the other side just a few seconds until lightly browned. Stack the crêpes on a plate until ready to fill (they won't stick together). Cover with a cloth. Brush the crêpe pan with oil or butter as needed.

For the sauce, heat the olive oil in a large saucepan. Add the onions, celery, and garlic and sauté until the onions are almost translucent. Add the herbs and stir. Drain the juice from the canned tomatoes into the saucepan. Squeeze the whole tomatoes in your hands to crush them and add them to the sauce. Cook about 10 minutes. Add salt and pepper. Do not allow the sauce to cook much longer than 10 minutes; it should have a fairly thin consistency.

For the filling, heat the olive oil in a large skillet or saucepan. Add the onions and garlic and sauté until the onions are translucent. Add the chopped spinach and sauté until the spinach is wilted.

Combine all the cheeses in a large mixing bowl. Stir in the nutmeg, salt, pepper, and the onion-spinach mixture.

Preheat the oven to 375°.

Spread a cup of two of sauce over the bottom of a large shallow baking dish. Place a large spoonful or two of the filling on each crespelle and roll it up. Place the filled pancakes, folded side down, close together in a single layer in the baking pan. Cover the crespelle with another cup of sauce. Bake for about ½ hour or until heated through.

Heat the remaining sauce. Serve the crespelle hot from the oven in the baking dish. Pass the tomato sauce.

*Note: The filling can also be used to stuff large tubular pasta such as manicotti or cannelloni.*

# *About Pasta*

Most Italians eat pasta at least once a day. Pasta is the most usual first course *(primo piatto* or *minestra)*. Ordinarily, pasta is served with sauce *(past'asciutta)* for lunch and in a broth *(pasta in brodo)* for dinner. Despite regional differences, the passionate love of pasta is pan-Italian.

The Italian appetite for pasta has a long history. Pasta may be as old as pre-Roman Etruscan times (there are fourth-century B.C. Etruscan bas-reliefs that may depict pasta-making), and the Romans had a version of gnocchi or dumplings, but pasta isn't securely documented in Italy until 1279, when it was listed as a valuable on an estate inventory. This contradicts the notion that pasta was brought to Italy from China by Marco Polo since the inventory predates his journey by several years. The first published recipes for pasta appear in a thirteenth-century cookbook. By 1400, pasta was produced commercially.

In early times, the drying of pasta was an important means of preserving the wheat crop. The sunniest, windiest coastal areas afford the best conditions for drying pasta, and so it was around Naples that the pasta industry developed in the eighteenth century. English tourists to Naples reported seeing pasta everywhere, hung to dry like laundry. Street vendors set up enormous boiling cauldrons and sold nourishing meals that were enthusiastically consumed on the street by lifting handfuls high and dropping them into the upraised mouth. In the 1930s, drying tunnels replaced sea breezes, enabling factories to make pasta all over Italy and not just where it was climatically suitable.

Pasta can be divided into two categories—fresh and dried. Recently there has been a popular notion, reinforced by many restaurants, that fresh pasta is superior, somehow classier, than dried. This is just silly; fresh and dried pasta are two quite different things —neither is better than the other. I actually prefer the taste and texture of dried; it has more bite.

Fresh pasta, which is usually homemade, is always an egg pasta made from somewhat soft, all-purpose flour. The dough is usually rolled flat and cut into noodles or pinched into flat shapes, like farfalle. Fresh pasta is fun to make, especially for filled pastas, such as ravioli or tortelli, using your own specially invented fillings. Delicate, fresh pastas are usually offset by smooth, mild-flavored sauces.

Dry pasta *(pasta secca)* is made with semolina flour, the grits from hard durum wheat, and water. Most dried, extruded pastas are made in factories and cannot be duplicated at home. The stiff dough is forced at high pressure through holes in dies (this used to be done with a screw mechanism turned by two men or a horse). The shape of the die determines the shape of the pasta—little round holes for spaghetti, larger notched holes with pins suspended in the center for hollow, ridged penne. The extruded ribbons or tubes are cut at desired lengths and dried.

A strong case can be made for the superiority of Italian-made commercial dried pastas over pastas made by U.S. manufacturers. In Italy, the national government imposes rigid standards on the pasta-making companies—standards that are not met by the U.S. industry. Law requires that dried commercial Italian pasta be made with pure durum flour without artificial additives, that colored pastas be made with natural vegetables, and that egg pasta contain at least five whole eggs per two pounds of flour.

In the United States, there are no legal restrictions on the type of flour used. Flour is usually overrefined and then enriched, and ordinary soft flour may be added to the semolina flour to make a dough easier to work. Frozen or powdered eggs in egg pastas are the norm, and pastas are usually colored with vegetable dyes—or at best, powdered, dehydrated vegetables.

Italian companies (many family owned and operated) tend to have a smaller production using slower extrusion machines with bronze dies that create a slightly rough, porous surface on the pasta for better sauce absorption. The kneading time is long, the temperature of the dough is kept low, and the drying is slow. American companies become financially successful by producing a large volume in an extremely efficient way. Their extrusion machines use teflon dies, making a smooth, glossy surface on the pasta. Kneading is fast and the dough is sometimes under enough pressure to create temperatures high enough to denature the proteins in the semolina (making a softer cooked pasta). Then the pasta is dried in high speed, high temperature drying tunnels where, again, there is risk of denaturing the protein. I recommend that you spend a little more and buy Italian pastas.

The health virtues of pasta have recently been reappraised. Pasta is low in sodium and fat, and many pasta dishes can be noncholesterol. Pasta is high in B vitamins, iron, and protein, with half the calories of an equal amount of lean meat (there are certainly fewer obese people in Italy than in the United States). Some recent studies have shown a lower incidence of heart disease and cancer in an Italian-American community with a diet high in pasta and olive oil. Complex carbohydrates, such as pasta, are an important component in healthy nutrition, and they give energy and satisfy appetites better than most other foods. So here's a case where science is just catching up with art.

## PASTA BASICS

In Italy, the pasta itself is so good that it is never subordinate to the sauce, which is just an enhancer. Pasta is sparingly anointed with a sauce or vegetable or cheese and never disguised or overpowered.

There are hundreds of shapes and sizes of pastas, which provide a variety for Italians who eat pasta every day. The choice of which pasta to use with a particular sauce should be neither arbitrary nor interchangeable. There are good reasons why one pairing will work better than another. In general, long strands are preferred in combination with most tomato sauces or pestos. Short, thick, tubular shapes (such as penne) are a good choice for a robust spicy sauce because these pastas are placed neatly in the mouth without too much contact between the hot spices and sensitive skin of the lips. Hollowed-out pastas, such as shells, work well with chunky vegetable sauces because the shape catches and holds the vegetable pieces. Use very short pasta with peas or beans. Fresh pasta and flat dried pastas and the shapes made from them (such as farfalle) are paired with cream and cheese sauces and delicate, smooth vegetable sauces.

## HOW TO COOK PASTA

Because pasta is the dominant attraction, it is important that it be cooked well. This is not hard to do, following basic guidelines:

1) For one pound of pasta, bring 4 or 5 quarts of water to a rapid boil (use a large amount of water so that it will quickly return to a boil once the pasta is added, and so that the pasta will have room to float freely). Add salt if you wish, but there is no reason to add oil.

2) I estimate portions of about ¼ pound of pasta per person. Allow a larger portion of fresh pasta than dried, because it contains more water and so weighs more before cooking. Add the pasta to the boiling water, stir it with a wooden spoon to ensure that it does not stick to itself, and cover the pot so that the water will quickly return to a boil. When water is once again boiling, remove the lid and stir again.

3) Because of all the variables, it is impossible to give an absolute cooking time. Don't count on the time suggested on pasta boxes—it's usually too long. The only way to know when pasta is properly cooked is to taste it. Fresh pasta cooks almost immediately. Start to test dried pasta (by biting) after only a few minutes and then test again every minute or so until pasta is al dente (tender, but with a firm bite). Don't expect fresh pasta to be al dente. If you're not sure, it's better to undercook, as pasta continues to cook as long as it's hot.

4) As soon as it is al dente, drain the pasta in a colander; don't let it drain enough to dry. Never rinse with cold water. Transfer dripping wet, hot pasta to the serving bowl (preferably heated) and toss it with just enough sauce to coat the pasta. Another technique, useful for thin wine- or stock-based sauces (which don't coat pasta readily), is to drain the pasta before it's al dente and add it to the hot sauce to finish cooking for the last minute. The flavor of the sauce will be absorbed by the pasta as it finishes cooking.

5) Not every pasta dish benefits from the addition of cheese—the flavor of some would become unnecessarily confusing. When cheese is served, it should be freshly grated. Use a cheese mill or small Italian cheese grater or the fine side of an all-purpose hand grater.

6) Now, trot to the table. Good pasta is served steaming hot.

# HOW TO EAT PASTA

Finally, to the question of how to eat pasta the proper Italian way. Italians wisely serve pasta in wide, shallow bowls with sloping sides, which helps to keep the pasta warm and also provides a place to twirl pasta onto a fork (twirling pasta onto a fork with the help of a spoon is for children or novices—use just the fork, but only pick up two or three strands at a time). Put the forkful of pasta in your mouth and, with conviction, slurp up the dangling ends. Pasta should be eaten fast so that it stays hot. Posted in Italy's Spaghetti Historical Museum in Pontedassio, near Genoa, is Sophia Loren's advice on pasta etiquette, "Spaghetti can be eaten successfully if you inhale it like a vacuum cleaner."

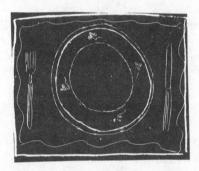

You could eat pasta every day of the year without repeating a dish. The following seven recipes will give a week's worth of easy pastas to get you started. The sauces can all be prepared in the same amount of time or less than it takes to cook the pasta.

# Shells with Broccoli

·

# Maccheroni con Broccoli

This recipe is from Puglia and Calabria (the heel and the toe of the boot) and couldn't be simpler. The broccoli topping sautés while the pasta cooks and all is ready in about 20 minutes. But even if it were more difficult, I would still make this dish frequently; it's that addictive. It's also an easy recipe to cut down and make for just one.

SERVES 4

*1 pound pasta (shells are best, but any short, chunky pasta such as ziti or penne is fine)*
*5–6 broccoli stalks, finely chopped (4 cups chopped)*
*6 garlic cloves, minced*
*½ cup olive oil*

*freshly ground black pepper*

---

*¾ cup freshly grated Pecorino Romano (or to taste)*
*extra-virgin olive oil for drizzling (optional)*

Heat a large covered pot of water. When the water comes to a rapid boil, add the pasta, stir, and cover the pot until the water boils again.

Meanwhile, in a large cast-iron skillet, sauté the broccoli and garlic in olive oil until the garlic is golden, but not brown, and the broccoli is bright green and crisp-tender. Add plenty of freshly ground black pepper. Pour a couple of spoonfuls of pasta water into the skillet to steam the broccoli.

When the pasta is al dente, drain it and put it into warmed serving dishes. Top it with the broccoli mixture and the grated cheese. Drizzle on a little extra-virgin olive oil, if you like. Serve immediately.

# Saffron Butterflies

•

# Farfalle allo Zafferano

This is a subtle-tasting, golden-colored pasta to use as a *primo piatto*. Most of Italy's saffron grows in the harsh and mountainous Abruzzi—a region known for its rugged and wild beauty. It is pleasing to think of these delicate and sophisticated butterflies gracing tables there.

### SERVES 2 TO 4

*½ pound farfalle (butterfly or bow-tie pasta)*

*2 tablespoons butter*

*a few threads of saffron (about ¼ teaspoon, crumpled)*

*½ cup heavy cream*

*3 ounces grated Bel Paese or freshly grated Parmesan (see note)*

Bring a large covered pot of water to a rapid boil, add the pasta, stir, and cover the pot until the water returns to a boil.

Meanwhile, in a saucepan large enough to hold the cooked pasta, melt the butter. Add the threads of saffron and cook them for a minute. Using the back of a spoon, push the saffron threads against the side of the pot to crush them a bit. Add the cream. Heat the sauce on low heat. Do not boil.

When the pasta is al dente, drain it and add it to the saucepan. Add the grated cheese. Toss until the cheese melts and the pasta is thoroughly coated. Serve immediately.

Try Stuffed Eggplant Provençal (see page 551) as a second course to follow Saffron Butterflies.

*Variations*

Top with finely chopped fresh tomato.

Add about ⅔ cup of fresh or frozen peas to the pasta pot a few minutes before you expect the pasta to be done. Drain the peas and pasta and add them as above.

> *Note: With Bel Paese, you get a creamy, mild sauce with the taste of saffron predominating, while Parmesan will produce a drier and sharper sauce.*

# Pasta with Porcini Mushroom Sauce

·

## Maccheroni Integrali al Sugo di Porcini

Dried porcini have a concentrated woodsy taste that can stand up to whole wheat pasta. Use elbow macaroni or ribbed penne if this is to be the main dish and perhaps use fettuccini if this is to be the pasta course in a more elaborate dinner party, in which case serve smaller portions. Misura and DeCecco both make fine whole wheat pastas.

### SERVES 2 AS A MAIN DISH

*1 ounce dried porcini mushrooms (about ⅔ cup)*

---

*2 tablespoons butter*
*1 small onion, diced*
*½ teaspoon chopped dried rosemary*
*¼ cup marsala*

---

*1 tablespoon tomato paste*

*1 cup heavy cream*
*1 tablespoon chopped fresh parsley*
*salt and freshly ground black pepper to taste*

---

*½ pound whole wheat pasta*
*¼–½ cup freshly grated Parmesan cheese*

Break each mushroom into two or three pieces. Soak them in one cup of hot water for at least 20 minutes. Meanwhile, heat a large covered pot of water. Melt the butter in a saucepan large enough to hold the cooked pasta. Sauté the onions and rosemary in the butter for several minutes, until the onion is translucent. Mix in the marsala and cook for 2 minutes more.

Drain the mushrooms through a coffee filter or several paper towels and reserve the liquid. Add ½ cup of the mushroom water, all of the mushrooms, and the tomato paste to the sautéed onions. Simmer. Mix the cream and parsley into the mushroom sauce and lower the heat to a gentle simmer. Don't allow the sauce to boil. Add salt and pepper to taste.

When the water in the large pot comes to a rolling boil, stir in the pasta and cover the pot until the water returns to a boil. When the pasta is al dente, drain and add it to the mushroom sauce in the saucepan. Add the cheese and toss everything to coat the pasta evenly. Serve immediately.

*Variations*
Top with chopped fresh tomato.
Add about ⅔ cup peas. Add the peas to the pasta water a couple of minutes before you
 expect the pasta to be al dente.

# Summer Corkscrew Pasta

·

## Fusilli Estevi

This dish is filled with the tastes of summer: lightly sautéed zucchini; fresh, uncooked tomatoes and herbs; the fruity flavor of extra-virgin olive oil; a hint of lemon; and a mild cheese only beginning to melt.

SERVES 4

*1 pound fusilli (short corkscrew pasta)*

*8–10 tiny finger-sized zucchini (or 2 medium zucchini)*
*3 garlic cloves, minced*
*⅓ cup pine nuts*
*2 tablespoons olive oil*

*3 large tomatoes, cut into ½-inch cubes*

*¼ cup chopped fresh parsley*
*¼ cup chopped fresh basil*
*1½ cups ½-inch cubes Bel Paese or mozzarella cheese (about ¼ pound)*
*2 tablespoons fresh lemon juice*
*2 tablespoons extra-virgin olive oil*
*freshly ground black pepper to taste*

*freshly grated Parmesan*

Bring a large covered pot of water to a rapid boil. Add the fusilli, stir, and cover the pot until the water comes to a boil again.

Meanwhile, cut tiny zucchini into whole rounds or cut medium-sized zucchini into half or quarter rounds about ¼ inch thick. In a heavy skillet, sauté the zucchini, garlic, and pine nuts in olive oil until the garlic is golden and the zucchini is barely tender, for just a few minutes. Put the zucchini into a large, wide serving bowl and add the tomatoes, parsley, basil, cheese, lemon juice, and extra-virgin olive oil. Add black pepper to taste and mix well.

When the pasta is al dente, drain it and add it to the serving bowl. Toss everything and serve immediately. Pass the Parmesan.

# Sun-Dried Tomato Pesto

•

## Pasta al Pesto di Pomodoro Secco

In Grottaglia, my mother's hometown in southern Italy, you can still see bright strings of tomatoes put out in the sun to dry, not just on farms, but also along the old streets in the center of town. The drying tomatoes festoon doorways and balconies. This is an important way to preserve the summer harvest into the winter all over Italy.

In recent years, sun-dried tomatoes have come into vogue here, and they are now widely available all year. This seems best as a winter pasta dish, although my favorite variation combines the pungent briny taste of the pesto with chopped fresh tomatoes and steamed green beans.

This pesto will keep for weeks in a sterilized jar in the refrigerator. Top the pesto with a thin coating of oil to seal it. Then next time, all you'll have to do is boil water.

### YIELDS ABOUT 1½ CUPS (12 SERVINGS)

**PESTO**

¾ cup oil-packed, sun-dried tomatoes (6½ ounces), drained

¾ cup pitted black olives (California, Italian, or Kalamata)

2 garlic cloves, pressed

1 packed cup chopped fresh parsley (Italian flat-leaf parsley if you can get it)

½ cup pine nuts

½ cup olive oil (use a little of the very flavorful but salty oil from the tomatoes)

¼ pound pasta per serving (whole wheat spaghetti or linguini is my first choice but any pasta shape will do)

**TOPPINGS (OPTIONAL):**

steamed green beans or steamed, chopped cauliflower

chopped fresh tomato

freshly grated Parmesan or crumbled goat cheese or feta

Heat a large covered pot of water.

Meanwhile, put all of the pesto ingredients into a blender or food processor and coarsely blend them so that the pesto is still a bit chunky—not completely puréed. If using a blender, you will probably need to stop the blender several times to stir the contents with a spatula. Set aside.

When the water comes to a boil, add the pasta, stir, and cover the pot until the water returns to a boil. If you are topping the pasta with green beans or cauliflower, put them into a colander hanging over or in the boiling water and steam or boil them until just tender, for about the same amount of time as the pasta needs to cook.

When the pasta is al dente, drain it and toss it with pesto. Use only about a tablespoon or two of this pesto per serving. It is not a sauce but rather a light coating of intensely flavored paste. Top the pasta with any or all of the steamed vegetables, fresh tomatoes, and/or cheese, if you like, and serve immediately.

## Variations

Add a few tablespoons of this pesto to your regular tomato sauce.

Lightly steam zucchini in place of the green beans or cauliflower.

Top the pasta with thinly sliced onion sautéed in olive oil.

# Ziti with Chard

•

# Ziti con Beitole

What a delicious way to eat chard. What a delightful way to eat pasta.

SERVES 4

1 large bunch red or green chard (about
    1–1½ pounds), washed
4 garlic cloves, minced
½ cup olive oil
salt and ground black pepper to taste

1 pound ziti

TOPPINGS (OPTIONAL):
freshly grated Asiago, Pecorino, or
    Parmesan cheese
chopped fresh tomatoes
fresh lemon juice and extra-virgin olive
    oil

Heat a large covered pot of water for the pasta. Remove and discard the tough ends of the chard and then chop it finely. In a large heavy skillet, sauté the chard and garlic in olive oil, stirring frequently, until the chard is limp but still bright green. The chard will reduce dramatically in volume. Add a little salt and plenty of black pepper.

When the water comes to a rapid boil, add the pasta and stir. Cover the pot until the water returns to a boil. When the pasta is al dente, drain it and divide it into serving bowls. Top it with chard. Sprinkle on cheese and add chopped tomatoes, lemon, or oil, if you wish. Serve immediately.

# Fettuccini with Creamy Gorgonzola Sauce

•

## Fettuccini al Gorgonzola

This creamy and delectable sauce is very easy and quick to prepare. With a sauce this thick and smooth it is important that the pasta has a bit of a bite, so be sure to buy a good imported brand of dried fettuccini and take care that it is cooked al dente. If you prefer fresh pasta, this is a classic sauce to top it.

### SERVES 4

*1 pound fettuccini*

*2 tablespoons butter*
*½ cup heavy cream or milk*
*4 ounces Gorgonzola cheese, cut into*
  *small pieces*

*4 ounces cream cheese, cut into ½-inch*
  *cubes*
*freshly ground black pepper*

*½ cup freshly grated Parmesan*

Bring a large covered pot of water to a boil. Add the fettuccini, stir, and cover the pot until the water returns to a boil.

In a saucepan large enough to hold the cooked pasta, melt the butter. Mix in the cream or milk and heat carefully, never allowing it to boil. Add the Gorgonzola and cream cheese, stirring frequently, until they are melted and the sauce is fairly smooth. Add freshly ground black pepper.

When the pasta is al dente, drain it and mix it into the sauce. Toss well to coat the pasta and serve immediately. Pass the grated Parmesan at the table.

### Variations
Top with chopped roasted walnuts.

Top with strips of roasted red pepper.

Add puréed spinach to the sauce. Steam about 12 ounces of spinach in a colander over the boiling pasta water. Increase the cream to one cup. Purée the wilted spinach with the cream in a blender or food processor. Proceed as directed. Top with chopped fresh tomatoes.

# Shrimp in Garlic-Wine Sauce

·

# Gamberetti in Aglio e Vino

This is a very flavorful and sprightly shrimp for all seasons. Preparing the shrimp for cooking can take a bit of time but can be finished beforehand. The last-minute cooking is done in a flash.

### SERVES 4 TO 6

2 pounds fresh shrimp

1/4 cup olive oil
4 garlic cloves, finely chopped
1/2 cup packed chopped fresh parsley

1/2 cup dry white wine
salt and freshly ground black pepper

lemon wedges

Clean and devein the shrimp.

In a large heavy skillet, heat the oil and garlic on medium-low heat for about 3 minutes. Add the parsley and shrimp and cook for about 2 minutes on medium-high heat.

Add the wine and cook the shrimp until done, about 3 to 5 minutes. The shrimp will be orangey-pink and white. Be careful not to overcook, so the shrimp will remain tender and succulent. Add salt and black pepper to taste.

Serve on rice or with hunks of Italian bread to sop up the juices. Garnish with lemon wedges.

# Spinach with Pine Nuts and Raisins

•

# Spinaci alla Romana

 This fast and interesting preparation of spinach is found all over the Mediterranean and shows the influence of Saracen (Persian) cooking. The spinach may be steamed ahead of time, but the sautéing must be done at the last minute. Chard and escarole are also excellent prepared this way.

SERVES 4 TO 6

3 tablespoons raisins (golden raisins look wonderful)

2 pounds fresh spinach

3 garlic cloves, sliced into thin rounds
3 tablespoons pine nuts
¼ cup olive oil
salt and freshly ground black pepper to taste

Soak the raisins in hot water to cover until you're ready to add them to the spinach.

Remove the coarse stems from the spinach, rinse the leaves well, and shake off the excess water. Place the spinach in a large pot. Steam on high heat for 2 or 3 minutes, tossing the leaves several times. The spinach should be bright green and the leaves still retaining some of their shape, although the volume reduced. Drain well.

Sauté the garlic and pine nuts in the olive oil for a few minutes, until golden. Add the spinach. Stir in the drained raisins. Toss to coat the spinach with the hot oil. Add salt and pepper and serve immediately.

# DOLCE

There are beautiful, elaborate pastries displayed in pasticcerie all over Italy. Bakeries develop reputations for particular artistry with special regional confections, and fine professional pastry chefs are considered artists. (Carême once classified confectionary as the chief branch of architecture, and, indeed, Bernini's Baldachino over the High Altar in Saint Peter's, Rome, rather resembles an elaborate meringue torte.) Pastries and fancy cakes are served with coffee or wine in cafés, and Italians buy them at pasticcerie to take home for holidays or for special occasions. But these sophisticated creations of the pasticcerie are not often attempted by busy home cooks.

Sweets made at home for family meals are usually quite simple and often traditional. They might be a nostalgic taste of something made exactly the same as Nonna made it or simply a favorite use of an abundant fruit, for example. Pesche Ripiene falls in this category.

Gelato (Italian ice cream) is a category in itself. Italians usually enjoy an ice cream cone at night during a stroll around the piazza. They have strong opinions about where to find the best gelato. Pity the poor tourist who must stop every few blocks to sample another cono in hope of experiencing the culture most fully.

Pastries and fancy cakes are occasional treats, not part of everyday meals. Italians almost always end their meals with fruit, sometimes fruit and nuts, or fruit and cheese, even if there is a more elaborate dessert. Each fruit—strawberries, cherries, apricots, figs, tangerines—as they appear in season is anticipated and relished. Ripe, fresh fruit is usually served whole and unadorned. Sometimes it is served chilled—grapes or melon wedges might be served on a bed of ice; berries, apricots, and peaches brought to the table in a bowl of water and ice—but most often fruit is served at room temperature. Guests may give as much praise to fruit as to a painstakingly prepared dish; and restaurants proudly display their selection of whole fresh fruits as an enticement.

Bel Paese, Fontina, Pecorino, Gorgonzola, Asiago, and Taleggio are common table cheeses to serve with fruit. Some combinations of fruit and cheese have become standard and classic. Taleggio goes well with grapes. The juicy sweetness of pears is offset by the tang of blue-veined Gorgonzola or the dry sharpness of Pecorino. There is an old Italian proverb from the time when landowners and peasants divided up the harvest. "Al contadino non far sapere, quanto è buono il formaggio con le pere," which translates "The peasants don't want the padrone to find out how good pears and Pecorino taste."

In Italy, the most common cheese for a last course is Parmigiano Reggiano. The mellowed, nutty flavor and firm texture of Parmigiano especially complement fall fruits such as apples, plums, figs, pears, or grapes.

Sometimes fruits are combined simply with wine. Strawberries, raspberries, or sliced peaches are often marinated in white wine or maybe in a sparkling wine such as Asti Spumonti. Dried figs soaked in marsala are delicious. Fruit salad (macedonia) made with any combination, a bit of sugar, and white wine or fruit juice is popular at home as well as in restaurants.

# Almond Meringue Cookies

•

## Amaretti

Italian almond meringue cookies, called Amaretti, have a hard crisp bite followed by a light, airy texture that quickly dissolves in the mouth. Amaretti are made all over Italy and many variations exist, usually with fewer almonds and more sugar than are in this recipe. In Italy, a small amount of bitter almonds would probably be included, but bitter almonds are very difficult to find in this country, so we've left them out. Traditionally, the almonds are blanched before grinding, but we find the darker, nuttier-tasting cookies made with unblanched ground almonds to be quite acceptable, possibly preferable, and much quicker. So that's what we recommend. But if you're making these to serve to your Italian grandmother, The Food Critic, you'd better blanch the almonds.

Amaretti are made in a couple of sizes and shapes. We prefer the larger long ovals that are designed for dunking into a glass of dessert wine such as vin santo or a cup of espresso. The baking time varies depending on the size of the cookies, the heaviness of the baking sheet, and the dryness of the whipped egg whites. To be sure that the cookies do not overbake on the bottom, place the prepared cookie pan inside another one to give a double thickness.

Amaretti will keep for months stored in an airtight container, so you may want to double or triple the recipe so that you'll have some on hand, but keep in mind that you'll need two or three baking sheets for the cookies to rest on before baking. If you'd like to make a bigger batch but only have one or two baking sheets, the solution is to form the cookies on buttered and floured sheets of aluminum foil, which can be lifted onto the baking sheet.

3 egg whites

½ cup sugar

1 teaspoon pure almond extract

2 cups almonds, blanched if desired,
   and finely ground

_____

butter, cornstarch, flour, or baking
parchment

In a large mixing bowl, whip the egg whites until stiff peaks form. Gradually add the sugar, while continuing to whip, until the egg whites are very stiff and glossy. Gently fold in the almond extract and the ground almonds.

Butter a large baking sheet and dust it with cornstarch or flour, or cover it with parchment. Spoon the meringue mixture onto the baking sheet in balls or long ovals about an inch apart. Set aside to rest at room temperature for one hour.

Preheat the oven to 300°.

Bake the Amaretti for 30 to 45 minutes or until very lightly browned. Turn off the oven and leave the cookies in for another 15 minutes to dry. Remove them from the baking sheet. Cool completely before storing in an airtight container.

## TO BLANCH ALMONDS

_TO blanch almonds, drop them into a pan of boiling water and cook for 30 to 45 seconds; drain in a colander. Cool with cold water. Remove the almond skins—they will slip off easily when the almonds are squeezed between your fingers. Dry the blanched almonds on a baking sheet in a 375° oven for 2 or 3 minutes. Cool the almonds before grinding._

# Baked Stuffed Peaches

•

## Pesche Ripiene

This is a typical, homey, not-too-sweet dessert from Piedmont, where peaches grow abundantly. It's a good dish to make the day after you have made Amaretti as it gives you an opportunity to use up the leftover egg yolks and some of those cookies. You can use commercially prepared Amaretti, however, with satisfactory results. The flavor and crusty texture of the almond filling perfectly complements the smooth lushness of the ripe peaches. At Moosewood, this seasonal dessert is always eagerly anticipated and then fondly recalled after a too-brief appearance.

SERVES 6

¾ cup ground almonds
¾ cup ground Amaretti (see page 373)
¼ cup sugar
2 egg yolks or 1 whole egg, beaten

6 freestone peaches
butter
½ cup marsala

Combine the almonds, Amaretti, and sugar. Stir in the beaten egg slowly, a bit at a time. Add just enough egg so that the crumbly, sticky mixture holds together. Don't let the mixture become too wet to hold its shape. Form the mixture into twelve balls about the size of whole walnuts.

Butter a shallow baking dish. Cut the peaches in half around the midline. Remove the pits. Peel the peaches if you wish. Place the peach halves close together in the dish, cut side up.

Press a ball of the almond mixture into the cavity of each peach half. Dot the tops with butter. Pour the marsala over all.

Bake at 375° for about 30 minutes until the almond mixture is crusty and golden. Serve warm or chilled.

ANDI GLADSTONE

# *Japan*

# INTRODUCTION

*I am one*

*Who eats breakfast*

*Gazing at morning-glories.*

*Bashō*

There were no breakfasts gazing at morning-glories for me when I began living in Japan in 1965. In fact, when I first arrived, I couldn't find Bashō anywhere in my busy life. I was a foreign exchange student at Kobe Public High School and a new member of the Kitamura household, a two-working-parent family who lived in a rapidly developing area on the outskirts of Kobe City. At first, there were only crowded streets; long, exhausting school days; lots of standing in packed, moving vehicles; and late-night silliness with equally exhausted friends and family members. No temple bells tolling in the distance, no quiet ponds with frogs jumping in. But then it changed. Even in my busy life, I began to discover the "spirit of Bashō," that Japanese spirit that ritualizes and elevates even the most ordinary activity. I discovered it in small, unexpected places. It began with the food.

A Japanese meal begins not with the first taste, but with the first look. In the country that created the Tea Ceremony, an exquisite ceremony in which it takes four hours to prepare and serve a cup of tea, planning a meal demands as much attention to presentation as to flavor. Whether it is the precooked ingredients of a seafood and vegetable cooked-at-the-table hotpot dish like Mizutaki, or the already prepared, tasty and delicate Hiyashi Somen, the meal is first received, and often judged, visually.

The ingredients for any Japanese meal must be prepared and arranged with great attention to shape and color, and often vary with the dish and season. The carrots may be matchsticks in the delicate summer dish Tofu Shira-ae, or the six-sided carrot chunks in the heartier and savory winter stew, Oden. Even for the simplest dishes, Japanese cooking is detailed and labor intensive.

Japanese flavors are simple and delicate. Traditionally, Japanese cooking rarely used oil or sautéed garlic or ginger, although these flavors are now often associated with it.

The more traditional flavors of Japanese cooking, the ones I have chosen to emphasize in this chapter, are soy sauce, miso, sake, mirin (a sweet rice wine), sometimes vinegar or lime juice, and most important, *dashi*.

*Dashi* means stock. It can be any stock but is commonly either a seafood or seaweed stock. These dashi can often be used interchangeably. In these recipes I have most often used konbu (seaweed) dashi, sometimes combining it with seafood and/or shiitake (black mushroom) dashi to enhance the flavor. Dashi is what makes Japanese cooking your own. I have given basic dashi recipes, but once you have become familiar with Japanese flavors, you may want to modify your dashi for certain recipes—make it stronger or lighter, emphasize konbu dashi in one dish, shiitake dashi in another.

Japanese people love their food and are hearty eaters. I always seem to put on a pound or more on every extended visit to Japan. But how can that be, ask my Moosewood compatriots, when portions are so scant? There are two simple answers. First, we eat several dishes in a Japanese meal. Although there may be one main dish, we often serve several side dishes alongside of it. Or else, even more often, our meal consists of as many as eight or nine side dishes. We have a "scant" portion of many different dishes. Rice is the second reason. In Japanese the word *gohan* means both "rice" and "meal." They are only differentiated by the context in which they are used. All other food is called *okazu*, or, as defined by *Kenkyusha Japanese Dictionary*, "subsidiary articles of diet." Rice is our meal. Everything else—all the dishes in this chapter that you will prepare with such care and attention to flavor and presentation—are only "subsidiary articles of diet." But they are such delectable subsidiary articles, you won't regret your efforts.

Sake is made from rice. In the same way that we usually do not eat rice and noodles together, in a Japanese meal we also do not have rice and sake together because they are both, in essence, rice. We begin our meal slowly, with sake and *okazu*, and when we have had enough sake, we stop drinking and slowly begin to eat rice with *okazu*.

In general, all *okazu* is served at the same time, and only miso soup and pickles are served later as a separate course. Once we have finished *okazu*, we eat miso soup and pickles with our remaining rice, often replenishing the rice so that it lasts throughout miso soup and pickles. Then, after everything, we end our meal with a steaming cup of green tea.

There are, of course, some variations. Gomoku Soba is not served with rice because we don't combine rice with noodles, and we also don't serve miso soup with Gomoku Soba because it is served in a broth of its own. But in this chapter, with the exception of noodle dishes and Okonomiyaki (Japanese pizza), these dishes should be eaten in the traditional sake, rice, *okazu*, miso soup and pickles combination.

Because Japanese food is basically either rice, noodles, or *okazu* without the more familiar appetizer, soup, salad, main course, dessert categories, there is still the question, "What goes with what?" It really is a matter of taste and aesthetics. Just as you will be able to experiment with your dashi as you become more familiar with it, you will also be able to put your own meals together as you become more familiar with the recipes. But here are a few combinations to get you started.

## Side Dishes with Main Dishes

If we look at Gomoku Soba we see that it has lots of vegetables, broth, noodles, and is very light. But since the only protein is a hard-boiled egg, we might want to serve a side dish of Gomoku Soy Beans, add a little richness with Zucchini in Walnut Sauce, and maybe spice up our meal with Kinpira Gobo. Because our portions are small, these four dishes together would give us a satisfying and varied meal.

Mizutaki, on the other hand, has almost everything in it and really doesn't need anything else (except rice and sake, of course). If I were going to add anything to Mizutaki from these recipes, I would choose Chawan Mushi because it is small and delicate (not to compete with the exquisitely arranged ingredients of Mizutaki that will definitely be dominating your table), it is warming and soothing to eat (in keeping with the winter-warming Mizutaki experience), and it is an egg custard, egg being one of the few things Mizutaki does not have in it.

Tempura might need something simple and cleansing like Spinach Nori Rolls, some Cucumber Ume-ae, and/or Caviar Oroshi. However, Sake-Braised Spinach Crowns, Tofu Shira-ae, Chawan Mushi, and Su-no-Mono would also be good—you decide!

Oden is a little like Mizutaki in that it has almost everything in it, but you might want to add some Caviar Oroshi, Zucchini in Walnut Sauce, and/or a little serving of Su-no-Mono.

Because Hiyashi Somen is for hot days when no one wants to eat too much, I would suggest just serving some Tofu Shira-ae with it to augment the protein in the meal.

Okonomiyaki is definitely a lunch dish and goes very nicely with a simple tossed salad with Japanese Salad Dressing.

Of course everything except the noodle dishes and Okonomiyaki is served with rice, pickles, and miso soup.

## Side Dishes as a Meal

It is when you start making meals of your side dishes that you can really be creative. Think about color, texture, taste, nutrients, and the season. Think about your table, your dishes, your tablecloth, the picture on the wall, the view outside your window. Almost anything is possible, but here is a place to begin·

Junco's Delicious Potatoes Braised in Sake and Butter
Cucumber Ume-ae (Cucumbers in Pickled Plum Sauce)
Kinpira Gobo (Spicy Sautéed Burdock Root)
Tofu Shira-ae (Tofu Sesame Pâté)
Gomoku Soy Beans (Soy Beans Simmered with Vegetables and Seaweed)
Sake-Braised Spinach Crowns
Rice, Miso Soup, Oshinko (Pickled Daikon)
Green tea

This will make a complete, aesthetically pleasing meal that will also be manageable to prepare, because only the potatoes and burdock root have to be served immediately. The spinach crowns can be made at the last minute, but it is also fine to do them ahead of time and serve them at room temperature.

Japan is an island country with rich soil and a temperate climate. In the not-too-distant past, before industrialization, Japan was a place where almost anything would grow and the ocean was fertile and accessible. It was a country abundant in food supply, so even with the Buddhist dietary rule of "nothing with four legs," a rich and varied cuisine developed. For this reason, I found it difficult to choose from among many delicious dishes that would best represent the essence of Japanese cooking. I want to thank Junco Tsunashima, my good friend and a great cook, who helped me make these choices. I hope that you will find them pleasing to both eye and palate, and that you will have leisurely, quiet, and joyful meals.


## BASICS


Before we get to the Japanese recipes, here are instructions for making Japanese rice and for dashi, which is an essential ingredient in many of the dishes that follow.

# Japanese Rice

In Japanese cooking, if the rice is wrong, the meal is wrong. Rice is simple and basic and often taken for granted, but it must be good.

Rice is served in individual servings in special rice bowls that vary in color and design but are almost universal in shape and size. Pick up your rice bowl and eat the rice with chopsticks. Find your own comfortable rhythm of eating a mouthful of *okazu,* a mouthful of rice, *okazu,* rice. . . .

The rice must be just glutenous enough so that it stays together in bite-sized clumps taken with chopsticks without any individual grains of rice falling where they shouldn't. In other words, those nice, individual grains that Uncle Ben talks about are not what one wants in Japanese rice. At the same time, the rice should achieve a pleasing texture so that the individual grains can be tasted.

It is best to use a Japanese electric rice cooker, which has all amounts clearly marked and also keeps the rice warm throughout the meal. But you can also make delicious rice in a simple saucepan or pot. Here is how to do it.

## Brown Rice

### YIELDS 3 CUPS

*1 cup short-grain brown rice*           *2½ cups water*

Rinse the rice well and drain it. Place the rice and the water together in a pot. Bring to a boil on high heat in the uncovered pot, then lower the heat, cover, and simmer until all of the water has cooked away. Depending on how low the heat is, this should take about 40 to 50 minutes. Remove the rice from the heat and let it sit, covered, for at least 3 minutes before serving.

## White Rice

### YIELDS A GENEROUS 2 CUPS

*1 cup short-grain white rice*           *2 cups water*

Follow the same procedure as for brown rice. White rice should simmer for 14 to 20 minutes before all of the water cooks away.

# Konbu Dashi

Konbu is a deep-sea kelp that is gathered in cold northern oceans and then sun dried. It is used in cooking to enhance flavors, as a natural tenderizer (which is why it is often used in bean dishes), and, more commonly, for making dashi or soup stock, which is the basis of much of Japanese cooking.

Here is the konbu dashi recipe we like best.

### YIELDS ABOUT 7 CUPS

*½ ounce dried konbu*                    *8 cups water*

Bring the konbu and water to a boil. Turn the heat down, cover, and simmer for 20 minutes. Pour through a strainer to remove the konbu. The remaining liquid is the dashi. If not using right away, let cool and then refrigerate. Konbu dashi will keep for four to five days.

# Shiitake Dashi

Shiitake Dashi is also fundamental to Japanese cooking. It will be used frequently in the recipes throughout this chapter.

### YIELDS 7 CUPS

*16 dried shiitake mushrooms*            *8 cups boiling water*

Place the shiitake mushrooms in a soup pot. Add the boiling water, cover, and let sit for about 30 minutes. Remove the shiitake mushrooms and reserve the liquid as dashi. Shiitake dashi will keep refrigerated and tightly sealed for four or five days.

# Mizutaki

·

## Seafood and Vegetable Hotpot with Pungent Dipping Sauce

 Mizutaki is one of many wonderfully social, winter hot-pot dishes in Japanese cuisine. It is social because it is cooked at the table with lots of guest participation ("We need to add more scallops soon," "Are these scallions done yet?" "More mushrooms, please"). It is best served in winter because you actually do get warm from the continually simmering hot pot in the middle of the table.

The dipping sauce should be prepared ahead of time and the raw ingredients should be arranged on platters (beautifully, of course) and put on the table. For cooking, use a large, unseasoned, shallow pan about 10 inches in diameter. Four or five inches high is ideal, deep enough to cook an adequate amount, but still easy for your guests to reach into with their chopsticks to select cooked ingredients. You might also keep a slotted spoon handy so that guests can serve themselves more easily.

Be sure your hot plate is powerful enough to boil water. The main cook should use long cooking chopsticks or tongs, although as the meal goes on it is perfectly acceptable for guests to add ingredients to their own liking to give the cook a break and a chance to eat, too. Each diner is given an individual bowl of dipping sauce.

As with most Japanese meals, serve this dish with sake. Then, when you have had enough sake, serve individual bowls of rice to accompany the rest of your Mizutaki.

### SERVES 4

**DIPPING SAUCE**
*½ cup fresh lime juice*
*⅔ cup tamari soy sauce*
*1 tablespoon sake*

*½ cup finely grated daikon*
*2 teaspoons finely grated peeled fresh*
*  ginger root*
*½ cup chopped scallions*

## MIZUTAKI

2 medium Chinese cabbages cut into
  1/2 x 2-inch pieces
4 bunches scallions, cut into 2-inch
  pieces
3 leeks, well rinsed, tender white parts
  cut into rings 1/4 inch wide
1 pound mushrooms, stemmed and
  halved

1/2 pound spinach, washed and stemmed
1 cake tofu, cut into 1/2-inch cubes
1 pound scallops
1/2 pound shrimp, shelled and deveined

3 cups water
8-inch piece dried konbu

4 servings cooked rice

For the dipping sauce, combine the lime juice, soy sauce, and sake in a saucepan and heat on low heat. In each of four individual small bowls, put 1 tablespoon of grated daikon, 1/4 teaspoon of grated ginger root, and 1 tablespoon of chopped scallions. To each bowl add 3 tablespoons of the soy sauce mixture. Some extra dipping sauce and garnishes will be left to freshen the bowls during the meal.

To make the Mizutaki, arrange all the vegetables, tofu, scallops, and shrimp on platters, prettily.

In a large, shallow pan on a hot plate in the center of the table, heat the water and konbu until it begins to boil. Let it boil slowly for 2 minutes. Remove the konbu.

When the guests are seated, begin cooking, adding the scallops and shrimp first, then the leeks and tofu, then the Chinese cabbage and mushrooms, then the scallions, and finally, just when everything is ready to eat, add the spinach.

Dilute each guest's bowl of dipping sauce with Mizutaki broth to taste. Each diner then selects things from the hot pot to dip and eat. As the dipping sauce gets diluted, keep adding remaining dipping sauce ingredients to keep it flavorful.

Keep the hot pot going and continue adding more ingredients. Try to keep the cooked ingredients on one side and the new ingredients on the other. Adjust the temperature of the hot pot to your pace of eating.

*Note: If you are lucky enough to have some Mizutaki left over in the pan and/ or on the platter, you will be in for a real treat. Continue to cook everything at the table, add the remaining dipping sauce and condiments to the pan, and reheat it the next day for a wonderful Japanese bouillabaisse. If you want a change from rice, cook some Japanese udon noodles (see page 685) and add them to the reheated Mizutaki just before serving.*

# *Tempura*

Tempura is everyone's favorite, and here is a recipe that will work at home. The key to a light and successful tempura is to organize everything you need before you begin cooking and then watch your temperatures (batter and oil) as you cook. If the cook wants to eat with everyone else, the tempura could be cooked a little ahead and kept warm in the oven, but tempura really is best when eaten immediately. So this is one of those meals in which the cook usually keeps cooking during the meal and eats later. Feel free to substitute any of your favorite vegetables for the ones I have chosen here.

## SERVES 4

### TEMPURA PIECES
*8 shiitake mushrooms (fresh or dried)*
*1 carrot*
*½ eggplant*
*1 sweet potato*
*8 scallions*
*2 red or green bell peppers*
*12 jumbo, fantail shrimp*

### DIPPING SAUCE
*½–⅓ cup konbu dashi (see page 385)*
*2 tablespoons tamari soy sauce*
*2 tablespoons sake*

*1 teaspoon apple cider or apple juice*
*½ teaspoon honey*
*¼ cup grated daikon*
*½ teaspoon grated peeled fresh ginger*
  *root (or to taste)*

### BATTER
*1 egg*
*¾ cup chilled water*
*1 cup sifted unbleached white flour*
_____
*2 cups vegetable oil*

Prepare the tempura pieces as follows:

Shiitake: If dried, soak in boiling water for 20 to 30 minutes, until soft. Trim off and discard the stems, and use the caps whole.

Carrot: Peel, cut in half lengthwise, and then cut into 2½-inch pieces. So that the carrots will cook better, make a couple of ½-inch-deep cuts in both ends of each piece.

Eggplant: Peel and cut into ½-inch slices (half rounds, if the eggplant is large).

Sweet potato: Peel and cut into ¼-inch slices.

Scallions: Remove the roots and wilted tops and then cut into 4-inch lengths.

Bell peppers: Cut into quarters, lengthwise, and then remove the seeds and stem.

Shrimp: Shell and devein, leaving the tails attached. Rinse if needed and pat dry.

To make the dipping sauce, combine the dashi, soy sauce, sake, apple cider or juice, and honey in a saucepan. Simmer for about 5 minutes and set aside. In each of four dipping sauce bowls, put 1 tablespoon grated daikon and a pinch of grated ginger.

For the batter, handling as little as possible, gently stir the egg until the yolk is just barely mixed with the white. Gently stir in first the water and then the flour, until just barely mixed. It is important to handle the batter as little as possible; some lumps are okay. Keep the batter in a bowl surrounded by ice so that it will stay cold. (Cold batter in hot oil equals light and crisp tempura.)

To cook, in a wok or heavy pan, heat the oil to 350°–375° and, as you cook, try to keep the oil this temperature. Use one utensil for dipping the vegetables into the batter and dropping into the oil and a different utensil for taking them out of the oil. I use long cooking chopsticks, but the tempura can also be removed with a Chinese strainer or a slotted spoon.

Cook the tempura in batches, several pieces at a time. Dip each piece of vegetable or shrimp in the batter until lightly covered. Don't let it sit in the batter. Drop it into the hot oil and deep-fry until the batter becomes slightly translucent. Remove and drain on paper towels. If when you first put a piece into the oil little pieces of batter come off, this means the oil temperature is good. These little pieces should be strained out as you cook.

When the first batch is done, pour the dipping sauce over the daikon and ginger in the individual bowls. Serve the hot tempura immediately, dipping it in sauce and eating it as you deep-fry more.

# Gomoku Soba

•

## Noodles and Vegetables in a Flavorful Broth

Slurping hot noodles when you eat really does cool them off, so learn to make noise as you eat this steaming bowl of noodles and vegetables in a flavorful broth.

SERVES 4

8 dried shiitake mushrooms
2 cups hot water
3½ cups konbu dashi (see page 385)
5 tablespoons tamari soy sauce
½ cup sake

_____

½ large carrot, sliced into thin rounds
8 scallions, cut into 2½-inch lengths

2 cups sliced Chinese cabbage, ½ inch
    thick

_____

1 pound soba noodles (see page 680)

_____

4 hard-boiled eggs, peeled and halved
chopped scallions
hot red pepper flakes to taste (optional)

Soak the shiitake in 2 cups of very hot water for 20 to 30 minutes. Reserving the liquid, remove the soaked shiitake, trim off and discard the stems, and slice the caps into strips. There should be 1½ cups of shiitake dashi left. Combine this with 3½ cups of konbu dashi (or however much konbu dashi it takes to make a total of 5 cups). Add the soy sauce, sake, and shiitake. Simmer. Briefly cook each vegetable in the broth as it simmers, one vegetable at a time so that everything is just barely cooked—or, just barely undercooked. Remove the cooked vegetables from the stock and set aside for later.

Continue to simmer the broth as you cook the soba in a separate pot. After the soba is cooked and drained, in each of four big bowls place approximately a fourth of the noodles. Then arrange, as prettily as possible, the vegetables and two halves of a hard-boiled egg. Pour a generous cup of broth over everything in each bowl. The broth must be very hot so it can reheat the vegetables and egg. Garnish with chopped scallions and, if desired, hot red pepper flakes to taste.

*Variation*   Snow peas, spinach, and mung sprouts are also very good in this dish. Snow peas should be briefly cooked with the other vegetables. Add uncooked spinach or sprouts to the serving bowl before pouring the hot broth over everything.

# *Oden*

•

## *Winter Stew*

"With food like this, I hardly miss meat at all!"

—Ruthie Gladstone, my German shepherd mix (lover of Japanese leftovers)

### SERVES 4

**DASHI**
- *4 cups water*
- *3-inch square konbu*
- *8 dried shiitake mushrooms*
- *3 tablespoons sake*
- *5 tablespoons tamari soy sauce*
- *3 tablespoons mirin*

**STEW**
- *4 hard-boiled eggs, peeled*
- *1 cake tofu, cut into 1-inch cubes*
- *3 medium carrots, peeled and cut in 1-inch rounds, then edged to make 6-sided shapes*

- *3 medium turnips, peeled and cut into quarters*
- *2 medium potatoes, peeled and cut into quarters*

---

- *12 scallions, cut on the diagonal into 4-inch pieces*
- *3 ounces spinach leaves*
- *½ bunch watercress leaves*
- *hot mustard*

To make the dashi, heat the water and konbu in a medium saucepan. Just before it boils (when small bubbles begin to appear), remove it from the heat. With a strainer or slotted spoon, remove and reserve the konbu. Soak the shiitake in the hot liquid for 20 to 30 minutes. Trim off and discard the stems. Set the caps aside. Add the sake, soy sauce, and mirin to the dashi.

Place the reserved konbu on the bottom of a large saucepan. Then arrange the eggs, tofu, carrots, turnips, potatoes, and shiitake caps to fit snugly into the pan. It is nice to place the eggs in the center and surround them with the vegetables.

Gently pour in the flavored dashi. Heat until bubbles begin to form and then simmer for 30 minutes, partially covered. It is best to use a cover from a smaller pot so that some of the liquid is exposed, but if not, then just don't cover it tightly. After 30 minutes, turn off the heat, uncover, and let cool about 15 minutes. Then refrigerate or put in a cool place for at least 2 hours, preferably overnight.

Just before serving, bring Oden to a simmer on medium heat. Simmer for 2 minutes, covered. Lay the scallions across the top and simmer, covered, for another minute. Add the spinach leaves and simmer, covered, for one more minute. Add the watercress, cover, and turn off the heat. Wait a moment before serving to allow the watercress to wilt slightly.

Serve Oden in individual shallow soup bowls. Be sure to arrange each serving nicely by color and shape. Top each serving with one of the hard-boiled eggs, sliced in half lengthwise, and a little of the broth. Finish with a dollop of hot mustard.

# Hiyashi Somen

·

## Chilled Somen Noodles with Spicy Dipping Sauce

Here is a light and delicious and very pretty summer dish for the days when it's so hot you just can't think about eating. You will rediscover your appetite when you eat Hiyashi Somen.

### SERVES 4

**DIPPING SAUCE**
1 cup shiitake dashi (see page 385)
2 cups konbu dashi (see page 385)
⅔ cup tamari soy sauce
1 cup sake
¼ cup mirin
1 teaspoon grated peeled fresh ginger
    root

½ cup finely grated daikon
½ cup chopped scallions

3 tablespoons finely grated fresh wasabi
    (1 tablespoon wasabi powder)

½ red bell pepper
½ cucumber
2 cups sliced Chinese cabbage
16 snow peas
1 egg
2 tablespoons water
1 sheet nori (about 8x7 inches)
1 pound somen noodles

In a medium saucepan, combine the dipping sauce ingredients. Simmer, uncovered, for about 30 minutes. Remove from heat and set aside to cool to room temperature.

Meanwhile, combine the daikon and the scallions and set aside. If using wasabi powder, make a paste by thoroughly mixing a tablespoon of wasabi powder with 2 tablespoons of cold water. Cover the wasabi after grating or mixing.

Slice the red pepper half into thin strips. Peel and seed the cucumber half and cut into matchstick pieces. Cut the Chinese cabbage into ½-inch slices. Stem the snow peas.

Blanch the Chinese cabbage in boiling water for 2 minutes and the snow peas for 1 minute. Set aside to cool.

Whisk the egg and the water. Pour into a moderately heated, lightly oiled skillet and cook for 1 minute. This will be crêpe-like, a flat pancake. Remove from the skillet in one piece, cool, and then cut into thin strips and set aside. Toast the nori by waving it over a flame until it stiffens slightly, but be careful—it burns easily. Crumble it into little pieces and set aside.

Boil the somen in 8 cups of water in a large pot for 3 minutes or according to the directions on the package. Place the drained somen in a bowl of cold water and ice cubes and let sit until completely cooled. Add more ice if necessary. Drain the somen.

To serve, mound the cold somen in the middle of the platter. Arrange the vegetables around the somen, paying great attention to color. Sprinkle the egg strips and crumbled nori on top of the noodles. In individual serving cups, put ⅓ to ½ cup of dipping sauce, 1 tablespoon daikon, 1 tablespoon scallions, and ½ teaspoon wasabi or to taste. Dip each bite of somen and vegetables into the dipping sauce. Keep freshening each sauce cup with more dipping sauce and condiments, as needed.

# *Okonomiyaki*

•

# *Japanese Pizza*

Like pizza, okonomiyaki is kids' food—which adults also love —snack food, quick-meal food. It was definitely the most popular food at Kobe High School in 1965.

1 sheet nori (about 8x7 inches)

SAUCE

¼ cup catsup

1½ tablespoons Worcestershire Sauce
   (see page 686)

¼ teaspoon Dijon mustard

2 tablespoons sake

1 teaspoon tamari soy sauce

OKONOMIYAKI

2 eggs

1 cup unbleached white flour

1 cup water

2 tablespoons sake

pinch of salt (optional)

2 cups shredded cabbage (1½-inch
   strips)

¼ cup shredded carrot (1½-inch strips)

4 whole scallions, cut in half lengthwise
   and into 1-inch strips (about 1 cup)

_____

¼ cup vegetable oil

½ cup cooked shrimp, cut in ½-inch
   pieces (or cooked crabmeat or seitan,
   thinly sliced)

Toast the nori by waving it over a flame until it stiffens slightly, but be careful—it burns easily. Crumble into little pieces and set aside.

Combine all the sauce ingredients in a small saucepan and simmer for 30 seconds, stirring constantly. Remove from the heat and cool to room temperature.

Beat the eggs in a large bowl. Add the flour and water and continue beating until you have a batter the consistency of pancake batter. Add the sake and salt. Fold in the cabbage, carrots, and scallions. Be sure to mix the batter and vegetables together evenly. Each okonomiyaki will use ¼ of this mixture.

Heat 1 tablespoon of the oil in a standard 10-inch skillet. Spoon ¼ of the batter onto the hot skillet (like a pancake) making sure the vegetables are evenly distributed. Then sprinkle ¼ of the shrimp, crabmeat, or seitan on top. Cook each side on medium heat for 2 minutes, until lightly browned. Reduce the heat to low and cook, covered, for another 5 minutes, occasionally turning and gently pressing the okonomiyaki with a spatula. Prepare three more okonomiyaki as above. Keep the finished pancakes warm in a low oven while making the rest, or use two skillets and make two okonomiyaki at a time.

Serve hot with the sauce to taste—I recommend 1 tablespoon per okonomiyaki— and top with a sprinkling of toasted nori.

## SIDE DISHES

# *Caviar Oroshi*

·

# *Caviar and Grated Daikon*

 This tasty little condiment should be presented in individual, dark-colored serving cups (preferably perfectly preserved, 400-year-old beautiful black lacquer cups with all four seasons represented in gold inlay—but if not, just any dark-colored little custard cups will do).

### SERVES 4

*¾ cup finely grated daikon*
*4 teaspoons salmon roe*

*1 teaspoon finely chopped scallion greens*
*tamari soy sauce to taste*

In each of four cups, mound 3 tablespoons of grated daikon. On top of that, put a 1-teaspoon dollop of salmon roe; sprinkle on ¼ teaspoon of minced scallion. Serve.

Tell your guests that before eating they should mix all this together and add soy sauce to taste.

# Sake-Braised Spinach Crowns

Spinach crowns are the base of the spinach plant, the little part tinged with pink where all the stalks originate. When we talk about spinach, we usually think about spinach leaves, so the crowns are often what gets thrown out. But the crowns are the sweetest part of the spinach plant and should not be missed. Don't throw them away. Use them just like this.

### SERVES 4

3 cups cleaned and trimmed spinach
  crowns (about 1/2 pound)

1/3 cup sake
1 1/2 tablespoons tamari soy sauce

Wash the spinach crowns, cut the stems to about one inch, and remove the roots.
In a saucepan, bring the sake and soy sauce to a simmer. Place the spinach crowns in the pan, crown down (stem end up). Cover and simmer for 3 or 4 minutes, until tender. Serve hot or at room temperature.

# Zucchini with Walnut Sauce

### SERVES 4

1/2 cup konbu dashi (see page 385)
2 tablespoons tamari soy sauce
2 tablespoons sake
1 teaspoon honey
1/2 teaspoon finely grated peeled fresh
  ginger root
1/2 teaspoon white miso

1 cup walnuts, toasted
3 medium zucchini, cut into
  2x1/2-inch matchsticks
  (about 6 cups)

_____

1 teaspoon sesame seeds, toasted

In a saucepan, combine the dashi, soy sauce, sake, honey, and ginger. Simmer for 10 minutes. Add the miso and turn down to very low heat, keeping the sauce warm, with no bubbles breaking at the surface. In a food processor or blender, grind the walnuts to a meal, not a paste, and stir into the sauce. Lightly steam the zucchini matchsticks—they should be crunchy (see page 681). Drain and toss with the sauce.

Serve hot or cold, depending on the season, and garnish with the toasted sesame seeds.

# Tofu Shira-ae
•
# Tofu and Sesame Pâté

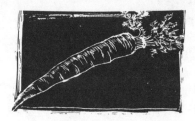

Best on a hot summer night with cold sake, but also good on a cold winter night with hot sake.

### SERVES 4 TO 6

3 dried shiitake mushrooms

2 cups hot water

2 tablespoons sake

2 tablespoons tamari soy sauce

1 small carrot, cut into 2-inch
matchsticks (about ½ cup)

8 green beans or snow peas, cut into
2-inch matchsticks (about ½ cup)

2 cups water

12-ounce cake tofu

½ cup white sesame seeds, toasted

3 tablespoons mirin

¼ teaspoon salt

2 tablespoons sake

Soak the shiitake in the hot water for 15 minutes, then remove them, reserving the liquid. Trim off and discard the stems, and cut the caps into matchsticks. Add 2 tablespoons of sake and soy sauce to the shiitake dashi and heat to a simmer. Simmer the shiitake mushrooms and the carrots in the dashi for one minute, then add the green beans and cook for a minute more. Remove the vegetables from the dashi and set aside to cool.

In a medium saucepan, bring 2 cups of water to a boil, then crumble in the tofu. Bring the water back to a boil and cook until the tofu begins to surface. Remove from the heat. Drain the tofu in a strainer by gently pressing it with your hands. Allow the tofu to cool for about 15 minutes.

In a blender or food processor, combine the tofu, sesame seeds, mirin, salt, and 2 tablespoons of sake. Process until almost smooth. It should retain a bit of texture. If the tofu stays crumbly and doesn't become smooth, it means you squeezed out too much water. Just add more water until it becomes smooth. In a bowl, toss the tofu-sesame pâté with the vegetables. Cool. Serve in individual small bowls.

# Junco's Delicious Potatoes Braised in Butter and Sake

 These potatoes will give you a taste of what happens when a Western food concept is adapted into Japanese cuisine. This dish was inspired by my good friend Junco Tsunashima.

Rice is served at most Japanese meals. Although in America we do not serve rice and potatoes together because we think of them both as starches, in Japanese cooking potatoes are a vegetable, rice is a grain, and they go very nicely together. But Japanese cuisine aside, this is also an interesting variation on hash browns.

### SERVES 4

4 medium potatoes
2 tablespoons butter

½ cup sake
2 tablespoons tamari soy sauce

Peel and quarter the potatoes. Cover them with water and bring them to a boil. Boil until tender, about 10 minutes. Drain.

Melt the butter in a heavy skillet. Add the potatoes and gently toss until each piece is coated with butter. Add the sake and cook on high heat, uncovered, stirring regularly, until the sake has almost evaporated. Add the soy sauce. Lower the heat and continue to cook about 5 minutes, stirring occasionally, until the potatoes are covered with a thick, brown sauce.

Serve hot.

# Su-no-Mono

•

## Light Cucumber Marinade

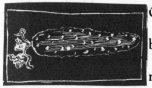Cellophane noodles can be slippery on chopsticks, so this might be a good time to mention that in Japanese table etiquette it is not only acceptable but even desirable to pick up the dish from which you are eating. In other words, because each person has several small serving dishes, it is easier and more polite to pick up one of yours and then, holding it close to your mouth, eat with chopsticks, than it is to leave your bowl on the table and risk dropping your noodles on your lap.

SERVES 4 TO 6

| | |
|---|---|
| *¼ cup sake* | *2 tablespoons mirin* |

---

| | |
|---|---|
| *1½ ounces cellophane noodles (mung bean thread) (see page 658)* | *2 medium cucumbers* |
| | *½ teaspoon salt* |
| | *2 ounces cooked crab meat (or 4 tablespoons coarsely chopped red bell pepper)* |
| *⅓ cup mild rice vinegar* | |
| *2 tablespoons tamari soy sauce* | |

In this dish, we use boiled sake because we want the flavor without the alcohol. Bring about ¼ cup of sake to a boil, immediately remove from heat, and cool. Reserve 2 tablespoons of boiled sake. (Use the leftover boiled sake in other recipes.)

Cook the bean threads according to the directions on the package (usually, boil for 3 minutes). Drain and place the noodles in a bowl of cold water. Run more cold water over the noodles until they are completely cool.

Combine 2 tablespoons of the sake with the vinegar, soy sauce, and mirin. Cool.

Peel the cucumbers, cut in half lengthwise, remove the seeds, and slice as thinly as possible. Place in a bowl, sprinkle with salt, and allow to sit for a few minutes. Squeeze the salted cucumber slices. Rinse well, squeezing out all of the excess water after rinsing.

In a (beautiful) bowl, place the noodles and then the cucumbers. Sprinkle on the crabmeat or red bell pepper. Pour the marinade over all and serve.

# Spinach Nori Rolls

Special equipment: a bamboo rolling mat, called a "sudare."

### NORI ROLLS

*1 pound spinach, washed and stemmed*
*½ medium carrot, cut into 1-inch*
  *matchsticks*
*3 sheets nori (8x7 inches)*

### DIPPING SAUCE

*¼ cup tamari soy sauce*
*4 teaspoons fresh lemon juice*
*2 tablespoons finely grated fresh wasabi*
  *(2 teaspoons wasabi powder)*

In a large pot, bring ½-inch of water to a boil. Add the spinach, lower the heat, cover, and simmer for just 2 minutes. Remove the spinach from the water and cool.

In a smaller pot, bring ½-inch of water to a boil. Add the carrots, lower the heat, cover, and simmer just 1 minute. Remove the carrots and cool.

After the spinach has cooled completely, wring out all the excess water. Pack it together and squeeze hard to get as much liquid out as possible. Pat the spinach dry with a paper towel. Also pat the carrot sticks dry.

Cut the sheets of nori in half to make six sheets, 8x3½-inches each. Place a sheet of nori on the bamboo rolling mat so that the 8-inch side is horizontal. Spread about ⅙ of the spinach evenly along the 8-inch length over the bottom 2 inches of nori. Put 2 rows of carrot matchsticks horizontally across the spinach about halfway up the spinach. Now, pick up the bottom edge of the mat and begin to roll toward the top using firm and steady pressure to shape a tight roll. Spinach might be squeezed out the sides, but this can be corrected later. The nori should seal with the moisture from the spinach, but if it doesn't, moisten the top edge of the nori sheet with a little water. Repeat this procedure with the remaining ingredients.

With a sharp knife, trim off the ragged edges of the nori rolls. Cut each roll in half. Then cut each half into thirds or quarters, making six or eight little rolls per nori sheet. Arrange the nori rolls on a platter with the cut side up.

For the dipping sauce, mix together the soy sauce and lemon juice. Pour into individual little saucers with wasabi added to taste. If using fresh wasabi, grate it finely. If using wasabi powder, make a paste by mixing 2 parts wasabi with one part water. Start with 2 teaspoons of wasabi and 1 teaspoon of water. Add the paste to the dipping sauce, a little at a time, until the hotness is right for you.

Serve immediately while the nori is still crisp.

# *Simmered Squash and*
# *Green Beans*

### SERVES 4

*1½ cups konbu dashi (see page 385)*
*2 tablespoons tamari soy sauce*
*1 tablespoon sake*
*2 teaspoons honey*
*1½ tablespoons grated peeled fresh*
   *ginger root*

*¾ pound butternut squash, peeled and*
   *cut into 1-inch chunks*
*¼ teaspoon salt*
*⅓ pound green beans, ends snipped off*
*1 tablespoon cornstarch dissolved in*
   *2 tablespoons water*

In a saucepan, gently bring 1 cup of the dashi, 1 tablespoon of the soy sauce, the sake, 1 teaspoon of the honey, and the ginger to a simmer. Add the squash and simmer, covered, 8 to 10 minutes, until just tender. Remove the squash from the broth with long cooking chopsticks or a slotted spoon and set aside.

Add the remaining ½ cup of dashi, the salt, and ½ teaspoon of the honey to the contents of the saucepan and return to a simmer. Add the green beans and simmer, covered, for several minutes until barely tender. Remove the beans. To the broth add the remaining tablespoon soy sauce and ½ teaspoon honey to taste. (If the squash seems very sweet you may prefer to omit this last ½ teaspoon of honey.) Return to a simmer and stir in the cornstarch mixture to thicken the broth. Add the squash and green beans and reheat gently.

Serve hot in a deep serving dish.

# Kinpira Gobo

•

## Spicy Burdock Root Sauté

Gobo, or burdock root, is eaten a lot in Japan, for its crunch and tasty flavor as well as its nutritional value. Besides vitamins and minerals, burdock root is high in fiber and has almost no calories. A medium burdock root is longer and thinner than an average carrot.

Gobo can be purchased at Japanese groceries, farmers' markets, or some healthfood stores. Use cultivated burdock root. It's quite different from the wild backyard variety that shows up in some areas. If you can't find gobo, you can use turnips or rutabagas, but they will not have the same texture or nutritional qualities as the gobo.

### Serves 3 to 4

| | |
|---|---|
| *3 medium gobo (burdock roots)* | *1½ teaspoons honey* |
| | *1 tablespoon dark sesame oil* |
| *½ carrot* | *¼ teaspoon hot red pepper flakes* |
| *1 tablespoon tamari soy sauce* | |
| *1 teaspoon sake* | *2 teaspoons toasted sesame seeds* |

Wash the gobo under running water to remove the sand and dirt. Scrape off the skin with a stiff brush or a knife. Because gobo turns black in the air as soon as the skin is removed, have a bowl of cold water handy and immerse the gobo in it as soon as it is peeled. Cut the peeled gobo into 2-inch matchsticks and soak it in cold water for one hour, changing the water every 20 minutes. The water will turn brown as the gobo soaks. This soaking process helps to remove the bitterness from the gobo.

While the gobo is soaking, peel the carrot and cut it into 2-inch-long matchsticks.

In a little cup, stir together the soy sauce, sake, and honey.

Heat the sesame oil in a wok or large heavy skillet. Stir-fry the matchsticks of carrot and gobo for 2 or 3 minutes, until the gobo is no longer raw, but still crunchy. Sprinkle in the red pepper flakes and continue tossing for another 30 seconds. Add the soy sauce–sake-honey mixture and stir-fry until the liquid is gone, about one minute.

Serve hot or cold, garnished with toasted sesame seeds.

# Gomoku Soy Beans

·

## Soy Beans Simmered with Vegetables and Seaweed

SERVES 4 TO 6

*½ cup dry soy beans*
*½ teaspoon salt*

_____

*4 dried shiitake mushrooms*
*1 cup hot water*
*1¼ medium carrots*

*10 water chestnuts*
*4-inch-square piece wet konbu (a piece left over from making dashi can be used)*
*2½ tablespoons tamari soy sauce*
*1½ tablespoons mirin*

Soak the soy beans overnight. Discard any beans that float to the top (see page 652).

Bring the soy beans to a boil in fresh water. Reduce to a simmer, add salt, and simmer for 2 hours. Add water if necessary to keep the beans always covered with an inch of water.

Soak the shiitake in the hot water for 20 minutes. Then drain the shiitake and reserve the dashi. Trim off and discard the stems and cut the caps into ¼-inch cubes.

Cut the carrots, water chestnuts, and konbu into ¼-inch cubes.

Drain the soy beans and put them in a medium-sized pot with the diced carrots, water chestnuts, konbu, and shiitake. Pour in the shiitake dashi. Add just enough water to barely cover the ingredients. Bring to a boil. Add the soy sauce and mirin. Reduce the heat and simmer for 15 minutes. Remove from the heat, cool to room temperature, and serve.

# *Japanese Salad Dressing*

Although tossed salads are not a traditional Japanese food, they have become popular and are served often in Japanese restaurants, usually with some variation on this "Japanese" salad dressing.

*1 small garlic clove, minced or pressed*
*¼ medium onion, minced (about 2 tablespoons)*
*½ medium carrot, grated (about ¼ cup)*
*1½ tablespoons grated peeled fresh ginger root*
*¼ teaspoon powdered mustard*

*1 teaspoon tamari soy sauce*
*1 teaspoon apple cider or apple juice*
*½ teaspoon dark sesame oil*
*½ cup vegetable oil*
*¼ cup mild rice vinegar (see note)*
*salt and freshly ground black pepper to taste*

In a food processor or blender, whirl the garlic, onion, carrot, and ginger for about 30 seconds. Add the rest of the ingredients, except the salt and pepper, and process until thickened. Stir in salt and pepper to taste.

Japanese Salad Dressing will keep for four or five days refrigerated in a tightly sealed jar.

---

*Note: If you can't get mild rice vinegar, use apple cider vinegar, but first bring it to a boil and then let it cool.*

---

# Cucumber Ume-ae

•

## Cucumber and Pickled Plum Salad

Umeboshi are pickled plums and are known to help digestion and stimulate appetite. This delicate salad is a perfect dish to aid a sluggish appetite on hot summer days. In cooler seasons, umeboshi can be eaten with hot rice or dissolved in hot water to make tea.

**SERVES 4 TO 6**

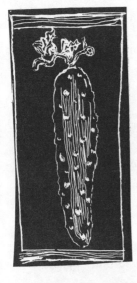

4 teaspoons umeboshi paste (or finely
  chopped umeboshi)
4 teaspoons mirin
¼ cup chopped scallions

¼ cup chopped parsley
2 cucumbers, peeled, seeded (unless the
  seeds are small and tender), and cut
  into half moons

Mix together the umeboshi paste, mirin, and chopped scallions and parsley. Toss the cucumbers with this mixture until they're evenly coated. Garnish with more chopped scallions or parsley, if you like.

This dish should be served soon after tossing it together or it will become watery.

# Chawan Mushi

•

## Light Vegetable Seafood Custard

SERVES 4

4 dried shiitake mushrooms
1½ cups hot water

8 snow peas (tender, small ones about
   2½ inches long are nice)

---

½ teaspoon salt
½ teaspoon tamari soy sauce
1 teaspoon sake
8 thin round slices carrot

2 eggs
4 shrimp, cooked, shelled and deveined
   (optional)
4 teaspoons minced scallions

Soak the dried shiitake in the very hot water for 20 to 30 minutes. Remove the shiitake and trim off and discard the stems. Reserve the liquid, which is the dashi.

In a saucepan, combine the dashi, salt, soy sauce, and sake and bring to a boil. Parboil the shiitake, carrot, and snow peas in separate batches until just tender. The shiitake will take about 5 minutes, the carrot 2 to 3 minutes, and the snow peas one minute. If the dashi has reduced to less than a cup during the parboiling, add hot water to make 1 cup. When all the vegetables are cooked, cool the dashi to room temperature.

Preheat the oven to 375°.

Mix the eggs together gently to avoid forming bubbles. Stir in 1 cup of dashi.

Fill each of four ovenproof cups with ½ cup of the dashi-egg mixture. In each cup, arrange as prettily as possible one shiitake cap, whole or sliced, 2 snow peas, and one cooked shrimp.

Place the cups in a shallow pan. Add ⅓ inch of boiling water to the bottom of the pan and bake for 10 to 12 minutes. Remove from the oven and add two carrot slices to each cup. Sprinkle 1 teaspoon of minced scallion on top of each cup. Bake 5 more minutes or until the custard is barely firm. Serve hot.

# *Miso Soup*

Tazio Asta's favorite.

SERVES 4

---

4 dried shiitake mushrooms
1¼ cups hot water
⅓ medium daikon (3 inches)
⅓ medium carrot (2 inches)
4 ounces tofu
5 cups konbu dashi (see page 385)
1 teaspoon honey
1 teaspoon tamari soy sauce
¼ cup sake
2 tablespoons white miso
2 tablespoons red miso

chopped scallions
WINTER
8 spinach leaves, stemmed
4 cooked shrimp
SUMMER
12 watercress leaves
FALL
1 medium potato
4 green beans
SPRING
8 snow peas

---

Soak the shiitake in the hot water for 20 minutes. After they are soft, trim off and discard the stems and cut the caps into ¼-inch strips.

Peel the daikon and carrot and cut into 1-inch cylinders. Then cut each cylinder lengthwise into ½-inch strips.

Cut the tofu into ½-inch cubes. It should make twelve pieces.

In a medium saucepan, combine the konbu dashi, honey, soy sauce, and sake. Bring to a simmer. Add the shiitake, daikon, and carrot. Simmer for 15 minutes. While this is simmering, prepare one of the following seasonal additions:

Winter: Steam spinach leaves for 30 seconds or until just barely wilted. In each of four serving bowls, place one cooked shrimp and 2 steamed spinach leaves.

Summer: Place 3 watercress leaves in each serving bowl.

Fall: Peel and boil one medium potato. Cut it into 8 pieces. Steam 4 green beans for 2 minutes. Cut them in half. Place 2 pieces of potato and 2 pieces of green bean in each serving bowl.

Spring: Steam 8 snow peas for one minute and place 2 snow peas in each serving bowl.

When the broth has simmered for 15 minutes, prepare the miso mixture. In a small bowl combine ½ cup of the broth and the white and red misos. Mix until all the miso is dissolved. Add the tofu cubes to the broth in the pot and simmer one minute. Then add the miso mixture and heat on low heat until the soup and tofu are hot, always keeping the broth below a simmer with no bubbles.

Ladle the broth into the four bowls prepared according to season. Sprinkle with chopped scallions.

# *Oshinko*

•

# *Pickled Daikon*

Traditionally in Japanese cuisine, the meal ends with a course of rice, miso soup, and pickles. Here is one popular pickle, a staple in Japan.

YIELDS 1 TO 1 ¼ CUPS

⅔ medium daikon (about 6 inches long)

¾ teaspoon salt

½ cup water

2-inch-square piece of wet konbu (a piece left over from making dashi can be used)

¼ cup finely chopped peeled fresh ginger root

2½ tablespoons tamari soy sauce

2 tablespoons mirin

½ teaspoon hot red pepper flakes (or to taste)

red bell pepper strips

Peel the daikon and cut it into ¼-inch slices. Place it in a deep, flat-bottomed bowl or pan. Sprinkle the salt evenly over the daikon and then squeeze the daikon pieces with your hands. Add ½ cup of water. Place a flat-bottomed dish or pan, such as a cake pan, that can be set on top of the daikon within the rim of the bowl. Put a weight (a brick or two, a heavy can, or stack of plates) on top of the cover and let it stand for 3 hours.

Cut the konbu into ⅛-inch strips with kitchen scissors. Set aside.

In a small saucepan, combine the ginger, soy sauce, and mirin and bring to a boil on medium heat. Once it comes to a boil, remove it from heat and let it cool.

Drain the daikon and then rinse so that any salt that has not been absorbed is removed. Wash the bowl.

Return the daikon to the clean bowl and mix in the konbu and red pepper flakes. Pour the ginger sauce over the daikon and replace the pan and weight. Let it stand in a cool place for 6 to 24 hours. It's hard to predict how soon the pickles will be ready, so after 6 hours, stir and taste them every couple of hours until you think they taste spicy and flavorful. Then rinse the daikon to remove the ginger, konbu, and red pepper flakes.

Garnish with strips of raw red pepper and sprinkle with soy sauce if desired. Store in a tightly covered container in the refrigerator. Oshinko will keep for a week refrigerated in a tightly sealed container.

*After the chrysanthemums,*
*Besides the daikon*
*There is nothing.*

> *Bashō*

W Y N E L L E   S T E I N

*Jewish*

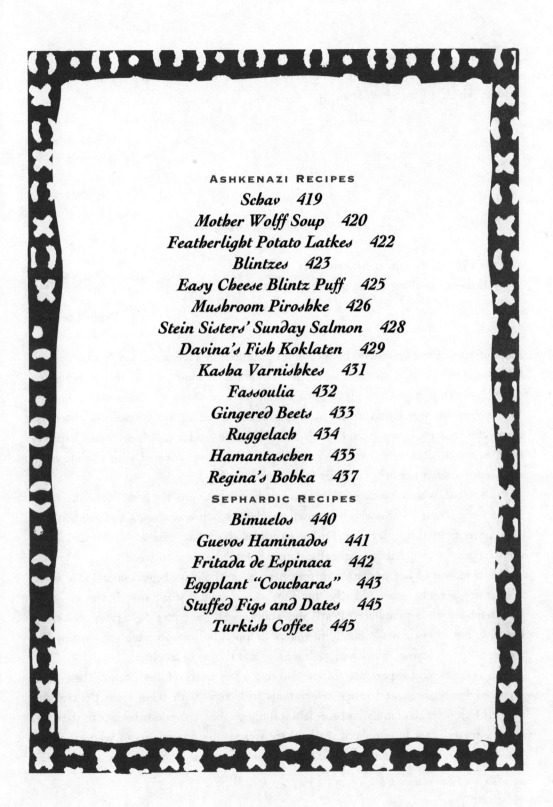

The recipes in this chapter reflect two major styles of Jewish cooking. The chapter is divided between the Ashkenazi tradition from Central and Eastern Europe and Sephardic cuisine, which originated in Spain and Portugal.

# Ashkenazi Recipes

**Az s'iz nito in top, iz nito in teller.**
"If there's nothing in the pot, there's nothing on the plate."

—Yiddish proverb

Some of my fondest childhood memories are captured in a treasured family photograph. It shows my great-grandmother, Rose, my grandmother, Molly, my mother, Davina, my sisters, and me, four generations of Jewish women at one of our countless family dinners. As the firstborn grandchild in my mother's family, I was always fawned over by these wonderful women. They would pinch my cheek and exclaim, *"Shana punim!"* (pretty face), as we children were being led to a big table that was covered with a white cloth and set for at least twenty. Then the feast would begin.

While Rose, whom we called Bubba, was still alive, she was the head cook. She was a Russian immigrant widow who had raised six children while sewing in a sweatshop, five days a week. In those days, on Friday mornings she would rise at 4 A.M. and begin preparations for the Shabbos (Sabbath) dinner before she went to work.

My memories of her preparations for Shabbos and holidays begin about 1955, when Bubba was seventy years old. By this time she shared a small row house in South Philadelphia with her daughter, Pearl. She would spend the entire day Friday cooking in her tiny, hot kitchen while family members dropped by for some tea and gossip. The atmosphere was joyous, filled with rich aromas and shouts of laughter.

This was a typical experience for an Ashkenazic Jew in the United States. The recipes prepared for Shabbos and other celebrations had come with them from Central and Eastern Europe. Each family had specialties influenced by the countries where they had lived, sometimes for hundreds of years. There were family legends about who baked the best strudel and who could make the lightest blintzes and matzoh balls. My grandmother served the finest gefilte fish and my mother, the tastiest blintzes. Rose, who only spoke Yiddish, would proclaim, *"Na"* (here) as she'd set before me the best apple strudel I've ever tasted.

My mother kept those legends alive for me by re-creating, as best she could, her mother's and her grandmother's recipes and secret ingredients. She had begged Bubba to teach her how to make strudel, but Bubba would only reveal so much. She would teach by saying, "And you will know it is right by the feel of the dough." Unfortunately, the art of her strudel-making died with her.

The pride of those women taught me the first lesson about good cooking. They always used the freshest ingredients, often creating imaginative dishes from inexpensive foods. It was clear that they loved this food that they were presenting to family and friends.

It's no wonder I felt right at home when I began working at Moosewood Restaurant many years later, though this was a very different time and place. This little haven in upstate New York was generations and miles away from my great-grandmother's kitchen, but for me the feeling was the same: a close-knit group of people working with extreme pride and love for the food that they were serving. Another familiar ingredient was alive in this place: the humor. Here, in a hot, cramped, busy kitchen, people were laughing, kibitzing, and gossiping, just like in my grandmother's kitchen. I knew I was home.

After a while, I learned that there were others at Moosewood who had backgrounds similar to mine. While cooking in the Moosewood kitchen, someone might remember a hilarious Yiddish phrase and then teach it to a co-worker, who might be a Catholic from the Midwest. I found there a shared appreciation of Jewish people and their foods, culture, and language.

Once, while I was working with David Hirsch (who can always make me laugh), he took out a large bowl and a hand-held chopping blade (in Yiddish, a *hockmesser*) and began miming someone furiously chopping. He said, "Winnie, what am I doing?" Immediately I remembered. We had often seen our grandmothers doing this frantic chopping while preparing gefilte fish. I remembered my mother telling me that when she was a girl, every Friday morning the air in her neighborhood was filled with a cacophony of chopping sounds, as the housewives prepared gefilte fish for Shabbos.

Because Moosewood highlights the vegetarian dishes prepared by different ethnic groups and cultures, many Jewish specialties have always been served. Potato and lokshen kugel, latkes, beet borscht, piroshki, and Jewish honey cake have been greatly enjoyed by our customers, many of whom had never before heard of these things.

There has traditionally been a strong vegetarian component to Jewish cuisine. The strictness of the dietary laws (kashrut) governing the preparation and kind of meat, fish, and dairy foods resulted in a cuisine rich with vegetarian possibilities. There is a school of thought that proposes that the difficulty of following kashrut was to eventually lead the Jews to a higher consciousness about eating, in other words, to become vegetarian. Jewish cooking can hardly be characterized as "vegetarian," but because the mixing of meat and dairy is prohibited by kashrut, Jewish people often serve what is called a "dairy" meal, which is meatless. Many dairy restaurants were created, especially in New York City, and they serve the best loved of these dishes. These Ashkenazic meals feature a hearty soup like Mother Wolff, or Schav, a heaping plate of Blintzes, Piroshki, or Potato Latkes, served with side dishes of beets and applesauce.

Jewish cuisine is from ancient traditions. It has been transported to many parts of the world and influenced by many cultures. What I have offered in this chapter are family recipes and some that I've created. I've also given a sampling of Sephardic cooking, which is a world of its own, quite different in origin from Ashkenazi cuisine.

*L'chayim!* (To your health!)

# Schav

•

## Sorrel Borscht

This is a tart and refreshing summer soup, always included in collections of Jewish recipes. It is traditionally prepared with sorrel, which is also called "sour grass" and "spinach rhubarb."

This perennial plant has long been prized by gardeners in Europe, which is where my family became acquainted with it. Look for sorrel in supermarkets that offer a good selection of greens, at farmers' markets, or ask your gardener friends for some. If all fails, substitute spinach, which tastes almost as good, though it lacks sorrel's distinctive sour flavor. Serve Schav with Blintzes (see page 423) for a traditional and delicious summer meal.

SERVES 6

4 cups water

2 medium potatoes, diced

2 sprigs fresh dill (a scant teaspoon dried)

3 scallions, chopped

_____

1 pound sorrel or spinach, washed, stemmed, and finely chopped

¼ cup fresh lemon juice (or to taste) (see note)

¾ teaspoon salt (or to taste)

½ teaspoon ground black pepper (or to taste)

2 tablespoons brown sugar

_____

2 eggs

1 cup cold water

_____

1 cup sour cream

chopped fresh dill or scallions

chopped cucumbers or hard-boiled eggs (optional)

In a soup pot, bring the water, potatoes, dill, and scallions to a medium boil and cook for 5 minutes. Add the chopped sorrel or spinach and the lemon juice, salt, pepper, and

Note: If using spinach, add more lemon juice to taste.

sugar. Simmer for about 10 minutes, until the potatoes are tender. Remove the pot from the heat and remove and discard the sprigs of dill.

In a large bowl, beat the eggs with the cold water until light. Very slowly pour 2 cups of the hot soup stock into the egg mixture while stirring constantly to prevent curdling. Then pour the egg mixture back into the soup pot, stirring thoroughly.

Chill until very cold, for at least 3 hours.

Just before serving, whisk in the sour cream and garnish with dill or scallions. You might also like Schav topped with chopped cucumbers or hard-boiled eggs.

## *Mother Wolff Soup*

This filling and homey soup, inspired by a recipe from *Jewish Cookery,* by Leah Leonard, can be served as a main course. My mother remembers her grandfather, Charles Klein, a fine Jewish baker, enjoying a version of this soup at midafternoon with thick slices of his fresh pumpernickel bread and beets or a baked apple. Prepare this soup while spending a long morning baking, especially on a cold winter day, and you will satisfy the soul.

### SERVES 8 TO 10

4 quarts water
½ cup dried lima beans, soaked overnight with water to cover, or brought to a boil and then soaked for 1 hour
½ cup uncooked rice (or 1 cup cooked rice)
½ cup barley
3–4 large garlic cloves, minced
1 tablespoon dried dill weed
1 bay leaf

1 cup diced onions

1 cup chopped celery
2 tablespoons vegetable oil
1 tablespoon sweet Hungarian paprika
1 cup diced potatoes
1 cup diced sweet potatoes or carrots
½ teaspoon salt
several pinches of ground black pepper
1 cup green beans or peas (fresh or frozen)

1 cup chopped tomatoes (fresh or canned) or tomato sauce
¼ cup chopped fresh parsley (optional)

In a large soup pot, combine the water, limas, rice, barley, garlic, dill, and bay leaf and bring to a boil. Lower the heat, cover, and simmer for 1½ hours, adding more water if needed as the limas and barley absorb liquid.

When the soup has been simmering for about an hour, prepare the vegetables. In a large frying pan, sauté the onions and celery in the oil for a few minutes. Sprinkle in the paprika. Add the potatoes, sweet potatoes or carrots, salt, and pepper. Cover and cook for a few minutes, stirring frequently. Stir in the green beans or peas and continue to cook, covered, for a few more minutes until just tender. Set aside.

Stir the soup and remove the bay leaf. Add the sautéed vegetables, the tomatoes, the parsley, if desired, and more salt and pepper to taste. Simmer, covered, on very low heat for 1½ to 2 more hours, stirring occasionally to prevent sticking.

To serve, ladle out generous bowls of this tasty soup. Leftovers will keep for several days, refrigerated. When reheating, add boiling water if the soup has become too thick.

# *Featherlight Potato Latkes*

At Channukah time, I've made these with my son Aaron's grade school class. Ithaca has quite an international community—Aaron's classmates are children from upstate New York, Laos, Cambodia, and Chile. I've made new latke fans of them all.

This method of blending the ingredients in a food processor or blender makes the work easy and creates extremely light, crisp latkes. Get busy, or as my grandmother would say, "Stop lying there like a latke."

YIELDS 15 LATKES, 2 ½ INCHES IN DIAMETER
SERVES 4

*6 medium potatoes*
*1 small onion, peeled and quartered*

*pinch of baking powder*
*freshly ground black pepper to taste*

---

*2 large eggs*
*¼ cup unbleached white flour (or*
  *matzo meal)*
*½ teaspoon salt*

*vegetable oil for frying*

---

*sour cream*

Grate the potatoes in a food processor or on the largest grating side of a hand grater. Drain the grated potatoes in a colander, pressing out the liquid.

Finely chop the onion using the steel blade in the processor or grate on the smallest grating side of a hand grater.

If using a food processor, return the potatoes to the bowl, add all of the other ingredients, except the oil and sour cream, and process until just smooth and evenly colored. If using a blender, it will be easier to mix the ingredients in two batches. Put an egg and half of the other ingredients (except oil and sour cream) in the bottom of the blender with the grated potatoes and onion on top. Whirl on high speed until well blended. Repeat this with the remaining ingredients. If you do not have either machine available, combine the grated potatoes and onion with the other ingredients in a mixing bowl. Handmade latkes will have a more traditional texture.

Heat ⅛ inch of oil in a large heavy skillet, preferably cast iron, until a drop of batter sizzles on the surface. Drop a large spoonful of batter into the skillet and flatten it with the spoon to make a thin pancake. Fry the latkes on both sides until brown and crisp, adding more oil if necessary. Drain the latkes on paper towels and keep them warm, in a single layer in a 200° oven, until all the latkes are made.

Serve immediately, topped with sour cream and with a side of applesauce and/or Gingered Beets (see page 433). My son likes them drizzled with maple syrup or with a "schmear" of jam.

# *Blintzes*

Blintzes are the ultimate Jewish delicacy. When I was growing up, I often ate blintzes with chilled beet borscht on hot summer evenings. My grandmother would make at least a hundred and send a heaping plateful to each of her children's households. It was a much loved gift that her grandchildren gobbled up in no time.

This family recipe combines my mother's delicate pancakes with Grandmom Rae's savory filling. It will serve six for breakfast, lunch, or dinner. Arrange a bountiful plate of blintzes and serve them at your next party alongside salad and fruit.

### YIELDS 20 BLINTZES

**FILLING**

*1½ pounds farmer cheese*
*½ pound cottage cheese*
*2 eggs*
*2 bunches scallions (green parts only),*
 *finely chopped*
*salt and ground black pepper to taste*

**PANCAKE BATTER**

*4 large eggs*

*2½ cups water*
*2 teaspoons salt*
*2½ cups unbleached white flour*

———————————

*butter for frying*
*sour cream (optional)*

For the filling, combine ingredients and set aside until the pancakes are made.

The pancake batter can be mixed in a blender or food processor or by hand. If using a blender or processor, just purée the batter ingredients until smooth. If mixing by hand, in a large bowl, beat the eggs well with the water. Stir in the salt and flour. The mixture will be lumpy. Put the batter through a colander twice, stirring with a rubber spatula, until all the batter is forced through and fairly smooth.

The batter should be thin enough so that it will "sheet" off a spoon. If it does not seem thin enough, add one tablespoon of water and mix well. You might need to do this again during cooking if the batter thickens while standing.

To fry the pancakes, lightly butter an 8-inch crêpe or frying pan. Heat the pan until it is hot enough that the pancake forms immediately when the batter is poured. Pour about 3 tablespoons of batter into the hot pan and tilt it quickly to coat the bottom. The pancake should be very thin. Cook for about a minute, until the edges start to curl and the bottom is lightly browned, and then turn it out onto a flat surface, fried side down, to cool. Repeat until all the batter is used. It should make about 20 pancakes. Be sure the pan stays hot. Add a little more butter after making each pancake. You may want to use 2 crêpe pans simultaneously to speed the process.

To fill the blintzes, spread one heaping tablespoon of filling along the bottom edge of the cooked side of each pancake. Roll the pancake up over the filling once. Fold the sides in and continue to roll it into a neat, egg roll–like package.

Melt 2 tablespoons of butter in a large frying pan. Fry the blintzes until golden brown on each side, adding more butter if necessary. Serve hot with a dollop of sour cream if desired.

Serve blintzes preceded by a first course of chilled Cherry Soup (see page 262) for a wonderful brunch or dinner.

*Variation* Omit the scallions and top with fruit preserves.

---

*Note: If you want to make blintzes ahead of time, refrigerate or freeze them after rolling them up. Then fry them just before serving. Frozen filled blintzes need not be thawed, but will need to fry a bit longer.*

---

# Easy Cheese Blintz Puff

This dish is close in taste to blintzes, but requires less time to prepare. Fast and delicious, it will serve eight or more as a brunch entrée or dessert. The source of this recipe is from *The Jewish Holiday Cookbook: An International Collection of Recipes and Customs* by Gloria Kaufer Greene.

At Moosewood, we often host benefit brunches for local organizations, and Easy Cheese Blintz Puff, served topped with blueberries and strawberries, has become one of our favorite offerings.

### SERVES 8 AS AN ENTRÉE

**BATTER**

*4 large eggs*
*1¼ cups milk*
*2 tablespoons sour cream or plain*
    *yogurt*
*¼ cup melted butter or margarine*
*¾ teaspoon pure vanilla extract*
*1⅓ cups unbleached white flour*
*1 tablespoon sugar*
*1¼ tablespoons baking powder*

**FILLING**

*about 1 pound farmer cheese*

*1 pound ricotta cheese*
*2 large eggs*
*2 tablespoons sugar*
*2 tablespoons fresh lemon juice*

**TOPPINGS**

*dollop of sour cream or yogurt (plain or*
    *vanilla)*
*applesauce*
*blueberries, strawberries, or cherries*
    *heated with sweetener or fruit*
    *conserve and a dash of cinnamon*

Preheat the oven to 350°.

With a blender or mixer, combine the batter ingredients until very smooth. Pour 1½ cups of the batter into a buttered 9x13-inch baking pan. Bake for about 10 minutes or until set.

Meanwhile, combine the filling ingredients and mix well.

When the bottom layer of batter has set, remove the baking pan from the oven and smoothly spread the cheese filling over it. Briefly remix the remaining batter and then gently pour it over the filling, covering it completely. Return the pan to the oven and continue to bake for 45 to 50 minutes or until the top is puffed, set, and browned.

Remove the Blintz Puff from oven and allow it to rest for 10 minutes before cutting it into squares.

Serve immediately, plain or with toppings.

*Variation* For a savory Blintz Puff, omit the vanilla and sugar from the batter and the sugar from the filling. Add one bunch of finely chopped scallions to the filling and serve topped with sour cream or yogurt and additional chopped fresh scallions.

# *Mushroom Piroshke*

My friend and co-worker, Sara Robbins, and I created this dish with our fathers' Russian-Jewish heritage in mind. We share their love of rich, hearty food, served up with lots of laughter and much controversial conversation: our idea of a perfect meal.

### YIELDS 8 PASTRIES

**DOUGH**

1 package dry yeast (about 1 tablespoon)

1 teaspoon honey

1 cup lukewarm water

1½ cups whole wheat flour

1½ cups unbleached white flour

⅓ cup vegetable oil

1 teaspoon salt

**FILLING**

1 cup finely chopped onions

2 garlic cloves, minced

2 tablespoons vegetable oil

½ ounce dried mushrooms (wild, shiitake, porcini, or any other interesting variety), soaked in hot water until soft

1 cup finely chopped fresh mushrooms

salt to taste

3 ounces cream cheese, softened

½ cup chopped scallions

1 teaspoon dried dill weed

½ teaspoon freshly ground black pepper

2 slices pumpernickel bread

1 cup cottage cheese

3 hard-boiled eggs, finely chopped

---

1 egg yolk beaten with 1 tablespoon water

poppy seeds for sprinkling on top

To prepare the dough, dissolve the yeast and honey in the warm water and set it aside for about 10 minutes. Combine the flours. Mix the oil, salt, and 2 cups of the flour into the dissolved yeast. Stir for 100 strokes. Let this batter sit for half an hour, until it bubbles (this is called a "sponge"). Mix in the remaining cup of flour, turn the dough out onto a floured surface, and knead it for 10 minutes. Place the dough in a lightly oiled bowl, cover it with a damp cloth, and let it rise in a warm place until doubled in size, about one hour.

To prepare the filling, sauté the onions and garlic in the oil for 5 minutes. Meanwhile, drain the soaking dried mushrooms and chop them coarsely. Add these and the fresh mushrooms to the pan, sprinkle with salt, and continue to sauté, covered, for 7 more minutes. Pour the hot mushroom mixture over the softened cream cheese. Add the scallions, dill, and pepper. Stir thoroughly. Crumble the bread into the cream cheese–mushroom mixture. Mix in the cottage cheese and eggs. Adjust the seasonings.

To assemble the piroshke, preheat the oven to 375°. Punch down the dough and divide it into eight equal pieces. Flatten each piece with your hands and then roll it out into a 6-inch square, about ⅛ inch thick. Place ½ cup of the filling in the center of each square. Bring the 4 corners of each of the squares to the center and pinch tightly along the top edges. Place the piroshke on a lightly oiled baking sheet.

Brush the tops of each piroshke with the egg yolk–water mixture and sprinkle with poppy seeds. Bake for 30 minutes, until golden brown.

Serve with Mother Wolff Soup (see page 420) and a side of Gingered Beets (see page 433) for a warming winter meal. For a buffet à la Russe, serve with heaping bowls of Kasha Varnishkes (page 431), fresh applesauce, and Sweet and Sour Red Cabbage (see *New Recipes from Moosewood Restaurant,* page 209).

# Stein Sisters' Sunday Salmon

During an early morning walk on the beach while visiting my sister, Joyce, in Newport, Rhode Island, we began to reminisce about our childhood Sunday breakfasts of smoked fish, bagels, and cream cheese. We began to crave those tastes, so we went to her favorite fish market, where the salmon was wonderfully fresh, and then home where we made up this tasty baked frittata. It features the tastes of both lox and fresh salmon. We served it for brunch with bagels and fresh fruit. Serve it for supper with dark pumpernickel bread and a green salad with a tart dressing.

## SERVES 4 TO 6 AS A MAIN DISH OR 6 TO 8 AS A SIDE DISH

4 medium potatoes, thinly sliced

2 medium onions, chopped

2 tablespoons butter

¼ pound lox (Nova Scotia or salty), cut into pieces

2 tablespoons minced fresh dill

salt and freshly ground black pepper to taste

½ pound fresh salmon steak

1 tablespoon fresh lemon juice

6 ounces cream cheese, cubed

4 eggs

1¼ cups milk

sweet Hungarian paprika

Parboil the potato slices for 5 minutes. Drain them and set aside.

Meanwhile, sauté the onions in the butter. When the onions are just translucent, add the lox and dill and continue to sauté for a few minutes more. Season with salt and pepper.

While the onions and lox are cooking, boil about an inch of water in the bottom of a saucepan. Place the fresh salmon steak in a steamer rack or colander that fits inside the pan. Sprinkle the salmon with lemon juice, and steam, covered, for 5 to 8 minutes, until it flakes easily.

Skin and bone the steamed salmon and flake it into a large bowl. Stir in the lox mixture.

Butter a 9x9-inch baking dish. Line the bottom with the potatoes. Sprinkle on the cubes of cream cheese and then spread on the onion-lox-salmon mixture. Beat together the eggs and milk with more salt and pepper and pour it over the other ingredients in the pan. Lightly dust the top with paprika.

Bake at 375° for about 40 minutes, until puffed, golden, and firm. Serve immediately, cut into squares.

## *Davina's Fish Koklaten*

*Koklaten* is Yiddish for a very generous patty. Generosity has always been the rule at my mother's table; this is her recipe for fish cakes that are well seasoned, savory, light, and golden brown.

Cracker meal or matzo meal creates the light outer coating for the fish cakes. Look for it in the grocery store next to bread crumbs or make your own (see note, page 430).

### YIELDS 4 TO 6 MAIN DISH SERVINGS OR 2 DOZEN APPETIZERS

*2 large potatoes, peeled and quartered*

*1 medium onion, quartered*

*1 large carrot, cut into chunks*

*1 teaspoon salt*

*1 teaspoon freshly ground black pepper*

*1 tablespoon butter*

---

*1 pound firm white fish fillets, such as cod, scrod, haddock, or hake*

---

*1 large egg*

*1 tablespoon mayonnaise*

*2 teaspoons Dijon mustard*

*1 garlic clove, pressed or minced*

*couple dashes Tabasco or other hot sauce*

*1/2 teaspoon sweet Hungarian paprika*

*2 teaspoons dried dill weed*

*salt and freshly ground black pepper to taste*

---

*cracker meal or matzo meal*

---

*oil for frying (half vegetable, half olive is best)*

---

*2 lemons, cut into wedges*

In a large saucepan, place the potatoes, onion, carrot, salt, pepper, and butter in water to cover. Bring to a rolling boil and then lower the heat, cover, and simmer until the vegetables are almost tender, 15 to 20 minutes. Add the fish, return to a simmer, and cook for about 8 minutes, until the fish flakes with a fork and the vegetables are very soft. Drain in a colander, reserving the liquid if desired, and set aside to cool. (The liquid can be used for fish stews or soup.)

In a large bowl, mash the drained vegetables and fish with a potato masher or fork until quite thoroughly mixed. Add the egg, mayonnaise, mustard, garlic, and seasonings and mix vigorously.

Coat the bottom of a large plate with a layer of cracker or matzo meal. Pat and shape the fish mixture into six large, rounded cakes. Gently roll each cake in the meal until thoroughly coated.

Heat ¼ inch of oil in a frying pan until it sizzles. Fry the cakes 4 to 5 minutes on each side, until golden brown. Drain well on paper towels. Or, if you prefer not to fry the koklaten, bake them on an oiled pan at 350° for about 45 minutes or until browned.

Serve with lemon wedges. For a simple and easy meal, serve with green salad or Fassoulia (see page 432). Koklaten are also delicious with Kasha Varnishkes (see page 431) and Gingered Beets (see page 433).

*Variation* Prepare as an appetizer by shaping the fish mixture into about 2 dozen little cakes 1½ inches in diameter. Fry or bake them until browned. Serve them with lemon wedges and homemade dill mayonnaise (See *New Recipes from Moosewood Restaurant*).

---

*Note: You can make cracker or matzo meal with a food processor, blender, or by hand. Whirl good quality crackers or matzo in either machine, or place them in a paper bag or between two sheets of waxed paper and crush with a rolling pin.*

---

# Kasha Varnishkes

*Kasha* is the Russian name for buckwheat, which is not a member of the wheat family as might be expected, but a relative of the rhubarb plant. Its seed is treated as a grain and roasted, which produces a food very high in protein and vitamins, with a nutty, rich flavor. Kasha was the nutritious daily fare of the poorer Jews of Russia; Kasha Varnishkes was prepared for special occasions. Sometimes I double this recipe and take it to potluck dinners, where it is always enjoyed for its simple, good taste.

## SERVES 4 AS A MAIN COURSE OR 6 TO 8 AS A SIDE DISH

*1 cup roasted buckwheat groats (kasha)*
*(see page 655)*
*1 beaten egg*
*2 cups vegetable stock (see page 685) or*
*water*
*½ cup chopped onions*
*1 cup sliced mushrooms (optional)*

*2 tablespoons butter or margarine*
*½ teaspoon salt*
*¼ teaspoon ground black pepper*

---

*8 ounces bow-tie or square egg noodles*
*(usually found in pasta or kosher*
*section of a supermarket)*

In a small bowl, stir the kasha into the beaten egg and set aside. Meanwhile, heat the stock or water to a simmer.

In a large, heavy skillet, lightly sauté the onions and mushrooms, if used, in the butter until the onions are lightly browned. Add the egg-coated kasha and, on high heat, stir and chop the kasha with a fork or wooden spoon for about 3 minutes, until the egg has dried and the kasha kernels are mostly separate. Quickly and carefully add the hot liquid, leaning away from the skillet to avoid being splattered. Stir in the salt and pepper. Cover with a tightly fitting lid, reduce the heat to low, and steam the kasha for 10 to 15 minutes. Check to see if all the liquid has been absorbed. If not, steam for a few minutes more.

Meanwhile, cook the noodles in boiling salted water until tender; drain and set aside. When the kasha is done, add the drained noodles to the skillet and toss, adding more butter, salt, and pepper to taste. Serve piping hot.

Serve Kasha Varnishkes with Gingered Beets (see page 433) and fresh applesauce for a complete winter supper.

# Fassoulia

•

## Sephardic Green Beans

This ancient Sephardic dish includes allspice, which reveals a more recent Turkish influence. The allspice is added to a "bouquet garni" (a clean piece of cheesecloth, or, in Yiddish, a *schmate,* filled with spices or herbs). The beans stew until very tender in an aromatic broth, along with sweet pearl onions, and can be served on couscous as a main course or alone as a tasty side dish.

I've included this in the Ashkenazi section because it can serve as a tasty cross-cultural companion to Davina's Fish Koklaten (see page 429) or Mushroom Piroshke (see page 426), or serve Kasha Varnishkes (see page 431) as the main course and Fassoulia as a side dish for a filling, unusual dinner.

### SERVES 4 TO 6 AS A MAIN DISH OR 6 TO 8 AS A SIDE DISH

12–15 pearl onions (fresh or frozen)
2 pounds fresh green beans
1 teaspoon whole allspice
¼ teaspoon whole black peppercorns

3 garlic cloves, pressed or minced

2 tablespoons vegetable oil
2 tomatoes, coarsely chopped
1 teaspoon salt
1 cup water
pinch of brown sugar (optional)

If using fresh pearl onions, drop them whole into boiling water and boil for 3 minutes, then plunge into cold water. This makes peeling the onions much easier. Carefully cut off the stem ends and slip off the skins. Set aside.

Remove the tip ends and stems of the green beans and cut each bean in half on the diagonal.

Make a bouquet garni by placing the allspice and peppercorns in a small piece of cheesecloth, any clean porous fabric, or a coffee filter. Tie to close with string or thread.

In a large saucepan, sauté the garlic in the oil for a minute, stirring to prevent burning. Mix in the tomatoes, onions, beans, and salt. Continue to sauté for a couple more minutes. Add the water, sugar, if desired, and the bouquet garni. Bring to a boil, and then reduce the heat, cover, and simmer for 30 minutes or until the beans are very tender. Remove the bouquet garni and adjust the salt and pepper to taste.

If you serve Fassoulia as a main dish, try it on couscous, topped with chopped almonds.

## *Gingered Beets*

Beets abound in Jewish (Ashkenazi) cooking. Often served as a first course, Beet Borscht and Russian Cabbage Borscht are featured in any basic Jewish cookbook. As a favorite for many years at the restaurant, they are also featured in the *Moosewood Cookbook*. This side dish, however, jazzes up the humble beet with the zing of ginger and mustard, and makes a colorful companion to Featherlight Potato Latkes (see page 422), Davina's Fish Koklaten (see page 429), or Mushroom Piroshke (see page 426). See the note at the end of this recipe for a simple way to prepare the delicious, nutritious beet greens.

### SERVES 4 TO 6

| | |
|---|---|
| *3 large beets* | *1–2 tablespoons brown sugar* |
| _____ | *¼ teaspoon salt* |
| *1 tablespoon butter* | *1½ teaspoons ground ginger* |
| *1 tablespoon unbleached white flour* | *¼ teaspoon dry mustard (or to taste)* |
| *2 tablespoons fresh lemon juice* | |

Cut off the beet greens, leaving 1-inch stems, and set aside. Scrub the beets well and place them, whole and unpeeled, in a saucepan with salted water to cover. Cook at a medium boil for about 45 minutes or until the beets can be easily pierced with a knife.

Drain the cooked beets, reserving ½ cup of the beet liquid (save the rest for borscht or soup). When the beets are cool enough to handle, slip off the skins and cut away the stems and roots. Slice the beets into ¼-inch rounds and then cut into strips.

In a medium saucepan, melt the butter. Whisk in the flour and brown it slightly, stirring often. Add ½ cup of beet liquid and whisk until smooth. Stir in the other ingredients and the beet strips. Heat through on low heat for 3 to 5 minutes.

> *Note: To simply prepare beet greens, thoroughly wash, drain, and coarsely chop them. Steam without any additional water in a covered pot for 5 minutes. Drain and toss with butter, or 2 tablespoons of olive oil in which a minced garlic clove was sautéed. Add salt and pepper to taste and serve topped with toasted sesame seeds.*

# Ruggelach

These little rolled pastries are sometimes known in German as *schnecken.* Bountiful plates of these delicacies are served on Rosh Hashanah (the Jewish New Year) to ensure a sweet year. They are also served at Channukah in memory of the legend of Judith, a daughter of the Maccabees. She served cheesecakes to General Holofernes along with much wine. When he became drunk she killed him, and her people were saved.

Traditionally, ruggelach are made with a raisin filling. My mother's chocolate-chip filling is a delicious, modern variation.

### YIELDS 6 DOZEN PASTRIES

PASTRY
1 cup unsalted butter, softened
2 3-ounce packages cream cheese,
  softened
2¾ cups unbleached white flour
¼ teaspoon salt

RAISIN FILLING
½ cup sugar
⅔ cup finely chopped raisins
½ cup finely chopped walnuts
2 teaspoons cinnamon

CHOCOLATE-CHIP FILLING
¾ cup semi-sweet mini chocolate pieces
¾ cup finely chopped walnuts
½ cup sugar
1 tablespoon unsweetened powdered
  cocoa
½ teaspoon cinnamon

GLAZE
1 beaten egg yolk
¼ cup water
¼ cup sugar

For the pastry, in a large mixing bowl, cream the butter and cream cheese until light and fluffy. Add the flour and salt and knead the dough lightly until well mixed. Wrap the dough in waxed paper or plastic and chill for at least 2 hours.

Meanwhile, prepare the filling of your choice by combining all of the ingredients. Set aside.

When the dough has chilled for a couple of hours and you're ready to bake the ruggelach, divide the dough into nine equal pieces. Work with one piece at a time and keep the rest refrigerated. Roll each piece of dough into an 8-inch circle. Sprinkle the dough all over with about one-ninth of the filling. Gently press the filling into the pastry. Cut the circle into eight pie-shaped wedges. Starting at the base of each wedge, roll to the point to form little horn-shaped pastries. Place each ruggelach, point-side down, on an unoiled baking sheet. Continue with the rest of the dough. When you have almost finished forming all the ruggelach, preheat the oven to 375°.

Combine the egg yolk with the water. Brush the tops with the beaten egg yolk mixture and sprinkle with sugar. Bake for 15 minutes or until golden brown.

> *Note: This is a very soft dough. For easier handling, roll the dough out on a piece of waxed paper.*

## *Hamantaschen*

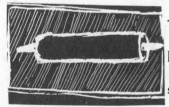

These yummy pastries, traditionally filled with poppy seeds and honey, are served during Purim, a holiday that celebrates the story of Queen Esther of Persia. She helped bring down wicked Haman, who had planned to kill all Persian Jews. Jewish people worldwide remember this story with special foods. German Jews make little triangular pastries, shaped like Haman's tricornered hat. Italian Jews have a variation called "Haman's Ears," after his ears, which were supposedly shaped like a donkey's. In Holland, Jews make a Haman gingerbread man, and the Sephardim have a pasta dish called "Haman's Hair."

Jewish history is often transmitted through a particular food. Special local celebrations have sometimes been created to commemorate some averted disaster within a particular

Jewish community. Prune-filled Hamantaschen are said to have been created in 1731 in Bohemia where a man named David Brandeis was falsely accused of selling poisonous plum jam but was later proven innocent. Hence a town holiday called "Brandeis Purim" resulted, and now prune-filled Hamantaschen are a holiday pastry served all over the world.

### YIELDS 40 HAMANTASCHEN

**DOUGH**

*1 cup butter, softened to room*
  *temperature*
*2 cups sugar*
*2 eggs*
*4 teaspoons baking powder*
*5 cups flour*
*4 teaspoons orange juice*
*2 teaspoons pure vanilla extract*

**FILLING**

*1 cup pitted prunes*
*⅔ cup raisins*
*1⅓ cups prune butter (see note)*
*½ cup unsweetened grated coconut*
*⅔ cup chopped walnuts*

For the dough, cream the butter and sugar until smooth. Add the eggs and mix well. In a separate bowl, stir the baking powder into the flour until well distributed. Add the flour mixture and juice alternately to the creamed mixture. Stir in the vanilla. Refrigerate for at least ½ hour.

Meanwhile, for the filling, put the prunes and raisins into a saucepan with water to cover. Bring to a boil, turn down the heat, and simmer for 5 minutes. Drain. Immediately purée the hot prunes and raisins with the prune butter in a food processor or blender. Be careful not to overprocess. If you use a blender, you'll need to stop it often to push down the prunes and raisins. Mix the purée with the coconut and nuts.

To make the filling by hand, finely mince the prunes and raisins and then, in a mixing bowl, combine with the prune butter, coconut, and nuts.

*Notes: Hamantaschen freeze very well. Put them in a plastic bag when they're cool and then into the freezer. When ready to serve, thaw them at room temperature for an hour or two. Truly, it's as if they were never frozen.*

*Prune butter is found in supermarkets shelved near apple butter.*

Allow the filling to cool to room temperature.

Preheat the oven to 375°.

Work with half of the chilled dough at a time. On a well-floured surface, roll the dough out to ¼-inch thickness. Cut into circles with a 3-inch cookie cutter or glass. Put one teaspoon of filling in the center of each circle. Pull 3 points of the circle of dough up over the filling to the center to form a triangle. Pinch the dough together along the top seams. Place the filled Hamantaschen about 2 inches apart on a buttered baking sheet. Rework the scraps of dough to get about 20 pastries from each half of the chilled dough.

Bake for 20 to 25 minutes, until lightly browned.

## *Regina's Bobka*

Penny Goldin Condon, a much-loved Moosewood worker and teacher extraordinaire, shared this family recipe with me. This luscious Romanian coffeecake was made in her mother Regina's family bakery in Newport, Rhode Island. The bakery was just around the corner from Touro Synagogue, which was founded 250 years ago by Spanish Jews and is the oldest continuous place of worship in the United States. George Washington spoke there about religious freedom, and later it became a refuge as part of the underground railroad. Many people visiting this historic landmark would stop in to the Goldin's bakery to buy wonderful cakes like this one.

Prepare the dough the night before and the next day bake one of the best coffeecakes you've ever tasted.

YIELDS 8 TO 10 SERVINGS

**BATTER**
*½ pound butter*
*½ cup milk*

---

*2½ cups unbleached white flour*
*¼ teaspoon salt*
*2 tablespoons sugar*

---

*2 packages dry yeast (about 2 tablespoons)*
*¼ cup warm water*

*3 eggs, separated*
**FILLING**
*1 cup water*
*½ cup sugar*
*1 cup chopped walnuts*
*1 cup golden raisins*
*grated rind of 1 lemon*
*1 teaspoon cinnamon*

---

*½ cup sugar*

For the batter, heat the butter and milk just until the butter melts. Set aside to cool.

Sift the flour into a large bowl with the salt and sugar. Dissolve the yeast in the water and mix in the egg yolks. Stir the cooled milk and butter mixture into the flour and then add the yeast mixture. Mix well and refrigerate, covered, overnight or for at least 12 hours. Refrigerate the egg whites.

For the filling, combine the water and ½ cup of sugar in a saucepan and bring to a boil. Add the rest of the filling ingredients and cook on low heat until thick, about 10 minutes. If you make the filling in advance, refrigerate it.

To assemble the bobka, bring the egg whites to room temperature. Beat the whites until foamy, and, while still beating, slowly add ½ cup sugar until peaks form.

Preheat the oven to 350°.

Remove the dough from the refrigerator just before you roll it out. Divide the dough in half. On a well-floured surface with a floured rolling pin, roll each half into a 12x24-inch rectangle. Work quickly because the dough becomes softer and more difficult to handle as it warms up. Spread half of the meringue and then half of the filling on each rectangle to within 1 inch of the sides. Roll the long side up like a jelly roll and seal the short ends together. Place one roll inside a buttered 10-inch tube or bundt pan. Lay the other roll on top.

Bake for 45 to 60 minutes, until firm and almost bread-like on top. Let the bobka cool. Turn it out onto a plate, put a serving plate on top, and reverse the cake to its original position.

# Sephardic Recipes

During the Spanish Inquisition in the fifteenth century, Jews in Spain and Portugal were given the choice of converting to Christianity or leaving the country. They had lived on the Iberian peninsula, which in Hebrew is Sephard, for nearly a thousand years and many held prominent positions as teachers, doctors, poets, and scholars. Nevertheless, many chose to migrate to Turkey, Greece, Italy, north Africa, the Balkans, the Middle East, and later to as far away as Mexico and the United States, bringing with them their ancient traditions and Mediterranean tastes. Today, many Sephardim still speak Ladino, a cross-cultural Spanish that has been altered during their migrations, in the same manner in which Yiddish was created as the Ashkenazim moved through northern, central, and eastern Europe.

It is told that during this migration the Sephardim took eggplant and fennel to Italy, forever changing that country's cuisine. At the same time, Sephardic cooking was influenced by the countries where the Sephardim found asylum. The presence of feta cheese, pine nuts, mint, raisins, and couscous in many Sephardic dishes, for instance, reflects a Middle Eastern influence. But basic culinary tastes remain: a love of eggplant, olive oil, and garlic, and the frequent use of tomatoes, peppers, and rice. Their use of matzoh in many dishes unites the Sephardim and Ashkenazim to their ancient origins.

My personal introduction as an Ashkenazic Jew to Sephardic cuisine began when, as a young girl, I met my lifelong friend, Janice Weltman, whose mother's family are Turkish Jews. The Crespi family brought Turkish rugs, coffeepots, and brass serving platters along with them to New York City, as well as a wonderful collection of Sephardic specialties. I had the opportunity to sample many of the recipes at Desayuno, a breakfast or brunch served on holidays, on the Sabbath after Synagogue, or on any special occasion that brings the family together. Some of these dishes are traditionally served at Passover. With the help of Janice's mother, Mary Crespi Weltman, I was able to compile recipes for some Desayuno dishes.

In the Crespi family tradition, the Desayuno includes Fritada de Espinaca, a baked spinach cheese soufflé, "Coucharas," eggplant au gratin appetizers, Bimuelos, fried matzo pancakes with ground walnuts, and Borekas, cheese-filled filo triangles (see *New Recipes from Moosewood Restaurant*). Also offered would be Guevos Haminados (eggs hard boiled in coffee), plates of feta cheese and olives, melons and grapes, and a sweet tray (Dulces) of crescent-shaped almond cookies, halvah, Jordan almonds, Stuffed Figs and Dates, and beautiful little marzipan fruits. The meal ends with mint tea or demitasse of Turkish coffee.

The following collection of recipes only touches on the vast cuisine of a culture spread throughout the world. I hope these recipes will inspire you to offer Desayuno to your friends and family.

## *Bimuelos*

The Ashkenazim serve fried matzo at Passover time, made either as a single large pancake (matzo brie) or scrambled and topped with jam. This Sephardic version of individual pancakes includes ground walnuts and is topped with an aromatic syrup. Serve for breakfast or as an unusual dessert.

YIELDS 4 SMALL PANCAKES (1 SERVING)—MULTIPLY BY THE NUMBER OF PEOPLE YOU'RE COOKING FOR

PANCAKES

*1 sheet matzo (egg matzo is especially good)*

*1 beaten egg*

*2 teaspoons ground walnuts*

*salt and freshly ground black pepper to taste*

*oil for frying*

SYRUP

*5 tablespoons honey*

*1 tablespoon orange juice*

*grated rind of 1 orange*

*1 teaspoon cinnamon*

Break up the matzo and place it in a bowl. Cover it with warm water, soak it for a minute or so, and then squeeze out all the water. Combine the softened matzo with the remaining pancake ingredients.

Coat the bottom of a heavy frying pan with about ¼ inch of oil. Heat it until a bit of batter sizzles on the surface. Drop tablespoonfuls of batter into the hot oil. Fry until crisp and browned on each side. Drain on paper towels.

Heat all of the syrup ingredients in a saucepan for a few minutes. Drizzle a tablespoon of syrup over each serving of pancakes. This makes enough syrup for 16 pancakes. Leftover syrup will keep for several weeks, refrigerated, stored in a tightly sealed jar. Reheat before serving.

## *Guevos Haminados*

·

## *Hard-Boiled Eggs, Sephardic Style*

This centuries-old Sephardic method of cooking hard-boiled eggs results in caramel brown eggs with a creamy texture and a light coffee flavor. The traditional method of cooking the eggs overnight intensifies the flavor. Save some onion skins and try a batch.

These eggs are a must as a part of the Sephardic Passover Seder meal and are also prepared overnight for the Sabbath Desayuno. Serve them, peeled and cut into wedges, with Greek olives and cubes of feta cheese for a snack or appetizer. Guevos Haminados are good warm from the oven for breakfast, alone or with Bimuelos (see page 440).

YIELDS 12 HARD-BOILED EGGS

*outer skins from 6 yellow onions*   *1 teaspoon salt (optional)*
*12 eggs*   *2 tablespoons olive or vegetable oil*
*⅓ cup ground coffee*

Oven method: Line a casserole dish with the onion skins. Place the eggs on top and cover with another layer of onion skins. Sprinkle on the coffee and salt. Drizzle on the oil. Pour in enough water to cover the eggs. Cover tightly and cook in a slow 225° oven for 6 hours or, preferably, overnight.

Stove method: Place all the ingredients in a saucepan with a tightly fitting lid and add water to cover. Bring the eggs to a boil, cover, and lower the heat to a simmer. Simmer for about 6 hours, adding more water as necessary.

## *Fritada de Espinaca*

•

## *Spinach Soufflé*

This Sephardic version of a baked omelet is cut into squares and served cold by Turkish Jews on Saturday morning after Synagogue. It is traditionally made with kashkaval cheese, a sharp yellow cheese used in the Balkans and the Middle East. If you can find it at the market or a Middle Eastern food store, use it in place of the cheddar and Romano. I serve this fritada, warm or cold, as a main dish, side dish, or appetizer. For a tasty summer brunch, serve with slices of melon, Guevos Haminados (see page 441), and Paklava (see page 86).

*1 1/2 pounds fresh spinach (or 2
    10-ounce packages frozen chopped
    spinach, defrosted)*

*1/2 cup matzo meal or bread crumbs*
*2 cups grated sharp cheddar cheese*
*6 eggs, thoroughly beaten*
*1 pound cottage, pot, farmer, or feta
    cheese (or a mixture)*

*1/2 cup grated Romano or Parmesan
    cheese*
*2 tablespoons olive oil*
*salt and freshly ground black pepper to
    taste*
*1/4 teaspoon nutmeg, preferably freshly
    grated*

Preheat oven to 350°.

If using fresh spinach, wash and stem it and then steam it (see page 681) until just soft. Drain it, squeezing out the excess liquid, and then chop it. If using frozen spinach, simply squeeze out all the excess liquid.

Set aside 1/4 cup of the matzo meal or bread crumbs and 1/4 cup of the cheddar cheese. In a large bowl, mix the spinach thoroughly with the rest of the ingredients.

Oil a 9x13-inch baking pan. Dust the bottom of the pan with the reserved matzo meal. Spread the spinach mixture evenly in the pan. Sprinkle the top with the reserved cheddar. Bake at 350° for 45 minutes to an hour, until the top is golden and firm to the touch.

## Eggplant "Coucharas"

This tasty eggplant gratin is baked on "spoons" of steamed eggplant skins. They often are served with Fritada de Espinaca (see page 443) and Fassoulia (see page 432) at a Passover meal.

If kashkaval cheese is available, use it in place of the cheddar and Romano. I've served this dish as an appetizer by cutting each eggplant into sixteenths instead of eighths, which makes enough for a party. Any leftovers (quite unlikely) taste wonderful cold.

YIELDS 16 COUCHARAS

*2 medium eggplants with smooth skin*

*3 garlic cloves, minced*
*3 eggs, beaten*
*2½ cups grated cheddar cheese*
*½ cup grated Romano cheese*

*¼ cup matzo meal or bread crumbs*
*2 tablespoons olive oil*
*salt and freshly ground black pepper to*
*taste*

*freshly grated nutmeg (optional)*

Stem the eggplants and cut each in half lengthwise. Cut each half crosswise into four pieces. In a covered saucepan, simmer the eggplant chunks in water to cover for 15 minutes, until the pulp is tender. Drain the eggplant in a colander and set them aside to cool. When you can comfortably handle the eggplant, use a teaspoon to separate the pulp from the skins, taking care not to tear the rectangles of skin. Reserve the skins. Should any of the skins tear apart, save them anyway, because you can overlap two torn pieces to form a single piece and the filling will hold them together.

In a bowl, vigorously mash the eggplant pulp with the garlic, or do this in a food processor or a blender. Mix in the remaining ingredients, except for ½ cup of the cheddar cheese and the nutmeg, and combine thoroughly. Add more matzo meal if the mixture seems too thin.

Place a skin, shiny side down, in the palm of your hand. Mound it with the eggplant mixture about an inch thick. Place it on a well-oiled baking sheet. Continue until all the skins and mixture are used. Sprinkle a little of the reserved cheddar and a bit of nutmeg onto each couchara. Bake at 350° for 20 minutes or until golden brown on top.

The preparation can be done ahead of time and the coucharas baked just before serving.

*Variation* Make eggplant fritada by adding 8 ounces of cottage cheese to the eggplant filling mixture. Line a 9x13-inch oiled baking dish with the eggplant skins, shiny side down. Pour the mixture evenly on top of the skins. Sprinkle the top with the reserved cheddar and a dusting of nutmeg. Bake at 350° for about an hour until golden brown. Cut into squares and serve as an appetizer or an entrée. The fritada may be eaten warm or cold and is nice with a green salad or tomatoes vinaigrette.

# Stuffed Figs and Dates

Stuffed figs and dates are lovely arranged on a platter with fresh fruit. They also make a delicious garnish, often used to decorate the serving dishes for Desayuno.

You can make ten or a hundred of these—just be sure to have as many walnut halves as you do figs and dates.

*figs, preferably Smyrna or Black Mission*
*pitted dates*

*shelled walnut halves*
*unsweetened shredded coconut*

Cut out the center of each fig and place a walnut half inside. Cut open the dates and do the same. Roll each stuffed fruit in shredded coconut.

# Turkish Coffee

My friend Janice remembers her grandmother, a Turkish Jew, serving her guests this sweet, potent coffee, and then turning over the cups and reading their fortunes from the grounds.

YIELDS 4 SERVINGS

*2 teaspoons sugar*
*2 heaping teaspoons Turkish coffee*

*2 (demitasse-sized) cups plus 2 tablespoons water*

Place the ingredients in a *jezveh,* a long-handled brass coffeepot, and stir to combine. Bring to a boil, letting the coffee foam up almost to overflowing. Remove from the heat and tap the *jezveh* gently on a surface away from the heat, to settle the grounds. Repeat the boiling and tapping process two more times.

Pour into demitasse cups and serve.

LISA WICHMAN

# *Mexico*

# INTRODUCTION

Mexico is a huge country that stretches almost 2,000 miles from north to south and almost 2,000 miles along its northern border with the United States. It encompasses mountain ranges, broad plateaus, jungle lowlands, and miles of coastline. Mexico is a country rich with the history and traditions of many different cultures, and abundant with plant and animal life.

Mexico's early inhabitants are thought by some to be related to the same peoples who long ago came to the Americas, probably from Asia via the Bering Strait. As some of these ancient tribes migrated southward, they developed degrees of knowledge in agriculture, astronomy, poetry, handcrafts, and political organization unknown to their northern relatives.

By the sixteenth century, most tribes—Mayas, Toltecs, Oaxacans, and many others—were either in alliance with or subjugated by the Aztecs, a warrior race led by the Great Emperor Montezuma.

In 1519 the Spanish conquistadores, led by Cortés, left the island of Cuba to explore new lands and landed on the Yucatan peninsula at a point now called Chalchiuh Cuecan. Cortés and his men founded the first Spanish community on the hemisphere mainland and named it Real Villa Rica de la Santa Veracruz. They were intrigued by stories that the local Indians told about the far away, rich empire of the Aztecs. In the Aztec capital, Tenochtitlan (near present-day Mexico City), Montezuma learned of the arrival of these "strange white men," and he remembered the legend of a golden-haired god who had sailed off to the east. Fearful that the god had returned, Montezuma sent gifts of gold and silver. These gifts motivated the Spanish to travel farther north.

When the conquistadores arrived at the Aztec capital, they must have been virtually awestruck by its size and splendor. The population was more than 100,000, larger than the city of Constantinople, which at that time was considered to be the cultural center of Europe. Tenochtitlan was a patchwork of islands with interconnected waterways and floating gardens. Montezuma, attended by slaves and elaborately dressed royalty, treated the Spanish guests to a splendid reception and sumptuous banquet, including food brought from great distances by relays of runners. The Spanish, overcome by greed, demanded to know the hiding place of all of the gold and jewels. The rest is well known. Spain, using her military might, began her subjugation of Mexico. This history, so laden with bloodshed and greed, has at least given us a positive blending of cultures in the formation of a new, exciting cuisine.

Spain, with its own experience of occupation and rule by the North African Moors, had one of the most elegant cuisines of Europe at that time, due partly to Moorish influence. The Spanish had many sophisticated techniques and ingredients, such as nut-thickened sauces, rich desserts, rice sautéed in fat before cooking, and spices to color and flavor the food. They introduced sugar cane, dairy products, citrus fruits, and pork to Mexico.

The Aztecs, with their highly developed agriculture, were growing maize, tomatoes, beans, and cacao. These, as well as other plants indigenous to Mexico such as vanilla, chiles, avocados, squash, pineapple, potatoes, and papaya, were to change or add to many cuisines of the world. When tomatoes were first introduced to Spain, they were considered quite suspect. Some people thought that they were dangerous to eat and some thought that because of their reputed aphrodisiac properties they should be forbidden to women. But by 1740 or so, they were firmly established in Spanish cooking.

This interchange of various foods and ways of cooking gave rise to a new cuisine. For example, the Aztecs made a special drink reserved for the royalty, with chocolate and chiles. The Spanish sweetened it with sugar, added cinnamon, and omitted the chiles. The result of this blending, to our present-day delight, is Mexican hot chocolate.

I first tasted Mexican food in 1966 when I moved from the East Coast to California. It was quite exciting to discover the old city in Los Angeles with its open-air markets, Spanish missions, and Mexican restaurants. There I savored my first tortillas, chiles, and avocados. My desire for hot, spicy foods and my enjoyment and appreciation of the taste of cumin, coriander, cilantro, lime, and the many other ingredients so necessary to Mexican cooking has increased as my repertoire has expanded.

In this chapter I have tried to be true to the essence of Mexican cooking while feeling free to experiment and incorporate my own style. Undoubtedly, after a decade of cooking at the restaurant, I've added a Moosewood touch as well. These recipes are a result of my vegetarianism and desire to explore new tastes and to try new things.

# ABOUT CHILES

*CAPSICUM PEPPERS, the family that includes bell peppers, paprika, and hot chiles, have been used for millennia in the Americas. Archaeological evidence has established that as early as 6500 and 5000 B.C., the indigenous peoples of Peru and Brazil ate capsicums, which grew wild. By the time of the Aztec civilization, many varieties had been cultivated and were favored foods. The chile, as many members of the capsicum family are called, was precious in Mexico where it was part of the tribute paid to the city of Tenochtitlan (today's Mexico City) by conquered peoples.*

*Peppers are almost impossible to classify, because their names change from region to region and new varieties are constantly being discovered as a result of cross-pollination. Chiles have certainly spread in popularity and have become important to cuisines around the world as well as integral to Mexican cooking.*

*Mexican cookbooks list a seemingly infinite number of chiles that are available fresh or dried (whole, flaked, or ground). But here in Upstate New York, the availability of chiles is limited mostly to jalapeño, serrano, and occasionally poblano. It is my suggestion that you experiment with those you find in your area.*

*What I have learned from personal experience is that chiles vary widely in their piquancy, or hotness, even among those on the same plant. The first summer I grew chiles, I joyfully went out to my garden to pick the first jalapeños of the season. I then proceeded to prepare a meal for my family that was so hot we couldn't eat it. I learned that about half of one of those chiles was all any dish needed. Later that summer, from the same plants, I had to pick and incorporate several chiles into any dish to get the desired hotness. The same is true with the fresh chiles that we use at Moosewood. One week they are fiery hot, the next, quite mild.*

*My suggestion for the following recipes is to use less chile than the recipe calls for if you can't tolerate or don't like hot, spicy food and use more if you want it really hot. For dinner parties or for the undecided, offer one of the salsas at the table; make it very hot and let each person adjust the food accordingly. Mexican food is not just meant to burn your mouth, but is a rich blend of flavors and spices. Don't be afraid to experiment.*

*When preparing chiles, never touch your face or eyes. The result of doing so could be a nasty burning sensation that for some people can be quite extreme. If you are particularly sensitive, you should think about wearing rubber surgical gloves when working with chiles. Luckily, I've never found that necessary, but I always wash very thoroughly with soapy water after handling them. If your fingers start to burn, try soaking them for a few minutes in milk*

or very salty water. Before cutting a chile you can rub your fingers with cooking oil and if you experience any burning, it can be neutralized by rubbing sugar onto your oiled fingers. You might sometimes experience a slight irritation from breathing the fumes of chiles as they cook; in my experience this has been very minor and temporary.

Capsaicin is the substance in chiles that burns your mouth. It is concentrated mainly in the seeds and the white tissue inside the chile pod. The flesh contains less of this mouth-burning substance, so remove the ribs and seeds to diminish the heat. If you get a bite that is too hot, don't drink water or other liquid because that only spreads the capsaicin around in your mouth. Instead, take a bite of rice, tortilla, bread, banana, avocado, or potato. A tolerance for and enjoyment of hot spicy food can usually be cultivated. My children can give testimony to this fact.

Chiles add spice to your food, but that's not all. Ounce for ounce, they contain more vitamin C than oranges, although it is hard to imagine eating a whole orange's worth of chiles. Capsaicin promotes the secretion of saliva and gastric juices and helps to speed food through the digestive system. It may also have some antibacterial effect and may decrease clotting of blood. In fact, there have been many medical claims made for chiles over the years, ranging from its ability to prevent hair loss to its reported aphrodisiac qualities. The most recent I've heard is that chiles might help prevent depression.

## SOPAS
### S O U P S

*Soup, or sopa, is an important prelude to a traditional Mexican meal. There are two kinds of sopas: sopas aguadas, or liquid soup, and sopas secas, or dry soup. The liquid soup is usually served first and in restaurants is called caldo. The second "soup" course is in fact a rice, pasta, or tortilla dish. Soups are often served twice a day at the midday and evening meals. For this reason, Mexican cooks have become quite adept at making a variety of soups using a multitude of ingredients.*

# Sopa de Lima

·

# Tomato, Lime, and Tortilla Soup

 This soup originated in the Yucatan peninsula, renowned for its special lime trees. Recipes for sopa de lima, which appear in many cookbooks, most often call for chicken and chicken stock. This one is made with vegetable stock and is brimming with fresh tomatoes, lime juice, and chiles. Cilantro seems to be an acquired taste, so try this soup with and without it.

### SERVES 4 TO 6

*1 cup chopped onions*

*4 large garlic cloves, minced or pressed*

*3 tablespoons vegetable oil*

*1–2 minced chiles (1 inch long) (or to taste)*

*1 teaspoon ground cumin seeds*

*½ teaspoon dried oregano*

*3½ cups chopped fresh tomatoes*

*3 cups vegetable stock (see page 685)*

*⅓ cup fresh lime juice*

*salt to taste*

_____

*grated Monterey Jack cheese*

*tortilla chips, crumbled (see note)*

*chopped fresh cilantro (optional)*

In a medium soup pot, sauté the onions and garlic in the oil until the onions are translucent. Add the chiles, cumin, and oregano, and sauté for a few more minutes. Add the chopped tomatoes and sprinkle with a little salt. Cover the pot and cook gently until the tomatoes begin to release their juices. Stir occasionally. This will take longer with winter tomatoes than with summer ones. Add the stock and simmer, covered, for about 15 minutes. Add the lime juice and salt to taste.

Serve topped with grated cheese and crumbled tortilla chips. Garnish with finely chopped cilantro, if desired.

---

*Note: You can either purchase tortilla chips, or to be more traditional: cut tortillas into strips and fry them quickly until crisp in very hot oil, about one inch deep. Drain on paper towels.*

# *Crema de Elote*

•

## *Creamy Corn Soup*

One warm summer evening, my head filled with images of Mexico and thoughts of chiles, maize, and tomatoes, I "invented" this soup using what was ripe in my garden. It makes for a delicious light summer meal with cornbread and salad.

### SERVES 6 GENEROUSLY

*1 cup chopped onions*
*1 large garlic clove, minced or pressed*
*3 tablespoons butter or vegetable oil*
*1 teaspoon ground coriander seeds*
*1 teaspoon ground cumin seeds*
*1 tablespoon minced chiles (or to taste)*
*1½ cups chopped fresh tomatoes*
*2 cups diced potatoes*
*1 green or red bell pepper, chopped (a combination of red and green peppers is nice)*

*2 cups vegetable stock (see page 685) or water*
*2½ cups cut corn (fresh or frozen)*

_____

*1 cup milk*
*½ cup grated Monterey Jack cheese*
*salt and ground black pepper to taste*

In a soup pot, sauté the onions and garlic in the butter or oil on low heat for about 10 minutes, until the onions are very soft. Add the coriander, cumin, and chiles. Sauté for 2 minutes and then add the chopped tomatoes and cook until they are juicy. Add the potatoes, bell peppers, and stock or water. Cover and simmer until the potatoes are tender, about 10 minutes. Add the corn and heat thoroughly.

In a blender, purée about half of the soup with the milk and cheese. Stir the purée back into the soup pot. Add salt and black pepper to taste. Heat slowly until the soup is hot, but not boiling.

# Gazpacho a la Guadalajara

•

## Chilled Avocado-Tomato Soup

This soup is quite refreshing and delicious on a hot summer day, especially if you serve it with a big spoonful of spicy Salsa Mexicana Cruda (see page 458).

SERVES 6 TO 8

2 cups cut corn, fresh or frozen
4 cups tomato juice
1 cucumber, peeled and cubed (seeded, if the seeds are large)
2 ripe avocados, peeled, pitted, and cubed
4 tablespoons fresh lime or lemon juice

1 large garlic clove, minced or pressed
1½ teaspoons ground cumin seeds
¼ teaspoon ground red pepper
salt to taste

_____

chopped fresh cilantro (optional)

Cook the corn in boiling water until just tender and drain well. Combine with the rest of the ingredients. Chill for one to 2 hours or until very cold.

## *Salsa Mexicana Cruda*

•

## *Fresh Tomato Sauce*

### YIELDS ABOUT 2 CUPS

2 medium tomatoes, chopped (about 2
  cups)
2 tablespoons chopped fresh cilantro
2 tablespoons minced chiles (or to taste)

2 tablespoons fresh lime juice
salt to taste

In a small bowl, mix together all of the ingredients. Serve immediately. Leftover salsa may be stored refrigerated in a well-sealed container for three to four days.

# Salsa de Tomate Verde Cocida

•

# Tomatillo Sauce

The main ingredient of this sauce is tomatillos, which are small, round, light green, slightly sour fruits with a distinctive flavor. They turn yellow when they ripen but are usually used green. Tomatillos are becoming more readily available in large grocery stores or specialty markets where they might be called Mexican green tomatoes, tomates verdes, tomates de cascara, or fresadillas. It is worth the effort to try to find them. You can buy extra and freeze them for future use after puréeing.

### YIELDS 1 TO 1 ½ CUPS

*12–14 fresh tomatillos*

*1 small onion, chopped (about ½ cup)*
*1 large garlic clove, minced or pressed*
*1 serrano or other chile, minced (or to taste)*

*1 teaspoon ground coriander seeds*
*2 tablespoons vegetable oil*
*¼ teaspoon sugar*
*1 teaspoon chopped fresh cilantro*
*salt to taste*

Remove the papery husks from the tomatillos and rinse. Place them in a medium saucepan and cover them with cold water. Bring to a boil, reduce the heat, and simmer gently for about 5 minutes or until the tomatillos are tender and can be easily pierced with a fork. Drain. Purée the tomatillos in a blender or food processor.

In a small cast-iron skillet, sauté the onions, garlic, chile, and coriander in the oil for 5 to 10 minutes, until the onions are very soft. Stir in the puréed tomatillos and cook gently for 5 minutes more. Add the sugar and cilantro. Salt to taste.

# SALADS

*The following easy vegetable side dishes should challenge the notion that Mexican food is heavy, fast-food fare consisting only of rice and beans.*

# Ensalada Esmeralda

•

## Zucchini-Avocado Salad

SERVES 4

2 cups cubed zucchini, lightly steamed
   (see page 681)
1 avocado, peeled, pitted, and cubed
¼ cup vegetable oil

2 tablespoons fresh lemon juice
1 small garlic clove, minced or pressed
salt to taste

Combine all the ingredients. Chill at least one hour.

# Ensalada Mixta

•

## Beets and Carrots in a Lime Vinaigrette

SERVES 4

2 medium beets, peeled and cubed
2 medium carrots, sliced diagonally
1 cup fresh or frozen peas
1 medium cucumber, peeled, seeded,
   and cubed

DRESSING
6 tablespoons vegetable oil
3 tablespoons fresh lime juice
2 tablespoons chopped fresh cilantro
1 small garlic clove, minced or pressed
salt to taste

Lightly steam the beets, carrots, and peas in separate batches until just tender, but still bright in color (see page 681). Mix them in a large bowl and add the cucumber. Combine the dressing ingredients. Toss the vegetables with the dressing and chill.

# ENTRÉES

# *Cheese and Pepper Enchiladas*

### SERVES 4 TO 6 GENEROUSLY

2 medium onions, chopped

1 to 2 large garlic cloves, minced or
pressed

1 tablespoon minced chiles

2 teaspoons ground cumin seeds

3 tablespoons vegetable or olive oil

2½–3 cups chopped bell peppers (use
two or three colors: red, green, and
yellow)

8 ounces cream cheese

1½ cups grated cheddar cheese

½ cup cottage cheese

salt to taste

_____

8 corn tortillas

vegetable oil for frying

HOT SAUCE

2 cups undrained canned tomatoes

½ green bell pepper, coarsely chopped
(about ½ cup)

1 small onion, coarsely chopped

2–3 tablespoons minced chiles (or to
taste)

1 teaspoon ground coriander seeds

1 teaspoon ground cumin seeds

salt to taste

_____

4 to 6 servings cooked brown rice (see
page 676)

In a large cast-iron skillet, sauté the onions, garlic, chiles, and cumin in the oil for 5 to 7 minutes, until the onions are soft. Add the chopped peppers, cover, and cook on low heat for about 10 minutes, until the peppers are tender. Remove from the heat and immediately stir in all the cheeses. Add salt to taste and set aside.

Preheat the oven to 350°.

Corn tortillas need to be softened a little in order to fill them more easily and to prevent them from cracking while baking. The easiest way to do this is to fry them individually in about an inch of hot oil for a few seconds on each side. You just want them to soften, not to crisp, so don't leave them in too long. Drain well on paper towels. Then place a tortilla on a flat surface. Spoon ¼ to ½ cup of the cheese and pepper filling onto the half of the tortilla closest to you. Roll and place, seam side down, in an oiled baking pan. Bake, tightly covered, for 20 to 25 minutes.

While the enchiladas are baking, prepare the hot sauce. Purée the tomatoes, bell peppers, onion, chiles, coriander, and cumin in a blender until smooth. Simmer, uncovered, on low heat for at least 20 minutes, stirring occasionally. Add salt to taste.

Serve the enchiladas on a bed of rice and top with the hot sauce.

# *Black Bean Tostada*

This is a very colorful dish well worth the effort of layering. The black beans are even more flavorful the next day, so make them ahead of time if it's convenient.

### SERVES 4 TO 6

*8 corn tortillas*
*vegetable oil for frying*
**BLACK BEANS**
*1⅓ cups dried black beans*

_____

*3 medium onions, chopped (about 2*
*  cups)*
*3 garlic cloves, minced or pressed*
*1½ teaspoons ground cumin seeds*
*1½ teaspoons ground coriander seeds*
*1 teaspoon minced chiles*
*¼ cup vegetable oil or butter*
*1 medium tomato, chopped*

*juice of 2 oranges*
*salt to taste*
**GUACAMOLE**
*2 large ripe avocados*
*1 large garlic clove, minced or pressed*
*  (or to taste)*
*juice of 1–1½ lemons (or to taste)*
*salt to taste*

_____

*shredded lettuce*
*grated cheddar or Monterey Jack cheese*
*sour cream (optional)*
*Salsa Mexicana Cruda (see page 458)*

Cook the black beans (see page 653).

Pour vegetable oil into a small skillet to about ½-inch depth. Heat until the oil is hot enough that when you drop in a tiny piece of tortilla, it quickly rises to the surface. Fry the tortillas, one at a time, for about one minute on each side until they are crisp. Drain the tortillas on paper towels and set aside.

To make the black beans, sauté the onions, garlic, cumin, coriander, and chiles in the oil using a large skillet or medium saucepan until the onions are soft and translucent, 5 to 10 minutes. Drain the cooked black beans and add them to the skillet. Mash with a potato masher or spoon until most of the beans are mashed. Add the tomatoes and orange juice. (Throw in the orange halves after squeezing out the juice if you like. Just remember to remove them before serving.) Cover and simmer on very low heat for 5 to 10 minutes, stirring frequently to prevent sticking. Add salt to taste.

For the guacamole, slice the avocados in half. Remove the pits and scoop out the avocado flesh with a spoon. In a mixing bowl, mash the avocado until fairly smooth. Add the garlic, lemon juice, and salt to taste. Or use a food processor for a very smooth guacamole.

Now it's time to layer the tostadas. You can make them for your guests or have them make their own. For each serving, start with a crisp tortilla, cover it generously with shredded lettuce and then black beans, topped with grated cheese, guacamole, and Salsa Mexicana Cruda. Top with sour cream, if desired.

# Mole de Olla

•

## Kettle Stew

*Mole* means "mixture" in Spanish. This word crops up in recipes that have nothing to do with the well-known traditional chocolate mole sauce. *Olla* is a big, fat-bellied clay pot—hence the name of this hearty stew, which is good served with cornbread for lunch or a light dinner.

SERVES 4

1 cup chopped onions
1 large garlic clove, minced or pressed
1–2 tablespoons minced chiles
3 tablespoons vegetable or olive oil
½ teaspoon cinnamon
¼ teaspoon ground cloves
4 small potatoes, cut into chunks (about 2 cups)
3 cups undrained canned tomatoes, chopped (28-ounce can)

2 cups cut green beans
1 small zucchini, sliced (about 2 cups)
2 cups cut corn (frozen or fresh)
1–2 tablespoons chopped fresh cilantro (optional)
salt to taste

grated cheddar cheese or sour cream

In a stewpot or large saucepan, sauté the onions, garlic, and chiles in the oil for about 5 minutes. Include the seeds from the chiles if you like a hotter stew, discard them if you don't. Add the cinnamon, cloves, and the potatoes and cook, covered, for another 5 minutes. Stir in the tomatoes and the green beans, cover, and cook 5 minutes more. Add the zucchini and corn. Simmer, covered, on low heat until all the vegetables are tender. If the stew seems too dry, add tomato juice or water. Add cilantro, if desired, and salt to taste.

Serve topped with plenty of grated cheese or sour cream.

# Chiles en Nogada

•

## Stuffed Green Peppers with a Creamy Walnut Sauce

The signing of the Treaty of Cordoba in 1821 marked the end of Spanish domination of Mexican territories. To celebrate independence, many dishes were created with ingredients chosen to match the green, white, and red colors of the Mexican flag.

Chiles en Nogada is a vegetarian version of a famous dish that incorporated green peppers, a white sauce, and red pomegranate seeds for garnish. I have substituted frozen, grated tofu for the ground beef in the traditional recipe. Its texture is similar and readily absorbs the flavors of the herbs and spices. You should also try these peppers topped with sour cream and the blender hot sauce in the recipe for Cheese and Pepper Enchiladas (see page 462).

SERVES 6 TO 8

2 cakes tofu, frozen, thawed, and
  shredded (see page 684)

1 medium onion, chopped (about 1 cup)
1 large garlic clove, minced or pressed
1/4 teaspoon cinnamon
1 teaspoon ground cumin seeds
1/4 teaspoon ground red pepper
3 tablespoons vegetable oil
2 large tomatoes, chopped (about 1 1/2
  cups)
1 small apple, cored and chopped
  (about 1/2 cup)
1/3 cup raisins
1/3 cup finely chopped almonds
1 tablespoon vinegar

salt to taste

6 large bell peppers (a mixture of green
  and red is nice)
1 cup tomato juice

WALNUT SAUCE
1/2 cup sour cream
1/2 cup lightly toasted walnuts
1/3 cup cream cheese
1/4 cup milk
1 teaspoon cinnamon
1/4–1/2 teaspoon ground red pepper

6 servings cooked brown rice (see page
  676)

Prepare the tofu.

In a large heavy skillet, sauté the onions, garlic, cinnamon, cumin, and ground red pepper in the oil until the onions are soft. Add the chopped tomatoes, apple, and raisins. Cover and simmer on low heat for 5 to 10 minutes, until the apple is soft. Add the shredded tofu, almonds, and vinegar and simmer for another 10 minutes, stirring occasionally. Salt to taste.

Cut the peppers in half lengthwise and remove the seeds. Leave the stems on if you can, which will help the peppers hold their shape during baking. Fill each pepper half with the tofu mixture and place it in a glass or porcelain baking pan. Add the tomato juice to the bottom of the pan and cover tightly with aluminum foil. Bake at 350° for 30 to 45 minutes, until the peppers are tender.

While the peppers are baking, purée together all of the walnut sauce ingredients in a blender until smooth. The sauce should be served at room temperature, but if you're making it ahead of time, refrigerate it.

Serve the peppers on a bed of rice with some of the tomato juice spooned over them, and a large dollop of the walnut sauce.

## Pompano Tampico

·

## Flounder Rolls with Tomatoes, Almonds, and Cilantro

### SERVES 4 TO 6

¾ cup sun-dried tomatoes
1 cup boiling water
½ cup chopped, toasted almonds
2 medium fresh tomatoes, chopped
3 tablespoons chopped fresh cilantro
salt to taste

1 large garlic clove, minced or pressed
¼ teaspoon ground red pepper or
    cayenne (or to taste)
¼ cup butter, melted
3 tablespoons fresh lemon juice

2 pounds flounder, in 2- or 3-ounce
    fillets

In a small bowl, soak the sun-dried tomatoes in the boiling water for 10 minutes. Drain the tomatoes and then chop them. Combine them with the almonds, fresh tomatoes, and cilantro. Add salt to taste. This filling can be used immediately, but it becomes even more flavorful if you refrigerate it for 2 or 3 days.

Rinse the flounder. Place each fillet, skin side up, flat on a board. Spoon some filling on one end of each fillet and then roll it up. Place the rolled fish into a buttered baking pan. If small fillets are unavailable, this dish can be made with scrod, haddock, or other firm-fleshed fillets. Place the larger fillets skin side down in the baking pan and spread the filling on top.

Sauté the garlic and red pepper or cayenne in the butter for a few minutes on very low heat. Add the lemon juice and pour the mixture over the fish. Bake, covered, at 375° for 20 to 25 minutes, until the fish is tender and flaky.

# *Arroz a la Mexicana*

•

# *Mexican Rice*

There are many versions of "Mexican rice," which in turn are all variants of pilaf, the presautéed rice of the Middle East, probably brought to Spain by the Moors. My friend and fellow cook, Linda, told me about a simple rice dish she had enjoyed while vacationing in the Yucatan. This recipe is the result.

Annatto or achiote seeds are collected from the pods of a small tree that grows in the Yucatan. They are used to add color and a subtle flavor. I love seeing the beautiful reddish orange color that the seeds turn the oil. It is one of those magical moments of cooking. In general, the smaller Haas avocado, grown in California and Mexico, is more flavorful and should be used whenever possible.

### SERVES 6 AS A SIDE DISH OR
### 4 FOR LUNCH OR A LIGHT SUPPER

*1 tablespoon annatto seeds*
*2 tablespoons vegetable oil*

_____

*1 small onion, chopped*
*1–2 large garlic cloves, minced or*
  *pressed*
*1½ cups uncooked brown rice*
*3 cups water*
*1 cup peas (fresh or frozen)*
*2 tablespoons fresh lime juice*

*salt to taste*

_____

*2 or 3 ripe avocados*
*lemon or lime wedges*
*grated cheddar or Monterey Jack cheese*
  *(optional)*
*sour cream (optional)*
*Salsa Mexicana Cruda (see page 458)*
  *(optional)*

In a very small skillet or saucepan, heat the annatto in the oil on medium heat for 4 to 5 minutes, until the oil turns a bright red-orange color. Strain the oil and discard the seeds.

In a medium saucepan, sauté the onion and garlic in the oil for 5 to 6 minutes. Add the rice and sauté another 2 or 3 minutes. Add the water and bring to a boil. Reduce the heat, cover, and cook until the water is absorbed, 35 to 45 minutes. Just before the rice is done, add the peas, but do not stir. The steam will cook them and they will remain bright green. Stir in the lime juice and salt to taste.

Serve garnished with slices of avocado and lemon or lime wedges. If desired, top with grated cheese and/or a dollop of sour cream, or try it with Salsa Mexicana Cruda.

## *Spicy Green Beans*

### SERVES 4

*1 medium onion, thinly sliced (about ½ cup)*
*1 large garlic clove, minced or pressed*
*1 tablespoon minced chiles (or to taste)*
*2 tablespoons vegetable oil*

*2 cups stemmed, halved green beans*
*1 fresh tomato, chopped (about ¾ cup)*
*½ cup water*
*salt to taste*

In a medium saucepan or skillet, sauté the onions, garlic, and chiles in the oil until the onions are translucent. Add the beans, tomatoes, and water. Cover and simmer on medium heat until the beans are tender, 5 to 15 minutes. Stir occasionally. Add salt to taste.

# *Tortilla Casserole*

This is a very simple, fast side dish or luncheon entrée, delicious served plain or topped with salsa.

SERVES 4 TO 6

*1 medium onion, chopped*
*1 garlic clove, minced or pressed*
*¾ teaspoon dried oregano*
*3 tablespoons vegetable oil*
*3 medium tomatoes, chopped*

_____

*10 6-inch corn tortillas*

*½ pint heavy cream*
*⅓ cup grated Parmesan cheese*
*salt and freshly ground black pepper to
    taste*

_____

*½ cup grated Monterey Jack cheese*

In a large skillet, sauté the onion, garlic, and oregano in the oil for 5 to 10 minutes, until the onions are translucent. Stir in the chopped tomatoes, cover, and simmer about 5 minutes, until the tomatoes are soft and juicy.

Cut the tortillas into ½-inch-wide strips and stir them into the tomato mixture with the cream, Parmesan cheese, and salt and pepper.

Bake, uncovered, at 375° in a buttered one-quart casserole dish for 30 minutes. Top with the grated Monterey Jack cheese and return to the oven until the cheese is thoroughly melted, about 5 minutes more.

If you like, top with Salsa Mexicana Cruda (see page 458) or Salsa de Tomate Verde Cocida (see page 459).

# DESSERTS

*Desserts are an important part of Mexican cuisine. This is due partly to the influence of the Spanish nuns who supported their convents by preparing and selling sweets. The nuns brought the tradition of using dairy products, eggs, sugar, and almonds with them to Mexico. By including indigenous fruits as well as that crucial dessert ingredient, chocolate, they enhanced and increased their repertoire and consequently our present-day enjoyment.*

## *Torta del Cielo*

•

## *Almond Torte*

Torta del Cielo is often made for holidays and special occasions. The almonds should be very finely ground. It works well to coarsely chop and then grind them in a blender.

### YIELDS 12 SERVINGS

*1 1/2 cups finely ground almonds*
*2/3 cup unbleached white flour*
*1/4 teaspoon salt*

———————————————

*6 egg yolks*
*3 tablespoons Amaretto (almond liqueur)*
*1/4 teaspoon pure vanilla extract*

*1/3 cup sugar*

———————————————

*6 egg whites*
*1 teaspoon cream of tartar*
*1/3 cup sugar*
*strawberries (fresh or unsweetened frozen)*
*whipped cream*

Preheat the oven to 325°. Butter and flour a 10-inch bundt pan.

Stir together the almonds, flour, and salt. Set aside.

Beat the egg yolks at high speed with an electric mixer for about 6 minutes or until they are thick and lightly colored. Add the Amaretto and vanilla. Gradually add ⅓ cup of the sugar, beating until it is dissolved. Set this mixture aside.

Wash and dry the beaters thoroughly. In a large bowl, combine the egg whites and the cream of tartar and beat until soft peaks form. Gradually add ⅓ cup sugar, beating until stiff peaks form. Gently fold the yolk mixture into the whites. Then gently fold in the flour mixture, about a third at a time.

Pour the batter into the bundt pan and bake for 45 to 55 minutes or until a knife inserted in the center comes out clean. Invert the pan onto a plate. After about 30 minutes, loosen the sides of the cake from the pan with a knife and remove the pan.

Serve topped with strawberries and whipped cream.

# Mexican Hot Chocolate

## SERVES 3 TO 4

| | |
|---|---|
| 2 ounces unsweetened chocolate | ½ teaspoon cinnamon |
| 2 cups milk | |
| 1 cup heavy cream | 1 egg |
| 6 tablespoons sugar | 1 teaspoon pure vanilla extract |

Melt the chocolate in the top of a double boiler. In a separate pot, heat the milk and the cream on low heat until hot but not boiling. When the milk is hot, slowly add a little bit of it to the chocolate until you have a thin paste. Then stir in the rest of the milk and cream, the sugar, and the cinnamon.

In a bowl beat the egg and the vanilla with a rotary beater. Add a very little of the hot chocolate to the egg (you don't want to "fry" the egg in the hot chocolate) and then stir the egg mixture into the hot chocolate. With the double boiler still on low heat, beat the chocolate with a rotary beater for about 3 minutes. Serve immediately.

This recipe is for chocolate lovers. It's like drinking a candy bar! Serve with Polvorones de Canela (see page 475).

# Flan

•

## Caramel Custard

 Mexican cookbooks are not complete without at least one rec-
ipe for flan, a delectable caramel custard. This is a more health-
ful version of a traditional flan, because I have substituted 2
percent milk for the usual heavy cream or evaporated milk.

Instructions for making flan vary considerably, and I found myself quite intimidated,
especially by the description of the technique for melting the sugar. After a few tries, I
discovered that if I used a pot with a heavy bottom, it was far better to stir very little if
at all until the sugar actually started to melt. And to my amazement, it really did melt!

**SERVES 8**

*3 cups milk (whole or 2 percent)*

*3 whole eggs*
*3 egg yolks*

*¾ cup maple syrup*
*½ teaspoon pure vanilla extract*

*½ cup sugar*

Preheat the oven to 350°.

In a heavy saucepan, heat the milk to just below the simmering point, stirring
occasionally. In a blender, whirl the eggs, egg yolks, and maple syrup until creamy and
then slowly pour in the hot milk. You may need to do this in two batches. Add the
vanilla. Set aside.

In a heavy saucepan, slowly heat the sugar until it starts to melt, at least 5 minutes.
When it starts to steam and turn brown, stir from time to time until it becomes a
smooth light brown syrup. Divide this syrup among eight custard cups. It sets almost
immediately, so you need to work quickly. There will be just enough syrup to thinly
coat the bottom of each custard cup.

Pour the custard mixture into the cups. Place the cups in a large baking pan and pour
very hot water into the pan about halfway up the sides of the cups. Bake for about 50
to 55 minutes, until the custards are set.

Remove the custard cups from the baking pan to cool. When cool, unmold the custards by running a knife around the edges and then overturning onto rimmed plates or into small bowls. Serve well chilled.

> *Note: Soak the custard cups in warm water for at least an hour or two before washing them and the caramel will be much easier to remove.*

# *Polvorones de Canela*

•

## *Cinnamon Cookies*

Polvorones are small, round Mexican shortbread cookies. They may be flavored with cinnamon or orange and are often made with ground nuts. Traditionally they are rolled in confectioners' sugar while still warm from the oven. I find it preferable to roll them in the sugar mixture before baking. They are great with Mexican Hot Chocolate (see page 473).

### YIELDS ABOUT 30 COOKIES

*1 cup butter*
*½ cup confectioners' sugar*
*½ teaspoon cinnamon*
*¼ teaspoon salt*
*1 teaspoon pure vanilla extract*

*2 cups unbleached white flour*

_____

*1 cup confectioners' sugar*
*1 teaspoon cinnamon*

With an electric mixer, cream the butter and sugar. Add the cinnamon, salt, and vanilla. Fold in the flour, making a stiff dough. Chill for an hour or two.

When you're ready to bake the cookies, preheat the oven to 350°. Form the dough into one-inch balls. Mix together 1 cup of powdered sugar and 1 teaspoon of cinnamon. Roll the balls in the cinnamon-sugar mixture.

Bake the cookies on a buttered baking sheet for about 15 to 20 minutes, until nicely browned. Cool on a wire rack.

MAGGIE PITKIN

# New

# England

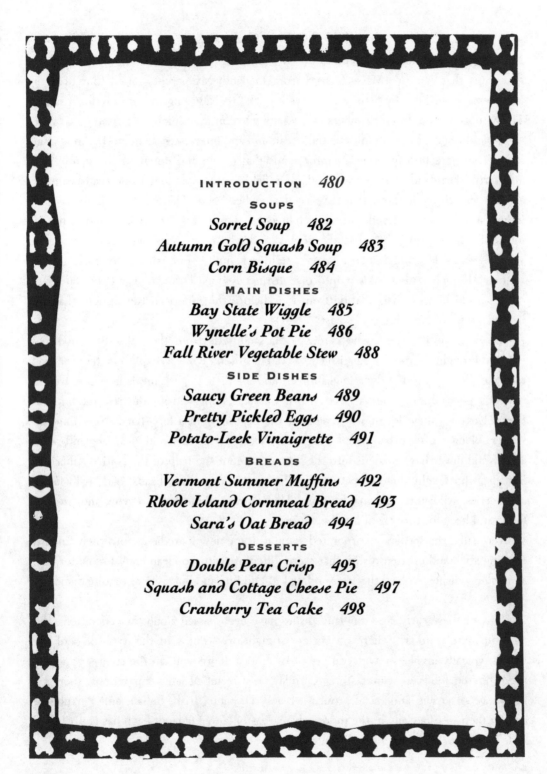

# INTRODUCTION

New England is almost like home to me. My ancestors go way back there to one of the first ships that came to Massachusetts from England. My parents raised four of us in New Jersey, but little by little we all "went back" to New England, if only for a while. Today more than a dozen members of my family live in the region, so I often go to visit.

In New England everything but the ocean and the interstates seems to be on a small scale. There are little winding country roads that go up and down among gentle hills and fertile farmland. There are woods and fields with more old stone walls running around and through them than I've seen anywhere else. There are small towns and industrial cities all scattered with church steeples. To the east, the Atlantic coast has all kinds of beaches; smooth and sandy, pebbly, and wild rocky ones too. There's so much variety—New England is like a crazy patchwork quilt—but with a common thread running through it that joins it into one distinct region. Throughout all six states are beautiful old houses, many dating from long before the American Revolution, that are living legacies of New England's past.

The first white settlers who came to Massachusetts from the cities and towns of England brought customs of English cookery. They didn't come as explorers; they wanted to settle down, continue their English lives, and eat their English meals in peace, free of religious persecution. They arrived, worn out and hungry from the trip, and found themselves in a huge forest wilderness, at the beginning of a long harsh New England winter. Being mostly urban people, they weren't ready for this wild New England place and would never have made it into the winter without the help of the Native American Indians, who taught them to eat corn and cornmeal, squashes, beans, oats, wild leeks, cranberries, wild nuts, and maple syrup. They showed them how to grow and prepare foods and how to store them for the winter.

Eventually, the settlers incorporated some of these new ingredients into their English cooking style and created dishes that were different, with no clear English counterpart, and so new dishes evolved that were related to Old England but were also quite distinctly of the New World.

Many of these early New England dishes have been passed along for generations and are still popular today. There's a certain straightforwardness to this type of cooking, which typically involves a wide variety of fresh local ingredients in the summer and the more limited foods in winter storage. Today, as a result of later emigrations, there's a full range of ethnic and racial groups—Black, Hispanic, Irish, Italian, and Portuguese among them—especially in the more urban areas of New England. Each has contributed style and flavor to New England's cuisine.

## *Sorrel Soup*

Sorrel grows wild all over New England, but use the kind found at green grocers or herb shops if you have none growing wild. Traditionally made with heavy cream, this is a lighter version using milk.

### SERVES 6

2 cups well-packed, washed and
    stemmed sorrel leaves
1 medium onion, chopped
3 tablespoons butter
1 tablespoon unbleached white flour
3 cups vegetable stock (see page 685)

2 egg yolks
1 cup milk or half-and-half
salt and freshly ground black pepper
dash of Tabasco or other hot sauce
    (optional)

Finely chop the sorrel leaves. In a medium saucepan, sauté the onion in the butter until translucent. Stir in the flour. Mix in the sorrel and cook it for a minute or so, just until it wilts. Add the vegetable stock. Bring the soup to a low simmer and cook for about 3 minutes.

Beat the egg yolks and milk in a medium mixing bowl. Slowly add 2 cups of the hot soup while stirring constantly. Stir this soup-egg mixture into the soup pot. Reheat the soup gently but don't let it boil. Add salt and pepper to taste and a dash of Tabasco, if you like.

# Autumn Gold Squash Soup

This hearty soup is wonderfully flavorful and satisfying. A dollop of sour cream in each serving is delicious and provides a bright contrast to the soup's crisp, deep color.

### SERVES 6 TO 8

*1 medium to large butternut squash
  (about 2 cups cooked pulp)*

---

*1 large Spanish onion, chopped (about
  3 cups)*
*2 tablespoons vegetable oil*
*¼ teaspoon nutmeg*
*¼ teaspoon cinnamon*
*¼ teaspoon dried thyme*

*2 bay leaves*
*1 medium carrot, diced*
*2 celery stalks, chopped*
*1½ cups water*

---

*1½ cups tomato juice*
*1 cup apple juice*
*1 cup orange juice*
*salt and ground black pepper*

Bake or boil the squash. To bake, halve the squash and scoop out the seeds. Place the squash halves cut side down on an oiled baking sheet and cover loosely with aluminum foil. Bake at 350° until tender, about one hour. Scoop out the pulp and discard the skin. To boil, peel the squash, halve it, and scoop out the seeds. Cut it into chunks and place them in a saucepan with water to cover. Bring the water to a boil and cook until the squash is tender, about 15 minutes. Drain and reserve the liquid.

Meanwhile, sauté the chopped onion in the oil with the nutmeg, cinnamon, thyme, and bay leaves until the onion is translucent. Add the diced carrot and celery and the water (if you boiled the squash, use the reserved liquid). Cover and simmer until the carrots are tender. Remove the bay leaves.

In a blender or food processor, purée the cooked squash, the onion-carrot mixture, and the juices in batches. Gently reheat the soup. Add salt and pepper to taste.

# Corn Bisque

A tasty summer treat, this soup borrows from an old New England recipe by boiling the corn cobs "to cook the sweetness out." Not overly rich, its fresh flavor goes well with Vermont Summer Muffins (see page 492).

### SERVES 6

8 ears corn (to yield about 4 cups cut corn)
5 cups water
1 teaspoon salt
1 bay leaf

_____

2 medium Spanish onions, chopped
2 tablespoons vegetable oil
½ teaspoon dried marjoram

⅛ teaspoon dried thyme
1 large carrot, peeled and chopped
2 celery stalks, chopped
1 medium potato, chopped

_____

¼ cup cream cheese
1 cup milk
salt and freshly ground black pepper

First make a stock using the corn cobs. Husk the corn, removing any silk that clings to the ears. Cut the corn from the cobs and set the kernels aside. In a large pot, bring the corn cobs, water, salt, and bay leaf to a boil. Reduce the heat and simmer, covered, for 15 to 20 minutes. Discard the cobs.

Sauté the onions in the oil until translucent. Stir in the marjoram and thyme and the remaining vegetables. Add the corn-cob stock, cover, and simmer until the vegetables are tender. Discard the bay leaf.

In a saucepan, lightly cook the reserved corn kernels in a cup of water for about 5 minutes and set aside.

Meanwhile, using a blender or food processor, purée in batches the vegetables, stock, cream cheese, and milk. Pour the purée back into the pot and stir in the corn kernels and their cooking liquid. Add salt and pepper to taste. Reheat gently, if necessary.

# *Bay State Wiggle*

Most commercial shrimp comes from the coastal regions of Virginia and south, but shrimp also are abundant along the New England coast. Five of the six New England states have Atlantic coastlines where a wide variety of seafood is always fresh and available.

This creamed asparagus with shrimp is delicately flavored with white wine. Served on toast, it has the comforting, cozy touch of some old English dishes. It's versatile and makes an easy, tasty supper for the whole family to enjoy. Or, for an elegant brunch, serve it with dry white wine or champagne.

### SERVES 4

*1 pound fresh asparagus*

*3 tablespoons butter*
*¼ cup unbleached white flour*
*2 cups milk, heated*
*salt and freshly ground black pepper to taste*

*1 tablespoon butter*

*1 pound medium raw shrimp, peeled and cleaned*
*2 tablespoons dry white wine*

*French or Italian bread, thinly sliced and toasted*
*dash of sweet Hungarian paprika*
*sprigs of fresh dill*

Snap off the tough bottom part of each asparagus spear. Cut the spears into bite-sized pieces. Lightly steam the asparagus for 3 to 4 minutes, drain, and set aside (see page 681).

In a saucepan, melt 3 tablespoons of the butter. Whisk in the flour. Simmer on low heat for a minute or two, stirring constantly. Gradually add the milk, while stirring. Continue to stir until the sauce thickens, about 5 minutes. Add salt and pepper to taste.

In another pan, melt the remaining tablespoon of butter, add the shrimp, and sauté briefly until they begin to turn pink. Stir in the white wine and simmer just a couple of minutes. Remove the shrimp from the cooking liquid and set them aside. Stir the cooking liquid into the white sauce. If the sauce seems too thin, let it cook gently for a few minutes more to reduce.

Arrange slices of toasted bread on each plate. Then add the shrimp and asparagus to the sauce and ladle it over the toast.

Garnish with a sprinkle of paprika and a fresh sprig of dill.

# Wynelle's Pot Pie

Long ago, Yankee cooks were known to bake two or three different types of pie for each meal. In addition to a substantial main course, it was customary to serve meat pies, fruit pies, and even an occasional vinegar pie.

Warm yourself on a cold winter's night with this pie. It's good served with applesauce and Harvard beets.

**SERVES 6**

CRUST
1 ½ cups unbleached white flour (up to
   ¾ cup whole wheat flour may be
   substituted)
½ cup chilled butter
3 tablespoons ice water
½ teaspoon salt (optional)
FILLING
1 large onion, chopped
3 tablespoons vegetable oil
2 medium carrots, diced

1 medium potato, diced
½ teaspoon sweet Hungarian paprika
½ teaspoon dried basil
½ teaspoon dried marjoram
½ cup diced red bell pepper
1 cup sliced mushrooms
½ cup green peas (fresh or frozen)
½ cup corn (fresh or frozen)
salt and ground black pepper to taste

| ROUX | TOPPING |
|---|---|
| 2 tablespoons butter | 1 tablespoon butter |
| 2 tablespoons unbleached white flour | ⅔ cup bread crumbs (garlic bread |
| 1 cup milk | crumbs are nice) |
| 1 teaspoon Dijon mustard | ¼ teaspoon dried marjoram |
| ¼ teaspoon nutmeg | ¼ teaspoon dried basil |
| 2 cups grated cheddar cheese | dash of sweet Hungarian paprika |

To make the crust, sift the flour into a mixing bowl. Cut in the butter using a pastry cutter or your fingertips until the mixture resembles a coarse meal. Sprinkle the ice water over the flour, a little at a time, as you turn the dough with a wooden spoon until a ball of dough forms. Add a little more ice water if the dough fails to come together. Chill the dough until firm, 30 to 60 minutes, or roll it out immediately on a lightly floured board. Place the dough in a 10-inch pie pan and crimp the edges.

To make the filling, in a large saucepan, sauté the onions in the oil until soft. Add the carrots, potatoes, paprika, basil, and marjoram. Cook, covered, on medium heat, stirring frequently, for about 10 minutes. Stir in the bell pepper, mushrooms, peas, and corn. Add salt and pepper to taste. Cover and continue to cook until the carrots begin to become tender, about 5 to 10 minutes.

For the roux, in another saucepan, melt the butter. Add the flour and stir constantly on low heat for 3 to 5 minutes. Whisk in the milk, mustard, and nutmeg. Continue to stir on low heat until the mixture is hot and lightly thickened, but do not let it boil. Remove the roux from the heat and whisk in the grated cheese until well blended.

Preheat the oven to 375°.

For the topping, in a small skillet, melt the butter on low heat. Add the bread crumbs and herbs, stir to coat them with the butter, and sauté them for about 3 minutes or until the crumbs are very lightly crisped.

Check the sautéed vegetables. If there is any liquid in the bottom of the pan, drain the vegetables.

To assemble the pie, spoon the drained vegetables into the waiting pie crust. Pour the roux over the vegetable filling and poke a spoon down into the vegetables in several places to encourage the roux to seep in. Sprinkle on the bread crumbs and, if you like, a few pinches of grated cheddar cheese. Bake for 40 minutes.

*Note: The pie will be easier to cut and serve if it sits for 10 to 15 minutes before cutting.*

# Fall River Vegetable Stew

Along the New England coast there's a large Portuguese population. Although meat and fish are common in Portuguese cooking, vegetarian dishes are also popular. Many of the Portuguese have wonderful backyard gardens where every available space seems to be planted with vegetables, herbs, fruit trees, and grapes.

This hearty, full-flavored dish is my version of a New England Portuguese stew. Serve it with crusty bread, cheese, and a leafy green salad.

### SERVES 5 OR 6

*1 large Spanish onion, chopped*
*4 garlic cloves, pressed*
*3 tablespoons olive oil*
*5 small potatoes, cut into chunks*
*2 large carrots, cut into ¹/₂-inch rounds*
*2 tablespoons sweet Hungarian paprika*

*1 cup water or vegetable stock (see page 685)*

*28-ounce can whole tomatoes, crushed*
*2 bay leaves*
*1 cup dry red wine*

*1 generous handful green beans (about ¹/₂ pound), trimmed and halved*
*3 cups sliced mushrooms*
*1 cup corn, fresh or frozen*
*salt and ground black pepper to taste*

In a large soup pot, sauté the onion and garlic in the olive oil until the onion softens. Stir in the potatoes, carrots, and paprika and sauté for 3 or 4 minutes, being careful not to let the paprika burn.

Pour in the water or stock, tomatoes, bay leaves, and wine. Cover and simmer on low heat for about 10 minutes.

Add the green beans and mushrooms and continue to simmer, covered, for about 30 minutes. Stir occasionally. Mix in the corn and simmer for about 15 minutes more or until the potatoes and carrots are tender. Add salt and pepper to taste. Remove the bay leaves.

## SIDE DISHES

# *Saucy Green Beans*

A tasty little side dish that's as American as apple pie.

### SERVES 4

½–¾ pound green beans
1¼ cups salted water
1 large onion, thinly sliced (about 1 cup)

_____

1 tablespoon butter
2 tablespoons unbleached white flour

¼ cup sour cream
1 teaspoon fresh lemon juice
1 tablespoon chopped fresh dill (1½ teaspoons dried)
salt and freshly ground black pepper to taste

Rinse and trim the green beans and cut them in half. Bring the water to a rolling boil. Drop the onion slices into the boiling water. After a couple of minutes, add the green beans. Cook until the beans are tender. Drain, reserving the liquid.

In a separate saucepan, make a roux. Melt the butter on low heat. Whisk in the flour and continue cooking for a minute or two, stirring constantly and taking care not to burn the roux. Whisk in about one cup of the reserved liquid, the sour cream, and the lemon juice. Add 2 teaspoons of the dill. Salt and pepper to taste.

Place the beans in a serving dish and pour the sauce over them. Serve sprinkled with the rest of the dill.

# Pretty Pickled Eggs

This is fun to make and the results are beautiful—the eggs turn magenta on the outside while their centers stay bright yellow and pure white.

YIELDS A QUART OF PICKLED EGGS AND VEGETABLES

*1 beet, trimmed and cut in half*
*1 carrot, sliced diagonally*
*1 red bell pepper, sliced*

*1 teaspoon fresh dill (¹/₂ teaspoon dried)*
*1 teaspoon fresh oregano (¹/₂ teaspoon dried)*

*¹/₃ cup vinegar*
*2 tablespoons brown sugar*

*4 hard-boiled eggs, peeled*

In a small saucepan, bring the beet halves to a boil in water to cover. Cook, covered, until tender, about 25 minutes. Remove the beets from the cooking water and set them aside. Keep the cooking water simmering, and add the carrot slices. Cover and simmer until almost tender, about 6 minutes. Add the red pepper, cover, and cook for about 4 minutes more. Remove the carrots and peppers from the cooking water and set them aside. Meanwhile, slip the skins off the beet halves and slice them.

Stir the vinegar, brown sugar, and herbs into the cooking water and bring it to a boil. Return the cooked vegetables to the broth, simmer for a minute or two, and then remove the pan from the heat.

Layer the vegetables and the hard-boiled eggs in a one-quart wide-mouth canning jar. Pour the vinegar mixture in to cover. Add more boiling water if necessary to fill the jar. Seal the jar tightly and refrigerate for 12 to 24 hours before serving. These pickled eggs will keep for up to a week in the refrigerator.

To serve, cut the eggs into wedges. Arrange them with the beet, carrot, and pepper slices on a bed of lettuce.

# Potato-Leek Vinaigrette

Leeks are fairly hardy. My mother grows them in Massachusetts and pulls them up as she needs them, right into the winter. By banking them with dry autumn leaves, she protects them from the cold.

The varied green tones of the leeks, mixed with the red pepper and white potatoes, make an appealing combination.

**SERVES 4**

4 leeks
4 medium potatoes
1 red bell pepper
**VINAIGRETTE**
½ cup vegetable oil

¼ cup vinegar
1 garlic clove, minced or pressed
1 ½ teaspoons finely chopped fresh dill
salt and freshly ground black pepper to
  taste

Wash the leeks well (see page 667). Slice the bulb and the tender green parts into ½-inch pieces. Drop the sliced leeks into boiling water, cook them for about 5 minutes, drain, and set aside to cool.

Cut the potatoes into 1½-inch chunks. Drop them into boiling, salted water and cook them until tender, but firm, about 10 minutes. Drain and set aside.

Slice the red pepper into 1-inch strips.

Whisk together the vinaigrette ingredients. Then combine the leeks, potatoes, and peppers in a serving bowl. Pour on the vinaigrette and chill well before serving.

# *Vermont Summer Muffins*

 In New England's northern regions the summers are short but intense, so things grow very fast. I remember visiting my cousin in Vermont during July when the fields were deep with hay,

the maple trees were lush and shadowy, and the garden was spewing out vegetables at full throttle. To keep up with the high production rate, some nights we'd eat a mountain of sautéed zucchini or a pot full of steamed green beans for our supper.

These wonderful muffins incorporate some of summer's bounty.

### YIELDS ABOUT 18 MUFFINS

*3 cups unbleached white flour*
*4 teaspoons baking powder*
*½ teaspoon baking soda*
*1½ teaspoons salt*

*1 cup grated sharp cheddar cheese*
*1 cup grated zucchini*
*3 tablespoons chopped fresh parsley*

*2–3 tablespoons chopped scallions*
*1 tablespoon chopped fresh dill (2 teaspoons dried)*

*2 eggs*
*1 cup buttermilk*
*¼ cup melted butter*

Preheat the oven to 350°.

Sift the dry ingredients into a large bowl. Add the cheese, zucchini, parsley, scallions, and dill and toss lightly to mix.

In another bowl, beat the eggs and then whisk in the buttermilk and melted butter. Add the wet ingredients to the flour-zucchini mixture and stir just enough to blend.

Spoon the batter into buttered muffin tins, filling them about ¾ full. Bake for about 30 to 35 minutes or until golden.

# Rhode Island Cornmeal Bread

This is a deliciously chewy bread with a nice subtle corn flavor. It's great served hot from the oven with soup or stew. It also makes a delightful toast for breakfast the next day.

1½ cups cornmeal

3 tablespoons butter

1¾ teaspoons salt

1½ cups boiling water

1 package dry yeast (about 1
   tablespoon)

¼ cup lukewarm water

½ cup water or milk

3½–4 cups unbleached white flour,
   more for kneading

Place the cornmeal, butter, and salt into a large mixing bowl. Add the boiling water and stir well until the butter has melted. Set aside to cool until just warm.

Meanwhile, dissolve the yeast in ¼ cup of lukewarm water. Stir the dissolved yeast into the cornmeal mixture and blend well. Stir in ½ cup water or milk and add the sifted flour, one cup at a time, blending well to form a dough.

The dough may be a little sticky, so flour your hands, and then gather the dough and turn it out onto a lightly floured board. Knead the dough for 5 to 10 minutes, using more flour as necessary to keep the dough from sticking. Place the dough in a lightly oiled bowl, cover it with a damp cloth, and let it rise in a warm place for about an hour, until it has doubled in size (see note). Then, punch it down and knead it for about 5 minutes. Return it to the bowl, cover it, and let it rise until doubled again. Knead the dough once more for a minute or two. Place the dough in a buttered 9x13-inch or a 3-inch deep, 9-inch round baking pan. Cover it and let it rise for about 40 minutes or until doubled in size.

> *Note: To create a warm, draft-free place where the dough can rise undisturbed, set the bowl of dough in a larger container that has about one inch of very hot water in it. Invert a saucer or shallow bowl in the water and set the bowl of dough on top so it sits just above the water. Wrap a thick bath towel over and around the whole setup to maintain the warmth.*

When the dough has almost risen, preheat the oven to 350°.

Bake for about 45 or 50 minutes, until the bread pulls away slightly from the sides of the pan. Cool the bread in the pan.

# Sara's Oat Bread

When Sara Robbins' husband, John, was a newspaper boy, one of his customers regularly offered him a slice of her favorite homemade bread as a treat. John loved the bread so much that his mother finally asked for the treasured recipe, and eventually passed it along to Sara. And now here it is from me to you.

If you follow this recipe exactly, you'll have a wonderfully light and tender bread.

### YIELDS 2 LOAVES

2 cups boiling water

2 cups rolled oats

1 tablespoon butter, oil, or margarine

_____

1 package dry yeast (about 1 tablespoon)

½ cup lukewarm water

½ cup brown sugar

4 cups unbleached white flour

1–1½ teaspoons salt

In a large bowl, pour the boiling water over the oats and butter and stir until the butter has melted. Set aside to cool.

Dissolve the yeast in the lukewarm water. Then stir the dissolved yeast into the cooled oat mixture. Add the brown sugar and 1 cup of the flour. Beat 100 strokes. Cover the bowl with a damp cloth and set it aside to rise in a warm place until the mixture bubbles, about 45 minutes. This batter is called a "sponge."

Stir in the salt and the remaining 3 cups of flour and mix well. Turn the dough out onto a lightly floured board and knead until it is elastic. This dough is sticky, so be patient. Oil your hands if necessary and try not to add much extra flour.

Oil the bowl. Return the dough to the bowl, and turn it over to coat it with oil. Cover the bowl with the damp cloth and set it aside in a warm place until the dough has doubled in size, 45 minutes to an hour.

Punch down the dough, turn it onto a lightly oiled board, and cut it in half. Form two loaves and place them in oiled one-pound loaf pans. Cover them and let them rise again in a warm place until doubled in size.

Preheat the oven to 350°. When the loaves have risen, bake them for about 40 minutes or until golden. Turn the loaves out of their pans. They should sound hollow when tapped on the bottom. Cool them on a wire rack. Brush the tops of the loaves with butter if desired.

## DESSERTS

## *Double Pear Crisp*

The taste of juicy, fresh pears is intensified by the concentrated flavor of dried pears in this simple, wholesome dessert. This dish, garnished with whipped cream, is always popular at Moosewood.

### SERVES 6

*6 ounces dried pears*
*1 cup bottled pear juice*
*4 cups chopped fresh pears (4 or 5 medium pears)*

*½ cup butter*
*¼ cup light brown sugar (or ⅓ cup maple syrup)*

*2 cups rolled oats*
*1 teaspoon cinnamon*
*½ teaspoon nutmeg*

*ice cream or whipped cream*

Preheat the oven to 375°.

Cut out and discard any stems and hard cores from the dried pears and then chop them into ½-inch pieces to yield about 1 cup. In a small saucepan, bring the dried pear pieces and the pear juice to a boil. Reduce the heat and simmer until the pears are tender, about 10 minutes. Meanwhile, core the fresh pears, chop them into bite-sized pieces, and place them in a 1½-quart or 8-inch square baking dish.

Melt the butter in a large saucepan and remove it from the heat. Add the brown sugar, oats, cinnamon, and nutmeg. Stir to coat the oats evenly.

When the dried pears are tender, pour them with their cooking liquid over the fresh pears in the baking dish. Top with the oat mixture.

Bake uncovered for 45 minutes or until the topping is browned and crisp.

Serve warm or cool with ice cream or fresh whipped cream.

# Squash and Cottage Cheese Pie

This is a great pie. The cottage cheese makes it a little lighter than most, and it's very quick to make if you use frozen squash purée. If you use fresh squash, I recommend butternut or delicata because they are easiest to peel. Some cottage cheeses are saltier than others, so add salt accordingly.

YIELD 6 SERVINGS

CRUST

1 cup unbleached white flour (up to ½ cup whole wheat flour may be substituted)

⅓ cup chilled butter

2 tablespoons ice water

½ teaspoon salt (optional)

FILLING

2 cups puréed winter squash (1 medium fresh squash or 2 10-ounce packages frozen squash purée)

1 cup cottage cheese

¾ teaspoon powdered ginger

1 teaspoon cinnamon

1 teaspoon salt (or to taste)

¼ cup sour cream

2 eggs

½ cup milk

1 tablespoon dry sherry

½–⅔ cup honey

To make the crust, sift the flour into a mixing bowl. Cut in the butter using a pastry cutter or your fingertips until the mixture resembles a coarse meal. Sprinkle the ice water over the flour, a little at a time, as you turn the dough with a wooden spoon until a ball of dough forms. Add a little more ice water if the dough fails to come together. Chill the dough until firm for about 45 minutes or roll it out immediately on a lightly floured board. Place the dough in a 9-inch pie pan and crimp the edges.

To prepare fresh squash, peel and seed a medium winter squash. Cut it into cubes. In a saucepan, cook the squash in about an inch of water, covered, until tender. Drain the squash, mash it lightly, and allow it to cool for a few minutes.

If using frozen squash, thaw it and drain it lightly.

Preheat the oven to 450°.

Using a blender or food processor, purée all of the ingredients until smooth. Pour the filling into the pie shell and bake for 10 minutes. Lower the heat to 350° and continue to bake for 30 to 40 minutes, until the pie is set.

# *Cranberry Tea Cake*

This cake is easy to make with consistently good results. The recipe comes from Moosewood's friend Pat Cerretani, who has been making variations of this cake for special occasions since she was ten years old.

The cranberries we use in this country are native to North America. Most of them are grown on Cape Cod in Massachusetts. The Indians of New England ate them fresh and also dried them for the wintertime.

I love baking with cranberries. Their showy, red color and crisp, tart flavor are great in muffins, coffeecakes, quick breads, and pies.

### YIELDS 8 SERVINGS

*2 cups fresh cranberries*
*½ cup brown sugar*
*½ cup finely chopped almonds*
*2 teaspoons cinnamon*
*¼ teaspoon nutmeg*

———————————————

*½ cup butter*
*1 cup sugar*
*1 teaspoon pure vanilla extract*

*½ pint sour cream*
*2 eggs, beaten*

———————————————

*2 cups unbleached white flour*
*1 teaspoon baking soda*
*1 teaspoon baking powder*
*pinch of salt*
*confectioners' sugar*

Preheat the oven to 350°.

Whirl the cranberries in a food processor or in a blender in small batches until coarsely chopped.

In a bowl, mix together the chopped cranberries, brown sugar, almonds, cinnamon, and nutmeg and set aside.

In a large mixing bowl, cream the butter and sugar. Add the vanilla, sour cream, and eggs and blend them well.

Sift together the flour, baking soda, baking powder, and salt. Stir the flour mixture into the butter mixture. Blend until just combined.

Pour half of the batter into a buttered bundt pan or an 8-inch round cake pan. Distribute half of the cranberry mixture over the batter. Pour on the rest of the batter and top with the remaining cranberry mixture.

Bake for 50 to 60 minutes. When the cake is done, remove it from the pan and cool it on a cake rack. Sprinkle the cake lightly with confectioners' sugar.

FOUAD MAKKI

# North Africa and the Northeast African Highlands

# INTRODUCTION

Exile, whether forced or voluntary, tends to produce moments rich in memories. Selective though they may be, memories are sometimes one's only link with the past. In preparing many of the recipes assembled in this chapter, I constantly found myself returning to the many wonderful moments of my childhood days. The aromas of many of these dishes have brought back distinct and vivid images of friends and family coming together to share food. I remember large quantities of bright red chiles spread out on straw mats and left out to dry before being ground and mixed with other spices into *berbere,* and the hustle and bustle in the house around lunch or dinner time. Writing this chapter has made me realize the role meals played in bringing members of my large extended family together, and has made me profoundly aware of the cultural and emotional significance of food. So the recipes assembled in this chapter are the embodiment of some of those nostalgic moments, of my childhood days in Addis Abeba, Asmara, and Massawa, and of times spent cooking together with friends from Morocco, Libya, and Tunisia.

These recipes are representative of countries with striking geographic, climatic, and social contrasts. For culinary purposes, they can be conveniently viewed as three distinct, but interconnected, regions. The countries of North Africa: Egypt, Libya, Tunisia, Algeria, and Morocco, the highlands of Ethiopia and Eritrea, and the lowlands and coastal regions of Eritrea.

## *North Africa*

The North African countries share a common history, language, and culture. Libya and those to its west are known as the Magreb or Arab west, while Egypt is considered part of the Mashreq, or Arab east. The territory covers a large part of the African continent, stretching from the Atlantic all the way across the Mediterranean to the Red Sea. It is set against the magnificent background of the Atlas mountain range with its rugged cliffs and peaks. It is home to the Berber and Arab peoples, and the Arabic language, in its various dialects, is spoken throughout the region. Islam is the major religion of North Africa, although small communities of Jews and Christians can also be found in almost all its constituent countries.

The development of North African cuisine reflects the history of its people, with influences brought about by conquests, mass immigration, and religious prohibition. The early origins of this cooking can be found in the Bedouin and peasant dishes of the Berbers and Arabs. In the case of Egyptian cuisine, one can find dishes dating from the times of the pharaohs.

Centuries before the Dutch East India Company attempted to monopolize the spice trade, the region served as a spice route between the Far East and Europe, and between central Africa and Europe. As a result, many spices became integrated into the cuisine.

Later, with the victorious wars waged by the followers of Mohammed in 632 A.D. and the establishment of the Islamic Empire, North Africa experienced another major development of its cuisine. In its golden age, the Islamic Empire stretched from Morocco to China and trade in foodstuffs among the countries of the empire thrived. Later, the area was occupied by the Ottoman Turks, who brought not only their cuisine but also foods of other regions of their empire, further enriching North African cooking.

The culmination of these diverse influences is today's cuisine of beautiful and elaborate dishes. The influence of both Arabs and Berbers is unmistakable. An infinite variety of stuffed vegetables, soups, stews, filo pastries, and salads makes North African cooking varied and interesting. Olive oil, which is relatively cheap and abundant, is widely used. Couscous, made from finely milled semolina wheat, is a contribution of the Berbers and is used today throughout the Middle East. Along with an assortment of breads, it serves as the basic accompaniment to other dishes. The most common drink with this rich cuisine is a sweet tea steeped with mint and renowned for its strong digestive powers. A variety of pastries, cakes, and fruit desserts completes most meals.

## The Highlands of Northeast Africa

The highlands of Northeast Africa form a vast area of complex mountains and high plateaus with altitudes ranging from 7,800 to 15,000 feet. It is crisscrossed with deep ravines and valleys and is the source of the Blue Nile, which merges with the White Nile at Omdurman, in the Sudan, to form the Nile River and eventually flow into the Mediterranean Sea. The region enjoys a temperate climate and a three-month rainy season, which promote the growth of diverse vegetables and fruits. *T'eff,* a member of the millet family and a basic ingredient in the region's cuisine, requires just such a climate. This makes this region of Northeast Africa one of a very few places around the world where *t'eff* is grown.

The highlands run through most of northern Ethiopia and southern Eritrea. This region was home to some of the world's most ancient civilizations, and early in the spice trade, it served as a transit stop for Arabian and Persian traders. After the decline of the Axumite Civilization in the seventh century, the region became relatively isolated. The mountains made a natural barrier to the outside world, further entrenching the area's isolation. In this setting, a very distinct cuisine has developed that is not found in other parts of Africa or the Middle East. The major religions of the area—Coptic Christianity and Islam, and the small Jewish community of Ethiopian Falashas—have affected the cuisine with their strict dietary rules. In Ethiopia, for instance, a wide range of vegetarian dishes have been developed because millions of Coptic Christians abstain from meat for some 200 days a year. The lentil w'et in this chapter is an example of such a dish.

The cooking of the highlands of Ethiopia and Eritrea is unique and delicious. Its variety is partly derived from the subtle blending and balancing of the spice flavors. The most common dishes, called *w'et* in Ethiopia and *zigne* in Eritrea, are stews that may include fish, vegetables, legumes, or meat. Most of the w'ets can be prepared as k'eyi w'et, which has the hot red spice berbere in it, or as alit'cha, which does not. These colorful and spicy stews are usually accompanied by *injera*—a flat, slightly fermented round bread made of *t'eff*, which provides for a delicious complementary contrast. Yogurt or cottage cheese is usually served alongside the stews. Fresh vegetable salads, soups, and a variety of baked breads add to an extensive and rich menu. With the traditional meal one would normally drink *t'ej*, a kind of honey wine or mead, or the local beer called *t'ella*. Almost every meal is then followed with a pot of richly brewed coffee, which is only natural since Ethiopia is the original home of the coffee bean.

## The Eritrean Lowlands

Unlike the central highlands, which have a cuisine similar to that of northern Ethiopia, the Eritrean lowlands constitute a slightly different cultural and historic region. Situated right at the Bab al Mendeb, the mouth of the Red Sea, it has been subjected to foreign occupation for the past three and a half centuries. The manifold administrations that came ashore with the tide have left their particular imprints on the culture and people of the coastline. As my parents were from the port city of Massawa, my family's history was also closely tied to that of the Red Sea coast.

The Ottoman Empire, which stretched all the way into Eritrea, linked the lowlands to the countries of North Africa and beyond for some 300 years. This allowed for a close development of food styles between the North African countries and the Eritrean lowlands. The proximity to the central highland regions of southern Eritrea and northern Ethiopia, on the other hand, enabled a constant interaction and culinary exchange. The result has been a singular blending of cuisines that at once makes the lowlands food style distinct as well as similar to both North African and Ethiopian cooking.

Today the lowlands are part of the Red Sea territory of Eritrea. With a population of over three and a half million, Eritrea has an area of approximately 119,000 square kilometers. The territory stretches for some 800 kilometers along the Red Sea coast. The topography includes the mountainous central and northern highlands, with an escarpment descending to the rich soil of both the western plains and the long eastern coastal strip.

A former Italian colony, Eritrea became federated to Ethiopia by the United Nations in 1952. The federation lasted for ten years, when in 1962 Ethiopia annexed Eritrea and abolished the federal arrangement. Since then, a protracted war has been fought by the Eritreans against Ethiopia. The war has ruptured Eritrean society, displacing tens of thousands of people internally and forcing over half a million others to flee into exile.

## Social and Culinary Aspects

Despite differences in names and methods of preparation, there is an underlying similarity in some of the dishes of the three areas. The highlands of Northeast Africa and the countries that border the Mediterranean coastline have preserved the tradition of sophisticated spicy stews, and both areas prize herbed clarified butter as the most desirable cooking oil. Practically every town has a spice street with little shops or open markets where the vendors fill paper cones with all sorts of spices and herbs. Each country seems to have its favorite combinations of spices or herbs, but cumin, coriander, cinnamon, ginger, turmeric, chiles, marjoram, and fresh mint are widely used. Sesame seed, caraway seed, anise, and fennel flavor breads and desserts. Saffron is used most extensively in Morocco, but it is highly valued throughout the region. Some "spices," like Ethiopia's berbere, are in fact combinations of several spices.

The activities of cooking and eating reflect many subtle and intricate facets of the region and the people's way of life. Meals are intensely social and representative of centuries of local culture, art, and tradition. Weddings, birthdays, religious holidays, and other important social events are always marked by the presentation of food. Some dishes such as Sambussa and the North African Harira are only made during the month of Ramadan, the ninth month of the Islamic calendar, when millions of Muslims fast from dawn to dusk. Throughout the region, hospitality is a cherished tradition, and guests are always welcomed and offered food.

In both North and Northeast Africa, lunch is the main meal of the day. People usually eat from a common tray of food and use their hands rather than utensils, so washing hands is part of the ritual of dining. In the northeastern highlands, the meal is normally served on a *mesob*—a cross between a basket and a table—with the injera spread out in several layers and the various w'ets spooned onto it. In North Africa, meals are served on large metal trays resting on a type of low round wooden stool. The trays themselves are made of copper, brass, or silver and are decorated with ornate patterns or phrases. Traditionally, people sit around these tables on cushions.

Although forks and knives have been increasingly adopted for eating some foods, the delicate and highly refined art of eating with one's fingers is still dominant. In Ethiopia, for instance, when eating injera and w'et, one has to learn how to fold the injera around the stew and eat without touching one's fingers either to the stew or the mouth.

As with all good food, that of North and Northeast Africa is always in flux and subject to constant experimentation. Improvisation within the bounds of tradition is common, which allows for the creation of unique and exquisite dishes. I am convinced that the traditional cuisine can sometimes be enhanced by unorthodox additions or deletions. So trust your own tastes and experiment if you wish. You might be delightfully surprised.

# Berbere

•

# Hot Spice Mixture

This is the hot and exotic spice mixture that gives Eritrean and Ethiopian cooking its characteristic flavor. The traditional method of preparation is lengthy and uses some spices and herbs not readily available here. The mixture presented below is a close adaptation, and it keeps well for months refrigerated.

Berbere is called for in my w'et recipes. It can also be used in other recipes in this book that call for a hot spice.

### YIELDS ABOUT ⅓ CUP

2 teaspoons cumin seeds
4 whole cloves
¾ teaspoon cardamom seeds
½ teaspoon whole black peppercorns
¼ teaspoon whole allspice
1 teaspoon fenugreek seeds
½ teaspoon coriander seeds

_____

8–10 small dried red chiles

_____

½ teaspoon grated fresh ginger root (1 teaspoon dried)
¼ teaspoon turmeric
1 teaspoon salt
2½ tablespoons sweet Hungarian paprika
⅛ teaspoon cinnamon
⅛ teaspoon ground cloves

In a small frying pan, on medium-low heat, toast the cumin, whole cloves, cardamom, peppercorns, allspice, fenugreek, and coriander for about 2 minutes, stirring constantly. Remove the pan from the heat and cool for 5 minutes.

Discard the stems from the chiles. In a spice grinder or with a mortar and pestle, finely grind together the toasted spices and the chiles. Mix in the remaining ingredients.

Store Berbere refrigerated in a well-sealed jar or a tightly closed plastic bag.

# Niter Kebbeh

·

## Spiced Clarified Butter

 Niter Kebbeh has been prized in Ethiopia as a cooking oil and a seasoning for a very long time.

Without careful packaging and proper refrigeration, butter easily spoils. Furthermore, because of the milk solids it contains, butter has a low scorching temperature, which limits its usefulness in cooking. However, the milk solids can be removed from butter by the process of clarifying it. Clarified butter keeps well, even at room temperature. Niter Kebbeh adds flavor to North African foods and is a must in Ethiopian cooking.

### YIELDS ABOUT 1 CUP

1 pound unsalted butter
¼ cup chopped onions
2 cloves garlic, minced or pressed
2 teaspoons grated peeled fresh ginger
   root
½ teaspoon turmeric
4 cardamom seeds, crushed

1 cinnamon stick
2 whole cloves
⅛ teaspoon nutmeg
¼ teaspoon ground fenugreek seeds
1 tablespoon fresh basil (1 teaspoon
   dried)

In a small saucepan, gradually melt the butter and bring it to bubbling. When the top is covered with foam, add the other ingredients and reduce the heat to a simmer. Gently simmer, uncovered, on low heat. After about 45 to 60 minutes, when the surface becomes transparent and the milk solids are on the bottom, pour the liquid through a cheesecloth into a heat-resistant container. Discard the spices and solids.

Covered tightly and stored in the refrigerator, Niter Kebbeh will keep for up to 2 months.

# Fatima's Salad

This colorful and delicious vegetable appetizer, which I have named after my mother, was a favorite in our house. It can be served as an appetizer or as a salad plate with bread or soup.

### SERVES 4 TO 6

2 medium potatoes, boiled and cut into
  thick slices
2 beets, boiled, skinned, and sliced
4 carrots, cut into ½-inch rounds
1 green bell pepper, seeded and sliced
1 red bell pepper, seeded and sliced

leaf lettuce

**FATIMA'S SALAD DRESSING**
⅓ cup olive oil
2½ tablespoons vinegar
salt and freshly ground black pepper to
  taste
2 tablespoons chopped fresh parsley

4 hard-boiled eggs, peeled and
  quartered
black olives
freshly ground black pepper

Prepare the potatoes and beets. In a pot of boiling water, cook or steam (see page 681) the cut carrots and peppers separately, until tender. On a platter, arrange all of the vegetables on a bed of lettuce.

In a blender, whirl the dressing ingredients until creamy. Pour the dressing over the salad.

Decorate the salad plate with the hard-boiled egg quarters and a few black olives. Sprinkle freshly ground black pepper on the eggs.

# Sambussa

•

# Savory Pastries

 These savory deep-fried pastries are always made during the Islamic month of Ramadan.

To make the preparation of Sambussas easy, I have substituted wonton wrappers for the traditional pastry dough. Sambussas can be served as appetizers or with Mahshi Filfil (see page 517) and Crisp Cooked Vegetable Appetizer (see page 513) for a satisfying meal.

## YIELDS 16 PASTRIES

| | |
|---|---|
| *1 cup brown lentils* | *¹/₂ teaspoon cayenne* |
| *1¹/₂ cups water* | *1 teaspoon cinnamon* |
| | *¹/₂ cup diced green bell pepper* |
| *³/₄ cup finely chopped onions* | *salt and ground black pepper to taste* |
| *2 garlic cloves, minced* | |
| *3 tablespoons olive oil* | *8 wonton wrappers (see page 686)* |
| *2 teaspoons sweet Hungarian paprika* | *1 egg yolk beaten with a tablespoon of* |
| *1 teaspoon grated peeled fresh ginger* | *water* |
| *root* | |
| *1 teaspoon ground coriander seeds* | *oil for deep-frying* |

Rinse the lentils and bring them to a boil in the water. Reduce the heat, cover, and simmer for 45 minutes.

Meanwhile, sauté the onions and garlic in the olive oil until the onions are translucent. Add the spices and chopped green peppers and simmer, covered, for 3 minutes, stirring often. Remove the pan from the heat. When the lentils are tender, combine them with the sautéed vegetables. Season with salt and pepper.

Cut the wonton wrappers in half to form rectangles. Place a wrapper vertically on a flat surface and brush it with the beaten egg mixture. Put a rounded tablespoon of the filling on the lower end of one of the rectangles. Fold the left bottom corner up and over the filling until it meets the right edge of the wrapper and forms a triangle. Next, flip the filled triangle up and over, folding along its upper edge. Then fold it over to the left on the diagonal. Continue folding until you reach the end of the wrapper and have formed a neat triangular package. Repeat this process with the other wonton wrapper rectangles.

Deep-fry each pastry until golden in 2 or 3 inches of oil heated to 360°. You can keep the fried sambussas in a warm oven until they are all prepared and ready to be served. Sambussas are best eaten hot.

## *Crisp Cooked Vegetable Appetizer*

### SERVES 4

¾ cup finely chopped onions

2 garlic cloves, pressed or minced

2 tablespoons olive oil

1 tablespoon sweet Hungarian paprika

¼ teaspoon cayenne

2 cups cubed eggplant (½-inch cubes)

2 cups cubed yellow squash (½-inch cubes)

1 cup chopped green and red bell peppers

1 cup chopped fresh tomatoes

**DRESSING**

3 tablespoons olive oil

2 tablespoons fresh lemon juice

2 tablespoons finely chopped fresh parsley

salt and freshly ground black pepper to taste

_____

leaf lettuce

Sauté the onions and garlic in the olive oil, adding the paprika and cayenne after a few minutes. Continue to sauté for about 5 minutes, until the onions are tender. Add the eggplant and squash and cook, covered, for about 10 minutes, stirring occasionally. Mix in the peppers and tomatoes and continue to cook for a few more minutes, until the vegetables are tender but still firm. Drain and set the vegetables aside.

To prepare the dressing, mix together the olive oil, lemon juice, half of the parsley, and the salt and pepper. Prepare a bed of lettuce on a large platter and mound the sautéed vegetables on top. Drizzle the dressing over the salad and garnish it with the rest of the parsley. Serve hot or at room temperature.

# *Harira*

•

## *North African Vegetable Soup*

A great favorite in North Africa, Harira is served during Ramadan, the ninth month of the Muslim calendar year. Ramadan is
a time of fasting during daylight hours, and this hearty soup,
full of vegetables and legumes, is the traditional way of breaking the fast. Harira is
considered the national soup of Morocco and can be eaten as a meal on its own. Our
Moosewood customers enjoy this soup year-round, not just for breaking fasts.

### SERVES 6 TO 7

1 cup finely chopped onions
2 celery stalks, diced
3 tablespoons vegetable oil
1 teaspoon turmeric
1 teaspoon ground coriander seeds
½ teaspoon cinnamon
⅛–¼ teaspoon cayenne (or to taste)
1 small potato, chopped
1 small carrot, diced
4 small tomatoes, chopped
1 cup tomato juice
4 cups vegetable stock (see page 685),
    liquid from cooking chick peas, or
    water (or a combination)

1 small zucchini, finely chopped
½ cup curly vermicelli, crumbled
1 cup canned or cooked chick peas (see
    page 663)
¼ cup fresh lemon juice (or to taste)
salt and freshly ground black pepper to
    taste

_____

chopped fresh parsley
fresh mint leaves
red bell pepper or pimiento strips

In a soup pot, sauté the onions and celery in the oil until the onions are translucent. Add the spices, potatoes, and carrots and cook for 5 minutes, stirring often. Mix in the chopped tomatoes, tomato juice, and chick pea liquid or stock and simmer until all of the vegetables are almost tender.

Add the zucchini and vermicelli and simmer for about 5 minutes longer. Mix in the chick peas, lemon juice, and salt and pepper to taste.

Garnish with chopped parsley, mint leaves, and strips of red bell pepper or pimiento.

# Split Pea and Rice Soup

### SERVES 4

| | |
|---|---|
| 1 cup dried split peas | ½ teaspoon ground cardamom |
| 3 cups water | |
| | 2 cups vegetable stock (see page 685) |
| 2 cups chopped onions | 2 teaspoons fresh lemon juice |
| 2 large garlic cloves, minced or pressed | ½ cup cooked rice |
| ¼ cup olive oil | salt and freshly ground black pepper to |
| 2 bay leaves | taste |
| 1 teaspoon ground cumin seeds | ¼–¾ cup chopped fresh parsley |
| ½ teaspoon cinnamon | |
| ¼ teaspoon cayenne | pimiento strips |

Rinse the split peas. Put them in a soup pot with 3 cups of water and bring them to a boil. Reduce the heat, cover, and simmer for 45 minutes to an hour.

Meanwhile, sauté the onions and garlic in the olive oil until the onions are translucent. Mix in the spices and sauté for 5 to 10 minutes more, stirring frequently to prevent burning. Set aside.

When the split peas are cooked, stir in the onion mixture along with the vegetable stock. Add the lemon juice and the cooked rice and season with salt and freshly ground black pepper. Stir in the parsley and gently reheat, if necessary.

Garnish each bowl with a thin strip of pimiento.

# Ful Nabed

·

## Egyptian Bean and Vegetable Soup

A popular Egyptian soup, Ful Nabed is simple and nutritious.

**SERVES 5 TO 6**

*1 cup chopped onions*
*2 garlic cloves, pressed*
*¼ cup olive oil*
*1 teaspoon ground cumin seeds*
*1½ teaspoons sweet Hungarian paprika*
*¼ teaspoon cayenne*
*2 bay leaves*
*1 large carrot, chopped*
*1 cup chopped fresh tomatoes*

*3½ cups vegetable stock (see page 685)*
*2 cups canned or cooked fava beans (see page 663)*
*¼ cup chopped fresh parsley*
*3 tablespoons fresh lemon juice*
*Salt and freshly ground black pepper to taste*
*fresh mint leaves (optional)*

In a large soup pot sauté the onions and garlic in the olive oil until the onions are translucent. Add the cumin, paprika, cayenne, bay leaves, and carrots and cook on medium heat for 5 minutes. Stir in the chopped tomatoes and vegetable stock and simmer until the carrots are tender, about 15 minutes. Finally, add the cooked fava beans and the parsley and lemon juice. Add salt and pepper to taste.

Ful Nabed can be served with pita bread and garnished with fresh mint leaves.

# Mahshi Filfil

•

# Stuffed Peppers with Feta Cheese Sauce

In North Africa, stuffed vegetables are called *mahshi* and are great family favorites. Each country has its own variation. This Moosewood version is unique because it uses brown rice and is topped with a creamy feta cheese sauce.

Normally, Mahshi Filfil are made with green peppers, but I think it is very attractive to make them with a combination of green, yellow, and red peppers.

## SERVES 4

1 cup chopped onions
3 garlic cloves, pressed
2 teaspoons dried dill weed
¼ cup olive oil
¼ cup pine nuts
3 tomatoes, chopped
3 cups cooked short-grain brown rice
¼ cup chopped fresh parsley
1½ tablespoons chopped fresh mint
freshly ground black pepper to taste

_____

4 large green, yellow, or red bell
   peppers

½ cup tomato juice
**CREAMY FETA SAUCE**
1¾ cups milk
¼ cup butter
¼ cup unbleached white flour
½ teaspoon dried dill weed
1–1½ tablespoons chopped fresh mint
¾ cup grated feta cheese
salt and freshly ground black pepper to
   taste

_____

4 fresh mint leaves

Sauté the onions, garlic, and dill in the olive oil until the onions are translucent. Add the pine nuts, and when they begin to color, add the chopped tomatoes and simmer, covered, for 3 minutes. Add the rice and mix well. Stir in the parsley and mint. Add salt and pepper to taste. Remove the pan from the heat.

Cut the peppers in half lengthwise and remove the seeds. Leave the stems on, so the pepper halves will hold their shape better during baking. Stuff the peppers with the rice mixture and place them in an oiled baking dish. Pour the tomato juice into the bottom of the dish. Tightly cover, and bake at 375° for 30 minutes.

To make the sauce, heat the milk in a small saucepan and stir occasionally to prevent scorching. In another saucepan, melt the butter. Stir the flour into the butter and cook it for a few minutes. Pour in the hot milk, stirring continuously, until the mixture thickens. Add the dill, mint, and feta. Heat gently until the feta is melted. Season with black pepper to taste.

Serve the stuffed peppers topped with the feta sauce. Garnish with fresh mint leaves.

# Vegetable Tajine

•

# Moroccan Stew

Stews are one of the finest features of North African cooking. There, this exotic and fragrant dish is cooked to perfection in a cone-shaped ceramic pot called a *tajine*. Saffron gives it a uniquely Moroccan taste. Vegetable tajines can be served with bread or on a bed of couscous.

### SERVES 4 TO 6

1½ cups chopped onions
3 garlic cloves, pressed
⅓ cup olive oil
1 teaspoon dried thyme
3 cups cubed potatoes
1 cup chopped green beans
1 red bell pepper, chopped
2 cups cubed fresh tomatoes
3 cups vegetable stock (see page 685)

13-ounce can artichoke hearts, drained
    and halved (reserve the brine)
½ cup pitted black olives, halved
pinch of saffron
¼ cup fresh lemon juice
¼ cup chopped fresh parsley
salt and ground black pepper to taste

_____

toasted, chopped almonds

Sauté the onions and garlic in the olive oil until the onions are translucent. Add the thyme, potatoes, green beans, bell pepper, and tomatoes and cook on medium-high heat for 3 minutes, stirring occasionally. Add the vegetable stock and the brine from the artichokes and simmer, covered, until the vegetables are tender, about 20 minutes.

Stir in the halved artichoke hearts, the black olives, and a pinch of saffron. Continue to simmer gently for another 5 to 10 minutes. Add the lemon juice, parsley, and salt and pepper to taste.

Serve with bread or on couscous and top with chopped almonds.

# Eggplant Marrakech

## SERVES 4

2 medium or large eggplants

---

1 cup finely chopped onions

2 garlic cloves, pressed or minced

$^{1}/_{4}$ teaspoon ground red pepper or
    Berbere (see page 509)

1 teaspoon sweet Hungarian paprika

1 teaspoon ground cumin seeds

$^{1}/_{4}$ teaspoon ground cloves

3 tablespoons olive oil

2 tomatoes, chopped

---

2 tablespoons olive oil

$^{1}/_{2}$ cup vermicelli, broken into short
    pieces

1 cup water

1 cup cooked brown rice

1 cup canned or cooked chick peas (see
    page 663)

$^{1}/_{2}$ cup raisins

3 tablespoons fresh lemon juice

$^{1}/_{4}$ cup chopped fresh parsley

salt and freshly ground black pepper to
    taste

---

$^{1}/_{2}$ cup grated feta cheese

pimiento strips

Leaving the stems on, slice the eggplants in half lengthwise and place them, cut side down, on an oiled baking sheet. Cover them with aluminum foil and bake at 375° for about 45 minutes, until tender.

Sauté the onions, garlic, and spices in 3 tablespoons of olive oil until the onions are translucent. Stir often to prevent the spices from burning. Add the chopped tomatoes and simmer, covered, for 3 or 4 minutes.

Meanwhile, in a separate pot, heat 2 tablespoons of olive oil. Toss the vermicelli in the hot oil for a couple of minutes until the color changes to golden-brown. Immediately add a cup of water, bring it to a boil, and simmer, covered, for about 5 minutes, until the water is absorbed; remove from the heat. Add the rice, chick peas, and raisins. Stir in the sautéed onion-tomato mixture, the lemon juice, and parsley. Add salt and pepper to taste.

Turn the baked eggplant halves over in the baking pan. With a fork or spoon, mash the pulp a little, taking care not to break the skin. Push aside some of the pulp to make a hollow. Mound a quarter of the filling on each half. Bake, covered, at 375° for 20 minutes.

Sprinkle with feta cheese and garnish with pimiento strips.

# Fish Kebabs

This is a very colorful and tasty arrangement of marinated and then skewered and grilled vegetables and fish. The marinade, called *chermoulla,* is a blend of fragrant seasonings, oil, and lemon juice. In this version I've suggested my favorite vegetables for kebabs. You should choose your own favorites; some other good choices are eggplants, mushrooms, and onions.

### SERVES 4

Special equipment: skewers (see note)

CHERMOULLA
*4 small garlic cloves, minced*
*1 teaspoon ground cumin seeds*
*½ teaspoon sweet Hungarian paprika*
*⅛ teaspoon cayenne*
*generous pinch of saffron*
*¼ cup chopped fresh cilantro*
*¼ cup fresh lemon juice*
*¾ cup olive oil*
*salt and black pepper to taste*

*1 pound monk fish or other firm fish*
*1 yellow squash*
*1 green bell pepper*
*1 red bell pepper*
*cherry tomatoes*
*bay leaves*

_____

*cooked brown rice or pita bread*
*lemon wedges*
*sprigs of mint*

Combine the ingredients for the chermoulla. Cut the fish into 1-inch cubes. Similarly, cut the vegetables into 1-inch cubes. Place the fish and vegetables in the chermoulla and marinate, refrigerated, for 2 hours.

When you are ready to assemble the kebabs, soften the bay leaves in boiling water for several minutes. Alternate the tomatoes, peppers, yellow squash, and fish on skewers. Place a bay leaf occasionally on the skewers next to the fish. Reserve the chermoulla.

Cover the broiler pan with foil and place the kebabs on it about an inch apart. Broil for 15 to 20 minutes, basting with the reserved chermoulla, and turning frequently to cook evenly.

Serve on rice or in pita bread and garnish with lemon wedges and sprigs of mint.

*Note: If you are using bamboo skewers, soak them in water for about ½ hour and fill them out to the ends so the skewers won't burn.*

# Yemiser W'et

•

## Spicy Lentil Stew

This spicy dish is one of the many stews made in Ethiopia. Yemiser W'et, made with berbere and niter kebbeh, an Ethiopian clarified butter, has a unique flavor and is traditionally vegetarian.

**SERVES 8**

*1 cup dried brown lentils*

---

*1 cup finely chopped onions*
*2 garlic cloves, minced or pressed*
*¼ cup Niter Kebbeh (see page 510)*
*1 tablespoon Berbere (see page 509) (to taste)*
*1 teaspoon ground cumin seeds*
*1 tablespoon sweet Hungarian paprika*
*2 cups finely chopped tomatoes*

*¼ cup tomato paste*
*1 cup vegetable stock (see page 685) or water*
*1 cup green peas (fresh or frozen)*
*salt and freshly ground black pepper to taste*
*3 batches Injera (see page 525) (to taste)*
*plain yogurt or cottage cheese*

Rinse and cook the lentils (see page 653).

Meanwhile, sauté the onions and garlic in the niter kebbeh, until the onions are just translucent. Add the berbere, cumin, and paprika and sauté for a few minutes more, stirring occasionally to prevent burning. Mix in the chopped tomatoes and tomato paste and simmer for another 5 to 10 minutes. Add 1 cup of vegetable stock or water and continue simmering.

When the lentils are cooked, drain them and mix them into the sauté. Add the green peas and cook for another 5 minutes. Add salt and black pepper to taste.

To serve Yemiser W'et, spread layers of injera on individual plates. Place some yogurt or cottage cheese alongside a serving of w'et on the injera and pass more injera at the table. To eat, tear off pieces of injera, fold it around bits of stew, and, yes, eat it with your fingers.

# Yetakelt W'et

•

## Spicy Mixed Vegetable Stew

 Try making this dish and Yemiser W'et for the same meal. In Ethiopia, it is customary to offer several stews at one time, and people eat some of each kind.

SERVES 4 TO 6

1 cup finely chopped onions
2 garlic cloves, minced or pressed
1 tablespoon Berbere (see page 509)
1 tablespoon sweet Hungarian paprika
¼ cup Niter Kebbeh (see page 510)
1 cup green beans, cut into thirds
1 cup chopped carrots
1 cup cubed potatoes
1 cup chopped tomatoes

¼ cup tomato paste
2 cups vegetable stock (see page 685)
salt and freshly ground black pepper to
   taste
¼ cup chopped fresh parsley

_____

2 batches Injera (see page 525)
plain yogurt or cottage cheese

Sauté the onions, garlic, berbere, and paprika in the niter kebbeh for 2 minutes. Add the beans, carrots, and potatoes and continue to sauté for about 10 minutes, stirring occasionally to prevent burning. Add the chopped tomatoes, tomato paste, and vegetable stock. Bring to a boil and then simmer for 15 minutes, or until all of the vegetables are tender.

Add salt and pepper to taste and mix in the parsley.

Serve with injera and yogurt or cottage cheese following the same serving and eating procedure as for Yemiser W'et (see page 522).

# Vegetarian Lahmajun

•

# North African Pizza

This is a vegetarian version of North African pizza. Here tofu replaces the traditional lamb. Make sure to freeze the tofu the day before. Vegetarian Lahmajun can be served as an appetizer or as a main dish.

SERVES 6 TO 8

CRUST

1 package dry yeast (about 1
   tablespoon)
1 cup warm water
1 teaspoon salt
¼ cup olive oil
3–3½ cups unbleached white flour
   (approximately)

TOPPING

¾ cup chopped onions
1 garlic clove, pressed

¼ cup olive oil
1½ teaspoons dried basil
freshly ground black pepper
2 cups chopped fresh tomatoes
1 cake tofu, frozen, thawed, and
   shredded (about 2 cups) (see page
   683)
½ cup chopped fresh parsley

_____

2 cups grated feta cheese

    To make the crust, dissolve the yeast in the warm water in a large bowl and let it rest for about 5 minutes. Add the salt and olive oil. Stir in 2 cups of flour and beat well. Gradually add enough of the additional 1½ cups of flour to form a soft dough. When the dough pulls away from the sides of the bowl, turn it onto a lightly floured board. Knead it for about 10 minutes, adding additional flour as needed, until the dough is smooth and elastic. Place the dough in an oiled bowl, turn it over to coat it with oil, and cover it with a damp cloth. Let the dough rise in a warm place until doubled in bulk, about 1½ hours.

While the dough is rising, make the topping. In a skillet, sauté the onions and garlic in the olive oil until the onions are translucent. Add the basil, black pepper, and chopped tomatoes and sauté for 5 minutes. Stir in the grated tofu and cook for 3 to 4 minutes. Add the chopped parsley and set the filling aside.

When the dough has doubled, preheat the oven to 400°. Punch down the dough and knead it slightly in the bowl. Oil a 12-inch round pizza pan or 9x13-inch baking sheet. Press and stretch the dough into the pan.

Bake the dough for 10 minutes. Remove it from the oven, spread the topping evenly over the dough, sprinkle it with the grated feta, and return it to the hot oven. Bake for another 15 to 25 minutes.

Lahmajun can be served hot or at room temperature.

# B R E A D

## *Injera*

•

## *Ethiopian Flat Bread*

Injera is a pliable, slightly fermented flat bread unique to the highlands of Eritrea and Ethiopia. It is an indispensable accompaniment to *w'et,* the Ethiopian stew. Made of *t'eff,* a member of the millet family, injera is light, with a somewhat spongy texture. *T'eff* is not readily available here, so I have substituted wheat flour. Although an imitation, this recipe approximates the real thing and is well worth the effort and the advance preparation.

1¾ cup unbleached white flour

½ cup self-rising flour

¼ cup whole wheat bread flour

1 package dry yeast (about 1
  tablespoon)

2½ cups warm water

_____

½ teaspoon baking soda

½ teaspoon salt

Combine the flours and yeast in a ceramic or glass bowl. Add the warm water and mix into a fairly thin, smooth batter. Let the mixture sit for three full days at room temperature. Stir the mixture once a day. It will bubble and rise.

When you are ready to make the injera, add the baking soda and salt and let the batter sit for 10 to 15 minutes.

Heat a small, nonstick 9-inch skillet. When a drop of water bounces on the pan's surface, take about ⅓ cup of the batter and pour it in the skillet quickly, all at once. Swirl the pan so that the entire bottom is evenly coated, then return to the heat.

The injera is cooked on only one side and the bottom should not brown. When the moisture has evaporated and lots of "eyes" appear on the surface, remove the injera. Let each injera cool and then stack them as you go along.

If the first injera is undercooked, try using less of the mixture, perhaps ¼ cup, and maybe cook it just a bit longer. Be sure not to overcook it. Injera should be soft and pliable so that it can be rolled or folded, like a crêpe.

Serve with Yemiser W'et (see page 522) or Yetakelt W'et (see page 523).

DESSERTS

# Sweet Bastela

•

## Creamy Layered Pastry

This legendary pastry of crisp filo layered with ground almonds and egg custard is a delicious and attractive dessert. Bastela is similar to the French pastry Napoleon.

YIELDS 6 SERVINGS

2 cups milk
¼ cup sugar
4 eggs
1 teaspoon pure vanilla extract
1 teaspoon cinnamon

_____

10 filo pastry sheets

3 tablespoons butter, melted

_____

2 tablespoons raspberry or strawberry
   conserve
½ cup coarsely chopped almonds
confectioners' sugar

In a heavy saucepan, heat the milk and sugar to scalding. Whirl the eggs in a blender while slowly pouring in the hot milk. Add the vanilla and cinnamon. If the custard doesn't thicken enough to coat a spoon, return it to the pan and reheat it gently, stirring constantly until it thickens. Should the custard curdle slightly while thickening, simply blend it again. Refrigerate the custard.

Using a 7- or 8-inch plate as a guide, cut two circles from each sheet of the filo. On buttered baking pans, stack the filo sheets, four sheets to a stack, brushing every second sheet with melted butter. Bake at 350° for about 20 minutes, until the filo is golden brown.

Assemble the bastela. Begin with one pair of filo circles. Spread all of the conserve evenly over this bottom layer of filo and sprinkle on a few of the chopped almonds. Add another pair of filo circles, some almonds, and some of the egg custard. Continue to layer the filo, almonds, and custard until all of the ingredients are used. End with a pair of filo circles.

Sprinkle the pastry with confectioners' sugar, cut it into six wedges, and serve immediately.

> *Note: Bastela is best served right after it is prepared, but if necessary to delay serving, refrigerate it and then cut it into wedges just before serving. It will keep for one or two days in the refrigerator.*

# Moroccan Date Cake

½ cup butter

¼–½ cup sugar

4 eggs

1 teaspoon baking powder

1 cup unbleached white flour

1 teaspoon cinnamon

1 teaspoon nutmeg

½ teaspoon ground cloves

½ cup milk

½ teaspoon pure vanilla extract

1 cup pitted, chopped dates

½ cup chopped walnuts

_____

fresh whipped cream

Preheat the oven to 325°.

Cream together the butter and sugar. Beat in the eggs. Combine the baking powder, flour, cinnamon, nutmeg, and cloves. Add the dry ingredients to the egg mixture, beating well. Mix in the milk and vanilla. Beat well. Add the chopped dates and walnuts and stir again to distribute them evenly.

Butter and flour a 9-inch cake pan. Pour the batter into the pan. Bake for about 30 minutes, until a knife inserted into the center comes out clean.

Serve with fresh whipped cream.

KIP WILCOX

# *Provence*

# INTRODUCTION

*Breathing I draw the air to me*[1]
*that I feel coming from Provence;*
*everything that comes from there rejoices me,*
*so that when I hear good of it*
*I listen smiling, and for every word demand a hundred,*[2]
*so fair to me is the hearing.*[3]

When the itinerant troubadour, Peire Vidal, sang these lyrics at a festive dinner in the fourteenth century, he was participating in a 300-year tradition that began in Provence. At feasts and banquets in courts throughout southern France, troubadours sang of political, religious, and moral issues. Above all, they sang of courtly love, or how to transform carnal desire into a ritual of polite seduction.

The culture of Provence, its landscape, weather, character, history, and cuisine, reflects this incongruity of passion and subtle seduction. Provence remains diverse, contradictory, elusive, alluring. It is a land of harsh and lavish beauty, of warmth and bone-chilling winds, of sea and rocks, of gnarled olive trees that yield tender, succulent fruit, of pungent herbs and sweet orange blossoms. Its inhabitants are descendants of the contrasting cultures that surround the Mediterranean. As the Saracens celebrated their victories with saffron and wine, and the Greeks rolled their barrels of olive oil ashore, and the Romans built their temples and aqueducts, and the Pope set up court in Avignon, Provence became an eclectic culture of its own, not quite French, and as intricate as the myriad twists in the olive tree.

For many years, Provence kept to itself, an unwilling compatriot of France. Then, in the nineteenth century, as more and more northern Europeans sought the sunny and mild Mediterranean climate for holidays and respite, they became aware of the history and culture of this southern province, but remained unaware of its changeable nature. The sudden wintry mistral winds took them by surprise. Even the most reserved Englishman was affected by the mistral, blaming it, in typical Romantic fashion, for his sudden emotional outbursts!

[1] Vidal, Peire, "Ab l'alen tir vas me l'air," translated by Ezra Pound, c. 1910, *Ezra Pound and the Troubadors,* Stuart Y. McDougal (Princeton, N.J.: Princeton University Press, 1972) 4.

[2] Vidal, Peire, translated by Frederick Goldin, *Lyrics of the Troubadors and Trouveres* (Garden City, N.J.: Anchor Books, 1973) 253.

[3] Pound, 3.

The beloved poet-chronicler, Frederic Mistral, who was perhaps named after these chilly winds, revived the language of Provence into literary usage in the nineteenth century. Soon poets, novelists, linguists, artists, and tourists began flocking to this somewhat mysterious part of France. Alphonse Daudet wrote short stories; Jean Giono wrote fierce novels; Cézanne painted Mt. Ste. Victoire; Van Gogh captured the brilliant starry skies, sunflowers, cypress, and twisted olive trees in his paintings; and English tourists wrote travelogues. Ezra Pound learned Provençal and translated the medieval lyrics of the troubadours. Georges Brassens wrote and sang contemporary lyrics.

Visitors discovered the history of Roman architecture, Celtic stonework, and the Greek origins of grapevines, and olive and almond trees. They tasted the exciting flavor of bouillabaisse, the freshness of a salad made with *mesclun,* the light pervasive taste of olive oil, and the wines harvested from grapes grown in the formerly salty marshes of the Carmargue. This alleged land of gypsies, exiles, and marauders became known for its poetry, paintings, architecture, food, and wine. The name Provence became fair to the hearing.

When the olive trees and grapevines took root in Provence, they grew as if they had always belonged there. Today it is difficult to imagine what the landscape would look like without them. From the bountiful fruits, vegetables, garlic, almonds, sweet and pungent herbs, fruits de la mer, and wine, a cuisine has evolved that contrasts with the "haute cuisine" of the north. Provence has remained faithful to its earthy and briny roots. Its ethnic dishes combine the natural and exotic flavors of its gardens, vineyards, orchards, and coastal waters.

Creating vegetarian dishes from a Provençal garden is both tempting and convenient. For, in their obsession with fresh produce, the French plant gardens everywhere: in small backyard plots, window boxes, terraces, and doorsteps. Vegetables are considered not only healthful, but essential to a meal. Used in hors d'oeuvres, entrées, and soups, they accompany, accentuate, and substantiate various dishes. A dish is not complete without fresh herbs from the garden. Salads are made of fresh greens, both wild and cultivated, without elaborate garnishes, and dressed in a simple vinaigrette. Garden vegetables, picked when they are young and tender, are usually cooked in as little water or stock as possible by braising, parboiling, and "refreshing," or glazing. Hearty or fanciful dishes are created by stuffing, stewing, and combining vegetables in various ways.

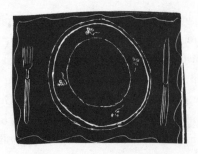

# APPETIZERS

*A French meal is both ceremonial and tradition bound. Each course is served* comme il faut *or "as it should be." A typical main meal begins with an hors d'oeuvre, a French word meaning, literally, "outside the main work." An hors d'oeuvre should be tasty and light, its purpose being to stimulate the appetite and to introduce the rest of the meal. An hors d'ouevre may consist of an egg or cheese dish, such as a tart or omelet, stuffed eggs or vegetables, vegetables marinated in a vinaigrette dressing, a light salad such as Salade Niçoise, or simply bread with butter and thinly sliced crisp radishes. These "appetite teasers" or appetizers are often served with a cool light wine.*

# Chick Pea Crêpe

•

## Socca

Socca is a chick pea flour crêpe sold as street food on the Côte d'Azur. Its name probably harkens back to the old language of Provence. I first read about Socca in *A Mediterranean Feast*, by Paola Scaravelli and John Cohen. This recipe is an adaptation using thyme or rosemary-flavored olive oil.

### SERVES 4 TO 6

*½ teaspoon dried rosemary (or ¼ teaspoon dried thyme)*
*2 tablespoons olive oil*

---

*1 cup unbleached white flour*
*1 cup chick pea flour (see page 657)*

*1 teaspoon salt*
*¼ teaspoon coarsely ground black pepper*
*1½ cups warm water*

---

*oil for frying*

Gently heat the dried rosemary or thyme in the olive oil for 2 minutes on very low heat. Set it aside to cool for 2 to 3 minutes. If using rosemary, pour the oil through a strainer and reserve. It is not necessary to strain the thyme.

Mix both of the flours with the salt and pepper. Add the water to the flour mixture and beat it with a whisk until smooth. Beat in the rosemary oil or the olive oil and thyme. Allow the batter to sit for 20 minutes.

Heat a small cast-iron skillet or crêpe pan on medium heat. Oil lightly. Pour about ¼ cup batter into the pan, tipping it so the batter thins out into about a 6-inch circle. Cook for about 30 seconds until the crêpe is golden-brown on the bottom; then, with a spatula, flip the crêpe over and cook about 10 or 15 seconds. Remove the crêpe onto a plate. Continue this procedure until the batter is used up. You should have enough batter to make about twelve crêpes. Cover the crêpes with a cloth until ready to use.

Roll the crêpes into cylinders for dipping or fill them with Garlic-Olive-Caper Spread (see page 539) or Herbed Chèvre Spread (see page 542) and serve with fresh crisp crudités.

# Roasted or Grilled Vegetables

•

## Légumes Rôtis ou Grillés

Grilling honors the essence of vegetables; their sweetness and distinctive flavors are enhanced by roasting in the oven or grilling outdoors at a high temperature with only a little salt, pepper, and olive oil. Because the presentation of a dish is as important as its flavor, a French cook would, no doubt, arrange each vegetable meticulously on individual plates or on an attractive platter.

### SERVES 4 TO 6

*Select any or all of the following vegetables according to season, availability, and preference:*

*1 carrot, cut in two and then sliced lengthwise into ¼-inch sticks*

*2–3 potatoes, cut into 1-inch pieces, or sliced, if grilling*

*1 large onion or 2 small onions, cut into lengthwise pieces*

*1 red bell pepper, cut into large pieces*

*1 green bell pepper, cut into large pieces*

*12 large garlic cloves, peeled*

*1 zucchini or yellow squash, cut in half and sliced lengthwise*

*12 asparagus stalks, trimmed (in season)*

———————————

*olive oil*
*salt and coarsely ground black pepper*

First, parboil the carrot and potato pieces by dropping each vegetable, in separate batches, into boiling water for 2 minutes. Drain them and let them cool.

To roast: Heat the oven to 500°. Brush three baking sheets with olive oil. Arrange the vegetables in a single layer on the sheets. Brush the vegetables with olive oil and sprinkle them with salt and black pepper. Bake them on the top shelf of the oven. Carrots, potatoes, onions, peppers, and garlic will take about 20 minutes. Zucchini and asparagus will take about 10 minutes.

To grill: Prepare a charcoal or wood fire and remove the grill. On a large tray or cookie sheet, brush the vegetables with olive oil. When the flames have died and the coals are white, spread aluminum foil over the grill. Poke small holes into the foil and brush it lightly with oil. Spread the vegetables on the foil and sprinkle them with salt and black pepper. Put the grill over the coals. The cooking time will vary according to the temperature of the coals and the height of the grill. In general, zucchini and asparagus will take about 20 minutes and the other vegetables about 30 minutes.

If you prefer to broil the vegetables rather than roast them in the oven, place the vegetables on a foil-covered broiler rack. Brush liberally with olive oil and sprinkle with salt and black pepper. Peppers and zucchinis will take about 7 minutes. Onions, asparagus, and mushrooms will take 8 to 10 minutes, and carrots and potatoes will be tender in about 12 minutes.

Roasted or Grilled Vegetables is a tempting side dish for Potato Cake (see page 555), Pissaladière (see page 554), or Stuffed Eggplant Provençale (see page 551).

# Garlic-Olive-Caper Spread

•

## Tapenade

"Tapenade" refers to any spread made with garlic. This is one of the most traditional—garlic mashed with olives and capers, though I've replaced the usual anchovies with pine nuts. Serve it as a stuffing in deviled eggs, in omelets, or on bread and crackers. It is delicious served on Chick Pea Crêpes (see page 537).

### YIELDS 1 ½ TO 2 CUPS

*1 cup Niçoise or Greek olives, rinsed and pitted*
*2 tablespoons capers*
*1 garlic clove, pressed*
*½–1 cup pine nuts*

*1 tablespoon olive oil*
*1 tablespoon fresh lemon juice*
*½ teaspoon dried thyme or basil*
*¼ teaspoon freshly ground black pepper*
*1½–2 cups stemmed parsley*

Using a mortar and pestle or food processor, blend all of the ingredients until the tapenade is just smooth enough to spread without becoming a paste. Tapenade will keep a week in the refrigerator and the flavor will intensify with age.

# Stuffed Tomatoes

•

# Tomates Farcies

In Provence, where eggplant, tomatoes, zucchini, and artichokes grow like weeds, stuffing them is a convenient and popular preparation. The vegetables themselves are perfect containers for favorite herbed fillings.

SERVES 4

4 small, firm, ripe tomatoes
salt and freshly ground black pepper

¼ cup olive oil
8 garlic cloves, minced

¼ cup chopped fresh basil and/or
  parsley
1 cup bread crumbs, fresh or dry
½ cup freshly grated Parmesan cheese

Cut the tomatoes in half and remove the stems. Arrange them, cut side up, in an oiled baking dish. Sprinkle with salt and pepper.

Heat the olive oil in a heavy skillet and carefully sauté the garlic for 2 to 3 minutes, stirring constantly and taking care not to brown. Add the basil and stir briefly. Add the bread crumbs and stir until the oil is evenly distributed. Remove the mixture from the heat and stir in the Parmesan.

Spoon the topping onto the tomatoes. Bake, uncovered, at 350° for 30 minutes.

Serve as a side dish for soup, Salade Niçoise (see page 550), or Potato Cake (see page 555).

# Whole Braised Garlic

•

## Ail Braisé

Who would imagine that garlic could be sweet and creamy? When it is slowly baked in its skin and basted with butter and olive oil, a transformation takes place. Pop it out of its skin and spread it on fresh warm sourdough or French bread. Try it on bread first slathered with creamy Herbed Chèvre Spread (see page 542).

### SERVES 6 TO 8

*4 whole heads fresh garlic*
*¼ cup butter*
*¼ cup olive oil*
*½ teaspoon minced fresh thyme (¼*
*teaspoon dried)*

*salt and freshly ground black pepper*

*a few sprigs fresh parsley and thyme*

Preheat the oven to 300°.

Carefully remove the papery outside layers of skin that cover the garlic heads. Leave only the innermost layer, which will hold the cluster of garlic cloves together during baking. Place the heads in a small, ovenproof dish that will just contain them. Melt the butter with the olive oil and thyme. Brush the garlic heads generously with the butter mixture. Sprinkle them with salt and pepper. Cover the dish with aluminum foil or a lid and bake for one hour, basting occasionally with the oil and butter. Remove the cover and bake for 20 minutes more. When poked with a sharp knife, the garlic should be tender and the skins should crinkle.

Remove the garlic heads from the baking dish and whisk a little water into the baking juices to make a light sauce. Pour the sauce over the baked garlic, garnish with sprigs of parsley and thyme, and serve.

At the table, squeeze the softened part of each clove from its skin onto buttered French bread and dip the bread into the sauce. Baked garlic is delicious with crisp radish slices, tomato slices, and Greek olives.

# Herbed Chèvre Spread

•

# Chèvre aux Herbes

SERVES 6

4 ounces soft chèvre
4 ounces cream cheese
1 tablespoon chopped fresh parsley
1 tablespoon chopped fresh marjoram
   (2 teaspoons dried)

2 teaspoons chopped fresh dill
   (1 teaspoon dried)
freshly ground black pepper to taste
olive oil

Combine the ingredients well.

You may pack the cheese spread into an earthenware or glass dish and drizzle a little olive oil over the top, just enough to coat the cheese so that it won't dry out. Or you may form the cheese spread into a ball and roll it in chopped, toasted walnuts or almonds or coarsely ground peppercorns. Store covered and refrigerated.

Serve with dark pumpernickel, sourdough, or French bread and Whole Braised Garlic (see page 541). Garnish with thin slices of crisp, fresh radishes.

# SOUPS

*Soup may be the second course in an elaborate meal, or it may be served for a light supper with bread, a simple egg or vegetable dish, and dessert. Americans are accustomed to soup for lunch and for light, quick suppers. Both of the following substantial soups fulfill this tradition. They can be made on the weekend, served for weekday meals, or frozen and served later.*

## Cream of Leek and Zucchini Soup

·

## Crème de Courgettes et Poireaux

A creamy soup, partially blended, partially textured with delicately sautéed leeks and zucchini.

### SERVES 6

3–4 leeks, rinsed well and chopped (see page 667)

1 large onion, chopped

1½ tablespoons olive oil

1½ tablespoons butter

3–4 medium zucchini, chopped

1 teaspoon salt

1 garlic clove, minced or pressed

1 tablespoon dried tarragon

1–1½ teaspoons ground fennel seeds

freshly ground black pepper to taste

3 tablespoons flour

3 cups vegetable stock (see page 685)

_____

1 cup heavy cream, half-and-half, or milk

In a medium soup pot, on medium heat, sauté the leeks and onions in the olive oil and butter until the onions are translucent, about 10 minutes. Stir in the zucchini, salt, and garlic. Sauté for 10 more minutes, until the zucchini is tender. Add the tarragon, fennel, and black pepper. Cook for a couple of minutes. Remove half of the vegetables and set aside.

Sprinkle the flour into the soup pot, stirring, until the vegetables are well coated. Whisk in the stock. Heat, stirring frequently, until the soup begins to thicken. Remove it from the heat. When the soup has cooled a little, purée it in a blender or food processor and return it to the pot.

Add the reserved vegetables and heat the soup to simmering. Stir in the cream or milk. Heat very carefully, using a flame tamer if you have one. Take care not to let the soup boil.

# *White Bean and Garlic Soup*

•

## *Purée de Haricots Blancs et d'Ail*

This soup is flavored with a "bouquet garni"—seasonings tied in a piece of cotton cheesecloth that can be easily retrieved from the soup. In this case, a cluster of cloves, bay leaves, and fresh or dried sprigs of rosemary and thyme are used. Traditionally, the soup contains a whole unpeeled bulb of garlic, which cooks with the beans. The pulp is then removed and squeezed back into the soup. I found it much easier to peel the cloves of garlic at the start rather than fishing them out later. This soup may be served with or without the addition of cream.

1½ cups pea beans, soaked overnight, drained, and rinsed

2 quarts water or vegetable stock (see page 685)

1 whole bulb garlic, separated into cloves and peeled

1 bouquet garni—tie the following herbs and spices into a piece of cheesecloth:

½–1 teaspoon rosemary, fresh or dried

1 teaspoon dried thyme (2 sprigs fresh)

½ teaspoon whole fennel seeds

1 bay leaf

4 whole cloves

1 cup chopped potato

_____

1 cup chopped onions

¼ cup olive oil

1 cup chopped carrot

salt and freshly ground black pepper to taste

1 cup milk, heavy cream, or half-and-half (optional)

1 cup chopped fresh parsley

Place the soaked, rinsed pea beans in a pot with 1 quart of the stock or water. Add the peeled garlic cloves and the bouquet garni and simmer for one hour. Then add the chopped potato and continue to simmer for another half an hour, until beans are soft.

In a separate pan, sauté the onions in the olive oil until translucent. Add the carrots and sauté until tender. Add these vegetables to the beans, along with the remaining quart of stock or water. Simmer for 15 to 20 minutes.

Remove the bouquet garni. Purée half the soup in a blender or food processor until smooth. Stir the purée back into the soup and reheat it gently. Add salt and pepper to taste. For extra richness or creaminess, add milk, cream, or half-and-half. If the soup seems too thick and you don't wish to add milk or cream, thin with a bit more stock. Stir in the parsley.

Serve with Stuffed Tomatoes (see page 540), a green salad, and fresh bread.

# ENTRÉES

*This principal course of the meal is more than a taste to stimulate the palate and more elaborate than a soup. It is important that the seasonal flavorings and vegetables complement the main dish and each other. In Provence, a red or white full-bodied wine is the typical accompanying beverage. Sparkling water might be served as well.*

# *Basic Fish Stock*

This clear, light bouillon gives flavor and depth to fish stews, seafood pilafs, and chowders, or can be served on its own accompanied by steamed vegetables and bread. Fish scraps are the distinguishing ingredients in this recipe. Use heads, tails, and collars of fresh, white-fleshed sea fish (ones that aren't too oily or too fishy such as salmon or mackerel). Scraps are usually available for the asking at your local fish store or supermarket fish counter.

### YIELDS 2 QUARTS

*5–6 cups water*
*¾–1 pound fish scraps*
*½ large onion, coarsely chopped*
*1 medium carrot, thickly sliced*
*1 teaspoon whole black peppercorns*
*1 bay leaf*
*3 unpeeled garlic cloves*
*shells and heads from cleaned shrimp*
   *(optional)*

*potatoes and potato peels (optional)*
*untrimmed green beans (optional)*
*zucchini (optional)*
*scallions (optional)*
*leeks (optional)*
*shallots (optional)*

Combine all the ingredients in a large soup pot, bring to a boil, and then reduce to a simmer. Cook for 30 to 45 minutes. Strain through a fine-meshed sieve or a sieve lined with cheesecloth.

Refrigerated in a tightly capped glass jar, fish stock will keep for five days.

# Bouillabaisse with Rouille

Bouillabaisse is probably the most versatile dish indigenous to Provence. It may be a humble fish stew created from the catch of the day or an elegant combination of carefully selected fish and shellfish. In Marseille, where this dish originates, conger eel, prawns, and tiny crabs are added to the pot, and the dish is served garnished with whole lobster. The only rule is that whatever seafood is chosen must be absolutely fresh, so that its aroma and taste are fragrant and delicate.

In southern France, some soups are often served over slices of bread. Bouillabaisse is traditionally served with rouille, a thick, peppery sauce made from fresh bread crumbs, olive oil, and spices. The rouille may be served on the side and passed at the table or stirred into the stew just before serving. Rouille is also delicious on poached fish, vegetables, or potatoes.

## SERVES 6

### BOUILLABAISSE

2 leeks, washed thoroughly and sliced (optional) (see page 667)

1–2 Spanish onions, sliced (use only 1 if you use leeks)

3 tablespoons olive oil

4–6 garlic cloves, peeled and chopped

2 bay leaves

2 carrots, peeled and coarsely chopped

plenty of freshly ground black pepper

6 medium potatoes, cut into large cubes

1/2 teaspoon ground fennel seeds

2 slices orange peel, about 3 inches long

4–6 sprigs fresh thyme (1 teaspoon dried)

6–8 sprigs fresh marjoram (2 teaspoons dried)

3 cups Basic Fish Stock (see page 547) (or 2 cups clam juice [see note] and 1 cup water)

2 ripe tomatoes, chopped

juice of 1 lemon

3 pounds assorted fish and shellfish (bluefish, cod, orange roughy, mussels, shrimp, clams), washed and drained, with fish cut into large chunks

generous pinch of saffron

1 cup chopped fresh parsley

salt to taste

## ROUILLE

2 cups bread crumbs

1 cup freshly grated Parmesan cheese

1/8 teaspoon cayenne (or more depending on its potency)

1/2 cup water

1/4 cup chopped fresh basil (1 tablespoon dried)

1/4 cup chopped fresh parsley

3 tablespoons olive oil

Tabasco Sauce or other hot sauce

For the bouillabaisse, sauté in a soup pot the leeks and onions in the olive oil for about 5 minutes, until they are soft. Add the garlic, bay leaves, carrots, and black pepper and sauté for another 5 minutes.

Stir in the potatoes, fennel, orange peel, thyme, and marjoram. Sauté for 10 minutes. Add the stock or clam juice and water, tomatoes, and lemon juice. Simmer for 15 minutes or until the carrots and potatoes are firm, but cooked.

Mix in the fish (but not the shellfish), saffron, and parsley and simmer for 5 minutes. Then add the mussels, shrimp, and clams. Simmer for 2 minutes or until the mussels and clams open and the shrimp is pink and firm. Add salt to taste.

While the bouillabaisse is simmering, but before you add the seafood, make the rouille. Mix together the bread crumbs, Parmesan, and cayenne. Add the water and blend into a paste. Stir in the basil, parsley, and olive oil. Add Tabasco for more spice. Rouille should be hot and flavorful.

As soon as the seafood is done, serve the bouillabaisse topped with rouille. Crisp French bread and a green salad make this a complete meal.

> *Note: If you are using clam juice, look for Doxsee or other all-natural brands that have no preservatives or additives.*

# Salade Niçoise

 This refreshing salad may be served as an appetizer to a grand feast, as an entrée, or as a luncheon or light supper dish. It should be served at room temperature. Don't worry about leftovers; they are even more delicious the next day!

I have used flounder as a substitute for tuna because of its delicate flavor and texture. Although tuna is traditional, I avoided it here because of current environmental issues.

## SERVES 4 AS A LUNCHEON OR LIGHT DINNER ENTRÉE

**VINAIGRETTE**

¼ cup vinegar (cider, wine, or herbed)
½ cup olive oil
1 teaspoon Dijon mustard
1 garlic clove, pressed
salt and freshly ground black pepper
2 tablespoons fresh dill or basil leaves
    (1 teaspoon dried)

———————————————

1½ pounds firm, white, fish fillets
    (flounder is recommended)
juice of ½ lemon
freshly ground black pepper

———————————————

2 carrots, cut into 2-inch strips
2 cups green beans, trimmed and halved
2 potatoes, cut into 1-inch cubes

1 cup mushrooms, halved
1 cup thinly sliced red or green bell
    peppers
1 cup cauliflower florets

———————————————

6 canned artichoke hearts (packed in
    brine), cut into quarters
2 tomatoes, cut into small wedges
2 tablespoons capers
12–16 Niçoise or Greek olives (or
    California black olives)

———————————————

bed of lettuce
lemon wedges
sprigs of fresh basil or dill

Blend together the vinaigrette ingredients and set aside.

Place the rinsed fish in a baking dish oiled with olive oil. Sprinkle with lemon juice and black pepper. Cover and bake at 325° for 20 minutes. Set the fish aside to cool.

Bring 2 quarts of water to a rolling boil and blanch the vegetables separately in the following order: carrots, 4 minutes; green beans, 5 minutes; potatoes, 5 minutes; mushrooms, 2 minutes; peppers, 2 minutes; cauliflower, 3 minutes. When each vegetable is done, lift the pieces out of the boiling water with a slotted spoon and spread them out in a large baking pan to cool, allowing as much steam as possible to escape, or "refresh" them under cold water.

When the blanched vegetables have cooled, toss them in a large bowl with the artichoke hearts, tomatoes, capers, olives, and ½ cup of the vinaigrette. Drizzle the rest of the vinaigrette over the baked fish.

The dish may be served at room temperature or chilled. Serve the fish and the salad on a bed of lettuce garnished with lemon wedges and sprigs of fresh basil or dill. Salade Niçoise is delicious with Stuffed Tomatoes (see page 540), warm crisp sourdough or regular French bread, and dry white wine or sparkling water.

*Variation* Pan Bagnat: Everywhere along the coast of France a "pique-nique sur mer" is a popular family outing. Pan Bagnat, which means, literally, "bathed bread," is almost always taken along with the bathing suits. Made with Salade Niçoise, Pan Bagnat is a favorite, whether packed for a picnic, lunch, or evening meal. To prepare Pan Bagnat, slice a loaf of French bread lengthwise and warm it in a 300° oven for about 10 minutes, until it is crisp. Cut it into four pieces. Press down the soft inner bread or scoop a little out to make boats. Brush on some olive oil, fill with Salade Niçoise, and close up. Serve right away or wrap each sandwich individually for a picnic.

# *Stuffed Eggplant Provençal*

•

## *Aubergines Farcies à la Provençale*

These savory stuffed eggplants are distinguished by the addition of sweet, buttery pine nuts. In summer, make the sauce with sun-ripened tomatoes. The Parmesan cheese in the topping may be omitted for a nondairy entrée. Served with Roasted or Grilled Vegetables (see page 538), a green salad, and fresh sourdough or dark rye with Herbed Chèvre Spread (see page 542), Stuffed Eggplant Provençal will become a memorable harvest meal.

SERVES 6

3 medium or large eggplants
¼ cup olive oil
salt

**STUFFING**
¼ cup olive oil
2 cups chopped onions
2 garlic cloves, minced
2 carrots, peeled and diced
1 red or green bell pepper, diced
1 cup diced zucchini or yellow squash
¼ pound mushrooms, chopped
½ cup pine nuts
2 tablespoons currants
1 teaspoon dried marjoram (1 tablespoon fresh)

½ teaspoon dried thyme (about 1 tablespoon fresh)
salt and freshly ground black pepper to taste

**TOPPING**
½ cup olive oil
2 garlic cloves, pressed or minced
2 cups fresh or dried bread crumbs
1 cup freshly grated Parmesan cheese

**SAUCE**
Provençal Tomato Sauce (recipe follows) or Herbed Crème Fraîche (recipe follows)

Preheat the oven to 500°.

Slice the eggplants in half lengthwise, without detaching the stems. Brush the eggplant halves generously with olive oil and sprinkle them with salt. Bake, cut side down, on oiled baking sheets for about 20 minutes, until tender inside but still firm outside. Remove them from the oven and allow to cool. Reduce oven temperature to 350°.

For the stuffing, heat the olive oil in a large, heavy skillet. Sauté the onions for about 10 minutes, until translucent. Add the garlic and carrots and sauté for 10 minutes more. Add the rest of the stuffing ingredients and sauté for another 15 minutes. Set aside.

To make the topping, heat the olive oil in a skillet. Sauté the garlic for a couple of minutes, stirring. Add the bread crumbs and continue to sauté, stirring, until the oil is absorbed. Remove the skillet from the heat and stir in the Parmesan.

To stuff the eggplant halves, place them, cut side up, on an oiled baking sheet. Push the flesh to the sides. Spoon the vegetable stuffing equally into the cavities of the eggplant halves and pat into mounds. Top with the bread-crumb mixture. Bake for 30 minutes.

Serve topped with one of the sauces.

# Two Sauces for Stuffed Eggplant

•

## Provençal Tomato Sauce

⅓ cup olive oil

1 cup finely chopped onions

2 garlic cloves, minced

2 bay leaves

6 cups chopped fresh tomatoes (about 6
 tomatoes)

salt and freshly ground black pepper

4–6 sprigs fresh thyme (about ¼
 teaspoon dried)

2 tablespoons fresh marjoram (2
 teaspoons dried)

2 tablespoons tomato paste

Heat the oil in a heavy pot. Add the onions and sauté for 10 minutes, until translucent. Add the garlic and bay leaves and sauté for another 5 minutes. Add the tomatoes, salt, pepper, and herbs. Simmer for 20 minutes. When the tomatoes have cooked down, add the tomato paste and simmer for 10 minutes. Remove the bay leaves. Ladle the sauce over the eggplants just before serving.

## Herbed Crème Fraîche

2 tablespoons chopped fresh parsley

2 tablespoons chopped fresh basil

½ teaspoon freshly ground black pepper
 (or to taste)

2 cups unsweetened Crème Fraîche (see
 page 562)

Stir the fresh herbs and pepper into the Crème Fraîche. Spoon about ¼ cup of the sauce over each stuffed eggplant half just before serving.

# Pissaladière

A variation on pizza, Pissaladière contrasts the typical Provençal flavors of sweet onions, pungent thyme, and robust brined olives.

### SERVES 6

CRUST

1 package dry yeast (about 1
   tablespoon) (or 1 ounce fresh)

1 cup warm water

1 teaspoon salt

2 tablespoons olive oil

2 cups unbleached white flour (up to 1
   cup whole wheat flour may be
   substituted)

additional 1–1½ cups unbleached
   white flour

additional 2 tablespoons olive oil

TOPPING

3 large Spanish onions, thinly sliced

3 tablespoons olive oil

1 teaspoon freshly ground black pepper

1 teaspoon dried thyme

---

2 cups packed grated mozzarella

1 cup freshly grated Parmesan cheese

16 Niçoise or Greek olives, halved

For the crust, mix the yeast and water in a large bowl and set aside for about 5 minutes until dissolved. Mix in the salt and olive oil. Stir in 2 cups of flour and beat well. Gradually add enough of the additional 1½ cups of flour to form a soft dough. When the dough pulls away from the sides of the bowl, turn it onto a lightly floured board. Knead it for about 10 minutes, until smooth and elastic.

Wash out the bowl and oil it with 1 tablespoon of olive oil. Place the dough in the bowl, turn it over to coat with oil, and cover the bowl with a damp cloth. Let the dough rise in a warm place until doubled in bulk, about 1½ hours or overnight in the refrigerator.

Just before you're ready to use the dough, preheat the oven to 400°.

Now make the topping by sautéing the sliced onions in the olive oil until translucent and beginning to brown, about 15 minutes. Add the black pepper and thyme. Sauté for 5 more minutes.

Punch down the dough and knead it briefly in the bowl. Oil a pizza pan or baking sheet with the remaining tablespoon olive oil. Press and stretch the dough to cover the pan and form a ridge around the edge.

Sprinkle the grated cheeses over the dough. Top with the sautéed onions and the olives. Bake for 30 to 40 minutes, until the crust in the center is firm and springy. Serve immediately with a green salad and Roasted or Grilled Vegetables (see page 538) or with a soup.

# Potato Cake

•

## Gâteau de Pommes de Terre

I have heard of a potato dish in the south of France made only of milk and freshly dug potatoes and baked until the milk is absorbed into the potatoes and caramelizes. It is extolled as a light and creamy creation. This Potato Cake is a bit heartier, fortified with cheese and onions and flavored with nutmeg and basil. It is a perfect luncheon or light supper dish, delicious with a green salad, Stuffed Tomatoes (see page 540), Roasted or Grilled Vegetables (see page 538), and cider or white wine.

### SERVES 6

6–8 medium potatoes, thinly sliced
1 large Spanish onion, sliced
2 bay leaves
¼ cup olive oil
½ pound Swiss cheese, grated
½ teaspoon freshly grated or ground
    nutmeg

salt to taste
lots of coarsely ground black pepper
¼ cup chopped fresh basil (2 teaspoons
    dried)

In a bowl, toss the sliced potatoes, onion, and bay leaves in the olive oil. Spread them on a baking sheet, cover it with aluminum foil, and bake at 350° for 20 minutes. Remove the foil and bake another 10 to 15 minutes, until the potatoes are fully cooked.

Mix together the cheese and seasonings.

In an oiled 9-inch round baking dish, layer the potatoes with the cheese mixture, ending with cheese sprinkled on top. Cover the dish and bake for 15 minutes at 350° until the cheese is melted and bubbling.

*Variations*
Add 4–5 minced or pressed garlic cloves to the potatoes before the initial baking.
Use half Swiss and half Parmesan cheeses.
Use a teaspoon of chopped fresh rosemary or ½ teaspoon dried rosemary in place of the basil.

## S A L A D

*The French believe flavors and textures must be featured separately in a meal. And they are characteristically concerned about digestion. For cleansing the palate and avoiding heartburn after a hearty entrée, a green salad is served.*

# Salade Verte

The *salade verte* is made from greens that are dry and crisp. In Provence, wild as well as cultivated greens, called *mesclun,* are gathered from gardens, fields, backyards, and road-sides. Lettuces, endive, escarole, chicory, arugula, dandelion greens, watercress, purslane, lamb's-quarter, sorrel, spinach, and fresh herbs are picked when they are young and tender.

First, a large wooden salad bowl is ceremoniously rubbed with crushed garlic, or sometimes a piece of bread rubbed with garlic is tossed with the salad and removed before serving. Then salt, freshly ground black pepper, vinegar, and a bit of Dijon mustard are placed in the bowl. Next, oil is whisked in, a few drops at a time. This thick vinaigrette is then tossed with *mesclun* or seasonal greens and served immediately.

If herbs are added, they should be fresh and complement the preceding entrée. If fresh herbs are unavailable, dried may be used, but should first be softened in the vinegar. Olive oil, a combination of olive and light vegetable oil, or walnut oil are all delicious. For a heartier salad following a light entrée, warmed chèvre and toasted hazelnuts are a favorite sweet-salty addition. Just be sure to keep the salad simple and light, a dénoue-ment to the rest of the meal.

# Classic Vinaigrette

YIELDS ABOUT ½ CUP

2 tablespoons wine vinegar, cider
   vinegar, or fresh lemon juice
¼ teaspoon Dijon mustard

salt and freshly ground black pepper
¼ cup virgin olive oil (or half olive oil
   and half vegetable oil)

Combine the vinegar or lemon juice, mustard, salt, and black pepper in a bowl or blender. Whisk or purée as you slowly drizzle in the oil.

Serve on fresh crisp greens, topped with croutons and thinly sliced red onions, if you like. For a more elaborate salad, I recommend a small piece of warm chèvre and a few chopped toasted hazelnuts, but only if the other dishes in the meal are relatively simple.

# DESSERTS

*Dessert at the end of a French meal usually consists of fresh fruit in season accompanied by cheese. Pastries and other sweets are served on special occasions, holidays, or at Sunday dinners.*

*To eat a piece of fruit "à la française," place it on a small plate and carefully cut each bite with a knife. This little ritual may seem fussy, but you will savor the fruit more than if you just bite into it "à l'américaine." And it definitely lasts longer. Usually the end of the loaf of bread is served with the cheese, which may be a creamy Camembert or Brie, a salty chèvre, or a musty bleu or Roquefort.*

*Even in more elaborate desserts, the freshness and integrity of the fruit are carefully considered. In the following recipes, crushed and puréed fruit as well as whole fruit are used.*

# Poached Peaches with Raspberry Sauce

•

# Confiture de Pêches à la Sauce de Framboises

**PEACHES**

1 quart peach or apple juice

2 cups water

2 cinnamon sticks

6 whole allspice berries

12 whole cardamom seeds

6 firm ripe peaches

**RASPBERRY SAUCE**

1 cup water

½ cup sugar

2 cups fresh or frozen unsweetened
 raspberries

¼ teaspoon orange blossom water
 (optional) (see note)

To prepare the peaches, in a 2-quart saucepan or deep soup pot, bring the juice, water, and spices to the boiling point. Choose a pot narrow enough that the liquid will cover the fruit. Drop the peaches into the liquid and poach them for 10 minutes. Remove the peaches, cover them with cold water, and slip off the skins. Cut each fruit in half and remove the stone. Place the peach halves in a glass or porcelain bowl. The poaching liquid may be saved and reused.

For the sauce, mix the water and sugar in a small saucepan, heat to a low boil and then simmer until the liquid has reduced by half.

In a blender or food processor, purée 1 cup of the raspberries and ¼ cup of the sugar syrup. Store the remaining syrup in a glass jar in the refrigerator. Stir the orange blossom water and the remaining cup of berries into the purée.

Serve the peach halves, rounded sides up, in a pool of raspberry sauce and garnish with fresh edible nasturtiums or day lilies and whipped cream or Crème Fraîche (see page 562) on the side.

The raspberry sauce is equally delicious on ice cream, pancakes, or pound cake. It can also be served on Marzipan Cake (see page 563) instead of glaze. The sauce will keep up to five days in the refrigerator.

*Note: Orange blossom water is available in the gourmet section of many supermarkets or in Greek or Middle Eastern groceries. It is commonly found in 3-ounce or 10-ounce bottles and is quite inexpensive. The orange blossoms come from an inedible species of bitter orange and are processed to produce orange blossom water, which is mostly used to flavor desserts.*

# Summer Blueberry Tart

•

## *Tarte aux myrtilles d'été*

This is the simplest of tarts, made of slightly tart, ripe berries.
It can become a wintertime treat made with frozen blueberries.

SWEET PASTRY CRUST
(PÂTE BRISÉE)
1½ cups unbleached white flour
2 tablespoons sugar
½ cup chilled butter, cut into small
  pieces
1 egg yolk
1 tablespoon fresh lemon juice
1–2 tablespoons cold water

FILLING
5 cups fresh or frozen blueberries
2 tablespoons water
⅓ cup sugar
1 tablespoon cornstarch dissolved in 2
  tablespoons water

½ pint heavy cream, whipped (optional)

For the Pàte Brisée, stir the flour and sugar together in a mixing bowl. Cut the chilled butter into small pieces and drop them into the flour. With your fingers, lightly and quickly rub the butter and flour together until the mixture becomes crumbly, or cut it in with a knife or pastry cutter. Whisk together the egg yolk, lemon juice, and 1 tablespoon of water. Sprinkle the liquid over the butter-flour mixture and continue to stir or rub this mixture between your fingers until a ball of dough forms. Be careful not to overwork the dough. If the mixture is crumbly, add up to one more tablespoon water, sprinkling it over the dough and lightly kneading it into a ball.

On a floured board and with a floured rolling pin, roll out the dough into a large circle. Gently lift it into a 9- or 10-inch pie plate or tart tin. Patch any holes in the crust with bits of dough and trim the edges. Flute the crust. Chill for 2 hours.

Preheat the oven to 375°.

Place a sheet of aluminum foil in the bottom of the crust and fill it with dried beans or rice to weigh it down during baking. Bake for 15 minutes. Remove the crust from the oven and carefully lift out the foil and beans. Bake for 5 minutes more. Cool.

To make the filling, heat in a small saucepan 2 cups of the blueberries, 2 tablespoons of water, and the sugar. Crush a few berries with a spoon to release some juice. When the berries have softened and become juicy, add the cornstarch mixture. Simmer on low heat for about 10 minutes, stirring occasionally, until the mixture thickens. Remove it from the heat and fold in one more cup of blueberries. Pour the berry mixture into the baked pie shell. Top with the remaining 2 cups of blueberries. Cool for at least one hour.

Serve plain or topped with fresh whipped cream, if desired, or sweetened Crème Fraîche (see page 562).

# *Winter Pear Tart Frangipane*

Frangipane is an almond custard traditionally baked with pears. In this recipe the pear slices are first caramelized in butter and brown sugar, then arranged in a pastry shell on top of the custard. When baked, the custard puffs up, leaving bits of jeweled pear glistening through the top. Both the pears and the custard can be prepared a day in advance and stored in the refrigerator.

### YIELDS 8 SERVINGS

| | |
|---|---|
| *1 unbaked 9-inch Sweet Pastry Crust (see page 560)* | *½ cup butter, softened* |
| | *2–3 drops pure almond extract* |
| CARAMELIZED PEARS | *2 eggs* |
| *2 tablespoons butter* | *2 teaspoons unbleached white flour* |
| *2 tablespoons brown sugar* | |
| *¼ cup water* | |
| *5 pears, washed, cored, and sliced* | *½ cup toasted slivered almonds (optional)* |
| FRANGIPANE (CUSTARD) | |
| *7 ounces almond paste, softened* | |

Follow the instructions for Sweet Pastry Crust but do not bake the crust.

To make the caramelized pears, heat the butter and brown sugar in a heavy saucepan or skillet until the sugar dissolves. Then add the water and stir briefly. Add the pear slices and sauté them for 10 minutes, covering the pan when not stirring. Remove the pears and set them aside. Cook down the caramel sauce on medium heat for a couple of minutes, stirring constantly. It is the right thickness when the spoon leaves a trail on the bottom of the pan.

For the frangipane, beat together the almond paste and butter. Add the almond extract. In another bowl whisk together the eggs and flour and then blend them into the butter mixture.

Preheat the oven to 325°.

Smooth the custard into the pie shell. Arrange the pear slices on top. Top with the slivered almonds, if desired.

Bake for 30 to 40 minutes, until the top is golden and the custard is firm. If the crust browns too quickly, cover the tart loosely with aluminum foil.

# Crème Fraîche

Crème Fraîche is a thick cultured cream, sweeter than sour cream. Its setting time varies from four to twenty-four hours, depending on the warmth of the environment. Store-bought crème fraîche is also now widely available.

YIELDS 1 CUP

CRÈME FRAÎCHE (PLAIN, UNSWEETENED)
1 cup heavy cream
1 teaspoon fresh lemon juice
1 tablespoon buttermilk

CRÈME FRAÎCHE (SWEETENED)
1 cup heavy cream
1 tablespoon maple syrup
1/2 teaspoon pure vanilla extract
1 teaspoon fresh lemon juice
1 tablespoon buttermilk

Combine the ingredients in a small glass jar. Cover it loosely and let it sit in a warm place for 4 to 24 hours. When the cream has thickened to the consistency of sour cream, refrigerate. It will keep for one week in the refrigerator.

Crème Fraîche may be used to enrich sauces and soups or to make a dip for raw vegetables by adding herbs and freshly ground black pepper. It is delicious as a topping for Stuffed Eggplant Provençal (see page 551). Use sweetened Crème Fraîche on fresh berries or poached fruit.

# Marzipan Cake

•

# Gâteau d'Amandes

This dense, moist cake was inspired by the "Calissons d'Aix," a fifteenth-century confection made in Aix-en-Provence and traditionally served three times a year—on Christmas, Easter, and September 1 (in honor of Saint Giles, a renowned hermit-monk who founded a monastery in Provence during the eighth century). To ensure a moist, chewy consistency, remove the cake from the oven when golden brown and glaze it while still warm.

### YIELDS 8 SERVINGS

*7 ounces almond paste*
*¼ cup butter, softened*
*½ cup sugar*
*1 cup ground almonds*
*2 eggs*
*¼ teaspoon pure almond extract*

*1 cup unbleached white or pastry flour*
*1 teaspoon baking powder*

_____

*2 tablespoons water*
*¼ cup apricot conserves*

Preheat the oven to 350°. Butter and flour a 9-inch cake pan.

Cream together the almond paste, butter, and sugar. Mix in the ground almonds. In a small bowl, beat the eggs lightly with the almond extract and add them to the creamed mixture. Combine the flour and baking powder and stir them into the liquid ingredients. Mix together in as few strokes as possible. Pour the batter into the cake pan and bake for 20 to 25 minutes. Do not overbake. The cake should be fairly dense, very moist, and golden brown on top.

In a small saucepan, stir the water into the conserves and gently heat until it's thin enough to easily brush on the top of the warm cake.

*Variation* Omit the apricot glaze and serve with Raspberry Sauce (see page 559).

B O B   L O V E

*Southeast*

*Asia*

# INTRODUCTION

I lived in the Philippines and stayed in Indonesia and Thailand for almost seven years of my young adult life. I never lived in a major city and always spoke the local languages of the places I lived. This did not make me an expert on Southeast Asian culture or food, but it did stimulate lots of thoughts and feelings about all the wondrous foods and the ways in which they connect to the rich and various cultures of the region. My intention here is to give you a sense of what it's like to be an amateur eater in the Southeast Asian world of deadly serious good cooking.

Picture yourself sitting with family and friends in a circle on the ground with banana leaves spread out before you. You each have a bowl of rice in front of you, but the rest of the food is in communal bowls or on platters in the center. Reach for the food with your hand, or with a large spoon if it's juicy, and place it on your rice. Mix it up a bit and eat it with your hand. Do this on the floor of a small thatched hut, on rocks near a stream where blossoms of the jade vine float by, or on a white sandy beach where coconut palms lean out over the crystal blue waters.

You have entered a travel-poster picture that's a little bit unreal. Educated, citified Southeast Asians cherish this same nostalgic, romantic picture and rural people who are forced to leave share this longing. What are they longing for? It's not just the swaying palms or flowing streams. It is a longing for food shared around a circle. It is a longing for *ramai* and *slamet*.

## *Ramai*

*Ramai* is an Indonesian word (and Philippine and Thai languages have cognates for it) that foreigners quickly pick up on, not only because they hear it so often, but also because it has no equivalent in Western languages. *Ramai* means crowded, noisy, and chaotic, as well as lively and bustling. Whatever the shade of meaning, its connotation is always desirable. *Ramai*'s opposite is "alone"; if you are alone then you must be lonely, and if you are with others, especially in the midst of a bustling crowd, then you are not, and cannot be, lonely.

As a teacher in the Philippines I lived with five boys in their late teens who were my students. Our house was in a somewhat isolated area right on a small bay of the Pacific Ocean. Sometimes I would hear the boys discussing under their breaths what they were going to do about me if they were to go out for the evening. The hassle was this: given that no one would ever want to stay alone, which one would stay back to be my companion? I would try to intervene by saying that I could damn well stay by myself for once, and their desire to go was so great that they'd give in. But, oh, the guilt it provoked! Sometimes I'd allow myself to be dragged along to the party just to solve the dilemma, or some young neighbor kids would be asked to stay with me for the evening so that I would not be alone. To be alone is to be, or to run the risk of becoming, unsocial or even antisocial: a social if not psychological pathology. And the corollary of course is simple: the more the merrier.

This is why food is so crucial; it is the ultimate social connector. To share food, to make gifts, offerings, or exchanges of food, is to connect oneself to family, friends, superiors, inferiors, spirits, and gods. Gods and spirits can no more refuse offerings of food than guests can. To do so would be to disconnect, to choose to be alone, which is to say, to be crazy. Food connects and makes things *ramai,* which comes to mean social and therefore human.

## *Slamet*

From the Arabic *salaam* and related to the Hebrew *shalom, slamet* in the Malay/ Indonesian world means tranquility, to be at peace, to be in a state of equilibrium or balance. To maintain this state of harmony with one's fellows and with the world of the spirit, it is customary to offer food to creatures of both worlds on all occasions that might provoke an upset of the harmony: births, circumcisions, marriages, deaths, any passage for which a little help might be needed to ease the transition from one state to the next.

I often wondered if this might be the reason why it is such a strong custom to eat before and after traveling, as though one's state or status had changed because of having changed one's physical position. I must eat before I leave my house in Gubat. Why? Because I'm traveling. I travel for half an hour by bus to the provincial capital and my hosts on the other end must feed me, even though they know how short a distance I've come and that I probably just ate in Gubat. It's not just "good old Philippine hospitality," because these same people do it themselves, even if it means stopping at a diner at the other end of the trip. We are somehow different after we have traveled and must reestablish our connectedness.

In Southeast Asia, tranquility *(slamet)* is possible only when one is surrounded by the bustling, the gossiping, the play-making, the sharing of family and friends. *Ramai* (chaos) and *slamet* (peace) might seem contradictory to us but not to the peoples of Southeast Asia. Human beings cannot be at peace if they are disconnected. Do they know something we have forgotten?

## Lamentation and Invocation

Near the temple complex at Angkor Wat there once stood a banyan tree two or three times the size of our little restaurant in Ithaca, New York. This tree was also a restaurant, for under its several dozen trunks there stood a small kiosk out of which came a most amazing assortment of spicy Cambodian dishes, crusty French breads, and red wines. The diners were seated at small tables nestled among the side trunks of the great banyan, protected from sun and light rains by the banyan's layers and layers of branches and leaves.

Virtually no tree standing in Cambodia today can be cut down by mechanical means without great damage to the saws caused by the masses of shrapnel embedded in the trunks from fragmentation bombs dropped by U.S. war planes. Since the bombing of Cambodia I often think about that restaurant and that tree. Do patrons still watch processions of monks from the temple next door as they pass by on Buddhist holidays? Do these monks still set forth one by one each morning with their alms bowls to gather food from citizens eager to gain spiritual merit by feeding them? Can the sanity and civility represented by the little restaurant under the great banyan or by those food offerings ever be restored? What kind of *slamet-an* or ritual offering of food to the community of people and spirits could be made to atone for the upset of people and the disturbing of nature?

It is with a sense of longing that I offer to share with you this food. Please share it in turn with friends and family and make the gathering a little noisy, a little chaotic. Have on hand too much food and perhaps even a few more people than you'd usually invite. Sit in a circle and feed one another generously in the hope that *slamet* can be restored, that food shared between peoples can still serve as communion.

# Rice

In Southeast Asia, those who can afford it eat rice at all meals. All other food is thought of as the accompaniment to the rice. The word viand is often used to translate the Indonesian *lauk-pauk* or the Philippine *bá-on,* words that mean "that which goes with the rice."

White rice is rice that has been polished at the mill, and because it has been milled it is considered prestigious to serve. One can ask at the mill that it be more or less polished, and frequently the nutritious outer layers of the rice kernels removed in polishing are fed to the mill owner's chickens or pigs. In many remote, rural areas, the poor have no access to rice polishing machines and must pound their rice in large mortars with pestles. This leaves the rice unpolished, and the resultant "brown" rice is more nutritious as well as more aromatic and flavorful.

There are thousands of varieties of rice in the world but fewer and fewer rices from which to choose, even in Southeast Asia. A few of the modern "miracle" rices have been bred for flavor, but many have not, and it is now quite common throughout Southeast Asia to see rice in the market that has neither taste nor nutritional value. Usually, when I was a guest in someone's home, the family would make sure I got the whitest, most modern (read tasteless) rice available, just as surely as they would hide the locally grown coffee and send out for a jar of instant coffee for the foreign guest.

It is commonly said that lowland paddy rice is the preferred rice for flavor and aroma, and as far as I know that may have been true at one time. But I was fortunate enough to eat upland, broadcast rice for a period of about one year, and there is nothing like it in the world. I was living in the home of a ninety-year-old woman named Aling Isay, who had run a carry-out restaurant for much of her life. Years before, Aling Isay decided that she was old enough and had worked hard enough to deserve one little luxury: the only rice she ate was this particular barely polished rice. Sown principally for flavor, this rice had an aroma and texture that made it all but impossible to want to adulterate it with the viands that were to accompany it. Once I moved away from Aling Isay's home I went into severe withdrawal.

In the United States, you can of course find highly polished, nutrition-free rices that are just as bland as those so widely used in Southeast Asia. Or you can opt for brown rice. Some of it is rather coarse-tasting and some of it isn't well cleaned, but it has the virtue of retaining the nutritional value, the aroma, and the bite of rice that has been pounded with a mortar and pestle. I use short-grain or fat-grain rice, even though long-grain rices are more common in Southeast Asia, for its texture and because it's easier to cook without turning to mush. (We tell you a lot more about rice in The Guide, page 649.)

## Fingers, Tablespoons, and Chopsticks

The preferred way to eat much of Southeast Asian food is with the fingertips of one, usually the right, hand. A lot of ritual surrounds this, however, which means that there are right ways and wrong ways of eating with the hands. Above all, never allow the food to go below your fingertips and never lick your fingers. In some places, finger bowls are provided. Once you get the hang of it, it's a great way to eat; the food tastes better because you can mix sauces and spices together in just the right proportion with the rice.

City people are more likely to use a fork and tablespoon. Hold the tablespoon in your eating hand and push the food onto it with the back of the fork. This way you can scoop up juices that might otherwise be lost. It makes no sense to eat Southeast Asian food with only a fork.

In parts of northern Southeast Asia, and of course in all of Southeast Asia's many Chinese communities, chopsticks are used. Soup dishes with noodles, for example, are best eaten with chopsticks. It's perfectly proper to lift the bowl to your mouth.

## Some Menu Ideas for Southeast Asian Meals

Serve everything except the dessert at the same time or, if you prefer, serve the soup first followed by the rest.

Beer and soft drinks are the beverages most often served with meals in Southeast Asia. Beer particularly hits the spot because of its strong, clear taste. Usually, however, I serve sparkling cider, fruit juices, or spritzers as well. In the Philippines, water is customarily served only at the end of meals, whereas in Thailand, a very weak tea is served with meals (apparently to prove that the water has been boiled and, therefore, safe to drink). Throughout Southeast Asia, coffee is served at breakfast and during midmorning and midafternoon snacks, but rarely with meals.

For anyone new to Southeast Asian cooking, the ingredients are different enough and the preparation complicated enough that the composition of a whole meal in the style of a Southeast Asian family or restaurant can be quite daunting. For this reason, I have chosen dishes that, with one or two exceptions, are quite easy to prepare. I have given you main course dishes that can stand on their own or be served with rice and perhaps one condiment. I have tried to keep the number of exotic ingredients to a minimum. Where that was not possible, as in Tom Yam Kung (Thai Hot-and-Sour Shrimp Soup), I have provided lots of information in The Guide and given every permutation of its name that I can think of to make marketing simpler. Will the search be worth it? Everyday life contains few peak experiences: Tom Yam Kung can be one of them.

Following are a few sample menus to which I add this suggestion: photocopy pages of this chapter and send one recipe to each guest as part of your invitation to a Southeast Asian dish-to-pass. The result will be a feast to which all guests have contributed. All you'll have to do is perhaps the main dish and, if you've got the wrong kind of friends, all the clean-up.

## *Sample Menus*

### A SIMPLE THAI MEAL

*Thai Hot-and-Sour Shrimp Soup*
*or*
*Thai Fish Soup with Coconut Milk*
*Thai-Style Fried Rice*
*Fried Fish, Southeast Asian Style (optional)*
*Nouc Mam Sauce (optional for drizzling on the fried rice and the fried fish)*
*Fresh fruit for dessert*

### A SIMPLE PHILIPPINE MEAL

*Steamed rice*
*Philippine-Style Fish Steaks in a Clear Hot Sour Broth*
*Philippine Mung Beans in Coconut Milk or Fried Sweet Potatoes*
*(see page 41)*
*Leche Flan*

### SOUTHEAST ASIAN LIGHT MEAL

*Steamed rice*
*Fried Fish, Southeast Asian Style (with the suggested sauce or with one of the*
*two sambals, bajag or kechap)*
*Ward and Leslie's Burmese Pumpkin or Butternut Squash*
*Shallot Chutney (optional)*
*Fresh fruit*

### A LARGE MEAL FOR GUESTS; NOT QUITE A FEAST

*Either soup that contains coconut milk (Thai Fish Soup with Coconut Milk or*
*Indonesian Squash and Spinach Soup)*
*Fried Fish, Southeast Asian Style (with the suggested sauce or with one of the*
*two sambals, bajag or kechap)*
*Steamed rice*
*Greens Adobo (use green beans)*
*or*
*Indonesian Fried Tofu with Cucumbers and Sprouts*
*or*
*A fresh spinach salad served with Nouc Mam Sauce and rings of red onion*
*Leche Flan or fresh tropical fruits for dessert*

### SOUTHEAST ASIAN FEAST

*Fresh Spring Rolls*
*Thai Hot-and-Sour Shrimp Soup*
*Indonesian Egg or Tofu Curry*
*Several of the suggested sauces or condiments*
*Steamed rice*
*Indonesian Rujak or Thai Yam Polomai (Fresh Fruit Salad with a*
*Difference)*
*Greens Adobo*
*Fresh papaya with lime wedges or fresh mangoes or Leche Flan for dessert*

# Simple Fish Stock for East Asian Dishes

The ideal is a clear, clean-tasting stock.

When I want fish scraps for stock I ask at our supermarket in Ithaca for the heads, tails, and/or collars of any fresh white-fleshed sea fish that isn't too oily or strong-tasting. Scraps from salmon or mackerel, for instance, would be too strong. Very few fish are shipped to the markets with their heads on, which is a pity, so there is usually little choice. In cities where there are still fishmongers, this will be easier. I know it's hard to think of fish as having necks, but a collar is just what you'd guess it is.

### YIELDS ABOUT 1 QUART

*¾–1 pound fish scraps (see discussion above)*

*5–6 cups water*

*½ large onion, coarsely chopped*

*2–3 slices fresh ginger root, ¼ inch thick*

*½ cup chopped celery (top leaves are good)*

*1 teaspoon whole black peppercorns*

OPTIONAL:

*a few unpeeled garlic cloves*

*a few small pieces carrot*

*bay leaf*

*shells and heads from cleaned shrimp*

Rinse the fish scraps in cold water and place them in a large pot with all the other ingredients. Bring to a boil and then simmer on very low heat for 30 minutes or so, skimming off any film that appears on the top. Once off the heat, allow the stock to sit, covered, for another 30 minutes to enrich the flavor.

For a very clear stock, such as you'd need for Thai Hot-and-Sour Shrimp Soup or Philippine-Style Fish Steaks, place a double layer of moistened cheesecloth in a strainer and pour the stock through. For soups that are to be thickened, such as Thai Fish Soup with Coconut Milk or other rich Asian soups, just passing the stock through a strainer will be sufficient.

## *Thai Hot-and-Sour Shrimp Soup*

•

## *Tom Yam Kung*

The quintessential central Thai dish. More than any other, this dish has converted people to Thai food.

Makrut, also called Kaffir lime leaves and *bai ma good,* are the perfumed leaves of the *Citrus hystrix* tree. They are available dried in one-ounce packages in East Asian groceries and are worth looking for, even if you only use them for this dish. Please consult The Guide for information on lemon grass, laos root, and cilantro root. Once you've stocked your pantry with the exotic ingredients, this dish is a snap to prepare.

Andi Gladstone, who tested this recipe for me, said, "I loved making it. I felt like a wise old woman using magic herbs and spices."

This soup should be quite spicy hot and quite sour. The cilantro and lime add a cool, refreshing balance. Get your kicks by making it hotter than you think you can tolerate. You won't regret it. My number is unlisted and my address unknown.

### SERVES 5

6 cups water

2 tablespoons dried lemon grass

2 large slices of dried laos root (see page 666)

¼ teaspoon whole peppercorns

4 makrut (see note above) leaves (optional)

_____

3 large garlic cloves, minced

1 tablespoon cleaned and minced cilantro root

_____

3 tablespoons vegetable oil (a bit more if you have the shrimp heads)

12 ounces unshelled shrimp (preferably purchased with the heads on), heads removed, shelled, and deveined (reserve the shells and heads)

_____

2 tablespoons fish sauce (see page 664)

¼ cup fresh lime juice

2 tiny fiery chiles, chopped (or substitute tiny dried ones, but reconstitute first by simmering 10 minutes or so in ½ cup water)

_____

fresh cilantro, chopped

3 limes, cut into wedges (optional)

In a large soup pot, bring to a boil the water, lemon grass, laos root, peppercorns, and makrut, if used. Simmer for at least 20 minutes.

Meanwhile, mix the minced garlic and cilantro root together and set aside.

In another large soup pot, heat the oil and stir-fry the shrimp shells (and heads) for a few minutes until they turn quite pink. Add the lemon grass broth directly from the other pot and return it to a boil; simmer for 10 minutes.

Rinse out the first pot and strain the broth back into it. Just before you're ready to serve the soup, add the garlic and cilantro root mixture and the cleaned shrimp. Simmer for 3 minutes or until the shrimp are just done. Stir in the fish sauce and lime juice. Add the chopped chiles, a little at a time, until the soup is as spicy as you like. Taste for sourness and hotness (spiciness). Adjust seasonings if necessary.

Serve piping hot, garnished with chopped fresh cilantro. Serve lime wedges on the side, to be squeezed into each bowl of soup to taste at the table.

# Thai Fish Soup with Coconut Milk

•

## Tom Yam Pla

I called for a range of three to six chiles because they vary in hotness and each person's taste is different. This dish should be sweet, sour, salty, and spicy hot—all at once.

### SERVES 6

*¼ cup dried lemon grass*
*4 slices dried laos root (see page 666)*
*3 cups Simple Fish Stock (see page 575), vegetable stock (see page 685), or water*
*2 14-ounce cans coconut milk*
*3–6 small red chiles, cut into rounds (or to taste)*

*3 scallions, minced*
*2 tablespoons chopped fresh cilantro*
*¾ pound white fish fillets, cut into large bite-sized chunks*

*juice of 2 limes*
*3 tablespoons fish sauce (see page 664)*

In a small saucepan, simmer the lemon grass and laos root slices in 1 cup of the stock or water for ½ hour. Add more liquid as necessary to retain 1 cup.

Meanwhile, in a large saucepan, simmer the coconut milk and the remaining 2 cups of stock, uncovered, for 5 minutes (covering the pot may cause the coconut milk to curdle). Add the chiles, scallions, cilantro, and the fish. Strain the lemon grass and laos mixture and add the liquid to the pot. Simmer, uncovered, until the fish is just cooked. Remove from the heat.

Stir in the lime juice and the fish sauce. Taste and adjust the flavor for tartness and saltiness by adding more lime juice and/or fish sauce.

Serve hot.

# Indonesian Squash and Spinach Soup

A soup that's a light meal. The curry leaves can be purchased at Indian or East Asian groceries. They are a little smaller than bay leaves and taste like what the name implies.

SERVES 6

1 teaspoon coriander seeds
1 teaspoon cumin seeds
1 teaspoon turmeric
2 small dried chiles
15 blanched almonds (or macadamia or
    candlenuts)

———————————

2 slices dried laos root (see page 666)
    (optional)

———————————

1 large onion, diced
2 large garlic cloves, minced
3 tablespoons vegetable oil

2 teaspoons grated peeled fresh ginger
    root
1 teaspoon salt
2 cups vegetable stock (see page 685) or
    water
a few whole small curry leaves
    (optional)
14-ounce can coconut milk
4 cups peeled and cubed butternut or
    acorn squash
6 small handfuls fresh spinach, coarsely
    chopped
fresh lime or lemon juice

Grind the coriander, cumin, turmeric, chiles, and nuts in a small spice grinder, with a mortar and pestle, or with about ½ cup of water in a blender.

If using the laos root, simmer it in 1 cup of water for at least 20 minutes, replenishing with water as necessary to maintain ½ cup of liquid. When the laos root is soft, chop it into bite-sized pieces and reserve it along with the ½ cup of cooking liquid.

In a soup pot, briefly sauté the onion and garlic in the oil. Add the ginger and salt and continue to sauté until the onions are translucent. Add the stock and the ground spice mixture to the pot and simmer for 5 minutes. Add the laos root and curry leaves, if using.

Stir in the coconut milk and the squash and gently simmer, uncovered, for about 40 minutes, until the squash is tender. Stir in the chopped spinach and allow it to just wilt. Remove the pot from the heat, squeeze in lemon or lime juice to taste and serve at once.

Note: Many variations are possible. Keep to the basic idea, though, of one chunky and one leafy vegetable. Among the chunky choose eggplant, summer squash or zucchini, or large cucumbers, seeded; among leafy choose Chinese cabbage, beet greens, Swiss chard, or kale.

A delicate, hard vegetable such as zucchini probably wants the company of a delicate, leafy one such as Chinese cabbage. A heartier hard vegetable like eggplant is best with spinach, beet greens, or chard. Follow your instincts about which ingredients will be most compatible. The procedure remains the same: just stir in the dark green leaves at the end.

# *Thai-Style Fried Rice*

·

# *Kao Pad*

Ordinarily, fried rice is made with leftover rice. If you are making the rice specifically for this dish, make it a day ahead. To ensure that the rice isn't gummy, stir it thoroughly and leave it uncovered overnight in the refrigerator. Fresh tomatoes, raw scallions, limes, fish sauce, and, of course, its spicy hotness distinguish Thai fried rice from Chinese.

### SERVES 4 TO 5

*Choose 3—4 of the following to equal
    2½ cups:*
    *diced carrots*
    *green peas (fresh or frozen)*
    *green beans, sliced diagonally in
        1-inch pieces*
    *red or green bell pepper, cut into
        short strips*
    *bean sprouts blanched for 5
        seconds, cooled, and drained*

*¼ cup vegetable oil*
*½ tablespoon minced fresh ginger root*
*2 tablespoons minced garlic cloves*

*small fresh or frozen shrimp (3—4 per
    person), shelled and deveined
    (optional)*

*6 cups cooked rice (preferably short
    grain)*
*2 eggs, lightly beaten*
*1 cup chopped fresh tomatoes*
*2 tablespoons Thai sriraja chili sauce or
    other fresh hot chili paste or a few
    tiny chiles cut into small circles*
*2 tablespoons fish sauce (see page 664)
    (or substitute light soy sauce)*
*juice of ½ lime*

*½ lime, cut into thin wedges*
*scallions, whole or cut on a severe
    diagonal into 1-inch pieces*
*tiny chiles (optional)*

Choose and prepare the vegetables. Select a combination with a variety of colors.

In a wok, heat the oil and stir-fry the ginger and garlic until golden. Remove them with a slotted spoon and set them aside for later. In the same oil, stir-fry the vegetables and shrimp until just cooked (add the harder ones like carrots first, then the shrimp, and finally the sprouts). Remove the vegetables and shrimp from the wok and set aside.

Most of the oil will now be gone, but never mind, just add the rice to the wok and heat thoroughly. With your wok spoon, make a hole through the rice down to the wok and put in the eggs. Stir until they are pretty well set before you mix them into the rice. The more you cook the eggs before stirring them into the rice the drier the dish will be, which is the way I like it. Add the tomatoes, the reserved ginger and garlic, and the stir-fried vegetables and shrimp. Finally, mix in the chili sauce, fish sauce or soy sauce, and the lime juice.

Either serve one whole scallion per person to chomp on with the fried rice, or top each serving with thin slices of scallion. Have lime wedges available for squeezing on top and more fresh chiles for the foolhardy. A side dish of something tangy (Nouc Mam Sauce, see page 605), sweet (Philippine Mung Beans in Coconut Milk, see page 587), pungent (Shallot Chutney, see page 607), or crunchy (Thai Fresh Cucumber Salad, see page 600) makes a nice complement to the dish.

# My Favorite Philippine Breakfast

 . . . or quick lunch or dinner. Fried eggs on garlicky fried rice, topped with coarse salt and fresh chiles in white vinegar: the sense of smell is a great stimulator of memory, and the aroma of this dish sends me back to the Philippines faster than any other.

Use crushed rock sea salt or at least Kosher salt, and fresh, whole, small fiery chiles that have soaked for at least a day or two in white vinegar. If you can't get fresh chiles, simmer a few whole dried chiles in half a cup of water just to soften, then chop and soak in white vinegar. For the rice use leftover, but not gummy, rice.

SERVES 2

1 tablespoon vegetable oil
1 large garlic clove, sliced thinly, crosswise
1½–2 cups cooked rice
2 eggs (or more if you're hungry)

coarse salt to taste
a few whole chiles plus the vinegar they're preserved in (see explanation above)

Heat the oil in a wok and fry the garlic pieces until barely golden. Remove the garlic and reserve. Stir-fry the rice until hot and well coated with the oil. Reduce the heat to low while you fry some sunny-side-up eggs in another pan. Mix the fried garlic pieces into the rice.

Serve the fried rice in individual shallow bowls. Place the eggs on top. Sprinkle on some coarse salt. Spoon on the peppery vinegar as you go along, eating as many of the chiles as you can tolerate.

# *Indonesian Egg or Tofu Curry*

•

# *Sambal Goreng Telor Atau Tauhu*

 I prefer to serve Sambal Goreng as one of many dishes at a large meal since it is a bit rich and heavy on its own. (See sample menus, page 573.) However, if you'd like to serve it as a main course with rice, top it with a steamed green vegetable, such as snow peas, sugar snap peas, green beans, or asparagus for a contrast in flavors and textures.

SERVES 6

*4 pieces dried laos root (see page 666)*
*1 heaping tablespoon dried lemon grass*
*3 curry leaves (see page 579) (optional)*
*½ cup water*

*1 tablespoon hot chili paste*
*1 cup chopped onions*
*3 garlic cloves, peeled*
*8 peeled almonds (drop in boiling water*
  *for a minute and the skins will pop*
  *right off)*

*2–3 tablespoons vegetable oil*

*1 teaspoon salt*
*1½ teaspoons brown sugar (optional)*
*14-ounce can coconut milk*

*6 hard-boiled eggs, peeled (or 1 pound*
  *steamed or fried tofu triangles, see*
  *page 591)*
*scallion greens, sliced on a severe*
  *diagonal*

Simmer the laos root, lemon grass, and curry leaves, if used, in the water until the liquid is reduced to ¼ cup.

Purée the chili paste, onions, garlic, and almonds in a blender or food processor, drizzling in just enough oil to keep things happening.

In a wok, cook the above two mixtures until "the oil comes out," which means until the liquid has evaporated and the oil begins to exude or "return." This can take a while, so keep a watchful eye and stir frequently. Add the salt, sugar if desired, and coconut milk and bring to a boil. Reduce the heat and simmer for 5 minutes. Finally, add the whole hard-boiled eggs or the steamed or fried tofu triangles and allow to simmer for another 10 minutes.

To serve, spoon one egg or several tofu pieces and some of the curry sauce on individual servings of rice. Top with steamed vegetables, if you choose. Garnish with scallions.

# Thai Noodle Salad

Cool, refreshing, light, so soothing it seems almost familiar, yet it's quite a unique blend; note the unusual presence of both sesame oil and coconut milk. You can use Chinese or other Asian wheat noodles, of course, but I use good old Italian linguini and it's great.

**SERVES 6**

1 pound linguini
SAUCE
3 tablespoons minced fresh basil
¼ cup minced fresh spearmint
8 ounces coconut milk
2 tablespoons dark sesame oil
1 tablespoon grated peeled fresh ginger root
1 tablespoon minced garlic
¾ teaspoon salt
2 tablespoons fresh lime or lemon juice
⅛ teaspoon cayenne (or to taste)
2 tablespoons minced scallions
VEGETABLES
Choose any of the following to equal 4 cups:
    small carrots, julienned 1 inch long

asparagus spears, cut into 1½-inch lengths
red bell peppers, cut into 2-inch strips
snow peas, cut in half
green peas or snap peas
mung bean sprouts, blanched and chilled
scallions, cut into 1-inch diagonal pieces
sliced water chestnuts
GARNISH
lime wedges
roasted peanuts, roughly chopped
minced fresh cilantro leaves (optional)

Cook the linguini in plenty of boiling salted water, drain, and then cool completely.

While the linguini is cooking, make the sauce. In a bowl, combine all the sauce ingredients and mix well.

Any combination of vegetables is fine: let color and contrasting textures be your guide. Prepare the vegetables as follows and set aside in a separate bowl. Drop carrots into boiling water and cook until barely tender. Do the same with asparagus. Blanch peppers, peas, and mung bean sprouts; plunge immediately into cold water and drain. Add scallions and water chestnuts to the other vegetables and set the bowl aside to cool.

Combine the noodles, vegetables, and sauce. Refrigerate until cool, then serve at once. If you must refrigerate the salad longer, keep in mind that noodles absorb flavor like crazy and so you'll need to readjust the seasonings before serving. Thai Noodle Salad will keep for about 2 days.

Each diner should have a wedge or two of lime to squeeze on top just before eating. Pass the chopped peanuts and, if you like, some fresh cilantro.

# Philippine Mung Beans in Coconut Milk

•

## Guinataang Munggo

A great complement to rice for a one-course meal. Easy, delicious, and, if you cook the beans ahead, very quick.

**SERVES 6**

1½ cups dried mung beans (see note)

1–1½ cups finely chopped onions
2 tablespoons vegetable oil
½ teaspoon salt
2 tablespoons finely minced peeled fresh
   ginger root
1–2 tiny fresh or dried chiles, minced
5–6 garlic cloves, minced

14-ounce can coconut milk
¾ cup cleaned small shrimp (optional)

1 tablespoon soy sauce
2 cups finely chopped fresh greens (beet
   tops, chard, mustard greens, rappini,
   spinach, or any other strong-tasting
   green)

Soak the beans in plenty of water for several hours, drain, then cook them in fresh water until soft, about 1 hour. Drain.

When the mung beans are almost done, sauté the onions in the oil with the salt. When the onions are translucent, add the ginger, chiles, and garlic and simmer on low heat several minutes. Add the coconut milk and simmer for 5 minutes. Add the shrimp, if used, and cook until just pink.

In a large pot, combine the shrimp mixture and the beans. Add the soy sauce and the greens and stir until the greens just wilt. Remove the pot from the heat at once. Taste for saltiness and add more soy sauce, if needed.

Sambal Bajag (see page 604), Sambal Kechap (see page 606), or Shallot Chutney (see page 607) provide a sharp contrast to this somewhat rich dish.

> *Note: The mung beans can be cooked up to a day in advance. Drain them and refrigerate until ready to use.*

# Fresh Spring Rolls

•

## Lumpiang Sariwa

This Philippine classic is more like a crêpe than a Chinese egg roll. The spring roll wrappers can be made from either wheat flour or cornstarch. The wheat wrappers are more healthful and a bit heavier, and so are easier to handle. The cornstarch wrappers are lighter and more authentic, but more apt to tear (see note).

Making spring roll wrappers from scratch is a snap if you have a good nonstick crêpe pan. Mine is cast iron, 9 inches in diameter, and I use it for crêpes of all kinds, especially these.

### YIELDS 6 TO 8 SPRING ROLLS

WHEAT WRAPPERS
*1 egg*
*1 cup unbleached white flour (up to ½ cup whole wheat pastry flour may be substituted for the same amount of white flour)*
*1 cup water*
*¼ teaspoon salt*
*oil for frying*

CORNSTARCH WRAPPERS
*1 egg*
*⅔ cup water*
*⅔ cup cornstarch*
*¼ teaspoon salt*
*oil for frying*
SAUCE
*1 cup water*
*⅓ cup brown sugar*

> *Note: Commercially available Vietnamese rice paper wrappers are a possible, but fussy, substitute. Look in the freezer section of East Asian groceries for wrappers about 8½ inches in diameter. Use a pastry brush dipped in warm water to soften each side. To stack, you must blot each wrapper very dry with a dishcloth. Remove the ribs from the lettuce leaves lest they tear these delicate wrappers. It's actually far easier to make your own wheat or cornstarch wrappers.*

2 teaspoons cornstarch
2 tablespoons light soy sauce
3 tablespoons white vinegar
2 tablespoons Thai sriraja chili sauce or
  ketchup with a dash of any liquid
  Asian hot sauce

FILLING
3 tablespoons vegetable oil
1/2 cup finely minced onions or shallots
2 tablespoons minced garlic cloves
1/2 teaspooon salt
1/2 teaspoon freshly ground black pepper

2 cups diced potatoes (substitute 1 cup
  canned hearts of palm or bamboo
  shoots, cut into thick strips, for 1 cup
  of the potatoes) (see note)
1 cup cut snow peas or string beans (cut
  1/4 inch thick on an extreme
  diagonal)
6–8 soft lettuce leaves (Boston, butter
  crunch, or curly leaf lettuce)

TOPPINGS (OPTIONAL)
chopped garlic cloves
chopped salted peanuts

To make the wrapper batter, using a blender, food processor, or whisk, mix either set of wrapper ingredients into a smooth batter, taking care that all the lumps are broken up.

Allow the batter to stand for 15 minutes or so while you make the sauce.

For the sauce, bring the water and sugar to a boil in a heavy saucepan. Allow it to cook down for about 5 minutes on moderate heat. Dissolve the cornstarch in the soy sauce. Lower the heat and add the cornstarch mixture. Stir until the sauce thickens slightly. Turn off the heat and mix in the vinegar and hot sauce.

Oil a crêpe pan as lightly as possible. I dip a wedge of paper towel in cooking oil, squeeze it out, and coat the entire cooking surface of my crêpe pan so lightly that not a single drop of oil is left to drip out. If necessary, use another piece of paper towel to wipe out the excess. A pastry brush is also good. If the pan is well seasoned it may not be necessary to re-oil it in between for just six to eight wrappers.

Heat the pan. When hot, pour in just enough batter to coat the whole bottom. Swirl it around very quickly and pour out any excess batter. When the batter is set on one side, turn the wrapper over with a metal spatula or your fingertips and cook for a few seconds on the other side. Remove. Stack the cooked wrappers and cover with a dry cloth.

Note: If you can get your hands on a fresh heart of palm or a fresh bamboo shoot, use that in place of all of the potatoes. The canned versions of these vegetables do add a nice tang, but their textures leave too much to be desired to stand on their own.

For the filling, in a wok or heavy skillet, heat the oil and stir-fry the onions and garlic until they are limp. Add salt, pepper, and the potatoes and cook until the potatoes are tender. Stir frequently to prevent sticking. Add the hearts of palm or bamboo shoots if you are using them. Mix in the snow peas or string beans and cook until they are barely tender, half a minute for snow peas, several minutes for string beans. Transfer to an attractive serving bowl and keep warm.

Arrange the spring roll wrappers and lettuce leaves attractively on a platter. Place the sauce, the filling, and the toppings in separate bowls.

You can assemble the fresh spring rolls for your guests just before they're ready to eat them, but I think it's more fun to let them do it themselves.

Construct a fresh spring roll by placing a lettuce leaf on top of one of the spring roll wrappers. Add 2–4 tablespoons of the filling in a line along the middle and roll up the wrapper. Fold up one end an inch and a half so the sauce can't drip through. Now drizzle some sauce into the open end. Sprinkle peanuts on top, if you like, and eat the spring roll with your fingers.

## Variations

Half a cup of finely shredded cabbage would be nice and so would half a pound of chopped shrimp (stir-fried after the potatoes are cooked), but this dish does very well without the pork or shrimp that Filipinos would ordinarily add.

Leftover filling is great in an omelette.

# Indonesian Fried Tofu with Cucumbers and Sprouts

•

## Tauhu Goreng Kechap

With rice, this is a quick one-dish meal. For a large dinner, serve Tauhu Goreng Kechap with a side dish of fried yams or sweet potato, steamed or fried whole sea fish, and Sambal Kechap (see page 606) or Sambal Bajag (see page 604) along with the rice.

### SERVES 4 TO 5

SAUCE
²/₃ cup light soy sauce
3–4 medium garlic cloves, minced
2 tablespoons minced onion, shallot, or
   scallions
1–2 small chiles, minced (seeded if you
   want less harshness)
¼ cup fresh lemon or lime juice
½–1 teaspoon sugar (optional)

2 cups mung bean sprouts

3 cakes tofu, pressed and patted dry (see
   page 684)
vegetable oil for frying
4–5 servings cooked rice
1–2 small cucumbers, cut in half
   lengthwise, seeded and sliced about
   ¼ inch thick on a severe diagonal
toasted peanuts, chopped

In a small bowl, mix together the sauce ingredients and taste to get a pleasing balance of hot, salty, and sour. Sweeten with the sugar if you like. Everything else in this dish is bland, so the sauce should be intense.

Blanch the mung sprouts by placing them in a strainer and pouring boiling water over them. Immediately plunge them into a bowl of very cold water. When the sprouts are cold, drain thoroughly.

Cut each cake of pressed tofu horizontally into thirds, and then cut each piece diagonally both ways to form four triangles. Pat the tofu dry again. Heat about 1 inch of oil in a wok or ½ inch in a shallow frying pan and, when it is hot, fry the tofu, a few pieces at a time, until golden brown. Drain on paper towels. The advantage of a wok is that you can use less oil, but you will fight to keep the pieces from sticking to one another. In a skillet you use more oil, but the tofu pieces won't stick together. If they stick to the bottom, just scrape them up with a thin metal spatula.

On a platter or individual plates, place first some rice and then the fried tofu with a drizzle of the sauce. Add the cucumber and mung sprouts and pour on some more of the sauce. Reserve some sauce to pass at the table. When you are ready to serve the dish, garnish it with a sprinkling of peanuts.

## Variations

Instead of the cucumbers and sprouts, substitute thin broccoli spears or green beans or long Chinese beans dropped into boiling water and cooked very quickly until just done. Or, keep the sprouts and substitute raw or barely steamed spinach for the cucumbers.

Use water instead of oil for cooking the tofu. *Easy method:* Place the cut-up pieces of tofu in plenty of boiling water and allow them to simmer for a minute or two, stirring to prevent them from sticking together. *Better method:* Use a Chinese bamboo steamer. Place it over water in a wok and arrange the tofu pieces on the steamer so they are not touching. Loosely cover the tofu and steam it for about 5 minutes at a high simmer until the pieces are moist but firm.

*Note: It would be a shame to ruin a well-seasoned carbon steel wok by using it as a steamer. I suggest you buy an extra cheap wok, like I did, expressly for steaming fish, tofu, and delicate greens and for making savory or sweet custards such as Leche Flan (see page 608).*

# Philippine-Style Fish Steaks
## in a Clear Hot Sour Broth

•

## Sinigang Na Isda

The cooking in the Tagalog-speaking region of the Philippines displays an incredible range of sour flavors. This superb but ridiculously simple fish preparation should be only moderately spicy but quite sour. In the Philippines, any number of unripe tropical fruits might provide the flavor, but here radishes and lemon juice do the trick quite well. Whole green beans or Chinese long beans, cut into 3-inch lengths, could be used instead of spinach. Add them just before the fish.

### SERVES 6

6—7 cups strained Simple Fish Stock (see page 575) or vegetable stock (see page 685)

2 small onions, cut lengthwise into long very thin strips (to make 2 cups)

2 cups sliced daikon radish, cut diagonally ½ inch thick (or use whole tiny icicle radishes or even the red ones cut in half)

½ cup fresh lemon juice

1 long (6—8 inches) chile, quartered lengthwise (seeded if you want it less harsh)

6 fish steaks, such as swordfish, cod, scrod, haddock, bluefish, or sea bass

2 cups chopped fresh tomatoes

5 ounces spinach, chopped

2 tablespoons fish sauce (see page 664)

¼ teaspoon freshly ground black pepper

1 tablespoon white vinegar (optional)

_____

chopped scallions (optional)

In a large soup pot, bring the stock and onions to a boil. Lower the heat, add the daikon or other radishes, the lemon juice, and the chile. Simmer for 10 minutes.

Add the fish and tomatoes and cook until the fish is just done, about 5 minutes. Turn off the heat and just before serving stir in the spinach. Then season with the fish sauce and black pepper. Taste for sourness and add a tablespoon or so of white vinegar to taste.

To serve American style: Place each fish steak into a warmed wide, shallow bowl and ladle the vegetables and broth over. Serve with crusty French bread and butter.

To serve Philippine style: Place each fish steak on individual plates of steamed rice. Serve the vegetables and broth in separate bowls. Fried Sweet Potatoes or Plantains (see page 41) complement this quintessential Philippine dish, as does Philippine Mung Beans in Coconut Milk (see page 587). Or serve Sinigang with rice as a meal in itself and treat yourself to a rich Leche Flan (see page 608) for dessert.

# Fried Fish, Southeast Asian Style

Here are some general guidelines for how to prepare fried fish. As far as I know, most cuisines in the world use this technique, but only Southeast Asia has fish sauce to provide both saltiness and that inexplicable added spark. Most often, I serve this fish as a side dish with commercially available fish sauce or Nouc Mam Sauce. However, when I serve it as an entrée, I serve it with the more substantial sauce suggested below.

A small, cleaned, whole fish is what we're looking for here, but a headless one will do if that's all that is available.

*whole fish, cleaned, small enough to fry whole (sea bass, trout, snapper, or other firm-fleshed sea fish, or something you've caught in your pond)*

*peanut oil (or other bland oil that reaches a high temperature before smoking)*

*fish sauce (see page 664) or Nouc Mam Sauce (see page 605) or my Informal Little Sauce suggestion (see note)*

Rinse the fish and pat with paper towels until very dry.

On each side of the fish, make three diagonal slits through to the bone.

Heat a skillet or wok. Add oil, to about ½ inch in a wok or ¼ inch in a skillet, and heat it to just below its smoking point. Fry the fish, one at a time in a wok or well separated in a skillet, until golden brown on one side, then flip the fish and do the same on the other side. Remove from the pan.

Sprinkle immediately with the sauce of your choosing. Somehow fish sauce and fried fish are a dynamite combination.

Serve Fried Fish with rice, tiny bird's-eye chiles, coarse salt, and more fish sauce on the side. It goes with just about any dish (except maybe more fish) that you find in this chapter.

> *Note:* **An Informal Little Sauce suggestion for Fried Fish:** *In a small skillet, sauté a small, minced onion and some minced garlic in oil. Add a cup or so of chopped fresh tomatoes and a splash of water, cover, and cook down to a thin sauce. Add freshly ground black pepper and fish sauce to taste.*

# Greens Adobo

*Adobo* to Filipinos seems to mean any dish cooked with garlic, soy sauce, black pepper, and vinegar: a strong flavoring yet one that allows the other ingredients to shine through. In fact, almost anything can be cooked *adobo,* and it's a particularly good way to use the tops of root vegetables such as beet greens. Greens Adobo makes a good accompaniment to steamed, blanched, baked, or fried tofu pieces.

### SERVES 4

*3 garlic cloves, sliced*

*2 tablespoons vegetable oil*

*5 cups chopped greens (beet tops, chard, mustard greens, rappini, or spinach, for example), washed and well drained*

*2 tablespoons light soy sauce*

*1 tablespoon white vinegar*

*freshly ground black pepper to taste*

In a wok, stir-fry the garlic pieces in the oil until golden. Remove with a slotted spoon and reserve.

Add the greens to the wok and toss over high heat until wilted. Turn off the heat. Stir in the soy sauce and vinegar and grind some pepper on top. Return the fried garlic pieces and stir them in. Serve at once.

Do this as quickly as possible so the greens will retain their bright color and most of their vitamins. A red pepper ring makes a pretty garnish.

*Variation* A hard green vegetable such as Chinese long beans, green beans, broccoli spears, or sugar snap peas can also be prepared *adobo,* but will require the addition of a bit of water, stock, or coconut milk to finish off the cooking.

# Fresh Fruit Salad with a Difference

•

## Indonesian Rujak or Thai Yam Polomai

I implore you to try this dish! Surely you came to Southeast Asian cooking in the hope of finding something exotic. Well, look no further. Fruit combined with fish sauce, chiles—maybe even shrimp! Fully ripe fruits are fine in this dish, but underripe, sour ones are even better. Since most of the fruit we find in the supermarket isn't ripe anyway, why not make a virtue of necessity?

### SERVES 4

*Choose 3–4 of the following:*
*grapefruit or pomelos, sectioned*
*oranges, sectioned*
*tangerines, sectioned*
*underripe pears, thinly sliced*
*firm papayas, thinly sliced*
*underripe mangoes, thinly sliced*
*tart apples (Greening, Mutzu,*
*    green MacIntosh, Northern Spy,*
*    etc.), thinly sliced*
*red grapes, halved and seeded*

**INDONESIAN RUJAK DRESSING**
*2 tiny chiles, cut into thin circles or*
*    deveined, seeded, and chopped for a*
*    milder taste*
*1 tablespoon brown sugar*
*1 tablespoon fresh lemon or lime juice*
*1 tablespoon water plus 1 tablespoon*

*fish sauce (see page 664) or*
*Vegetarian Fish Sauce Substitute (see*
*page 603)*

**THAI YAM POLOMAI DRESSING**
*2 tablespoons oil*
*1 large shallot, peeled and sliced*
*    lengthwise into thin strips*
*3 garlic cloves, sliced crosswise*
*1/2 teaspoon salt*
*juice of one lime or lemon*
*pinch of brown sugar (optional)*

---

*1 tiny chile, seeded and sliced into long,*
*    thin slivers (for Thai Yam Polomai)*
*2–3 medium cooked shrimp per person*
*    (optional, but especially nice with*
*    Thai Yam Polomai)*
*chopped toasted peanuts (optional)*

Select some beautiful fruits from the list, but be sure to include grapefruit and something that's unripe like a green pear, tart apple, unripe mango, or firm but not quite ripe papaya.

For Indonesian Rujak, simply mix the ingredients together in a bowl, stirring to dissolve the sugar. For Thai Yam Polomai, heat the oil in a small pan and sauté the shallot and garlic with the salt until just translucent. Drain off the oil and stir the lime or lemon juice and the optional brown sugar into the shallot mixture.

Put together the salad by arranging the thinly sliced fruit artfully on a platter. Scatter the grapefruit and other citrus sections around and top with the dressing, the chile strips (if it's Yam Polomai), the shrimp, and, at the last minute, the chopped toasted peanuts.

*Variation* Use the same treatment with raw vegetables. For example, use chopped celery with some of the top leaves, seeded cucumber slices, shredded cabbage, spinach, lettuce, or quickly blanched mung bean sprouts. Top with one of the dressings and be sure to include some toasted peanuts. This is much tamer than unripe fruit with shrimp and chiles, and definitely less exotic.

# *Ward and Leslie's Burmese Pumpkin or Butternut Squash*

Here is a recipe an Indian woman in Burma frequently cooked for my friends Ward and Leslie. It's just onions and squash, but the magic is in the method. Asian cooks often give such a twist to the technique to make very ordinary ingredients come out tasting terrific. When selecting the squash, the darker orange, the better.

2 tablespoons vegetable oil

1 small onion, chopped

_____

1 small onion, quartered

1 garlic clove

1 tablespoon grated peeled fresh ginger
  root

½ teaspoon shrimp paste (see note)

1 fiery green chile, sliced in half
  lengthwise (remove the veins and
  seeds for a milder effect)

_____

4 cups cubed peeled butternut squash or
  pumpkin (1-inch cubes)

_____

chopped fresh cilantro leaves

In a wok, heat the oil and stir-fry the chopped onion until it's nicely browned but not burned.

Liquefy the quartered onion, garlic, ginger, and shrimp paste in a food processor or blender. Add this mixture to the chopped onion in the wok and stir-fry "till the oil comes out"—until you've cooked away all the liquid. When this happens, you'll see it. It may take as long as 10 minutes. Stir in the chile halves.

Add the cubed squash and a cup of water. Reduce the heat and cover. Add more water as it's needed to prevent sticking, but just enough so that the water will have cooked away as soon as the squash is just tender, and the dish will be "dry." Then it's done.

Top with chopped fresh cilantro leaves and serve at once.

---

*Note: Much more of an acquired taste than fish sauce, shrimp paste has an offensive odor to those not accustomed to it. Cooking it removes that odor from the dish but not from the kitchen. I've tried this dish without the shrimp paste without success, so be bold, but turn on an exhaust fan or open the window. Shrimp paste is available in Asian groceries, the Thai varieties being the most common. Stored well sealed in several layers of plastic, shrimp paste will keep for several weeks.*

# Thai Fresh Cucumber Salad

•

# Taeng Kwa Brio Wan

Asian cooks perform many tricks to get rid of the bitter juice around cucumber seeds. In this recipe, you salt the cucumbers and then squeeze them—so forcefully, in fact, that if your cheesecloth is weak, it will rip. The result is that the cucumbers are less bitter and, oddly enough, more crisp. Serve with fried fish and rice or as an accompaniment to dishes rich in coconut milk.

## YIELDS 4 TO 5 CUPS

3 medium cucumbers, sliced as thinly as possible (peel the cucumbers only if they are waxed and even then leave on a few strips of green)
salt

_____

½ teaspoon dried hot pepper flakes

1 tablespoon sugar dissolved in ¼ cup hot water
4 tablespoons white vinegar
2 tablespoons minced red onion (or 1 tablespoon minced scallions) (optional)

In a bowl, generously salt the sliced cucumbers. Allow to sit for at least 30 minutes, stirring occasionally.

Combine the other ingredients.

Squeeze out as much of the cucumber juice as you can, by wringing a handful at a time in a double layer of cheesecloth or a dish towel. Twist until you can extract no more juice.

Combine the squeezed cucumbers and the sauce in a serving bowl and refrigerate until ready to serve.

# CONDIMENTS
# AND SAUCES

## *Southeast Asian Condiments*

At a Southeast Asian meal many condiments and sauces accompany the rice and the viands. Wedges of lemons or limes and tiny bowls of soy sauce, fish sauce, coarse salt, or small chiles floating in white vinegar all might appear, along with whole scallions and minced fresh cilantro. Many prepared hot sauces, pickled chiles, fish sauces, and even Southeast Asian soy sauces are now available in the United States. Serve any combination of these prepared sauces or mix some of the following and place them on the table in separate bowls. The more little bowls, the more you can play with your food.

- *fish sauce and fresh lemon or lime juice (with or without minced cilantro leaves)*
- *light soy sauce and fresh lemon or lime juice*
- *white vinegar and minced garlic (salt optional)*
- *white vinegar, minced garlic, and soy sauce*
- *white vinegar, minced garlic, soy sauce, and hot pepper flakes or fresh chiles cut into thin rings*
- *white vinegar and fresh or dried chiles (with or without cilantro leaves)*

Taste for saltiness, hotness, and sourness. Adjust accordingly. Dilute with a splash of water if that seems appropriate.

# About Fish Sauce

Called *nouc mam* in Vietnamese, *nam pla* in Thai, *tuk trey* in Khmer, *patis* in the Philippines, and *ngan pya ye* in Burmese, fish sauce is the characteristic Southeast Asian condiment. Because it is made by fermenting anchovies, it takes a little getting used to. But you must believe me when I tell you it's a taste very worth acquiring.

If it is true that nothing unlocks memories more readily than aromas, it's also true that the aromas of food stir up powerful feelings. This was the case with American GIs when they first encountered the ubiquitous *nouc mam* in Viet Nam. Many of them looked down on the Vietnamese for the mere fact of being fish sauce–eaters. To the new arrivals, GIs who were long-termers or re-uppers had "gone native" if they had taken to using it on their food. But soon enough, military rations forced all but the hard core to try a little fish sauce themselves.

Now, all across the United States you'll find Viet Nam vets who crave the stuff. It's not just that the aroma brings back memories of Viet Nam. Fish sauce adds a depth of flavor to foods that salt alone cannot do. It is also a very important source of protein in all of Southeast Asia, except in parts of Indonesia where (even stinkier) shrimp pastes and locally made light and sweet soy sauces are used instead.

There are several things to know about bottled fish sauces. First, be assured that much of the odor cooks away, leaving only the rich flavor which, like salt, brings out the other flavors in a dish. Second, there are a number of brands from which to choose, some better than others. Squid Brand fish sauce from Thailand is good, and it is widely available in Asian specialty stores in the United States. I like it better than Rufina *patis* from the Philippines. The Vietnamese fish sauces are generally the finest, but they are expensive and hard to find.

If you're lucky enough to find a Vietnamese fish sauce with the words *"phu quoc"* written on the label, it may or may not be from the island of Phu Quoc (the "Burgundy Region" of fish sauces), but it will probably be quite good—too good, perhaps, to cook with. Use it for serving at the table as a dipping sauce either alone or with the addition of garlic, lime juice, chile circles, a little sugar, or in combination with any or all of these. You'll know that you've gone native when you start craving fish sauce on unripe mangoes, a passion food if there ever was one!

If you do not eat fish, use the concoction that follows or substitute light soy sauce for fish sauce in recipes. But please realize that the resulting dish, while no doubt still tasty, will in many cases not be authentically Southeast Asian.

# Vegetarian Fish Sauce Substitute

I have experimented a lot to find a vegetarian substitute for fish sauce. This is the best I've come up with so far, better even than light soy sauce in some cases.

This substitution works only when fish sauce is called for as a seasoning for a recipe, not as a dipping sauce that stands on its own.

Make a strong vegetable stock that is heavy on onions and black peppercorns. For each 2 tablespoons of fish sauce called for in a recipe, substitute 2 tablespoons of the stock plus ½ to 1 teaspoon of salt.

# Sambal Bajag

•

## Fiery Indonesian Spice Paste

 This is my favorite, number one, all-time killer hot sauce. If it's not hot, it's not right.

As with Sambal Kechap, which follows, I have used dried chiles because they are always available in Asian specialty shops. The shorter the chile, the hotter it is, which makes it also more authentic; less than 1½ inches is usual. Tiny, hot bird's eye peppers are about ½ inch long and are the best, but are seldom seen here. Pizza parlor dried hot pepper flakes are fine too.

*3 tablespoons oil*
*¼ cup minced onions*
*1–2 tablespoons minced garlic cloves*
  *(2 sounds like a lot, but it's not too*
  *much)*
*4–6 teaspoons red hot pepper flakes or*
  *crushed tiny dried red chiles (do not*
  *stint; be bold)*

*⅓ cup finely minced fresh tomato*
*1 scant teaspoon salt*
*2 teaspoons sugar*
*2 teaspoons molasses (4 teaspoons dark*
  *brown sugar can be substituted for*
  *the sugar and molasses)*

In a small frying pan (I use a 6-inch cast-iron one) or in a wok, heat the oil and stir-fry the onions and garlic. After a minute or so add the hot pepper flakes. Reduce the heat and stir constantly lest the pepper burns. As soon as the flakes darken a little, add the rest of the ingredients and, on the lowest heat, cook the sambal until most of the moisture has evaporated and, as they say, "the oil returns"—about 15 to 20 minutes. The final product should be so well cooked that you can't really detect the tomatoes.

Sambal Bajag, like most sambals, should be so fiery hot that you just dip the tip of a teaspoon into the sambal and then mix that into a bit of your rice, stir it into your soup, or whatever. There is virtually no Southeast Asian meal that will not be enhanced by this condiment.

Note that this recipe only makes a small amount, which is all you'll need. Refrigerated, Sambal Bajag will keep for months.

# Nouc Mam Sauce

•

## Vietnamese/Cambodian Dressing with Fish Sauce

This sauce is for eating with rice alongside almost any Southeast Asian dish, especially fried fish. Also to be used as a dressing for tossed salads including spinach, savoy, Chinese or white cabbage, carrot curls, rings of red onion, and the like.

YIELDS ⅔ CUP

3 tablespoons white vinegar

3 tablespoons fish sauce (see page 664) or Vegetarian Fish Sauce Substitute (see page 603)

1–2 fresh chiles, minced (or 1–2 small dried chiles reconstituted by simmering in ½ cup water until soft and then minced)

2 tablespoons fresh lemon or lime juice

sugar to taste (optional)

minced garlic (optional)

_____

a few strands of long, very fine carrot julienne

Combine and taste. Too salty or sour? Add a little water until it's just right.

# Sambal Kechap

This sauce is supposed to be fiery hot. Indonesians might use a whole tablespoon of dried hot pepper flakes for this amount of soy sauce. The idea is to add tiny amounts of Sambal Kechap at a time to what you are eating: soup, fried fish, plain rice, or whatever.

*¼ cup light soy sauce*
*1 small garlic clove, pressed*
*1–1½ teaspoons dried hot pepper flakes*
*    or crushed tiny dried chiles*

*½ teaspoon dark molasses*

Mix the ingredients and allow to sit for at least half an hour.

Cover any leftover sauce tightly and store in the refrigerator. It will keep a long time, perhaps even indefinitely.

# Shallot Chutney

If this condiment were spicy hot, it might be called a sambal, but because it's mild, let's call it a chutney, which it most closely resembles. To sweeten it, you could add unsweetened, toasted, shredded coconut, but I prefer it plain.

*½ pound shallots, cut in half, peeled, and sliced paper thin (or substitute red onion)*
*2 tablespoons vegetable oil*
*2 tablespoons golden raisins*
*2 tablespoons coarsely chopped cashews, blanched almonds, or macadamia nuts, or whole pine nuts*

*½ teaspoon ground cumin seeds (or to taste)*
*grated peel of 1 lemon (or to taste)*
*½ teaspooon salt*

Place the sliced shallots between several layers of paper towels and pat to remove excess moisture.

Heat the oil in a small skillet or wok. Add the shallots and stir-fry on medium heat until golden brown. Add the raisins, nuts, cumin, lemon peel, and salt. Cook a while longer, until the shallots are an even darker brown. Taste and adjust cumin and lemon flavors.

Cool before serving with rice and any of the main dishes in this chapter. Chutney may be stored in the refrigerator in an airtight container and will keep for a long time.

# DESSERT

## *Leche Flan*

A perfect flan is smooth and uniform throughout, neither rubbery nor eggy. A perfect flan is also a rare thing. Nevertheless, this recipe always works for me, perhaps because, like me, it's a bit fussy.

My Filipina friend Natalia asked me to try maple syrup instead of caramelized sugar. It works fine but provides a slightly less contrasting flavor. If you prefer the traditional caramel, see Mexican Flan (see page 474).

It's worth buying a bamboo steamer and an extra "el cheapo" wok and wok ring to reserve for steaming. They're endlessly versatile. You'll be more than adequately rewarded even if you only use it for this indescribably elegant dessert.

*½ cup maple syrup*
*12-ounce can evaporated milk*
*2½ cups fresh whole milk*

*12 egg yolks*
*⅔ cup sugar*
*grated rind of 1 lime*

In a heavy pot, heat the maple syrup to bubbling and, stirring constantly, cook it down a bit to thicken. It can be reduced to as little as ¼ cup, but be careful not to go too far or it will turn into maple sugar. Pour the syrup into the bottom of a glass or stainless steel medium loaf pan, tilt to cover the whole bottom, and allow to cool.

Warm the evaporated and whole milks. Remove from the heat before bubbles form.

In a large bowl, beat the egg yolks. Stir in the sugar and lime rind. Mix in the warm milk. If a film has formed on the surface of the milk, strain it as you pour it into the bowl. Pour the custard mixture into the loaf pan. Try to disturb the syrup as little as possible. The custard should be about 1½ inches deep.

Steam or bake the flan.

Steaming method: If you have a Chinese-type steamer and wok, this is the best way to make a flan that is smooth, rich, and creamy without being rubbery. Pour 3 inches of water into the wok. Place the steamer in the wok, carefully balance the loaf pan in the center, and cover however you can. Most likely, neither your steamer lid nor your wok lid will fit, so use aluminum foil or whatever, but be sure to leave an air hole to allow some of the steam to escape. Steam over moderate heat for about 45 minutes, replenishing the water in the bottom of the wok with hot or boiling water whenever necessary, until a knife inserted into the center of the flan comes out clean. Pay no attention to any extraneous juices you may see floating around; some thin syrup will probably separate from the flan.

Baking method: Preheat the oven to 325°. Place the loaf pan of flan into a larger pan and pour hot water to a depth of 1½ inches into the larger pan. Bake for 1 to 1½ hours, until a knife inserted into the center of the flan comes out clean. Replenish the water in the outer pan, as necessary, with very hot or boiling water. If the top of the flan begins to brown before it is cooked through, cover it with aluminum foil to prevent a crust from forming.

When the flan is done, allow it to cool before loosening the sides with a wet knife and inverting it onto a platter. Serve at room temperature. Spoon any thin syrup that separated from the flan onto the slices of flan as you serve them.

S A R A   R O B B I N S

# Southern United States

# INTRODUCTION

My mother, Anne Wade Robbins, was born and raised in rural Georgia. She married a Yankee and settled in the North, but even after thirty-odd years, she never lost her Southern accent or her Southern way with food. I was raised on Southern cooking.

While she cooked, Mom would often tell stories of her childhood growing up on a farm in rural Georgia with five sisters and three brothers. The food was a meaningful connection to the past for her, and it remains so for me. My mother died in 1984, and often I cook her recipes conjuring the aromas and spirit of the past in my own kitchen.

We traveled South a lot when I was a child, visiting family or vacationing. Often we drove the thousand miles from our home in New York to Atlanta, and I remember these trips as great adventures into another culture, almost like going to another country, complete with foreign language, customs, and, of course, native cuisine. Crossing the Mason-Dixon line was a spiritual experience for my mother, accompanied by much teasing and singing of "Dixie" by the Yankee side of the family.

We would stop at the first Stuckey's we came to and feel we had arrived—we were really in the South now! We would load up on Southern treats: coconut milk, praline, and divinity fudge, boiled peanuts, and, of course, Coca-Cola. We would fill the car with food and cruise on down the highway, chocolate-covered coconut patties melting in our mouths.

My mother's family was large and the Southern hospitality was genuine. There were many aunts, uncles, and cousins to see, and eating was a major feature of a visit. The Wade family had (and still has) some great cooks and a real appreciation for sharing good food. I remember Aunt Minnie's coconut cake, Aunt Emma's perfect biscuits, Aunt Sara's homemade peach ice cream, Uncle Claude's fish fry, Aunt Mildred's snap beans, and Uncle Hoyt's Brunswick stew, to name just a few.

Having been raised in the North with its short summers, I was always impressed by the abundant gardens in the South. Every relative had a garden, and many of the vegetables were hard to find up North. When the relatives came to visit us, they would bring frozen homegrown butter beans, lady peas, and baby limas packed in dry ice as a special treat. Southern cooking brings to my mind a distinctive selection of ingredients: sweet potatoes, rice, okra, grits, sweet corn, white cornmeal, collards, mustard and turnip greens, kale, pecans, peanuts, bell peppers, black-eyed peas, lima beans, lady peas, coconuts, peaches, watermelon, all types of summer squash, string beans, eggplants, and glorious tomatoes, red and green.

My mother was a brilliant cook but undisciplined, measuring by a "pinch" of this,

"some" of that. I learned by watching and listening, because very little was written down. Some of the best meals I ever had were the garden meals my mother would prepare. First we would walk through the garden, Northern or Southern, depending on where we were, and pick whatever was ripe: some tender green beans, a zucchini, a red and green tomato or two. And then Mom would whip up a batch of hoecake, my favorite type of cornbread, which is actually fried cornmeal mush. She'd boil the green beans until just tender, top with chopped ripe tomato, flour and fry the green tomatoes, sauté the zucchini with onion and lots of black pepper, and we would feast.

We rarely ate in restaurants in the South. I remember going to a famous barbecue joint to buy a quart of their sauce and trying to copy it at home. Impossible! And once Uncle Bud took us to a wonderful all-you-can-eat fried catfish with hush puppies restaurant. But for the most part, Southern cooking as I experienced it was home cooking: simple unpretentious food using very fresh ingredients.

When I first considered cooking the food of the Deep South at Moosewood Restaurant, I was stumped. Authentic Southern food is drenched in pork fat, and fried chicken seemed essential. I had to redefine Southern cooking in order to present it without meat, and in rethinking it I discovered a wealth of ingredients that are authentic and vegetarian. Combined grains such as rice, corn, or wheat and beans like limas or black-eyed peas provide complete proteins. The traditional smoky flavor of many Southern dishes can be provided by smoked cheeses: cheddar, Swiss, or gouda in place of bacon or ham. I've tried to cut down on the use of fats and fried foods associated with Southern cooking to present a lighter, more healthful variation.

So fix a bunch of cornbread, cook up a mess of greens, dish up that Hoppin' John, and enjoy!

# *Okra Gumbo Soup*

This soup is very popular at Moosewood. The famous Louisiana chef Paul Prudhomme calls onion, celery, and bell pepper "the holy trinity" of Creole cooking, and it blesses this.

### SERVES 4 TO 6

*1 cup chopped onions*
*2 tablespoons vegetable oil*
*½ teaspoon dried oregano*
*½ teaspoon dried thyme*
*½ teaspoon dried basil*
*2 bay leaves*
*2 celery stalks, finely chopped*
*1 green or red bell pepper, chopped*
*1 medium carrot, diced*
*1 cup chopped potatoes*

*2 cups chopped fresh tomatoes (or 16-ounce can of tomatoes, chopped, with juice)*

*3 cups vegetable stock (see page 685) or water*

*1 cup corn, fresh, frozen, or canned (with liquid)*
*1 cup sliced fresh okra (or 10 ounces frozen)*
*1 tablespoon cider vinegar*

*salt and ground black pepper to taste*
*Tabasco or other hot sauce to taste*
*1 teaspoon Worcestershire Sauce (see page 686) (optional)*

Sauté the onions in the vegetable oil until just translucent. Add the herbs, celery, bell pepper, carrot, and potatoes and cook for about 10 minutes on medium heat, stirring to prevent sticking. Add the tomatoes and stock and simmer for 10 minutes. Add the corn, okra, and vinegar and simmer until the okra is tender. Remove the bay leaves. Add the remaining seasonings to taste.

 ## *Pimiento Cheese Bisque*

This recipe was inspired by the pimiento cheese spread I ate as a child. My Southern aunts would always have a jar of this homemade treat in their refrigerators. Sweet potato provides the sweet golden background for the bright taste and color of the pimiento.

**SERVES 4 TO 6**

*2 celery stalks, chopped*
*1 cup chopped onions*
*2 tablespoons vegetable oil*
*1 medium sweet potato, diced (about 2 cups)*
*1 medium white potato, diced (about 2 cups)*
*4 cups vegetable stock (see page 685) or water*

*1 cup sharp or extra sharp cheddar cheese, grated or chopped*
*3 ounces cream cheese, cubed*
*4-ounce jar pimientos, chopped*
*salt and ground black pepper to taste*

In a heavy saucepan, sauté the celery and onion in the vegetable oil, stirring occasionally. When the onions are translucent, about 10 minutes or so, add the sweet potato, white potato, and stock. Simmer until the vegetables are soft, for about 20 minutes.

Remove the soup from the heat, add the cheddar and cream cheeses, and allow it to sit a few minutes to soften the cheese. In a blender or food processor, purée the soup with half of the pimientos. Add salt and pepper to taste. If the soup is too thick, thin to the desired consistency using milk, water, or vegetable stock. Stir in the remaining pimientos. Reheat gently, but do not boil.

# Cocola Salad

This is not a joke. It is a healthful adaptation of a salad/dessert presented at potlucks all over the South. This two-layer fruit concoction is a good introduction to agar agar, a vegetarian "gelatin." Refreshing and light, Cocola Salad is especially good served in hot weather or after a rich meal.

### SERVES 6 TO 8

16-ounce can cherries in juice or water
16-ounce bottle natural cola (or other cola choice)
1½ cups cherry or apple-cherry juice
4 tablespoons agar agar flakes (see note) (do not substitute agar agar powder)

5 tablespoons maple syrup, honey, or sugar
3 ounces cream cheese
½ cup toas. d. chopped pecans

First layer: Drain the cherries, saving the juice. Add enough of the cola to the reserved cherry juice to make 2 cups of liquid. Pour this and 1 cup of the cherry or apple-cherry juice into a saucepan and sprinkle on 3 tablespoons of the agar agar flakes. Heat until boiling. Reduce the heat and simmer gently, stirring often, for 5 minutes, or until the agar agar is dissolved. Remove from the heat and stir in the cherries and 2 tablespoons of the sweetener. Pour into a 10-inch glass pie plate or a nonmetallic quart mold or casserole dish. Chill for 1 hour in the refrigerator or 20 minutes in the freezer.

Second layer: In a saucepan, combine the remaining ½ cup of cherry juice, ½ cup of the cola, and 3 tablespoons of syrup, honey, or sugar. Stir in 1 tablespoon agar agar flakes and simmer for 5 minutes, or until the agar agar is dissolved.

Cut the cream cheese into little bits and put them in a blender or food processor. Pour in the hot agar agar mixture and purée until creamy. Gently pour this over the chilled first layer and sprinkle the pecans on top.

Cover with foil, plastic wrap, or a plate and chill thoroughly for at least 2 hours.

*Variation* Substitute an equal amount of the fruit juice of your choice for the cola. Use any fruit that you like. Omit the cream cheese layer or substitute lowfat yogurt for the cream cheese, and increase the agar agar by 2 teaspoons.

> *Note: Agar agar is made from seaweed and used as a gelatin. It is available in Asian and healthfood stores and often in the ethnic section of supermarkets. It is important that agar agar be completely dissolved, so simmer and stir for at least 5 minutes. The general formula is one tablespoon agar agar flakes to one cup liquid.*

# Vidalia Onion and Bell Pepper Salad

Vidalia onions grown in Georgia are famous for their sweetness. Use at least two varieties of bell peppers to create a colorful salad.

### SERVES 6 TO 8 AS A SIDE DISH

*1 medium Vidalia (see note) onion, thinly sliced into circles (about 1 cup)*

**MARINADE**
*1 garlic clove, minced*
*½ teaspoon freshly ground black pepper*
*salt to taste*
*¼ cup cider vinegar*
*¼ cup vegetable oil*

*⅛ teaspoon dried thyme*
*2 tablespoons chopped fresh parsley*

*4 medium or 3 large red, green, yellow, and/or orange bell peppers, sliced lengthwise into ½-inch strips (about 4 cups)*

Place the sliced onion in a large bowl. Mix together all of the marinade ingredients and pour over the onions.

Blanch the bell pepper strips in boiling water for about 2 minutes. Drain the peppers and let them cool. Add them to the onion mixture and toss well. Chill for one hour before serving. This salad is a nice complement to Cheese Grits (see page 632).

> *Note: If Vidalia onions are not available, use any sweet red or white onion.*

# *Hoppin' John*

It is a Southern tradition that Hoppin' John, usually flavored with ham hocks, brings good luck when eaten on New Year's Day. In this meatless version, rice and beans provide complete protein.

### Serves 6 to 8

4 cups fresh black-eyed peas (or 2 10-ounce packages frozen)

3 cups water

¾ teaspoon salt

1 cup finely chopped onions

2 garlic cloves, minced

2 tablespoons butter or vegetable oil

pinch of ground allspice

pinch of cayenne

1½ tablespoons tamari soy sauce (optional)

plenty of freshly ground black pepper to taste

_____

3 cups cooked brown rice

_____

1 large ripe tomato, chopped (about 1 cup)

½ cup chopped scallions

chopped fresh parsley (optional)

sour cream or grated smoked cheddar cheese

Cook the black-eyed peas in the water and salt for about 20 minutes or until tender. Drain, reserving the liquid.

Sauté the onions and garlic in the butter or oil until golden, about 10 minutes. Add the allspice, cayenne, and soy sauce. Stir this mixture into the cooked peas with enough of the reserved liquid to make it juicy and simmer gently for about 20 minutes to allow the flavors to marry. Stir often.

To serve, top the warm rice with the black-eyed peas and then the chopped fresh tomato, scallions, and parsley. Add sour cream or grated smoked cheddar cheese as well, if you like.

# Vegetarian Brunswick Stew

Many families in Georgia have their own versions of Brunswick stew. My uncle Hoyt Adamson gave me his own special recipe, which was the inspiration for my meatless adaptation. Thick and spicy, sweet and sour, the whole garden appears in this one. Because it must be made in large batches, freeze some for later. Corn and beans provide complementary proteins.

### SERVES 6 TO 8

*2 cups chopped onions*

*2 garlic cloves, minced*

*3 tablespoons vegetable oil*

*1 cup chopped carrots*

*1 cup chopped zucchini or summer squash*

*1 cup chopped potatoes*

*2 cups chopped fresh tomatoes (or 16-ounce can whole tomatoes, with juice)*

*4 cups vegetable stock (see page 685) or water*

*1½ cups sliced fresh okra (or 10 ounces frozen)*

*1½ cups fresh cut corn (or 10 ounces frozen or 10-ounce can with liquid)*

*2 cups fresh lima beans or black-eyed peas (or 10 ounces frozen)*

*3 tablespoons Worcestershire Sauce (see page 686)*

*½ teaspoon Tabasco or other hot sauce*

*3 tablespoons molasses or brown sugar*

*1½ tablespoons vinegar*

*salt and freshly ground black pepper to taste*

*3 tablespoons catsup or barbecue sauce (optional)*

---

*1 tablespoon cornstarch dissolved in ¼ cup water (optional)*

---

*Tabasco to taste*

*grated smoked Swiss or cheddar cheese*

*chopped scallions*

In a large stewpot, sauté the onions and garlic in the oil, stirring often, until golden. Add the carrots and sauté for 3 more minutes, stirring to prevent sticking. Add the zucchini or summer squash, potatoes, tomatoes, and stock. When this begins to simmer, add the okra, corn, and limas or black-eyed peas. Season with Worcestershire Sauce,

Tabasco, molasses, vinegar, salt and black pepper, and catsup or barbecue sauce, if desired.

Simmer carefully, using a flame-tamer if needed, for at least 30 minutes or until all the vegetables are tender. You cannot overcook this stew, but you can burn it.

Thicken with the cornstarch mixture if you like. Add more Tabasco to taste and garnish with the cheese and scallions.

Serve with Sayra's Cornbread (see page 634), a mess of Sayra's Greens (see page 627), and Mocha Pecan Pie (see page 637). Y'all come!

# *Jambalaya*

This adaptation of the classic Creole dish contains no ham or shrimp, but it does capture the essential flavors of Creole cooking and is beautiful as well. The brown roux used here is a bit tricky but worth the trouble.

## SERVES 8

### STEW

3 tablespoons olive or vegetable oil

1 cup chopped onions

2 garlic cloves, minced

2 bay leaves

1 cup carrots, sliced diagonally, 1/8 inch thick

1 cup chopped celery

2 cups coarsely chopped red and green bell peppers (about 1 of each color)

2 teaspoon dried basil (2 tablespoons fresh)

1/4 teaspoon dried thyme

2 cups coarsely chopped tomatoes, fresh or canned

10 ounces frozen whole baby okra (or 2 cups fresh whole baby okra)

3 cups vegetable stock (see page 685) or water

*⅛ teaspoon ground allspice*
*⅛–½ teaspoon cayenne (or to taste)*
*salt and freshly ground black pepper to*
  *taste*

**ROUX**
*¼ cup vegetable oil*
*⅓ cup unbleached white flour*

**TOPPINGS**
*chopped fresh parsley*
*chopped scallions*
*grated smoked Swiss or cheddar cheese*

Jambalaya is more quickly prepared if you cook the stew and the roux at the same time. The roux does require about 30 minutes of close attention, but happily the stew cooks for about the same amount of time, with just occasional attention. So I suggest that you get all the ingredients chopped, measured, and ready, and start the stew. Then begin the roux while you finish the stew.

For the stew, in a large stew pot, heat the oil. Add the onions, garlic, and bay leaves and sauté, stirring occasionally, until the onions are translucent. (Start the roux now.) Stir in the carrots, celery, bell peppers, basil, and thyme. Sauté, stirring occasionally, for about 5 minutes. Add the tomatoes, okra, stock, and remaining spices. Cover and simmer gently for about 20 minutes, until the vegetables are tender.

For the roux, in a heavy skillet, preferably well-seasoned cast iron, heat the vegetable oil. The oil should be hot but not smoking. Test the temperature of the oil by carefully sprinkling a pinch of flour onto the hot oil. If it smokes, it's too hot, so lower the heat and wait a minute; if the flour floats away, not burning, it's a good temperature. Whisk in all the flour, to form a smooth paste. Lower the heat so that the roux gently simmers. Stir almost constantly, stopping only to attend to the stew. The roux will very slowly darken, so be patient and keep stirring. The flavor is wonderful; it's worth the effort. Cook the roux for 20 to 30 minutes, until it turns a nutty brown. Don't let it burn.

When the stew vegetables are tender, adjust the seasonings and stir in the roux. Simmer the stew on low heat for about 10 minutes more, taking care not to scorch. Remove the bay leaves before serving.

Serve on rice, topped with parsley, scallions, and grated smoked cheese.

*Variation* Don't abandon Jambalaya if you don't want to make the roux. It's still delicious. Just make the stew and when the vegetables are tender, if it hasn't thickened enough, stir in 2 tablespoons of cornstarch dissolved in ¼ cup of cold water. You won't get the same rich, dark flavor, but you will save time.

# "Not Fried" Catfish

Catfish has a distinctive taste and is very popular in the South. Old Bay Seasoning, regional to the Chesapeake Bay in Maryland, originated as a seasoning for steamed seafood. Here it flavors baked catfish, an alternative to the usual fried version.

## SERVES 4 TO 6

2 pounds fresh catfish fillets (or any
    firm, white, fish fillets, such as cod,
    perch, or monkfish)
2 tablespoons fresh lemon juice
salt and cayenne pepper to taste
½ teaspoon Old Bay Seasoning or
    Homemade Southern Seafood
    Seasoning (page 628)

2 garlic cloves, minced or pressed
4 tablespoons olive or vegetable oil
2 cups finely crumbled cornbread
    (⅓–½ recipe Sayra's Cornbread,
    page 634)
4 tablespoons finely chopped fresh
    parsley

Preheat the oven to 350°. Lightly oil a 9x13-inch baking pan.

Rinse the fish fillets and place them in the baking pan. Sprinkle the fish with lemon juice, salt, cayenne, and Old Bay Seasoning.

In a heavy skillet, sauté the garlic in the oil for a couple of minutes. Stir in the cornbread crumbs and continue to cook, stirring frequently until the crumbs are golden and crisp. Stir in the parsley. Spoon the seasoned crumbs evenly over the fish.

Cover and bake for 15 minutes. Uncover and continue to bake for 10 to 15 minutes more, until the fish is tender and the topping is crisp.

# Stuffed Vegetables with Spinach and Artichoke Hearts

This is a delicious, unusual entrée or side dish. Moosewood's customers simply love it when they see this on the menu.

SERVES 4

10 ounces fresh spinach, cleaned and
    stemmed
4 ounces cream cheese, at room
    temperature
14-ounce can artichoke hearts, drained
    and chopped (about 1½ cups)
½ cup minced scallions
½ cup grated sharp cheddar cheese

½ cup chopped toasted pecans
salt and freshly ground black pepper to
    taste

4 medium firm ripe tomatoes (or 2
    large zucchini or summer squash,
    about 7 inches in length)

Steam and drain the spinach. Chop it well and place it in a large bowl. Stir in the cream cheese and allow it to soften in the heat from the spinach. Stir in the artichoke hearts, scallions, cheddar cheese, pecans, salt, and black pepper.

Preheat the oven to 350°.

Prepare the vegetables. If you're going to stuff tomatoes, core them and scoop out the insides, leaving a shell. If you are using squash, scrub them and slice them lengthwise and scoop out the pulp, leaving a shell ¼ to ½ inch thick.

Stuff the vegetables with the filling and place them in a buttered baking dish. Pour ½ inch of water in the bottom of the pan to help steam the vegetables.

Bake, covered, for 20 minutes or until the vegetables are tender and the filling is firm on top. Uncover the dish and bake a few minutes more to lightly brown the filling.

Serve on a bed of rice with collard greens (see page 627) and Sayra's Cornbread (see page 634).

*Variation* You may also like to try this filling in bell peppers or prebaked eggplant halves (see page 551). See also Cornbread Stuffing (page 631).

# Fried Green Tomatoes

This unusual, tangy side dish was popular in my family. Try it while you're waiting for the tomatoes in your garden to ripen. Use only tomatoes that are entirely green and unripe.

## SERVES 6 TO 8

*3 large or 4 medium unripe tomatoes
  (very green—not red at all)*
*salt and freshly ground black pepper to
  taste*
*cayenne, Tabasco, or other hot sauce
  (optional)*

*⅓ cup unbleached white flour*
*2 tablespoons white or yellow cornmeal*
*¼ cup vegetable oil*

Slice the tomatoes into quarter-inch slices. Discard the ends. Spread the slices out on a platter or cutting board and sprinkle generously with salt, black pepper, and, if desired, cayenne or Tabasco. Turn the slices over and season the other sides.

In a shallow bowl, combine the flour and cornmeal. Dredge the tomato slices in the flour mixture, one at a time, covering each side thoroughly. I find using 2 forks to do this job keeps your hands neat. Shake any excess flour off the tomato slices.

Heat the oil in a heavy frying pan, preferably well-seasoned cast iron. When the oil is hot but not smoking, fry the slices in batches; don't overcrowd the pan. Fry for about 3 or 4 minutes on each side or until golden brown. Drain on paper towels. Serve immediately.

# *Sayra's Greens*

Greens are essential to Southern cooking. Although many Southerners overcook their greens and season them with pork fat, I like them best when cooked until "just tender" and seasoned with the bright flavor of Hot Pepper Vinegar.

SERVES 6 TO 8

*3 pounds fresh greens (collards, mustard, turnip, or kale) (see note)*

*salt and freshly ground black pepper to taste*

*Hot Pepper Vinegar (see page 629) to taste*

*butter (optional)*

Carefully clean the greens by soaking and rinsing well. Make sure that any sand or grit is removed. Remove any yellowed leaves or tough spines. Coarsely chop the greens. Place them in a large pot and cover them with cool water. Simmer for 10 to 30 minutes, until the greens are as tender as you like.

Drain the greens. Save the cooking liquid, or "pot liquor," if you wish; some people serve this as a broth. Place the greens in a bowl and season with salt, black pepper, and Hot Pepper Vinegar to taste. Top with a pat of butter, if desired.

Serve with Sayra's Cornbread (see page 634). Greens are a delicious, healthful side dish to complement any Southern meal.

---

*Note: If fresh greens are not available, frozen may substitute. Use two 10-ounce packages of frozen chopped greens for 6 to 8 servings.*

---

# Annie Wade's Sweet Potato Soufflé

This special holiday side dish, always present at Thanksgiving and Christmas dinners, was my mother's most frequently requested recipe.

SERVES 6

3 cups mashed cooked sweet potatoes
    (about 2 large sweet potatoes, peeled)
¼ cup brown sugar
3 tablespoons butter

4 eggs, beaten
¼ cup light rum
¼ teaspoon cinnamon

Preheat the oven to 350°.

Combine the mashed sweet potatoes with the rest of the ingredients. Beat well by hand or with an electric mixer. Fold into a buttered 2-quart baking dish.

Bake for 45 to 50 minutes or until a knife inserted into the center comes out clean and the top is firm and golden.

# Homemade Southern Seafood Seasoning

Old Bay Seasoning is manufactured by the Baltimore Spice Company, Baltimore, Maryland 21208. It contains celery salt, pepper, mustard, pimiento, cloves, laurel leaves, mace, cardamom, cassia, paprika. This is an essential ingredient in "Not Fried" Catfish (see page 624), and other Southern seafood dishes.

1 tablespoon celery seed

1 tablespoon whole black peppercorns

6 bay leaves

½ teaspoon whole cardamom

½ teaspoon mustard seed

4 whole cloves

1 teaspoon sweet Hungarian paprika

¼ teaspoon mace

In a spice grinder or small food processor, combine all of the ingredients. Grind the spices well and store the mixture in a small glass jar. Although this will keep indefinitely on your spice shelf, spices become less potent over time, so it's better to use this freshly ground. Use to season fish or vegetables.

# Hot Pepper Vinegar

Here's a quick and easy way to make this classic Southern table condiment, an essential topping for collard, mustard, or turnip greens. All of my aunts kept a cruet of Hot Pepper Vinegar in their cupboards.

YIELDS 1 CUP

1 cup apple cider vinegar

¼ teaspoon–1 tablespoon Tabasco or
    other hot sauce (or ⅛–1 teaspoon
    cayenne, or to taste)

In a cruet or glass jar, combine the vinegar and hot pepper sauce or cayenne to taste. Shake before using. Hot Pepper Vinegar keeps indefinitely, refrigerated or not.

# Creole Sauce

This sauce is easy, quick, and delicious, and you can use it as a topping for stuffed vegetables or rice or to make shrimp or fish creole.

### SERVES 4 TO 6

1½ cups chopped onions

3 tablespoons vegetable oil

½ teaspoon salt

1 cup chopped celery (about 3 stalks)

1½ cups chopped bell pepper (red or green or both)

2 tablespoons minced fresh garlic cloves

1 bay leaf

½ teaspoon freshly ground black pepper

½ teaspoon dried thyme

1 teaspoon dried basil

½ teaspoon Tabasco or other hot sauce

1 cup vegetable stock (see page 685) or water

1½ cups chopped, peeled tomatoes (fresh or canned)

¾ cup tomato sauce or purée

1 teaspoon sugar

¼ cup finely minced fresh parsley

In a nonreactive 2-quart saucepan, sauté the onions in the oil on high heat for one minute. Sprinkle in the salt and cook, stirring often, for several minutes, until the onions are translucent. Add the celery and bell peppers and lower the heat to medium. Continue to cook, stirring as needed to prevent sticking, for 5 minutes.

Stir in the garlic, bay leaf, black pepper, thyme, basil, Tabasco, and vegetable stock or water. Simmer for 5 minutes. Add the tomatoes, tomato sauce or purée, and the sugar. Simmer gently for 15 minutes. Taste the sauce and adjust the seasonings. Stir in the parsley. Remove the bay leaf before serving.

Serve on rice, with stuffed vegetables, or use to make one of the following:

Shrimp Creole: Stir 1¾ pounds peeled, cleaned, raw shrimp into the cooked Creole Sauce. Cover and simmer for about 5 minutes, until the shrimp are just cooked. Do not overcook the shrimp. Serve on rice.

Baked Fish Creole: Place 2 pounds of firm, white, fish fillets in a shallow, oiled baking dish. Top with enough Creole Sauce to cover. Save the rest to serve on the side. Cover the baking dish and bake at 350° for about 20 minutes, until the fish is tender. Serve on rice.

# Cornbread Stuffing

Although traditionally served with poultry, this stuffing stands alone beautifully. Or try stuffing an eggplant or winter or summer squash with this for a holiday meal. Delicious with Annie Wade's Sweet Potato Soufflé (see page 628).

**YIELDS 10 CUPS**
**SERVES 6 AS A SIDE DISH**

*1 pan Sayra's Cornbread (see page 634)*
*2–3 slices whole wheat bread, toasted*
*2 eggs, lightly beaten*
*2 cups vegetable stock (see page 685) or water*
*2 tablespoons tamari soy sauce*
*3 tablespoons poultry seasoning*

*salt and ground black pepper to taste*

*3 celery stalks, diced (about 1 cup)*
*2–2½ cups finely chopped onions*
*3 tablespoons butter or vegetable oil*
*pinch of salt*

Butter a 9x13-inch baking pan or a 2-quart casserole dish. Preheat the oven to 350°.

In a large bowl, crumble the cornbread and whole wheat toast. Stir in the eggs, stock, soy sauce, and seasonings. Mix well.

In a heavy skillet, sauté the celery and onions in the butter or oil on medium heat with a pinch of salt. Stir often and sauté until the vegetables are tender and juicy but not mushy, about 7 minutes. Add the celery and onions to the bread-crumb mixture and stir well. Add more salt if needed.

Spoon the stuffing into the baking pan or casserole dish and bake for 20 minutes or until somewhat firm and crisp on top. Don't overbake.

To stuff a squash: Cut 3 medium acorn or butternut squash in half and scoop out the seeds. Place the cut sides down in an oiled baking pan. Add ½ inch of water and bake, covered, at 350° for about 40 minutes. When tender, turn them over and mound with cornbread stuffing. Continue to bake, uncovered, for 15 to 20 minutes more.

To stuff an eggplant: Slice 3 medium eggplants in half lengthwise. Place the cut sides down on an oiled baking sheet and bake, covered, at 350° for 20 to 25 minutes, until the flesh is tender when pricked with a fork. Turn the eggplants over and mash the flesh to create a hollow in each eggplant. Stuff carefully with about 1½ cups of the cornbread mixture, mounding it as high as you can. Bake for 15 to 20 minutes uncovered.

# *Cheese Grits*

The smoked cheese lends an authentic Southern flavor to this hearty, rich casserole.

### SERVES 4 TO 6

3¾ cups water
1 cup hominy grits
1 teaspoon salt
¼ teaspoon freshly ground black pepper
1 large egg

½ cup milk
½–¾ cup shredded cheddar cheese
½ cup shredded smoked Swiss or
    cheddar cheese

Boil the water in a heavy saucepan. Slowly pour in the grits, stirring constantly to avoid lumps. Add the salt and black pepper. Cook, stirring often, on low heat until thick and smooth, about 7 minutes. Remove the pan from the heat.

In a bowl, beat the egg and milk together. Fold the egg mixture into the grits. Add half the cheese and mix well. Pour the grits mixture into an oiled 2-quart baking dish. Top the casserole with the remaining cheese.

Bake, uncovered, at 375° for 20 to 30 minutes or until the top is golden. Remove the dish from the oven and allow it to set for 5 minutes before serving.

Delicious topped with Creole Sauce (see page 630) or sprinkled with Tabasco.

## QUICK BREADS

# *Buttermilk Biscuits*

Savory, rich biscuits are a Southern tradition. Inspired by memories of my Southern aunts' buttermilk biscuits, I developed my own version, with variations that follow. Try them all! Your family and friends will love them. Serve them for breakfast, lunch, dinner, and even dessert!

### YIELDS 12 LARGE BISCUITS

*2 cups unbleached white flour*
*½ teaspoon salt*
*4 teaspoons baking powder*

*½ teaspoon baking soda*
*6 tablespoons butter (about ⅓ cup)*
*¾ cup buttermilk*

Preheat the oven to 450°.

Sift all of the dry ingredients into a large bowl. Cut in the butter using a knife, a pastry cutter, or your fingers, until the mixture resembles coarse cornmeal. Quickly, but gently, stir in the buttermilk, just until the dough holds together. Don't overstir or the biscuits will be tough.

Turn the dough onto a lightly floured board and knead gently with floured hands. Press the dough into a ball, cut it in half, place one half on top of the other and press down. Repeat three or four times. Then roll out the dough to about ½-inch thickness. Cut rounds with a biscuit cutter or glass, or cut rectangles with a knife. Place the biscuits on an ungreased baking sheet leaving a little space between them.

Bake for 15 to 18 minutes, until the biscuits are golden. Serve warm with butter, preserves, or plain.

## Variations

Wheat Germ Biscuits: Reduce the flour to 1¾ cups and add ¼ cup wheat germ. Proceed as directed.

Cornmeal Biscuits: Reduce the flour to 1¾ cups and add ¼ cup stone ground white or yellow cornmeal. Proceed as directed.

Pecan Biscuits: Stir ¼ cup ground toasted pecans into the sifted dry ingredients. Proceed as directed.

Red Pepper–Cheese Biscuits: After cutting the butter into the sifted dry ingredients, stir in ½ cup grated sharp cheddar cheese and a pinch or two of cayenne pepper. Mix well. Proceed as directed.

Shortcake Biscuits: Add 2 tablespoons of sugar to the dry ingredients and 2 teaspoons vanilla extract to the wet ingredients. For a shortcake biscuit deluxe, add ¼ cup of ground pecans as well. Proceed as directed.

# Sayra's Cornbread

Bread is an essential part of a Southern meal—perfect for sopping up the "pot liquor" from greens. My mother's cornbread was not sweet, but you can make it that way if you like.

Mom enjoyed leftover cornbread crumbled in her buttermilk. I freeze the leftovers to use in "Not Fried" Catfish (see page 624), Cornbread Stuffing (see page 631), and other recipes.

### YIELDS 1 9-INCH SQUARE OR 10-INCH ROUND PAN OF CORNBREAD

2 eggs
1 cup milk or buttermilk
¼ cup cooking oil
¾ teaspoon salt
¼ cup brown sugar (optional)
4 teaspoons baking powder

1 cup white or yellow cornmeal (preferably good quality stone ground)
1 cup unbleached white flour (or half whole wheat, half white)

Preheat the oven to 400°.

In a large bowl, beat together the eggs, milk, oil, salt, and brown sugar (if desired) until well blended. Sift in the baking powder and whisk until foamy. Quickly mix in the cornmeal and flour. Beat until the batter is smooth. Pour into an oiled 9-inch square or 10-inch round baking pan. Bake for 20 to 25 minutes, or until a knife inserted in the center comes out clean.

# *Huguenot Torte*

This is a South Carolina Low-Country recipe, a gift from the Huguenots who fled France in the late seventeenth century seeking religious freedom.

*2 eggs*
*¾ cup sugar*

_____

*¼ cup unbleached white flour*
*2 teaspoons baking powder*
*¼ teaspoon salt*
*2 teaspoons pure vanilla extract*

*1 cup coarsely chopped apples*
*1 cup chopped, toasted pecans*
*1 teaspoon fresh lemon juice*

_____

*½ pint heavy cream*
*2 tablespoons maple syrup or sugar*
*8 pecan halves, toasted*

Preheat the oven to 325°.

In a large bowl, beat the eggs by hand or with an electric mixer until fluffy. Slowly add the sugar, while beating, until the mixture is very thick.

In a separate bowl, sift the flour, baking powder, and salt. Gradually add the dry ingredients to the eggs and sugar, stirring just enough to combine them thoroughly. Gently fold in the vanilla, chopped apples, pecans, and the lemon juice. Pour the batter into a buttered 10-inch round or 9-inch square baking pan.

Bake for 35 to 40 minutes or until the top is brown and crusty. As the torte cools, the bottom layer will be soft and the top layer will become cookie-like and crunchy.

Just before serving, whip the heavy cream with the syrup or sugar. Cut the torte into wedges or squares and top each serving with a dollop of whipped cream and a pecan half.

# Mocha Pecan Pie

This is an adaptation of my mother's pecan pie recipe. The blender technique makes it very easy to prepare. Mocha Pecan Pie is extremely rich and decadent.

### YIELDS 1 9-INCH PIE

**CRUST**

⅓ cup butter

1 cup unbleached white flour

3 tablespoons ice water (approximately)

**FILLING**

¾ cup sugar

½ cup maple syrup or dark corn syrup

2 tablespoons coffee liqueur (or brewed
    strong black coffee)

2 tablespoons butter

2 tablespoons unbleached white flour

3 large eggs

½ cup semi-sweet chocolate chips

———————————

1 cup toasted pecans

Preheat the oven to 400°.

For the crust, cut the butter into the flour with a knife, a pastry cutter, or your fingers until the mixture resembles coarse cornmeal. Add about 3 tablespoons of ice water and combine until the dough clings together in a ball. Roll it out on a lightly floured board. Place the crust in a 9-inch pie plate and crimp the edges.

To make the filling, place all of the filling ingredients except the pecans in a blender or food processor and purée until the chocolate chips are completely ground up and everything is smooth. If you don't have a machine, melt the chocolate and butter on very low heat, cool it, and beat it with all of the other filling ingredients except the pecans. Pour the filling over the pecans in a bowl and stir just enough to coat the nuts.

Pour the filling into the unbaked 9-inch pie shell. Bake at 400° for 10 minutes, then reduce the heat to 350° and bake for another 30 minutes or until the filling is set but still moist. Cool completely before cutting.

Serve with whipped cream or vanilla ice cream.

# Best Peach Cobbler

There is a story my mother once told me about a favorite aunt of mine who is now deceased. Aunt Minnie had attended a funeral, and afterwards the family gathered to grieve and, of course, to eat. At that time in her life my aunt was no longer young and had grown quite hard of hearing. A neighbor stopped by with her condolences and a covered dish. When she left, someone remarked, "Last week that woman made the best peach cobbler I ever ate!" And others agreed, "Yes, she makes an excellent peach cobbler," "What a cook," "How nice of her to think of us," and so on.

All my aunt heard of this exchange was "best peach cobbler" and so she assumed that it was a cobbler sitting on the table. She asked one of the younger cousins to bring her a plate of the neighbor's dish, and she sat back in anticipation.

The cousin brought a plate over and my aunt took a bite. She almost choked. She swallowed and blinked. She took a breath and tried again. Once again she almost gagged on the food and, thoroughly confused, yelled out to the group, "Best peach cobbler? Best peach cobbler? Why, y'all don't know what the hell you're talking about! That's the worst peach cobbler I ever ate!"

No one understood why Minnie was so upset until they uncovered the questionable peach cobbler and found baked beans there instead. Everyone laughed long and hard at this, except poor Aunt Minnie, who immediately went home, embarrassed and disappointed.

It was in memory of her that I developed my own "Best Peach Cobbler," which I hope will not disappoint.

*1 recipe Buttermilk Biscuits, shortcake variation (see page 633)*

---

*6 cups peeled, sliced, fresh ripe peaches*
*¾–1 cup sugar (or ½–¾ cup honey or maple syrup)*

*1 tablespoon unbleached white flour*
*¼ teaspoon cinnamon*
*1 tablespoon fresh lemon juice*
*sugar for sprinkling*

Preheat the oven to 375°.

Prepare the dough for the shortcake variation of Buttermilk Biscuits. Set the dough aside.

In a large bowl, mix the peaches with the sugar, flour, cinnamon, and lemon juice until well combined. Generously butter a glass or ceramic 10-inch round deep baking dish or a 9x12-inch baking dish. Pour the fruit into the buttered baking dish. On a lightly floured board, roll out the dough. Lay the dough on top of the peaches, taking care to cover them completely. Sprinkle the top with sugar.

Bake for 30 to 40 minutes or until the top is golden and the shortcake dough is baked through. The dough is ready when a knife inserted in the center comes out clean. If the biscuits begin to brown too quickly, cover them loosely with aluminum foil until the last 5 minutes of baking time.

Serve warm or at room temperature with sweetened whipped cream or vanilla ice cream.

*Variation* Peach Melba Cobbler: Use 4 cups of peaches and 2 cups of fresh raspberries. Actually any combination of fruit and berries will do—plums, blueberries, blackberries, strawberries, etc.

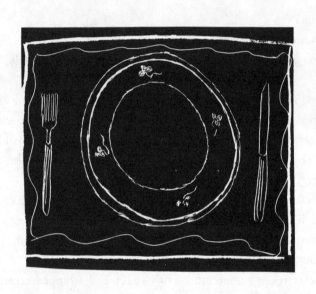

# *Menu Planning*

We encourage you to mix and match recipes from the different cuisines presented in this book. Following are a few guidelines for planning harmonious yet varied menus.

You might begin by combining dishes from cuisines that use similar seasonings and ingredients. While the historical influences on any one cuisine may be far-reaching and complex, we see certain groups of cuisines as related, and we have grouped them together because their foods are compatible. You will notice that several cuisines fit into more than one group.

Menus that combine dishes from related cuisines afford the cook a wide variety of choices but minimize the risk of unappetizing clashes.

# Related Cuisines

### MEDITERRANEAN/MIDDLE EASTERN INFLUENCE

*Provence*
*Italy*
*North Africa and the North African Highlands*
*Armenia and the Middle East*
*Jewish (Sephardic dishes in particular)*
*Eastern Europe (Balkan dishes in particular)*

### NORTHERN AND EASTERN EUROPEAN INFLUENCE

*Jewish (Ashkenazic dishes in particular)*
*Eastern Europe*
*Finland*
*British Isles*
*New England* } *(dishes from European*
*Chile*        *immigrants)*

### THE AMERICAS—NATIVE AMERICAN, LATIN, AND AFRICAN INFLUENCES

*New England (Portuguese and Native American)*
*Southern United States (Native American and Creole)*
*Caribbean (African, Latin, and Native American)*
*Mexico (Native and Latin)*
*Chile (Native and Latin)*

### TROPICAL—AFRICAN AND INDIAN INFLUENCES

*Africa South of the Sahara (with Indian influences)*
*Southern United States (African influence)*
*Caribbean (African and Indian)*
*India*
*Southeast Asia (with Indian influence)*
*Mexico*

## ASIA

*India*
*Southeast Asia*
*China*
*Japan*

Menus should offer contrasting yet complementary foods: rich with light, spicy with mild, chilled with hot. The menu should provide a variety of colors, textures, and flavors.

The menu should be suited to the season and the setting. Take advantage of the freshest foods in season and plan menus that feature them. Consider whether the meal will be served formally or informally, indoors or out; avoid serving juicy, potentially messy dishes at buffets or parties where guests must stand.

Limit the number of assertive, highly flavored dishes to produce a pleasing balance. As you become familiar with our recipes you will be able to draw on your own experience and good judgment. Check the ingredient lists to avoid the excessive use of items such as cayenne, extra-virgin olive oil, cilantro, rosemary, oregano, cumin, sweetenings, etc. Seasonings like these can dominate the palate, and while they are wonderful flavors, a concentration of too many of them can be distracting or upsetting.

Be aware of your time constraints and if possible select some dishes that can be prepared in advance, freeing you to concentrate on others that require last-minute attention.

## Sample Menus from Related Cuisines

\* Contain fish or seafood and can be optional or replaced on these menus.

| MEDITERRANEAN | CHAPTER |
|---|---|
| Crisp Cooked Vegetable Appetizer | North Africa |
| Serbian Cucumber-Pepper Salad | Eastern Europe |
| Risotto with Dried Porcini | Italy |
| Bouillabaisse with Rouille* | Provence |
| Fritada de Espinaca | Jewish |
| Paklava | Armenia and the Middle East |
| Turkish Coffee | Jewish |

## NORTHERN EUROPEAN

| | |
|---|---|
| Cheddar and Parsnip Soup | British Isles |
| Stein Sisters' Sunday Salmon* | Jewish |
| Potato-Leek Vinaigrette | New England |
| Croatian Mushroom-Stuffed Tomatoes | Eastern Europe |
| Finnish Rye Bread | Finland |
| Kuchen de Manzanas | Chile |

## THE AMERICAS

| | |
|---|---|
| Autumn Gold Squash Soup | New England |
| Tomates Claudia | Chile |
| Bay State Wiggle* | New England |
| Empanadas de Papas | Chile |
| Sayra's Greens | Southern United States |
| Mocha Pecan Pie | Southern United States |

## TROPICAL—AFRICAN INFLUENCED

| | |
|---|---|
| Okra Gumbo Soup | Southern United States |
| Fried Green Tomatoes | Southern United States |
| Senegalese Seafood Stew* | Africa South of the Sahara |
| Arroz a la Mexicana | Mexico |
| Sweet Potato Balls | Caribbean |
| Classic Rum Punch | Caribbean |

## ASIA

| | |
|---|---|
| Thai Hot-and-Sour Shrimp Soup* | Southeast Asia |
| Cauliflower Pakoras with Sweet-and-Sour Tamarind Sauce | India |
| Fresh Spring Rolls | Southeast Asia |
| Batter-Fried Fish with Garlic Sauce* | China |
| Junco's Delicious Potatoes Braised in Butter and Sake | Japan |
| Chawan Mushi* | Japan |
| Tamari Roasted Nuts | China |
| Bancha or Spiced Tea | India |

## ASIA

| | |
|---|---|
| Indonesian Squash and Spinach Soup | Southeast Asia |
| Patrani Machi* | India |
| Su-no-Mono | Japan |
| Zucchini with Walnut Sauce | Japan |
| Almond Cookies | China |

(The cuisines of Asia have all influenced each other, yet each is curiously self-contained. These menus alter those boundaries.)

## THE AMERICAS

| | |
|---|---|
| Sorrel Soup | New England |
| Escoveitche de Pescado* | Caribbean |
| Torta de Papas | Chile |
| Pebre | Chile |
| Avocado Ahdi | Caribbean |
| Best Peach Cobbler | Southern United States |
| Coffee with Rum | |

## TROPICAL—INDIAN INFLUENCED

| | |
|---|---|
| Curried Avocado Soup | Caribbean |
| Baked Paneer | India |
| Colombo de Giromon | Caribbean |
| Banana Chutney | Africa South of the Sahara |
| Thai-Style Fried Rice* | Southeast Asia |
| Shallot Chutney | Southeast Asia |
| Cheese and Nut Dessert Balls | India |
| Ginger Soft Drink | Africa South of the Sahara |

## A MEDITERRANEAN/MIDDLE EASTERN BUFFET

| | |
|---|---|
| Puréed White Bean Dip | Armenia and the Middle East |
| Topig with Tahini Dressing | Armenia and the Middle East |
| Rosemary Focaccia | Italy |
| Mushrooms Roasted with Pine Nuts | Italy |
| Chick Pea Crêpe | Provence |

| | |
|---|---|
| Garlic-Olive-Caper Spread | Provence |
| Herbed Chèvre Spread | Provence |
| Rounds of French Bread | |
| Pita Bread | |
| Sambussa | North Africa |
| Fresh Fruit | |

## A TROPICAL BUFFET

| | |
|---|---|
| Fried Sweet Potatoes or Plantains | Africa South of the Sahara |
| Tomato-Apricot Chutney | India |
| Zucchini-Tofu Koftas | India |
| Minted Cucumber-Yogurt Refresher | Africa South of the Sahara |
| Ensalada Mixta | Mexico |
| Philippine Mung Beans in Coconut Milk | Southeast Asia |
| Indonesian Egg or Tofu Curry with Rice | Southeast Asia |
| Savory Stuffed Bread | India |
| Fresh Fruit Salad with a Difference* | Southeast Asia |
| Yellowman's Banana Lime Bread | Caribbean |

# *Sample International Menus from Divergent Cuisines*

* Contain fish or seafood and can be optional or replaced on these menus.

Once you have prepared dishes from several divergent chapters, you will probably find that rather unorthodox combinations begin to occur to you. Follow the guidelines above and your own experience and good taste will give you all the confidence you need to make some daring, cross-cultural meals. Here are some menus from divergent cuisines to get you started.

| | |
|---|---|
| Salade Verte | Provence |
| Haddock with Sorrel and Onions* | British Isles |
| Oven-Roasted Vegetables | Armenia and the Middle East |
| Torta del Cielo | Mexico |
| | |
| Sopa de Camarones | Chile |
| Marinated Tomato Salad | Italy |
| Potato Cake | Provence |
| Spinach with Pine Nuts and Raisins | Italy |
| Polvorones de Canela | Mexico |
| | |
| Split Pea and Rice Soup | North Africa |
| Romanian Marinated Mushrooms | Eastern Europe |
| Fettuccini with Creamy Gorgonzola | |
|    Sauce | Italy |
| Fassoulia | Jewish |
| A Proper Trifle | British Isles |
| | |
| Sopa de Ajo | Chile |
| Thai Noodle Salad | Southeast Asia |
| Spinach Nori Rolls | Japan |
| Mango with Yogurt | India |

| | |
|---|---|
| Sopa de Lima | Mexico |
| Fish Kebabs* | North Africa |
| Rice Pilav with Orzo | Armenia and the Middle East |
| Hot Pepper Green Beans | China |
| Ukrainian Almond Crescents | Eastern Europe |
| Spearmint Tea | |
| | |
| Lebanese Vegetable Soup | Armenia and the Middle East |
| Vidalia Onion and Bell Pepper Salad | Southern United States |
| Macedonian Sweet-and-Savory Strudel | Eastern Europe |
| Thai Fresh Cucumber Salad | Southeast Asia |
| Winter Pear Tart Frangipane | Provence |
| | |
| Pimiento Cheese Bisque | Southern United States |
| Hungarian Pumpernickel Bread | Eastern Europe |
| Gingered Beets | Jewish |
| Shepherd's Pie | British Isles |
| Saucy Green Beans | New England |
| Marzipan Cake | Provence |
| | |
| White Bean and Garlic Soup | Provence |
| Mushroom Piroshke | Jewish |
| Grated Turnip and Apple Salad | Finland |
| Dried Fruit Pudding | Finland |
| | |
| Root Vegetable Purées | Finland |
| Casamance Stew* | Africa South of the Sahara |
| Ensalada de Porotos Verdes | Chile |
| Cranberry Tea Cake | New England |

WRITTEN AND
COMPILED BY
JOAN ADLER

# Guide to

# Ingredients,

# Techniques,

# and

# Equipment

**Allspice** Our childhood memory of allspice was the tin of brown powder in the cupboard that we assumed was a blend of "all the spices" in gingerbread and pumpkin pie. It came as a minor revelation to learn that this pungent seasoning, redolent of cloves, nutmeg, and ginger, is in fact a berry that grows on the West Indian allspice tree. Allspice also holds the distinction of being the only spice commonly used, indigenous to, and exclusively grown in the Western Hemisphere. At Moosewood, we use it whole in vegetable stock and mulled cider, and powdered in savory dishes and desserts that call for something spicy and exotic yet not as acrid as its sister spice, cloves.

**Almond Paste** Almond paste is a mash of ground, blanched almonds, sugar, and liquid glucose. It is sold, ready made, in 3½- and 7-ounce plastic packages and in small cans at European groceries and gourmet food shops. Almond paste is used in Byzantine and Central and Eastern European cakes and confections.

**Annatto (Achiote Seed)** A hard red seed used in Latin American cooking that imparts a subtle flavor and a beautiful yellow-orange coloring to dishes. Best results are obtained by sautéing the seeds in oil, discarding the seeds, and using the oil in which the seeds have been heated. Place 1 tablespoon whole achiote seeds and 3 to 4 tablespoons of vegetable oil in a very small pot or skillet. Maintain a medium heat until the oil turns a bright reddish-orange, approximately 3 to 4 minutes. Strain and discard the seeds. Annatto is available in stores specializing in Latin American foods.

**Artichoke** Look for artichokes that are bright green with firm, tightly packed leaves. Artichokes with brown streaks or spots are either old or frost-bitten, but still may be good to eat if the inner parts of the leaves are green and tender.

*TO PREPARE* Place the artichoke on its side and cut the stem off evenly so that the artichoke will stand on its base. Cut off ½ to ¾ inch from the top of the cone. Peel away any small leaves at the bottom, and with kitchen scissors trim away the barbed tops on the rest of the leaves. This trimming isn't absolutely necessary because the prickles soften when cooked. Artichokes should be thoroughly washed in running water or soaked in salt water before cooking to draw out any bugs lurking inside.

*TO COOK* Place the artichokes in a deep pot large enough to hold them all standing upright. Add water to a little more than half the height of the artichokes. Salt, a splash of vinegar, whole cloves of garlic, whole fennel seeds, and/or a tablespoon of oil may be added to the pot. Cover, bring to a rapid boil, reduce to a simmer. Cooking takes from 30 to 45 minutes. Check the water level every 10 minutes, adding boiling water when needed. The artichokes are done when their bases are tender when tested with a fork. The leaves should pull off easily, but if they fall off, the artichokes are overdone.

Drain the artichokes upside down. Serve upright on individual plates with a bowl of lemon-butter or other sauce for each person. Remember to provide an empty bowl for the discarded outer leaves and the chokes.

*TO EAT A WHOLE ARTICHOKE* Pull off the leaves one at a time, dip the bottom edge of each leaf into the sauce, and then scrape off the fleshy part with your teeth. Discard the rest of the leaf. After you've eaten the outer leaves, you'll come to smaller inner leaves which are very tender. Under the very small leaves is the feathery, inedible choke. With a spoon, gently scrape off the choke, down to the hollowed, firm surface of the most delicious part of the artichoke, the heart. Cut the heart into bite-sized pieces, dip into the sauce, and eat.

*Artichoke Heart* The rich, succulent center of the artichoke. Canned or jarred artichoke hearts are available in most supermarkets. They are packed in brine or a marinade. When our recipes call for artichoke hearts, use those packed in brine. Canned, brined artichoke hearts are what we regularly use for flavor and convenience. We make the most of their tang and texture in a variety of dishes including soups, stews, and savory strudels.

*Asian Hot Sauce* Any sauce that will add fire to your fare. Options include Chinese Chili Paste with Garlic (see page 657), Sriraja Chili Sauce (see page 681) for a sweet and hot taste, and Chili Oil (see page 657), used by Chinese and Southeast Asian cooks. When using chili oil add extra cayenne or chopped chiles so your dish will be hot enough but not too oily.

*Asparagus* Fresh asparagus is available from February until early summer. Look for young green spears that are uniform in size. They should be firm, and the tips should have tight buds. Avoid asparagus that appears dried or shriveled. Short, thick stalks and long, thin ones may be equally tender. Remove any sand that clings to the stalks by rubbing them gently under cool, running water. Snap off the tough, white base of each stalk before cooking.

*Avocado* A creamy, rich tropical fruit that transcends its food group because of its high fat, high protein content. About 500 varieties of the fruit are grown in tropical climates from South America to Australia. The most widely available avocados are from Florida and California: our favorite avocado is the California Haas. It is about the size and shape of a pear, has a green-black lizardy skin and, when ripe, is light green and yellow inside, with a custard-smooth texture and buttery taste. Florida avocados are larger and rounder and can often be identified by their bright green, smooth-skinned peels; the flesh is more watery, less creamy.

Most avocados are picked unripened, not, as might be assumed, so they can ripen during shipping, but to prevent bruising when they fall prematurely from the tree. Avocados ripen at room temperature, or more speedily in a closed paper bag with a banana or banana peel. The paper bag traps a gas released by the banana that accelerates ripening. An avocado is ripe when it yields slightly to pressure but is overripe if it collapses under the weight of a thumb.

*Barley* Barley is a sweet, low-starch grain. The barley seed itself is quite dense, requiring more water and greater cooking time than most grains.
TO COOK  Bring 1 cup barley and 5 to 6 cups water to a boil. Reduce to a simmer and cook about 1¼ hours. Drain any excess water. One cup of raw barley yields 3¾ cups of cooked barley.

*Basil* Basil, either the familiar green or

dark purple, is easy to grow and increasingly available in markets. Freshly cut basil keeps in the refrigerator for several days. The whole leaves can be wrapped in plastic and frozen for up to 6 months. Alternatively, it can be dried but its aroma and flavor are diminished and altered. Even so, we use dried basil frequently in winter.

***Bay Leaf*** Soups, stews, and sauces are the mainstays of vegetarian cuisine, and whole bay leaves find their way into most of our pots, adding warmth, depth, and a sweet, peppery scent. Long considered to possess the power to render witches and devils helpless, this strongly scented herb is still used, in a way, as a hex. Importers of figs and confections ward off weevils by packing their crates with bay leaves, which act as a fumigant. In the household, crushed bay leaves, tied in cheesecloth, may be stored with grains to help repel insects; the phenol in bay oil is released when the leaves are crushed. If you can pluck your bay fresh from a laurel tree, it is said that a week of drying time allows the herb's full flavor and fragrance to develop. When purchasing dried bay leaves, buy from a reliable merchant or company in bulk or in clear bottles so that you can examine what you are buying. Bypass leaves that are brown, brittle, and chipped. A good leaf is green or gray-green and smells clean and sweet.

***Beans (Canned)*** We recommend cooking dried beans to avoid the chemicals added to most canned beans. Disodium EDTA and calcium chloride are commonly added to beans to retain their shape and color. Also, the "hidden" salt in the disodium EDTA, together with the table salt added to all canned beans, make for a very salty product. The convenience of precooked beans is indisputable, however, so we list below some rare brands of beans free of additives and preservatives:

| | |
|---|---|
| Chick peas (garbanzo beans) | Sahadi |
| Canellini (white kidney beans) | Goya |
| Black turtle beans | Goya |
| Pinto beans | Eden Foods |
| Great northern beans | Eden Foods and Randall |

***Beans (Dried)*** Most dried beans and peas must be softened by soaking in water before they are cooked. No soaking is necessary, however, for small beans like lentils, split peas, and mung beans, or for beans cooked in a pressure cooker. Before soaking or cooking unsoaked beans, sort through the beans. Check for pebbles and remove any beans that are shriveled or discolored. Next, immerse the beans in cool water to rinse them of dust and to allow any debris left from shelling and harvesting to rise to the top. Pour off this water. You may have to repeat this step depending on how dirty the beans are.

***To soak beans***
METHOD 1 Cover beans with 2 to 3 times their volume in water and soak them overnight or for at least 12 hours. Because beans ferment easily, avoid soaking them on a burner or near the burner's pilot light. In the summertime, in an unair-conditioned home, the only safe place is the refrigerator.
METHOD 2 Cover the beans with 2 to 3 times their volume in water and bring the water to a vigorous boil in a covered pot; boil for two minutes. Remove from the heat and let the beans soak for one or two hours.

| Variety | Water-Bean Ratio | Cooking Time | Cooked Equivalent of 1 cup dried |
|---|---|---|---|
| Black turtle beans | 5:1 | 2½ to 3 hours | 3 cups |
| Red kidney beans | 3:1 | 1 to 1½ hours | 2¾ cups |
| Navy pea beans | 3:1 | 1 hour | 2¾ cups |
| Pinto beans | 3:1 | 45 minutes | 3¼ cups |
| Lentils | 3:1 | 30 minutes | 3 cups |
| Red lentils | 2:1 | 15 to 20 minutes | 2⅔ cups |
| Chick peas (garbanzo beans) | 6:1 | 2⅓ to 3 hours | 3 cups |
| Split peas (green) | 3:1 | 45 minutes to 1 hour | 1¾ cups |
| Split peas (yellow) | 3:1 | 30 minutes | 2¼ cups |
| Soy beans | 5:1 | 3 hours | 2¾ cups |
| Mung beans | 4:1 | 45 minutes | 3 cups |
| Fava beans (see page 663) | | | |
| Canellini (white kidney beans) (see page 656) | | | |

After either method, pour off the remaining soaking liquid and rinse the beans before cooking. This reportedly removes some of the raffinose, the offending carbohydrate responsible for the flatulence associated with beans. Method 2 may also lessen this problem.

TO COOK BEANS Use the chart above for the correct amount of water and cooking time for specific beans. Bring the beans to a boil and then reduce the heat to a simmer. Begin timing once the heat has been lowered. Periodically check the water level. Replenish with water to cover until the beans are thoroughly cooked.

**Bell or Sweet Pepper** Bell peppers are the mild salad peppers familiar to most of us as "green peppers." In Mexico, Spain, and Hungary sweet peppers are essential to the flavoring of the cuisines. We encourage you to sample the increasingly popular and available red, yellow, and purple varieties. They are superb roasted, braised, and broiled and are beautiful to work with. Instructions for roasting peppers can be found on page 349.

**Berbere** An Ethiopian hot spice mixture. See page 509 for our recipe.

**Blanching** At Moosewood we blanch vegetables and sometimes nuts. The purpose is twofold. First, a quick immersion in boiling water takes the edge off raw vegetables and intensifies their colors. Blanching also removes the peels of thin-skinned vegetables and nuts such as tomatoes and almonds. To blanch, submerge food in rapidly boiling water for a short time. Then transfer immediately to cold water to halt the cooking process. Drain. Blanching time depends on the hardness of the vegetable. It can range from a quick hot water dip for sprouts, snow peas, and mushrooms, to 2 to 3 minutes for carrots, broccoli, or string beans. Blanching time also depends on how thickly or thinly the vegetable is cut. This is a good technique for pickles and crudités.

**Bok Choy**  See Chinese Cabbage.

**Bouquet Garni**  A bouquet garni is an array of dried or fresh herb sprigs tied together and added to the simmering broth of a soup, stew, or sauce and retrieved before the dish is served. A bouquet is used when subtlety is sought; it perfumes and flavors without altering texture or appearance. While classic bouquet garni is composed of thyme, parsley, and bay leaves, we consider that just one bouquet among many. If fresh or dried herb sprigs are unavailable, ground or flaked dried herbs can be tied in a cheesecloth sachet or enclosed in a teaball.

**Bread Crumbs**  The bread crumbs we use in our recipes are simply stale or toasted whole wheat bread pulverized in a food processor or blender. Large chunks of bread can also be hand grated. It is not necessary to remove crusts from the bread. We never do.

### Bread-Making (Basic)

*YEAST*  One tablespoon of dry yeast equals one cake of compressed yeast or one package of dry yeast. One package of dry yeast will raise as much as 8 cups of flour. For faster rising, as much as one package of dry yeast

to each 3 cups of flour may be used. This bread will taste "yeastier."

It is important that yeast be fresh. If it isn't fresh and alive, the bread won't rise. Keep yeast refrigerated or frozen.

*ACTIVATING THE YEAST*  To activate dry yeast in preparation for bread-making, dissolve the yeast in warm water. The temperature of the water should be between 100° and 115°, a temperature that feels comfortably warm on the inside of your wrist. A little honey or sugar (½ teaspoon) will nourish the yeast cells as they divide and grow, but you will not want to add a sweetener to all breads. After about 5 minutes, the yeast should begin to foam or bubble. Compressed yeast takes a little longer. If the yeast doesn't foam, it won't raise bread, so start again with new yeast.

*PREPARING THE DOUGH*  Add the other liquid ingredients to the activated yeast and then gradually stir in the flour until the dough has a consistency that can be kneaded, dry enough that it doesn't stick to your floured fingers or the bowl.

*GLUTEN*  Essential to all yeast breads is the gluten found in wheat flours. Gluten is a protein that makes bread dough strong and elastic. As the yeast releases its gases, the gluten allows the dough to stretch and form thousands of air pockets.

*KNEADING*  Kneading the dough distributes the yeast evenly and gives it a smooth texture. To knead the dough, push the heels of your hands into the dough and then fold it over, occasionally sprinkling more flour on the surface of the dough and the board to prevent sticking. Give the dough a quarter turn and repeat. Continue this procedure for about 10 minutes or until the dough is satiny and springs back when pressed with a finger.

*RISING* Place the dough in a large, buttered bowl and brush the top lightly with oil or melted butter, or simply flip it over so all sides get coated, to keep a crust from forming. Cover it with a damp cloth and place it to rise in a warm, draft-free spot such as: in an oven with a pilot light; with pots of steaming water in an electric oven; on top of a warm refrigerator, or on a chair over a warm furnace grate.

Rising times will vary from recipe to recipe, but a general rule is that the dough should be allowed to rise until it is doubled in volume, an hour or two. To test, make a small indentation in the dough; if it fills back in within a few minutes, allow the dough to continue rising. If the indentation does not disappear, the dough has finished rising.

Now comes one of the most satisfying moments in bread-making—punching down the dough. After punching it down, knead the dough until it is smooth. Form the deflated dough into loaves or rolls and allow them to rise until almost full size. The second rising will take less time than the first. The final fullness will be achieved during baking. This part of the process can vary depending on specific recipes.

*BAKING* Bake the loaves for the full time recommended. To test for doneness, tip a loaf out of its baking pan and lightly tap the bottom of the loaf. If the bread is done, there will be a distinctly hollow sound. If it doesn't sound hollow, turn the bread back into the pan and bake it a short time longer.

**Buckwheat** Also called kasha, buckwheat is a noncereal cereal. Although it is treated as a grain, it is botanically a fruit in the rhubarb family and for centuries has served as a

hearty, high-protein, vitamin-rich source. Buckwheat today has a small but loyal following, which may stem from its social history. It is a hardy plant that grows quickly, even in poor soils, and cooks quickly, saving fuel. Until the turn of the century, impoverished cultures from Eastern Europe to the Deep South depended on buckwheat for porridge and as an extender for costly wheat flour. Today, its appeal is more discretionary than necessary, and as with other specialty items, it is now more expensive than other grains. Buckwheat can be eaten as a cereal, a side dish, or incorporated into a main dish. Unless cooking it for cereal, always use roasted buckwheat. Unroasted buckwheat for cereal is most often sold in bulk in natural food stores. It can however be dry-roasted in a skillet. Already roasted buckwheat is also available in natural food stores and in the Jewish food section of supermarkets. Cream of buckwheat cannot be substituted. Buckwheat offers an alternative to those who are wheat sensitive or allergic. For our recipe, see page 431.

**Bulghur** A quick-cooking form of wheat widely used in Balkan and Middle Eastern countries. Bulghur is the end result of wheat berries that have been precooked, dried, and cracked. Available at natural food stores, Middle Eastern groceries, and often in the international or gourmet food sections of supermarkets, it comes in two textures, fine and coarse.

*TO COOK* Place the bulghur in a bowl with an equal amount of boiling water and a dash of salt. Cover and let sit for 20 to 30 minutes. Stir to fluff. If the bulghur is still too firm or chewy, add another ¼ cup of boiling water, cover, and let sit for 10 minutes more. One cup of dry bulghur yields 2½ cups of cooked bulghur.

**Buttermilk**   This modern misnomer derives from a buttermilk of the past—the liquid runoff remaining after cream has been soured and churned to butter. Today's version, lowfat milk, thickened and soured by the addition of a special culture similar to yogurt, is still creamy, tart, and low in fat. Sweeter and lighter than yogurt, buttermilk is an excellent substitute for cream and sour cream in soups and salad dressings. On its own, buttermilk is often a principal ingredient in many baked goods and is enjoyed by many as a creamy and refreshing beverage.

**Cannellini**   A white variety of kidney beans used in Italian cooking. Cannellini are reportedly imported from Italy in canned and dried form. However, we have only found canned cannellini, available in the Italian section of the supermarket. If you wish to use dried beans and cannot find cannellini, great northern or navy beans may be substituted.

**Capers**   The small, green, pickled buds of a flowering Mediterranean plant. They come packed in brine and have a distinctive flavor. Capers are used mainly as a piquant condiment or garnish for soups, stews, sauces, and vegetable and fish dishes. Capers are usually available in the gourmet food sections of supermarkets.

**Cardamom (Cardamon)**   Cardamom is a sweetly pungent, aromatic spice native to India. Its popularity is also well established in Indonesian, Scandinavian, German, and Middle Eastern cuisine. In some countries it is used commonly as a breath sweetener. Next to saffron, cardamom is the most expensive spice, as each pod must be hand picked. Fortunately, the seeds are highly aromatic and only a small amount is required to add flavor and fragrance to a dish. Ground seeds give a stronger flavor to a dish; it is preferable to grind your own just before using, as the ground spice quickly loses its essential oils. Cardamom is available in pods or as seeds, whole and ground in the spice sections of most supermarkets.

**Cayenne**   Ground dried chiles named for a pepper native to the Cayenne Island, capital of French Guiana. Today, cayenne also has become the generic name for finely ground dried red pepper made from chiles from many localities. Cayenne is best known for heating up savory foods, but we've found that a pinch will also wake up the other flavors in a dish. Cayenne varies greatly in hotness, so as a general rule of thumb, start by using ⅛ teaspoon for four servings of food. When you want to add cayenne at the end of cooking, harshness can be avoided by sautéing it briefly in a little oil before adding it to the pot. Cayenne can be found in the spice section of the supermarket.

**Celery Cabbage**   See Chinese Cabbage.

**Cellophane Noodles**   The name of these noodles derives from their transparency. Made of mung bean flour, cellophane noodles are used in Asian cookery in soups, stir-fries, and hot pots. When deep-fried, they become a nest for fragile toppings. Cellophane noodles can be found in Asian food stores and in the Asian section of supermarkets.

**Cheesecloth**   Used to finely strain liquids from solids, and vice versa—for example, when a smooth soup or clear broth is sought, or in cheese-making to separate the curds from the whey. To use, place a sieve or strainer over a bowl or pot and line it with two to three layers of cheesecloth. Strain your preparation through the cloth. Cheesecloth can be found alongside other kitchen supplies or where automotive supplies are sold.

**Chick Pea Flour (Besan Flour)** The meal of ground raw dried chick peas (also known as garbanzo beans). This sweet flour is predominantly used in Indian and North African cooking but has surfaced in European cuisines long influenced by those cultures. See Chick Pea Crêpe (page 537), à la Provence. Chick pea flour is available at Indian food stores. Or it can be ground at home in a bread mill. Avoid lightweight grinding gadgets; we've found the blades of coffee mills and blenders too weak to do the job.

**Chiles (Hot Peppers)** To choose and use chiles, fresh and dried, see page 452.

**Chili Oil** A red oil colored and flavored by hot, red peppers. Use chili oil (sparingly!) as a hot spice in Chinese and Southeast Asian cooking. Available at Asian food stores, chili oil is also easily made at home: heat 1 cup of peanut or vegetable oil until hot but not smoking. Stir in about 2 dozen small dried red hot peppers or 3 tablespoons red pepper flakes, or 1 tablespoon cayenne. Cover, cool completely, and strain.

**Chili Paste with Garlic (Szechuan Chili Paste)** A spicy condiment made with chiles, salt, and garlic. Chili paste is available in Asian food stores. It will keep almost indefinitely when refrigerated.

**Chinese Cabbage** No one has to tell Chinese people to eat their vegetables; in China, reportedly, a pound is consumed per person per day. And, of that pound, half is from the cabbage family. In this country, the numerous varieties of Chinese greens are not specifically translated into English and many simple bear the name Chinese cabbage. Two types of Chinese cabbage are used in this book, bok choy and celery cabbage. We encourage you to become familiar with these two varieties and not be misled by the generic "Chinese cabbage" label.

BOK CHOY (PAK CHOI, BOAK CHOI, CHARD CABBAGE, CHINESE WHITE CABBAGE, SHIRONA) One of the most popular of the Chinese cabbages, bok choy looks like a cross between celery and Swiss chard. Like celery, its stalks rise from a single base, but they branch out to become wide, smooth, and lustrous white, ending in broad, dark green, chard-like leaves. Both stalks and leaves are tasty and therein lies bok choy's charm. It is at once soft, crunchy, bitter, and sweet. Its stalks are dulcet, juicy, and crisp with leaves that are soft and slightly bitter. Together they give multiple interest to a stir-fry. Separately the greens can become tangy ribbons in a rich salty broth, the stalks, refreshing counterpoints when cooked with seafood or pickled. More fragile than domestic cabbage, bok choy will keep for about four days if wrapped in perforated plastic and stored in the vegetable crisper of the refrigerator. However, all greens, with the exception of spinach, keep much longer when wrapped in a damp cloth, sealed in a plastic bag, and refrigerated. Bok choy will keep for about ten days this way.

Available in Asian markets and some super-markets.

*CELERY CABBAGE (NAPA CABBAGE, TIENTSIN CABBAGE, MICHIHLI CABBAGE, HAKUSAI)* A delicate, crinkled-leaf cabbage widely used in Chinese, Japanese, and Korean cooking. Celery cabbage is claimed to be the most popular leafy green in southern China. It is also the cabbage of kim chee, Korea's national pickled condiment and daily staple. Celery cabbage was presumably named for its pale green color, mild taste, and elongated stalks growing upward from its base. The leaves do not top its stalk but grow from it as a midrib. There are two varieties of celery cabbage grown in the U.S. One has leaves that broaden as they grow up the stalk, fanning out at the top like leaf lettuce. The other variety which is mostly stalk, is very tall and straight with crisper, shorter uniform-sized leaves that grow inward rather than curling out. To further confuse matters, the most common celery cabbage on the market today is a variety called Napa, which appears to be a cross of the two. Napa is squat with full leaves that grow inward. It is nearly white and very tender. Celery cabbage is at home in soups, stir-fries, and fried rice and noodle dishes. Uncooked, it has a radishy edge and is a superb salad addition when shredded. See bok choy, page 657, for storage instructions.

**Chinese Strainer or Skimmer** A shallow strainer with a long handle used for removing foods safely from hot oil or boiling water. We prefer wooden handles because they don't require a pot holder. Available where Asian kitchen supplies are sold.

**Chutney** East Indian condiment made of cool fruits, hot spices, sweet vegetables, and tart flavorings. Small batches of these sweet-and-sour side dishes can be easily made, or large batches can be prepared and canned like jam. Once opened, store-bought or home-made chutney keeps for at least two weeks if refrigerated. A variety of prepared chutneys are available in stores and markets where gourmet foods are sold.

**Cilantro (Spanish or Chinese Parsley, Coriander Leaf)** These fresh green leaves of the coriander plant are used in many cuisines, including East Indian, Asian, and Central and South American. The dried seed of the plant, called coriander, is a spice with a very different taste and cannot be used interchangeably. Many people think that cilantro has a "soapy" flavor, but this is an herb you can learn to love. In fact, cilantro, with its global popularity, is consumed more than any other herb in the world. Do not substitute dried cilantro for fresh; when dried, this heady herb becomes nondescript in color, aroma, and taste.

Fresh cilantro can usually be found in Asian and Hispanic markets and often in the fresh herb section of your supermarket's produce department. It often comes with the root still attached and will keep for about a week in the refrigerator if the roots are submerged in a jar of water and the leaves loosely covered with plastic, though its flavor will fade. For more information, see page 289.

**Cilantro Root (Coriander Root)** The root of the coriander plant, famous for its cilantro leaves (see page 289), and coriander seeds (see page 289), is used by Thai cooks as an herb in its own right. Whenever Bob Love can find coriander with the roots on, he buys a bunch and cuts off the roots for freezing. Then, when the mood strikes, he can make Thai Hot-and-Sour Shrimp Soup (see page 576) without—er—rooting around for ingredients. Produce vendors and supermarkets frequently do leave the roots on. Let your supplier know that you have a use for those "useless" roots.

**Cinnamon** A delicate, sweet, and pungent spice that is one of the world's oldest seasonings. Its use was recorded in China as early as 2500 B.C. As with many ancient spices, cinnamon's popularity is based on function as well as flavor. Its essential oils contain phenol, a bacterial deterrent. Thus, while cinnamon primarily flavors cakes and desserts in the West, it is an ingredient of long standing in savory and meat dishes in the hot countries of the East, its place of origin. Literally, what we know as cinnamon is actually a close relative called cassia. Cassia, sturdier and more pungent than cinnamon, travels and keeps better. It is also more crudely processed, making it a less expensive and a more salable product than cinnamon. In countries where the two spices are plentiful, cinnamon's delicacy is reserved for sweet dishes while the more pungent cassia is used in heartier concoctions. Both cinnamon and cassia are the shaved bark from branches of several evergreen trees in the laurel family. The sun-dried bark naturally curls into scrolls called "quills" or sticks from two to ten inches or more in length. Stick cinnamon is hard to grind at home but fortunately packaged ground cinnamon holds its flavor better than other ground spices.

**Clarified Butter** Clarified butter is butter from which the water and milk solids have been removed. It has a much higher burning point than ordinary butter and will keep much longer without spoiling. It also has a rich and distinctive taste. As pure butter fat, it is richer, ounce for ounce, than butter—so you may choose to use less as a result. Clarified butter is easily made at home. It can also be found at Indian and specialty food stores, though it is quite expensive.

GHEE is India's clarified butter. Its taste is rich and strong, just the thing to carry those intense Indian spices. See page 294 for a discussion of ghee and a foolproof recipe.

NITER KEBBEH is the spiced clarified butter of Eritrea and Ethiopia, see page 510.

**Cloves** Cloves are highly aromatic and have long been valued both for their fragrance and their flavor. However, they must be used sparingly in order to complement other flavors. Often just one or two whole cloves, or a pinch of ground cloves, is enough to season a dish. We grind the whole spice for baked desserts but use whole cloves in poaching liquids and beverages, and strain them before serving. Cloves, whole and ground, are on your grocer's spice shelf. Whole cloves will keep almost indefinitely if tightly wrapped and stored in a cool, dry spot.

**Coconut, grated** When a recipe calls for grated coconut, either fresh or dried will suffice but avoid sweetened coconut found in the baking section of your food store. A fresh coconut can be grated easily by first cracking the shell open with a hammer, recracking it into manageable pieces, and then shredding it on a hand-held grater. Unsweetened, shredded, dried coconut is available at natural and Asian food stores.

**Coconut Milk**   Coconut milk is richly flavored, slightly sweet, and smooth. It is used in Southeast Asian and Pacific cuisines in sauces, soups, curries, and desserts. Coconut milk can be made from fresh or dried coconut (see above) or purchased canned or bottled. Commercial coconut milk varies greatly in sweetness, flavor, and ingredients, so when using it in a recipe, be aware that the results may vary. There is canned coconut milk from Malaysia called "Tropical Coconut Milk" that is worth looking for because it has no preservatives. Coconut milk is available in Asian and natural food stores. The coconut "milk" or "mix" that is intended for use in mixed drinks is very sweet and different and should never be used as a substitute.

*HOMEMADE COCONUT MILK:*   If using fresh coconut, cut the coconut meat into 1-inch pieces and place equal amounts of coconut and hot water in the food processor or blender. Purée at high speed for a couple of minutes. Let steep for 30 minutes. Then pour the purée into a strainer set over a bowl. Press on the pulp and squeeze by the handful to extract as much milk as possible. Pour the milk through a fine-mesh strainer. One cup of coconut meat combined with 1 cup of hot water yields about 1 cup of coconut milk.

Or, combine 1 cup of unsweetened, dried, shredded coconut with 1½ cups of hot tap water. Allow to stand for 5 minutes. Purée for one minute and proceed as above. This yields a little more than 1 cup of coconut milk. Coconut milk will keep for up to three days, if covered and refrigerated, and indefinitely, if frozen.

**Conserves**   See Fruit Conserves.

**Coriander**   When we call for coriander, we are referring to the spice—the dried, round, light brown seeds of the coriander plant. Cilantro, also known as coriander leaf, is the green leafy part of the coriander plant. It is very different in taste and aroma from the dried seeds and cannot be substituted. Coriander imparts a delightful aroma and sweet flavor and is best when freshly ground. While seeds remain fresh for up to two years, ground coriander should be used within a few months. It is available in most supermarkets and health and specialty food stores.

**Coriander Root**   See Cilantro Root.

**Couscous**   A staple food of North Africa, couscous is essentially tiny pearls of pasta made of finely milled semolina wheat. We use the quick-cooking variety. The traditional variety is longer cooking; refer to a good Moroccan cookbook or the couscous package for cooking directions. Couscous is available in Middle Eastern, Greek, and natural food stores and in the international foods sections of supermarkets. Whole wheat couscous, which is heartier, is now also available at many natural food stores.

*TO COOK*   One cup of dry couscous yields about 2½ cups of cooked couscous. The traditional North African method of cooking couscous is to steam it over a simmering stew or soup. We use the following methods to cook quick-cooking couscous.

*STEEPING METHOD*   Place equal amounts of dry couscous and boiling water with a little salt in a bowl. Cover and let sit 10 to 15 minutes, stirring frequently to fluff. If it is still a little crunchy, add another ¼ cup of boiling water, stir, cover, and let sit another 5 minutes.

STEAMING METHOD  Place the couscous in a fine-meshed sieve or a colander lined with cheesecloth. Rest the sieve on the rim of a deep pot so that the bottom of the sieve is a couple of inches above the pot bottom. Pour several cups of boiling water over the couscous, making sure to dampen all the grains. Using foil, tightly cover the pot to seal in the steam. After 5 minutes, stir the couscous to fluff. If the couscous is still crunchy, pour in some more boiling water, making sure that the water doesn't reach high enough to touch the bottom of the sieve. Cover the pot again and check the couscous after 5 minutes. Stir to fluff. When the couscous is ready, place it in a serving bowl and stir in salt to taste and some butter or a little oil.

Use the steaming method to reheat leftover couscous.

**Croutons**  Croutons are best made from bread just past its peak of freshness but not stale. We regularly use whole wheat bread. Preheat the oven to 350°. Cube the bread. Spread the cubes on an unoiled baking sheet and bake them, stirring occasionally, until crisp, about 10 to 15 minutes. Meanwhile, melt some butter. Sauté a good amount of minced or pressed garlic in the butter until it is golden. Add a pinch of herbs, such as thyme, summer savory, oregano, or marjoram, if you wish. Toss the bread cubes and garlic butter well in a bowl. Serve croutons warm or at room temperature. Croutons will keep up to 2 weeks in an airtight container.

**Cumin**  The aroma of cumin dominates much of Mexican and Indian cookery. If you're wild for those cuisines, chances are cumin is your spice. Cumin also figures prominently in the cooking of Latin America, North Africa, the Middle East, and Spain. Cumin seeds are light brown and shaped like caraway. Traditionally, the seeds are rubbed vigorously between the palms of one's hands to release flavor and are then used whole or ground. We roast the whole seeds briefly in a skillet or a toaster oven to achieve the same effect. Whole and ground cumin are available in the spice section of your market, but freshly ground whole seeds are most flavorful.

**Currants**  The currants our recipes call for are dried from a variety of tiny raisin grapes principally grown, dried, and exported from Greece. The name "currant" derives from Corinth, their city of origin. Dried currants are unrelated to the tart red or black currants that grow in temperate climates and are used, fresh, primarily in jellies and wines. Many of us at Moosewood prefer currants to raisins because they are not as intensely sweet. Also, raisins, when cooked, plump up and lose color, whereas currants remain small and dark, providing a lovely jeweled effect in any stew or pilaf. Currants are also much used in baking.

**Curry Powder**  A mixture of untoasted spices used to give food an East Indian or curried flavor. Curry powders bought in spice shops or Indian food stores vary greatly in flavor, aroma, and "hotness." Curry powders bought in supermarkets are fairly consistent but are considered uninteresting by those enthusiastic about Indian food. Curry powder may also be mixed at home. At Moosewood we use a small coffee grinder to grind whole curry spices. Following is a curry powder mixture we like. Experiment to find a combination you find pleasing.

> 2 teaspoons ground cumin seeds
> 2 teaspoons ground coriander seeds
> 2 teaspoons turmeric
> ½ teaspoon cinnamon
> ¼ teaspoon nutmeg
> ¼ teaspoon cayenne
> ¼ teaspoon ground black pepper
> ¼ teaspoon ground cloves
> ¼ teaspoon ground cardamom

Unless you've roasted the spices before grinding, curry powder should be cooked briefly in a little butter or oil to enhance its flavor before it is added to foods.

**Daikon** Known in Japan as the "giant white radish," daikon is a sturdy, versatile winter radish. The average healthy daikon is between 1 and 2 feet long, has a satiny sheen, and is firm, not spongy. It will keep for at least 2 weeks refrigerated. As with other radishes, daikon makes a crisp and pungent salad addition. It also figures in Japanese cuisine as a serious and sometimes solo component in stews, soups, condiments, and pickles.

Daikon is traditionally served simmered in a flavored broth or miso soup, and is also grated raw. When grated, it has a nice, full, cleansing flavor that provides a crisp counterpoint to salty food. Look for daikon in the produce section of Asian food stores, natural food stores, and in the international section of your supermarket's produce department.

**Dashi** Traditional dashi is a broth of simmered konbu (see page 666), water, and dried fish flakes called bonita. There are also vegetarian versions, such as the konbu and shiitake dashis on page 385 in our Japanese chapter. Dashi is the virtual basis of Japanese cuisine, the starting point for soups and hot pots, a flavoring for savory custards, and an addition to marinades for grilled meats and fishes. A dash of dashi gives depth to dipping sauces and salad dressings. The konbu, shiitake mushrooms, and fish flakes are available at Asian food stores and at natural food stores where macrobiotic foods are sold.

**Dates (Dried)** Moist, and almost too sweet, the date's reigning popularity in this country has been in baked goods and confections. But historically, dates have played a much more central role in diet. In addition to being an especially high energy food (54 percent sugar in composition), dates are 7 percent protein and high in iron. They were long a staple food for the Arabian Bedouins along with the milk and meat from their camels and sheep. In the middle ages, dates were often the "sweet" in their much favored sweet and savory meat and game dishes. Dried dates are available in many forms, whole or chopped, with pits or pitted and sold as a brick of undifferentiated date. Because dried dates are sticky they are sometimes chopped and coated with oat flour or coconut for easier measuring and handling. Such date pieces are appropriate for cooking and baking. When stuffing dates (see page 445), the pitted variety are convenient. However, unpitted dates can be sliced, opened, and pitted with little damage to the fruit. Chopped or whole dates are available in the baking section of the supermarket. Whole dates can also be found in the section where other dried fruit and nuts are sold and in fancy food stores, specialty fruit and nut stores, and natural food stores.

**Day Lily Buds**  See page 190.

**Deep-frying**  See page 40.

**Dill**  A green, feathery annual herb that is popular in the cuisines of northern and Eastern Europe and the fertile crescent of Greece, Turkey, Armenia, and Iran. Dill is especially good on fish, with winter vegetables, and in rice and nut pilafs. Fresh or dried, the dill in our recipes is dill weed. Dill seed, another part of the dill plant, has a different taste and is not a substitute. Dill, when dried, retains much of its flavor but also takes on a haylike quality. We find it always a second choice when fresh is available. Both fresh and dried dill should be added at the end of cooking, because its flavor fades quickly when heated. FRESH DILL  is often available in supermarkets throughout the year. It can be frozen to preserve much of its summertime taste by forming into a ball, wrapping in aluminum foil, and freezing. To use, remove from the freezer, unwrap, and slice off the quantity desired; rewrap and return immediately to the freezer. DRIED DILL WEED  is always available in the spice sections of supermarkets.

**Dried Fruit**  Most cold-climate peoples have sweetened their winters by preserving and drying fruits. At Moosewood, we regularly use raisins, currants, dates, and dried apricots in our fruit salads, desserts, and chutneys. For our ethnic nights and at holiday times, we also stock dried apples, pears, and figs for fruitcakes and compotes. Whenever possible, we avoid sulphured fruits for flavor and health reasons. While sulphured fruits retain their midsummer colors, the chemical leaves a residual taste, and can even cause illness. Unsulphured dried fruit is often available at natural food stores. Suppliers are required to inform the consumer when sulphur has been added to a product.

**Dutch Oven**  A large, heavy pot with a tight-fitting lid, recommended for hearty soups, stews, and casseroles, or for any dish that depends on its liquid and long cooking for its flavor. The thick walls of a Dutch oven and its close-fitting lid prevent liquids from escaping as steam and permit slow, even cooking without burning or drying out food. Such cooking also promotes a particularly rich exchange of juices from the slow release and breakdown of the ingredients' flavors, fats, and sugars. Foods cooked in this way are sweeter, richer, thicker, and more flavorful. Recommended ovens are available in cast iron and ceramic-coated cast iron. The advantage of the ceramic oven is that it won't interact with acidic fruits and vegetables or discolor your ingredients.

**Farmer Cheese**  See Pot Cheese.

**Fava Bean (Horse Bean, Broad Bean)**  A legume popular with the peoples of Italy, the Middle East, North Africa, and northern China. Although fresh favas can be found at some Asian markets, they are not available in Ithaca, so we have never used them. Also, the coarse, brown dried favas available in our markets have tough hulls and cook unevenly. So we experimented with canned favas—with good results. Canned favas can be found at Italian and Middle Eastern outlets. If you wish to try fresh or dried fava beans, most Middle Eastern and Italian cookbooks offer detailed instructions on their preparation.

**Fennel Seed** Licorice-flavored fennel seeds are similar to anise but are milder, sweeter flavored, and plumper. Fennel is the distinguishing flavor in some Italian sausages, and when we use it in lasagna or savory strudels, the flavor often prompts the remark, "This is vegetarian?" Fennel seeds are used whole or ground.

**Feta Cheese** A soft, white, Greek or Balkan cheese made from the milk of sheep or goats. The brine in which it is stored both preserves the cheese and gives it its characteristic salty taste. Feta is often sold loose in its brine in the delicatessen department of supermarkets or wrapped in small, well-sealed packages in the dairy case.

**Figs (Dried)** Figs are perhaps the most snackable of dried fruits, neither leathery nor too sweet. Still, it is hard to eat one absentmindedly. When bitten, the calloused skin gives way to a soft, syrupy, seedy interior that is winey, bittersweet, rich, and complex. A dried fig looks like a chocolate kiss. Its body bulges then tapers toward a curled stem. Its colors range from taupe to burnt orange. Figs grow in Greece, Turkey, North Africa, and California. The most popular fig for drying is the Smyrna. In Ithaca, there is a California variety of Smyrna called Calimyrna that we have found to be superior in flavor and freshness to a Turkish Smyrna, possibly because it didn't have to travel as far. We also tasted a fig called Black Mission. It was smaller, drier, less sweet, and less interesting than the Smyrna. Packaged dried figs are available in supermarkets in either the produce department, ethnic food section, or delicatessen department. They can also be found in fancy food stores and at natural food stores where they are often stocked in bulk.

**Filo Pastry Dough (Phyllo)** These very thin sheets of dough are used to make flaky, crisp pastries and strudels. Packaged filo dough is available refrigerated or frozen in many supermarkets and in Mediterranean or Middle Eastern food stores.

**Fish Sauce** Fish sauce is an extract of fermented fish that is used as a basic flavoring in the cuisines of Thailand, Viet Nam, the Philippines, and China. It has a distinctive flavor and a strong odor that disappears when the fish sauce is cooked. It is available in Asian food stores. Check the labels; some fish sauces contain additives you might wish to avoid and others have no additives. For more information on this classic condiment, see page 601.

**Fish Stock** For a basic recipe see page 547; for an Asian version see page 575.

**Folding in** When it is desirable that a dish such as a soufflé be light, fluffy, and puffed up, skillful folding in may be the key to success. Folding in is the process used to gently but thoroughly combine an airy ingredient such as whipped egg whites or whipped cream with a heavier mixture, such as a pudding base, sauce, or batter. The air pockets in these whipped ingredients begin to deflate almost immediately, so work swiftly (whip your eggs or cream just before they are to be folded in). To fold in, pile the lighter mixture on top of the heavier one. Using a rubber spatula, cut into the layers and slide the flat side of the spatula along the bottom of the pan or bowl, lifting the heavier layer up from the bottom and over the lighter layer. Move the spatula to another area of the pan and repeat the process. Continue this procedure until there are no longer two layers but a single, fluffy, uniform mixture.

**Fruit Conserves** Traditionally, a conserve is a sugar-sweetened preserve of two or more whole fruits. Here, we mean specifically the fruit-sweetened jams, marmalades, and spreads that now sit beside their sugared counterparts on your market's shelves. Sorrel Ridge, Polaner's All Fruit, Woodstock, Just Fruit, and Knudsen's are all reliable brands. This is a "natural food" that has gone mainstream. The same items cost almost twice as much in natural food stores.

**Galanga** See Laos Root.

**Garam Masala** For a discussion and recipe, see page 293.

**Garlic** The entire garlic bulb is called a head, and its sections, cloves. When buying garlic, look for heads that feel firm and have good-sized cloves.

Heads of garlic vary greatly in intensity of flavor and size of cloves, so the amount of garlic called for in recipes should be adjusted for those two factors as well as for personal taste. The way garlic is cooked also determines the strength of its flavor. Whole garlic cloves simmered in soups or sauces lend a mild fragrance and flavor. The flavor imparted by sautéed minced garlic is half as strong as that of pressed garlic. Raw garlic is strongest. Take care when sautéing garlic by itself, because it burns quickly and becomes bitter. The flavor of dried garlic cannot be compared to the real thing, and we never use dried or powdered garlic in any form.

To peel garlic easily, lay each clove on its side on a chopping board. Place the side of a large broad-bladed knife flat on the clove. Hold the knife firmly with one hand and whack the blade of the knife just over the garlic clove with the base of your other palm. Once you successfully "squish" the garlic clove, the papery skin will slip right off. When pressed garlic is called for, we mean garlic crushed in a garlic press.

**Ghee** An Indian clarified butter; see page 294.

**Ginger Root** Fresh ginger is a knobby root with light brown papery skin. Healthy ginger is firm and unblemished. When cut, the inside should be juicy and yellow with a clear, fresh scent and a hot, spicy taste. Ginger root is usually prepared by grating it on the finest surface of a hand-held grater or by mincing it finely. If the ginger is young and fresh, the skin will be thin and unnecessary to peel. If the skin is tough or shriveled, peel it with a paring knife. Some cooks always peel ginger; this is a personal preference. Fresh ginger root is available in the produce sections of many supermarkets and in Asian food stores. It will keep stored in a plastic bag in the refrigerator for about 2 weeks. For longer storage, peel the ginger root and keep it in a jar of sherry in the refrigerator. The ginger-flavored sherry can be used for cooking also. Powdered or dried ginger, used primarily in baking, has a completely different flavor and cannot be substituted for fresh ginger. Also different are pickled ginger, a well-known sushi condiment, and crystallized ginger, a popular ingredient in Chinese desserts and confections.

**Heat Diffuser**   A heat diffuser is a round metal plate that sits between the burner and cooking pot. It serves both to reduce the heat and to distribute it evenly. Heat diffusers, also called flame-spreaders and flame tamers, are available where kitchen supplies are sold and through some kitchenware catalogs.

**Hoisin Sauce**   A Chinese condiment; see page 190.

**Hot Peppers (Chiles)**   To choose and use hot peppers, fresh and dried, see page 452.

**Jerusalem Artichoke (Sunchoke)**
The Jerusalem artichoke is a tuber native to the Americas and one that was avidly cultivated by native Americans. The name is said to derive from a mispronunciation of the Italian word for sunflower, *girasole,* a cousin of the tuber, and from the taste, which resembles artichokes. The root's sweet and nutty taste and crisp, clean texture evoke a quality so elusive that it has been compared to chestnuts, water chestnuts, salsify, and new potatoes, as well as artichoke hearts. Jerusalem artichokes are funny-looking roots, closely resembling ginger root, but knobbier and of a flat grayish-tan color, sometimes flecked with red. Select artichokes that are smooth and firm; avoid those that are blotchy and tinged with green. The peak season is fall and winter. Thinly sliced, raw Jerusalem artichokes can be pickled or added raw to salads. Or, like new potatoes, the tubers can be roasted, fried, or puréed. Jerusa-

lem artichokes are available in gourmet food stores and in the produce department of many supermarkets. The roots will keep for a week, wrapped in plastic and refrigerated.

**Ka (Kha, Kar)**   See Laos Root.

**Konbu (Kombu, Kelp)**   This seaweed is perhaps better known to Westerners in its powdered form, although it is used regularly by the Japanese as a whole sea vegetable available in pressed sheets. Discovered to be a natural form of MSG, konbu's enduring popularity no doubt relates to its unique flavor-enhancing and tenderizing qualities. The Japanese use konbu either in large pieces in stock or dashi (see page 385), as wrappers for filling, or cut into strips of varying widths in soups and stews. Konbu is available at Asian food stores and at natural food stores where macrobiotic foods are sold.

**Laos Root, Dried (Galanga, Ka, Kar, Kha, Thai Ginger, Lengkuas, Galingale, Chinese or Siamese Ginger)**   Dried laos root is the preserved form of galanga, an underground rhizome or stem resembling ginger. Like ginger, it is used medicinally and tastes hot, although its flavor is quite different. Much of Southeast Asia, notably Indonesia, Laos, and Thailand, use laos root in the ways the rest of Asia uses ginger. In Ithaca, we've only been able to find laos root in dried slices, packaged in 1-ounce cellophane bags. The slices do not need to be presoaked before they are floated in your stock or soup but remove them before serving. The texture of dried laos root is woody and its taste bitter. Powdered dried laos root should not be substituted for the dried slices. Available at Asian food stores.

**Leek**  Leeks, members of the onion family, have cylindrical white bulbs and long, ribbon-shaped green leaves but are milder in flavor and strength than onions. To prepare, cut off the roots and tops, leaving 8 to 10 inches of bulb and lower leaf. The tops of the leek leaves are tough and should be discarded or used in stock. Leeks are grown in sandy soil and must be washed carefully. Slice the leek down the middle almost to the root and, holding it under running water or immersed in a basin of water, gently pull each layer away from the bulb, rinsing well. Drain or shake dry. Slice or chop according to recipe directions.

**Lemon Grass**  A citrus-flavored herb used in Southeast Asian cooking. Dried lemon grass is available at Asian food stores, frequently sold in one-ounce cellophane packages. In many areas you may also find it fresh. Don't hesitate to ask, since fresh lemon grass will likely be kept in the refrigerator and perhaps out of sight; it is far and away the better choice. Fresh lemon grass is a tall stalk 1½ to 2 feet long. Only the bottom 6 inches are tender enough to be eaten, but the rest of the stalk can be boiled to release the wonderful, lemony flavor. Dried lemon grass should be similarly treated as a flavoring for your dish that must be removed before serving. Enclose the dried herb pieces in a teaball or cheesecloth pouch.

**Long Beans**  Pencil-thin and 18 inches long, these beans are truly long. Although green, long beans do not belong to the green bean family, but are kin to the black-eyed pea. When simply prepared, they taste starchy, not juicy, and bland, but their texture and receptivity are the long bean's vir-

tues. They maintain their integrity through such rugged cooking techniques as braising, deep-frying, and long cooking. In stews, long beans remain firm and chewy and become a sponge for potent flavorings. A healthy long bean is flexible, falling somewhere in between crisp and limp. There are purple, dark green, and pale green varieties. Long beans will keep for 2 to 3 days refrigerated in the vegetable crisper.

**Mace**  Mace is the aril—an accessory to the outer covering of a seed—of the nutmeg, and the nutmeg's is notably lovely. Fresh, mace is a red filament that laces around the nutmeg. Dried, it becomes the color of coffee-with-cream. Mace tastes slightly of nutmeg but is distinctive. In the United States it is used primarily in cakes and pastries, but it flavors savory dishes in other parts of the world. The British seem to have a particular fondness for it as do Africans living south of the Sahara. Scraping your own mace from a nutmeg is perhaps worth the taste, possibly the experience, but doubtfully the effort, given the small amount of mace a single nutmeg yields. Proceed directly to the supermarket for this ground spice.

**Mango**  Eating a good mango is an all-absorbing, almost ceremonial event. Mangoes are the kind of good thing, like Christmas for some, that you wouldn't want to overdo. So, it is hard to believe that for half the world this tropical fruit is a staple item. Some are grown in Florida, though most sold in the United States are imported from Mexico and Haiti. Mangoes are round, oval, or kidney shaped, have green leathery skins, and weigh from ¾ to 3 pounds. The flesh is golden or apricot, creamy, and smoothly sweet. Its taste is a flirtation with peach, melon, and orange with just a hint of musk. Its delicacy is as perfect in combinations—in fruit salads and chutneys, purées, and parfaits—as it is alone, simply eaten with a spoon. Mangoes also make sweet and exotic upside-down cakes and quick breads. There are mangoes that are stringy and resinous, but the odds are better than decent that you'll pick a good one. Ripeness helps. Skin color may or may not be an indicator. Many varieties, when ripe, have turned various shades of yellow and rose and may be speckled, or not. Some, however, remain green. A more telling sign is the fruit's "give." Your thumb should meet a bit of resistance, it should not disappear into the flesh of the fruit. Aroma is another clue. Look for a sweet, fruity fragrance at the stem end. Unripe mangoes will ripen at room temperature. Chill when ripe.

*Margarine* Hydrogenated vegetable oil. Although we prefer the taste of butter, we use margarine for savory strudels, tarts, and turnovers that we wish to keep dairy-free. We recommend Willow Run brand margarine, a soy margarine free of additives and preservatives. Many natural food stores carry this or similar brands. Happily, our town's most responsive supermarket was willing to begin carrying it. Your local supermarkets might respond favorably as well. Try asking for it.

*Marjoram* Marjoram is a delicate herb with a sweet and mild flavor. Even dried, it is best added toward the end of cooking.

*Matzo* Square, unleavened wheat crackers available in the kosher food section of the supermarket. Finely ground matzo is referred to as matzo meal (see note, page 430) and is frequently used in Jewish dishes in place of flour or bread crumbs.

*Millet* A round, yellow seed-like grain that cooks into a fluffy cereal like couscous. In fact, the couscous of Africa is a variety of millet. Millet is high in protein, iron, magnesium, and potassium. It is available at natural food stores and wherever bulk, whole grains are sold. More perishable than other grains, always store millet in a tightly capped glass jar in the refrigerator. For more information and cooking instructions, see page 34.

*Mint* We respond to the call for mint in various ways, depending upon the supply and the season. When the weather turns warm, perennial herb patches around our homes and in nearby fields and streams flourish madly, yielding spearmint, peppermint, and loads of hybrids. Such, it appears, is the indiscriminate nature of the species. We use the fresh herbs, to taste, since different types, and different plants within types, can vary decidedly in strength. We also delight in having mint available as a garnish. Nothing sets off a brownie so well as a slice of orange and a sprig of mint. Store fresh mint refrigerated, immersing the stems in water and covering the leaves loosely with plastic. When our supply of fresh mint disappears, we use herbal mint tea, fresh from the package or tin. We add it to our pot or vinaigrette as we would any other dried herb. Within our ranks some cooks prefer peppermint over spearmint, and vice versa. Choose for yourself.

*Mirin* A golden, sweet-cooking wine made from sake (see page 678), sweet rice, and rice malt. Mirin's alcohol content evaporates in the cooking process, leaving a subtle and unique sweetness. If mirin is not available, substitute ⅔ cup dry sherry plus ⅓ cup sugar for 1 cup mirin. Or, if using honey, substitute ¾ cup dry sherry and ¼ cup honey. Mirin can be found in Asian markets and natural food stores.

**Miso**   Miso is a fermented soy bean paste that originated in Japan over 2,000 years ago. Salty, high protein, and good for the digestion, it imparts a rich, full flavor to food. It ranges in color from dark brown to light golden and has a consistency similar to peanut butter. There are many different kinds of miso, each with its own aroma, flavor, color, and texture. Miso is made by crushing boiled soy beans; adding barley, rice, or wheat; injecting the mass with a culture; and allowing it to mature for a few months to three years. In the United States, the three best-known varieties of miso are rice miso, barley miso, and soy miso. Rice miso, also called light miso or white miso, is yellow to amber in color and relatively sweet. Barley miso, also called red miso, is darker colored and very savory. Soy miso is usually thickest and strongest in flavor. Within these three varieties there are countless offshoots of flavor from salty to sweet.

At Moosewood, we primarily use an unpasteurized rice miso made by the Onozaki family on their farm in Japan. It has a full, slightly sweet flavor. We like it in soups, stews, spreads, and salad dressings. Care should be taken not to boil miso or reportedly the digestion-aiding enzymes produced during the fermentation process will be destroyed.

Miso will keep indefinitely if refrigerated.

It is available at some supermarkets and most Asian and natural food stores.

**Mung Bean Thread Noodles**   See Cellophane Noodles.

**Mung Beans**   These humble, olive-green beans are best known to us as the slender, silvery bean sprout of Chinese cuisine. Throughout Southeast Asia and China, however, there exists a tradition of sweet and savory dishes that use the whole, unsprouted bean. In India, for example, mung bean dals (spicy bean side dishes) are standard fare. When cooked, the mung bean is rich, starchy, and sweet, similar to split peas. Mung beans are available at Indian, Asian, and natural food stores. See page 653 for cooking instructions.

**Mushrooms, Dried**   See Porcini and Shiitake mushrooms.

**Mustard**   America seems to be in the midst of a mustard renaissance. This once-simple condiment is now offered to us spiced, sweetened, and soused. Ethnic cooks have also discovered that this ancient spice has a variety of cultural adaptations. Listed below is a quartet of mustards that have served us well over the years.

*DIJON MUSTARD*   is a type of prepared mustard made with water, vinegar, spices, and white wine. The name derives from its French city of origin, though the biggest selling brand in the U.S. is a domestic product. Dijon mustards are available in most supermarkets and gourmet food stores.

*HOT MUSTARD (CHINESE MUSTARD)*   is the "exotic" mustard you may have initially sampled with your first eggroll. Though available commercially, we make our own simply by mixing ground yellow mustard seeds with small amounts of water until a prepared mustard consistency is achieved. Vinegar, salt, and a little sweetener can be added to taste.

YELLOW MUSTARD SEEDS are from the mustard plant native to India and China. They are the basis for prepared "ball park mustard" and are available whole and ground on the spice shelf of the supermarket. We use ground yellow mustard seeds to enliven sauces, salad dressings, marinades, and curries. Mustard seeds are primarily used whole as a pickling spice and in some Indian dishes, such as chutneys. When ground mustard is called for, we suggest grinding your own for a more pleasantly piquant flavor and adjusting the amount used to your taste.

BLACK MUSTARD SEEDS are widely used in Indian cooking. See page 288 for a complete discussion.

**Niter Kebbeh**  An Ethiopian spiced clarified butter; see page 510.

**Nonreactive Cookware**  Metals like aluminum and cast iron interact with acidic fruits and vegetables, imparting a metallic taste to these foods and everything else in the pot. Cast iron also causes nonacidic vegetables to discolor. Safer cookware choices include stainless steel, glass, ceramic-coated cast iron, lined copper, and a new material, anodyzed aluminum. Anodyzed aluminum has the dual attributes of noninteraction with foods and a nonteflon, nonstick surface.

**Nori (Laver)**  Dark green or purplish seaweed. Nori is sold dried in thin sheets packaged in cellophane or in cans and available in gourmet or Asian food stores. Nori is used to wrap fillings as in sushi rolls or, crumbled, as a seasoning for foods. The flavor of nori is enhanced if you "toast" it just before use by very briefly passing it over a gas flame until it becomes greenish and crisp. It is best stored at room temperature well wrapped.

**Nutmeg**  Nutmeg from the Spice Islands of Indonesia found its way to the hospitable soil of the West Indies during the sixteenth-century heydey of spice trading. Nutmeg is a super-large seed, slightly rounder and smaller than an unshelled pecan with a similar mahogany color. Once grated, its aroma fades fast, so it is best to grate it fresh, as needed, and directly into your pot or tureen right before serving. Specialized nutmeg graters exist, but whole nutmeg can be easily hand-grated on the fine side of a standard kitchen grater. Store whole or partially grated nutmeg in a tightly capped jar. Fresh nutmeg smells sweet and elusive. Mildly pungent, it beautifully complements white sauces and spinach, but the key is restraint or nutmeg will overwhelm. Whole nutmeg is available in gourmet food stores and spice shops.

**Nuts and Seeds, to Toast and Grind**  Nuts and seeds can be toasted in a conventional oven, skillet, or toaster oven. When using a conventional oven, spread nuts on an unoiled baking sheet and bake at 350°. Stir occasionally until they are browned and fragrant. When using a skillet, heat nuts on a low to medium heat, stirring frequently. At Moosewood, we toast nuts and seeds effortlessly and effectively in an everyday toaster oven. To toast walnuts, almonds, and sesame seeds, set the dial for "medium-colored toast" and toast the nuts twice. Small quantities of nuts and seeds can be ground in a spice or coffee grinder (see page 680). For larger quantities we use the bowl of a food processor.

**Okra**   Like tapioca, battle lines are drawn when it comes to okra. And, it appears, for the same reason: slipperiness. Elizabeth Schneider has dubbed us a nation having "a horror of slipperiness in food." To other cultures, textural variety is considered essential to a meal's balance and aesthetic. This slipperiness has its place in the universe—next to something crisp. A classic Japanese side dish combines wakame, a slimy seaweed, with crunchy cucumber. And, slippery cellophane noodles in Chinese broths are often topped with crisp-fried noodles. So for you tapioca lovers (and whoever else is still with me) okra is also a sweet and succulent vegetable. It is the signature ingredient in Creole gumbo, and its tropical origins render it particularly compatible with other hot weather vegetables such as tomatoes, eggplants, and peppers. Because of okra's viscosity it is a good thickener, highly valued as such by the canning industry for soups and stews.

Okra looks like a pod-shaped, miniature zucchini. Good fresh okra is hard to find in much of the U.S., but frozen baby okra is widely available, and it's a fine substitute. Frozen okra is easiest to slice or chop while it's frozen. If fresh is available, the sweetest and most tender are under 4 inches long with bright, dark, or light green exteriors. Look for those with firm, unspotted skins. Larger and limper versions will be tough and fibrous. Fresh okra will keep for one to three days, refrigerated. Store in a paper bag or perforated plastic. Always cook okra in ceramic, glass, or stainless steel since cast iron will discolor it.

**Olive Oil**   Everyone's talking about it, for a variety of reasons. Assimilation, affluence, tourism, and television have all inspired interest in ethnic foods. Abundance, availability, and leisure have also redefined food as re-creation. Sampling and cooking new and foreign foods is now entertainment and avocation. Lastly, current research claiming that olive oil and other monounsaturated fats may reduce cholesterol has made olive oil more than food; for many, it has become medicine, or at least an investment in longevity. Olive oil devotees consider oil from Italy to be the finest; very good oils are also produced in Spain and southern France. The three grades of oil produced are extra-virgin, virgin, and pure olive oil. Each has its place in the kitchen. See pages 330.

**Olives**   Olives are a staple at Moosewood. In cooking, they add interest and richness, and simultaneously "cut" rich foods with their saltiness and tang. In salads, olives provide both substance and contrast. The world of olives includes hundreds of varieties from different trees, soils, and climates, or cured with different herbs. Regrettably, access to exotica is limited in central New York State. Below are the olives we work with; but definitely experiment on your own.

CALAMATA OLIVES   These are our house olives. They are salty and sweet and have a meatiness that melts in your mouth. Their veneer is rich and glossy, with coloring that alternates between chocolate and eggplant. They give our salads depth and class. Calamatas are imported from Greece, unpitted. But their taste is so special that we encourage you to slice them away from their pits if ripe olives are called for in a dish, especially in Mediterranean and North African classics.

*PITTED CALIFORNIA RIPE OLIVES*   The black, pitted, canned variety on our supermarket shelves. They are tasteless compared to their Mediterranean kin, but they add succulence, salt, and a hint of olive when chopped into fillings, on top of tostadas, or added whole to stews. M. F. K. Fischer, epicure/pragmatist has even taught these "jumbo monsters" to comport themselves as antipasto or salad olives: she warms them, rolls them in garlic and a good olive oil, and finishes them off with a splash of Tabasco.

*PIMIENTO-STUFFED SPANISH OLIVES*   Unripened or green olives, stuffed with pickled sweet red pepper. We use these olives in enchilada and burrito fillings, and at times in gazpacho and egg salads. Available in the supermarket.

*NIÇOISE OLIVES*   Niçoise olives are not part of our working repertoire, but they are worth seeking out. Small, egg-shaped, and purple-black or green, the Niçoise is a milder-tasting olive than the Calamata. Niçoise olives originate in Nice, in the south of France. Look for them in specialty food stores and gourmet delicatessens.

**Orange Blossom Water**   See page 559.

**Oregano**   Fresh oregano is a sweet and mild herb that is not widely grown in this country. The generic dried herb with which we are most familiar has the drawback of pizza-fying whatever's in the pot with the least bit of overuse. Though types of oregano abound—Greek, Italian, Spanish, Mexican varieties, dried oregano is a seasoning that easily dominates, so it should be used with

care. We discovered that a variety native to Greece, Origanum heracleoticum, is sweeter, milder, and less bitter than its Italian kin. For the freshest-tasting herb, purchase any oregano in leaf, not powdered, form. Greek oregano is available by mail from Frontier Cooperative Herbs, Norway, Iowa 52318.

**Papaya**   The papaya is a tropical fruit that has the look of a smooth-skinned, miniature melon. Hundreds of varieties exist. The one that ships best from Hawaii, our major supplier, is pear shaped and weighs about ¾ pound. A perfectly ripe papaya of this variety has a yellow skin and the resiliency of a ripe avocado. Don't let skin spots trouble you if the color and "give" are good. The delicate flavor of a ripe papaya quickly fades, so much so that it is best to choose one that is partially green, unless you will be using it immediately. A green papaya will ripen in a dark place at room temperature, but only if there is some trace of yellow apparent. Papayas are sometimes picked so green that they will never mature. The ripening process can be hastened by putting it in a closed paper bag with a banana. Once ripe, a papaya should be chilled and eaten within a day or two.

**Paprika**   We recommend using sweet Hungarian paprika, which is made from dried, ground, sweet red peppers. To ensure retaining the delicate flavor, avoid scorching. Hot paprika is pungent and fiery and can be used in place of cayenne.

**Parsley**   When we call for parsley, we're referring to the fresh, curly, or flat-leaf Italian variety. Dried parsley is so faded in flavor and color that we never use it. Bunches of fresh parsley sprigs can be kept for a week in the refrigerator. To store, immerse the stems in water, cover leaves loosely with plastic, and refrigerate.

**Parsnip**   For those unfamiliar with the parsnip, a common first reaction is that it looks like a bleached carrot. The parsnip's sweet and pungent taste, however, is anything but colorless. Its varying intensity dictates discretion when adding parsnips to soups or stews. More often, the parsnip solos in soups and purées, where it is mellowed by cream or cheese (see Cheddar and Parsnip Soup, page 105), or baked with orange juice, where it is balanced by the acid. A root vegetable, parsnips are sold loose in the fall and early winter, and after that in single-pound plastic bags. If you choose your parsnips by hand, select those that are firm, have unblemished white skin, and are no more than 6 inches long. The cores of larger parsnips become woody and can taste medicinal. Brown spots on the exterior may mean the entire root is rotten.

**Pastry Brush**   A pastry brush is handy for buttering strudel leaves, oiling pans, and glazing breads and pastries. We've discovered that the best pastry brush is actually your average 2-inch paintbrush. The "pastry brush" that is sold as a kitchen supply is frustratingly narrow, usually no more than 1 inch wide, and sparsely bristled. Alternatively, paintbrushes come in a variety of widths and are more deeply bristled, providing a quicker, smoother, and more even application. Nylon- or natural-bristle paintbrushes can be purchased in paint or hardware stores for half the price of the designer model. To keep your brush soft and pliable, immerse it in hot, soapy water as soon after

use as possible; all buttered brushes gum up quickly.

**Pastry Dough**   See Pie Crust.

**Peanut Butter**   We use unhomogenized peanut butter without sweeteners, preservatives, or stabilizers and have found that this type works best for cooking. After stirring thoroughly, refrigerate to preserve its freshness and to keep the oil distributed evenly. For easier handling, bring the peanut butter to room temperature before using it; restir if the oil separates. Unhomogenized peanut butter is available in natural food stores and most supermarkets.

**Peanut Oil**   A flavorful oil that is especially good for deep-frying (see page 40) because it has a high burning point and does not absorb flavors as readily as other oils. Refined peanut oils are available at the supermarket. Cold-pressed, aromatic ones can be found at some Asian markets, natural food stores, and some supermarkets.

**Peppercorns**   All peppercorns start as the berry of the tropical vine *piper nigrum.* Whether they are black, white, or green depends on when they are picked and how they are processed.

BLACK PEPPERCORNS   are unripe, unhulled, green berries that turn black when dried. Once ground, these peppercorns become the familiar black pepper that is a constant on our tables and in most classic dishes because it is a complement, an accent, and a fulfillment. It balances salt and sharpens the flavors of other ingredients. It can draw a dish, subtly, to a satisfying resolution. When added to a stockpot, a handful of peppercorns will mildly season a broth. However, when peppercorns are ground they also become a pungent spice that must be used with discretion. For cooking and table use, grind pepper fresh from peppercorns and add it to your pot or plate at the last minute. The difference between freshly ground pepper and preground pepper is enormous; besides having lost its flavor and aroma, commercially ground black pepper may also be adulterated with ground date stones and other spices. Black peppercorns are available at the supermarket and in specialty food stores. Peppermills for grinding the corns are affordable and available wherever kitchen supplies are sold.

WHITE PEPPERCORNS are ripened berries of the pepper plant. Their pulp and matured pink or red hulls are separated from the seed by a process of fermentation. The white seed is whole white pepper and is less aromatic than black. It is often called for in Chinese dishes and can be used instead of black to keep white or light sauces pristine. White peppercorns are available in specialty food stores. Ground white pepper can be found at the supermarket and is a satisfactory substitute for freshly ground white peppercorns.

GREEN PEPPERCORNS are unripe, unhulled berries that stay green because they have been canned in brine rather than dried. Green peppercorns have a fresh taste that is not as hot as black pepper. They are usually cooked, whole, with fish, meat, and poultry.

**Pesto** Loosely translated, pesto means "pounded" in Italian, and refers to the age-old method of preparing a paste by pounding and grinding the ingredients together with a mortar and pestle. Today, pesto refers to a class of rich sauces usually served with pasta, but it can admirably complement a variety of vegetables including carrots, green beans, zucchini, and potatoes. It gives a luscious twist when added to mayonnaise, particularly in potato or seafood salads. While not absolutely authentic, we've had delicious results with the careful use of a food processor or blender.

The most well-known pesto is pesto Genovese, a paste of fresh basil, pine nuts, garlic, olive oil, and Parmesan cheese. Other pestos exist, combining other nuts, herbs, and ingredients. At Moosewood we make a creamy hazelnut pesto, and our Italian chapter offers one made with sun-dried tomatoes (see page 365). Experiment with different ingredients or mixtures of ingredients: use fresh tarragon, or mix fresh mint with basil. Try almonds, walnuts, or sunflower seeds. We make a good, dairy-free pesto Genovese by substituting tofu, lemon juice, and salt for Parmesan cheese. *Pasta al Pesto* is one of the quickest, most satisfying, and indulgent meals we know. One cautionary word: pesto is practically a concentrate, so start with a spoonful, not a ladleful.

**Pie Crust** For a basic dough see pages 637 and 497. For a rich crust see page 276. For a sweet dessert crust sample the one on page 560.

**Pine Nuts (Pignoli)** Pine nuts, the edible seeds of pine trees, have been harvested and eaten throughout the world from Roman times to the present. Until recently, native pine nuts, called Indian Nuts, were a commodity here. The nuts were named after the Native American gatherers, who, alone, could scale the tall, Southwestern two-leafed pine trees for the nuts. Because all pine nuts, to a greater or lesser degree, taste like turpentine, the pine nut of culinary choice comes from the stone pine grown along the Mediterranean and Black Sea coasts. The stone pine nut is a smooth, cream-colored, bean-sized nut with the softness of a seed and the patina of satin. It tastes rich and delicate and its hint of resin evaporates quickly when cooked. Not surprisingly, pine nuts predominate in cuisines where the nuts are plentiful: North Africa, the Middle East, Spain, and Italy. Pignoli are a star ingredient in the Italian classic, pesto Genovese. Imported pine nuts are very expensive, because shelling them without damaging the fragile seed is painstaking work. Fortunately, the richness of pine nuts provides its own restraint. Pine nuts are available at Italian, Spanish, and Middle Eastern food stores, gourmet food stores and departments, and wherever fine, fresh nuts are sold.

*Plantain* The plantain is a tropical fruit related to the banana, and obviously so. It looks like a long, thick-skinned banana and can range in color from very green to yellow to dark brown. Although officially a fruit, cooked plantains are widely used as a starchy vegetable. When choosing plantains to use as vegetables, select those that are green or yellow-green. The deep yellow and brown ones are reportedly used in sweet condiments and desserts. A few of us had a delicious introduction to plantains in Puerto Rico. Our gracious hostess, Carmen, soaked thickly cut plantain slices in salted lime juice with garlic, fried them, pounded them, and finally crisp-fried them. Plantains are sold in *bodegas,* or Spanish groceries, and in supermarkets in Spanish-speaking neighborhoods.

*Pomelo (Pummelo, Shaddock)* A strange fruit with an interesting past, the po-

melo is a sour, pulpy citrus fruit said to be the grandparent of the grapefruit. It is eaten with salt in Southeast Asia, and one pomelo could conceivably feed a small village at a single sitting. It is the world's largest citrus fruit, weighing in at a high of 22 pounds. The availability of this thick and rumpled-skinned fruit is currently limited to the west and southeast coasts of the United States. Perhaps with the steady influx of Southeast Asians and West Indians to our shores, we may soon be seeing pomelos and a host of other exotic foods.

*Poppadums* Thin, lentil-based wafers available in Indian and Asian groceries and many supermarkets. Cook them in an inch of hot oil for a few seconds before serving.

*Porcini* Porcini are Italian wild mushrooms that cluster under chestnut trees in the fall and spring. They are imported to this country, dried, but lose nothing in the transition because they are cut and dried at their peak of ripeness; in fact, the flavor intensifies. Porcini are traditionally used to flavor sauces, stews, and rice dishes (see Risotto, page 350). To choose, look for mushrooms that are fully opened, fleshy and whole, not broken. To use, soak porcini in warm water for 20 to 30 minutes, after which both mushrooms and soaking liquid become, for the Italians, unparalleled flavoring ingredients. As with most dried mushrooms, porcini are expensive, but a few go far. Available at Italian markets and gourmet food stores. Fresh porcini are also beginning to appear in the United States.

*Pot Cheese* Pot cheese is a primitive cheese; all dairy-eating cultures have their versions. These cheeses are made from milk fermented naturally, by organisms in the atmosphere. More complicated ripened cheeses are injected with bacteria or fungus. By definition, primitive cheeses are not difficult to make. Once milk has soured, it naturally thickens and separates into curds and whey. The cheesemaker drains off the liquid whey, and the remaining curds become the basis for a variety of primitive cheeses. The amount of liquid removed, of salt added, the addition of cream and special cultures, or whether or not the cheese is pressed into a shape, distinguish such cheeses from one another. For example, pot cheese is drier and less salty than cottage cheese. It is a subtle medium for strong flavors and textures and makes an especially good filling for turnovers and crêpes.

Unlike most ripened or aged cheeses, pot cheese or other cheeses of this type do not store well. Tightly sealed and refrigerated, it will keep for about a week. Once a staple foodstuff of Eastern European households, today pot cheese is sold mostly in specialty food shops, good Jewish delicatessens, and in some Eastern European groceries. Its drier cousin, farmer cheese, is a reasonable substitute and can be found in the dairy case of most supermarkets. Salt-free farmer cheese is also available.

*Purée*  This process is most easily accomplished in a blender or food processor, but reasonable results can also be achieved with a sieve when cooked ingredients are used. When using a blender or food processor, whirl the ingredients with a liquid until smooth. If a sieve is used, place the base ingredients in the sieve over a bowl or pot and push them through the mesh with the back of a large spoon or potato masher. Mix in the liquid last.

*Red Pepper Flakes*  Crushed, dried chiles. Available in the spice section of the supermarket.

*Rice*  After years of experience and experimentation, we've found brown rice to be the grain that pleases most of the people most of the time. When cooked correctly, it strikes a near perfect balance between sweetness, lightness, moistness, and heartiness. Some of our recipes call for Basmati rice, a long-grain rice with a distinctive taste. Brown rice is available in most supermarkets and all natural food stores. Brown Basmati can be found at many natural food stores.

TO COOK  Clean the rice by immersing it in cool water, swirling it around with your fingers, and pouring off the liquid that is often clouded by dust and debris. Repeat this process until the water runs clear. A heavy saucepan or pot with a tight-fitting lid is best for cooking rice, because it retains more moisture and is less apt to scorch the rice. Good rice can be made in a lighter pot with the use of a heat diffuser (see page 666).

When uncooked rice is sautéed briefly in oil before the water is added, it yields non-gummy, clearly separated grains of cooked rice. Before adding the water, sauté the rice in a little oil for a minute or two, stirring briskly. Add the water in a 2:1 water to rice ratio. Add a pinch of salt if you wish. Cover the pot and bring the rice to a boil. When you see steam escaping from the lid, turn the heat off for 5 minutes and then simmer the rice on very low heat for 25 minutes. Use a heat diffuser at this point if your pot is light or if the heat won't go very low. Honor a time-tested Asian practice: resist looking into the rice once it has come to a boil. Rice is always better steamed, and lifting the lid will spoil that.

After the simmer, let the rice stand off the heat for 10 minutes, then stir it well. One cup of raw rice yields about 3 cups cooked.

This recipe works for short-grain brown rice. Medium- and long-grain rice usually cooks in less time.

TO COOK BROWN BASMATI RICE   Clean the rice by immersing it in cold water, stirring it with your hands, then pouring off any debris or loose hulls that float to the top. At first the water will be cloudy. Repeat washings until the water rinses clear, two or three times. Bring 2¼ cups of water, 1 cup of rice, and ¼ teaspoon of salt (optional) to a rapid boil; stir once. Cover the rice with a tight-fitting lid, lower the heat, and simmer for 40 to 45 minutes. Remove the pot from the burner and allow the rice to rest, covered, for 10 minutes.

Refer to page 383 for the Japanese method of cooking brown and white rice.

**Rice Vinegar**   There are many varieties of vinegar made from different rice wines— clear, golden, red, or black, and Chinese or Japanese—but all are more delicately flavored than the cider, wine, or white vinegars more commonly used. The red and black varieties are often used by Chinese cooks as table condiments, while the mellow flavor of the clear and golden types are best suited to salad dressings and marinades.

For use in recipes in this book, buy a clear or golden variety, either Chinese or Japanese. The strength of the vinegar—hearty, me-dium to mild, very mild—is often marked right on the label. Avoid brands that contain added sugar, salt, or monosodium glutamate (MSG). Rice vinegar is available in Chinese and Japanese food stores, natural food stores, and many supermarkets.

**Rosemary**   Rosemary is a lush and fragrant Mediterranean bush that can grow to six feet tall. Its evergreen and white leaves have the look and smell of pine needles. It is an important commercial herb, cultivated for its essential oils for perfumes, shampoos, and herbal baths. In cooking, its piney aroma and sharp clean taste appear to be best supported by the saline richness of meat, game, or fish. However, rosemary has appeared throughout history on vegetables, in sauces, and in savory breads. At Moosewood we use rosemary carefully. Because it can easily dominate, we reserve its assertive scent and flavoring for simple vegetables and vinaigrettes that accompany rich entrées. Fresh rosemary is becoming increasingly available, but when it is not, the dried herb can be crumbled into dishes as they cook or tied in cheesecloth, added to the pot, and removed before serving.

**Rutabaga (Swede Turnip)**   Rutabagas are large, globe-shaped, yellow root vegetables available in the fall through midwinter. Some rutabagas, among them those grown on small and organic farms, have some purple shading and look like large, long turnips. One might speculate that the globe variety is easier to wax, which seems to be the case for all mass-distributed rutabagas. Peel the waxed skins before cooking. Rutabagas make a fine side dish simply steamed, drizzled with butter, and salted to taste. They turn a bright yellow-orange when cooked, making a colorful and hearty addition to a winter stew.

**Rye Flakes**  Rye flakes look like rolled oats, but slightly darker, and are processed in the same way. The rye berry kernel is cracked and flaked, creating a form that is easier and quicker to cook and easier to digest. Whole rye in berry or flaked form is worth investigating. Jane Brody, food and nutrition writer, contends that it has "more protein, phosphorus, iron, potassium, and B vitamins than whole wheat."

**Saffron**  This strongly aromatic spice imparts a bright yellow color and an elusive, exotic flavor when used with discretion. Saffron threads are the dried stamens of the saffron crocus of southern Europe. It takes 70,000 to 80,000 crocus flowers to yield one pound of saffron, making it a very expensive spice. Purchase saffron in strand form instead of powdered to ensure its purity. When stored in a cool, dark place, it lasts virtually forever. "Mexican saffron," sold in some Latin American markets, is actually safflower and should not be confused with true saffron.

**Sage**  Sage is a powerful herb with an evergreen smell that verges on camphor. This may explain why, historically, it has been paired with bland and fatty foods. Traditionally, it is used in stuffings for fatty fowl like goose and as a flavoring for sausage, eel, and potatoes. Our mostly vegetarian recipes have nudged sage to the back of our spice shelf. However, we resurrect it for holiday squashes dressed with rich wild rice and chestnut stuffings and also use it judiciously in some cheesy sauces and casseroles. Sage, like rosemary, has its ardent friends and foes. Experiment with it—it is not inherently an herb to be spurned by vegetarians. Peoples of the Middle East include fresh sage leaves in their salads and regularly add it to fava beans and other legumes. Fresh sage is superior to dried but is far less available. Dried sage can be found on the supermarket's spice shelf. Choose the dried leaf over powdered sage for a more fragrant herb.

**Sake**  Sake is Japanese rice wine, a beverage and a common ingredient in Japanese cooking. As with any wine, the longer sake is cooked the smoother and sweeter it becomes. Traditionally, sake's sweetness provides a balance in dishes where soy sauce is used. To give dishes an alcoholic bite, add sake at the end of cooking, or add it, uncooked, to dressings, marinades, and sauces.

**Salt, Coarse or Kosher**  Coarse salt's name derives from its large crystals. Because it is processed for cooking rather than for table use, it is a purer and tastier salt, processed without dextrose or the anticaking agents necessary for easy pouring. Available at supermarkets.

**Seitan**  Seitan is the end product of a lengthy process designed to extract the protein-rich gluten from the starch of wheat flour. Pieces of gluten are boiled in water, like dumplings, and then sautéed with soy sauce and ginger. The result is seitan. This chewy, meaty foodstuff can be a dead-ringer for beef in a vegetarian goulash. For instructions on home preparation, refer to *Macrobiotic Cooking* by Aveline Kushi. Seitan can often be found in natural food stores and in Japanese markets, where it might be called wheat gluten.

**Sesame Oil**   Thick, amber-colored, and wonderfully aromatic, this oil is made from roasted sesame seeds. We specify "dark" sesame oil, which is used for flavoring, so it will not be confused with paler cold-pressed sesame oil used for cooking. Dark sesame oil burns easily and loses its distinctive, nutty flavor when overheated. It is available in bottles and cans in natural and Chinese food stores.

**Sesame Paste**   See Tahini, page 682, or Chinese Sesame Paste, page 183.

**Shallots**   In size and voice, shallots appear to be the runt of the onion-garlic family. But in French kitchens, where one listens closely to subtle and delicate sounds, the shallot is an honored and essential guest. Craig Claiborne describes shallots as harboring the best of onions, garlic, and scallions. They have the mildness of spring onions with the bite, creamy texture, and full-bodied flavor of a cooked, whole garlic clove, but without its dominance. In appearance, shallots look like a cross between onion and garlic. Under a red-brown and papery skin, each shallot head is slightly larger than a bulb of garlic, separates into cloves, and looks, inside, like a miniature red onion. Shallots keep well when stored in a cool, dark, uncrowded place where air can circulate around them. A rack within a storage bin is recommended.

**Shiitake Mushrooms**   An unusually flavored Japanese mushroom, sold fresh or dried. Shiitake are expensive—but a very few will richly flavor a dish. To soften the dried mushrooms, submerge them in very hot water and soak for 20 to 30 minutes. After soaking, trim off and discard the stems, slice the caps thinly, and add them to sautés, stews, or soups. The soaking liquid (shiitake dashi) is an excellent addition to stocks or sauces. Dried shiitake mushrooms (and often fresh) are available at many Asian and natural food stores.

**Skillet**   We use the words "skillet" and "frying pan" interchangeably. The best skillets, we think, are cast iron, ceramic-coated cast iron, and stainless steel. The heavier iron cookware has much to recommend it. Foods cook in it more evenly and can cook longer without scorching or sticking. Slow cooking allows flavors to penetrate and marry. Throughout our book we call for small, medium, and large skillets. On page 691 we offer some specific pan sizes for these general categories.

**Smoked Cheeses**   We've recently incorporated smoked cheeses into our repertoire where the hickory flavoring of cured meats are signature ingredients of certain classic dishes and cuisines. Quiche Lorraine would be one example, German potato salad another. We use good-quality smoked cheddar and smoked Swiss cheeses, smoked in a smokehouse without chemicals. Liquid smoke or smoked salt are additives to avoid. Smoked cheeses are available at some natural food stores and at gourmet cheese shops.

**Snow Peas**   Snow peas are essentially edible pods housing embryonic peas. A healthy pod is medium green, translucent, soft, and flexible. Its stem looks like a perky elf's hat.

Avoid snow peas that are yellowing, have a dusty cast, or are cracked and leathery. Snow peas are most closely associated with Asian cooking but do splendidly as a light accompaniment to rich savory strudels and tarts. They add texture, color, and sweetness to marinated vegetable salads and rice salads of all persuasions. To prepare, stringing one seam will usually do. Start at the stem and pull the fibrous "backbone" down the length of the pod. For peas that are crisp, sweet, and colorful, steam, blanch, or stir-fry for no more than a minute or two. Snow peas are available at Asian markets, specialty food stores, and some supermarkets.

**Soba Noodles** Widely known as "Japanese pasta," these noodles are made of either 100 percent buckwheat flour or with varying percentages of buckwheat flour and whole wheat or white flour. Soba are brownish-gray and usually flat and thin. They vary in texture and density depending on the proportion and type(s) of flour used. Soba are traditionally used in broths like Gomoku Soba (see page 390), but they also adapt well to chilled Asian pasta salads. They can be found at Asian food stores and many natural food stores.

**Somen Noodles** A very thin, light, wheat noodle from Japan that is traditionally used in chilled noodle dishes served in summer. Available in most Asian food stores.

**Sorrel** Sorrel is an herb that has received regrettably little acclaim in this country. Its unique lemony taste and tanginess make it an ideal companion for fish. Sorrel's acidity has long been recognized by Europeans as a valuable complement to rich foods. Historically, there is a train of sorrel sauces for fatty meats, poultry, and fish, and it is the star customary flavoring in omelets and certain egg-rich soups as well: see Schav (page 419) and Sorrel Soup (page 482). Sorrel grows easily and abundantly here, but only its small tender leaves are recommended for snipping. French sorrel, a less acidic variety, is advised when using uncooked, as in salads.

**Soy Sauce** See Tamari Soy Sauce.

**Spice Grinder** Whenever possible, we use freshly ground dried herbs and spices. Flavors, freshly released, do more than season a dish, they bring it to life! Here, too, quality affects quantity. A smaller amount of a freshly ground seasoning will go farther than a packaged powder. Spices can be ground with a mortar and pestle, and there still are many cooks who prefer this method. In a restaurant, however, the time and effort required to manually crush large quantities of spices would limit our use of fresh flavorings. We use a spice grinder, a labor-saving device that exceeded our best small-scale personal efforts as well; now most of us have our own grinders at home. And, we were pleased to discover that nuts and seeds can be ground as easily as spices. The gadget we've dubbed a spice grinder is actually a 5- to 6-inch high electric coffee mill, available at department, hardware, and specialty stores. It is priced in the $15 to $30 range. If you already own a coffee mill, another one just for spices is worth the investment, unless you like cayenne in your morning coffee.

**Squash** See Summer Squash and Winter Squash.

**Sriraja Chili Sauce (Sriracha Sauce, Thai Sriracha Sauce)** A Thai condiment made of hot peppers, vinegar, salt, and sugar. Sriraja sauce has the consistency of thin ketchup.

**Star Anise** A strong-flavored, aromatic spice used in Chinese and Southeast Asian cooking. Star anise comes from brown pods in eight-pointed star-shaped clusters. To use, break off "points" (one or two are usually ample) from the whole cluster and tie them in a cheesecloth or place in a teaball to simmer in the cooking food. Chinese five-spice powder, which is sold in Asian food stores, includes star anise and is the only substitute we know for star anise that will impart a similar flavor.

**Steaming** There are specially made steamers, but you can also use a colander in a tightly covered pot of water or a bamboo basket over a wok. The water level should always be below the bottom of the steamer basket or colander to avoid sogginess. Bring the water to a boil, add the food to be steamed, and maintain heat at a medium boil. Vegetables can also be gently steamed in a small amount of water, using a heavy pot with a tight lid. If vegetables are for a chilled or room temperature salad, briefly plunge the cooked vegetables in ice water. This stops their cooking, cools them, and helps to maintain their bright colors.

**Sugar Snap Peas** These sweet wonders come to us by way of an arduous attempt to strengthen snow peas (see page 679) for commercial harvesting. Although peas with edible pods have been documented since the 1600s, sugar snaps, as we know them, hit the market

in 1979, a literal prizewinner in plant breeding circles. If you haven't been introduced, sugar snaps have stubby, crunchy, sweet, edible pods enclosing fat, sweet peas. Uncooked, the peas and their pods are crisp and delicious. When ever-so-lightly steamed or blanched, their color turns a dazzling emerald green and their sweetness is intensified. Before being eaten, sugar snaps must be strung on both seams. Whether this is done before or after cooking depends on the dish, the occasion, and personal preference, but it is necessary because cooking does not degrade the string's obstinate fiber. To store, wrap in plastic and refrigerate.

**Summer Savory** Summer savory is an herb whose flavor is similar to but milder than thyme, and it is often preferable to thyme for just that reason. It is used in stuffings, croutons, stews, soups, and in lentil and other bean dishes. It is available dried in natural food stores and supermarkets.

**Summer Squash** The thin-skinned, light-fleshed, quick-cooking squashes of late summer. When we call for summer squash in our recipes the choice is yours. Varieties that immediately come to mind are: crook-neck, yellow squash, zucchini and golden zucchini, and patty pan. For our purposes here, the only inappropriate summer squash would be the stringy spaghetti squash.

**Sun-Dried Tomatoes** Sun-dried tomatoes, packed dried or in olive oil, add a piquant and concentrated tomato flavor to salads, sandwiches, and pasta dishes. Before using the dry-packed tomatoes, soften them in hot water for 15 to 30 minutes. After soaking, these tomatoes like the ones packed in oil are ready to be diced or cut into thin slices. Save the packing oil or soaking liquid to enliven salad dressings and marinades. If you want to try drying tomatoes at home, see *Rodale's Basic Natural Foods Cookbook,* edited by Gerros, for clear and simple instructions for conventional oven and outdoor drying. Commercial sun-dried tomatoes are available in Italian groceries, gourmet food stores, and some supermarkets.

***Sweet Potato and Yam*** Well, what *is* the difference? Without question these are two distinct vegetables. Sweet potatoes are of the genus *Ipomoea batatas,* yams are *Dioscorea.* In the United States, though, whether these orange tubers are called sweet potatoes or yams, whether they are large or small, short or long, tan-colored or brick-red, all are botanically sweet potatoes. Sweet potato growers divide their crop into two types: dry flesh and moist flesh. The potatoes with the brick-red exterior belong to the moist flesh group and are the ones most often mislabeled yams. True yams are usually white fleshed. They grow only in tropical countries and are available solely through special arrangement with an importer. For a fuller discussion and description of yams, see page 21.

***Szechuan Peppercorns*** Although unrelated to black peppercorns (see page 673), these dried seed pods provide a similarly sharp (but not hot) accent to foods. To prepare, briefly toast the peppercorns in a dry, hot skillet until they begin to smoke. When cool, pulverize them in a spice grinder or peppermill or with a mortar and pestle. Any excess can be stored in a tightly capped jar, but freshly ground peppercorns have a superior aroma and flavor.

***Tahini*** A sesame paste made of hulled and toasted sesame seeds, tahini is beige in color and creamy in texture. Tahini should not be confused with sesame butter, a denser, stronger-tasting product made from roasted and pressed unhulled sesame seeds, or with Chinese sesame paste (see page 183). Tahini is widely used in Middle Eastern cookery and is available in natural food stores, Middle Eastern and Greek groceries, and, increasingly, in the ethnic sections of supermarkets. Refrigerate after opening.

***Tamari Soy Sauce*** Soy sauce is traditionally made with fermented soybeans, wheat, water, and sea salt. The natural foods industry has recently begun labeling their products "tamari soy sauce" to distinguish them from chemically processed soy sauces that often contain sugar, food coloring, and chemical additives. Although the terms "soy sauce" and "tamari" are often used interchangeably, tamari, a by-product of the miso-making process, is an entirely different product. Tamari is the liquid that rises to the top of the miso-making tubs and is then drawn off for use as a condiment. It is stronger in taste and must be used with care as a replacement for soy sauce. It is also wheat-free. Tamari soy sauce and tamari can be found in most Asian and natural food stores.

LIGHT SOY SAUCE is a variety not darkened by the addition of molasses. It is recommended over dark soy sauce for vegetarian and fish dishes. Light soy sauce should not be confused with "lite" or low-sodium soy sauces.

***Tamarind*** For information and preparation directions, see page 290.

**Tapioca**  The slippery tapioca pudding that as a child you either loved or loathed has exotic origins. Tapioca is processed from the cassava or yuca root, a staple vegetable for much of the tropical world. Outside of Hispanic and Asian neighborhoods this root comes to us as tapioca, a starch, in pearled and granulated forms. Pearled tapioca can be used like rice, pasta, or barley in soups, stews, or puddings. When granulated, it has the thickening properties of cornstarch or arrowroot and is so used in sauces and pie fillings. Tapioca will keep indefinitely, unrefrigerated. Look for it in the pudding section of your supermarket.

**Tarragon**  Fresh tarragon has a beguiling licorice taste that stands best on its own. It can literally "make" a vegetable vinaigrette —using the fresh herb or tarragon vinegar —and is a singular sensation with fish and in omelets and piquant sauces. It successfully combines with milder tastes as well, and the French have canonized *fines herbes,* a blend of tarragon, parsley, chives, and chervil. Fresh tarragon can be preserved by freezing. Dried tarragon retains the anise taste of the fresh herb, but it also takes on a musty and hay-like quality. Still, when used in cooking, it imparts a satisfying and somewhat mysterious flavor. Fresh or dried, heat intensifies the taste of tarragon, so use less in cooking. Look for it on the spice shelf of your supermarket.

**Tempeh**  A staple food of Indonesia, tempeh is a cultured whole soybean product, made more digestible by the culturing process. It can also be made of seeds, grains, and other beans. Tempeh is a unique "meaty" product and a good vehicle for strong flavors. When simmered in a tangy tomato sauce, it becomes a terrific barbecued tempeh. Marinate in soy sauce and sauté with spices and you won't miss the corned beef at all in Tempeh Reubens. If you're lucky, you'll find fresh tempeh, if not, it is available frozen in packaged squares or rectangles in most natural food stores. Thaw it before using, but slice or cube it when it is partially thawed to avoid the crumbling that sometimes occurs when cutting fully thawed tempeh.

**Thyme**  An assertive, aromatic herb that gives food depth and bouquet when judiciously used. Thyme has not always been a seasoning herb, or even primarily so. History records its cultivation for decorative, ceremonial aromatic, antiseptic, and medicinal purposes. The Egyptians embalmed with it; the Greeks bathed in it and burned it in their temples. Thyme, with rosemary and lavender, were the environmental perfumes of the Renaissance. Today, thyme is used in cough syrups. And, for centuries, it has been a charming and fragrant border plant and ground cover. Nonetheless, thyme's popularity as a flavoring herb is impressive. Along with bay and parsley, it is the third member of the trio composing classic bouquet garni. Thus, thyme is present in the legion of dishes that use this bouquet as a backdrop. Fresh thyme's gray-green leaves smell resinous and sweet and have a bright, sharp taste. Dried, it loses some of its fragrance and gains pungency. Fresh thyme is becoming increasingly available in food stores, and it is easy to grow. Dried thyme is available in the spice section of the supermarket. Choose leaf over powdered for a more fragrant and fresher herb.

**Tofu**  Tofu is a fresh soybean curd, a highly versatile and protein-rich food that has been a staple of Chinese and Japanese cooking for centuries. It is white, has the consistency of a firm custard, and is pressed into cakes. Plain tofu tastes bland, but it absorbs flavors readily. Smooth and soft-textured, it can be simmered, blanched, steamed, marinated, fried, deep-fried, baked, mashed, or puréed.

Tofu provides complete protein and is a source of iron, phosphorus, potassium, and other minerals and vitamins. Because of the solidifiers used in making it, tofu has 23 percent more calcium by weight than milk. It is low in calories (147 per 8 ounces) and unsaturated fats.

Commercial cakes of tofu vary in size and firmness, making it difficult to describe exact amounts used in recipes, but generally smaller cakes of tofu are also firmer and so about equivalent to the larger, softer cakes. We use 12-ounce cakes of medium-soft tofu.

TO PRESS TOFU Most recipes call for pressed tofu because pressing makes the tofu firmer and more absorbent. To press tofu, place the cakes of tofu between two flat plates or baking sheets. Weight the top with a bowl of water, a stack of plates, a heavy can, or whatever is handy. The sides of the cakes of tofu should bulge out a little but not split. Let stand for at least 30 minutes, remove the press, and pour off the water.

TO BLANCH TOFU When using tofu uncooked (marinated, mashed, puréed), blanch it after pressing and before continuing with the recipe. To blanch tofu, drop whole cakes or cubes of tofu into boiling water. Simmer for no more than 5 minutes, remove, and drain. Blanching firms tofu, makes it less likely to dilute a soup, stew, or sauce, and makes it more absorbent and digestible.

TO FREEZE TOFU The texture of tofu becomes chewy and sponge-like when frozen and thawed. In this form, it adds textural variety and high protein, lowfat bulk to casseroles and pastry and vegetable fillings.

Place the cakes of tofu on a tray or plate in the freezer, either uncovered or lightly covered with plastic wrap. In a couple of hours the tofu will be solidly frozen. Since frozen tofu keeps almost indefinitely, you may wish to always keep a couple of frozen blocks on hand. Thaw the tofu for about 24 hours in the refrigerator or for seven to eight hours at room temperature. The thawed tofu blocks resemble sponges. Gently squeeze the water out. Then, either grate the tofu by hand or in a food processor, or chop it finely with a knife. Tofu can also be hand crumbled. If using this method, work the tofu until it resembles bread crumbs. Larger pieces can be too chewy.

Tofu is available in Asian and natural food stores and most supermarkets. Submerged in frequently changed water and refrigerated, tofu will keep for about a week.

**Turmeric** Turmeric is a powdered spice derived from the rhizome of a plant in the ginger family. It imparts a golden color and mild, slightly musty flavor primarily to Indian and Middle Eastern cooking. It is quite inexpensive and sometimes substituted for saffron. However, besides similarly coloring the foods they season, the spices taste very different and are really not interchangeable.

**Turnip** A beet-shaped, white root vegetable that shades into purple toward its crown. Thinly sliced or grated, raw turnips are pleasantly pungent. They take to pickling and make a refreshing addition to salads and slaws. Cooked turnips can taste juicy, sweet, and mildly earthy or so strong that they dominate the pot. Young, very small turnips are the better choice, since as the vegetable matures, it is hit-or-miss as to its intensity and bitterness. But turnips, like beets, are a personal affair. To many, a strong turnip taste is the source of its majesty.

**Udon Noodles**  Wide, hearty wheat noodles. The Japanese serve udon in a broth similar to the Gomoku Soba broth (see page 390) or in winter hot pot cooking. Available in Japanese and natural food stores.

**Vegetable Oil**  We use light, "tasteless," polyunsaturated vegetable oils with no preservatives, generally soy and safflower oils.

**Vegetable Stock**  A broth made by simmering vegetables in water until they are soft and their flavors and nutrients have been released into the liquid.

The best vegetables to use in stock are carrots, peeled onions, celery, zucchini, potatoes, parsley, parsnips, sweet potatoes, and squash. We often throw in chunks of apples or pears to sweeten the stock a little. Do not include the strongly flavored vegetables of the cabbage family—broccoli, cauliflower, turnips, rutabagas, and kohlrabi—or those with bleeding colors—beets, red cabbage, and greens (unless you intend to make a borscht or cream of green soup). Green peppers and eggplant will make the stock bitter. Be cautious about adding lots of tomatoes or other acidic fruits or vegetables to the stock, because they may curdle the soup if milk or other dairy products are to be added afterward.

Wash the vegetables thoroughly, especially root vegetables. Making stock is the perfect solution for vegetables that are too unattrac-

tive to be used in other ways. Leftover carrot sticks, parsley stems, and unused halves of onion can all be tossed into the pot.

FOR 2 QUARTS OF VEGETABLE STOCK:  Put the following ingredients into a large pot, bring to a boil, and simmer, covered, for 45 minutes to an hour. Strain.

> 2 large unpeeled potatoes, quartered
> 2 large carrots, peeled and thickly sliced
> 1 large onion, peeled and quartered
> 1 celery stalk, chopped
> 1 apple or pear, seeded and chopped
> 1 bay leaf
> 12 peppercorns
> 10 cups water (2½ quarts)

For a more assertive stock, throw in some garlic cloves, skins and all, and a small amount of tomato. To add Asian flavors, include ginger, scallions, and shiitake mushrooms. Or, make it sweet for a carrot purée or hot fruit soup with the addition of sweet potato or winter squash.

**Wasabi**  A green Japanese radish with the assertive flavor and sinus-clearing effect you may have enjoyed in sushi.

DRIED WASABI is a powder that is usually packed in small tins. It can be found in Japanese and other Asian food stores and often in the Asian section of supermarkets. Mix the powder with water to form a smooth paste, cover it, and set it aside for a few minutes so that the taste fully develops. Some Asian stores have also begun to carry premixed wasabi paste. Wasabi is very pungent (hot!) and should be used sparingly, but it adds a wonderful bite to Spinach Nori Rolls (see page 401) and is an interesting addition to soy sauce and dipping sauces.

*FRESH WASABI* popularly known as Japanese horseradish, should not be confused with domestic horseradish. Wasabi is grown underwater, can reach a length of 6 inches, and is bright green inside. Its availability is currently limited to Japanese food stores in import meccas like New York City, Boston, and San Francisco.

**Watercress** Watercress looks a bit like parsley and a bit like clover. It grows wild in water and at times in stunning profusion, near clear brooks, streams, and rivers. Watercress is reportedly cultivated by some thirty farmers in the United States, who make it available in many supermarkets as well as at quality produce stands. The charm of watercress is in its multitalent as a nutritious food and flavorer. At its best, it is refreshing, nourishing, and has a peppery bite. Watercress is delightful in salads, soups, and sandwiches. To store watercress, immerse its stems in water and loosely cover the greens with a plastic bag.

**Winter Squash** If not specified in a recipe, a call for winter squash can include any one of the exotically colored and shaped edible gourds of autumn. Despite their widely diverse exteriors, the rinds of winter squash are consistently thick and their flesh pulpy and orange. Properly stored under cool, dark, and dry conditions, winter squash will last through most of the winter. Varieties include: butternut, buttercup, acorn, turban, and delicata. Small pumpkins, although botanically summer squashes, may also be used. Avoid the large, tasteless jack-o'-lanterns.

**Wok** A steel skillet with rounded sides used primarily in Asian cooking. Its contour and thin walls allow a large surface area to heat quickly, evenly, and intensely. This enables rapid yet thorough "stir-frying," a method that maintains the color and integrity of the food beautifully. Woks can be found in the housewares section of most department stores.

**Wonton Wrappers** Chinese cooks use these thin sheets of egg dough to envelope a variety of fillings; often they are made into dumplings that are either boiled or fried. Wonton wrappers are sold frozen, or vacuum-packed and refrigerated. Once opened or thawed, rewrap tightly and refrigerate to prevent them from drying out and becoming brittle. They will keep for 3 or 4 days under refrigeration. Available at Chinese markets and in some supermarkets that carry Asian foods.

**Worcestershire Sauce** The sauce that gives that "je ne sais quoi" to so many soups, stews, and marinades. This commercially prepared condiment was formulated by Victorian chemists Lea and Perrins under the direction of one of their patrons, an ex-Bengal governor. Displeased with the sauce, the governor abandoned it to the pharmacists who rediscovered it after it had "aged" for quite a while in the cellar of their Worcester store. The rest, as they say, is history. The formula remains a well-guarded secret, but we do know the Lea and Perrins product contains molasses, anchovies or sardines, sugar, garlic, tamarind, soy sauce, vinegar, and spices. Other condiment makers are also marketing Worcestershires, but a few include artificial flavorings and preservatives. There are some vegetarian adaptations, among them

Life brand, from Britain, which is additive-free (not all are).

*Yams*   See Sweet Potato.

*Yogurt*   The combination of milk's availability, perishability, and high food value has motivated societies for centuries to create palatable fermented milk products. The modern·"scientific" discovery that "souring" milk enhances its digestibility reinforces the endurance of soured milk products across cultures and through the ages. Yogurt made its first appearance as the soured milk of Central Asia and spread westward to the Balkans.

Our recipes call for unflavored or plain yogurt that can be purchased at most supermarkets. If you can find it, try Brown Cow Farm Yogurt. Unlike many other brands that add extra dried milk, stabilizers, and thickeners, Brown Cow is made only from milk—whole or lowfat—and yogurt cultures. The taste is fresh, not too tart, pleasantly rich, and uncomplicated. There are other such brands available, often regionally, that are worth seeking out.

# What We Mean When We Say, "One Medium Onion . . ."

| ITEM | AMOUNT, RAW & PREPARED | APPROXIMATE WEIGHT |
|---|---|---|
| **Vegetables and Fruit** | | |
| Apple (1 medium) | 1 cup, chopped | 4 ounces |
| Avocado (1 medium) | 1 cup, mashed | 8 ounces |
| Broccoli (1 stalk) | 2 cups florets | 6 ounces |
| Cabbage (1 large) | 10 cups, minced | 1 pound, 12 ounces |
| Carrots (2 medium) | 1 cup, diced | 8 ounces |
| Cauliflower (1 medium) | 2½ cups florets | 1 pound |
| Celery (3 stalks) | 1 cup, diced | 8 ounces |
| Eggplant (1 medium) | 4 cups, cubed | 14 ounces |
| Green beans | 1 cup | 5 ounces |
| Green peas, shelled | 1 cup | 5 ounces |
| Green peas, unshelled (1 pound) | 1 cup shelled | |
| Green pepper (1 medium) | ¾ cup; diced | 4½ ounces |
| Leek (1 medium) | ¾ cup, diced | 3 ounces |
| Lemon (1 medium) | 2 tablespoons juice 1 tablespoon grated peel | |
| Mushrooms | 1 cup, sliced | 3–4 ounces |
| Onion (1 medium) | 1 cup, diced | 4 ounces |
| Orange (1 medium) | ½ cup juice 2 tablespoons grated peel | |

| | | |
|---|---|---|
| Parsley (1 bunch) | 3½ cups, chopped | 4 ounces |
| Potato (1 medium) | 2 cups, diced | 8 ounces |
| | 1¼ cups, mashed | 8 ounces |
| Spinach (fresh) | 12 cups, loosely packed | 10 ounces |
| | 1 cup, cooked | 10 ounces (raw) |
| Tomato (1 medium) | ¾ cup, diced | 4½ ounces |
| Canned tomatoes | 3 cups with juice | 28-ounce can |
| | 1½ cups drained | 28-ounce can |
| Winter squash (1 medium) | 4 cups, cubed | 1 pound, 4 ounces |
| Zucchini (1 medium) | 2 cups, diced | 10 ounces |

## Cheeses (grated)

| | | |
|---|---|---|
| Bleu | 1 cup | 2 ounces |
| Cheddar | 1 cup | 3 ounces |
| Feta | 1 cup | 5 ounces |
| Gorgonzola | 1 cup | 2 ounces |
| Monterey Jack | 1 cup | 3 ounces |
| Mozzarella | 1 cup | 4 ounces |
| Muenster | 1 cup | 3 ounces |
| Parmesan | 1 cup | 3 ounces |
| Provolone | 1 cup | 4 ounces |
| Swiss or Jarlsberg | 1 cup | 3½–4 ounces |

## Nuts (whole)

| | | |
|---|---|---|
| Almonds | 1 cup | 8 ounces |
| Cashews | 1 cup | 6 ounces |
| Walnuts | 1 cup | 6 ounces |

## Sprouts

| | | |
|---|---|---|
| Alfalfa | 1 cup | ¾ ounce |
| Mung bean | 1 cup | 2 ounces |

## Other

| | | |
|---|---|---|
| Currants (dried) | 1 cup | 5 ounces |
| Raisins | 1 cup | 6 ounces |
| Tofu (1 cake) | 2 cups, ¼-inch cubes | 12 ounces |

## Utensils

Skillets:

| | |
|---|---|
| small | 6 inches |
| medium | 9 inches |
| large | 12 inches |

Saucepan:

| | |
|---|---|
| small to medium | 2 quarts |
| large | 3 quarts |
| Soup pot or kettle | 4 quarts |
| Dutch oven | 6 quarts |

# *Suggested Reading List*

# *— if you want to know*

# *more . . .*

## *Vegetarian Cookbooks*

*The Moosewood Cookbook,* Mollie Katzen. Ten Speed Press, Berkeley, 1977.
*New Recipes from Moosewood Restaurant,* The Moosewood Collective. Ten Speed Press, Berkeley, 1987.
*The Vegetarian Epicure,* Anna Thomas. Alfred A. Knopf, New York, 1972.

## *Africa South of the Sahara*

*The Africa News Cookbook,* African News Service Inc., ed. Tammi Hultman. Penguin Books, New York, 1986.

# Armenia and the Middle East

*The Best Foods of Russia,* Sonia Uvezian. Harcourt Brace Jovanovich, New York, 1976.

*The Best of Baghdad Cooking,* Daisy Iny. Saturday Review Press/E. P. Dutton, Inc., New York, 1976.

*A Book of Middle Eastern Food,* Claudia Roden. Alfred A. Knopf, New York, 1974.

*Armenia, Cradle of Civilization,* David Marshall Lang. George Allen & Unwin, London, Third Edition (corrected), 1980.

# The Caribbean

*Caribbean Cookbook,* Rita G. Springer. Evans Brothers Ltd., London, 1968.

*Caribbean Cookbook, Using the Foods We Grow,* Lisa Miller. Kingston Publishers Ltd., 1979.

*Caribbean Fruits and Vegetables,* Beryl Wood. Longman Caribbean Ltd., Trinidad, 1973.

*The Complete Book of Caribbean Cooking,* Elisabeth Lambert Ortiz. Ballantine Books, New York, 1973.

*A Merry Go Round of Recipes from Jamaica,* Leila Brandon. Golding Printing Service Ltd., Kingston, Jamaica W.I., 1963.

# China

*Asian Vegetarian Feast,* Ken Hom. William Morrow and Co., New York, 1988.

*Chinese Meatless Cooking,* Stella Lau Fessler. New American Library, New York, 1980.

*Classic Chinese Cooking for the Vegetarian Gourmet,* Joanne Hush. Smallwood and Stewart, New York, 1984.

# Finland

*Classic Scandinavian Cooking,* Nika Standen Hazelton. Scribner, New York, 1987.

*The Cooking of Scandinavia,* Dale Brown. Time-Life Books, New York, 1968.

*The Finnish Cookbook,* Beatrice Ojakangas. Crown Publishers, Inc., New York, 1964.

*The Great Scandinavian Baking Book,* Beatrice Ojakangas. Little, Brown and Company, Boston, 1988.

*Natural Cooking the Finnish Way,* Ulla Kakonen. Quadrangle, New York, 1974.

## *India*

*Classic Indian Cooking,* Julie Sahni. William Morrow and Co., New York, 1980.

*The Cooking of India,* Santha Rama Rau and the editors of Time-Life Books. Time-Life Books, New York, 1969.

*Classic Indian Vegetarian and Grain Cooking,* Julie Sahni, William Morrow and Co., New York, 1985.

*Indian Vegetarian Cookbook,* Tarla Dalal. St. Martin's Press, New York, 1983.

*Lord Krishna's Cuisine—The Art of Indian Vegetarian Cooking,* Yamuna Devi. E. P. Dutton, New York, 1987.

*A Taste of India,* Mary S. Atwood. Houghton Mifflin Co., Boston, 1969.

## *Italy*

*The Authentic Pasta Book,* Fred Plotkin. A Fireside Book, Simon and Schuster, New York, 1985.

*Classic Italian Cookbook,* Marcella Hazan. Alfred A. Knopf, New York, 1978.

*The Cooking of Italy,* Waverly Lewis Root. 1. Time-Life Books, New York, 1972; 2. Time-Life Books, New York, 1968.

*The Food of Southern Italy,* Carlo Middione. William Morrow and Co., New York, 1987.

*Honey from a Weed,* Patience Gray. Harper & Row/Prospect, New York, 1987.

*Modern Italian Cooking,* Biba Caggiano. Simon and Schuster, New York, 1987.

*Sunset Italian Cookbook,* editors of Sunset Books and Sunset Magazine. Lane Publishing Co., Menlo Park, California, 1981.

*The Tuscan Year,* Elizabeth Romer. Atheneum, New York, 1985.

## *Jewish*

*The Jewish Holiday Cookbook: An International Collection of Recipes and Customs,* Gloria Kaufer Greene. Times Books/Random House, New York, 1985.

## *New England*

*Native Harvests,* Barrie Kavasch, Vintage Books, New York, 1979.

# Provence

*The Complete Book of Pastry*, Bernard Clayton, Jr. Simon and Schuster, New York, 1981.

*The Cooking of Provincial France*, M. F. K. Fisher. Vintage Books, New York, 1983.

*The Cuisine of the Sun: Classical French Cooking from Nice & Provence*, Mireille Johnston. Random House, New York, 1979.

*Lyrics of the Troubadours & Trouveves*, Frederick Goldin. Anchor Books, Garden City, N.J., 1973.

*A Mediterranean Harvest*, Paola Scaravelli and John Cohen. E. P. Dutton, Inc., New York, 1986.

*Sun-Drenched Cuisine*, Marlena Speiler. J. P. Tarcher, Los Angeles, 1986.

*Two Towns in Provence*, M. F. K. Fisher. Vintage Books, New York, 1983.

# Southeast Asia

*The Best of Thai Cooking*, Chalie Amatyakul. Travel Publishing Asia Ltd., Hong Kong, 1987.

*Bruce Cost's Asian Ingredients: Buying and Cooking the Staple Foods of China, Japan and Southeast Asia*, Bruce Cost. William Morrow and Co., New York, 1988.

*The Complete Thai Cookbook*, Jennifer Brennan. Richard Marek, New York, 1981.

*Joys and Subtleties of Southeast Asian Cooking*, Rosemary Brissenden. Pantheon, New York, 1970.

*Pacific and Southeast Asian Cooking*, Rafael Steinberg. Time-Life Books, New York, 1970.

# Southern United States

*Chef Paul Prudhomme's Louisiana Kitchen*, Paul Prudhomme. William Morrow and Co., New York, 1984.

*Craig Claiborne's Southern Cooking*, Craig Claiborne. Times Books, a division of Random House, New York, 1987.

*The Prudhomme Family Cookbook—Old-Time Louisiana Recipes*, The eleven Prudhomme brothers and sisters. William Morrow and Co., New York, 1987.

# Guide to Ingredients, Techniques, and Equipment

*Bruce Cost's Asian Ingredients,* Bruce Cost. William Morrow and Co., New York, 1988.

*Cooking with Herbs,* Susan Belsinger and Carolyn Dille. Van Nostrand Reinhold Co., New York, 1984.

*The Cook's Encyclopedia,* Tom Stobart, ed. by Millie Owen. Harper & Row, New York, 1980.

*The International Wine and Food Society's Guide to Herbs, Spices and Flavorings,* Tom Stobart. McGraw-Hill Book Co., New York, 1970.

*The New York Times Food Encyclopedia,* Craig Claiborne, compiled by Joan Whitman. New York Times Co., New York, 1985.

*Uncommon Fruits and Vegetables: A Commonsense Guide,* Elizabeth Schneider. Harper & Row, New York, 1986.

## LIQUID AND DRY MEASURE EQUIVALENCIES

| Customary | Metric |
|---|---|
| ¼ teaspoon | 1.25 milliliters |
| ½ teaspoon | 2.5 milliliters |
| 1 teaspoon | 5 milliliters |
| 1 tablespoon | 15 milliliters |
| 1 fluid ounce | 30 milliliters |
| ¼ cup | 60 milliliters |
| ⅓ cup | 80 milliliters |
| ½ cup | 120 milliliters |
| 1 cup | 240 milliliters |
| 1 pint (2 cups) | 480 milliliters |
| 1 quart (4 cups, 32 ounces) | 960 milliliters (.96 liters) |
| 1 gallon (4 quarts) | 3.84 liters |
| | |
| 1 ounce (by weight) | 28 grams |
| ¼ pound (4 ounces) | 114 grams |
| 1 pound (16 ounces) | 454 grams |
| 2.2 pounds | 1 kilogram (100 grams) |

## OVEN TEMPERATURE EQUIVALENCIES

| Description | °Fahrenheit | °Celsius |
|---|---|---|
| Cool | 200 | 90 |
| Very slow | 250 | 120 |
| Slow | 300-325 | 150-160 |
| Moderately slow | 325-350 | 160-180 |
| Moderate | 350-375 | 180-190 |
| Moderately hot | 375-400 | 190-200 |
| Hot | 400-450 | 200-230 |
| Very hot | 450-500 | 230-260 |

# Index

Abidjan cabbage salad, 36
achiote seed (annatto), 650
acorn squash and spinach soup, Indonesian, 579–80
African cuisines, *see* North African cuisine; Southern
    Africa, cuisine of; sub-Saharan Africa, cuisine of;
    West African cuisine
ail braisé, 541
Albanian walnut cake with lemon glaze, 232–33
allspice, 650
almond(s):
    apricot bread, Slovenian, 237
    blanching, 374
    cookies, 199
    in creamy layered pastry, 527–28
    crescents, Ukrainian, 231–32
    flounder rolls with tomatoes, cilantro and, 466
    in frangipane, 561, 562
    in marzipan cake, 563
    meringue cookies, 373–74
    rusks, 45
    shortbread, 85
    torte, 472–73
almond paste, 650
amaretti, 373–74
Americas:
    menus based on foods of, 644, 645
    *see also* Chilean cuisine; Mexican cuisine; New
    England cuisine; Southern United States, cuisine
    of
anise rusks, 45
annatto (achiote seed), 650
Annie Wade's sweet potato soufflé, 628
antipasto, 331
    baked eggplant sandwiches, 339–40
    bread and tomato salad, 341
    marinated tomato salad, 340
    mushrooms roasted with pine nuts, 337
    polenta gnocchi with Gorgonzola, 347–48
    rosemary focaccia, 335–36
    Sicilian eggplant relish, 333–34
    stuffed artichokes, 338
    tomato and mozzarella, 341
    tomato crostini, 342
appetizers and first courses:
    baked eggplant sandwiches, 339–40
    baked paneer, 309
    baked tofu variations, 187–88
    black bean ful, 64–65

blue cheese balls, 257
Bosnian "meatballs" in yogurt sauce, 216–17
bread and tomato salad, 341–42
chick pea crêpe, 537
crespelle, 353–54
crisp cooked vegetable, 513
Davina's fish koklaten, 429–30
eggplant "coucharas," 443–44
ensalada Olimpica, 146
Fatima's salad, 511
in France, 536
garlic-olive-caper spread, 539
hard-boiled eggs, Sephardic style, 441–42
herbed chèvre spread, 542
marinated tomato salad, 340
mezze or maza, 57–60
mushrooms roasted with pine nuts, 337
North African pizza, 524–25
polenta gnocchi with Gorgonzola, 347–48
puréed white bean dip, 63
risotto, 350–51
roasted chile and tomato relish, 61
roasted or grilled vegetables, 538–39
rosemary focaccia, 335–36
savory pastries (sambussa), 512–13
sesame noodles, 183
Sicilian eggplant relish, 333–34
spinach nori rolls, 401–2
spinach soufflé, 442–43
stuffed artichokes, 338
stuffed eggs with mushrooms, 147
stuffed tomatoes (Chilean), 148
stuffed tomatoes (Provençal), 540
tomato and mozzarella antipasto, 341
tomato crostini, 342
vegetable pancakes, 185
vegetable pâté, 258
whole braised garlic, 541
wontons, 179–80
zucchini-tofu koftas, 310
*see also* pasta; salads; soups
apple(s):
    brown betty, 113
    cake, 279
    and carrot confetti, Czechoslovakian, 230
    coconut smoothie, 129
    grated turnip and, salad, 266
    in Huguenot torte, 636

in red pottage, 106
soaking, 652
soup, creamy Hungarian, 211–12
soy, simmered with vegetables and seaweed,
    404
and vegetable soup, Egyptian, 516
in vegetarian Brunswick stew, 621–22
white, and garlic soup, 544–45
white, dip, 63
*see also* chick pea(s); lentil(s)
bean thread, marinated vegetables and, 184–
    185
beer:
    as breakfast beverage in Great Britain, 95
    in Southeast Asia, 572
beet(s):
    and carrots in lime vinaigrette, 461
    in Fatima's salad, 511
    gingered, 433–34
    and horseradish salad, 265
    in Russian salad, 263
berbere, 509, 653
besan flour (chick pea flour), 657
beurek with parsley-cheese filling, 74–75
beverages:
    breakfast, in Great Britain, 95
    classic rum punch, 128
    ginger soft drink, 47
    hot spiced wine, 167
    in Japan, 381
    Mexican hot chocolate, 473
    in Southeast Asia, 572
    spiced tea, 321
    syllabub, 111
    tail of the monkey, 166–67
    tea, 95–96, 572
    Turkish coffee, 445
    Zemi's ginger smoothies, 129
bimuelos, 440–41
biryani, vegetable, 306–7
biscuits:
    buttermilk, 633–34
    cornmeal, 634
    pecan, 634
    red pepper—cheese, 634
    rusks, 44–45
    scones, 98
    shortcake, 634
    wheat germ, 634

bisque:
    corn, 484
    pimiento-cheese, 617
black bean:
    fermented, 186
    ful, 64–65
    tostada, 463–64
black bread, 238–39
black-eyed peas:
    in hoppin' John, 620
    and rice with tempeh, West Indian, 132–33
    in vegetarian Brunswick stew, 621–22
black mustard, 288
blanching, 653–54
    almonds, 374
    tofu, 684
blintz(es), 423–24
    cheese, puff, 425–26
blueberry:
    tart, summer, 560–61
    yogurt pie, 276–77
blue cheese balls, 257
bobka, Regina's, 437–38
bobotie, tofu, 32–33
bok choy, 657
borscht, sorrel, 419–20
Bosanske čufte, 216–17
Bosnian "meatballs" in yogurt sauce, 216–
    217
bouillabaisse with rouille, 548–49
bouquet garni, 654
Brazilian cuisine, 19
bread:
    in Finland, 248–49
    and tomato salad, 341–42
bread crumbs, 654
breads, quick:
    Christmas, 161
    coconut, 121
    oat bran muffins, 255
    roti, 130
    rusks, 44–45
    Sayra's cornbread, 635
    scones, 98
    Slovenian almond-apricot, 237
    sweet potato, 302–3
    Vermont summer muffins, 492
    Yellowman's banana-lime, 123–24
    *see also* biscuits

chilled:
avocado-tomato soup, 457
somen noodles with spicy dipping sauce, 393–94
Chinese cabbage, 657–58
in mizutaki, 386–87
in noodles and vegetables in flavorful broth, 390–91
Chinese cuisine, 169–99
almond cookies, 199
baked tofu variations, 187–88
basic elements of, 173–74
batter-fried fish with garlic sauce, 193–94
Buddha's garden, 196–97
dipping sauce, 181
duck sauce, 180
five-spice tofu, 189
ginger ice cream, 198–99
hot pepper green beans, 186
mandarin pancakes, 191–92
marinated vegetables and bean thread, 184–85
menu planning in, 174–75
methods and techniques of, 175–77
mu shu vegetables, 190–91
regional differences in, 172–73
seasoned chili oil, 197
sequence of dishes in, 175
sesame noodles, 183
spinach and leek soup, 182
stuffed tofu, 194–95
suggested reading on, 694
tamari roasted nuts, 198
vegetable pancakes, 185
vegetables emphasized in, 173
vegetable stock, 178
wontons, 179–80
wonton soup, 181
Chinese ginger, 666
Chinese mustard, 669
Chinese parsley, see cilantro
Chinese strainers or skimmers, 658
chocolate:
Mexican hot, 473
in ruggelach, 434–35
chopsticks, 572
Christmas bread, 161
chutneys, 658
banana, 43
coconut-cilantro, 307
shallot, 607
tomato-apricot, 317

cilantro, 289, 658
coconut chutney, 307
flounder rolls with tomatoes, almonds and, 466
cilantro root, 658–59
cinnamon, 289, 659
cookies, 475
clarified butter, 659
Indian-style, 294–95
spiced, 510
cloud ears, 190
cloves, 289, 659
cobblers:
best peach, 638–39
peach melba, 639
cocola salad, 618–19
coconut:
apple smoothie, 129
bread, quick, 121
cilantro chutney, 307
grated, 659
orange-pineapple smoothie, 129
coconut milk, 660
homemade, 660
mung beans in, Philippine, 587
Thai fish soup with, 578
coffee:
in Southeast Asia, 572
in tail of the monkey, 166–67
Turkish, 445
coffeetable, in Finland, 252–53
cola de mono, 166–67
colombo de giromon, 131
condiments:
banana chutney, 43
berbere, 509
caviar and grated daikon, 396
coconut-cilantro chutney, 307
fiery Indonesian spice paste, 604–5
fiery onion relish, 313
garam masala, 293–94
homemade Southern seafood seasoning, 628–29
hot pepper vinegar, 629
minted cucumber-yogurt refresher, 42
pebre, 158–59
roasted chile and tomato relish, 61
sambal kechap, 606
seasoned chili oil, 197
shallot chutney, 607
Sicilian eggplant relish, 333

cumin, 289–90, 661
currants, 661
curry(ied):
    avocado soup, 120–21
    Capetown fruit and vegetable, 31–32
    eggplant, red pepper, and spinach, 303–4
    Indonesian egg or tofu, 584–85
    vegetables, 131
curry powder, 661–62
custard, light vegetable-seafood, 407
custards, sweet, 112
    caramel, 474–75
    in creamy layered pastry, 527–28
    frangipane, 561, 562
    milk, 164
    in South African milk tart, 46–47
cutting techniques, Chinese, 175
Czechoslovakian cuisine, 207–8
    apple and carrot confetti, 230

daikon, 662
    grated, caviar and, 396
    pickled, 409–10
dal, 314–15
dashi, 380–81, 391–92, 662
    konbu, 385
    shiitake, 385
date(s), 662–63
    cake, Moroccan, 529
    stuffed figs and, 445
Davina's fish koklaten, 429–30
day lily buds, 190
deep-frying, 40
desserts:
    almond shortbread, 85
    almond torte, 472–73
    apple brown betty, 113
    apple kuchen, 165
    best peach cobbler, 638–39
    bimuelos, 440–41
    blueberry-yogurt pie, 276–77
    caramel custard, 474–75
    cheese and nut balls, 320
    Christmas bread, 161
    creamy layered pastry, 527–28
    crème fraîche, 562–63
    double pear crisp, 495–96
    dried fruit pudding, 278

easy cheese blintz puff, 425–26
fig and apricot conserve, 88
in France, 558
fruit and cheese, 371–72, 558
ginger ice cream, 198–99
halvah shortbread, 84–85
hamantaschen, 435–37
Huguenot torte, 636
in Italy, 331, 371–72
leche flan, 608–9
lime tart, 134–35
Macedonian pear and fig strudel, 234–35
mango with yogurt, 319–20
in Mexico, 472
milk custard, 164
mocha-pecan pie, 637
paklava, 86–87
peach melba cobbler, 639
pear pastries, 162–63
poached peaches with raspberry sauce, 559
proper trifle, 112
Regina's bobka, 437–38
ruggelach, 434–35
sorbet Caribe, 133
South African milk tart, 46–47
squash and cottage cheese pie, 497
stuffed figs and dates, 445
summer blueberry tart, 560–61
Ukrainian almond crescents, 231–32
winter pear tart frangipane, 561–62
see also cakes, sweet; cookies
diagonal slicing, 175
dicing, 175
Dijon mustard, 669
dill, 663
dip, puréed white bean, 63
dipping sauces, 181, 388, 389, 401–2
    pungent, 387
    spicy, 393
dolce, 331, 371–72
    almond meringue cookies, 373–74
    baked stuffed peaches, 375
dolma, 72–74
domaca gibanica, 219–20
domatene supa, 212–14
double pear crisp, 495–96
dressings:
    classic vinaigrette, 557

focaccia, rosemary (focaccia al rosmarino), 335–36
folding in, 664–65
forcemeat, tomatoes with, 99–100
frangipane, winter pear tart with, 561–62
French cuisine, *see* Provençal cuisine
fried:
    batilgian, 80
    batter-, fish with garlic sauce, 193–94
    fish, Southeast Asian style, 595
    green tomatoes, 626
    rice, Thai style, 581–82
    sweet potatoes or plantains, 41
    tofu with cucumbers and sprouts, Indonesian, 591–
        592
fritada:
    eggplant, 444
    de espinaca, 442–43
fruit:
    and cheese, as last course, 371–72, 558
    dried, 663
    dried, pudding, 278
    fresh, salad with a difference, 597–98
    and vegetable curry, Capetown, 31–32
    weights and measures of, 689–90
    *see also specific fruits*
ful:
    black bean, 64–65
    nabed, 516
funghi arrosti con pignoli, 337
fusilli estevi, 364

galanga, 666
galingale, 666
galletas de nueces, 163
gamberetti in aglio e vino, 369
garam masala, 293–94
garlic, 665
    dressing, 184
    feta dressing, 68
    olive-caper spread, 539
    sauce, 193, 194
    soup, 144
    and white bean soup, 544–45
    whole braised, 541
    wine sauce, shrimp in, 369
garnishes:
    stuffed figs and dates, 445
    tamari roasted nuts, 198

gâteaux:
    d'amandes, 563
    de pommes de terre, 555–56
gazpacho a la Guadalajara, 457
gelato, 371
ghee, 294–95, 659
ginger(ed), 290, 665–66
    beets, 433–34
    Chinese, Siamese, or Thai, 666
    crystallized, 198
    ice cream, 198–99
    smoothies, Zemi's, 129
    soft drink, 47
glazed onions, 274–75
glazes:
    for bread, 236, 251, 253
    lemon, 233
    for pie, 270
gluten, 196, 654
gnocchi, polenta, with Gorgonzola, 347–48
gombo, 37
gomoku:
    soba, 390–91
    soy beans, 404
Gorgonzola:
    polenta gnocchi with, 347–48
    sauce, creamy, fettuccini with, 368
grains:
    barley, 651
    barley, in Mother Wolff soup, 420–21
    bulghur, in little balls, 62–63
    bulghur pilav, 82–83
    cheese grits, 632
    couscous, 660–61
    millet, 668
    millet, steamed, 34–35
    *see also* brown rice; corn; cornmeal; rice
grated turnip and apple salad, 266
gravy, mushroom, 103, 104
green bean(s):
    in Fall River vegetable stew, 488
    hot pepper, 186
    in kettle stew, 465
    in Moroccan stew, 519
    in salade niçoise, 550–51
    saucy, 489
    Sephardic, 432–33
    simmered squash and, 402

spicy, 470
in spicy mixed vegetable stew, 523
in stewed batilgian, 79
and tomato salad, 159
in vegetable paté, 258
greens:
adobo, 596
Sayra's, 627
*see also* spinach
green tomatoes, fried, 626
grilled vegetables, 538–39
grinders, for spices, 680
grits, cheese, 632
groundnut stew, 27–28
guacamole, 463, 464
guevos haminados, 441–42
guinataang munggo, 587
gumbo soup, okra, 616–17

haddock with sorrel and onions, 108–9
halvah shortbread, 84–85
hamantaschen, 435–37
hard-boiled eggs, Sephardic style, 441–442
harira, 514–15
heat diffusers, 666
herb(ed) (s):
bouquet garni, 654
chèvre spread, 542
crème fraîche, 553
*see also specific herbs*
hernerakkaa, 259–60
high tea, 102
apple brown betty, 113
Brussels sprouts with horseradish, 104
cheddar and parsnip soup, 105
cheese pastries, 107–8
haddock with sorrel and onions, 108–9
orange and mushroom salad, 109
proper trifle, 112
red pottage, 106
rumpledethumps, 110–11
shepherd's pie, 103–4
syllabub, 111
hiyashi somen, 393
hoisin sauce, 190
holiday rye bread, 251–52
hoppin' John, 620

horseradish:
and beet salad, 265
Brussels sprouts with, 104
hot:
chocolate, Mexican, 473
sauce, Asian, 651
spiced wine, 167
spice mixture, 509
hot-and-sour shrimp soup, Thai, 576–77
hot pepper:
green beans, 186
vinegar, 629
*see also* chile(s)
hotpot, seafood and vegetable, with pungent dipping sauce, 386–87
huevos rellenos con callampas, 147
Huguenot torte, 636
Hungarian cuisine, 206
creamy bean soup, 211–12
pumpernickel bread, 235–36

ice cream:
ginger, 198–99
in Italy, 371
sorbet Caribe, 133
the imam fainted (imam bayildi), 77
incavolata, 344–45
Indian cuisine, 21, 281–321
baked paneer, 309
baked stuffed potatoes, 305
cauliflower pakoras, 311
cheese (chenna and paneer), 296–97
cheese and nut dessert balls, 320
clarified butter, 294–95
classic raita, 318
dal, 314–15
eggplant, red pepper, and spinach curry, 303–4
fiery onion relish, 313
garam masala (spice mix), 293–94
ghee (clarified butter), 294–95
lightly spiced tomato soup, 299
mango with yogurt, 319–20
mulligatawny, 298–99
patrani machi, 307–8
sautéed paneer, 309
savory stuffed bread, 300–301
spiced tea, 321
spices in, 284, 286–91

tofu shira-ae (tofu and sesame pâté), 398–99
visual qualities emphasized in, 380
zucchini with walnut sauce, 397–98
Jerusalem artichokes, 666
Jewish cuisine, 413–45
*see also* Ashkenazi cuisine; Sephardic cuisine
joululimppa, 251–52
Junco's delicious potatoes braised in butter and sake, 399
juurikasviksiakeitto, 260–61
juustotahna, 257

ka, 666
kaali ja tofu paalle riisi, 272–73
kachumber, tomato, 315
Kaffir lime leaves, 576
kale and bean minestra, 344–45
kao pad, 581–82
kar, 666
karpalokastike, 275
kasha (buckwheat), 655
varnishkes, 431
kasvipasteija, 258
kebabs, fish, 521
kelp, *see* konbu
kettle stew, 465
kha, 666
kidney beans, in red pottage, 106
kidney beans, white (cannellini), 656
and kale minestra, 344–45
kinpira gobo, 403
kirsikkakeitto, 262
kisela juha, 209–10
koftas, zucchini-tofu, 310
konbu (kelp, kombu), 666
dashi, 385
kroketi od sira-skute, 225–26
kuchen, apple (kuchen de manzanas), 165
kukkakaalialaatikko, 271
kurkkusalaatti, 264
kurkku-viili kastike, 267

lahmajun, vegetarian, 524–25
laos root, 666
Large Meal for Guests: Not Quite a Feast menu, 574
latkes, featherlight potato, 422–23
Lebanese vegetable soup, 69–70

leche flan, 608–9
leek(s), 667
cream of zucchini and, soup, 543–44
in mizutaki, 386–87
potato vinaigrette, 491
and spinach soup, 182
legumes:
black-eyed peas and rice with tempeh, West Indian, 132–33
dal, 314–15
in hoppin' John, 620
split pea and rice soup, 515
yellow split pea soup, 259–60
*see also* bean(s); chick pea(s); lentil(s)
legumes rôties ou grillés, 538–39
leipiā, 248–49
lemon glaze, Albanian walnut cake with, 232–33
lemon grass, 667
lengkuas, 666
lentil(s):
in Bulgarian red pepper stew, 217–18
in dal, 314–15
in savory pastries, 512–13
and spinach soup, Turkish, 70–71
stew, spicy, 522
light:
cucumber marinade, 400–401
vegetable-seafood custard, 407
lightly spiced tomato soup, 299
lima beans:
in Mother Wolff soup, 420–21
in vegetarian Brunswick stew, 621–22
lime:
banana bread, Yellowman's, 123–24
tart, 134–35
tomato, and tortilla soup, 455
vinaigrette, 461
little balls, 62–63
long beans, 667
lumpiang sariwa, 588–90
luncheon entrées:
baked eggplant sandwiches, 339–40
black bean ful, 64–65
bread and tomato salad, 341–42
kettle stew, 465
Macedonian cottage cheese croquettes, 225–26
Mexican rice, 469–70
rumpledethumps, 110–11

red pepper flakes, 676
red pottage, 106
Regina's bobka, 437–38
relishes:
fiery onion, 313
roasted chile and tomato, 61
Sicilian eggplant, 333–34
repollo relleno, 152–53
Rhode Island cornmeal bread, 493
rice, 676–77
cabbage and tofu over, 272–73
cooking, 676–77
and endive soup, 343–44
in hoppin' John, 620
in Japan, 381, 383–84
Mexican, 469–70
in Mother Wolff soup, 420–21
in my favorite Philippine breakfast, 583
and peas with tempeh, West Indian, 132–33
pilav with orzo, 83
risotto, 350–51
in Southeast Asia, 571–72
and split pea soup, 515
Thai-style fried, 581–82
in vegetable biryani, 306–7
white, 384
*see also* brown rice
rice vinegar, 677
riso e indivia, 343–44
risotto, 350–51
brown rice mock, 352
roasted:
chile and tomato relish, 61
mushrooms with pine nuts, 337
nuts, tamari, 198
red pepper sauce, 348–49
vegetables, 538–39
roll cutting, 175
Romanian cuisine, 207
carrots with sour cream, 229
marinated mushrooms, 226–27
root vegetable purées, 260–61
rosemary, 677
focaccia, 335–36
oil, 336
roti dough, 130
rouille, 548, 549
roux, 487, 623

ruggelach, 434–35
rujak, Indonesian, 597–98
rumpledethumps, 110–11
rum punch, classic, 128
rusks, 44–45
Russian cuisine, 246
Russian salad, 263
rutabaga(s), 677
and carrot soup, 260–61
sauté, spicy, 403
rye:
bread, Finnish, 249–50
bread, holiday, 251–52
cauliflower casserole, 271
rye flakes, 677

saffron, 290, 678
butterflies, 361
sage, 678
sake, 381, 678
-braised spinach crowns, 397
Junco's delicious potatoes braised in butter and, 399
salad dressings, *see* dressings
salades:
niçoise, 550–51
verte, 557
salads:
Abidjan cabbage, 36
avocado ahdi, 126
beet and horseradish, 265
beets and carrots in lime vinaigrette, 461
bread and tomato, 341–42
cocola, 618–19
cucumber and pickled plum, 406
cucumbers in yogurt, 65
cucumber—sour cream, 264
Czechoslovakian apple and carrot confetti, 230
ensalada Olimpica, 146
Fatima's, 511
fresh fruit, with a difference, 597–98
grated turnip and apple, 266
green bean and tomato, 159
marinated tomato, 340
marinated vegetables and bean thread, 184–85
orange and mushroom, 109
Russian, 263
Serbian cucumber-pepper, 228–29
Syrian, 66

stiff porridge, 35–36
stir-frying, 176
stocks:
    basic fish, 547
    Chinese vegetable, 178
    simple fish, for East Asian dishes, 575–76
    vegetable, 685
strainers, Chinese, 658
strudels:
    Macedonian pear and fig, 234–35
    Macedonian sweet-and-savory, 219–20
stuffed:
    artichokes, 338
    bread, savory, 300–301
    cabbage, 152–53
    eggplant (imam bayildi), 77
    eggplant Provençal, 551–52
    eggs with mushrooms, 147
    figs and dates, 445
    green peppers with creamy walnut sauce, 467–68
    peaches, baked, 375
    peppers with feta cheese sauce, 517–18
    potatoes, baked, 305
    tofu, 194–95
    tomatoes (Chilean), 148
    tomatoes (Provençal), 540
    tomatoes with mushrooms, Croatian, 214–15
    vegetables, 72–74
    vegetables with spinach and artichoke hearts, 625
stuffing, cornbread, 631–32
sub-Saharan Africa, cuisine of, 15–47
    Abidjian cabbage salad, 36
    banana chutney, 43
    Capetown fruit and vegetable curry, 31–32
    Cape Verde vegetable soup, 25
    Casamance stew, 30–31
    East African sweet pea soup, 26
    fried sweet potatoes or plantains, 41
    ginger soft drink, 47
    gombo (okra side dish), 37
    groundnut stew, 27–28
    ingredients in, 21
    maize pudding, 38
    minted cucumber-yogurt refresher, 42
    peanut sauce, 39
    rusks, 44–45
    Senegalese seafood stew, 28–29

    South African milk tart, 46–47
    steamed millet, 34–35
    suggested reading on, 693
    tofu bobotie, 32–33
    ugali (stiff porridge), 35–36
    West African peanut soup, 23–24
sugar snap peas, 681
summer blueberry tart, 560–61
summer corkscrew pasta, 364
summer savory, 681
summer squash, see squash, yellow summer; zucchini
sunchokes, 666
sun-dried tomato(es), 681
    flounder rolls with almonds, cilantro and, 466
    pesto, 365–66
su-no-mono, 400–401
suomalaisruisleipä, 249–50
Swede turnips, 677
Swedish cuisine, 246
sweet:
    bastela, 527–28
    bread, Finnish, 252–54
    pastry crust, 560
sweet-and-sour tamarind sauce, 312–13
sweet potato(es), 21, 681–82
    balls, 125
    bread, 302–3
    in Casamance stew, 30–31
    fried, 41
    in groundnut stew, 27–28
    soufflé, Annie Wade's, 628
    in tempura, 388–89
    in vegetable biryani, 306–7
Swiss cheese, in potato cake, 555–56
syllabub, 111
Syrian cuisine:
    fig and apricot conserve, 88
    salad, 66
syrup, orange-honey, 441
Szechuan chili paste, 657
Szechuan peppercorns, 682

tablespoons, eating with fork and, 572
taeng kwa brio wan, 600
tahini, 682
    dressing, 68
tail of the monkey, 166–67
tajine, vegetable, 519

tamarind, 290–91
    sauce, sweet-and-sour, 312–13
tamari soy sauce, 682
    roasted nuts, 198
tapenade, 539
tapioca 682
taratour sauce, 67
tarragon, 682–83
tarte aux myrtilles d'été, 560–61
tarts:
    lime, 134–35
    South African milk, 46–47
    summer blueberry, 560–61
    winter pear, frangipane, 561–62
tauhu goreng kechap, 591–92
tea (beverage), 95–96
    proper pot of, 96
    in Southeast Asia, 572
    spiced, 321
tea (meal), 97
    scones, 98
    shortbread, 101
    singin' hinnies, 98–99
    tomatoes with forcemeat, 99–100
    Welsh rarebit, 100–101
    *see also* high tea
tea cake, cranberry, 498–99
techniques:
    in Chinese cuisine, 175–77
    guides to, 697
    *see also specific techniques*
tempeh, 683
    with rice and peas, West Indian, 132–33
tempura, 388–89
tequila, in tail of the monkey, 166–67
Thai cuisine:
    fish soup with coconut milk, 578
    fresh cucumber salad, 600
    fried rice, 581–82
    hot-and-sour shrimp soup, 576–77
    noodle salad, 585–86
    sample menu for, 573
    sriracha sauce, 680
    yam polomai, 597–98
Thai ginger, 666
thyme, 683
tofu, 683–84
    baked, variations, 187–88

blanching, 684
bobotie, 32–33
    in Bosnian "meatballs" in yogurt sauce, 216–17
    and cabbage over rice, 272–73
    and corn casserole, 153–54
    curry, Indonesian, 584–85
    five-spice, 189
    freezing, 684
    Indonesian fried, with cucumbers and sprouts, 591–592
    in mizutaki, 386–87
    in North African pizza, 524–25
    pressing, 684
    and sesame pâté (tofu shira-ae), 398–99
    in shepherd's pie, 103–4
    stuffed, 194–95
    in stuffed green peppers with creamy walnut sauce, 467–68
    in vegetable pâté, 258
    in winter stew, 391–92
    in wontons, 179–80
    zucchini koftas, 310
tomates:
    Claudia, 148
    farcies, 540
tomatillo sauce, 459
tomato(es):
    apricot chutney, 317
    avocado soup, chilled, 457
    and bread salad, 341–42
    in Cape Verde vegetable soup, 25
    in classic raita, 318
    in crisp cooked vegetable appetizer, 513
    Croatian mushroom-stuffed, 214–15
    crostini, 342
    dal, 315
    in dolma, 72–74
    dumpling soup, spicy Bulgarian, 212–14
    in Fall River vegetable stew, 488
    flounder rolls with almonds, cilantro and, 466
    with forcemeat, 99–100
    fried green, 626
    and green bean salad, 159
    in jambalaya, 622–23
    kachumber, 315
    in kettle stew, 465
    lime, and tortilla soup, 455
    marinated, salad, 340

## *About the Authors*

Moosewood Restaurant is run by a group of 18 women and men who rotate through the jobs necessary to make a restaurant go. We plan menus, set long-term goals, and wash pots. Our ranks are bolstered by about half a dozen employees.

Major decisions are made collectively, and while democracy at work and at meetings has required effort and determination, the payoffs have been rich. Most of us have worked together for nearly ten years, and some of us since the restaurant's inception in 1973. Personally, we are an assortment of individuals who have become a family—caring deeply for one another, striving for fairness and consensus, and putting-up-with and letting-go-of various human foibles. Professionally, our collective process has worked well for seventeen years. Come visit!

If you have enjoyed *Sundays at Moosewood Restaurant,* you will want to read *The Moosewood Restaurant Kitchen Garden* by David Hirsch.